Advertising and Sales Promotion Strategy

Advertising and Sales Promotion Strategy

Gerard J. Tellis

University of Southern California

 ADDISON-WESLEY

An imprint of Addison Wesley Longman, Inc.

Reading, Massachusetts • Menlo Park, California • New York • Harlow, England
Don Mills, Ontario • Sydney • Mexico City • Madrid • Amsterdam

Sponsoring Editor: Michael Roche
Developmental Editor: Elaine Silverstein
Design, Composition, and Project Coordination: Elm Street Publishing Services, Inc.
Cover Design: Regina Hagen
Printer and Binder: World Color

Library of Congress Cataloging-in-Publication Data

Tellis, Gerard J., 1950-
    Advertising and sales promotion strategy / Gerard J. Tellis.
        p.   cm.
    Includes bibliographical references and index.
    ISBN 0-321-01411-1
    1. Advertising. 2. Sales promotion. 3. Marketing—Management.
  I. Title.
HF5823.T27   1997
658.8'2—DC21   97-20699
                                                              CIP

1 2 3 4 5 6 7 8 9 10 RNT 01 00 99 98 97

To Cheryl, Neil, Viren, Kethan and Sonia.
Gerard J. Tellis

PREFACE

Promotion, which consists primarily of advertising and sales promotion, is a vital business function that fashions and communicates a firm's offer to its consumers. It is a rich topic that integrates perspectives from a number of disciplines including marketing, economics, psychology, anthropology and operations research. It is also a dynamic area that is constantly changing as firms develop new media, appeals and methods to better compete with their rivals in a rapidly changing environment. This book is designed to communicate these aspects of promotions.

The book is the fruit of my experience teaching advertising and sales promotion over the last six years at the University of Southern California. There are many fine books on the market, but they did not fully meet what I considered to be important characteristics of a textbook for such a course. To begin with, the book must be rooted in the knowledge emanating from research in the field. However, the few books that provide such a perspective tend to be a little abstract for students. The book must help prospective managers understand the topic well enough to design successful strategies. For this reason the book's presentation must be practical, analyze a large number of relevant examples and describe creative strategies. Several advertising books that are rich in examples tend to lack theoretical depth. They may not appeal to the more advanced students. The current book is designed to fill a void in the market, for an exposition that is theoretically rigorous, rich with examples and useful for designing strategies.

FOCUS

Advertising became a major economic force in the United States around the middle of the nineteenth century, with the advent of the mass market for manufactured goods. Advertising helped develop this mass market by establishing branded products that stood for uniform quality at good prices. However, as markets matured with a proliferation of similar brands, sales promotion gained in importance. Sales promotion draws attention to a brand in a crowded field and helps to fine-tune a firm's offer to specific segments at specific time periods. Many textbooks, following the historical growth of the discipline, focus only on advertising. Others, realizing the breadth of the field, cover personal selling and publicity, in addition to sales promotion and advertising. This book focuses on advertising and sales promotion, and only these two topics, for the following three reasons.

First, over the last decade, firms have been spending a bigger fraction of the promotional dollar on sales promotions and a smaller fraction on advertising. Indeed, over a ten-year period from 1981 to 1992, the fraction of the promotional dollar spent on advertising fell almost in half, while that in trade promotion increased by the same amount. Currently, firms spend about three-fourths of the promotional budget on sales promotion, and one-fourth on advertising. Thus sales promotions have become a very important component of the promotional mix.

Second, advertising and sales promotion are closely interlinked. Expenditures on advertising have a direct bearing on expenditures on sales promotion. In many cases they are substitutable, while in some cases they are complementary. However, in every case the spending decision must be taken together. More importantly, the strategy and content of advertising must be closely linked to that in sales promotion. Thus, these two topics need to be treated jointly.

Third, personal selling and publicity may not be close enough to advertising and sales promotion to merit an in-depth treatment in the same book. While personal selling is related to promotion, it primarily involves the management of personnel. Thus it involves a substantially different science. Similarly, publicity involves the management of news, which is a slightly different science from advertising. A broad coverage of related topics may hinder an in-depth coverage of important core topics. Advertising and sales promotion are key promotional activities of the marketing department. They involve a number of content issues that are fully within the control of the firm and must be jointly addressed. Thus they need to be taught and discussed in a single course.

KEY CHARACTERISTICS

Advertising and Sales Promotion Strategy is designed to give students a deep understanding of advertising and sales promotion that will enable them to develop successful strategies in practice. Specifically, the book has the following characteristics:

- It focuses on advertising and sales promotion, two key areas of promotion. To cover these two topics thoroughly, the book does not consider the related areas of personal selling and publicity.
- It draws from the most recent research in the social sciences to ensure that students are exposed to the most current knowledge in the field.
- The discussion explains why phenomena occur, rather than merely describing them. Similarly, it tries to show why certain strategies succeed, while others fail, rather than merely identifying them.
- The book has a managerial orientation. Its purpose is to help prospective managers design successful strategies. The book uses contemporary examples to enliven the exposition and clearly communicate key points.
- The book explains theories, concepts and terms from first principles. It requires no particular prerequisites in business, marketing economics or psychology. Thus students in any discipline could pick up the book and follow its contents. Nevertheless, students with any one of those backgrounds are more likely to appreciate related aspects of the book. So instructors will need to complement the exposition and definitions in the book to match the specific backgrounds of their students.

- The writing is simple, direct and lively. It uses simple language even when explaining complex ideas.

ORGANIZATION OF CONTENT

This book is divided into four parts. The first part provides a background to the field. The second part covers communication, the core aspect of advertising. The third part discusses the concepts, principles and strategies of sales promotions. The fourth part explains how to use advertising and sales promotion to plan strategy.

Part I has three chapters. Chapter 1 defines the basic terms used in the field. It reviews the history of promotion and explains its relationship to marketing strategy. The historical review gives a deep understanding of the evolution of promotion. It helps students put in proper perspective various practices, trends and controversies in the field. The review of marketing strategy and its relationship to promotion is essential because advertising and sales promotion are intrinsic components of the marketing strategy of a firm.

Chapter 2 is probably unique among texts in the field, in its in-depth coverage of the regulation of both advertising and sales promotion. Advertising and sales promotion are heavily regulated because they have great potential for deception. Regulations are partly responsible for the form that the field has taken today. They also define the range of strategies that managers can adopt. Thus a good coverage of regulation is necessary fairly early in the course.

Chapter 3 explains the structure and working of the advertising agency, the single institution most closely tied to the function. The chapter also pays special attention to the role of creativity. While creativity is not solely the function of the agency, it is an institutional or personnel characteristic that must inspire every aspect of the discipline. For this reason, the book discusses the topic in Part I. In addition, a variety of creative styles can be effective. These styles have been developed by specific advertising practitioners and exemplified by certain agencies. A discussion of such issues is best covered in the context of the agency.

Part II covers the topic of communication in five chapters. Chapter 4 introduces the key concepts and principles of persuasion. Chapter 5 explains how to draw consumers' attention, which is a prerequisite of communication. The three most important routes of persuasion are argument, emotion and endorsements. The book is unique in that three separate chapters (6, 7 and 8), focus on each of these topics. Many people believe that emotion and endorsements are less important means of persuasion than information and argument. However, emotion is probably the most powerful means of persuasion, while information and argument probably the least powerful. Ads today probably rely at least as much on emotion or endorsements as on information and argument. The separate treatment of these topics does not imply that they must be used in exclusion. The theory and examples show how persuasion can be enhanced by use of multiple appeals.

Part III covers sales promotions. Changing price is one of the central aspects of sales promotions. Chapter 9 is a unique chapter among comparable texts in addressing this topic. It explains how consumers react to price changes, and the strategies that firms can legally and fairly adopt in response. The chapter draws heavily from recent advances in marketing, economics and decision science in understanding consumer decision making. The three important components of sales promotions are retail promotions, trade promotions and consumer promotions. Chapter 10, 11 and 12 cover these three topics, respectively. The book covers these topics in greater detail than other texts because of their growing importance in recent years.

Part IV covers planning. Goals are the targets of any plan and must be set at the start of planning. Chapter 13 addresses this important topic. Chapter 14 explains how managers can test the effectiveness of advertising and sales promotions. The variables used for testing depend on the goals of a firm. Thus this chapter follows the chapter on setting goals. One section of the chapter addresses the billion dollar question, whether advertising today affects sales. It reviews some of the most recent empirical studies to provide a coherent answer to the question. A central aspect of planning is the choice of an appropriate mix of media to carry the ads. The two major classes of media are mass media and direct media. Chapters 15 and 16 explain how to plan these two types of media. In contrast to other texts, these chapters do not detail the structural and operational aspects of each medium. Rather they focus on the comparative advantage of each medium for communicating messages and the principles involved in choosing a media plan. Chapter 17 explains how managers can determine the advertising budget and schedule it over time. The final chapter explains how a practicing manager needs to integrate the various components of advertising and sales promotion into effective strategies.

COVERAGE OF SPECIAL TOPICS

Many instructors and students are interested in special topics that have gained importance recently. Some of these topics are regulation, direct marketing, ethics, international strategy and brand equity.

Of these topics, regulation is probably the most important. A vast number of regulations cover almost every aspect of advertising and sales promotions. These regulations define the range of legal strategies that managers can adopt. Chapter 2 details the regulatory climate of the field.

Direct marketing is another topic that has gained enormous importance with changes in consumer behavior and advances in media technology. Chapter 16 covers this topic under the discussion of direct media. It pays special attention to the growth of new media such as the Internet.

Ethics is a field of growing importance to advertising. Federal and state regulations already encompass what most practitioners today would consider to be ethical behavior. As noted above, Chapter 2 discusses these regulations. In addition to Chapter 2, various chapters raise the ethical aspect of some sensitive issues. Because it is more appropriate to discuss such issues in the chapter in which they naturally occur, the following list indicates where instructors can engage students in a useful discussion of ethical issues:

- Truth in advertising and sales promotion, Chapters 2 and 6
- Subliminal advertising, Chapter 4
- Manipulation of consumers' emotions, Chapters 5 and 7
- Use of sex appeals in advertising, Chapters 5 and 8
- Characterization and casting of endorsers, Chapter 8
- Stereotyping in communication, Chapter 8
- Misuse of endorsers or role models, Chapters 2 and 8

- Fair pricing, Chapters 2 and 9
- Advertising and price inflation, Chapters 1 and 10
- Price discrimination, Chapter 9
- Deceptive pricing or promotion, Chapters 2 and 9
- Annoying or intrusive direct marketing, Chapters 2 and 16

Branding is a vitally important topic in advertising. A major goal of advertising is to develop a distinct brand that embodies a distinct image or position in consumers' minds. In this sense, much of the content of the book is directly or indirectly related to branding. A special chapter devoted to branding would be either too small for the topic, or too redundant with other material in the book. So the book does not contain a chapter on branding, but embeds the topic implicitly in the discussion of related issues.

Most of the material in the book is developed in the context of the U.S. market. Internationalization of the curriculum is very important today because markets are becoming global. However, the major difference when going from one country to another is the change in regulations. It is beyond the scope of this book to cover the regulatory environment of promotion of every country. Another major difference across countries is culture. Advertising as a form of communication is intricately linked with the culture of a people. Again, it is beyond the scope of this book to cover the differences in advertising due to different cultures. However, subject to cultural and regulatory differences, much of the knowledge covered in this book should apply to the international realm. For this reason, the book does not contain a special chapter devoted to international advertising. The book tries to use international examples wherever these are relevant.

SUPPORT MATERIAL

Advertising and Sales Promotion Strategy comes with an excellent teaching/learning ancillary package designed to aid the educational experience of the student and aid instructors in teaching their courses. The ancillary package includes an Instructor's Manual with Test Bank; a computerized testing program; a CD-ROM that includes most figures and tables from the book, as well as additional advertisements and examples of television advertisements; and an interactive CD-ROM for students.

Instructor's Manual and Test Bank

Prepared by Siva K. Balasubramanian, of Southern Illinois University, this extensive manual includes course syllabi for quarter-length and semester-length courses at both the undergraduate and MBA level; lecture outline and summary of key points for each chapter; answers to all questions and problems; test bank of 25 multiple choice, 10 true or false and 5–10 problem-type items per chapter and 2 Mid Term and 2 Final Examinations.

Test Generator/Editor

This computer program allows instructors to assemble their own customized tests from the items included in the test bank. If desired, the test items can be viewed on screen, edited, saved and printed. In addition, they can add questions to any test or item bank. A real time-saver, Test Generator/Editor is available to qualified adopters on compatible personal computers.

Instructor's CD-ROM

A cross platform instructional CD-ROM that includes all of the advertising images, figures and tables from the book as well as additional advertisements and television commercials is available to instructors for classroom presentation purposes, or for placement on a network for student use.

Student CD-ROM

Intel: A Multimedia Exercise in Advertising Management by John A. Quelch of the Harvard Business School is available packaged with this book for a nominal price. This dynamic simulation places the student in the role of marketing manager for Intel, the maker of microcomputer chips. The student/marketing manager must decide on market segments to target, select differing advertising strategies, establish budgets, conduct focus groups with prototype advertisements and select from the possible options. The simulation will take between four and ten hours to complete, depending on the instructional objectives and the extent to which teams are encouraged to work together.

ACKNOWLEDGMENTS

I wish to thank many people who helped me to prepare this manuscript. Anne Smith motivated me to start the book and provided critical support as I developed its outline and unique position. She took an active interest in the contents of the early chapters, providing editorial feedback, as well as examples and clippings to support specific points. Michael Roche was also editor during the latter period of development. He served as a valuable point of contact with the market, helping me complete the book to fill a market void. His experience helped me keep various components of publishing in proper context. Mary Claire McEwing took over as project manager when the book came under Addison Wesley Longman. I especially appreciate her unhesitating support and generous praise.

I would like to acknowledge the help I received from three editors, Stephen Perrine, Elaine Silverstein and Ingrid Mount. Stephen provided very detailed comments on some early chapters of the manuscript. Elaine Silverstein carefully scrutinized all the chapters for logic, consistency and proper composition. She provided valuable advice about the distribution and presentation of examples. Ingrid Mount supervised the final copyediting of the manuscript and the production process.

The book also benefited enormously from the comments of many reviewers. These include

Irfan Ahmed, *Texas A&M University*

Earl Andresen, *University of Texas—Arlington*

William E. Baker, *University of Vermont*

Vincent J. Blasko, *Arizona State University*

Janice L. Bukovac, *Michigan State University*

Hugh M. Cannon, *Wayne State University*

Marjorie J. Cooper, *Baylor University*

John Deighton, *Harvard Business School*

Charles Gulas, *Wright State University*

Jay L. Laughlin, *Kansas State University*

Darrel D. Muehling, *Washington State University*

Douglas Olsen, *University of Calgary*

Cornelia Pechmann, *University of California at Irvine*

Frank N. Pierce, *University of Florida*

S. P. Raj, *Syracuse University*

Douglas Robideaux, *Central Missouri State University*

Herbert J. Rotfeld, *Auburn University*

Alan G. Sawyer, *University of Florida*

David Schmittlein, *The Wharton School, University of Pennsylvania*

Deepack Sirdesshmukh, *Case Western Reserve University*

Douglas M. Stayman, *Cornell University*

Joel Steckel, *New York University*

James E. Swartz, *California State Polytechnic University at Pomona*

Brian Wansink, *Dartmouth College*

Mike Weigold, *University of Florida*

Alan Sawyer and Connie Pechmann, in particular, repeatedly served on the review panel, consistently provided insightful comments and did so in a most encouraging tone.

Several graduate students at the University of Southern California provided research assistance at various stages: Pattana Thaivanich, Rajesh Chandy, Lallit Saldanha, David Ackerman, Rajeev Kohli, Liesel Johnson and Om Narasimhan. In particular, Pattana Thaivanich spent many hours proofreading first drafts of each chapter, and researching the literature for appropriate references. Many individuals at Addison Wesley Longman provided editorial, research and administrative support at various states of the project. I would especially like to mention Arlene Bessenoff, Jay O'Callaghan, Nina Novak, Anne Bonacum, Lisa Pinto, Matthew Rohrer, Billie Porter, Gina Hagen, Ruth Berry and Karen Stevenson for their efforts.

My wife Cheryl, and children, Neil, Viren, Kethan and Sonia, enthusiastically supported me through all stages of the manuscript. Neil and Viren also helped out with clipping and filing articles during the holidays. Cheryl unhesitatingly helped out with proofreading, advice or feedback anytime I asked. My four children were an inspiration each time they spontaneously praised me for progress or innocently chided me for being late. I am fortunate to have a family that shared in the labors and joys of this project

Gerard J. Tellis

CONTENTS

PART I

Introduction to Advertising and Sales Promotion 1

1 Evolution of Advertising and Sales Promotion as Strategic Decisions 3

The Scope of Advertising and Sales Promotion 5
  Basic Definitions 6
  Principal Agents 6
History of Advertising and Sales Promotion 8
  Advertising from U.S. Independence to the Civil War 9
  Advertising from the Civil War to World War I 10
  Advertising from World War I to World War II 16
  Post–World War II Advertising 17
Fundamentals of Marketing Strategy 18
  Consumer Orientation 18
  Segmentation 21
  Targeting 24
  Positioning 26
Marketing and Promotional Planning 27
  Goals of Promotion 27
  The Process of Planning Promotions 29
Summary 31
Questions 32
Notes 32

2 The Regulatory Environment of Promotion 34

The Meaning of Truth in Promotion 36
  History of the Federal Trade Commission 36
  Evaluation of Truth 36
  Implementing FTC Policy 41
Regulation of Specific Forms of Advertising 43
  Comparative Advertising 43
  Endorsements 44
  Demonstrations 45
  Warranties 45
  Loans and Leasing 46

Regulation of Sales Promotions 46
  Price Discrimination 46
  Trade Allowances 47
  Deceptive Pricing 48
  Deceptive Value 48
  Contests and Sweepstakes 49
Regulation of Media 50
  Broadcast Media 50
  Mail 51
Regulation of Labeling 52
  Advertising of Ethical Drugs 52
  Labeling of Food 53
  Labeling of Alcohol, Tobacco and Firearms 53
Self-Regulation 54
  In-House Self-Regulation 54
  Self-Regulation by Business Associations 54
Summary 57
Questions 58
Notes 58

3 Advertising Agencies and the Creative Process 61

The Structure of Agencies 64
  The Market for Advertising Agencies 64
  Agency Functions 65
  Agency Types 68
  Agency Ownership 72
  Agency Organization 74
Choosing an Advertising Agency 75
  Locating the Advertising Agency 75
  Organizing the Advertising Function 76
  Selecting an External Agency 77
Compensating Agencies 80
  Commission 80
  Fixed Fee 80
  Cost Basis 82
  Performance Basis 82
  Conclusion: The Benefits of a Mixed Approach 82

Managing Creativity 83
    Processes of Thinking Creatively 83
    Fostering Creative Thinking 84
    Organizing for Creativity 85
    Creative Styles 86
    Emphasizing Content or Execution 88
Summary 93
Questions 93
Notes 94

PART II

Communication Strategy 97

4   Introduction to Persuasion 99

Classical Conditioning 101
    The Process of Conditioning 102
    Factors Favoring Conditioning 103
Repetition 104
    Mere Exposure 104
    Subliminal Advertising 105
    Message Repetition 106
Involvement 110
Elaboration 111
    The Elaboration Likelihood Model 111
    Stability of Persuasion by Processing Route 114
Integration 115
Summary 116
Questions 116
Notes 117

5   How to Win and Hold Consumers' Attention 119

The Dynamics of Consumer Attention 120
    The Principle of Selective Attention 120
    Consumers' States of Receptivity 121
Gaining the Consumer's Attention 123
    Methods of Gaining the Consumer's Attention 123
    Choosing a Method to Gain Attention 129
Designing Components of an Ad to
    Gain Attention 131
    The Components of the Ad 131
    Ad Placement 133
Summary 134
Questions 134
Notes 135

6   Persuasion with Information and Argument 136

How Consumers Process Information 137
    Perception: Making Sense of External Stimuli 137
    Cognition: Thinking about Incoming Messages 139
    Memorizing and Retrieving Information 142
Argument Strategy 145
    Comparative Argument 145
    Refutational Argument 150
    Inoculative Argument 152
    Framing 152
    Supportive Argument 153
Summary 153
Questions 153
Notes 155

7   Persuasion with Emotion: Use of Drama, Humor and Music 157

Emotion 158
    What Is Emotion? 158
    How Does Emotion Persuade? 160
    When Do Emotions Work? 165
Methods of Arousing Emotions 166
    Drama 168
    Humor 169
    Music 173
Harnessing Specific Emotions 175
    Irritation 175
    Warmth 177
    Fear 178
    Ennobling Emotions 180
Summary 181
Questions 182
Notes 182

8   Persuasion Using Endorsers 184

Types of Endorsers 185
    Experts 185
    Celebrities 186
    Lay Endorsers 187
Role of Endorsers 188
    The Source Credibility Model 188
    The Source Attractiveness Model 188
    The Meaning Transfer Model 190
    Application of the Models 191

The Use of Endorsers 192
  Audience Characteristics 192
  Communication Modes 193
  Cost Effectiveness 194
The Evaluation of Endorsers 194
  Q-Ratings 195
  Customized Research 196
Strategic Implications 196
  Matching Celebrities to Consumer Segments 197
  Overuse of Celebrity Endorsers 197
  Screening of Candidates for Endorsers 198
  Managing Endorsers 199
Stereotyping of Endorsers 200
  Gender Stereotypes 201
  Race Stereotypes 204
  Age Stereotypes 204
Summary 205
Questions 206
Notes 207

PART III

Sales Promotion Strategy 209

9 **Overview of Sales Promotions 211**

Key Dimensions of Sales Promotions 215
  Channel Characteristics 215
  Promotion Characteristics 216
Principles of Price Promotion 217
  Knowledge of Prices and Discounts 217
  Price Discrimination 219
  Periodic Discounting 219
  Random Discounting 220
  Qualifying and Second Market Discounting 222
  Consumer Response to Price Promotions 222
  Reference Prices 223
  Asymmetry in Response 225
  Perception of Fairness in Pricing and Promotion 227
  Dual Entitlements 227
Summary 229
Questions 230
Notes 230

10 **Retail Promotions 233**

Description of Retail Promotions 235
  Displays 235
  Features 237
  Price-Cuts 238
  Double Coupons 239
Analyzing the Effects of Retail Promotions 240
  Response to Retail Promotions 240
  Decomposing the Promotional Bump 242
The Profitability of a Price Promotion 244
  Analysis of Profitability 244
  Strategic Implications 246
  The Story Behind Sears's Pricing Strategy 248
Summary 249
Questions 249
Notes 250

11 **Trade Promotions 251**

Characteristics of Trade Promotions 252
  Goals of Trade Promotions 252
  Growth of Trade Promotions 253
  Dynamics of Trade Promotions 254
Description of Trade Promotions 256
  Price-Based Trade Deals 256
  Nonprice Trade Deals 258
  Informative Trade Promotions 259
  Motivational Trade Promotions 262
Problems of Trade Promotions 264
  Costs of Trade Promotions 264
  Efficient Consumer Response 266
  Benefits of Trade Promotions 266
Evaluating the Profitability of a Trade Promotion 267
  Analysis of Profitability 267
  Strategic Relevance 268
Summary 269
Questions 270
Notes 270

12 **Consumer Promotions 272**

Manufacturer Coupons 273
  Types of Manufacturer Coupons 273
  The Purpose of Coupons 275
  Coupon Redemptions 275
  Evaluating Coupon Strategy 279
  New Trends 280
Rebates 281
Price Packs 282
  Differential Benefits of Price Packs 282
  Regulation of Price Packs 283

Premiums 283
  The Logic of Premiums 283
  Goals of Premiums 284
Tie-ins 284
  Role of Tie-ins 285
  Bases for Tie-ins 285
  Management of Tie-ins 286
Bonus Plans 286
  Principles of Effective Bonus Plans 287
Sweepstakes and Contests 288
Sampling 289
  Types of Sampling 290
  Costs of Sampling 291
  Conditions Favoring Sampling 291
Comparing Methods of Price Promotions 292
Summary 292
Questions 293
Notes 293

PART IV
Planning Advertising and Sales Promotion 297

13 **Setting Goals for Advertising and Sales Promotion 299**

Characteristics of Well-defined Goals 302
  Goals Should Be Explicit 302
  Goals Should Be Precise 304
  Goals Should Be Inspiring but Attainable 305
  Goals Should Involve All Relevant Parties 305
Hierarchy of Effects 306
  Classification of Advertising Effects 306
  Models of the Hierarchy of Effects 308
  Use of Hierarchy of Effects 309
Summary 310
Questions 310
Notes 310

14 **Testing the Effectiveness of Advertising 311**

Advertising Effectiveness: Some Basic Definitions 313
Approaches to Researching Advertising Effectiveness 315
  Laboratory Experiment 315
  Field Approach 318
  Field Experiment 319
Collecting Data on Advertising 319
  Evaluating Methods for Collecting Data 320

  Tools for Collecting Data on Advertising 322
Standard Measures of Advertising Effectiveness 328
  Recall 329
  Recognition 330
  Inquiries 331
  Sales 332
How Advertising Affects Sales 335
  Major Studies on the Advertising-Sales Relationship 336
  Why Do Advertisers Continue with Ineffective Ads? 338
  Conclusion 339
Summary 340
Questions 341
Notes 341

15 **Planning Mass Media 344**

The Structure of the Media 346
  The Market for Media 348
  Organization of TV 350
  Pressure on Program Content 352
  Major Trends in Media 353
Media Planning 356
  Media Choice 357
  Focus 357
  Vehicle Choice 360
  Summary 370
Syndicated Data Sources 371
  The A. C. Nielsen Company 371
  Audit Bureau of Circulation (ABC) 372
  Simmons Market Research Bureau 372
  Mediamark 373
Summary 373
Questions 373
Notes 374

16 **Planning Direct Media 376**

Growth of Direct Media 378
Evaluation of Direct Media 379
  Advantages of Direct Media 379
  Disadvantages of Direct Media 380
The Major Direct Media 381
  Mail 381
  Telephone 383
  The Internet 386
Evaluating the Profitability of Direct Media 389
  Collecting Data 390
  Estimating Profits 391
Summary 392

Questions 392
Notes 393

17 **Budgeting: Setting the Level and Timing of Promotion Expenditures 394**

Methods for Determining the Promotion
    Budget 396
    Affordability 396
    Percentage of Sales 397
    Competitive Parity 397
    Objective and Task 402
    Profit Maximization 402
    Matching the Elasticity Ratio 404
Scheduling Advertising Expenditures 405
    Factors Affecting the Choice of Scheduling 406
    Goal of the Campaign 407
    Sales Pattern 407
    Optimal Ad Intensity Relative to Available
        Budget 408
    Dynamic Effects of Advertising 408
Summary 410
Questions 411
Notes 412

18 **Integrated Advertising and Sales Promotion Strategy 413**

Promotion Strategy over the Product Life
    Cycle 414

Promotion Strategy over Stages of the Product
    Life Cycle 419
Promotion Strategy over Successive Life
    Cycles 421
Promotion Strategy Depending on Speed of
    Takeoff 425
Integration of Advertising and Sales Promotion in
    Every Life Cycle Stage 427
    Trade-offs among Promotion Components 427
    Reinforcement among Promotion Variables 428
Integrating Promotion and Marketing for
    Defense 429
    The Defender Model 429
    Deflection 430
    Tit-for-Tat 431
    Counterattack 432
Summary 433
Questions 434
Notes 434

Glossary 437

Company Index 455

Name Index 461

Subject Index 467

I

Introduction to Advertising and Sales Promotion

During the 1984 Super Bowl, Apple Computer Company aired an ad called "1984" that changed the fortunes of the company, and greatly affected the perception of Super Bowl advertising. Why did the ad have such a major impact?

In 1983 Apple Computer Company was planning to introduce the Macintosh, a new line of personal computers. The Macintosh was designed to compete with IBM's personal computers. IBM was the leading producer of mainframe computers. It had a reputable brand name, strong

1

Evolution of Advertising and Sales Promotion as Strategic Decisions

sales force, excellent distribution, and stocks that were regularly rated as blue chip. Most important, IBM had just displaced Apple as the leader of the personal computer market, even though it entered late.

Apple chose a small West Coast advertising agency called Chiat/Day to do the introductory ad for the Macintosh, because of the agency's record for creative advertising. True to its reputation, the agency developed a 60-second com-

▼ EXHIBIT 1-1. Scenes from Apple's Macintosh ad, "1984."

Source: Courtesy of Apple Computer, Inc.

mercial costing $400,000, based on the theme of the Orwellian nightmare *1984*. The ad showed an executive lecturing an audience of zombielike listeners, from a giant screen (see Exhibit 1-1). The scene was a parody of IBM's domination of the computer market with customers at its mercy, reminiscent of the domination of Big Brother in the novel *1984*. In the midst of that scene, a woman athlete ran down the aisle carrying a mallet, and slammed it at the screen destroying Big Brother. As the screen crashed, a voice-over announced, "Introducing the Apple Macintosh. Why 1984 will not be like *1984*."

The ad was dramatic and forceful. When screened at Apple's sales meeting, the ad won an enthusiastic 15-minute standing ovation. Chiat/Day then booked two 60-second slots for the ad during the 1984 Super Bowl, for $500,000 each. Unfortunately, Apple's board of directors found the slots too costly, and the creative too controversial; they feared that it would offend IBM's business customers. The board asked Chiat/Day to sell off the two slots on the Super Bowl. However, because the agency was unable to sell one 60-second slot and argued for the ad, the board reluctantly agreed to air it.

The ad had the greatest impact of all the 1984 Super Bowl ads. It was widely covered by the media and universally praised by ad critics. Even though the ad aired just once, the publicity it won helped Apple sell 72,000 Macintosh units the first day, almost 50 percent above target. That year *Advertising Age* rated "1984" the ad of the decade, and Chiat/Day, the agency of the decade. Well into the 1990s, the ad was still considered by many to be the best TV commercial ever.

The ad also changed the perception of the Super Bowl, which already had one of the highest national and international audiences and advertising rates among all TV shows. In subsequent years advertising critics and news agencies closely watched Super Bowl ads for new advertising trends or consumer products. Advertisers in turn chose that vehicle to showcase their best ads and launch important new products.[1]

THE SCOPE OF ADVERTISING AND SALES PROMOTION

The introductory ad for the Apple Macintosh suggests the enormous potential of advertising. Chiat/Day developed a creative that was gripping, evocative and humorous. (The term **creative** is used in the ad industry as a noun to refer to the unique design of an ad.) Yet the creative clearly communicated a key benefit of the new product—empowering individuals with decentralized desktop computing. The dramatic ad fired up the sales staff and distributors to sell the product against those of a respected, well-entrenched competitor, IBM. The ad also stirred intense interest in the media that quickly transferred into consumer interest in the product. The success of the ad vindicated those in the agency who had vouched for it. The ad was a typical product of Chiat/Day, known for its bold, irreverent style of advertising. The ad vindicated those in the firm that chose the agency.

Yet, the story of the ad campaign also suggests the fragility of the advertising process. In advance, managers were sufficiently uncertain about the ad as to be willing to scrap it. They agreed to invest only a limited budget on the ad, which could well have washed out, had the ad not been as effective. They chose a medium and vehicle (TV's Super Bowl) without fully realizing its enormous potential. Numerous other ads aired during that Super Bowl. None was as compelling and many failed. Yet all of their sponsors probably believed in those ads at least as much as did the sponsors of "1984." Many of them may have hoped for as big an impact.

"1984" suggests an important principle of advertising—that it is partly the scientific judgment of managers, partly the native creativity of individuals, and partly luck. However, after centuries of advertising, and decades of intense research on its effectiveness, the scope of science in advertising has greatly increased. Today, much more is known about why and when advertising works, and what makes for great advertising. Within those confines, the role of creativity is in no way diminished. Science illuminates the path for advertising strategists, art directors and copywriters. Science does not substitute for creativity. Science does however, reduce the need to rely on luck.

For example, science could suggest whether managers should adopt a cool rational appeal or a hot emotional appeal. For each of those appeals creatives could generate 100 executions, only a few of which may be winners. Scientific pretests could separate promising winners from likely losers. But artists and copywriters could still enhance the selection with deft touches. Science may suggest how often to repeat an ad to persuade consumers, and which mix of media may be necessary to do so. Within those guidelines, the creative match of medium, program, ad and target segment can give an advertiser the edge over competitors.

A major premise of this book is that good advertising today requires science and creativity. The purpose of this book is to describe current knowledge regarding the science of advertising and sales promotion. To do so, the book draws on research accumulated in many disciplines especially advertising, marketing strategy, consumer psychology and market economics. It strives to integrate this knowledge into a structured whole that can enable a manager to develop an integrated campaign of advertising and sales promotion from start to finish.

The book is divided into four parts. The first part develops the background of the subject. It describes the history of advertising, the regulatory environment in which it takes place, and the role of the agency and creativity.

The second part gives an in-depth analysis of communication, which is the central function of advertising. One chapter gives an overview of the communication process and describes the principles of persuasion. Another chapter describes how to win and hold consumers' attention, a vital function in today's distracting environment. The next three chapters discuss the three principal routes of persuasion: the use of argument, emotion and endorsements.

The third part of the book provides an in-depth analysis of sales promotion. One chapter describes the various types of sales promotions and the principles involved in their use. Since sales promotion is closely tied to the price of the product, many of these principles revolve around consumers' perception of price and price changes. Separate chapters then delve into the three principal forms of sales promotions: consumer, trade and retail promotions.

The fourth part of the book shows how the knowledge gained thus far can be integrated into a promotional plan. Separate chapters cover goal setting, testing, planning mass media, planning direct media and budgeting. The final chapter describes how advertising and sales promotion need to be integrated.

This chapter first defines the basic terms of the field, and then introduces the key agents responsible for promotion. It then takes the reader on a tour of the salient historical events that have shaped advertising and sales promotion today. Developments in marketing strategy that have had the most impact on promotion strategy, are the subject of the next section. The final section completes the introduction to the field by providing an overview of the process of marketing and promotional planning.

Basic Definitions

The term **product** is used generically to refer to any good, service, idea, time or candidate that an individual or organization offers to another individual or organization. So *product* could refer to the Macintosh, a TV movie, safe driving, safe sex, Christian values, or Bob Dole's candidacy. The terms *firm* or *manufacturer* are used interchangeably to refer to any individual or organization that offers products to others. In the context of the above examples, the firms would be Apple Computer Inc., the Disney Channel, Mothers Against Drunk Driving, the State of California, the Lutheran Hour Ministries or the Republican Party. The terms **buyer, consumer** and **customer** refer to individuals or organizations who may potentially buy products from firms. The verb **market** refers to a set of related managerial tasks: identify needs of consumers and design, price, promote, distribute and sell products to meet those needs.

This book uses the term **promotion** to cover both advertising and sales promotion. **Advertising** is communicating a firm's offer to customers by paid media time or space. A **sales promotion** is a program that makes a firm's offer more attractive to buyers and requires buyer participation. Some authors also include two other functions when defining *promotion:* personal selling and publicity. **Personal selling** is communicating a firm's offer to consumers through the sales staff. **Publicity** is communicating a firm's message to consumers through unpaid news releases.

This book focuses only on advertising and sales promotion, rather than on all four functions for several reasons. First, a single book cannot adequately treat all four functions in sufficient depth. Second, advertising and sales promotion are very closely related, and involve trade-offs depending on a firm's products, competitors and consumers. Indeed, because of changes in markets in the last two decades, the promotion budget of firms has shifted substantially from advertising to sales promotion. Because of the inherent trade-off between these two functions, neither can be fully and satisfactorily treated alone. On the other hand, personal selling is closely related to sales management and can best be treated in that context. Publicity falls within the domain of public relations, and is often not within the marketing department. Thus it deserves a separate treatment.

Principal Agents

In 1995, U.S. expenditures on advertising totaled $161 billion. This figure included media and production costs, in all mass media, plus direct mail. It did not include expenditures on telemarketing. It also did not include expenditures on sales promotion. The overall level of advertising as a proportion of gross national product has been fairly steady in the United States over the last 30 years (see Exhibit 1-2). There are five principal agents involved in the trade of these resources: promoters, agencies, media owners, distributors and consumers.

The promoters are firms that wish to market products to consumers. Every individual person or organization is likely to be a promoter at some time or other. For example, most people run classified ads at one time or another to advertise their need for or desire to sell household goods. Also, most individuals at one time or another prepare a resumé, which is a statement promoting their ability to perform some work. However, a few firms with large shares of consumer markets consistently dominate as heavy spenders on promotion (see Exhibit 1-3). Consumers are sometimes subjected to the advertising or sales promotions of these firms even when they would prefer not to be. For this reason, advertising and sales promotion are sometimes associated as unwanted activities of giant corporations. The orientation of this book is primarily managerial. It seeks to explain how any individual or organization—students, workers, professionals, commercial firms, schools, welfare organizations, churches, state governments or political candidates—can use advertising and sales promotion to further its goals. The book is not an endorsement of the particular type or level of promotion of any one firm.

Agencies are the organizations that prepare or place ads or sales promotions for firms. Firms can always prepare their ads in-house. However, because of the advantages of specialization, a firm is better off focusing on producing or marketing its

▼ **EXHIBIT 1-2.** U.S. spending on advertising and sales promotion, 1960–1994.

Year	GDP Trillions of Dollars	GDP Percent Change	AD VOLUME* Billions of Dollars	AD VOLUME* Percent Change	AD VOLUME* Percent of GDP	TV AD VOLUME* Billions of Dollars	TV AD VOLUME* Percent Change	TV AD VOLUME* Percent of Ad Volume
1960	$ 0.5	4%	$ 12	7%	2.3%	$ 1.6	6%	13%
1961	0.5	4	12	–1	2.2	1.7	6	14
1962	0.6	8	12	5	2.2	1.9	12	15
1963	0.6	6	13	6	2.2	2.0	7	16
1964	0.6	7	14	8	2.2	2.3	13	16
1965	0.7	8	15	8	2.2	2.5	10	16
1966	0.8	10	17	9	2.2	2.8	12	17
1967	0.8	6	17	1	2.1	2.9	2	17
1968	0.9	9	18	7	2.0	3.2	12	18
1969	1.0	8	19	7	2.0	3.6	11	18
1970	1.0	5	20	1	1.9	3.6	0	18
1971	1.1	9	21	6	1.9	3.5	–2	17
1972	1.2	10	23	12	1.9	4.1	16	18
1973	1.3	12	25	8	1.9	4.5	9	18
1974	1.5	8	27	7	1.8	4.9	9	18
1975	1.6	9	28	5	1.8	5.3	9	19
1976	1.8	12	33	19	1.9	6.7	28	20
1977	2.0	12	37	12	1.9	7.6	13	20
1978	2.2	13	43	16	1.9	9.0	18	21
1979	2.5	12	49	13	2.0	10.2	13	21
1980	2.7	9	54	10	2.0	11.5	13	21
1981	3.0	12	60	13	2.0	12.7	10	21
1982	3.1	4	67	10	2.1	14.3	13	22
1983	3.4	8	76	14	2.2	16.8	17	22
1984	3.8	11	88	16	2.3	19.8	18	23
1985	4.0	7	95	8	2.3	21.0	6	22
1986	4.3	6	102	8	2.4	22.9	9	22
1987	4.5	6	110	7	2.4	23.9	4	22
1988	4.9	8	118	8	2.4	25.7	7	22
1989	5.3	7	124	5	2.4	26.9	5	22
1990	5.5	6	129	4	2.3	28.4	6	22
1991	5.7	3	126	–2	2.2	27.4	–4	22
1992	6.0	6	131	4	2.2	29.4	7	22
1993	6.3	5	138	5	2.2	30.6	4	22
1994	6.7	6	150	9	2.2	34.2	12	23

*Includes national syndication and cable.

Data Sources: U.S. Census Bureau, Statistical Abstracts of the United States: Washington, D.C., 1995. Darnay, Arsen J. (1992), *Economic Indicators Handbook*, MI: Gale Research, Inc. U.S. Census Bureau, *The Statistical History of the United States from Colonial Times to the Present*, New York, NY: Basic Books, Inc., 1976.

products, resorting to the expertise of agencies to prepare its ads. Chapter 3 discusses the role of the agency in depth.

Media are the means through which ads reach consumers. Television, newspapers, radio, magazines, mail and telephone are currently the major media, and carry the bulk of advertising and sales promo-tions. **Media companies** or **media owners** are the organizations that own one or more media, such as Times/Mirror or CBS. Chapters 15 and 16 explain the structure of the media, and how managers should choose the mix of media for their promotions.

The term **distributors** covers wholesalers, retail-ers and other agents who undertake the physical

▼ EXHIBIT 1-3. Ten leading national advertisers.

Firm	Total U.S. Promotional Spending (billions of 1994 dollars)	Percent Increase over 1993	1994 Rank	1991 Rank
Procter & Gamble	$2.7	13%	1	1
Philip Morris Co.	2.4	28	2	2
General Motors Co.	1.9	25	3	3
Ford Motor Co.	1.2	17	4	6
Sears Roebuck & Co.	1.1	12	5	4
AT&T Corp.	1.1	36	6	12
PepsiCo.	1.1	6	7	5
Chrysler Corp.	1.0	27	8	21
Walt Disney Co.	0.9	20	9	23
Johnson & Johnson	0.9	12	10	7

Data Sources: *Advertising Age* (1994), "100 Leading National Advertisers," January 3, 14; *Advertising Age* (1995), "100 Leading National Advertisers," September 27, 16.

transfer of goods from firms to consumers. Thus they play a critical role in the marketing of goods. Some advertising, and much of sales promotion is geared to motivating distributors to carry and promote products to consumers. Part III of the book, (especially Chapters 10 and 11) deals with these aspects of sales promotions.

The consumer is the *raison d'être* for the other four agents, and thus for all advertising and sales promotion. The only exception is the media, which provide entertainment and information to consumers, in addition to advertising. So the media could exist in the absence of advertising and sales promotion revenues. However, the vast majority of competing media have grown to be heavily dependent on promotion expenditures, and would shrink substantially in their absence.

HISTORY OF ADVERTISING AND SALES PROMOTION

▼ EXHIBIT 1-4. Early print ad for Procter & Gamble products.

Oils for lamps and machinery. A fine article of clarified Pig's Foot Oil, equal to sperm, at a low price and in quantities to suit buyers. Neat's Foot Oil ditto. Also No. 1 & 2 soap. Palm and shaving ditto. For sale by Procter & Gamble Co., east side Main Street 2nd door off 6th Street.
Source: *Cincinnati Gazette*, June 29, 1838

Procter & Gamble is the largest advertiser in the United States today, spending as much as $2.7 billion on advertising in 1994 (see Exhibit 1-3). It has a portfolio of well-established brands with enormous drawing power. Yet the company started off as a small, obscure maker of candles.

Procter & Gamble was founded by William Procter and James Gamble, immigrants from England and Ireland, respectively. The men met by marrying into the same Cincinnati family. In the early nineteenth century, they went into business together, buying a small candle works. Soap and lard were by-products of candle making, and harder to sell (see Exhibit 1-4). The company got a boost in sales from military purchases during the Civil War. By the end of the war, Procter & Gamble was a well-established producer of candles in Cincinnati. Still, soap amounted to only 25 percent of its revenues. Vision, innovation and luck combined to change that, just when Edison's electric lightbulb was rendering candle lighting obsolete.

At that time, soap consumption was limited because people bathed and washed infrequently. Less well-off and rural households made their own soap, while others bought it at the grocer. It was cut and sold by the bar. The major problem in soap making was durability. Soap that fell in the bathtub quickly turned to mush. Another problem was consistency. Homemade and much factory-made soap varied widely in firmness and purity, depending on the mixture of soda and fats that went into its production. With experience and research, Procter & Gamble succeeded in developing a fairly consistent product.

At that time, all soap served the same purpose. No manufacturer made distinctions in form or uses. There was one exception, "Castile." It was a pure white bar

▼ **EXHIBIT 1-5.** Evolution of Ivory soap.

Source: Courtesy of Procter & Gamble.

hired salesmen to push goods to wholesalers and retailers. Procter & Gamble changed all that. It began to buy space in available magazines and newspapers to sell Ivory, with ads that explained its unique attributes and vouched for its purity (see Exhibit 1-6).

The Ivory ads were successful right from the start. However, Procter & Gamble never gave up its commitment to research. It kept innovating with product improvements, line extensions and new products, even if they cannibalized the old ones. And it kept promoting with novel ads and sales promotions through new media. Its strategy of high-quality, innovative products, each uniquely branded with carefully designed advertising, led it to become the giant consumer products company it is today.[2]

of European soap, made of olive oil, and it sold at a premium in the United States. In 1875, Gamble hired a chemist to duplicate Castile. Three years later, the company succeeded. It called its new product P&G White Soap, and individually wrapped each bar to keep it dust free and give it an identity (see Exhibit 1-5). A few months later, the company began getting requests from distributors for the "soap that floats." The company's search indicated that one of its chemists working on a batch of white soap accidentally let it stir for a longer time than required. That error whipped up the soap mixture with more air so that it cooled to be lighter than water. When bathers dropped the soap in the bathtub, it immediately popped up to the surface—a great convenience when bathing was primarily in tubs. A year later Gamble thought of a better name for this white soap that floats—Ivory, from a passage in the Psalms that read, "All thy garments smell of myrrh and aloes and cassia out of ivory palaces. . . ."

Procter was convinced of the purity of his white soap, but he wanted proof. So he sent separate samples of Ivory and Castile for testing to a New York chemist. He was surprised to learn that Ivory was purer than Castile, and had only .56 percent impurities. From that emerged one of the greatest selling themes in advertising history: *"Ivory Soap . . . 99 and 44/100 percent pure."*

At that time advertising consisted primarily of regional ads indicating what products were available at which store. There was little national advertising. If manufacturers wanted to sell beyond their region they

A review of the history of advertising and sales promotion provides an excellent background to the field. It gives a good feel for how various products and advertising practices developed over the years. It also indicates the resilience of certain systems, suggests causes of certain phenomena and hints at future trends.[3]

While advertising and sales promotion have become the symbol of American capitalism around the globe, they existed much before the founding of the United States.[4] Indeed ads for slaves and household goods occur in the written records of early civilizations. However, the distinct form of advertising today developed along with capitalist markets in the United States. This development can, for convenience, be roughly divided into four periods by the major wars of the United States: (1) War of Independence to the Civil War, (2) Civil War to World War I, (3) World War I to World War II, (4) post–World War II. Major market developments, partly triggered by and partly simultaneous with these wars, suggest these periods, each with distinct characteristics. However, some historical developments evolved slowly over time spilling across successive periods. We review each period in turn.

Advertising from U.S. Independence to the Civil War

As soon as the United States won its independence from England, a tremendous drive for self-sufficiency sprang up among its citizens. People wanted to

▼ **EXHIBIT 1-6.** Sampling of early Ivory soap ads.

Source: Courtesy of Procter & Gamble.

buy goods made in America, and shun foreign goods, especially those of British origin. The U.S. economy was still primarily a local and regional one. There was relatively little mass production and transport of industrial goods across regions. Most products used daily were produced either at home or in the village or city in which a consumer lived. This arrangement applied to meats, fruits, vegetables, dairy products, cosmetics, medicines and toiletries. For example, households made a soft soap by melting together fat drippings, common salt and lye. Lye itself could be obtained by leaching ashes from the stove and fireplace. The process was messy and the soap of unpredictable grade, but it was inexpensive and ensured self-sufficiency.

Most of the advertising of that time focused on three principal items that were extensively sought and traded: land, runaway slaves and transport. Ads for transport primarily announced the arrival and departure of ships and stagecoaches with their cargoes. The rest of the advertising announced the availability of basic commodities such as coffee, salt, clothes, tools and medicines. The primary means of advertising were posters, handbills and newspaper ads. Posters were displayed mainly at storefronts and near public meeting places.

Only a few newspapers existed. They limited ads to the length of 1 to 3 inches without pictures, somewhat like the classified ads today (see Exhibit 1-7).

This limit was partly due to a shortage of newsprint, and partly to avoid any disadvantage to small merchants who could not afford larger ads. Newspapers themselves consisted primarily of ads sprinkled with a little news, more like a small regional news/advertising booklet rather than the national newspapers of our times. Some newspapers also limited the term of a particular ad to two weeks. Creativity in newspaper advertising was channeled into designing attractive lines or catchwords that could be repeated in the space of an ad. These lines were probably the forerunners of today's taglines and slogans.

Advertising from the Civil War to World War I

Of the four periods, this period probably witnessed the most dramatic changes in markets, and thus in the practice of advertising. The Civil War partly initiated and partly ran concurrently with some major changes in U.S. markets.

First, the need for vast amounts of military equipment and uniforms on short notice stimulated the mass production of industrial goods. Second, the employment of men in the military prompted women to do more of the shopping relative to what they did before, and reduced their reluctance to buy ready-made products which were otherwise produced at home. For example, households shifted to the purchase of ready-made bread, soap, crackers and clothes. Third, massive expansion of the U.S.

railroads facilitated the transport of mass-produced goods. Total rail lines expanded from 35,000 miles in 1865 to 193,000 miles in 1900.[5]

Fourth, the population of the U.S. itself expanded at a rapid rate, almost doubling from 40 million to 76 million in the last 30 years of the nineteenth cen-

tury.[6] Many of the new people were immigrants. The increase in population was a tremendous stimulus to the economy and created a huge demand for basic and new consumer products.

Fifth, innovation in the production of gadgets, cosmetics, foods and toiletries changed people's

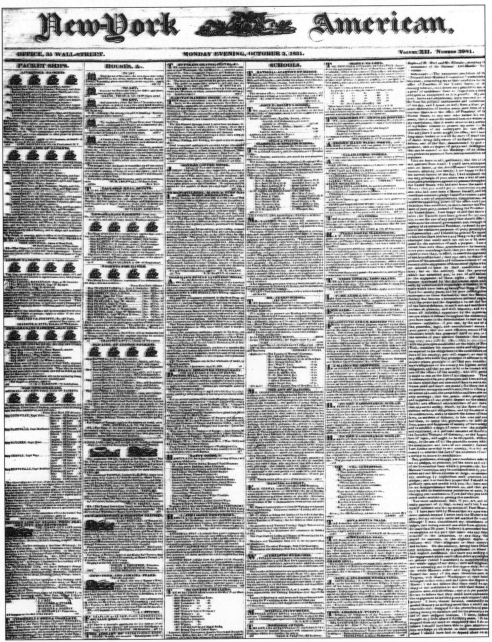

▲ **EXHIBIT 1-7.** Early newspaper ad.

▼ **EXHIBIT 1-8.** Ads for innovative new products.

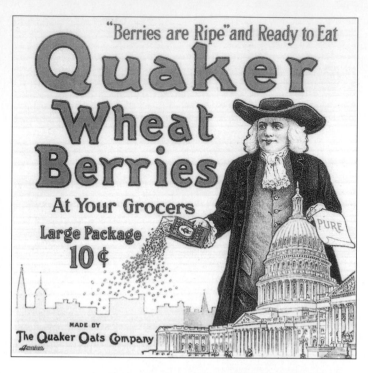

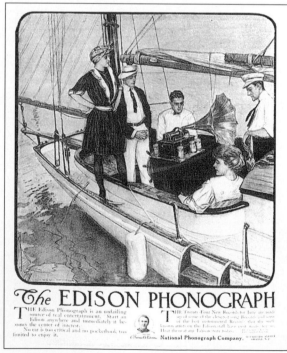

lifestyles radically (see Exhibit 1-8). For example, inventors were developing a number of gadgets that made office and household chores much more bear-able if not enjoyable. The sewing machine, type-writer, electric bulb, safety razor, Kodak camera, automobile, and some major kitchen appliances became popular during the second half of the nine-teenth and early decades of the twentieth centuries. Chemists formulated a number of basic but innovative cosmetics such as cold cream (Pond's), petroleum jelly (Vaseline) and talcum powder. These cosmetics together with the greater independence of women popularized the use, buying and marketing of cosmetics. Similarly, there were breakthroughs in the formulation and manufacture of foods and toiletries such as breakfast cereals, soft drinks, soaps and toilet tissue. These products transformed the lifestyle of consumers, and the structure of the economy.

These combined developments opened up the U.S. mass market for manufactured goods. The changes in the economy prompted radical changes in branding, media and advertising agencies.

Branding Mass production affected advertising in two important ways. First, with mass production came the ability of one manufacturer to serve huge markets. The mass producer could be immensely profitable even with a small margin on each item bought and sold. All the mass marketer needed was to produce an item a little superior to that of competitors, and for consumers to ask for that item. However, consumers would only ask for a particular item if the manufacturer could brand that item with a unique name. Thus, mass production and marketing could be very profitable if branded. The story of Ivory illustrates this point nicely.

Second, mass production required good packaging. Before that time, most items were sold generically at the local grocer's by units or weight as demanded by consumers. For example, crackers were sold by units from barrels, bacon in slabs cut to order, flour in paper sacks filled from bins and pickles individually from jars. The mass production of inexpensive paper and metal packages enabled manufacturers to wrap their products in sizes that matched household needs. That in turn enabled them to brand their packages with a unique design and name (see Exhibit 1-5). Advertising was the means to communicate to consumers the unique quality of products identified by unique packages and brand names.

The age of branding had begun. Some well known names today had their origins at that time: Borden's Eagle Brand Condensed Milk (1866), Campbell's Soup (1869), Coca-Cola (1886), Ivory Soap (1879), Levi Strauss Overalls (1873). That does not mean that every brand name of that time was guaranteed to survive. Probably hundreds of other names sprang up and died out as the years went by.[7]

Media This period saw radical changes in advertising in three media: magazines, mail catalogues and newspapers.

By the end of the Civil War, a few well-known magazines, such as *Harper's Illustrated Weekly*, existed. However, these magazines were primarily literary, providing an outlet for serialized novels. They were not open to advertising. F. G. Kinsman, a proprietary bottler of patent medicines in Augusta, Maine, realizing the potential of magazine advertising, began publishing weeklies and monthlies with the intent of carrying ads. By linking his periodicals to religion he was able to win quick circulation, and publish a large number of periodicals that appealed to different religious groups. Kinsman's success opened the literary magazines to advertising, and triggered entrepreneurs to publish many other types of magazines for the mass market. A new medium for advertising—magazines—had begun. By the end of the nineteenth century advertising accounted for two-thirds of the revenues of publishers. Newspaper advertising also accounted for about that proportion of newspaper revenues. However, the two media differed greatly in their sources of advertising revenue. For magazines, two-thirds of ad revenues came from national advertisers and one-third from local advertisers. For newspapers, the ratios were reversed.

Montgomery Ward was a traveling salesman for a Chicago dry goods store. From his experiences, he realized that if he could get a catalogue of available goods in the hands of individuals they would order their goods directly through the mail, eliminating salesmen and store owners. In 1872 with the help of $2,400 borrowed from a friend he issued his first catalogue, which measured 3.5" × 7" and had 100 pages. The idea worked as he had expected. With experience, Ward realized two important principles about print ads. First, an ad with a picture of the product increased sales relative to one with text only. Second, a color ad sold three times as many units as a black and white ad. Technology for mass printing in color was developed about that time. Ward not only pioneered modern catalogue advertising, but also introduced to advertising the important principles of including color and pictures of the product. The mailing of catalogues was facilitated by the establishment of inexpensive second-class postage in 1879 and rural delivery in 1890 by the United States Postal Service.

By the end of the nineteenth century, newspaper advertising had changed from the drab style of text announcements to the persuasive blend of copy and picture that we see today. This change was partly initiated by the freer availability of newsprint, and by the use of more vivid ads in magazines and catalogues.

Advertising Agencies Ad agencies of today had their origins in the advertising broker. In the mid-nineteenth century, as the market for goods and ads expanded beyond the narrow confines of the village and city, to the boundaries of states and the union, newspaper and magazine publishers needed to sell their space to a wider audience of manufacturers. The latter likewise needed to buy space in media outside of their own location. Ad brokers arose to fill this need. They booked advertising space in bulk, and promised publishers to sell it to advertisers at a set rate. Because brokers explicitly worked for the media, the latter allowed them a commission for their services. The brokers billed the advertisers the rate set by the publishers, but they paid the publishers only 85 percent of the billings. The remaining 15 percent was their commission. This was the beginning of the commission system. Note, that when calculated on the *publisher's revenues*, the 15 percent commission amounts to 17.66 percent.

As brokers gained in size and experience, and as manufacturers' needs became more sophisticated, brokers began to offer more services, including planning a mix of media for the ad, designing the ad, producing the ad and even providing some marketing research (see Exhibit 1-9). Thus they began to evolve into what are now called full-service agencies, working on behalf of advertisers rather than publishers. However, their compensation remained the commission system, creating a major conflict of interest in the agency: agencies worked for advertisers, ostensibly to maximize ad effectiveness; but their earnings were in proportion to the dollars spent on media space and time, as if they worked for publishers.

▼ **EXHIBIT 1-9.** Ad for an early advertising agency.

Source: Courtesy of N.W. Ayer & Sons, Inc.

Implications Tracing the history of advertising sheds light on some of the major controversies about the role of advertising in society today. This chapter cannot address all these controversies. However, it can evaluate the merit of the following criticisms of advertising:

- Advertising persuades people to buy products against their will.
- Advertising artificially differentiates products and creates brand loyalty.
- Advertising prevents new firms from entering the market.
- Advertising enables advertisers to raise prices relative to those of unadvertised products.

These criticisms or propositions about the role of advertising may be related. In particular, the first two may be causes of the latter two. For example, consumer loyalty may hinder new brands from entering the market. Lack of new market entrants may reduce competition and enable existing firms to raise the prices of their brands. Also, a consumer may be willing to pay a higher price for a brand to which he or she is loyal. So the higher price of advertised brands may be the result of the other propositions about advertising.

How valid are these criticisms of advertising? Well-designed experiments may be able to test the validity of these statements. However, conducting such experiments is difficult in the current environment because a researcher cannot easily remove the effects of firms' prior advertising from those of current advertising. Moreover, consumers' prior experience with these brands interferes with the effect of current advertising. Because of the difficulty of designing good experiments, these propositions are quite controversial, with adherents arguing for and against them. However, historical analysis can cast fresh light on these issues, because it shows how advertising evolved and affected various aspects of the economy. We focus on the last two issues, because they are important and probably effects of the first two.

While there may be some truth that advertising raises prices today, the claim is exaggerated and is based on a static analysis. It is indeed true that advertised products today are higher priced than unadvertised ones. So a naïve static analysis may deduce causality and conclude that advertising raises price. However, history reveals a different facet of advertising. In particular, history shows that advertising has three important characteristics that may not be visible from a static analysis.

First, advertising is a relatively inexpensive means by which a firm can announce to consumers the availability of a novel product. The Apple Macintosh ad is a good example. Indeed the history

▼ **EXHIBIT 1-10.** Sears, Roebuck and Co. ad.

SEE COLOR GALLERY

Source: Courtesy of Sears, Roebuck and Co.

of products in the United States is a riveting one in which new entrants constantly displace older ones that failed to innovate.[8] Thus rather than limiting entry, advertising is a force that helps innovative, superior products gain quick entry into markets. Some may argue that only large corporations can enter markets because of the heavy advertising required today. That is also inaccurate. Firms can enter on a small scale by using less expensive advertising media such as direct mail. That was the route used by the founders of Sears, Roebuck and Co. (Exhibit 1-10) in the late nineteenth century, as well as by Dell Computer Company 100 years later.

Second, large-scale advertising enables mass production which in turn enables a manufacturer to produce an item inexpensively. Advertising enables a small manufacturer in a small region to tap a huge national market. This large market enables the manufacturer to realize economies of scale. Such economies may enable a manufacturer of a superior product to sell it for less than an inferior rival product that has only a small regional market. It is such mass advertising combined with economies of scale in mass production that made safety razors, cameras, disposable diapers, personal computers, microwave ovens and hundreds of other products available to the mass market.

Third, advertising creates a brand identity for a manufacturer's product. Consumers then begin to demand that product, and retailers begin to stock it. The better the quality and advertising of the product, the more consumers demand it and the greater the firm's returns from advertising. As products are heavily advertised and demanded, retailers begin to compete among themselves to offer the product at a low price. They may even sell these products below cost, as **loss leaders,** to get people into stores. They may more than make up for the loss due to the extra profits from the traffic generated by the loss leaders. As a result, advertising could help to *reduce* the retail price of high-quality products, relative to what they would have been in the absence of advertising. Manufacturers also profit, in that they can sell more of the product, and charge retailers more for it. Thus advertised products lead to higher wholesale prices but lower retail prices. As a result, it is wholesalers and retailers whose margins are squeezed, and who may even be eliminated by advertising. However, consumers benefit overall.

Thus, the analysis of history throws light on an important facet of advertising, which may help to resolve some controversies about its role.

▲ **EXHIBIT 1-11.** Ad for a patent medicine.

cines worked primarily via the placebo effect, plus whatever temporary relief the alcohol and other sedatives provided. The makers of patent medicines were quick to realize that advertising was a means for them to become well known, distinguish themselves from competitors and gain a larger share of the market. By the beginning of the twentieth century patent medicines were one of the most heavily advertised categories.

Several developments changed the course of this industry. First, in the early part of the twentieth century, the patent medicine industry was thriving. However, the formula consisted primarily of alcohol with other ineffective or even dangerous ingredients. The ads for these medicines made numerous outlandish and untested claims. The U.S. government was concerned enough about the addictive and dangerous nature of these medicines that it passed the Pure Food and Drug Act in 1906. This act set standards for drugs, banned certain formulas, and was the first act to control certain forms of advertising. Second, advertisers realized that the outrageous claims of the medicine makers were giving advertising a bad name. Thus they initiated efforts at self-regulation. The Better Business Bureau, founded in 1912, is still the major body for self-regulation today. Third, state governments were also concerned about the spurious claims of the medicine ads, and they initiated laws for truth in advertising. Many of their laws were based on a model for state regulation of advertising, published by *Printer's Ink* in 1911, a leading advertising trade paper. Fourth, aspirin was introduced a little before World War I. For the first time U.S. consumers had an effective drug that was scientifically proven and easily experienced. Many of the claims of patent medicines seemed dubious in comparison. Under these multiple pressures, the patent medicine industry soon died out. But the regulatory climate it triggered became an integral part of U.S. advertising. Brands

Advertising from World War I to World War II

The most significant advertising development during this period was the growth of advertising regulation. Regulation was triggered primarily by the practices of the patent medicine industry. Patent medicines were one of the earliest categories to be mass marketed. The term *patent* did not mean that the product was formally protected with patents as is done today. Rather the term **patent medicine** was left over from colonial days, when an endorsement by the British crown was referred to as "a patent of royal favor." Because of the absence of well-tested drugs, makers of medicines sought credibility and distinction by obtaining royal approval. Thus as early as the eighteenth century, patent medicines began to be sold as cures for illnesses, aging and loss of appetite, or just as tonics for health and general well-being (see Exhibit 1-11). The medicines were extracts of roots and herbs in an alcohol base. Alcohol was used as a solvent or preservative, or for its temporary effects. Some medicines were harmless while others contained addictive substances such as cocaine, opium and morphine. The medi-

that survived had to resort to more careful advertising of substantiated claims (see Exhibit 1-12).

The 1930s witnessed the Great Depression, which ended when the economy geared up to meet the increased demands of World War II. Concern with the plight of consumers, some provocative books, as

▼ **EXHIBIT 1-12. Use of substantiated claims.**

Internal Revenue Service all created laws that controlled the practice of advertising.

Another major development was the start of systematic measurement of advertising. Before the late nineteenth century, most newspapers either did not know or did not reveal their real circulation. Figures that were revealed were often grossly inflated, or included unpaid issues delivered free or to consumers who had stopped their subscriptions. In 1914, the Audit Bureau of Circulation was founded to provide certified figures of circulation. The newspapers reluctantly agreed to cooperate. Also, due to the Great Depression, advertising revenues fell from $3.4 billion in 1929, to $1.3 billion in 1933. This shortfall in expenditures required a more efficient use of advertising resources, through greater precision in measuring audiences and ad effectiveness. At the same time, progress in communication technology made radio available to most American households. This was the first national medium for mass marketing and created a great opportunity for quickly introducing new products and developing brand names. However, the vastness of the medium required much better measuring systems than were previously available. These factors led to the development of commercial measurement systems. The most notable were A. C. Nielsen's indices of wholesale and retail sales, and of radio audiences, and George Gallup's polls of consumer sentiment.

Post—World War II Advertising

The U.S. economy expanded rapidly when World War II ended, as U.S. consumers made up for postponed purchases, and U.S. allies rebuilt their economies. Initially, advertising prospered with the good times. One of the major stimulants to advertising was the availability of national TV. This medium furthered many of the trends that had begun over a century ago. In particular, it made gaining access to the mass market,

well as some business excesses, triggered a new spate of regulations. The Pure Food, Drug and Cosmetic Act was passed in 1934, while the Wheeler-Lea Amendment to the Federal Trade Commission Act was passed in 1938. In addition, the Securities and Exchange Commission, the Post Office Laws and the Alcohol and Tobacco Tax Division of the

developing brand names, and introducing new products much easier. TV advertising was also much more effective at using two routes of persuasion, emotion and endorsements. The success of Apple Macintosh's "1984" ad is a testament to the power of emotional appeals in TV advertising.

Ten years or so after World War II, growth slowed. A large number of products reached maturity penetrating nearly 100 percent of the U.S. population. As technology became increasingly standardized, competitors found it hard to differentiate their products. They began price cutting, intense sales promotions, and overadvertising. The economy periodically suffered from recession. Pressures on the accountability of advertising increased.

These pressures increased the need for managers to more carefully evaluate advertising effectiveness and plan advertising expenditures. The age of research and testing had dawned. Advertising slowly became more of a science. A large number of research firms sprang up to more accurately measure the audiences of various media, to design the most effective advertising copy, and to test the effects of advertising on sales. Pressures mounted on advertising agencies to be compensated on performance rather than on their media billings. At the same time, greater expenditures on research in the natural and social sciences led to an explosion of knowledge. Knowledge gained in psychology, economics and marketing contributed to the scientific approach for practicing and evaluating advertising. Part II of the text draws on this knowledge to explain the science of communication; Part III to develop the principles of sales promotion.

Cultural developments also affected the practice of advertising. Most notably, there was greater sensitivity to stereotyping on the basis of race, gender, age, physical ability, country of origin and religion. In particular, advertisers realized that women were not the sole buyers of household goods such as appliances and groceries, while they were also buyers for so-called "male" products such as cars and beer (see Exhibit 1-13). Chapter 9 discusses these changes in greater depth.

During this period, perhaps the greatest impact on advertising arose from developments in marketing strategy. Managers realized that advertising was most effective when integrated into the marketing strategy of a product. Four major concepts of strategic marketing revolutionized the development of

marketing strategy: consumer orientation, segmentation, target marketing and positioning. Today these concepts pervade the practice of marketing, and are the foundation of advertising and sales promotion strategy.

FUNDAMENTALS OF MARKETING STRATEGY

Field of Dreams is a lyrical movie about a man's love for baseball. The movie's hero has a dream in which a baseball star tells him to build a baseball field in a beautiful but remote, and sparsely populated region. Will it attract players and spectators? The answer given by the baseball great is the alluring theme of the movie: "If you build it they will come." The theme echoes the words of Ralph Waldo Emerson: "If a man make a better mousetrap, the world will beat a path to his door."[9] In the movie, the hero gambles his few remaining resources to build the field, against the advice of bankers, family and friends. He meets with unexpected, heartwarming success, as baseball greats come to play in the field and thousands of spectators flock to it.

However, *Field of Dreams* is just that. A nice dream. A romantic story. A beautiful escape from reality. In the highly competitive, fast-paced and overcommunicated society of today, an attractive field will be no more than that. It will attract no one unless strategically marketed. Moreover, it will remain unknown unless cleverly promoted.

What makes for strategic marketing? It relies on four fundamental principles: consumer orientation, segmentation, targeting and positioning. The next section presents these fundamentals of marketing strategy and shows how they apply to promotion.

Consumer Orientation

Consumer orientation means setting consumer satisfaction as the primary goal of a firm, ahead of product design, sales, profits or any other goal. Why is such a priority important? The simple reason is that the consumer must want the product enough to buy it in order for the firm to make a sale. If the consumer does not want the product—or worse, does not know about it—the product will never sell. In the world today, spectators do not flock to beautiful but remote and unknown fields. Buyers do not beat a path to better but unknown mousetraps.

▼ **EXHIBIT 1-13.** The changing perception of women in advertising.

176   *THE SATURDAY EVENING POST*   *November 10, 1928*

SHE WANTS NO CLERKS... *to tell her what to buy...*

A nation-wide vogue in shopping that leaves women free to choose for themselves

"MOTHER steps out"—in these words a great magazine has pictured the woman of today, self-reliant as never before, sweeping aside old barriers, winning new freedom.

When she shops for foods, she wants to be *free to choose* for herself. Free to make her own knowledge count in giving her family more tempting food at lower cost. She needs no salesman to tell her what to buy.

And so, in a few swift years, she has made this special plan of shopping a nation-wide vogue. Only a few years ago the first of the Piggly Wiggly Stores was opened. Today they are being used by the women of more than 800 cities and towns.

Choice foods with prices plainly marked

Spread on the open shelves, the choice foods of the world are waiting for you to look over at Piggly Wiggly. There are no salesmen to urge you.

Slowly or quickly, just as you please, you examine this rich offering of delicacies and staples at Piggly Wiggly. Famous packages you know

Today 2,500,000 women come every day to Piggly Wiggly—to choose for themselves

of old—colorful fruits and vegetables, fresh and enticing.

You read the big square price tags that hang by every item. You compare values, you reach your own decisions purely on merit, uninfluenced by salesmen. And always, ideas for your menu come flashing, while you shop at Piggly Wiggly.

Less expense for groceries

Best of all you save money—regularly, certainly, on your groceries

when you deal at Piggly Wiggly. Lower prices are assured by our special economical plan of operation.

For dishes that please your family even more, for monthly savings that will astonish your husband—try this method of shopping. See for yourself why it has so swiftly become a nation-wide vogue. Visit the Piggly-Wiggly store in your neighborhood and choose for yourself.

Take what you please from the shelves at Piggly Wiggly. Just read the price tags and help yourself

The woman of today wants to choose for herself when she buys foods. With no clerks to persuade her, she makes her own decisions at Piggly Wiggly

More tempting foods—less expense! The choice foods of the world are waiting for you to examine at Piggly Wiggly

PIGGLY WIGGLY
STORES

The finest kinds of each food selected for you to choose from

A SERVICE NOW OFFERED IN OVER 800 CITIES AND TOWNS

© 1928. P. W. A. C.

Source: Piggly Wiggly Company, Memphis, TN.

This principle of consumer orientation is so basic that it might appear obvious to the reader. However, its importance comes from the fact that managers frequently forget about it. Some simple characteristics of human and organizational behavior lead marketers to overlook this apparently obvious principle: a self-serving bias, the success trap, or a product, sales and financial orientation.

Self-Serving Bias A **self-serving bias** is a misperception of reality that prompts individuals to believe that their own possessions are better than they really are. Firms are basically organizations of individuals. As such, the self-serving bias can also afflict managers of a firm, so that they have an inflated perception of their own products. Normally, a slightly inflated self-perception is healthy. However, the self-serving bias can hurt when managers think their products are more valuable than consumers think they are. Thus managers invest in these products in the mistaken belief that they will succeed in the market. Failure to test these beliefs against actual consumer perceptions will at some point in time, if not immediately, lead to products that fail to sell.

Success Trap At some time in the history of a firm, success may strike, leading to ballooning sales and profits. Success is a heady wine. It fills managers with pride and self-confidence and perpetuates the self-serving bias mentioned above. When a firm is on a roll with a hot product, managers tend to believe in their invincibility. They may not analyze the true causes of success; they may overestimate their own contribution, and underestimate the role of luck. Moreover, they can fall prey to the human tendency to project the present to the future, assuming that growth will continue for a long time. This response to success is called the **success trap.** However, growing markets draw many competitors and soon get crowded. Moreover, markets change, consumers can be fickle and growth does not last forever. Sooner or later, the market slows down. This is an immutable law of a finite world. Even though some managers realize these phenomena, the demands of rapid growth force them to pay too much attention to the exigencies of current demand, instead of scanning future consumer demand. When demand plateaus or shifts, managers who have not focused on consumers can be caught off guard with unfortunate results.

Product Orientation A **product orientation** is a focus on products as the key to success. This philosophy often afflicts managers in technological firms. These managers spend a huge amount of resources and time to keep abreast of technological progress but may fail to invest adequately in consumer research. It is consumers who buy products fashioned by technology. If consumers do not like or want the products, the products will fail, no matter how well engineered they are. Thus managers with a product orientation may end up with beautifully engineered products that no one wants. One reason that Apple was more successful early on, than many other manufacturers of personal computers, was the single-minded focus of Steve Jobs and his associates on consumer convenience rather than on technological power.

A *service orientation* may also afflict traditional service providers that cater to mental and spiritual development, such as educational and religious organizations. Such organizations may believe that the products they offer are so wholesome and desirable, that marketing them to their clients is unnecessary. Religious organizations may believe that marketing their services may dilute their message. However, failure to design services that fill clients' needs, and failure to communicate them to clients, may doom the service providers with a loss to their customers.

Sales Orientation A **sales orientation** is a focus on sales as the key to success. It can emerge from the pressures of competition, and managers' legitimate concern to motivate and reward productive sales staff. In many competitive markets, firms' survival depends on fighting for small fractions of the market from month to month, or even day to day. Managers often set up sales-based incentives, in order to reward sales staff who are productive, and motivate those who are not. Further, managers may set up complex bureaucracies to monitor incentive systems. As this orientation takes hold through the firm, managers may overlook the interests of the consumers who buy the product. In the long run, if consumers are unhappy or if their needs change, a firm with a sales orientation will fail to meet its sales targets, however great its incentives.

For example, in the mid-1990s, the state of California accused Sears of deceptive auto-service practices in which consumers were steered into unnecessary brake service. How did a company reputed for its honesty fall prey to such practices?

The root cause may have been an incentive system that rewarded auto service representatives for the sales generated, rather than for customer satisfaction. Overenthusiastic sales representatives probably talked trusting customers into repairs they never really needed.

Profit Orientation A **profit orientation** is a focus on short-term profits at the cost of long-term consumer welfare. Several factors lead managers to adopt a short-term orientation. First, managers are under constant pressure from shareholders to keep the firm's stock price high. For that purpose, managers need to keep margins high and costs low. Second, junior or middle managers are often rewarded by short-term sales or profits. Many do not even stay at a firm long enough to be motivated by long-term sales and profits. In this environment, managers might favor products and strategies that do well in the short term, but are not tailored to long-term consumer welfare.

For example, by the late-1970s IBM dominated the mainframe computer market with a line of highly respected and powerful products. The firm won a reputation for being a technological leader and a secure investment for the future. However, company managers were so eager to protect the sales and profits of mainframe computers that they were reluctant to enter the personal computer market. They ultimately did so only through an independent subsidiary, located in Florida, far from the parent company's headquarters. Even when the subsidiary successfully marketed personal computers, its progress was restricted for fear of hurting the sales and profits of mainframe computers. As a result, by the mid-1990s, IBM seemed like a giant rich with resources, but unable to match quick and innovative rivals who were tuned in to consumer demand.

Summary Our discussion suggests that when developing marketing strategy, attention to consumer needs must take precedence over attention to products, sales or profits. The consumer orientation is vital not only for marketing strategy, but also for promotional strategy. Thus when designing promotion strategy, focusing on consumers' needs must precede the development of the creative. Indeed, just as the glamour of technological sophistication can distract managers from the needs of consumers, the glamour of creative design can distract managers from communicating a coherent message that appeals to consumers.

Segmentation

As a market increases in size, it tends to get more diverse including a variety of consumers with different needs. It becomes more difficult for a firm to satisfy this market with a single homogeneous product. **Market segmentation** is the conceptual breakup of a market into groups of relatively homogeneous consumers, to better serve each of them. The opposite of market segmentation is **mass marketing,** where a firm sells a standard product to the whole market. Market segmentation is a natural outcome of a consumer orientation. Because consumers differ in their needs, a consumer orientation will try to identify these differences and satisfy them adequately. Better satisfied consumers provide firms with two other very important advantages. First, they provide a more loyal stream of future purchases that can better withstand attacks by competitors. Second, they are willing to pay a premium over the prevailing price for the product that better meets their needs.

The major question that managers face is how to determine market segments. There are five bases for segmentation: demographic, geographic, usage, psychographic and benefit segmentation. These bases are listed in order of increasing difficulty of use, and increasing reward for firms that do so.

Demographic segmentation includes variables such as gender, age, education, income, race or household size. This basis of segmentation is likely to be the most obvious to marketers. For example, a marketer is likely to design different styles of clothes for men, women, teens or children. Exhibit 1-14 presents a Gerber ad that describes different products for children of different age groups.

Geographic segmentation involves identifying differences in demand due to location. Geographic differences in demand may arise due to topography, climate, culture or nationality. However, differences can also exist at a more refined level such as between cities in a region, or even between stores within a city. The latter type of segmentation can be useful to a manager of a grocery chain who has to choose which one of thousands of categories to stock and promote each week (see Exhibit 1-15).

Geodemographic segmentation is a type of segmentation that is based on combined demographic

▼ **EXHIBIT 1-14.** Segmentation by age group.

Source: Courtesy of Gerber Products Company.

The most important of these schemes are ACORN, ClusterPLUS, PRIZM and MicroVision.

Usage segmentation involves identifying groups of consumers with distinct patterns of product usage. One rationale for usage segmentation is the finding that the majority of sales for a product come from a small segment of consumers (see Exhibit 1-16). Therefore, managers can use a firm's resources more efficiently by concentrating on those consumers rather than on the whole market. On the other hand, if a firm wishes to expand the market for its product because of an improvement in either features or price, it can focus its efforts on the large pool of nonusers. Another rationale for usage segmentation is the finding that a large fraction of consumers tend to be loyal to a single brand (see Exhibit 1-17), while others regularly switch among brands depending on price. Segmentation along these lines can be very useful for a firm, because defensive marketing (retaining loyal consumers) can be several times less expensive than offensive marketing (winning over loyal consumers of other brands). A third reason for usage segmentation is the finding that loyal consumers of a brand tend to be much more responsive to the brand's advertising than are those who are not regular users.[11]

Psychographic or **lifestyle segmentation** is based on people's lifestyles. The rationale for psychographic segmentation is that people from different regions and demographic backgrounds may still have certain similarities in things they value and the way they like to live their lives. These similarities create demand for distinct products and distinct methods of shopping for them. For example, Exhibit 1-18 on page 25, shows an ad for Jockey underwear designed for active women who might belong to a variety of races, age groups or professions.

The value of psychographic segmentation may be gauged from the example of General Motors. Beginning with the efforts of Alfred Sloan, General Motors segmented the U.S. auto market by socio-economic status, and differentiated cars on a price-status basis for each segment. The strategy led GM

and geographic data.[10] The data can be obtained from public data sources, such as the U.S. Census, or from periodic surveys developed for the purpose. The database contains demographic characteristics of households nested within geographic regions. The demographic information is used to characterize the geographic clusters and group them into segments. This type of segmentation is particularly useful for retail establishments and services in some way bound by location. It enables them to target regions most suitable for their product. The segmentation is also useful to any organization that wants to send a standard mailing to all households in a geographic location. Various market research firms now develop standard geodemographic segmentation schemes.

▼ **EXHIBIT 1-15. Segmentation by grocery store.** Micromarketers can now target a product's best customers and the stores where they're most likely to shop. Here's one company's analysis of three products' best targets in the New York area.

Hitting the Bull's-Eye

Brand	Heavy User Profile	Life style and Media Profile	Top Three Stores
Peter Pan Peanut Butter	Households with kids headed by 18- 54-year-olds, in suburban and rural areas	■ Heavy video renters ■ Go to theme parks ■ Below-average TV viewers ■ Above-average radio listeners	**Freedtown Super Market** 3350 Hempstead Turnpike Levittown, NY **Pathmark Supermarket** 3635 Hempstead Turnpike Levittown, NY **King Kullen Market** 596 Stewart Ave., Bethpage, NY
Stouffers Red Box Frozen Entrees	Households headed by people 55 and older, and upscale suburban households headed by 35- 54-year-olds	■ Go to gambling casinos ■ Give parties ■ Involved in public activities ■ Travel frequently ■ Heavy newspaper readers ■ Above-average TV viewers	**Dan's Supreme Super Market** 59-62 188th St., Flushing, NY **Food Emporium** Madison Ave. & 74th St., NYC **Waldbaum Supermarket** 196-35 Horace Harding Blvd., Flushing, NY
Coors Light Beer	Head of household, 21-34, middle to upper income, suburban and urban	■ Belong to a health club ■ Buy rock music ■ Travel by plane ■ Give parties, cookouts ■ Rent videos ■ Heavy TV sports viewers.	**Food Emporium** 1496 York Ave., NYC **Food Emporium** First Ave. & 72nd St., NYC **Gristodes Supermarket** 350 E. 86th St., NYC

Source: Michael McCarthy, "Marketers Zero In On Their Customers," *The Wall Street Journal*, March 18, 1991, B1. Reprinted by permission of *The Wall Street Journal*, © 1991 Dow Jones & Company, Inc. All rights reserved worldwide.

to dominate the U.S. auto market until the 1970s. However, management guru Peter Drucker argues that since then, U.S. consumers have bought cars to suit their varying lifestyles, rather than to fit their socioeconomic status. The success of sports utility vehicles and minivans are evidence of this trend. He attributes the decline of General Motors to its failure

to grasp this important shift in the basis of segmentation.[12]

Benefit segmentation involves determining market segments based on the unique benefits that consumers seek from the product. Consumers may have different primary motives in buying the same product. For example, one person may buy a toothpaste

▼ EXHIBIT 1-16. **Percentage of 1 month's sales due to heavy users.**

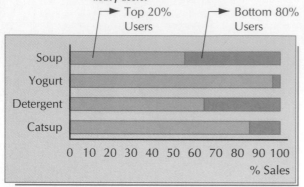

Source: Reprinted by permission Schmittlein, David C., Lee G. Cooper and Donald G. Morrison "Truth in Concentration in the Land of (80/20) Laws," *Marketing Science*, Vol. 12, No. 2, Spring, 1993, 167–183, figure based on article. © 1987, The Institute of Management Sciences and the Operations Research Society of America (currently INFORMS), 2 Charles St., Suite 300, Providence, RI 02904 USA.

to prevent cavities, another to maintain fresh breath, and a third to keep teeth white (see Exhibit 1-19). This is perhaps the most subtle basis for segmentation, but one that has the greatest potential for firms. The reason is that as products and consumers evolve, the benefits of those products and consumers' perceptions of them change. Over time, the product could take on new meanings or uses never intended by the original inventor. Keeping abreast of the market to find out these new benefits that consumers seek can give a firm a competitive advantage.

Just as in marketing, segmentation has become a fundamental concept in advertising strategy. However, the basis of segmentation in advertising is not very sophisticated. Segmentation is used primarily when developing the media plan. For that purpose, strategists primarily use a crude form of geographic and demographic segmentation. Thus there is great potential to use more sophisticated bases of segmentation such as psychographic, usage and benefit segmentation. Chapter

15 describes the current practice of segmentation in media planning, and how it can be improved by the use of more sophisticated methods.

Targeting

Once managers have identified market segments, they must decide whether to serve all segments, some segments or none at all. **Mass marketing** is a strategy in which managers market one standard product for the whole market. **Target marketing** is a strategy in which managers identify and market variations of a product to various segments. **Niche marketing** is a strategy in which managers identify and market a unique product to a very small segment or niche. What criteria should managers use to choose between these strategies? Three criteria are particularly important: segments should be measurable, of adequate size and accessible.

Measurable means that managers can identify variables to estimate the size and potential of demand, and the types of consumers in each segment. A convenient means of identifying segments is

▼ EXHIBIT 1-17. **Percentage of consumers who are loyal to one brand.**

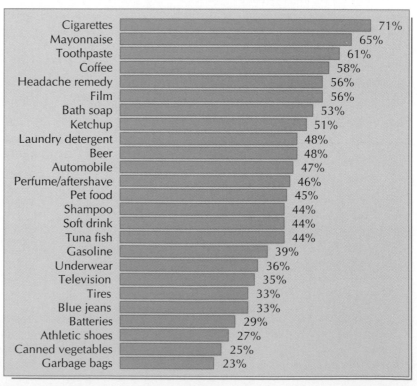

Source: Ronald Alsop, "Brand Loyalty Is Rarely Blind Loyalty," *The Wall Street Journal*, Oct. 19, 1989, p. B1. Reprinted by permission of *The Wall Street Journal*, © 1989 Dow Jones and Company, Inc. All rights reserved worldwide.

▼ **EXHIBIT 1-18.** Jockey ad based on psychographic segmentation.

Source: JOCKEY, JOCKEY FOR HER, and Half JOCKEY FIGURE DESIGN are trademarks of and used with permission of Jockey International, Inc.

based on multiple criteria, such as the one in Exhibit 1-15.

Adequate size means that the segment is large enough to enable profitable marketing. Marketing different products to different segments involves higher costs in terms of designing, producing, stocking and distributing a greater variety of products, each on a smaller scale. Marketing to different segments also involves higher costs in terms of developing a distinct image for each product and advertising it to each segment. Thus segmentation leads to diseconomies of scale. In contrast, a mass marketing strategy is less costly because it achieves economies of scale by marketing one standard product to the whole market. Such a strategy is especially useful during the growth stage of a product life cycle when demand is strong and undifferentiated. For example, it was the mass marketing strategy of Henry Ford's Model T that opened up the mass market for automobiles.[13] On the other hand, target and niche marketing are especially useful once a market matures or ceases to grow. Such a strategy can reduce competition, create customer loyalty and enable growth. It could thus lead to higher prices and sales for the company. Consider the following research findings:

- The narrower the niche, the lower the competition. Thus the firm would have to spend less on fighting the competition, and could charge a higher price. For example, one study found entrepreneurs profitably served very narrow markets, such as consulting on using rare granite for construction or selling premium makeup mirrors.[14]
- The narrower the niche, the more homogeneous the customer base. The firm would thus have better satisfied and more loyal customers, who

by demographics and brand usage. Note however, that using demographics to *measure* segments based on the other criteria (such as benefits sought) is not the same as demographic segmentation. For example, Lee Jeans uses demographic segmentation when it designs different jeans for boys and girls. However, it uses benefit segmentation when it designs better-fitting jeans to suit segments of consumers who distinctly prefer comfort, even if it uses age or gender to identify that segment. An ideal analysis should provide a profile of target segments

▼ **EXHIBIT 1-19.** A toothpaste brand offering benefits.

PEARL DROPS® TOOTHPASTE HAS A
TRIPLE ACTION WHITENING SYSTEM

If a tooth whitener doesn't get your teeth their whitest, what's the point?
PEARL DROPS toothpaste has a **Triple Action Whitening System** that
helps get your teeth their whitest. You can actually feel **PEARL DROPS** toothpaste help whiten your teeth.

A BURST OF WHITE YOU CAN ACTUALLY FEEL

would be willing to buy more of the product, or pay a higher price for it.[15]

■ Niches have a tendency to grow, sometimes even into large mass markets. Indeed, many standard consumer products today started off as specialty products marketed to narrow niches. Examples include diet soft drinks (to diabetics), disposable diapers (to travelers), video recorders (to professionals) and personal computers (to computer buffs).[16]

Accessible means that managers can reach the target segment with advertising using one or another medium of communication. Because of the immense size of the United States, the variety of media, and limited advertising budgets, efficiently accessing target segments is essential for success. Currently advertisers use a fairly simple method for choosing media to access segments. It involves the use of a few geographic, demographic and usage variables. For example, advertisers may determine that women aged 18 to 34 consume more yogurt, as well as watch more "Murphy Brown," so the latter TV program is chosen for an ad. However, this approach ignores other important factors, such as other users of yogurt, other viewers of "Murphy Brown," viewers' response to advertising and users' brand loyalty. Chapter 15 explains the current procedure and its limitations in greater depth, and shows some better methods for accessing target segments.

Positioning

Positioning is projecting a distinct image for the product in the consumer's mind.[17] Today a plethora of brands compete in every one of hundreds of categories. For example, pharmaceutical firms introduced 48 new products in a total of 85 different flavors or sizes in the category of cold or cough remedies in one year alone.[18] Thus for a consumer to **evoke** or spontaneously think of every brand name when choosing a product is quite impossible. Evoking a brand name is just the first step in the consumer's choice of brands. Yet getting consumers to take this preliminary step is a big challenge for managers in today's competitive and crowded market. To increase its chances of being evoked, a brand should have a unique image that stands for some unique benefits. For example, Avis is the rental car company that tries really hard to please consumers; Lee Jeans is the brand that fits; Dove, the gentle soap. Consumers are likely to think of the brand the moment they desire those benefits. How do managers identify such a unique position for a brand?

One approach for doing so is perceptual mapping. **Perceptual mapping** is a procedure for graphically depicting consumers' image of competing brands in the market, together with consumers' preferences or **ideal points**. Consumers with similar ideal points form a segment. The axes of the graph are called dimensions, and represent the key attributes of the product being analyzed. For example, taste (sweet to bitter) and calories (light to heavy) may be the key attributes of beer. Perceptual maps are very useful for marketers because they give a simple pictorial representation of a fairly complex market of competing brands that serve different consumer segments.

The key question is, how does one develop such perceptual maps? There are two ways to do so. A normative approach is to graphically portray what managers perceive to be the current situation. The problem with this approach is that it may just confirm managers' current biases, and may not provide any new insight. It may also be invalid. An alternative, better approach is a descriptive one based on consumer research and statistical analysis of research data. A standard technique for perceptual mapping is called *multidimensional scaling*. This technique uses a variety of data to represent in a single map consumers' ideal points, perceptions of brands and criteria for choosing a brand.

Good perceptual maps can reveal promising untapped consumer segments. In many established consumer markets, the most promising segments are likely to be small, because large segments are already crowded with competitors. So, discovering and targeting a narrow niche may ensure little competition and easy entry. Yet niches can grow to be hugely profitable. For example, when Procter & Gamble first promoted Ivory, it targeted a narrow market niche that wanted very pure soap. A hundred years later that niche had grown to become the $1.5 billion market for bar soap. In that time, Procter & Gamble dominated the market with brands such as Ivory (gentleness), Safeguard (deodorizing), Camay (moisturizing) and Zest (refreshing).[19] In 1991, when Lever Brothers wanted to expand its share of the market, it again targeted an untapped market niche that wanted a soap that was *both* moisturizing and deodorizing. The positioning was sharp, and the niche unexpectedly large. Within six months of introduction, Lever's new soap called Lever 2000 had won 8.4 percent of the market.[20]

The positioning that managers adopt for a brand is the foundation for the entire promotional program. The positioning must inspire the theme for the ad.

The unique selling proposition or *theme* of an ad is the message about the brand that managers wish to communicate to consumers. It is sometimes referred to as the tagline. Typically, but not always, the tagline is the last line of an ad and embodies the theme. The repetition of a theme over time can imprint the image of the brand in consumers' minds. For example, the tagline, "When E.F. Hutton talks people listen," established E.F. Hutton as a broker that commanded investors' respect for its insight into financial markets. It was so effective that the line is remembered long after the company collapsed in scandal.

A major danger during the process of developing ads is that art directors and copywriters strive so hard to be creative that they lose sight of the brand's positioning and the ad's theme. Creativity can make the difference between an ad's being either noticed or ignored among the hundreds of messages with which consumers are bombarded. Yet, a creative ad is fairly worthless if it does not embody the theme and clearly communicate the positioning of the brand. On the other hand, creativity can be very effective when based on a good positioning strategy. In 1994, Coca-Cola initiated a radically new ad campaign with 30 different ads, starring polar bears. Commentators praised the sheer creativity of the campaign. However, some criticized the variety of ads which could diffuse the image of Coke and confuse consumers. The critics overlooked the fact that beyond the variety, the ads portrayed a hip, trendy image for Coke, and were linked by a single tagline, "Always Coca-Cola. Always."[21]

MARKETING AND PROMOTIONAL PLANNING

This section outlines how managers should make marketing and promotion plans. It shows how the various concepts we have discussed fit together in a situation. It also shows where promotion fits in the overall process of marketing planning. The first subsection presents the various goals that advertising and sales promotion can achieve, while the next explains the process of choosing goals and developing strategy.

Goals of Promotion

Why do firms use advertising and sales promotion? What goals do they serve? It would take an entire book to fully answer these questions. However, a

▼ EXHIBIT 1-20. Goals of advertising and sales promotion.

Goal Category	Type of Response	Goal
Tactical	Cognitive	Attract attention
		Inform
		Remind
	Affective	Increase liking
		Improve attitude
	Conative	Persuade
		Reduce dissonance
		Instill loyalty
Strategic	Brand choice	Generate trial
		Trigger switching
		Establish repurchase
	Purchase intensity	Increase stockpiling
		Increase purchase frequency
		Increase quantity consumed
	Market	Grow, hold, harvest share of market
Ultimate	Accounting	Increase sales
		Increase price
		Increase profits

summary of the goals of advertising and sales promotion provides an excellent overview of their scope and potential. We can classify these goals into three broad categories: tactical goals, strategic goals and ultimate goals. Each in turn can be further broken down into subordinate goals (see Exhibit 1-20). The three categories of goals are related to each other by a certain hierarchy. *Hierarchy* means an order of importance in which a goal lower down is a means to meet one higher up. Thus each goal is not an end in itself but really a means by which managers can achieve a higher goal. The hierarchy listed in Exhibit 1-20 is probably the most plausible one. However, as Chapter 13 explains, the same hierarchy may not apply to all circumstances.

Tactical Goals The term *tactical* is used to refer to an immediate or short-term perspective. The tactical goals can be further divided into cognitive, affective or conative goals. The term *cognitive* means relating to thoughts, *affective* means relating to feelings, and *conative* means relating to action.

Cognitive Goals The cognitive goals of promotion are to draw attention to the brand or the ad, inform consumers about it, and remind them about it.

Drawing the attention of consumers is the very first step a promoter needs to take, and is the subject of Chapter 5. Much consumer decision making depends on how they use information, the subject of Chapter 6. These two chapters explain how managers can achieve the cognitive goals of promotion. The power of Ivory's first tagline, "99 and 44/100 percent Pure" was probably due to the fact that that one sentence met all three of these goals. It drew attention by making a bold, unusual claim; it was quite informative; and by repeating this terse assertion, it became memorable.

Affective Goals The affective goals are to increase consumers' liking for the brand and improve their attitude toward it. These two affective variables are not the most important ones. Indeed, Chapter 7 describes the wide range of feelings that ads can arouse in consumers. However, liking and attitude are often treated as important criteria that determine the likelihood of behavioral change; thus Chapter 14 describes how researchers measure these variables and use them to predict behavior change.

Conative Goals The conative goals are to persuade consumers of the merits of a brand, reduce dissonance about it and instill loyalty for the brand. For example, consumers need to be persuaded of the merits of a new or high-priced brand before they buy it. The term *dissonance* refers to doubts that a consumer may have about a brand. Such doubts may arise because of the price or performance of the brand, feedback received from friends, or information about rival brands. Promotions need to address and assuage such doubts. Most importantly, promotion needs to instill loyalty for a brand among new buyers, and retain it among regular buyers.

Strategic Goals A *strategic goal* is a moderate- to long-term goal based on a deeper understanding of the dynamics of the market, than that required by a tactical goal. Strategic goals can be further classified depending on whether they affect the pattern or intensity of consumer choices, or the position of a brand in the market.

In terms of pattern of choices, a manager may want to generate trial, trigger brand switching, or establish repurchase. *Trial* is a consumer's first purchase of the brand. Every subsequent purchase of the same brand is called a *repurchase*. The purchase of another brand from that purchased on the previous occasion is called a *switch*. The separation of pattern of choices into trial, repurchase and switching allows a manager to decompose a brand's appeal to consumers. Trial indicates the propensity of a consumer to experience a new brand, repurchase indicates the depth of consumer loyalty for a brand, while switching indicates a brand's pull relative to a rival's. For example, Lever Brothers was confident enough about the merits of its new Lever 2000 that it sent samples of the bar to half of U.S. households. The promotion paid off handsomely. In that environment, Lever's advertising had to aim for repurchasing among those who tried the brand, while Procter & Gamble's for a switch back to its brand.

In terms of the intensity of choice, a manager could use promotions to increase purchase frequency, stockpiling or consumption. These three ideas are distinct though not independent. *Purchase frequency* refers to how often a brand is purchased, *consumption* refers to how much is used up, and *stockpiling* refers to how much is stored in a time period. Higher consumption is clearly the most desirable of the three goals. Why would a firm have the other two goals? The reason may be their interdependence. More frequent purchases of a brand could lead consumers to keep a higher inventory which in turn may lead to higher consumption.[22] For example, consumers who have stocked up on crackers are more likely to snack on crackers than are those who have stocked up on potato chips. Indeed some health-conscious consumers may intentionally not succumb to promotions, even buying foods in smaller, less economic quantities to avoid overconsuming.[23] Even if consumers do not consume more of a product that they stockpile, their stockpiling of the brand causes a shift of inventory costs from manufacturer to consumers. Most importantly, stockpiling of a manufacturer's brand may preempt the purchasing and consuming of a rival's brand.

In terms of market position, a manager may use promotions to increase or hold market share relative to competitors'. The market share of a brand is the sales of a brand divided by the sales of all competitors in the market. Tracking market share is particularly important in mature categories when brands are very similar and the overall market is not growing. In that case, any improvement in a brand's position can only come at the cost of another brand's. In such circumstances, merely holding share may be an important goal. Increases in market share can be costly and lead to self-destructive wars among competitors. Moreover, because keeping a loyal consumer is several times less expensive than winning over a new consumer from a rival, promotion just to hold market share can be a wise goal.

Ultimate Goals When we sum up the choices of individual consumers at the level of the firm, we get the accounting measures of a firm's performance: sales, revenues and profits. The sum of all quantities of a product purchased by consumers within a particular time period gives *sales in units*. The product of unit sales and the price per unit gives *revenues*. *Profits* are revenues less costs. Managers often plan promotions to meet sales or profit goals rather than various strategic goals, because sales and profits are more easily tracked.

For most organizations, long-run profitability is theoretically the *ultimate goal*. For long-run profitability consumers must be sufficiently satisfied with a firm's product that they keep buying it. Managers can achieve this goal by increasing consumer satisfaction, increasing sales, or increasing price. For noncommercial organizations, profit may not be important, so consumer welfare and sales are the ultimate long-term goals of promotion. The term *sales* is used here broadly to encompass a variety of aggregate measures of change in behavior. For example, political organizations target votes, parks target visits, churches target attendance, schools target graduations, and traffic safety organizations target accident reductions.

The Process of Planning Promotions

Exhibit 1-21 shows the marketing planning process as a hierarchy of stages, in each of which managers must make certain decisions. The term *hierarchy* is used to mean an order of importance of decisions and not the strict sequence in which managers make those decisions.

As argued earlier, managers should begin the marketing process with research on consumer needs.

▼ EXHIBIT 1-21. Marketing planning process.

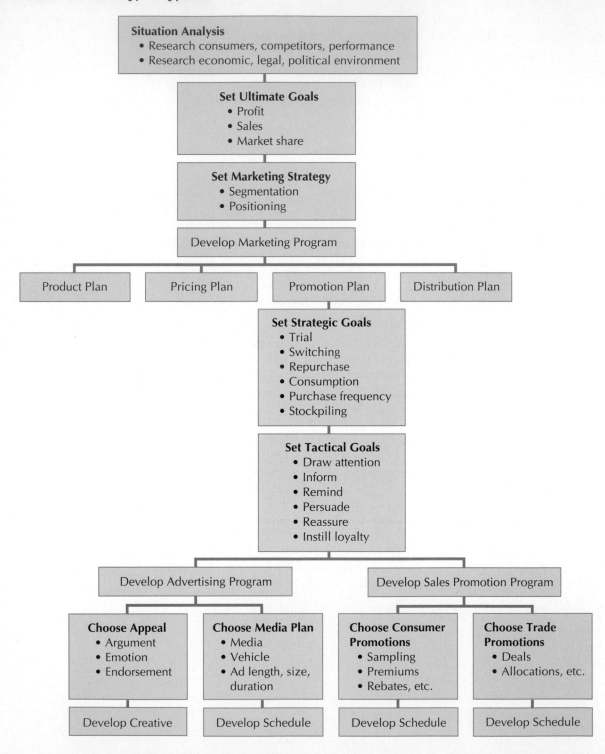

However, to get a complete grasp of the firm's options, managers should also include research on competitors; the firm's past performance; and the economic, legal and political environment. This set of research activities is called the *situation analysis*. A good situation analysis reveals the problems and opportunities that the firm faces, as well as its strengths and weaknesses. It then suggests the marketing plan that managers should adopt to overcome problems or exploit opportunities.

A manager's first step in planning is to set goals. Managers need to set the ultimate goals of the marketing plan in terms of profits and sales. They can then translate these goals into the share of the market and rate of growth they want relative to competitors. Those goals should then lead to the marketing strategy in terms of segmentation and positioning. The strategy should then prompt the appropriate marketing program.

The marketing program consists of four major managerial tasks: planning the product, price, promotion and distribution. Most marketing books give a good introduction to these four tasks. This book focuses on promotion only. However, because the promotion plan must be consistent with the other three parts of the marketing plan, the book explains the relationship between promotional planning and the rest of the marketing plan. Chapter 9 shows how promotional planning is closely related to the product's pricing strategy. Chapters 10 and 11 show how the promotional plan needs to be executed with and through the distribution system. Chapter 18 shows how promotion planning depends intrinsically on the product's life cycle.

The manager's first step in developing the promotional plan is to set strategic goals. The strategic goals are the pattern of trial, switching and repurchasing and the level of consumption, purchase frequency and stockpiling that the manager wants from consumers. The strategic goals influence the tactical goals which in turn influence the promotional program. The promotional program itself consists of two major components, the advertising program and the sales promotion program.

The advertising program involves choice of an appropriate appeal and media for the ad. The *ad appeal* is the type of persuasion that the manager uses to communicate the ad's message. Chapter 4 introduces the principles of persuasion. The three most important types of appeals are argument, emotion and endorsements. Chapters 6, 7 and 8, respectively, detail these three types of appeals. The ad appeal is the platform for developing the content of the ad, such as the copy, picture, sound and color. For the *media plan,* managers must decide where, when and in which media to place the ad, as well as

how long or how large to make it. Chapters 15 and 16 cover this topic.

The sales promotion program consists of choosing the mix of consumer and trade promotions, and their impact on retail promotions. These topics are covered in Chapters 10, 11 and 12. The final stage of the advertising plan is the manager's choice of a schedule and budget. The schedule is the frequency and time sequence in which the manager places ads. This topic is closely related to the advertising budget and is covered in Chapter 17.

This process of planning is an ideal one to which managers should aspire. It describes the hierarchy or importance of various activities, but not necessarily the sequence of actions. In any ongoing firm, the various stages of planning are not isolated activities that flow in a strict sequential fashion. Rather, they flow into each other, so that managers may revisit a higher stage decision after addressing one lower down in the hierarchy. Further, in many organizations, senior managers make global decisions while junior managers make specific decisions. However, plans are often sent up and down an organization, with junior and senior managers responding to feedback from each other. As such, the time order of decisions is not rigid. The hierarchy in Exhibit 1-21 shows the importance of various decisions and their likely impact on each other.

SUMMARY

Promotion consists primarily of advertising and sales promotion. Advertising is communicating a firm's offer to customers by paid media time or space. Sales promotion is a program that makes a firm's offer more attractive to buyers and requires buyer participation. The success of promotion strategy depends partly on the scientific judgment of managers, partly on the native creativity of individuals, and partly on luck. Science does not substitute for creativity. Rather it helps promotion strategists, art directors and copywriters use their creative skills productively. Science reduces the need to rely on luck. This book describes the science of advertising and sales promotion as best we know it today.

Promotion constitutes a $161 billion industry today and accounts for about 2 percent of the U.S. gross national product. The principal agents involved in promotion are promoters, agencies, media owners, distributors and consumers. Every individual person or organization is likely to be a promoter at some time or other. However, a few firms with large shares of consumer markets consistently dominate as heavy spenders on promotion.

While advertising and sales promotion existed much before the founding of the United States, the distinct form of advertising today developed along with U.S. capitalist markets. This development can, for convenience, be roughly divided into four periods by the major U.S. wars: (1) War of Independence to the Civil War; (2) Civil War to World War I; (3) World War I to World War II; (4) post–World War II. A review of the history of advertising and sales promotion provides an excellent background to the field. It gives a good feel for how various products and advertising practices developed over the years. It indicates the resilience of certain systems, suggests causes of certain phenomena and hints at future trends. It also sheds light on some of the major controversies about the role of advertising in society today.

One of the most important impacts on the role of promotion was the development of marketing strategy. Promotion can be most effective when it is integrated into marketing strategy. Four major concepts of marketing strategy are most relevant for the study of promotion: consumer orientation, segmentation, target marketing and positioning. Today these concepts pervade the practice of marketing, and they are the foundation of advertising and sales promotion strategy.

QUESTIONS

1. What was the impact of the Apple Macintosh "1984" TV ad? Why did it have such an impact?
2. What key events fashioned the mass market for consumer products in the United States?
3. How did branding make a difference in the pricing, advertising and distribution of goods in the nineteenth century?
4. Many critics of advertising claim that it artificially inflates the prices of branded products. Discuss the merits of this argument.
5. What is a consumer orientation? Why is it vital to marketing success?

6. Are the various bases of segmentation really different, or are they just different starting points for the same process? Explain.
7. Target marketing basically involves a trade-off between effectiveness and efficiency. Discuss.
8. Firms are often advised to go where the market is. In practice that means targeting large mass markets. Is this a good strategy? Why?
9. Is positioning a battle for the product, the market or the mind? Explain.
10. What goals can advertising and promotions achieve in the market today? How do these goals relate to each other?

NOTES

1 *Advertising Age*. (1995), "50 Years of TV Advertising" (Spring), 10–54; Fawcett, Adrienne Ward (1995), "The 50 Best," *Advertising Age* (Spring), 36; Bradley, Johnson (1994), "10 Years After '1984': The Commercial and the Product That Changed Advertising," *Advertising Age*, January 10, 12–14; Garfield, Bob (1994), "Breakthrough Product Gets Greatest TV Spot," *Advertising Age*, January 10, 14; Horton, Cleveland (1990), "Apple's Bold '1984' Scores On All Fronts," *Advertising Age*, January 1, 12.

2. Based on Goodrum, Charles, and Helen Dalrymple (1996), *Advertising in America: The First 200 Years*, New York: Harry N. Abrams; Swasy, Alecia (1993), *Soap Opera: The Inside Story of Procter & Gamble*, New York: Random House.

3. For example, see Tellis, Gerard J., and Golder, Peter N. (1996), "First to Enter, First to Market? The Real Causes of Enduring Market Leadership," *Sloan Management Review* 37, 2, 65–75.

4. This section borrows heavily from information in Goodrum and Dalrymple, *Advertising in America: The First 200 Years*; and Tellis and Golder "First to Enter, First to Market?"

5. Mueller, Frederick H. (1961), *Historical Statistics of the United States*, Washington, DC: Bureau of the Census with the the cooperation of the Social Science Research Council; Wattenberg, Ben J. (1976), *The Statistical History of the United States*, New York: Basic Books.

6. Brown, Ronald H. (1995), *Statistical Abstracts of the United States*, 115th ed., Washington, DC: U.S. Department of Commerce, Bureau of Census.

7. For example, see Golder, Peter, and Gerard J. Tellis (1993), "Pioneering Advantage: Marketing Fact or Marketing Legend," *Journal of Marketing Research* 30 (May), 158–170.

8. Tellis and Golder, "First to Enter, First to Market?"

9. Evans, Bergen (1968), *Dictionary of Quotations*, New York: Delacorte Press.

10. For a good exposition of this topic, see Curry, David J. (1993), *The New Marketing Research Systems*," New York: John Wiley & Sons.

11. Tellis, Gerard J. (1988), "Advertising Exposure, Loyalty and Brand Purchase: A Two Stage Model of Choice," *Journal of Marketing Research* 15, 2 (May), 134–144.

12. Drucker, Peter F. (1991), "The Big Three Miss Japan's Crucial Lesson," *The Wall Street Journal*, June 18, A18.

13. Carlson, Eugene (1989), "In Ford's Model T, The Timing Purred Perfectly," *The Wall Street Journal*, March 28, B2.

14. Gupta, Udayan (1990), "Narrowest Niches Can Yield Comfortable Profit Margins," *The Wall Street Journal*, September 26, B2.

15. Fornell, Claes (1992), "A National Customer Satisfaction Barometer: The Swedish Experience," *Journal of Marketing* 56 (January), 6–16.

16. Tellis and Golder, "First to Enter, First to Market?"

17. Ries, Al and Jack Trout (1985), *Positioning: Battle for Your Mind*, New York: McGraw-Hill.

18. Deveny, Kathleen (1996), "Copycat Cold Medicines Proliferate, Creating Confusion Among Consumers," *The Wall Street Journal*, February 1, B1.

19. Http://www.pg.com

20. Power, Christopher (1992), "Everyone is Bellying Up To This Bar," *Business Week*, January 27, 84.

21. Burke, Bill, Sr. (1994), "Brand Identity's New Math," *Advertising Age*, April 4, 32.

22. Folkes, Valerie S., Ingrid M. Martin, and Kamal Gupta (1993), "When to Say When: Effects of Supply On Usage," *Journal of Consumer Research* 20 (December), 467–477.

23. *Ibid.*

C
H
A
P
T
E
R

2

In 1989 the Federal Trade Commission (FTC) charged the Campbell's Soup Company with deceptive advertising of its Campbell's brand of soups. The firm's print ads claimed that its chicken noodle soup and "most of" its other soups were low in fat and cholesterol and helped reduce the risk of heart disease. The FTC said the ads were misleading because they failed to disclose the high sodium content in Campbell's soups. Sodium is a factor in high blood pressure, which can increase the risk of heart disease. The ads

The Regulatory Environment of Promotion

were part of Campbell's "Soup Is Good Food" campaign which appeared in women's service magazines throughout 1988.[1]

In August 1992, Campbell's Soup reached an agreement with the FTC, under which the company would disclose the sodium content of the soup and the recommended maximum daily limit on an individual's intake of sodium. The disclosure had to appear in ads that mentioned heart disease—directly or by implication—if the advertised products contained more than 500 milligrams of sodium, or more than the limit set for soups by the Food and Drug Administration (FDA).

In commenting on the settlement, Commissioner Mary L. Azcuenga said that she would have preferred that the settlement apply to all Campbell's products, but agreed to the limited version in the interests of reaching a settlement without further delay.

Wal-Mart became the largest retailer in the U.S. through its strategy of beating out competitors with low prices on food and convenience products. Its advertising slogan, "Always the low price. Always," captured its strategy and was a driving force in its expansion. However, by the early 1990s, competitors such as Target and Kmart, often had prices comparable to Wal-Mart's and sometimes had lower prices. Target ran an ad suggesting Wal-Mart's claim was deceptive, and also complained to the Better Business Bureau. Under this pressure, Wal-Mart changed a few letters in its slogan to read, "Always low prices. Always."[2]

Were these advertising claims really deceptive? Who should decide these matters? How should the determination be made? This chapter will help you answer these questions. The key to the answer is the meaning of *truth*. Advertising and sales promotions are means by which firms communicate their offers to consumers. If that communication has to be valuable to consumers and fair to competitors, it must be truthful. Thus the issue of truth permeates most aspects of the regulation of promotion.

The regulation of promotion in the United States can be classified into three groups: federal regulation, state regulation and self-regulation. **Federal regulation** consists of the laws of the federal government, the rules of various federal agencies, and

the rulings of federal courts. The action against Campbell's in the opening example came under the auspices of federal regulation. **State regulation** parallels that of the federal government but applies at the state level. Within the United States, federal regulation always takes precedence over state regulation when the two conflict.[3] Moreover, state regulation does not apply in a specific area in which the federal government has passed regulations. **Self-regulation** refers to control of promotion by promoters, as occurred for Wal-Mart in the opening example.

Despite the multiple forms of regulation, federal regulation forms the basis of all regulation in the United States for several reasons. First, because of the preeminence of federal laws, states do not even attempt to pass laws in areas covered by federal laws. When states do pass laws they often embody principles developed by federal laws or agencies. Moreover, federal departments or agencies generally have much greater resources than the states to implement the laws, so most states do not monitor promotion as closely. While self-regulation can exist independently of federal regulation, it is often adopted to preempt federal regulation, and its intensity is in proportion to the threat of federal regulation.[4] Self-regulation tends to wax and wane with actual or potential federal regulation. Moreover, self-regulation often follows the principles and concerns set by federal regulation.[5] Thus for all practical purposes, federal regulation sets the tone and tempo of the regulation of promotion in the United States. For this reason, the chapter focuses on federal regulation.

Several federal agencies are responsible for the regulation of promotion. Of these, the single most important is the Federal Trade Commission (FTC). It is responsible for two of the most important aspects of promotion: whether promotions are truthful and whether they are fair to competitors, distributors and consumers. Other agencies with responsibility over specific aspects of promotion include the antitrust division of the Justice Department, the Federal Communications Commission (FCC), the Food and Drug Administration (FDA), the U.S. Postal Service (USPS), and the Bureau of Alcohol, Tobacco, and Firearms (BATF). This section will discuss the role of the FTC in relatively greater detail, and that of the other agencies only briefly. Many other federal departments and agencies also have jurisdiction over various aspects of the marketing of products.[6] However, their jurisdiction is too narrow or specific to be covered in this chapter.

This chapter will first discuss the meaning of truth in promotion, because of the importance of this issue. It will then cover the regulation of four important areas of promotion: specific forms of advertising, sales promotion, labeling and media. The final section will discuss the nature and role of self-regulation.

THE MEANING OF TRUTH IN PROMOTION

As the two opening examples illustrate, no simple, objective test of truth is available. Campbell's could argue that its ads were truthful because its low-fat, low-cholesterol soups were more healthy than other soups at that time. Wal-Mart could argue that most consumers would understand that its slogan referred to its strategy of always *striving* to get the lowest prices for consumers. Thus truth in promotion is relative. It depends on the goals of the promoter, perceptions of consumers, prevailing meaning of words and prevailing social norms for honesty. In the United States, the FTC, which has been entrusted by the federal government with monitoring deceptive practices of business, is the key arbiter of truth in promotion. This section describes the history of the FTC, its standards for evaluating truth and its system for monitoring ads.

History of the Federal Trade Commission

The Federal Trade Commission (FTC) was set up in 1914 as an independent regulatory agency by the FTC Act of Congress. The FTC consists of a chair and four commissioners. Each commissioner is appointed by the president of the United States for a staggered 7-year term. As with other regulatory bodies, the chair reports to the president but is answerable to Congress for the FTC's policies and practices. The FTC has in addition hundreds of lawyers, economists and other professionals who help the commissioners implement its charter.

The original purpose of the FTC Act was to more effectively combat unfair trade practices than was then being done by the Sherman Act. Section 5 of the FTC Act contained the clause, "unfair methods of competition in commerce are hereby declared unlawful." At that time the FTC's charter was to control monopolistic practices that hinder competi-

tion, for the benefit of disadvantaged firms and consumers at large. Initially the FTC's charter did not explicitly cover promotion. But from the very beginning the FTC monitored these activities because unfair or deceitful promotion can injure small firms and competition in general.

However, in the 1931 *FTC v. Raladam* case, the Supreme Court held that deceptive trade practices, such as deceptive advertising did not fall under the FTC's jurisdiction since such practices did not injure competition when most major competitors indulged in them. While this ruling limited the FTC's jurisdiction, it was a blessing in disguise for consumers because it mobilized support for Congress's formal expansion of the powers of the organization. In 1938, Congress passed the **Wheeler-Lea Amendment** which changed Article 5 of the Sherman Act to read, "unfair methods of competition and unfair or deceptive acts or practices in commerce are hereby declared unlawful." This amendment extended the FTC's charter to explicitly include promotion. It also extended the FTC's jurisdiction to cover the promotion of food and drugs, though the marketing of those products falls under the jurisdiction of the Food and Drug Administration.

The FTC Act and the Wheeler-Lea Amendment are fairly broad in scope, in that they provide no specific definition of the term *deception* or penalties for deception. The meaning of and penalties for deception have evolved with the interpretation of these laws by the FTC commissioners, and by the judges who have ruled on cases.

In 1988, Congress amended the 1946 Lanham Act, enabling firms to sue rivals for false claims and win triple damages. Because competitors have better knowledge of and motivation to monitor competitors' promotions than does the FTC, the amendment opened up the potent force of competitor vigilance to ensure that ads would be truthful. Moreover, because the FTC has a limited budget and has at times not been very active, the new law ensures more thorough monitoring of truth in promotion.

Evaluation of Truth

This section first presents some criteria for truth, then discusses whether puffery, miscomprehension and unfairness are deceptive under these criteria. Finally it outlines how the FTC's interpretation of these criteria has changed over time.

Criteria for Evaluation What is truth? That simple, age-old question may elicit a simple answer from some people. But in the real world of complex communications, truth has many levels and involves a number of issues. Six of these issues are especially relevant to the regulation of promotion: explicit lie, misleading claim, significant audience, substantiation, materiality and injury. The first four may be considered increasingly stringent standards for truth, while the next two are legal standards for remedies.

Explicit Lie At the most basic level, the word *truth* means free of explicit lies. An **explicit lie** is a claim that unambiguously contradicts fact. The terms *explicit lie, falsehood,* or *explicit misrepresentation* are used synonymously. An example of an explicit lie is the universal claim by Wal-Mart that it has the lowest price *always*. Even a single instance of a lower price at a competing store can contradict that fact. Another example is a one-time practice of Savon Drugs, which advertised sale prices on some items, although consumers were charged higher prices at the checkout.[7] Most large, established firms do not resort to explicit lies because they would be quickly revealed. Savon may have adopted the pricing strategy due to the negligence or naiveté of a manager. Wal-Mart probably made its claim based on its historical experience as a price leader. In contrast, small fly-by-night operators profit from ads that contain explicit lies.

Misleading Claim A higher standard of truth than avoiding explicit lies, is providing full information so that the audience can fully understand the limitations of the claim. Failure to provide full information could lead to an understanding that runs contrary to fact. A **misleading claim** is one that by omission or choice of words suggests a meaning that contradicts fact. For example, the Campbell's Soup ad, while claiming to be healthful, did not disclose the high sodium content of the soup. One study identifies several types of misleading claims:[8]

Hedge: Rainbow toothpaste fights plaque. (It could also lose the fight!)

Elliptical comparative: Fibermunchies have more vitamin C. (Than what?)

Implied causation: Gainesburgers is rich in milk protein for your dogs. (Milk protein is not required for healthy dogs.)

Implied inferior competition: Wonder Bread builds strong bodies 12 different ways. (So do other brands.)

Incomplete statistics: FreshenUp mouthwash kills up to 50 percent of the germs in your mouth with one gargle. (Fifty percent is the maximum not the mean.)

As these examples show, a misleading statement contains an explicit claim that is true and an implicit claim that may be false. For this reason, a misleading statement is also called an *implicit lie, implicit falsehood* or *implicit misrepresentation*. The FTC considers misleading statements to lie on a continuum ranging from being almost explicitly untrue to being wholly ambiguous. For example, in one case FTC research found that Kraft's singles contain as much as 70 percent of the calcium in 5 ounces of milk. Now consider the following three of many possible claims that Kraft can make:

1. One Kraft slice has all the calcium in 5 ounces of milk. Five ounces.
2. One Kraft slice is made from 5 ounces of milk. Five ounces that are rich in calcium.
3. One Kraft slice is made from 5 ounces of milk that contains calcium.

The first is explicitly untrue. The second is potentially misleading. The third is ambiguous. When a claim is explicitly false, the FTC and the courts require only the copy of the claim and material evidence of the contrary to establish falsehood. They do not require any survey of consumers' understanding of the claim. However, in the case of implicit claims, the falsehood depends on the audience's interpretation of the claims. For that reason, as a statement is more ambiguous, the FTC and the courts are more likely to require surveys to determine what the audience understands from the claims.[9]

The question is, who is the audience and how many of them must be misled for the ad to be considered false? We address this topic next.

Significant Audience The audience of an ad is the population exposed to it. One standard of truth is to ensure that *the whole* audience must be misled by a claim for it to be false. This may happen with an explicit lie. A higher standard of truth is to ensure that *most* of the audience or *the average person* in the audience is misled by a claim for it to be false. However, the FTC and the courts use a still higher standard of truth. They consider a claim to be false if a *significant segment* of the audience is misled by the claim. The law contains no specific definition of a *significant segment*. The FTC has considered a proportion as low as 10 percent to be significant, while courts tend to use 15 percent as the rule.[10] The actual determination of significance depends on the case. In some cases, the concern may be with certain vulnerable segments even if they constitute a very small segment. For example, misleading ads targeted to seniors or children may justify scrutiny because these segments are vulnerable. In other cases the concern may be the damage or injury from the deception. Serious injury may suggest an ad is misleading, even if the proportion so misled is small. For example, consider an ad for an over-the-counter medication that leads some people to use it incorrectly and die as a result. The ad may be considered seriously misleading even if only one-tenth of one percent of the population is misled by it.

Substantiation An even higher standard of truth is that the advertiser must have substantiation for its claims. **Substantiation** means evidence from laboratory or field studies that provides reasonable support for a claim. Note that the focus at this level is not merely on the truth of the claim but on the promoter's possession of suitable evidence in support. For example, Campbell's Soup would have had no problem with its ad if it had conducted clinical studies showing that people who used its soups had a lower incidence of heart disease than those who did not. In an ear-

▼ **EXHIBIT 2-1.** Relevant copy from Firestone's "stops 25 percent quicker" ad.

Like the original Super Sports Wide Oval Tire. It came straight out of Firestone racing research. It's built lower, wider. Nearly two inches wider than regular tires. To corner better, run cooler, stop 25% quicker.

lier even stricter application of this principle, the FTC challenged a Firestone ad that claimed its Wide Oval tires stopped 25 percent quicker than regular tires (see Exhibit 2-1), even though Firestone had evidence in support based on ten runs on wet smooth concrete. The FTC's contention was that Firestone's claim was universal, while its evidence was based on one set of tests (ten runs), on one surface (wet smooth concrete), at one speed (15 m.p.h.) on the same day with the same tire pressure and load.[11] Exhibit 2-2

▼ **EXHIBIT 2-2.** Substantiation requirements emerging from FTC cases.

Documentation Required to Substantiate Claims	Claims	Product
Competent scientific tests	Safety and efficacy	Auto tires Cosmetics Hair care
	Comparative handling	Autos
Independent laboratory tests	Fuel economy	Autos
Competent and reliable scientific test or the opinion of experts	Cleaning	Dishwashers
Tests, including demonstrations, experiments, surveys, reports, and studies	Structural strength and quietness	Autos
	Dependability and reliability	Appliances
	Superiority	Appliances Sugar
Competent scientific engineering data	Air cooling power	Air conditioners
Competent and objective material available in written form that fully and completely substantiates safety or performance characteristics	Safety and performance	"All products" of a mail-order company
Opinion of a qualified person that competent tests or other objective data exists	Comfort	Denture adhesive
Written certification from a reliable source	Beautification	Wrinkle remover

Note: If tests are used for superiority claims, results must establish the comparative superiority which must be discernible or beneficial to the class of consumers to whom the representation is directed.

Source: Cohen, Dorothy (1980), "The FTC's Advertising Substantiation Program," *Journal of Marketing* 44 (Winter), 26–35. Reprinted with permission of the American Marketing Association.

lists cases where the FTC required substantiation by the firms. One study of these cases concluded that firms need substantiation for specific claims ("stops 25 percent quicker") rather than for general ones ("the super tires").[12]

Materiality and Injury A **material claim** is one that affects the purchase decision of a consumer. For example, the nondisclosure of sodium information in Campbell's advertising of the health benefits of its soups is material; the nondisclosure of cornstarch which may be used as a thickener is not material. A claim of inflated fuel efficiency in a car ad would be material. However, a claim about the location of the stereo speakers inside a car would be immaterial, because most consumers do not choose cars by the location of the speakers. Even if an advertiser's claim is deceptive, the FTC or the courts are unlikely to move against that advertiser if the claim is not material.

Injury refers to the harm that consumers suffer from deceptive promotion. Providing evidence of injury is necessary for awarding compensation to the injured party, and for determining the size of the award. Injury can have many degrees: **loss of benefits** (buying a product with inferior quality or features), **financial harm** (loss of property or money), or **physical harm** (damage to body or health). Misleading claims that endanger life or health are serious. For example, herbal remedies that claim to reduce blood cholesterol and high blood pressure without the need to diet may lead patients with arteriosclerosis to neglect their diets. The harm for such patients may be a progression of the disease and ultimately death. In contrast, books that promise to help you "breathe easier" and "live happier" are less likely to be dangerous if they contain vacuous information that causes only a monetary loss equivalent to the cost of the book. There are promotions—such as mortgage scams—where vulnerable consumers can suffer serious monetary loss due to misleading claims made by mail, phone or in person.

Strictly speaking, materiality and injury are separate but related issues. A material claim that is false does not imply that the claim would injure consumers. However in practice, proof of injury already implies materiality, while deception that does not injure is unlikely to be material. For this reason, both the FTC and the courts focus more on injury than on materiality.

Conclusion The FTC uses the term *deceptive* to describe ads that are not completely truthful. Based on the issues just discussed, an ad is **deceptive** if a *significant* segment's *understanding* of a *material* claim in the ad is not *substantiated*. Because the term *deception* is based on the audience's understanding of the ad's claim, it takes into account both explicit and implicit claims.

Deception versus Puffery, Miscomprehension and Unfairness An explanation of three related concepts—puffery, miscomprehension and unfairness—will help to further define the concept of deceptive promotion.

Puffery *Is puffery deceptive?* **Puffery** involves exaggerated, nonspecific claims. Examples would be, "Campbell's Soup tastes delicious," "Sleepwell is your dream mattress," you meet the "nicest people" in your Honda Civic, or Folgers instant coffee is "the ultimate one-cup coffee machine." Puffery is currently not considered deceptive if an average consumer is unlikely to perceive that the advertiser is guaranteeing a benefit in the claim. For example, a court threw out a suit brought by one man who claimed that he did not meet the nicest people in his Honda Civic as promised by the company's claim.[13] In practice, the criterion for deception is specificity of the claim. This specificity may arise due to numerical statements of price or performance ("17 grams of fat per serving"), clear comparison with rivals ("the best hamburger in town") or details of attributes ("Tylenol does not irritate the stomach"). If ads make specific claims, they require substantiation.

Miscomprehension *Can misunderstanding be an excuse for deception?* Studies have found that consumers miscomprehend as much as 30 percent of the information in ads.[14] Assuming the level of miscomprehension is truly that high, is that a good defense against deceptive advertising? Specifically, when miscomprehension is as high as 30 percent, can an ad that misleads only 15 percent of the population be considered deceptive? Such a defense of deception is not valid, because a deceptive statement tries to influence consumers to think *better* of the advertiser's offer, *a direction favorable to the advertiser*. Miscomprehension is a *random* process that may lead consumers to think better or worse of the advertiser's offer. Analysis of the copy can reveal the advertiser's intent, and consumer surveys can confirm if the errors are random (probably a misunderstanding) or directional (probably deceptive).

Consider the claim of FreshenUp cited earlier. A good way to evaluate the truthfulness of the ad is to survey the beliefs of consumers exposed to it. If the survey finds that a quarter of the respondents believe that FreshenUp is very effective at killing germs, while an equal proportion believe it is quite ineffective, then the ad may well have been misunderstood and is not deceptive. But if the proportion of respondents who believe the product is effective is ten times higher than those who believe it is ineffective, the ad does lead to an understanding very favorable to the company. This finding together with the lack of full disclosure suggests it is deceptive.

Unfairness *Is unfairness deceptive?* The term **unfair** is currently used to cover ads that can harm consumers but are not deceptive. Examples include an automobile ad showing a driver not wearing a seat belt, a motorcycle ad encouraging drivers to take risky turns at high speeds, or a gun ad claiming resistance to fingerprints. In each of these cases, the meaning that consumers get from the ad is exactly what the advertiser wants. So the ad is not deceptive. But the product may harm buyers or others if used the way it is advertised. In the 1970s, the FTC assumed jurisdiction over such unfair ads based on its general mandate to regulate unfair practices in industry. However, the FTC was unable to develop a clear definition of *unfairness*. In 1980, the U.S. Congress stripped the FTC's authority to develop rules about unfair ads for all firms and industries. It allowed the FTC to restrict or ban unfair ads on a case by case basis.[15]

Changes in FTC Criteria The intensity with which the FTC regulates promotion tends to be cyclical.[16] This pattern is evident in periods of close regulation of promotion followed by periods showing a laissez-faire attitude. The change in FTC attitude is partly due to changes in the U.S. president who appoints the FTC commissioners, and partly due to overreaction to the FTC practice in the previous period.

For example, in the late 1960s, the FTC came under pressure from consumer advocates such as Ralph Nader and the American Bar Association for not implementing its charter seriously. In response, in 1970 President Nixon appointed a new chair who set the FTC on a more aggressive path to monitor and control deceptive promotion. Among the changes, the FTC began requiring firms to substantiate all their claims in advance. The Firestone case was one of the first pursued under the new commissioner. That atmosphere prevailed for much of the 1970s. Then in 1980 Ronald Reagan was sworn in as U.S. president, partly on a platform to reduce government regulation. In 1981, President Reagan appointed an economist as chair, who sought to set the FTC on a less intrusive path, taking into account the costs and benefits of any action. This FTC policy was maintained through the Reagan-Bush administrations of the 1980s. However, under the more liberal administration of President Clinton, the FTC has pursued more active enforcement of its policies.[17]

Nevertheless, two important changes that the FTC instituted in the early 1980s, still influence FTC policy today.[18] By a 3 to 2 majority, the FTC ruled in 1981 that:

- Commercial communications would be evaluated on their probability to mislead, rather than merely their potential to mislead.
- The burden of proof for substantiation would rest with the FTC rather than with the defending firm accused of deceptive promotion.

In other words, the FTC would only investigate ads likely to mislead consumers, and it would no longer level a charge of deception until it had substantiation for such a charge. The logic behind the less stringent policy, as behind most deregulation, is that the market can more efficiently monitor firm performance than can any government body. Such monitoring takes two forms.

First, as firms resort to deceptive or misleading promotion, consumers become less trustful of such promotion. Indeed, one study found that consumers were so distrustful of "sales" and "discount" prices that they thought that regular prices were much higher than they actually were.[19] Another survey found that over 40 percent of survey respondents had trouble believing the claims for health in food ads.[20] Thus firms in their own interests need to be truthful or the public loses faith in promotion. The problem with this argument is that while the majority of consumers and firms behave as predicted, some firms may still cheat, and some vulnerable consumer groups may still suffer.

Second, competitors, consumers and the state governments step in as the FTC becomes more lax in monitoring promotion, while legislative bodies issue new laws to control deception. Thus the new FTC policy did not mean free license to firms to indulge in misleading promotion. Four forces moved in to partly compensate for the FTC's revised role.

- Some firms that were disadvantaged by the deceptive promotion of rivals sought relief by appealing to the courts on their own, albeit at their own cost.[21]
- Attorneys general of many states stepped in to tighten their own monitoring of truth in promotion. They also worked together to set general guidelines for advertisers, as will be discussed shortly.
- Some consumer groups became more active in filing suits against corporations they thought indulged in deceptive promotion.
- Many firms began to sue their competitors for misrepresentation of their products under the 1988 amendment to the Lanham Act.

As a result of all these cases, laws and precedents across the country, firms could still be held to the old stricter standards by various states and courts. They also faced a less uniform policy than before (see Exhibit 2-3 for some examples).

Implementing FTC Policy

If the FTC staff finds an example of deceptive promotion, it brings it to a commissioner's attention with a recommendation of action. The commissioner can then approach the promoter and informally request action or formally issue a remedial order. The promoter may consent or appeal the order before a hearing examiner. Each party can then present its case to the hearing examiner. The parties may then accept the ruling of the examiner or appeal it first to the panel of five commissioners and subsequently to the federal courts. The FTC can order one of four types of remedies: cease-and-desist order, affirmative disclosure, restitution and corrective advertising.

A **cease-and-desist order** requires the promoter to stop the promotion that was found to be deceptive. While this order is the least punitive, promoters still object to it and appeal it, either because they genuinely believe in their case or wish to delay any remedial action.

An **affirmative disclosure** requires the defendant to provide new, clear and conspicuous information to help consumers to make a good choice. This order is a little stronger remedy than the first. For example in the Campbell's Soup case, the firm agreed to disclose in future soup ads that made a health claim,

▼ **EXHIBIT 2-3.** **Some challenges to advertising claims.**

Complainant	Forum	Product	Complaint	Status
American Home Products	Federal district court	Johnson & Johnson's Tylenol	Ads imply that ibuprofen causes stomach irritation.	In discovery
Center for Science in the Public Interest	New York and Texas Attorneys General	Kraft's Cheez Whiz	Ads say the pasteurized processed cheese is real cheese.	Under investigation
New York Attorney General		McDonald's Chicken McNugget	Ads say 100% chicken without saying product is fried in animal fat.	Under investigation
General Foods (Oscar Mayer subsidiary)	National Advertising Division of Council of Better Business Bureau	Sara Lee's Bryan's bacon and bologna	Ads say that products are no. 1 in the South.	Under investigation
New York Attorney General	Internal investigation	VLI's Today contraceptive sponge	Ads say that the sponge has no side effects.	Advertising modified

Source: Christine Dugas, and Paula Dwyer, "Deceptive Ads: The FTC Laissez-faire Approach Is Backfiring," Reprinted from December 2, 1985 issue of *Business Week* by special permission, copyright © 1985 by the McGraw-Hill Companies, Inc.

▼ **EXHIBIT 2-4.** History of corrective advertising cases.

Company/Year	Product	Claim	Order Type	Disclosure Features
Amstar Corp. (1973)	Domino sugar	Sugar benefits	Consent	25% of ad costs
Beauty-Rama Carpet Center (1973)	Retailer	Prices	Consent	Firm used "bait and switch"
Boise Tire Co. (1973)	Uniroyal tires	Tire ratings	Consent	One ad
ITT Continental Baking (1971)	Profile bread	Caloric content	Consent	25% of one year's ads
Lens Craft Research (1974)	Contact lenses	Medical claims	Consent	Four weeks
Matsushita Electric of Hawaii (1971)	Panasonic TV sets	Hazard ratings	Consent	One ad
National Carpet (1973)	Retailer	Prices	Consent	Firm used "bait and switch"
Ocean Spray Cranberries (1972)	Cranberry drink	Food energy claim	Consent	One of every four ads
Payless Drug Company (1973)	Motorcycle helmets	Safety	Consent	Equal number to original ads
Rhode Island Carpets (1974)	Retailer	Prices	Consent	Firm used "bait and switch"
RJR Foods, Inc. (1973)	Hawaiian punch	Juice content	Consent	Every ad until effects are shown
Shangri La Industries (1972)	Swimming pools	Availability and terms	Consent	25% of one year's ads
STP Corp. (1976)	Oil additive	Effectiveness	Consent	One ad in 14 media
Sugar Information (1974)	Sugar	Sugar benefits	Consent	One ad in 7 media
Warner-Lambert (1975)	Listerine	Effectiveness claim	Litigated	Correction in $10 million worth of ads
Waserns Inc. (1974)	Waserns vitamins	Vitamin benefits	Consent	One ad over 7 insertions
Yamaha International (1974)	Yamaha motorcycle	Motorcycle safety	Consent	Corrective letter

Source: Wilkie, William L., Dennis L. McNeill, and Michael B. Mazis (1984), "Marketing's 'Scarlet Letter': The Theory and Practice of Deceptive Advertising," *Journal of Marketing* 48 (Spring), 11–31. Reprinted with permission of the American Marketing Association.

both the sodium content of the soup and the recommended maximum daily limit on sodium intake.[22]

An order of **restitution** requires compensation for damage caused by the deceptive promotion. The restitution could be paid directly to consumers by a refund, rebate or coupon if they can be conveniently identified. Alternatively, the money could be directed to a trust or a public organization that can use it for the benefit of consumers potentially harmed by the deceptive promotion. For example, in a Magic Wand case the FTC extracted a $550,000 settlement from the marketers of the product.[23]

Corrective advertising is advertising meant to correct any untruthful information or impressions that consumers may have gotten from some prior decep-

tive promotion. Corrective advertising has caused promoters much concern because of the ambiguity of the criteria, the costs involved and the potential for embarrassment. Exhibit 2-4 presents a brief history of corrective advertising cases assembled by one study. That study concluded that promoters' concern may be exaggerated. The FTC has not been overly aggressive in requiring corrective advertising, and some firms have even used such campaigns for positive publicity.

When evaluating truth in advertising, and assessing the need for and effectiveness of corrective advertising, the FTC prefers information obtained from consumer surveys rather than the testimony of experts.[24] These surveys can be conducted by professional research firms, independent consultants, professors or the firms involved in the dispute. The FTC puts more value on the studies provided by professional research firms rather than that done by other parties, because they are dedicated to this task and are generally more experienced. Actually, the more experienced the surveying company, the more faith the FTC puts in it.

REGULATION OF SPECIFIC FORMS OF ADVERTISING

The general principles of truth in promotion guide the regulation of all forms of advertising. The advantage of understanding these principles is that they make it easier to appreciate past decisions of the FTC and the courts, and to predict their future behavior. Moreover, an understanding of these principles better enables us to grasp the vast number of rules that cover specific forms of advertising. Five such forms of advertising merit special discussion: comparative advertising, endorsements, demonstrations, warranties and credit.

Comparative Advertising

In the mid-1990s, two acid-suppressing drugs entered the $1 billion over-the-counter antacid market to expand it by a massive 38 percent. Johnson & Johnson-Merck introduced Pepcid AC, while SmithKline introduced Tagamet HB. Both drugs were previously available only by prescription. Before they entered, the antacid market was dominated by Tums and Rolaids. The entries were accompanied by intense advertising battles, as the two brands quickly rose to leading positions in the market.

In August 1995, shortly after Tagamet's entry, SmithKline filed a lawsuit complaining that Johnson & Johnson-Merck exaggerated Pepcid's effectiveness with several false claims, including that it worked for 9 hours and provided heartburn relief all day. SmithKline also complained that another ad wrongly claimed that 8 out of 10 doctors and pharmacists recommended Pepcid over Tagamet. (The survey was done before Tagamet's entry.) Johnson & Johnson-Merck countersued over SmithKline's claim that Tagamet worked faster than Pepcid, and won seven times as many prescriptions as Pepcid. (This number included prescriptions before Pepcid was on the market.)

The judge deciding the case ordered both companies to withdraw all such ads until they could provide evidence to support their claims.[25]

The example shows the intensity of comparative advertising and the potential pros and cons for consumers. **Comparative advertising** refers to an ad that compares a brand to some competitive standard (see Chapter 6). Before 1970, comparative ads were rare, being discouraged by the FTC, and avoided by skeptical firms and agencies. Regulators feared that comparative advertising could confuse consumers and give large firms an advantage over small firms. Advertisers feared that comparative advertising would create legal problems for the advertised brands, while giving free exposure for the brand used for comparison. However, under pressure from consumer advocates, the FTC changed its policy in 1971 and began actively encouraging firms to use comparative advertising. The new thinking was motivated by a belief that specific, comparative information about brands would help consumers make more informed decisions. Small or new brands such as Pepcid could especially benefit from such advertising if they had more to offer than an established brand such as Tums.

When using comparative ads, advertisers have to be especially careful that their ads are truthful. The reason is that competitors have the right to sue advertisers for any misrepresentation in ads, under an amendment of the Lanham Act of 1946. In 1988, Congress amended the 1946 Lanham Act, enabling firms to sue rivals for false claims and win triple damages. (Previously courts had ruled that under the Lanham Act advertisers' misrepresentations about their own products were illegal, but misrepresentations about a competitor's products, however flagrant, were not illegal.[26]) Because competitors have greater expertise, resources, proximity and motivation than the FTC, their scrutiny of competing ads is likely to be more thorough. For example, SmithKline's legal action came within weeks of Tagamet's introduction, while Johnson & Johnson-Merck's reaction came within a week of SmithKline's. Also, both actions involved no direct major cost to the public.

When ruling on lawsuits filed by a firm (plaintiff) about a rival's (defendant's) advertising, judges follow the same general principles of determining deception as does the FTC, with one major difference. They generally require that the plaintiff incur the burden of proof about the deception. Further, if the rival's claims are ambiguous, the plaintiff must also give external evidence that consumers were misled by the rival's claims. When the FTC brings a case against an advertiser, the burden of proof could lie with the advertiser. Judges tend to lean toward deception if plaintiffs can show evidence that at least 15 percent of the target population was misled by the advertising.[27] Finally, if the plaintiff seeks damages from the rival's deceptive advertising, then it must provide evidence of the harm done. However, in the case of the antacid market, the judge required both firms to stop their comparative ads, because the intensity of rival claims and the incomplete information in their advertising did not help consumers to make better choices.

The 1988 amendment did not cover political advertising because of the concern that it might limit political debate of important issues. As a result, political ads frequently make claims or provide information of questionable veracity, that would not be allowed for branded products. The inability of candidates to sue rivals for untruthful claims leads to a multiplicity of claims and counterclaims and accentuates the intensity of negative political advertising. Overall, the lower accountability in political advertising may hinder voters from getting accurate information about candidates and issues and prevent them from making informed choices. For that reason, some critics are opposed to the exception. They argue that if brand advertising can benefit from the amendment, so can political advertising.

Endorsements

The FTC defines an **endorsement** as any advertising message that consumers are likely to believe reflects the opinions, beliefs, findings or experience of a party other than the sponsoring advertiser. That party may be an individual, group or institution and is called an *endorser* (see Chapter 8). The FTC has special guidelines for the use of endorsers, because this form of communication elicits greater trust from consumers and has greater potential to mislead. The guidelines differ depending on whether the endorser is a lay consumer, celebrity or expert. We consider the FTC's guidelines under each of these headings.

Lay Endorsers **Lay endorsers** are individuals who appear in ads and are neither well known to the general public, nor considered by the latter to be experts. The FTC requires that lay endorsers should be typical consumers. If the advertiser uses actors instead of typical consumers, then it should disclose that fact in

the ad.[28] Further, the experiences of the lay consumer shown in an ad must be substantiated by the advertiser as being the typical experiences that a significant proportion of actual consumers would have. Even a disclosure that "individual consumers may not get the same result" is not enough to compensate for advertising an atypical experience. Only a clear and conspicuous disclosure of the typical experience of consumers prevents the ad from being deceptive.

For example, suppose a Toyota ad portrays an owner of a Toyota Corolla who claims that his particular car never broke down in five years. The ad is not deceptive *only if* the company has evidence that a significant majority of consumers have a similar experience, or it clearly discloses the typical experience owners have with their Toyota Corollas.

Celebrity Endorsers **Celebrities** are individuals or characters known to a large portion of the general population, primarily because of the publicity associated with their lives. The FTC has the following guidelines about celebrity endorsements. The endorsement should reflect the honest belief, opinion or experience of the celebrity. If the endorser makes any claims, the advertiser must have substantiation for these claims according to the principles described above. The celebrity does not have to use the product. However, if the celebrity *claims* to have used the product, then that should be true. Both the celebrity and the advertiser are liable for any misrepresentation in this area. Moreover, the advertiser should ensure that the celebrity continues to use the product if the endorsement gives this impression.

For example, the singer Pat Boone once endorsed an acne remedy, giving the false impression that Boone and his family used the remedy. He had to contribute to a fund that made refunds to consumers of the acne remedy.[29]

Expert Endorsers The FTC defines an **expert** as an individual that the target population perceives as having greater knowledge about the advertised product than the average consumer, because of his or her experience, training or study. The FTC requires that experts only endorse within the area of their expertise. For example, former astronaut Gordon Cooper endorsed an automobile fuel economy device. The FTC found this endorsement deceptive because Cooper's expertise as an astronaut did not extend to automobile engineering.[30] Other requirements of expert endorsers are similar to those for celebrity endorsers. Experts need to use the product as conveyed in the endorsement, consumers should have the same access to or the same version of the product as the expert, and the advertiser must be able to substantiate the attributes that the expert endorses.[31]

Advertisers need to use seals of approval of various organizations in the same spirit as they use expert endorsers. In particular, because seals of approval imply that the organization approves of the product, the product should have been thoroughly inspected and evaluated by the organization.

Demonstrations

A **mockup** is a demonstration of a product benefit with artificial ingredients or unnatural props. For example, an ad for Mr. Clean uses resin to make the floor wax appear to splash (see Exhibit 2-5). Consider the following mockups for TV ads:

- To heighten the impression of solids in its soup, Campbell's Soup uses marbles in a bowl of soup.

- To demonstrate the strength of its cars, Volvo has a monster truck drive over a row of competitors' cars and its own Volvo 240 station wagon. The truck crushes all but the Volvo 240. However, the Volvo car has been structurally reinforced, while structural supports of competitors' cars have been severed.

- An infomercial for Magic Wand's handheld mixer shows the mixer crushing an uncut pineapple into pulp and whipping skim milk into a frothy dessert topping. The pineapple is precrushed and the milk is not skim milk.

- To show how consumers enjoy its ice cream, an advertiser uses mashed potatoes because ice cream does not stay solid under the heat of TV lights.[32]

Advertisers often resort to mockups in order to show certain product benefits. The purpose of these mockups is not always to deceive consumers.

Sometimes, as in the ice cream example, the mockup is essential to effectively convey the information through certain media. The FTC has ruled that mockups are deceptive when the mockup is intrinsically related to the attribute being communicated, and does not include a clear disclaimer. The examples of Campbell's Soup, Volvo and Magic Wand illustrate such a situation. However, the ice cream example is not deceptive, because the advertised attribute—enjoyment—is not one that depends on the presence of mashed potatoes. The FTC has

▼ **EXHIBIT 2-5.** Mr. Clean makes a splash with some help from resin.

Source: Courtesy of Procter & Gamble.

successfully defended its rulings in court, and has won compliance from advertisers.

Warranties

The FTC has specific guidelines about the advertising of warranties.[33] The spirit of these guidelines is that the ads should describe the precise warranty accurately in terms of item(s) warranted, duration of the warranty, the terms of a prorated warranty if any, and the money that will be refunded when applicable. For example, a lifetime warranty for a car battery is deceptive if the warranty is good only for as long as the car itself lasts. Similarly, a lifetime warranty on a car is deceptive if it applies only to the chassis and not to the other components. A product warranty for five years would be deceptive if the product normally lasts for less than that time. A warranty calculated on a discounted sale price is deceptive if the warranty is stated as being calculated on the original list price. Money-back warranties are deceptive if they do not include the fees of the transaction such as taxes, mailing and handling.

Despite all these restrictions on warranties, in early 1996, Goodyear Tire and Rubber developed a clever warranty program for a new tire called Infinitreds. The $32 million ad campaign launching the brand attracted a great deal of interest because it found a niche in a very competitive market.[34] Most tires are warrantied for 40,000 to 60,000 miles. Michelin warranties its XH4 tire for 80,000 miles. Goodyear also found that its Infinitreds last 80,000 miles. Since most cars need tire replacements around 40,000 miles, an 80,000-mile warranty will last till the car reaches 120,000 miles, well beyond a car's average lifetime of 80,000 to 100,000 miles. Thus Goodyear could offer an attention-getting lifetime warranty for the Infinitreds without risking many claims. Is the Goodyear warranty deceptive?

Loans and Leasing

The Federal Truth in Lending Act describes the terms under which firms may advertise loans. The act outlaws false and misleading advertising about the cost of a loan, and bait-and-switch advertising in which consumers are drawn to a vendor by a cheap loan and sold on a more expensive one. The act has several other requirements to ensure that consumers get a clear picture of the true cost of the loan in standard terms that are easy to compare across lenders. The act defines the "annual percentage rate" which is the only rate that can be listed in any ad. The advertising of certain aspects of the loan requires a full disclosure of the terms of the loan clearly and conspicuously in the ad. A full disclosure includes statement of the annual percentage rate, the down payment and the repayment terms.[35]

In the 1990s, many retailers began to offer zero-interest loans as a promotion. These loans waived interest for a period of time, such as three to six months. However, retailers manipulated these offers by either accumulating the interest which became payable after the zero-interest period, or making the zero interest contingent on monthly payments. In 1996, several states filed suit against major retailers for deceptive use of such promotions, and won settlements. Without admitting to deception, the retailers agreed to clearly announce the terms of all zero-interest loans, as well as reimburse the states for their legal and investigative costs.[36]

Another promotional tool that became popular in the 1990s was automobile leases. The lease lets a consumer use a car for a set period of time with a low down payment and low monthly payments. However, at the end of the lease period, the consumer had to pay a predetermined amount to own the car, or the car would revert to the dealer. Although firms advertised the fact that consumers were not obliged to buy the car and could take up another lease instead, they limited the mileage and the wear-and-tear that the car could accumulate without penalties. In 1996, the Federal Reserve Board announced new rules to make automobile leases clearer and let consumers compare rival offers. In particular, dealers had to prominently disclose the car's cost, down payment, monthly payments and charges for excess mileage and wear-and-tear.[37]

REGULATION OF SALES PROMOTIONS

Sales promotions are *temporary* changes in price, benefits or the product itself to make an offer more attractive to consumers. Price cuts are a common and effective form of sales promotions, and are called **price promotions**. They can be combined with other types of sales promotions. Firms may indulge in price promotions that are explicitly or implicitly deceptive. Thus regulation to ensure honest price promotions constitutes an important form of the regulation of promotion. To facilitate the discussion, we divide the regulation of sales promotions into five important topics: price discrimination, trade allowances, deceptive pricing, deceptive value and contests and sweepstakes.[38]

Price Discrimination

Price discrimination refers to the strategy of offering the same product to different customers at different prices, typically at the highest price each customer will pay. Price discrimination is a central aspect of price promotions, because all price promotions involve selling the same product at different prices to different consumers. However, certain forms of price discrimination are illegal based on the principle of unfairness, even if they do not involve any deception.

The basic law covering price discrimination is Section 2 of the Clayton Act (1914). The restrictions against price discrimination are further strengthened by the Robinson-Patman Act of 1936. The FTC and the Justice Department are responsible for implementing these laws. While these laws are not entirely explicit about the exact practices that are illegal, their implementation by government agencies and their interpretation enable us to arrive at some norms about what pricing strategies are illegal.

Price discrimination may be illegal under the two federal laws cited above, if it meets *all* of the following conditions:[39]

1. The company charges different prices within a reasonably contemporaneous time period. The actual time would vary by product category, but six months may be considered a good norm.
2. The differences in prices occur in interstate commerce. If sales are entirely within one state, these federal laws do not hold. Also, the laws hold only if the buyers are involved in commerce; i.e., are businesses. Price discrimination to individual consumers is not illegal.
3. The products sold under different prices are of like grade and quality. In applying this norm, regulators focus on the physical grade or quality of the product and not on the brand name or other nominal difference.
4. The discrimination is to injure competition at the seller, buyer or sub-buyer level.

The original law was intended to protect small retailers who were discriminated against in favor of large retailers. The large retailers forced their suppliers to lower the prices the retailers paid them for goods. The large retailers could in turn pass on the savings to their own consumers, or they could retain the savings for higher profits. Such arrangements worked to the competitive disadvantage of small retailers who lost market share to the larger retailers or had to make do with lower profits.

The laws allow for three defenses for price discrimination:

1. Price discrimination is legal if motivated by differences in cost. These differences may arise due to differences in quantity, geographical location or specifics in the order of the buyers.
2. Price discrimination is also legal if it is due to changes in the market. Such changes may be due to differences in demand or supply over time, the perishability of goods, or technological obsolescence.
3. Price discrimination is also legal if a seller lowers price to another buyer in a good faith attempt to meet similar prices offered by the competition.

These conditions and exemptions indicate that discriminatory pricing can be successfully used as a pricing strategy and is illegal in a fairly narrow range of circumstances.

Trade Allowances

Trade allowances are short-term cash or other benefits that a manufacturer makes to wholesalers, distributors or retailers so that they may buy more of the product, or promote it more heavily to consumers (see Chapter 11). Manufacturers could use trade allowances unevenly to favor large retail chains. Such a practice would hurt small retailers and would amount to price discrimination as discussed earlier. Accordingly, the FTC has specific rules to ensure that trade allowances are not discriminatory in that sense. The main rules are the following:[40]

1. The allowance may be made only for services rendered and may not be worth much more than the value of those services.
2. All buyers must be able to avail of the allowance.
3. All buyers must be duly informed of the allowance.
4. Buyers who cannot avail of the allowance must have access to alternate benefits.

5. The promoter must make clear the terms and conditions of the allowance.

Here again the rules are not unduly burdensome. They ensure that if firms use trade allowances, such promotions are fair to all their customers, especially the smaller ones.

Deceptive Pricing

Deceptive pricing refers to efforts by sellers to suggest that a price is different from what it actually is. Unlike price discrimination, federal laws are much less explicit about deceptive pricing. However, this topic is covered under the FTC's general mandate to restrict unfair or deceptive acts or practices of competition. Under this act, the FTC does not have to show that anyone is actually deceived, but only that the practice has the potential to deceive. To better help firms, the FTC has a publication titled *Guides Against Deceptive Pricing*.[41] This book lists several pricing terms that have the potential to misrepresent: *regular price, former price, comparable market price, suggested retail price, wholesale price, factory price* or *for a limited time only*.

Former or Regular Price When sellers offer a discount against a former or regular list price, the former price should be a genuine price. Thus the seller should make a good faith effort to sell at the regular price for a reasonable length of time. Raising a price merely to offer a discount, and then calling the former price a regular price would be deceptive. Also, over a long period of time, if sales occur only at the discount price and not at the regular price, then the latter loses its status as a regular price.

Comparable Market Price Retailers often state next to their own price the comparable price of the product in the market. The FTC requires that the retailer verify that price, and ensure that substantial sales occur at that price in the areas in which it operates.

Suggested Retail Price Some retailers suggest a price or discount below the manufacturer's suggested retail price. The FTC holds that many consumers believe that the manufacturer's suggested retail price is the price at which the product generally sells. If sales do not normally occur at the suggested retail price, then retailers may not use such a price as a reference price. Also, manufacturers who have a suggested retail price may be liable for deception if sales generally occur substantially below that price.

Wholesale or Factory Price Using terms such as *wholesale price* or *factory price* for prices that are not literally the prices paid by the wholesaler or ex-factory respectively, is deceptive. Further, this labeling may also be deceptive if the retail price happens to literally equal the wholesale price, but the retailer gets a trade allowance that lowers the effective price.

Limited Time Claiming a price is for *a limited time only* when it is really a regular price, is deceptive. Similarly, such a claim would be deceptive, if the retailer plans to reduce the price after the time period and not return to a higher price.

Bargains and Price Packs The FTC also warns against promoted bargains such as "buy one get one free" or "2 for 1." These offers are valid and not deceptive only if the price of the first item is the one at which sales normally occur.

Price packs are new packages on which a manufacturer effectively lowers the price to the consumer, such as "50¢ off" or "contains 25% more" (see Chapter 11). The FTC has established the following restrictions on the use of price packs.[42]

- Price packs may be used only with brands in distribution with established retail prices.
- Price packs are limited to three promotions a year.
- At least 30 days must elapse between consecutive price pack promotions.
- The volume sold in price packs must be less than 50 percent of the product's annual sales.
- The manufacturer must provide retailers with materials to display the price pack.
- The retailer must display the price pack in addition to the regular price.

All of these pricing strategies or pricing labels have a basic similarity. They implicitly suggest a norm or reference price by which consumers can evaluate the current price of the product. Deception occurs when that reference price does not correctly reflect the true norm in the market.

Deceptive Value

Many other forms of promotions are also deceptive if they violate the spirit of honest pricing described above. Three types of deceptive promotions are worth noting: introductory offers, economy size and bait and switch.[43]

Introductory Offers The FTC regulates the use of the term *introductory offer* because it connotes that the consumer can get a special bargain for a new product. For such an offer to be valid and not deceptive, it must meet three conditions. The product must be new or changed in a significant way. The introductory offer should hold no longer than six months, after which the product will be on regular terms that are less favorable. The marketer must intend to offer the regular terms for a substantial period after the termination of the introductory offer.

Economy Size The FTC regulates the use of terms such as *economy size*, *economy pack*, *budget pack* and *bargain size* because they connote saving from some other available size. For these terms not to be deceptive, three conditions need to be met. The marketer must sell the brand in some other size. The savings from this size must be at least 5 percent relative to the price of all other packages of the brand offered for sale. No other package of the brand should use the same term.

Bait and Switch **Bait and switch** is a promotional strategy by which a marketer draws customers into a store with an unusually low discount price on an item, and then encourages the consumer to buy a substitute item at a higher price, either through personal selling pressure or by not stocking the discounted item. The FTC requires that retailers not pressure customers to switch to costlier substitutes, stock enough of the discounted item to meet reasonable increases in demand, and offer rain checks if they run out of the discounted item.

Premiums A **premium** is a gift or reward that promoters give consumers for purchasing a product. Examples of premiums include a free Disney video for the purchase of a Nintendo machine, or a free cruise for examining a vacation condominium. The FTC considers a premium to be deceptive when a firm misrepresents its value, fails to disclose the qualifying conditions to obtain it, or falsely implies that a consumer has already won it.[44]

Contests and Sweepstakes

Contests and sweepstakes are regulated because of their similarity to lotteries and gambling.[45] In most states, the latter are either illegal or heavily regulated. A game is a lottery if it meets the following three conditions:

1. It offers a prize.
2. Winning depends on chance and not on skill.
3. A participant has to give up something of value to participate.

That something of value is legally termed **consideration.** Most sweepstakes and lotteries do meet the first of these two conditions. Therefore, they can avoid being considered a lottery only if they do not meet the third condition. For that reason, most contests and sweepstakes explicitly state that the game is free and requires no payment or purchase of the promoted product. However, what constitutes consideration is a gray area. Most states do not consider a consumer's visit to the store, filling out of forms, or provision of related material such as pictures to be consideration, despite the fact that these actions do involve consumer time, information and personal property. On the other hand, a strictly imposed one-entry-per-person (or per-visit) rule, could make a product purchase or store visit equal to consideration, and may trigger evaluation.

The FTC has strict disclosure rules for legal games that are not classified as lotteries, to protect consumers from deceit. The disclosure must state:[46]

1. The exact number of prizes and odds of winning.
2. The geographic area and total outlets in the contest.
3. The duration of the game.
4. Weekly lists of unredeemed prizes valued at $25 and over, if the game lasts more than 30 days.

In addition, the FTC requires that all game pieces must be dispersed randomly; successive games must be separated by at least 30 days or the duration of the previous game; the game cannot be terminated before the distribution of all game pieces; and more pieces cannot be added during the course of the game. Most states have rules patterned after these FTC rules.

REGULATION OF MEDIA

Two media have received careful scrutiny because of their potential for unfair competition, intrusiveness, fraud or deception. These media are the broadcast media and the mail. Congress has special rules to govern the broadcast media because of its intrusiveness and its power to affect people's lives and opinions. The postal service has always been carefully monitored because the distance and anonymity of the sender can facilitate fraud and unfair trade practices.

Broadcast Media

The broadcast media include radio, television, telephone and telegraph. Regulation of the broadcast media falls within the jurisdiction of the Federal Communications Commission. The FCC was established by the U.S. Congress in 1934. Its primary purpose is to license radio, TV, telephone and telegraph services to ensure that their broadcasts are suitable for the public. In particular, the FCC ensures that programs and ads are in good taste, fair and not deceptive. The FCC works closely with the FTC in matters of deception and restricts its supervision to the media, while the FTC supervises advertisers and agencies. This section covers four important areas of the regulation of broadcast media: sponsor identification, time devoted to ads, fairness doctrine and telemarketing. Like the FTC, FCC policies in these areas have changed over time.

Sponsor Identification The FCC supports the principle that consumers have a right to know when they are being exposed to advertising. In practice, this principle implies that broadcasters clearly indicate when any paid commercial or sponsored program is being aired, and who is paying for or sponsoring it. The principle applies to three important forms of advertising: product placements, program tie-ins and infomercials. These activities are now legal although they were discouraged or explicitly banned by the FCC before the 1970s.

Product Placement A **product placement** is a planned and paid appearance of a brand message in a movie or TV program. For example, one scene of the movie *True Lies* conspicuously displays the name "Marriott Hotels." The FCC's rule of sponsor identification did not apply to product placements in movies as long as they were not broadcast over TV. However, in 1963 the FCC waived this rule even for movies to be broadcast over TV, provided the placement showed a reasonable use of the product.[47] The FCC's move was probably to avoid the inconsistency between movies aired in theaters and on TV. Product placements became more popular after the rule change. The popularity was also fueled by the increasing cost and proliferation of commercials, and by movie producers' efforts to attract placements to defray costs of production.

Program Tie-In A **program tie-in** is an arrangement by which a program provides exposure to a particular brand in exchange for a commitment by the brand's owner to advertise during that program. Broadcasters sometimes prefer program tie-ins because the advertiser can substitute commercials with product placements, but not with program tie-ins. In the past, the FCC discouraged program tie-ins because broadcast stations may fail to identify the program's sponsor as required. The three networks had voluntarily avoided program tie-ins for the same reason.[48] However, in the 1980s, broadcasters relaxed their policy due to more competition among broadcasters, and more product placements.

Infomercial An **infomercial** is an ad that takes the form and time of a full-length program. Chapters 5 and 15 discuss this form of advertising in greater detail. The FCC greatly restricted the use of infomercials before the 1980s.[49] It held that the infomercial could lead consumers, especially children, to believe that the infomercial was a regular program, and thus trust it more than they would an ad. In 1984 the FCC relaxed its guidelines for the use of infomercials for two reasons. First, as long as competitors have the same access to this form of advertising, no single advertiser would have any overriding advantage in using infomercials. Second, if advertisers overused the infomercial, the overuse would undercut its appeal and reduce its effectiveness.

Nevertheless the FTC continues to monitor infomercials to ensure that they are not misrepresentative. In particular, infomercials have developed a reputation for promoting shoddy products with exaggerated claims to susceptible audiences.[50] The FTC may also prosecute the agencies that produce the ads, rather than the advertisers themselves. The agencies may be better established and have deeper pockets relative to some small firms that order infomercials to market their inferior products.[51]

Time Devoted to Ads The FCC no longer restricts the amount of time devoted to ads, except for TV programs. With the proliferation of TV channels, including channels that carry no ads, consumers can avoid channels that carry too many ads. For this reason, broadcasters themselves control the proportion of ads to program content on any program so as not to lose audiences. Some radio and TV stations even advertise their low level of ads relative to competitors to draw audiences. Advertising to children is currently covered by the Children's Television Act of 1991. It requires that advertising during children's programs be limited to 10.5 minutes per hour on weekdays, and 12 minutes per hour on weekends.[52] The regulation of children's advertising time can be justified on the premise that children have a smaller choice of programs and are less discriminating when choosing among them.

Fairness Doctrine The FCC no longer enforces the fairness doctrine. The **fairness doctrine** required broadcasters to provide time for opposing views on ads or programs that took a strong advocacy position. Before its ban in 1970 this doctrine required the airing of anti-smoking messages to match ads by cigarette and tobacco brands.[53] In the absence of FCC rules, many broadcasters do arrange for the airing of alternate viewpoints during news programs, documentaries or debates of controversial issues. However, many broadcasters do not accept ads advocating a particular position, especially on controversial issues such as abortion, the flat tax or welfare programs. Broadcasters do accept paid political ads without providing free time for rival politicians, provided those ads promote the politician's claim to office rather than his or her viewpoint.

Telemarketing Telemarketing is the promotion of any good or service through telephone lines. The FCC's control over marketing through the telephone media has been greatly expanded under the Telephone and Consumer Protection Act of 1991.[54] The act greatly restricts telemarketing, requires the FCC to create rules for orderly telemarketing, and provides consumers with recourse to claim damages through the courts for violation of the laws. Among the specific provisions, the law forbids:

- Calling residences that do not wish to be called.

- Calls made through automatic dialing or with prerecorded messages.
- Calls before 8:00 A.M. or after 9:00 P.M.
- Calls to emergency numbers or hospital rooms.
- Unsolicited faxes or unidentified faxes.

Consumers who receive such calls can sue the telemarketer for damages for monetary loss or a sum up to $500. Note that the laws do not ban all telemarketing. The purpose of the law is to protect consumers' privacy without restricting the First Amendment right to free speech and the right to market legal products over the telephone.

The FTC also has jurisdiction over telemarketing in that firms cannot use it for deceptive practices. For example, in early 1996, the FTC cracked down on "draft fraud." Draft fraud is a practice in which unscrupulous operators obtain the bank account numbers of consumers and then withdraw funds from their accounts using demand drafts. A demand draft stating that an individual has granted permission for a withdrawal, and bearing his or her name and account number is sufficient for a bank to release the funds. The FTC found that such operators in Georgia and Oklahoma had cheated consumers of several million dollars.[55]

Mail

The U.S. Postal Service (USPS) has jurisdiction over marketing through the mail through its responsibility for managing the postal service. The USPS is the oldest law-enforcement agency in the United States. Few people know it as such because the agency's law enforcement arm works quietly. But it is much feared in the underworld because of its thoroughness in investigations and its success in winning convictions.[56] The FTC also has responsibility over marketing through the mail from its charter to control unfair trade practices. The two agencies coordinate their efforts for the benefit of mail users. They especially monitor four areas: fraud, unordered merchandise, negative option mail and prompt shipping.[57]

Fraud The U.S. Postal Service tries to ensure that businesses do not use its mail service to profit from fraud. Over the more than 200 years of its history, the USPS has obtained convictions for myriad fraudulent schemes. Some examples include phony mail-order businesses, illegal lotteries, Ponzi schemes, fictitious charities, check kiting, chain letters, missing-heir swindles, and misredemption of promotional coupons and rebates.[58] The U.S. Postal Service also moves against businesses that advertise through other media but collect dues for a fraudulent scheme through the mail. Similarly, the service moves against consumers who misredeem rebates and coupons through the mail.

Unordered Merchandise Marketers may not mail unordered merchandise to consumers and then coerce or even request them to pay for the goods. The FTC considers this practice to be unfair. The exceptions to this rule are gifts or samples given free to the consumer. In such cases, the marketer must make it very clear to the consumer that the item is given freely and can be used by the consumer as he or she wishes. The rule frees consumers from having to pay for or return unsolicited merchandise. The mailing of unwanted materials, such as pornographic material, is also considered an illegal use of the mail service.

Negative Option Mail-Order Plans **Negative option mail-order plans** refer to the practice by which marketers send merchandise to consumers at regular intervals unless the consumer explicitly indicates he or she does not want it. The FTC devised specific rules for marketers who use this plan. At the start of the plan, they must inform consumers of all terms of the plan. They must also inform consumers of an impending shipment, and give consumers enough time and an appropriate form to reject the shipment. They must ship the requested merchandise within four weeks after they receive consumers' orders. Some well-known mail-order marketers go further by allowing consumers to return shipments they ordered, within a limited time period, if they are not satisfied.

Prompt Shipping The FTC has rules about prompt shipping by mail-order firms. Firms must ship all orders promptly on receipt. They must not solicit shipments unless they believe they can mail the goods within the time period promised in the solicitation, or within 30 days if no time period is given. In the event that they are unable to ship the goods within these time periods, the marketers must give consumers the option to cancel the order.

REGULATION OF LABELING

The Food and Drug Administration (FDA) is the federal agency most involved with the regulation of labeling and packaging. Although under the jurisdiction of the U.S. Health Department, the FDA receives its charter primarily from the Federal Food, Drug and Cosmetic Act of 1938.[59] It is best known as the agency that must approve new drugs for sale in the United States. Yet, its charter is much wider. The FDA is responsible for branding, licensing, packaging, labeling, grading and quality approval of foods (except those containing meat and poultry), cosmetics, drugs, medical devices, biological products, radiation-emitting products and medical laboratories.[60] Foods containing meat and poultry are regulated by the U.S. Department of Agriculture (USDA). Those containing fish and game are regulated by the FDA. The FDA is also responsible for the advertising of drugs. This section will cover the advertising of ethical drugs, the labeling of packaged food, and the labeling of alcohol, tobacco and firearms.

Advertising of Ethical Drugs

The FDA working with the FTC has very strict guidelines about the advertising of prescription drugs. In particular, the use of brand names, and the description of ingredients, effectiveness and side effects in ads have to meet FDA guidelines for the labeling and packaging of drugs.[61] Advertising of a prescription drug directly to consumers must include the full list of side effects.[62] The list of side effects is often so alarming that consumers might hesitate to take a drug even when it has been prescribed by a physician. Pharmaceutical companies might prefer not to disclose such information to consumers, even if that means not advertising the drug to them. However, companies do not have to mention side effects if the ad does not mention the drug by name. In such cases, the ad merely states the disease and the availability of a cure, urging consumers to ask their doctor about it. This approach makes sense only for patented drugs that offer a unique treatment for a disease, that is distinctly superior to that of rivals. In such situations, the doctor is likely to prescribe the drug even though the ad does not mention the brand name, and the consumer does not ask for it by name. Whenever a drug is not patented, advertising for it that does not include a firm's brand name helps all companies that supply the drug.

Labeling of Food

The FDA has been very active in the area of truthful labeling of packaged foods. Since eating healthy foods became a craze in the United States, the FDA has been concerned that consumers may misunderstand terms such as "low-fat" or "cholesterol-free." For example, a food containing a high proportion of coconut oil but no animal product may claim to be cholesterol free. However, coconut oil is rich in saturated fats which can promote the body's own production of cholesterol. Thus, consumers who need to be on a low-cholesterol diet may wrongly assume that such foods are good for them. Similarly, many consumers assume that the term "all natural" implies healthful. However, a food such as honey-roasted peanuts may contain all-natural ingredients, but still be low in fiber and high in fat and sugar. Thus it may be harmful for a consumer on a low-fat or sugar-free diet.

In 1990, the U.S. Congress passed the Nutritional Labeling and Education Act, which gave the FDA jurisdiction over food labeling that would preempt state regulations. It also allowed the FDA to set precise definitions for terms used in food packaging and advertising, such as *lean*, *low* and *high*.[63] Under the act, the FDA established a uniform system of labeling titled "Nutrition Facts" which every packaged food product had to adopt as of May 1994 (see Exhibit 2-6). This labeling ensured that all packaged food products list the key ingredients and nutrients in the food, using the same terms, and a standard format, so consumers could easily compare, choose and use such products. The FDA also ensures that all claims made on packaged foods, drugs and cosmetics are not misleading and are fully substantiated.

The FTC adjusted its rules for the advertising of food products to harmonize with the FDA's rules. In particular it adopted the same definitions of common health claims. However, the FTC did not require as

▼ **EXHIBIT 2-6.** An example of nutrition facts (Lipton Cup-a-Soup).

Source: Courtesy of Lipton.

much substantiation of food claims as did the FDA.[64] Similarly, the USDA adjusted its rules concerning the labeling and package claims of foods containing meat and poultry to be consistent with those of the FDA for foods containing fish and game.[65]

While the new rules greatly help consumers to better understand and not be misled by food claims and labeling, they prevent the use of new or creative claims about nutrition and food composition, unless firms first convince the FDA to accept such claims.[66]

Labeling of Alcohol, Tobacco and Firearms

On July 1, 1993, Gian Luigi Ferri using a TEC-DC9 killed eight people and wounded six others in a shooting spree in San Francisco.[67] The TEC-9 was also famous as the weapon used by drug dealers in the TV series "Miami Vice." In 1994, relatives of five victims filed suit against Intratec Firearms, maker of the TEC-9. The suit faulted the company for marketing and advertising the weapon to criminals. As evidence, the suit cited an ad for the product that clearly states the gun resists fingerprints.[68]

Is the ad deceptive or unfair? Who should regulate such ads?

The Bureau of Alcohol, Tobacco and Firearms (BATF), an agency within the U.S. Treasury Department, has responsibility over the manufacture, marketing, taxation and use of alcohol, tobacco and firearms. The role of this agency, and its location within the treasury department have been debated, especially after its confrontation with religious fanatic David Koresh, which led to the self-immolation of Koresh and many of his followers. The BATF also has some jurisdiction over the packaging, labeling, advertising and sale of products containing alcohol or tobacco, or involving arms or ammunition.[69] For these categories of products, the agency may determine where ads may appear, what information they may contain, whether that information is misleading, and how that information may be endorsed. The most important rule of the agency is the requirement that all cigarette ads and packages contain the warning that cigarette smoking is injurious to the smoker's health. A lesser known regulation of the agency is its ban on live athletes as endorsers for all beverages containing alcohol.[70]

The FTC also claims jurisdiction over the advertising of firearms, within its general mandate to regulate truth in advertising. However, one author claims that neither the FTC nor the BATF has been active in monitoring the advertising of firearms. As a result the author claims that firearm ads have become "notorious for playing up the suitability of their weapons for criminal use."[71] For example, the ad's statement that the gun resists fingerprints, an attribute of interest only for criminals. The situation depicts the problem of multiple agencies having overlapping responsibilities. It also shows the limitations of agencies with limited budgets monitoring the entire domain of advertising. However, if the courts rule in favor of consumers who bring suits against companies for unfair advertising, it may enable the market to regulate unfair advertising more efficiently than does the FTC.

SELF-REGULATION

As stated earlier, **self-regulation** refers to the control of promotion by advertisers themselves. In particular, such regulation may occur by the advertisers or their agencies in-house, or by business organizations for their members.

In-House Self-Regulation

As an organization increases in size and brand-loyal clientele, it has more to lose from the future stream of dissatisfied consumers, than it can ever gain from a single misleading ad or promotion. For example, a misleading Tide promotion could seriously compromise its reputation with consumers and its future sales and profits. Procter & Gamble's potential earnings from the well-established and highly respected brand name Tide are so great, that no single, deceptive promotion may ever match the gains from consumers' future purchases of the brand without such a promotion. In general, the stronger an organization's franchise with consumers, the more stringent is its own in-house regulation of promotions. Such organizations are also likely to maintain legal departments that scrutinize all promotions to ensure that they meet all federal, state and common laws, as well as all internal principles of ethical promotion. In addition, because advertising agencies are as responsible for deceptive advertising as the client for whom they work, and because such agencies have to protect their own reputations for good advertising, agencies also maintain in-house staff to regulate promotions before pitching them to their clients. Thus the possession of strong brand names encourages firms to self-regulate, reducing the government's burden of monitoring firms' practices.

Despite these precautions, deceptive promotions still slip through in-house regulators. The reason could be lax monitoring by the advertiser or its agency, the inexperience or naiveté of employees, or the pressure of meeting sales targets or combating aggressive competitors. Thus, although organizations may set rational, lofty standards of promotion, particular employees may break these rules in specific situations.

Self-Regulation by Business Associations

A vast number of business associations regulate the promotions of their member firms. For example, after the lifting of Prohibition in the United States, the Distilled Spirits Council adopted a policy against advertising distilled spirits on TV. That policy was flouted by Seagram in June 1995, when it began advertising on TV, in order to be on equal footing with the beer and wine industries which do not have such a ban.[72] As another example, until the mid-1980s, the television code of the National

Association of Broadcasters stopped lingerie advertisers from using live models in ads.[73] One study found 22 self-regulatory organizations which it classified into four groups: industry groups, advertising associations, media associations and trade associations (see Exhibit 2-7). (The order of the groups in this exhibit proceeds from the most broad to the most specific.) In addition, professional organizations such as the American Bar Association and the American Dental Association also regulate advertising by their professional members.

Self-regulation has several benefits. First, it serves as a less public, expensive and confrontational means of regulation than federal or state regulation. To follow government regulation, firms must frequently hire expensive lawyers, set up law departments, indulge in costly data gathering, and face public disclosure of violations and costly sanctions. Self-regulation can achieve compliance with codes in a less costly, cumbersome, public or confrontational manner. In some cases, trade or business organizations have resorted to self-regulation to assure governments of their good intentions, and preempt less desirable federal or state regulation.

Second, self-regulation serves to control undesirable forms of advertising such as distasteful or irritating ads, to reduce consumers' displeasure with advertising. Similarly, self-regulation helps to control new, indiscreet and deceitful advertisers so that consumers do not lose their trust in advertising in general.

Third, while self-regulation is enacted primarily in the self-interests of firms, it can benefit consumers by making advertising more honest, fair and tasteful. Indeed, one study that analyzed the codes of the 22 organizations

involved in self-regulation found that most address issues prominent in federal regulation (see Exhibit 2-8). This is by no means a duplication of effort. To the extent that such self-regulation preempts the enactment of further regulation or the scrutiny of

▼ **EXHIBIT 2-7. Business associations with advertising regulations.**

Association	Acronym	Year Code Created
Advertising Associations		
American Advertising Federation	AAF	1965
American Association of Advertising Agencies	AAAA	1924
Association of National Advertisers	ANA	1972
Business/Professional Advertising Association	B/PAA	1975
Special Industry Groups		
Council of Better Business Bureaus:	CBBB	1912
■ Household Furniture		1978
■ Automobiles and Trucks		1978
■ Carpet and Rugs		1978
■ Home Improvement		1975
■ Charitable Solicitations		1974
Children's Advertising Review Unit	CARU	1974
National Advertising Division/National Advertising Review Board	NAD/NARB	1971
Media Associations		
American Business Press	ABP	1910
Direct Mail/Marketing Association	DM/MA	1960
Direct Selling Association	DSA	1970
National Association of Broadcasters:	NAB	
■ Radio		1937
■ Television		1952
Outdoor Advertising Association of America	OAAA	1950
Trade Associations		
American Wine Association	AWA	1949
Wine Institute	WI	1949
Distilled Spirits Association	DISCUS	1934
United States Brewers Association	USBA	1955
Pharmaceutical Manufacturers Association	PMA	1958
Proprietary Association	PA	1934
Bank Marketing Association	BMA	1976
Motion Picture Association of America	MPAA	1930
National Swimming Pool Institute	NSPI	1970
Toy Manufacturer Association	TMA	1962

Source: LaBarbera, Priscilla A. (1980), "Analyzing and Advancing the State of the Art of Advertising Self-Regulation, *Journal of Advertising* 9, 4, 27–38. Reprinted with permission of the American Academy of Advertising.

specific agencies, it ensures a less costly means of regulation for businesses and for consumers who ultimately pay the bill for all government regulation.

For example, in February 1974, Texaco launched a $40 million advertising campaign for a new gasoline, CleanSystem3, with claims that it was "changing what gasoline can do," "a breakthrough in technology," and provided the "highest performance."[74] Rival Chevron Corp. spent $500,000 and found that those claims were false. When Texaco refused to alter its claims based on Chevron's research, the company took its case to the networks and the Better Business Bureau. The three major TV networks agreed with Chevron and stopped running some Texaco commercials while asking Texaco to tone down others. The National Advertising Division of the Better Business Bureau which arbitrates such disputes between advertisers also got Texaco to tone down the claims on TV and other media. For example, Texaco had to use "breakthrough in Texaco technology" instead of "breakthrough in technology," and "higher performance" instead of "highest performance." In this case, the public benefited because the self-regulatory efforts of business incurred the cost of research and determining the settlement.

Self-regulation is not always in the consumer's interests. Certain forms of self-regulation could harm consumers. Such harm occurs when self-regulation reduces competition through advertising, misjudges consumer welfare, or reduces the information consumers can get to make good decisions.

For example before 1970, professional organizations (such as the American Bar Association) banned all advertising by their members. The reasoning was that advertising was profit oriented and "commer-

▼ EXHIBIT 2-8. Subject matter addressed by self-regulatory codes.

Subject Matter of Self-Regulation	Percent of Occurrences in Codes of 22 Associations
Truth and accuracy	100%
Substantiation of claims	81
Testimonials and endorsements	62
Illustrations or television presentations	62
Comparative advertising	58
Disclosure of complete information	54
Price claims	50
Puffery	50
Taste	46
Guarantees and warranties	38
Young and immature markets	35
Bait advertising	35
Use of word *free*	31
Layout	31
Contests, prizes and other promotions	31
Credit	31
Health and safety	27
Placement and acceptance in media	27
Use of words conveying professional qualifications (*bonded, insured*)	23
Degradation of societal groups	19
Asterisks	19
Use of words implying low price (*factory, manufacturer, wholesaler*)	19
Fear appeals	12
Advertising frequency	12
Trade-in allowances	12
Abbreviations	8
Indication of the identity, age, or volume of business	8
Advertising space for public causes	4

Source: LaBarbera, Priscilla A. (1980), "Analyzing and Advancing the State of the Art of Advertising Self-Regulation," *Journal of Advertising* 9, 4, 27–38. Reprinted with permission of the American Academy of Advertising.

cial." As such, it clashed with the dignity of these professions. Further, organizations feared that the advertising of prices could compromise the commitment of professionals to providing quality service. However, in 1974 the U.S. Supreme Court ruled that commercial speech such as advertising was protected by the First Amendment guarantee of free speech, as long as it was truthful. The Supreme Court struck down the state of Virginia's ban on advertising of prices. Since then the FTC and the Justice Department have successfully brought cases against restrictions on advertising by over 17 professional groups such as the American Dental Association and the American Medical Association. In the same spirit, the U.S. Department of Justice successfully challenged a code of the National Association of Broadcasters that prohibited advertising more than one product in a 30-second commercial. The court ruled that such a prohibition forced advertisers to buy more airtime than they wanted.[75]

Besides violating the guarantee of free speech, restrictions on advertising may also not be in the public interest because they deprive consumers of valuable information on the availability and prices of services. Several studies have shown that after the removal of such restrictions the prices of professional services (such as filing for taxes or divorce) have fallen as professionals could advertise better deals, and consumers could make more informed decisions.[76] Restrictions on advertising can also violate the government's antitrust laws which were enacted to ensure that collusion among competitors would not hurt consumers and other competitors.

Thus the determination of whether self-regulation of advertising by an industry is potentially illegal depends on whether the regulation contains a broad ban on advertising, reduces competition among firms in an industry or restricts the flow of relevant product information to consumers. On the other hand, self-regulation that promotes the goals and spirit contained in the federal regulation of advertising is likely to be legal and beneficial to consumers and competitors. For example, a potential rule by the Motion Picture Association of America requiring all movie producers to limit advertising to $2 million per movie would be anticompetitive, because it would prevent a producer with a good movie from informing consumers of the merits of the movie. However, a rule by this organization requiring all movie ads to contain the rating of the movie would not be anticompetitive, because it provides consumers with key information useful for choosing movies.

The evaluation of self-regulation shows that self-regulation, just like advertising, is intrinsically neither bad nor good. It is the manner and context of its use that make it so. Self-regulation is most effective when it promotes competition and increases consumer information without compromising the guarantee of free speech.

Summary

The regulation of promotion in the United States consists of federal regulation, state regulation and self-regulation by businesses. Federal regulation forms the basis of all U.S. regulation because of the preeminence of federal laws and the extensive resources of the federal government to implement the laws. State regulation and self-regulation tend to be patterned on federal regulation.

Several federal agencies are responsible for the regulation of promotion. Of these, the single most important is the Federal Trade Commission (FTC). It is responsible for two of the most important aspects of promotion: determining whether promotions are truthful, and whether they are fair to competitors, distributors and consumers. The FTC was set up in 1914 as an independent regulatory agency to more effectively combat unfair trade practices. A subsequent amendment extended the FTC's charter to explicitly include the monitoring of promotion.

Truth in promotion is relative. It depends on the goals of the promoter, perceptions of consumers, prevailing meaning of words and prevailing social norms for honesty. In the United States, the FTC is the key arbiter of such truth. It takes into account six issues when considering the truthfulness of claims: explicit lie, misleading claim, significant audience, substantiation, materiality and injury. Based on the six issues, the FTC may consider an ad deceptive if a significant consumer segment's understanding of a material claim in an ad is not substantiated. If the FTC staff finds an example of deceptive promotion, it brings it to a commissioner's attention with a recommendation of action. The FTC can order one of four types of remedies: cease-and-desist order, affirmative disclosure, restitution and corrective advertising.

Puffery is currently not considered deceptive if an average consumer is unlikely to perceive that the advertiser is guaranteeing a benefit in the claim. Miscomprehension cannot be an excuse for deception, because miscomprehension occurs randomly, while deception is directional. The FTC does not have the authority to develop rules about unfair ads for all firms and industries, but it may restrict or ban unfair ads on a case-by-case basis.

In addition to its general guidelines for truth in promotion, the FTC has guidelines for specific forms of advertising. The FTC requires that comparative claims in ads be truthful just as any other claims. However, firms must also research and word comparative claims carefully, because competitors can sue for inaccurate claims. The FTC has special guidelines for the use of endorsers, because this form of communication elicits greater trust from consumers and has greater potential to mislead. The FTC has ruled that mockups are deceptive when the mockups are intrinsically related to the attribute being communicated, and do not include a clear disclaimer. The FTC's guidelines on warranties require that ads describe the warranty accurately in terms of item(s) warranted; duration of the warranty; terms of a prorated warranty if any; and the money that will be refunded when applicable. The Federal Truth in Lending Act describes the terms under which firms may advertise loans. In particular, the act outlaws false and misleading advertising about the cost of a loan, and bait-and-switch advertising in which consumers are drawn to a vendor by a cheap loan and then sold on a more expensive one.

The FTC closely monitors all forms of sales promotions, especially price promotions, because they elicit an immediate and strong response from consumers, and are prone to misrepresentation by promoters. An important principle in the FTC's guidelines about truthful price promotions is that a suggested reference price should correctly reflect the prices in the market. State and federal agencies regulate contests and sweepstakes because of their similarity to lotteries and gambling.

Two media have received careful regulation from the federal government because of their potential for unfair competition, intrusiveness, fraud or deception: the broadcast media and the mail. Special rules govern the broadcast media because of their intrusiveness and power to affect people's lives and opinions. Mail service has always been carefully monitored because the distance and anonymity of the sender can facilitate fraud and unfair trade practices.

The FDA working with the FTC has very strict guidelines about the advertising of prescription drugs. In particular, the use of brand names, and the description of ingredients, effectiveness and side effects in ads have to meet FDA guidelines for the labeling and packaging of drugs. The FDA has been very active in the area of truthful labeling of packaged foods in standard terms, both to avoid consumer deception and to make consumer comparisons easy.

QUESTIONS

1. Federal regulation has become the basis of all regulation of promotion in the United States. Discuss.
2. What is truth in promotion? How should one determine if ads are truthful?
3. How and why has the FTC's monitoring of truth in promotion changed over the decades?
4. What is comparative advertising? What is the current FTC policy about comparative advertising, and why did it change from that in the past?
5. How should one distinguish between puffery, miscomprehension, unfairness and deception in advertising?
6. Discuss the impact of the 1988 amendment of the Lanham Act.
7. Is the FTC's policy regarding endorsement, demonstrations, warranties and credit consistent with its general policy regarding truth in advertising? Explain.
8. When exactly is price discrimination illegal? Why did the government institute this policy?
9. Explain the FTC policy regarding truth in price promotions.
10. Why does the federal government regulate the broadcast media? Why has such regulation changed over the decades?
11. Critics claim that all government regulation is a waste of public resources and an unnecessary burden on businesses. Self-regulation can achieve the same goals at a lower cost. Discuss.
12. Can competitive vigilance compensate for federal regulation? Discuss.

NOTES

1. Key, Janet (1989), "FTC Takes Campbell Ad With Grain Of Salt," *Chicago Tribune*, January 27; *Advertising Age* (1992), "Campbell, FTC Settle Ad Dispute," August 24, 8.
2. Ortega, Bob (1993), "Wal-Mart Bows to Pricing Reality by Changing Four Letters," *The Wall Street Journal*, May 21, B1.

3. Stern, Louis W. and Thomas L. Eovaldi (1984), *Legal Aspects of Marketing Strategy*, Englewood Cliffs, NJ: Prentice-Hall.

4. Rotfeld, Herbert J. (1992), "Power and Limitations of Media Clearance Practices and Advertising Self-Regulation," *Journal of Public Policy & Marketing,* 11, 1, 87–92.

5. See especially Exhibit 2 of LaBarbera, Priscilla A. (1980), "Analyzing and Advancing the State of the Art of Advertising Self-Regulation," *Journal of Advertising* 9, 4, 27–38.

6. Stern and Eovaldi, *Legal Aspects of Marketing Strategy.*

7. Silverstein, Stuart (1990), "Savon Drug Settles False-Advertising Case," *Los Angeles Times*, September 1, D1; Gellene, Denise (1993), "Drug Price Cuts: Mystery Solved," *Los Angeles Times*, May 7, D3.

8. Harris, Richard Jackson, et al. (1986), "Language in Advertising: A Psycho-linguistic Approach," *Current Issues and Research in Advertising* 9, 1 and 2, 1–26.

9. Yao, Dennis A., and Christa Van Anh Veechi (1992), "Information and Decisionmaking at the Federal Trade Commission," *Journal of Public Policy & Marketing* 11, 2, 1–11. The FTC does not *need* to obtain external evidence. The courts do require plaintiffs who file suits against deceptive advertising to bring such external evidence.

10. Petty, Ross D. (1992), *The Impact of Advertising Law on Business and Public Policy,* Westport, CT: Quorum Books.

11. *Federal Reporter* (1974), "Firestone Tire & Rubber Company v. FTC," St. Paul, MN: West Publishing.

12. Cohen, Dorothy (1980), "The FTC's Advertising Substantiation Program," *Journal of Marketing* 44 (Winter), 26–35.

13. Ross, Chuck (1996), "Marketers Fend Off Shift in Rules for Ad Puffery," *Advertising Age*, February 19, 41.

14. Chapter 7 discusses the results of these studies in greater detail. Jacoby, Jacob, and Wayne D. Hoyer (1982), "Viewer Miscomprehension of Televised Communication: Selected Findings," *Journal of Marketing* 46 (Fall), 12–26; Jacoby, Jacob, and Wayne D. Hoyer (1989), "The Comprehension/ Miscomprehension of Print Communication: Selected Findings," *Journal of Consumer Research* 15 (March), 434–443; Jacoby, Jacob, and Wayne D. Hoyer (1990), "The Miscomprehension of Mass-Media Advertising Claims: A Re-Analysis of Benchmark Data," *Journal of Advertising Research* (June/July), 9–16.

15. Snyder, Wally (1994), "Does FTC Have An 'Unfair' Future?" *Advertising Age*, March 28, 20.

16. Richards, Jef I. (1991), "FTC or NAAG: Who Will Win the Territorial Battle," *Journal of Public Policy & Marketing* 10, 1, 118–132.

17. Gatty, Bob (1993), "FTC Cracks Down on Promotion Schemes," *Promo* 6 (October), 12.

18. Preston, Ivan L. (1987), "A Review of the Literature on Advertising Regulation, 1983–1987," *Current Issues and Research in Advertising* 10, 1 and 2, 297–326; Ford, Gary T., and John E. Calfee (1986), "Recent Developments in FTC Policy on Deception," *Journal of Marketing* 50 (July), 82–103.

19. Preston, "A Review of the Literature on Advertising Regulation, 1983–1987."

20. Fawcett, Adrienne Ward (1994), "Excuses Erode Adherence to Healthy Diet," *Advertising Age*, May 2, S-2.

21. Dugas, Christine, and Paula Dwyer (1985), "Deceptive Ads: The FTC Laissez-faire Approach is Backfiring," *Business Week*, December 2, 136.

22. "Campbell Soup Resolves FTC Charges Regarding Health Claims in Advertising," (1992) *The Bureau of National Affairs, Inc. Antitrust and Trade Regulation Report* 63 (August 27), 265.

23. Levine, Joshua (1993), "Entertainment or Deception," *Forbes*, August 2, 102.

24. Preston, "A Review of the Literature on Advertising Regulation."

25. This anecdote is based on Elyse, Tanouye (1995), "Heartburn Drug Makers Feel Judge's Heat," *The Wall Street Journal*, October 16, B8.

26. Keller, Bruce P., and David H. Bernstein (1993), "Don't Add An Insult to Injury," *New York Law Journal* (April 12).

27. Petty, *The Impact of Advertising Law on Business and Public Policy.*

28. Washington D.C.: Office of the Federal Register (1996), "Guides Concerning Use of Endorsement and Testimonials in Advertising," *Code of Federal Regulation*, 16, Chapter 1, Part 255.

29. Stern and Eovaldi, *Legal Aspects of Marketing Strategy.*

30. *Ibid.*

31. *Ibid.*

32. Examples taken from: Levine, "Entertainment or Deception"; Stern and Eovaldi, *Legal Aspects of Marketing Strategy*; Miller, Julia (1994), "Shoot Fast, 'Cut Back On Trickery,'" *Advertising Age*, October 17, 29.

33. Stern and Eovaldi, *Legal Aspects of Marketing Strategy.*

34. Nelson, Emily (1996), "Goodyear Hopes to Drive Home Lifetime Guarantee on New Tires," *The Wall Street Journal*, March 7, B14.

35. For details, see Stern and Eovaldi.

36. Gellene, Denise (1996), "Stores Settle Allegations On Zero-Interest Advertisements," *Los Angeles Times*, September 15, D1, D3.

37. Kristof, Kathy M. (1996), "New Fed Rules Aim To Make Automobile Leases Clearer," *Los Angeles Times*, September 19, D1, D3.

38. In addition to these three areas, a vast number of other regulations cover pricing activities. We do not cover the latter regulations because they are not related to promotions.

39. Inman, James E. (1984), *The Regulatory Environment of Business*, New York: John Wiley & Sons; Monroe, Kent B. (1990), *Pricing: Making Profitable Decisions*, 2nd ed., New York: McGraw-Hill Book Company.

40. Washington, D.C.: Office of the Federal Register (1995), "Guides for Advertising Allowances and Other

Merchandising Payments and Services," *Code of Federal Regulation*, 16, Chapter 1, Part 240, 34–40.

41. Washington, D.C.: Office of the Federal Register (1995), "Guides Against Deceptive Pricing," *Code of Federal Regulation*, 16, Chapter 1, Part 233, 19–22.

42. ANA *Consumer Promotion Seminar Fact Book,* 7.

43. Stern and Eovaldi.

44. Gatty, "FTC Cracks Down on Promotion Schemes."

45. This subsection is based on Stern and Eovaldi, *Legal Aspects of Marketing Strategy.*

46. Washington, D.C.: Office of the Federal Register (1995), "Games of Chance In The Food Retailing and Gasoline Industries," *Code of Federal Regulation*, 16, Part 418, 297–298.

47. Balasubramanian, Siva K. (1994), "Beyond Advertising and Publicity: Hybrid Messages and Public Policy Issues," *Journal of Advertising* 23, 4, 29–46.

48. *Ibid.*

49. *Ibid.*

50. Levine, "Entertainment or Deception?"

51. Lipman, Joanne (1990), "FTC Zaps Misleading Infomercials," *The Wall Street Journal*, June 19, B1.

52. *United States Code Service* (1995), Lawyers Cooperative Publishing, 278.

53. The Public Health Cigarette Smoking Act of 1970 banned the advertising of cigarettes on TV and radio.

54. *United States Code Service.*

55. Based on Salem, D'Jamila (1996), "U.S. Cracks Down on Telephone Con Artists' 'Draft Fraud' Tactics," *Los Angeles Times*, March 20, D1, D10.

56. Kahn, E. J., Jr. (1973), *Fraud: The United States Postal Inspection Service and Some of the Fools and Knaves It Has Known*, New York: Harper & Row.

57. Stern and Eovaldi, 99–102.

58. Kahn, *Fraud.*

59. Committee on Interstate and Foreign Commerce, U.S. House of Representatives (1974), *A Brief History of Food, Drug &*

Cosmetic Act, Washington D.C.: U.S. Government Printing Office.

60. Stern and Eovaldi.

61. Committee on Interstate and Foreign Commerce, U.S. House of Representatives, *Brief History of Food, Drug & Cosmetic Act.*

62. Washington, D.C.: Office of the Federal Register (1995), "Prescription Drug Advertising," *Code of Federal Regulation*, 21, Chapter 1, Part 202.

63. Ippolito, Pauline M., and Alan D. Mathios (1993), "New Food Labeling and Regulations and the Flow of Nutrition Information to Consumers," *Journal of Public Policy & Marketing* 12, 2, 188–205.

64. Colford, Steven (1994), "Congress May Nibble At Foods' Ad Claims," *Advertising Age*, May 30, 12.

65. Ippolito and Mathios, "New Food Labeling and Regulations."

66. *Ibid.*

67. Colford, Steven W. (1994), "Policing of Gun Ads Draws Blank," *Advertising Age*, July 7, 14.

68. *Ibid.*

69. United States Bureau of ATF (1990), *An Introduction to the Bureau of Alcohol, Tobacco, and Firearms and The Regulated Industries*, Washington, DC: U.S. Government Printing Office.

70. *Ibid.*

71. Colford, Steven W. (1994), "Policing of Gun Ads Draws Blank."

72. Goll, Beatty (1996), "Seagram Flouts Ban on TV Ads Pitching Liquor," *The Wall Street Journal*, June 11, B1–B6.

73. Rotfeld, "Power and Limitations of Media Clearance Practices and Advertising Self-Regulation."

74. Solomon, Caleb (1994), "Gasoline Ads Canceled; Lack of Truth Cited," *The Wall Street Journal*, July 21, B1, B7.

75. Petty, *The Impact of Advertising Law on Business and Public Policy.*

76. *Ibid.*

3

In December 1994, the board of Saatchi
& Saatchi, at that time one of the largest
advertising agencies in the world,
shocked the advertising community by
forcing out the chairman and cofounder
of the agency, Maurice Saatchi.[1] Maurice
and his brother Charles Saatchi founded
Saatchi & Saatchi in London in
September 1970, with a $60,000 invest-
ment[2] and nine employees. The more
flamboyant younger brother, Maurice,
managed the accounts while the older,

Advertising Agencies and the Creative Process

more reclusive brother, Charles, handled
the creative.

From the beginning, Maurice Saatchi
pursued clients aggressively and had
visions of building a large agency. In
1975 the company began merging with
or acquiring other agencies. By 1982 it
was the largest agency in the United
Kingdom. Acquisitions in the United
States and Europe followed, until it
became the fifth largest global advertising
holding company in 1994 and 1995 (see
Exhibit 3-1). The large multinational

▼ EXHIBIT 3-1. The world's largest advertising agencies, 1995.

Rank in 1995 (1994)	Holding Company	Agency Brands Owned	Gross Income, 1995 (billions of dollars)	Growth, 1992–1995 (%)
1 (1)	WPP Group	**Ogilvy & Mather Worldwide:** Cole & Weber; Ogilvy & Mather Direct; A. Elcolf & Co. **J. Walter Thompson Co.:** Brouillard Communications; J. Walter Thompson Direct; JWT Specialized Communications; JWT Direct **Other U.S. units:** Einson Freeman; Mendoza, Dillon & Associates	$3.2	13%
2 (2)	Omnicom Group	**BBDO Worldwide:** Baxter, Gurian & Mazzel; Frank J Corbett Inc.; Doremus & Co.: Larry/Wolf/Swift; Lyons, Leavey Nickel and Swift **DDB Needham Worldwide:** Bernard Hodes Group; Kallir, Philips, Ross **Other units:** TBWA Advertising; Alcons Marketing Group; Goodby, Silverstein & Partners; Merkley Newman Harty; Rainoldi Kerzner Radcliffe; Rapp Collins Worldwide; Harrison, Star, Weiner & Beitler	2.6	17
3 (3)	Interpublic Group of Companies	**Ammirati Puris Lintas:** Dailey & Associates; Messianu Lintas; Long, Haymes & Carr; C-E Marketing Communications; Ammirati Puris Lintas; Campbell-Ewald **Lowe Group:** Lowe & Partners/SMS; Lowe Direct; The Martin Agency; Gotham Inc.; Die Hager Group **McCann-Erickson Worldwide:** McCann Direct; McCann Healthcase; Anderson and Lembke	2.3	10

Continued

agency was especially useful to multinational corporations that wanted consistent and integrated service for their advertising around the world. For example, by 1995, Saatchi & Saatchi served Toyota in 20 countries and Procter & Gamble in 50 countries. While Saatchi & Saatchi's reach was impressive, it did not become famous for particularly bold or creative advertising.

At the same time, in its haste to acquire companies, Saatchi & Saatchi piled up more than $750 million in debt. By late 1989, crippling debt forced the company to bring in new management. Maurice Saatchi had to cede the chairmanship of the company to a financial expert, Robert Louis-Dreyfus, and later when Louis-Dreyfus left, to his right-hand man, Charles Scott. Maurice lived a flamboyant lifestyle, had expensive tastes, and was very costly for the company to support. His view of the company clashed with Scott's. The conflict between the two personalities started many public feuds. Ultimately, under pressure from lenders, on December 16, 1994, the governing

▼ **EXHIBIT 3-1.** (Continued)

Rank in 1995 (1994)	Holding Company	Agency Brands Owned	Gross Income, 1995 (billions of dollars)	Growth, 1992–1995 (%)
4 (4)	Dentsu Inc.	Dentsu Corp. of America	2.0	12
5 (5)	Cordiant	**Saatchi & Saatchi Advertising:** Saatchi & Saatchi/CMS; Saatchi & Saatchi Direct; Team One; Conill Advertising; Cliff Freeman & Partners; Klemtner Advertising; Saatchi & Saatchi Business Communications **Backer Spielvogel Bates Worldwide:** BSB/Dryden & Petisi; AC&R Advertising; Kobs & Draft	1.4	12
6 (6)	Young & Rubicam	Young & Rubicam; Chapman Direct; CMF&Z; Sive/Young & Rubicam; Sudler & Hennessey; Wunderman Cato Johnson Worldwide; Bravo Group	1.2	14
7 (9)	Hakuhodo	Hakuhodo Advertising America	1.0	24
8 (7)	Havas Advertising	**Euro RSCG:** MVBMS; Tatham Euro RSCG; Cohn & Wells **Havas Diversified Agencies:** Lally, McFarland & Pantello; Robert A. Becker Inc.; Hadley Group **Pampas**	0.9	12
9 (8)	Grey Advertising	Grey Advertising; Font & Vaamonde; Grey Direct Marketing Group; Gross Townsend Frank Hoffman	0.9	11
10 (10)	Leo Burnett Company, Inc.	Leo Burnett Company, Inc.	0.8	19

Source: "World's Top 50 Advertising Organizations" (1996), *Advertising Age*, April 15, S14.

board stripped Maurice Saatchi of the chairmanship of the holding company, Saatchi & Saatchi Co., and offered him the lesser job of chairman of Saatchi & Saatchi Advertising Worldwide. On January 3, 1995, Maurice Saatchi declined the offer and resigned from the company.

However, he did not leave quietly. On January 11, 1995, he founded a rival company called the New Saatchi Agency. He motivated three senior executives of the parent company plus his brother (who was president) to join the new company. Maurice Saatchi's departure also prompted many huge accounts to cancel their contracts with Saatchi & Saatchi, including the company's biggest

account, British Airways. Soon, the New Saatchi Agency won most of these big accounts including British Airways, Dixons Group PLC, Gallaher Tobacco Ltd. and Mirror Group Newspapers. By May 1995, Saatchi & Saatchi had a net loss in accounts worth $92 million or 8 percent of its revenues, while the New Saatchi Agency had won a total of $211 million in accounts in the four months since its inception. Saatchi & Saatchi also suffered a major loss in stock price, which by February 2, 1995, dropped to less than two-thirds of its price prior to the crisis.

The two advertising agencies and their employees were also locked in several lawsuits. Saatchi & Saatchi sued the new company and its employees for use of the name, theft of documents and breach of contract in trying to attract former clients. The executives had contracted with their former employer not to solicit its clients for two years after leaving the agency. The former executives and Maurice Saatchi also sued Saatchi & Saatchi over bonuses and other matters. After a judge passed a preliminary injunction in favor of the New Saatchi Agency, the two parties reached an out-of-court settlement. The New Saatchi Agency seemed to have won the best part of the settlement with the old company dropping its suits against its executives, changing its name to Cordiant, and paying $800 million for all legal costs of both sides. The New Saatchi Agency had to change its name to the M&C Saatchi Agency, and had to refrain from soliciting clients of Cordiant until December 31, 1995. Both requirements were considered small costs for the new agency.

The turmoil at Saatchi & Saatchi brings into focus a number of issues about the advertising agency. Why does an advertising agency exist? What functions does it serve? How do advertisers choose and compensate agencies? How do agencies develop creative ads? This chapter addresses these questions.

The previous two chapters provide the background for advertising: Chapter 1 describes the fundamentals of marketing strategy and the place of advertising in that strategy. Chapter 2 describes the regulatory environment that defines what types of advertising are legal. This chapter describes the structure and working of the advertising agency, the principal organization that helps advertisers develop ads. The chapter is divided into four parts that cover the important features of advertising agencies: their structure, selection, compensation and creativity.

THE STRUCTURE OF AGENCIES

The **advertising agency** is an organization that solicits clients, creates ads, or places ads in the media. It is the institution that is most closely associated with advertising in people's minds. As Chapter 1 explained, advertising agencies began in the mid-1800s as agents of the media, who sold space in local media to manufacturers from other regions. Today, the structure of an agency is driven largely by the market in which it operates. This section begins by discussing the market for agencies. It then discusses the functions, types, ownership and organization of agencies.

The Market for Advertising Agencies

Life in an advertising agency can be very exciting, with rapid changes in the market in which clients operate, frequent changes in clients' tasks and many changes in clients themselves. But one of the most typical characteristics of life in an agency is its competitiveness. Three factors account for its competitiveness.

First, advertising agencies provide a service that must change constantly in response to the needs and problems of clients. Agencies are under constant pressure to come up with creative solutions for their clients' communication problems. Thus agencies do not provide a standard service of known quality, such as a hamburger or a package of detergent, which has a loyal following. Their performance changes, sometimes deteriorates or just does not meet their clients' expectations. They can and frequently do lose their accounts. For example, despite a long tradition of outstanding advertising that includes such icons as the Marlboro Man and Tony the Tiger, and despite winning many new accounts in 1992 alone, Leo Burnett Company, Inc. had its Oldsmobile account reviewed that year because of its lackluster advertising. Similarly, despite outstanding creative for the Nike account, Wieden and Kennedy ultimately lost the account. One study indicates that over a five-year period, 67 percent of the clients of the 50 largest agencies moved part or all of their accounts to other agencies.[3]

Second, entry into this market is easy, requiring appropriate staff, but only minimal equipment and fixed assets.[4] The unique strength of a typical agency lies in its creative staff which produces the ads, or in its account staff which wins and services clients. Any individual or group of individuals with appropriate skills and contacts can form an agency. Groups of such individuals can decide to leave an employer and form a new agency of their own, increasing the number of agencies in the market and intensifying the competition, while weakening an established firm. The increasing sophistication of computer software for designing and producing ads has reduced the need for human artistic skills, and increased the ease with which new agencies can enter this market. As the opening example illustrates, Maurice Saatchi left the company he founded and built a new $200 million agency in three months. While established agencies have contract clauses that prevent their employees from breaking off and taking their clients with them, such clauses are difficult to enforce, as the example of the New Saatchi Agency indicates.

Third, because of easy entry into this market, a large number of agencies compete for clients. Competition in an industry intensifies as the number of competing firms increases.[5] For example, about 60 percent of the billings in this industry are controlled by as many as 500 agencies.[6] In comparison, in the soft drinks market, as much as 60 percent of industry sales are controlled by just two firms (Pepsi-Cola and Coca-Cola), while in the market for personal computer operating systems, as much as 77 percent of industry sales are controlled by just one firm (Microsoft).[7] Competition in the soft drinks and software markets is intense. So the reader can gauge how much more intense competition is in the market for advertising agencies.

As a result of this intense competition, agencies do not have enduring contracts with clients, face downward pressure on their compensation rates, and suffer considerable employee turnover. But the challenge of creating original ads continues to draw talent to this industry. The thrill of designing an outstanding ad that propels a brand into market leadership is one that fires up the people who work in this industry.

Agency Functions

In April 1995, Jay Chiat, the founder of Chiat/Day, a hothouse of creative ads, agreed to sell his agency to Omnicom Group Inc., a sedate agency holding company.[8] Jay Chiat founded the company with Guy Day, a writer, in 1968. Mr. Chiat was not a creative genius himself. His strength was in inspiring his colleagues and employees to produce great ads. The creative force at Chiat/Day was Lee Clow, who said of Jay Chiat, "Jay drove me to reach higher than I ever would have reached on my own. I wonder now, am I going to be able to force myself to reach even higher without Jay behind me?"[9] Under Chiat's inspiration and Clow's leadership, Chiat/Day became famous for its creative ads. Among its many achievements was the introductory campaign for Nissan's Altima, the Energizer Bunny, Reebok's U.B.U campaign and Apple Macintosh's "1984" introductory ad, which is often cited as the best ad in U.S. TV history (see Chapter 1). Based on its achievements, *Advertising Age* anointed Chiat/Day as the "Agency of the Decade."[10]

But Jay Chiat was not a genius at accounts management. The agency lost many well-known accounts, which one source attributed to its arrogance.[11] In the late 1980s and the 1990s, Jay purchased other businesses, diversified abroad and built a personal art collection. These activities may have distracted him from the important function of soliciting clients and managing accounts. The agency lost a number of accounts in the 1990s while at the same time it was saddled with debt from its acquisitions. It sold out to Omnicom to liquidate its debt and focus on its strength of developing creative ads.

The experience of Chiat/Day shows how designing creative ads led to success and fame, while poor accounts management quickly led to failure. These two functions, creative and accounts management, are the primary functions of an advertising agency. In addition, many agencies also offer two other important functions, media planning and market research. This section discusses these functions of the agency.

Creative The **creative** function involves the job of designing the ad. This function is also called design, or creative design, and the people responsible for the function are called **designers** or **creatives**. Designing itself consists of two tasks: art direction and copywriting. **Art direction** includes the development of the visuals and sound for the ad, which may be print, audio or video. The professionals who design the art are called **art directors**, while those who produce the art are commercial artists. **Copywriting** includes the development of the verbal

▼ **EXHIBIT 3-2.** Sampling of a Leo Burnett Company, Inc. ad.

Source: © 1959 by Kellogg Company. Reprinted with permission of Kellogg Company.

component of the ad, whether spoken or written. Art direction and copywriting are separate functions because the same individual is rarely both a good art director and a good copywriter. Nevertheless, specialists in either area contribute to the work of the other area. Moreover, these two tasks require close coordination, because the finished ad must involve a seamless integration of words, sounds and pictures. The need for this integration led William Bernbach to design the creative team consisting of an art director and copywriter.[12] Prior to his innovation, art direction and copywriting were housed in separate departments, leading to conflicts over resources and lack of coordination.[13]

Designing the creative is the most important service that an agency can provide an advertiser. It is one of the characteristics that distinguishes one agency from another, and is frequently the primary cause of the success of an agency. As the experience of Chiat/Day indicates, many agencies have grown from small operations to renowned agencies due to their outstanding creative.

Accounts Management The **accounts** of an agency are its clients who advertise. **Accounts management** involves the solicitation and servicing of these accounts. It may be considered the first function of the agency: if there are no accounts, the agency has no work. The role of an account executive is to try to understand the client, communicate its problem to the other departments in the agency, especially the design team, and then mediate between these departments and the client to develop the advertising campaign. If the design team has a strong feeling for taking the client in a new direction, the account executive may have to persuade the client about this direction. On the other hand, if the design team develops ads that are creative but either not suited to the client or not supported by marketing research, the account executive may have to persuade the design team about a different direction. Above all, the account executive must foster an atmosphere of loyal and wholehearted dedication to the client that motivates the entire staff to give their best to the client.

At Leo Burnett Company, Inc., outstanding creative together with dedicated service have been welded into a tradition of advertising that has survived for over 60 years and has grown a small Chicago operation into a $5.6 billion global advertising agency (see Exhibit 3-2). A hallmark of the agency is the staff's intense dedication to its clients. One study found that during one five-year period (1987–1992), the agency had the best loyalty among all agencies, retaining 76 percent of its clients. In contrast, the setback of Chiat/Day in the 1990s may be attributed to weakness at accounts management rather than any other factor. Similarly, Saatchi & Saatchi floundered in early 1995 because the board underestimated the importance of Maurice Saatchi's contact with clients, while it overvalued the financial side of the business.

Tension between the creative and accounts departments is common. Creatives feel that account executives do not appreciate their creativity, are unwilling to take risks and tend to water down their bold ideas.[14] On the other hand, account executives feel that creatives are unrealistic, do not understand their clients or are more interested in winning attention than in increasing sales. As a result, in some agencies these two functions do not work in unison, and one or the other may have the upper hand. Agencies in which designers play the most important role tend to produce creative, attention-getting ads, and to attract clients that need such ads. Agencies in which account executives play the most important role tend to establish a strong rapport with clients and maintain long-term relations with them. Advertisers with well-established brands that require good image maintenance, rather than attention-getting ads, may favor agencies that place a premium on accounts management rather than on creativity. For example, Nissan Altima, a new entry in the mid-size car market, chose the creative house Chiat/Day as its agency when it wanted to attack the market leaders, Toyota and Honda. But the leader, Toyota, retained the more sober agency, Saatchi & Saatchi (Los Angeles) as its agency.

Media Planning **Media planning** involves the design of the media plan and the purchase of media time and space. The **media plan** consists of a mix of time slots on and spaces in various media (see Chapter 15). **Media** is a collective term for the channels, such as TV and magazines, through which advertisers or programmers communicate with individuals. Media planning is one of the oldest functions of the agency. In the 1840s, agencies began primarily as media buyers.[15] At that time, newspapers restricted ads to small space, a few typesets and no pictures. Newspapers had to deal with hundreds of advertisers scattered all over their selling region, without the benefit of good transport and communication. Agencies made the task of the newspapers easy, by buying space in bulk and selling it to advertisers. For their service, agencies received a commission from the newspapers. That was the start of the agency business, and of the commission system of compensation.

As the agencies and advertisers grew in size, and as advertisers were allowed more variety in ads, agencies began to offer more services such as the design and production of ads. By the early part of the current century, agencies offered a full spectrum of services, becoming representatives of the advertisers. However, until recently they were paid by the media solely on the commission basis. Because most agencies still bill their clients a percentage of the amount the clients spend on media, the media buying department is an important source of revenues for the agency. The two important functions of the media buying department are to develop the media plan (see Chapter 15), and to buy media time and space for as low a cost as possible.

Market Research **Market research** involves obtaining information about the client, its customers, and its competitors to make good advertising decisions. It consists of five main activities: determining what information is needed, developing the research design, collecting data, analyzing data and interpreting the results. A full-fledged market research department would carry out all these five functions. However, an advertising agency's research department need not do so, because specialized market research firms are better equipped to carry out such research (see Chapters 14 and 15). Moreover, some advertisers themselves have in-house market research departments for such tasks.

The market research department of an agency needs to carry out just the first and last of the five research activities: determining what information is needed and interpreting the results. These two activities are the least time consuming of the five, but also the most valuable. Determining what information to collect also determines the scope and direction of research and the probability of hitting on the right solution for the advertiser. Interpreting the results involves translating technical findings into information that is useful to managers. It also involves filtering out what is actionable in the results, from what is noteworthy and what is trivial. To be performed well, these two research activities require staff with insight, experience and a good understanding of the statistical methods used for research.

For example, suppose the state of Iowa hires the agency Bozell Worldwide to develop an ad campaign to attract more manufacturing firms to the state. An important decision for the agency is to choose a theme for the campaign. The agency needs to research business managers' intentions to start new manufacturing plants, and their perceptions of locating those plants in Iowa versus other states. The agency's research department need not carry out the research to obtain this information. But it needs to define the precise issues on which it wants information. When the research results come in, the research department needs to explain to the agency's seniors and the client, how the findings suggest the appropriate theme for the advertising campaign.

Agency Types

In 1992, McCann-Erickson Worldwide all but lost creative responsibility for the Coca-Cola account, which it had held for almost 37 years, to a relatively small talent firm in Hollywood. How that came about is an interesting story in agency relations and creativity.[16]

McCann-Erickson first worked for the Coca-Cola account in 1955. Over the years it captured the accounts of many of Coca-Cola's brands in the U.S. and around the world (see Exhibit 3-3). It produced some memorable ads for the accounts, including the "It's the real thing" slogan of the 1970s. However, from about the mid-1970s, Coca-Cola suffered a massive onslaught of competitive advertising from Pepsi. Initially the campaign was based on the "Pepsi challenge," which suggested that consumers found that Pepsi tasted better than Coke in blind taste tests. In the 1980s and early 1990s Pepsi's attack was more subtle, taking the form of creative and youthful ads that appealed to a younger age group—the "Pepsi Generation." Despite many changes in campaign themes, McCann-Erickson's ads for Coke never seemed to get the better of Pepsi's in freshness or creativity.

In September 1991, Coca-Cola tried a radical alternative. It retained the consulting services of Creative Artists Agency (CAA), a premier talent firm in Hollywood. The consulting arrangement grew from a relationship between CAA founder and president Michael Ovitz and Coca-Cola president and chief operating officer Donald Keough. Ovitz's advice was well received by Coke and the market, and his agency soon displaced McCann-Erickson as Coca-Cola classic's primary agency. By 1993, CAA was responsible for 24 of 26 ads created for Coke, while McCann-Erickson was responsible for only 2.

CAA brought a radically new style to Coke's advertising. It used computer animation, Hollywood directors, and drama to create a multiplicity of ads that were immediately noticed, well remembered, and well liked, especially by younger consumers, who were the primary target. A particularly appealing and memorable image was that of computer animated polar bears relaxing with a bottle of Coke (see Exhibit 3-4). In a departure from the past, CAA also used quite different ad executions for different media outlets and target segments. As a Coke's senior vice president put it, "The campaign isn't one sight, one sell."[17] The most amazing aspect of CAA's work was that the agency had only four full-time staff members on the job. Most of the ad production was farmed out to production houses, and so was some of the creative. That strategy ensured that CAA had a stream of fresh ideas, minimal overhead and low costs. One senior vice president at Coke claimed that the cost for producing 26 ads at CAA was the same as that for 4 at McCann-Erickson. In terms of market share, Coca Cola classic gained .4 percent relative to Pepsi. For 1993, Coca Cola classic's market share rose by .1 percent to 20.1 percent, Pepsi's fell by .3 percent to 17.7 percent. Each 1 percent in market share equals about $500 million in sales.

The shift of the $350 million account of one of the world's major advertised brands, from a traditional full-service East Coast advertising agency to a Hollywood talent firm that did no advertising, was not lost on the advertising community. The shift came amid intense discussion in advertising circles of the problems with full-service agencies and the potential decline of traditional agencies. As one agency president put it, "America's biggest advertisers are realizing the only comfort for their brand in tough times is a huge idea, not a huge agency."[18]

The success of its experience with CAA led Coca-Cola to hire other small non–East Coast agencies, such as Fallon McElligott of Minneapolis and Wieden and Kennedy of Portland, Oregon. In 1994, CAA produced 23 ads for Coke, Fallon-McElligott produced 2 and McCann-Erickson only 1.

The example of McCann-Erickson and the rise of CAA brings into focus the different types of agencies, the roles they play and the nature of their competition for clients. In terms of the services they provide, agencies can be classified into two broad types: specialized agencies and full-service agencies.

Specialized Agencies **Specialized agencies** are organizations that do not perform all four functions of agencies. Typically, such agencies specialize in only one or part of one of the functions, such as design, production, representing talent (performers) or placing outdoor ads. A plethora of specialized agencies perform functions that span the entire spectrum of agency activities. **Creative boutiques** are small agencies that specialize in developing the creative for ads. They may work directly for advertisers who split their account among specialized agencies, or they may

▼ EXHIBIT 3-3. McCann-Erickson's worldwide accounts.

McCANN-ERICKSON WORLDWIDE

Clients:

Column headers — The Americas: U.S., Canada, Argentina, Barbados, Belize*, Bolivia*, Brazil, Caribbean**, Chile, Colombia, Costa Rica, Dom. Republic, Ecuador, El Salvador, Guatemala, Honduras, Jamaica, Mexico, Nicaragua*, Panama, Paraguay, Peru, Puerto Rico, Surinam*, Trinidad, Uruguay, Venezuela

Europe: Austria, Belgium, Bulgaria*, Croatia, Czech Repub., Denmark, Finland, France, Germany, Greece, Hungary, Ireland, Italy, Netherlands, Norway, Poland, Portugal, Romania*, Russia, Slovakia, Slovenia, Spain, Sweden, Switzerland, Turkey, U.K.

Clients listed:
Agfa
Air Canada
American Express
American Home Products
AT&T
Aviateca
Bacardi/Martini & Rossi
Bayer/Miles
BBC World Service
Bimbo Bread
Black & Decker
Boots Healthcare Intl.
Braun
BSN
Buitoni
Canon
Casio
Cathay Pacific
Cereal Partners Worldwide
Chesebrough-Pond's/Vaseline
Citibank
Coca-Cola
Columbia Tri-Star
Continental Micronesia
Delphi Auto Systems
Del Monte
Europcar
Exxon/Esso
Ferrero
General Motors
Gillette
Goodyear
Wm. Grant & Sons
Grundig
Heineken
Hitachi
Interbrew
Johnson & Johnson
Lee Jeans
Levi Strauss
London Intl. Grp. (Durex)
L'Oreal
Lotus Software
MasterCard
Mattel
McCormick
Motorola
MultiChoice
Nestle
Parker Pen
Perfetti
Reckitt & Colman
Riviana Pozuelo
RJR Nabisco
RJR Tobacco
San Miguel
Savoy
Scott Paper
Sega
SmithKline Beecham
Sony
Star TV
Texas Instruments
Tiffany & Co.
Unilever
UPS
Wash. State Apple Comm.
Waterman Pens
WD-40
World Gold Council
Yoplait

*Non-equity affiliation. **Caribbean includes Aruba, Bahamas, Bermuda, Grand Cayman, Guadeloupe, Guyana, Haiti and Martinique. ***Middle East consists of Bahrain, Iran, Israel, Jordan, Kuwait, Lebanon, Oman, Qatar, Saudi Arabia and United Arab Emirates.

Source: Reprinted with permission from the September 18, 1995, issue of *Advertising Age*. Copyright © 1995 Crain Communications, Inc.

▼ EXHIBIT 3-3. (Continued)

McCANN-ERICKSON WORLDWIDE — Clients:	Cameroon*	Egypt*	Ghana*	Ile de la Reunion*	Ivory Coast*	Kenya*	Mauritius*	Middle East***	Morocco*	Nigeria*	Senegal*	South Africa*	Tanzania*	Tunisia*	Uganda*	Zimbabwe*	Australia*	Cambodia*	China*	Guam*	Hong Kong*	India*	Indonesia*	Japan*	Malaysia*	Myanmar*	New Zealand*	Pakistan*	Philippines*	Singapore*	South Korea*	Sri Lanka*	Taiwan*	Thailand*	Vietnam*
Agfa												•					•		•		•			•									•	•	
Air Canada								•													•			•											
American Express					•																			•											
American Home Products																																			
AT&T												•												•											
Aviateca																																			
Bacardi/Martini & Rossi								•				•					•		•		•	•		•						•	•		•	•	
Bayer/Miles																								•											
BBC World Service			•						•			•	•		•	•																			
Bimbo Bread																																			
Black & Decker									•																		•								
Boots Healthcare Intl.												•					•																		
Braun									•										•		•		•	•					•	•	•		•	•	
BSN																																			
Buitoni																			•		•	•							•	•			•		
Canon																																			
Casio					•				•	•														•											
Cathay Pacific	•					•		•				•					•		•		•	•	•	•			•		•	•	•	•	•	•	•
Cereal Partners Worldwide					•									•							•			•					•	•			•		
Chesebrough-Pond's/Vaseline				•	•	•		•	•													•		•				•							
Citibank																																			
Coca-Cola	•	•	•	•	•	•	•	•		•	•				•		•	•						•			•	•	•	•	•	•	•		•
Columbia Tri-Star								•									•							•											
Continental Micronesia																	•			•	•			•								•			
Delphi Auto Systems																				•				•											
Del Monte																					•	•		•											
Europcar					•																														
Exxon/Esso					•		•										•		•	•		•	•							•			•	•	•
Ferrero												•					•		•		•			•	•					•			•	•	
General Motors		•		•	•	•	•	•		•	•	•		•	•		•		•	•	•	•		•	•		•		•	•			•		
Gillette	•	•		•	•	•	•	•	•	•	•	•	•	•	•		•	•	•		•	•	•	•	•		•	•		•	•		•	•	•
Goodyear																	•							•											
Wm. Grant & Sons												•					•		•		•			•					•	•			•	•	
Grundig																																			
Heineken			•																		•														
Hitachi								•									•				•			•					•						
Interbrew																																			
Johnson & Johnson								•	•								•		•		•	•	•	•	•		•		•	•	•		•	•	
Lee Jeans	•																																		
Levi Strauss								•									•				•	•		•	•					•			•		
London Intl. Grp. (Durex)								•	•		•		•				•							•									•		
L'Oreal	•							•	•								•		•		•	•	•	•	•		•		•	•	•		•	•	
Lotus Software												•																							
MasterCard			•	•				•	•						•																				
Mattel																						•	•							•	•				
McCormick																																			
Motorola																					•			•											
MultiChoice	•	•			•	•	•			•	•	•	•	•	•																				
Nestle	•		•		•	•	•			•	•	•	•	•	•		•	•	•		•	•	•	•	•	•	•		•	•	•	•	•	•	•
Parker Pen						•						•					•				•	•	•	•					•	•					
Perfetti																			•														•		
Reckitt & Colman																						•									•		•		
Riviana Pozuelo																																			
RJR Nabisco		•						•													•			•			•			•			•	•	•
RJR Tobacco	•	•			•					•	•						•	•	•		•			•	•	•	•	•					•	•	•
San Miguel																	•	•			•	•	•		•			•		•			•	•	
Savoy																																			
Scott Paper																	•		•		•			•	•			•	•	•	•		•	•	
Sega																																			
SmithKline Beecham		•			•		•	•		•					•																				
Sony																								•											
Star TV																			•		•	•	•							•		•			
Texas Instruments																	•		•		•			•						•	•		•		
Tiffany & Co.								•									•		•		•			•						•	•		•		
Unilever	•	•	•	•	•	•	•			•	•						•		•		•	•	•	•	•		•		•	•	•		•	•	•
UPS																	•		•		•	•	•	•	•		•		•	•	•		•	•	
Wash. State Apple Comm.																	•		•		•	•		•											
Waterman Pens									•						•		•		•		•	•	•	•					•	•	•		•	•	
WD-40																								•											
World Gold Council					•																			•							•	•	•		
Yoplait								•											•					•											

▼ **EXHIBIT 3-4.** CAA's polar bear icon for Coca-Cola classic.

Source: Courtesy of The Coca-Cola Company.

competition from other agencies, agencies often lose their contracts. To retain their flexibility, full-service agencies tend to contract out the more specialized tasks such as research and production. Then, if they lose an account, they can just terminate the contract of their suppliers without having to incur costly layoffs of their own employees. CAA's handling of the Coke account is a good example. Third, some large advertisers prefer to unbundle their accounts, contracting separately with creative boutiques, production houses and media-buying agencies, because of the flexibility and freshness associated with that approach. Coca-Cola's hiring of agencies in the 1990s is an example.

work for large agencies that need a fresh alternative to their own creative department. *Media-buying agencies* may serve advertisers directly, or they may serve other full-service agencies. Some media-buying agencies have very competitive rates relative to full-service agencies, charging as little as a tenth of their rate. *Market research firms* carry out research on various aspects of marketing and are discussed in Chapters 14 and 15. **Talent houses** are agencies such as CAA that represent endorsers, performers, and other artists. **Production houses** specialize in producing the final form of the ads. With the exception of market research firms, most specialized agencies tend to be small organizations with few employees. Indeed, a large number of specialized agencies consist of fewer than a dozen employees working in a small office. At the smallest level, there are **freelancers**, specialists who carry out small design or production jobs as the demand arises, frequently working out of their homes.

The proliferation of small specialized agencies occurs for several reasons. First, entry into this market is easy, so that anyone with the requisite interest and skills can acquire the minimal equipment necessary to set up shop and carry out such activities. Second, due to changes in the market and

Full-service Agencies **Full-service agencies** perform all of the four major agency functions, and have become the exemplar of the concept of the advertising agency today. McCann-Erickson Worldwide is a good example (see Exhibit 3-3). Most large advertisers use the service of at least one or more full-service agencies, rather than rely on several specialized agencies, for several reasons. First, it is much more efficient for an advertiser to deal with one agency rather than with several different agencies. Second, the development, execution and monitoring of an advertising campaign require coordination of various interrelated functions over time. Coordination is easier if it is carried out by the one agency handling the account, rather than distributed among several agencies. Third, an important function of the agency is buying time and space in various media. Agencies have greater buying power when they buy in bulk for several clients. In addition, they can plan the media purchase more efficiently if they also carry out the other functions of design, accounts management and marketing research for their clients. Fourth, an advertiser gets the attention and dedication of an agency in proportion to the advertising budget that the agency handles. By consolidating its accounts with a small number of agencies, the advertiser increases the advertising budget handled by each agency, and thus its importance to the agency.

Exhibit 3-5 depicts the general structure of a traditional full-service agency. It visualizes the agency as an institution that brings together the four important functions of creative design, accounts management, media buying, and market research, for the benefit of the client. However, full-service agencies need not carry out all of these tasks internally. Full-service agencies may use the services of specialized agencies for jobs that they need only occasionally, or for services that are fairly routine but highly technical, such as the production of final artwork or testing of advertising. Specialized agencies can perform such tasks more efficiently than can the full-service agency.

So what are the essential tasks that make an agency a full-service agency? The essential tasks of an agency are accounts management (soliciting accounts and servicing clients), and developing innovative and effective ads. Resources permitting, they may also carry out the media planning and marketing research. For example, CAA farmed out to specialized agencies even some of its creative work. What the agency provided to Coca-Cola was a fresh understanding of the role of advertising for its established, well-known brand, and a set of highly innovative ads to implement that understanding. More generally, a well-run full-service agency carries out internal services such as servicing accounts and the design of the creative, media plan and market research. It farms out to specialized agencies all other routine, technical or occasional services.

Full-service agencies may be general-purpose agencies that serve a wide spectrum of advertisers, or focused agencies that concentrate on serving specific industries or consumer markets. For example, *medical agencies* specialize in serving pharmaceutical companies, which require highly technical knowledge for developing promotional copy for pharmaceutical products. *Minority agencies* specialize in advertising to certain minorities, which have unique tastes, cultures and communication idioms.

Agency Ownership

Agencies in general, and full-service agencies in particular, can adopt any one of three ownership structures: independent agency brand, merged agency or advertising holding company. An **independent agency** is one that provides clients with some advertising service but is not owned by or has not merged with any other agency. Examples are CAA or Chiat/Day prior to its merger.

A *merged agency* is one in which two or more agencies join to form a new agency. The merger differs from an independent agency only while the merged agencies' operations and styles are not yet fully integrated. For example, on October 1, 1930,

▼ **EXHIBIT 3-5.** Structure of a full-service agency.

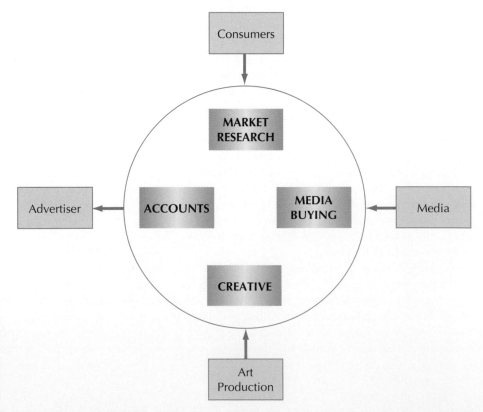

H. K. McCann Company, a large international agency, and The Erickson Company, a smaller agency with some large accounts, merged to become McCann-Erickson, Inc.[19] The merger was successful because the two original agencies had excellent reputations, no competing accounts, complementary strengths and dynamic leaders who worked well together. The merged company prospered and became the second largest agency brand in the world.[20] An **agency brand** refers to an independent or merged agency that is primarily involved in agency work and not in owning subsidiary agencies.

An advertising **holding company** (or advertising organization) is one that owns two or more agency brands. An example is the former Saatchi & Saatchi Co. As in the example at the beginning of the chapter, during the 1970s and 1980s the number of advertising holding companies greatly increased due to their acquisitions of independent and merged agencies. As a result, of the world's eleven largest advertising agencies, only one, the Leo Burnett Company, Inc., is an agency brand, while all the rest are holding companies (see Exhibit 3-1). What were the causes for this trend? What are the advantages of each of these three forms relative to the other two?

The agency merger formed by the integration of two independent agencies enjoys some advantages relative to each of the independent agencies. First, as companies grow in size nationally or internationally, they need agencies that can serve their broader needs. Because advertising is a culturally dependent activity, an agency cannot master the subtleties of advertising in diverse countries unless it has domestic offices or affiliates in those regions. For consistency in advertising strategy and execution, multinationals often prefer to work with one agency that has operations in the countries in which they operate. For example, in April 1994, IBM shifted its advertising accounts from more than 40 separate agencies to Ogilvy and Mather Worldwide, for greater efficiency and consistency.[21] In 1995, the New York agency N.W. Ayer & Partners lost the DeBeers Consolidated Mines account to JWT Worldwide, after 57 years of service, partly because the latter agency had greater international capabilities and served DeBeers's other international accounts.[22] These examples show that as their clients grow, small independent agencies may need to merge with other agencies with complementary skills or regional expertise to better serve their clients.

Second, when a small independent agency wins a big account, it needs to expand to fully serve that account. If the agency stays independent, the big account could constitute a major fraction of the agency's business, making its operation very risky. For example, despite a 127-year history, N. W. Ayer & Partners obtained more than half its revenue from serving three accounts: AT&T, Procter & Gamble, and General Motors.[23] In the 1950s the small but up-and-coming agency Ogilvy and Mather declined an invitation to compete for Ford's Edsel account because the account would have represented one-half of the agency's total billings.[24] The Los Angeles office of Saatchi & Saatchi obtains more than half its business from a single account, Toyota Motor Corporation. By merging with other independent agencies with similar skills, the agency becomes less dependent on a few large accounts.

However, a merger creates new risks and problems. First, an independent agency tends to develop a unique identity and creative style. Frequently, this unique style may be the single most important factor that attracts clients to the agency. When two independent agencies form a new organization, the new organization faces the problem of either operating with two different styles or losing the unique identities of each agency. Second, in the United States, agencies cannot serve two clients who are direct competitors in one or more markets because of a conflict of interest. For example, Cordiant cannot serve TWA and British Airways. Thus, a merger is restricted to agencies that do not serve competitors, or the newly merged agency must be willing to lose clients who are competitors.

The **holding company** is an organizational form that can overcome these limitations. Independent agencies that are purchased by a holding company operate as autonomous units. This arrangement does not require the units to integrate their unique creative styles. Also, because each agency within the corporation is fully autonomous, the potential for conflicts of interest is less.

However, holding companies also have disadvantages. Clients may be reluctant to stay with an agency purchased by a holding company that also serves a direct competitor, albeit through another autonomous acquisition. For example, in November 1994, Anheuser-Busch fired D'Arcy Masius Benton & Bowles, its agency of 79 years' standing, from its $110 million account for Budweiser plus another $25 million in business. The immediate reason was because the agency's subsidiary in New York, TeleVest, accepted a media-buying assignment from Budweiser's competitor, Miller Brewing Co., without informing either DMB&B or its client, Anheuser-Busch.[25] Another disadvantage of the holding company is that managing a conglomerate of autonomous agencies scattered around the world becomes difficult in itself, and can distract senior managers from their primary task of serving clients and designing winning advertising campaigns. A third problem with the holding company is that it often takes on debt to acquire the independent agencies. Servicing this debt can be expensive and distracting. These are some of the problems that plagued Saatchi & Saatchi and Chiat/Day in the 1990s.

Agency Organization

Agencies can adopt a variety of organizational forms. Perhaps no two agencies have the exact same organization. However, we can identify two prototypical organizational forms: functional and accounts based. These two forms parallel the functional and brand management organizational forms, respectively, prevalent among advertisers. These two forms are important because they are based on different assumptions about motivating staff and completing projects.

In a **functional organization,** the agency is divided into departments, each of which carries out one of the core functions of the agency. Responsibility for both personnel and their work rests with the senior managers within each department. The accounts department acts as the liaison between the client and the media, research and design departments in the agency. Senior managers within these departments assign work to the staff depending on their skills and availability. Thus each staff member might work on a variety of accounts.

In the **accounts-based organization,** the agency's staff are organized in teams, each of which serves one account. If the account is large with many brands, each team may work on only one or a few brands. Each team consists of an account executive, a creative director and a copywriter, plus staff from other departments, depending on the needs of the account. The account executive may serve as the leader and acts as the liaison between the team and the client. For example, MCA Advertising, a Connecticut agency, combines an art director, a copywriter and an account executive in a team that is responsible for an account from start to finish.[26]

The accounts-based organization may have been started by a London agency, Boase Massimi Pollitt, in 1968. By 1987 as many as 90 percent of British agencies had adopted the system.[27] It became popular in the United States after the rise of Chiat/Day, which was one of the early agencies to adopt the system.

The great appeal of the accounts-based organization is that the staff are more clear about the client's needs, more motivated to serve the client, and more loyal to the client, because they are permanently assigned to a team working for the account. For example, with the accounts-based organization, the Leo Burnett Company, Inc. is said to instill in its staff fanatic loyalty to its clients. The agency's staff who work on the McDonald's account wear McDonald's wristwatches and answer the phone by saying "McDonald's Group," rather than "Leo Burnett."[28] The accounts-based organization is also more convenient for the client, because the client's staff know who is assigned to the account and what role they play.

The disadvantage of the accounts-based organization is that the creative staff may not be able to develop new and bold ads because they constantly interact with account executives, who, like the advertisers they serve, tend to be more conservative. Indeed, some authors suggest that the functional organization may be better at allowing creatives to develop innovative ads independently of the account executives. The latter can then either accept or reject the ads.[29] Another disadvantage of the account-based organization is that teams within an agency may start to compete for new accounts. In general this organizational form does not provide for the efficient assignment of work, and the convenient recruitment and evaluation of staff. Further, in the accounts-based organization, staff may suffer from the stress of having dual allegiances, one to the department to which they are assigned, and the other to the accounts team on which they work.

However, advertisers and agencies prefer the accounts-based system and tend to implement it despite its costs. For example, in early 1990, Chiat/Day moved to a virtual office system, in which personnel did not have dedicated office space. They obtained equipment and office space depending on need, on a first-come, first-served basis each day. Even then, the company valued the accounts-based organizational system so highly that each account team was given one of the few dedicated office spaces where team members could meet, work and store account-specific materials.

Choosing an advertising agency

The advertiser must make three major decisions about the agency service that it wants: the location of the agency, the structure of its own advertising department, and the choice of the external advertising agency. The first two decisions are basic ones, which, once made, are not revisited frequently. On the other hand, the selection of the agency is a dynamic decision because the advertiser must constantly evaluate the agency's performance and consider alternatives, either explicitly or implicitly. We now turn to the issues involved in these decisions.

Locating the Advertising Agency

The decision regarding the location of the advertising department refers to whether the advertiser should use the services of an internal or external agency. An **external agency** is an independent organization that carries out one or more of the four advertising functions as described above. An **internal agency** is a department or business unit within the firm that carries out these functions. While external agencies are the norm among large advertisers, some major advertisers, such as Benetton and Calvin Klein, use internal ad agencies.

The primary advantage of an internal agency is cost savings. Many agencies charge 15 percent of the cost of media purchases for their service. (However, because of the intense competition in this industry, advertisers can drive down this rate.) The agency's fees cover the direct and overhead costs of its services, plus an allocation for profits. To the extent that an internal agency could carry out the same function as the external agency for the same or lower direct and overhead costs, the advertiser could save the amount that covers the profits of the agency. Because an internal agency requires some minimum investment in terms of personnel, office space, and equipment, a small advertiser may not break even on the fixed costs of using an internal

agency. However, a large advertiser with a $500 million budget could save a sizable sum of money by doing so. This amount could then be used to buy additional media time and space.

Another advantage of an in-house agency is the freedom to develop a unique style or tradition of advertising that is not available in the market, and which the advertiser does not wish to have replicated. For example, Benetton's in-house agency, United Colors Communication, has produced controversial ads that have drawn widespread attention and criticism (see Exhibit 3-6).[30] Calvin Klein's in-house agency, CRK Advertising, has produced sexually provocative ads, some of which have won awards while others have been withdrawn in a whirl of controversy.[31] In general, an internal agency ensures greater confidentiality in advertising strategy, and greater control over proprietary marketing information and advertising methods.

A third advantage of in-house agencies is the control they provide over communication of technical information. Firms that need to communicate such information need to rely on their own technicians to ensure that the information is correct and up to date. Working with outside agencies could increase the odds of random errors or biases in copy.

Against these advantages, hiring an external agency provides many benefits to the advertiser. The primary benefit is flexibility. Each agency tends to have a distinct style of designing ads and serving clients, and tends to develop expertise in certain markets or for certain types of brands. As the market changes, a brand may require a different style or expertise. Sometimes the current agency can make this change. At other times it cannot. Designing an ad is also a creative task that is a challenge for an agency to perform consistently over time. Using an external agency allows advertisers the flexibility to change agencies to respond to market changes or to achieve a higher performance goal. It would be difficult to change an internal agency as easily.

A second advantage of an external agency is its breadth of experience. An internal agency is limited to the brands of the advertiser. In contrast, an external agency services a variety of competitors in a variety of markets. This practice provides the agency personnel with a wealth of experience across numerous situations. This benefit is especially true for consumer goods manufacturers. Among all categories of

▼ EXHIBIT 3-6. Controversial ad by Benetton's United Colors Communication.

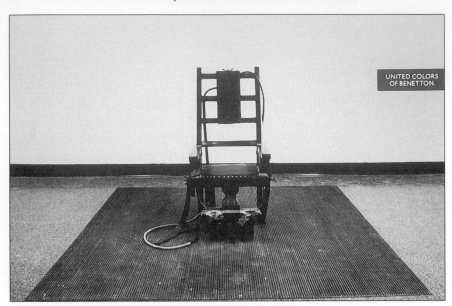

Source: Courtesy of United Colors of Benetton.

advertisers, the latter have the highest fraction of firms using external agencies.[32]

A third benefit of the external agency is that it enables the advertiser to focus on its core competencies, rather than on managing the advertising agency within the firm. So a car manufacturer can concentrate on the critical tasks of researching, designing and manufacturing cars, rather than on researching, designing and producing the ads for those cars.

A fourth benefit is that an external agency may provide a more independent or less biased point of view than an internal agency that tends to adopt the advertiser's perspective.

These four benefits of using an external agency can be summed up by the general principle *against* vertical integration in the presence of a competitive market of suppliers.[33] According to this principle, whenever a competitive market exists for a firm's suppliers or a firm's buyers, competition will ensure that the prices and quality of the suppliers in that market are better than the firm can obtain by owning these suppliers. In the current context, advertising agencies constitute a market that is very competitive due to the low costs of entry and the presence of a large number of agencies. The advertiser is better off picking an agency from the wealth of agencies in the market, rather than trying to develop one internally.

Organizing the Advertising Function

The advertising function within a firm can take the form of a stand-alone advertising department or it can be integrated with other marketing or managerial functions. A **stand-alone department** is a separate department with its own cost structure and a department head who reports to a marketing or divisional manager. On the other hand, the advertising function can be integrated with that of marketing management or brand management. In the latter case, staff involved with advertising may report to the brand manager, or the brand manager may report to the advertising manager. The choice among these two alternatives depends on the location of the advertising agency, the importance of advertising within the firm and the number of brands.

The stand-alone structure is especially useful for firms that use internal agencies. In that case, the advertising staff constitutes a separate entity with a clear mission and a clearly defined cost structure against which their performance can be evaluated. With a stand-alone structure, the advertising department that serves different departments or brand managers within the firm can develop expertise in advertising in the same manner as can an external agency. Further, the separation of the department from line responsibilities, such as sales, allows it to provide the brand or marketing manager with an independent perspective on the value and design of the advertising campaign.

The disadvantage of the stand-alone advertising department is that it has little final authority on the design of the campaign. The advertiser that owns a number of complementary or substitute brands, each with a unique identity, needs someone with responsibility to coordinate the advertising among the brands. This need is greater if advertising plays an important role in fashioning the independent images of these brands. Further, coordination may be required not only on matters of image, but also on matters of the advertising budget, the scheduling of ads, the buying of media time and space and the scheduling of associated promotions. A stand-alone advertising department does not have such responsibility.

There are two important reasons for the integrated advertising setup. First, if the firm uses an external, full-service advertising agency, then it needs little or no internal advertising staff. In that case integrating the advertising function with the brand or marketing management function is more efficient. Second, if the firm has a large number of complementary or substitute brands with unique images that are dependent on advertising, then integrating the advertising function with the brand management function can ensure coordination in the advertising strategy across brands. One good integrated setup is for all brand managers of substitute or complementary brands to report to the advertising manager. The advertising manager then coordinates the advertising function among the different brands. This is the organization that Procter & Gamble uses (Exhibit 3-7).

Selecting an External Agency

Given the proliferation of advertising agencies, the advertiser rarely lacks choice. However, the task of choosing an agency is by no means simple. Among the many decisions involved, the advertiser has to decide whether or not to continue with the current agency and how to select the new agency.

Continuing the Current Agency's Contract Should an agency resign or be fired from an account because of an error, careless or otherwise? Consider the following two examples:

D'Arcy Masius Benton & Bowles probably tried to save some time or money in preparing an ad for its former client, Qantas. The ad's headline read, "You'll feel like you're in Australia as soon as you're on Qantas." Unfortunately, the beach shown in the ad was Hawaiian, and the picture featured two well-known rocks. The advertiser terminated the agency's contract.[34]

A Continental Airlines ad in the *Boston Herald* offered a one-way fare to Los Angeles for $48. The actual fare was supposed to be $148; the typo was made by the airline's agency, Wells Rich Greene BDDP. At the urging of the U.S. Department of Transportation, Continental Airlines honored the advertised fare until midnight of the day the ad ran. It reportedly lost $4 million on the error. Three months later it switched its account to Richards Group.[35]

These examples bring into focus the fragility of an agency's contract. An agency with a long-term relationship and a strong record may well survive a small error. Or an error may be the last straw in a weakening relationship. More generally, what are good grounds for an advertiser to end an agency's contract? An advertiser should consider changing an agency for the following reasons:

- The brand has been doing badly, and none of the alternatives tried by the agency has worked.
- The market has changed and the brand needs a new style that is inconsistent with that of the current agency.
- The current agency has merged with another that serves a competitor.
- The advertiser has expanded into new regions or countries in which the agency does not have the required expertise.
- The key personnel responsible for the brand or for past successes have left, and their replacements do not have comparable credentials.
- The agency has been going downhill or self-destructing.
- A personality conflict has developed between the account executive and the brand manager.

An advertiser should not consider changing agencies merely because the agency has been around for a long time, competitors have changed agencies, competitors have larger or better known agencies, or personnel at the advertiser or at the agency have changed. None of these are adequate grounds for changing the agency as long as the agency is performing. Moreover, a long-term relationship may ensure that the agency is dedicated to the account and is able to retain staff who understand the advertiser well. In this case, an advertiser who wants a change of style can sometimes get that merely by asking the agency to assign new

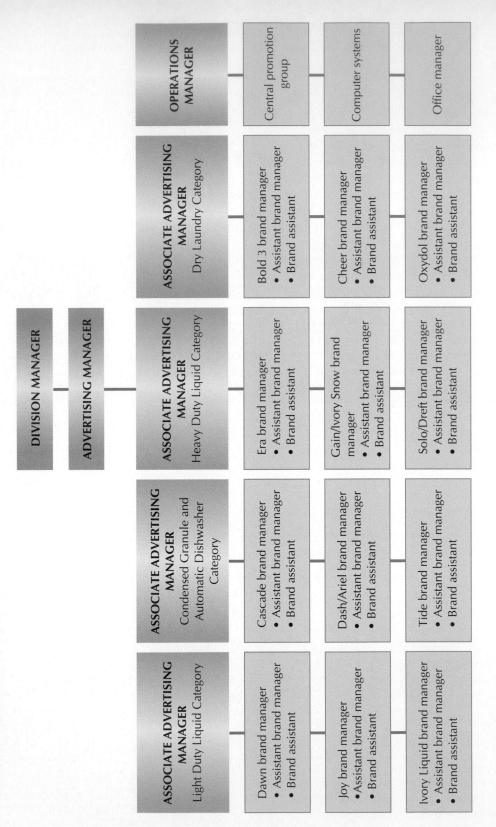

▶ EXHIBIT 3-7. Procter & Gamble's organization for advertising.

DIVISION MANAGER

ADVERTISING MANAGER

ASSOCIATE ADVERTISING MANAGER
Light Duty Liquid Category

Dawn brand manager
• Assistant brand manager
• Brand assistant

Joy brand manager
• Assistant brand manager
• Brand assistant

Ivory Liquid brand manager
• Assistant brand manager
• Brand assistant

ASSOCIATE ADVERTISING MANAGER
Condensed Granule and Automatic Dishwasher Category

Cascade brand manager
• Assistant brand manager
• Brand assistant

Dash/Ariel brand manager
• Assistant brand manager
• Brand assistant

Tide brand manager
• Assistant brand manager
• Brand assistant

ASSOCIATE ADVERTISING MANAGER
Heavy Duty Liquid Category

Era brand manager
• Assistant brand manager
• Brand assistant

Gain/Ivory Snow brand manager
• Assistant brand manager
• Brand assistant

Solo/Dreft brand manager
• Assistant brand manager
• Brand assistant

ASSOCIATE ADVERTISING MANAGER
Dry Laundry Category

Bold 3 brand manager
• Assistant brand manager
• Brand assistant

Cheer brand manager
• Assistant brand manager
• Brand assistant

Oxydol brand manager
• Assistant brand manager
• Brand assistant

OPERATIONS MANAGER

Central promotion group

Computer systems

Office manager

Source: Quelch, John (1983), "Procter and Gamble (B)," Cambridge, MA: Harvard Business School Case Clearing House, No. 9-584-048.

78

▼ **EXHIBIT 3-8.** Long-term advertiser-agency relationships.

Advertiser	Agency	Year Ended	Duration of Relationship
Unilever	J. Walter Thompson	Active	92 years
Sunkist Growers	Foote, Cone & Belding	Active	87 years
AT&T	N. W. Ayer & Partners	Active	86 years
Exxon	McCann-Erickson	Active	82 years
Hammermill Paper	BBDO	1996	81 years
Anheuser-Busch	D'Arcy Masius Benton & Bowles	1994	79 years
Kraft	J. Walter Thompson	Active	70 years
Kraft	D'Arcy Masius Benton & Bowles	1995	66 years
Johnson & Johnson	Young & Rubicam	Active	64 years
General Foods	Young & Rubicam	Active	62 years
DeBeers	N. W. Ayer & Partners	1995	57 years
Kellogg	Leo Burnett Company, Inc.	Active	42 years

Sources: Based on Goldman, Kevin (1995), "Kraft Is Dropping D'Arcy Masius, Ending Relationship of 66 Years," *The Wall Street Journal*, October 3, B10–B11; Lipman, Joanne (1992), "Study Shows Clients Jump Ship Quickly," *The Wall Street Journal*, May 21, B8; Ogilvy, David (1992), "We Sell. Or Else," *The Advertiser*, Summer, 21–24; Teinowitz, Ira (1994), "Why A-B Bounced Bud," *Advertising Age*, November 21, 1.

staff to the account. This change is far less costly and time consuming to all, and could enable an advertiser to continue a long-standing relationship with its agency. Indeed, some advertisers have had a relationship with their agency that has spanned many decades (see Exhibit 3-8).

Selecting the New Agency If an advertiser has a current agency, it can start the selection process with an **account review**, a full-scale evaluation of the current agency against the record or proposals of prospective new agencies. David Ogilvy, speaking on behalf of agencies, has this to say about account reviews:

> ". . . It is like telling your wife that you are going to put your marriage under review—by sleeping with some other women on the off-chance that one of them may turn out to be a better lover. If none of them do, you will continue to live with your wife. . . . If you get fed up with your agency, get another. A clean-cut divorce. But don't subject your agency to the public indignity of trying out some other agencies for size and releasing their names to the press. . . ."[36]

Ogilvy makes a strong case against the account review. However, it is not clear that all agencies would feel the same way. Clearly, an agency would prefer a continuation of its contract to an account review or a termination. But faced with the choice of an outright termination versus an account review,

many agencies would prefer the latter. In an account review, they have a chance to remind the client about their past contributions, make changes to avoid repeating past failures, and develop proposals for the future. The account review also allows the advertiser to evaluate the proposals from new agencies against what the current agency can offer. Moreover, the announcement of an account review is so serious that it forces the agency to take the advertiser more seriously. The agency may make radical changes in its organization, increase resources devoted to the client, or even assign top managers to service the account. The advertiser also gets an opportunity to determine how other agencies in the market measure up. For example, in 1992, General Motors Corporation's Oldsmobile division put its $140 million account, which was served by Leo Burnett Company, Inc., up for review.[37] Most agencies do not end up retaining their client under these circumstances. But Leo Burnett did. The agency took the review seriously and made several radical changes to satisfy Oldsmobile. These changes included closing its large Michigan office that handled the account; doing all creative work at the head office in Chicago; opening a small, new, strategic office near Oldsmobile's headquarters in Michigan; and having the agency's chief executive and president oversee the account.[38]

Once the advertiser has decided between terminating its current agency or conducting an account review, it must decide how to evaluate prospective agencies. Typically advertisers do so in three steps. The advertiser first invites interested agencies to submit names. It then develops a "long list" of agencies. It may evaluate the record of the agencies on this long list, visit their facilities, or interview potential members of the accounts team. It then develops a short list of two or three agencies. The advertiser evaluates these agencies more closely, and may ask them to submit a speculative campaign, which may be paid for by the advertiser. This exercise gives the advertiser a firsthand experience of how the agency operates.

David Ogilvy has this to say about advertisers calling for speculative campaign proposals:

"Whatever you do, don't ask the candidates for your account to submit speculative campaigns. When I was running Ogilvy & Mather, I refused to do that—and for seven years we won every account for which we competed.

"Creating speculative campaigns costs a lot of money—money which would be better spent on the agency's present accounts. Worse, they divert the time of the best people in your agency to speculations. . . .

"How would you like it if your agency spent the commission it earns in your services on competing for other clients?"[39]

Ogilvy makes a convincing case against speculative campaigns. Even if the advertiser pays for the campaign, there are still hidden costs. For example, the time of the agency's best talent is diverted to work on the speculative account instead of on the current accounts. Further, the advertiser has no guarantee that the same staff who designed the speculative campaign would be assigned to the account, or that they would be as good or lucky in the future in designing good campaigns. The past record of the agency is a better indicator of its future performance. Despite these problems, advertisers continue with the practice of speculative campaigns, in the quest for more information when committing to a new agency. Agencies comply because the business is so competitive.

COMPENSATING AGENCIES

In the early 1990s, Home Depot and Admarketing terminated their client-agency relationship over a compensation dispute. When interviewed, Joe Roth, president of Admarketing, said that Home Depot's "style of operation is negotiate, negotiate. For two years now, they've been haranguing us for special deals and we've resisted." Roth did not discuss the compensation cut, but said, "Even if they put 2% on the table, we wouldn't have taken it." Roth further claimed that the senior vice president of marketing for Home Depot "told us we had to cut our commission or else. I asked him, didn't he want a strong agency on the account? He said they don't need a strong agency anymore 'because the chain is doing so well.'"

Home Depot was established in 1978 to sell a wide assortment of do-it-yourself needs to consumers. The chain was very successful and expanded rapidly due to its wide selection of items and its low costs. In 1992 it had 214 stores, and expected to have 516 stores by 1996. In 1992 sales had doubled over the previous two years, and profits had shown a 46 percent compounded growth rate.[40]

The dispute between Home Depot and Admarketing brings into focus the question of a fair compensation for an agency's service. Was Home Depot right in pressing Admarketing to lower its compensation rate, just as it reduced its costs in other areas? If not, what is a fair method for compensating agencies? What is the prevalent practice?

Currently, most agencies work for or represent advertisers. However, agencies began as representatives of the media. They brought business from advertisers to the media, and prepared the ads for the media. The media paid them a 15 percent commission for their services, which became the traditional rate. In the twentieth century, agencies began to represent the advertisers. However, the 15 percent rate stuck, and has begun to be replaced by other methods only in the last decade or two. Currently, we can identify three important methods of compensation besides the commission: fixed fee, cost basis and performance basis. This section discusses the pros and cons of each and recommends one compromise method.

Commission

In the **commission** method, the advertiser pays the agency a fixed percentage of the media bill for its services. The *media bill* is the amount that the advertiser spends to buy media time or space. The method works as follows. Suppose the agency buys $100,000 of media space on behalf of the advertiser, for a 15 percent commission. In a traditional arrangement, the media charge the agency $85,000, the agency bills the advertiser $100,000 and retains the $15,000 as its commission. In effect, the advertiser lets the agency keep the commission that the media grants the agency. Note that the commission rate of 15 percent on media bookings of $100,000 is actually 17.65 percent when computed on the $85,000 that the agency bills the advertiser.[41]

Some media may not grant a commission. In that case, the advertiser lets the agency **gross up** the media bill by its commission rate. For example, suppose the cost of media time and space is $170,000, and the media charge the agency the same amount (no commission). Then the agency grosses up that amount by 17.65 percent to $200,000 when billing the advertiser.[42] The agency pays the media $170,000, retaining $30,000, or 15 percent of the $200,000, as its commission. Thus the commission rate is always calculated on the total amount the *advertiser* pays for the media time and space.

The primary advantage of this method of compensation is its clarity and simplicity. There is a set procedure and formula for computing the commission. A second advantage of the method is its proportionality to the advertiser's advertising outlays. The cost of buying media time and space is the single most important item in the advertising budget. By linking their service charges to the level of media purchases, agencies can tailor their compensation and services to the advertising outlays of the advertiser. Advertisers with large media budgets would pay more, but these are firms that can afford to pay more in return for better service.

However, the commission method of compensation has several disadvantages. First, it ignores agency performance. For example, using the same media plan, one agency may produce a stellar campaign that vaults a brand into the first place in the market, while another agency may produce a mediocre campaign that gets lost in the noise in the market. The commission method rewards both agencies at the same rate. Second, there is a conflict of interest on the part of the agency. On the one hand it must design an advertising campaign that best serves the client. On the other hand, its compensation is based on the media purchases it advises the client to make, not on its design of the advertising campaign. Third, the agency's compensation varies with the cost of media rather than with the performance of the ad campaign that it designs.

During years when media costs rise, agencies could earn higher revenues without any improvement in performance. On the other hand, when media costs remain stable or fall, agencies could see a drop in their revenues without any decline in the quality of their service.

Fixed Fee

Under the **fixed-fee** method, the advertiser negotiates with the agency a fixed payment for its services. The fee normally applies for an advertising campaign, or for a certain time period. This method avoids the conflict of interest and the linkage to media expenditures prevalent with the commission method. However, like the commission method, it still does not reward performance. In addition, it does not provide a guideline for the level of compensation. The client and agency must negotiate a mutually agreeable fee. In the absence of an explicit rule for compensation, both parties are likely to resort to the commission as the basis of comparison. Advertisers are likely to reduce the fee from what the agency would have earned by the commission approach, probably because they find that approach too generous. On the other hand, the agency is likely to use the commission as its reference rate, and perceive any lower compensation as a "sacrifice" to win or retain the client. Thus the fee approach is not a true alternative to the commission, and can deteriorate to a means by which advertisers harangue agencies for a lower compensation rate than the commission method.

The dispute between Home Depot and Admarketing shows how fee negotiations can break down when the advertiser's sole concern is to get the lowest rate from its agency. Such an approach may be consistent with the management philosophy of a company like Home Depot, which strives relentlessly to lower costs and prices for consumers. Also, the approach may work for a company that thrives on low costs rather than on creative advertising. But for companies that depend on advertising, the creativity, health and cost structure of the agency should be matters of concern. David Ogilvy once pointed out that if an advertiser increases an agency's commission by 1 percent, from 15 percent to 16 percent, it may well double the agency's profit.[43] The agency could then put greater talent, effort and resources at the advertiser's disposal. Agencies today cannot pay their employees as well as consulting firms, partly because of the relentless pressure from advertisers for lower commissions and fees. Thus agencies may not be able to attract as good talent as the consulting firms. In the long run, poorer talent will hurt agency creativity.

Cost Basis

In the **cost-basis** method, the agency charges the advertisers an amount that covers its costs plus an agreed-upon profit, which could be related to the margin the advertiser earns on the advertised brand. The advantage of this method is its apparent fairness. It compensates the agency in proportion to the cost of its services. Also, to the extent that the agency's compensation is linked to the profits of the advertised brand, the agency is motivated to work for the brand's success. The problem with this method is that it requires detailed accounting by the agency. This accounting becomes problematic when the agency works for a number of clients over different time periods under different compensation schemes. For example, how should an agency allocate the cost of data collected some years earlier for another client and covered by its commission? In addition, the agency may find it difficult to price intangibles such as its experience and creativity. A second problem of this approach is that the agency has no motivation to keep costs down, and may inflate costs to increase revenues. Most importantly, like the previous two approaches, this method does not compensate the agency directly for its performance.

Performance Basis

The **performance basis** involves compensating an agency to the extent its advertising campaign helps meet specific sales goals. In principle, this is the best method for compensating an agency, because it makes the agency accountable for the advertised brand's performance. An advertiser chooses an agency to achieve certain goals, and it pays the agency to the extent that it does so. The ultimate goal of most advertisers is increased sales or some comparable behavioral measure. So it is reasonable to base agency compensation on that measure. However, the problem with this method is determining the sales effectiveness of advertising. The measures for this purpose are partly ambiguous and often debated, because the effects of advertising on sales are not instantaneous, and occur in conjunction with the effects of a number of other variables, such as price, distribution, quality and sales promotions. Chapter 14 explains how one can evaluate the sales effectiveness of advertising. The agency and advertiser have to agree on the measures and models to estimate the sales effectiveness of advertising in order to rely on this method as the sole means of determining the compensation.

Conclusion: The Benefits of a Mixed Approach

As can be seen from the above discussion, no single approach for agency compensation is ideal. A good approach may be a hybrid of two or more of the above methods. One solution would be for the advertiser to offer the agency a tiered commission, where the compensation rate declines for each increase in media expenditures. The rationale for this method is that the agency's work does not increase much as the media bill increases. In 1991, Quaker Oats Co. instituted such a plan which had two components.[44] First, the commission rate was set at 15 percent for the first $10 million in billings, 13 percent for the next $10 million and 10 percent for any amount above $20 million. Second, if the company cut its budget during the year, the agency was guaranteed 90 percent of the original budget. Another solution would be for the advertiser to start off with a commission-based approach, but at a negotiated level below the traditional 15 percent. It then could provide further compensation based on some performance indices. It could also set upper and lower limits to the total compensation, so that the total fee earned by the agency does not fall to a level that is unfairly low relative to the agency's costs, or unfairly high relative to the advertiser's profit margin.

Even though such hybrid methods have not yet caught on in the industry, advertisers have moved away from the traditional 15 percent commission method of compensation. One survey indicated that the traditional compensation method had fallen from being the most popular in 1992 to being the third most popular in 1995 (see Exhibit 3-9). For example, Coca-Cola cut its commissions rate to between 9 and 12 percent in 1994.[45] The decline in the popularity of the traditional method is probably motivated by advertisers' concern about accountability, their reduced spending on advertising, and

▼ **EXHIBIT 3-9.** Trends in agency compensation.

	PERCENTAGE OF ADVERTISERS USING VARIOUS COMPENSATION METHODS			
Year	15% Commission	Commission < 15%	Fee	Other
1992	33%	26%	32%	9%
1995	14	45	35	7

Note: Totals do not add up to 100% in original source.

Source: Selinger, Iris Cohen (1995), "Big Profits, Risks with Incentive Fees," *Advertising Age*, May 15, P3. Based on the 1995 Association of National Advertisers' Trends in Agency Compensation study.

the recent trend to split media purchases and creative design among several agencies. Coca-Cola, for example, had split its creative among a number of smaller agencies, and needed a means of compensating each of them.

MANAGING CREATIVITY

We can define **creativity** as productive divergence. Both these terms, *productive* and *divergence*, are essential to the definition. We consider something to be creative if it *diverges* from the norm, or is different from what is currently done or believed. Creative advertising must be different from usual advertising. For example, Michael Somoroff, a director of television commercials, follows this motto when shooting for commercials, "If you've seen it before, don't shoot it."[46] But being different alone is not enough. Difference can be fruitful or fruitless, helpful or harmful, constructive or destructive. We consider the difference creative if it has at least some redeeming value which renders it *productive*. Difference is important, and is the starting point of creativity. But being productive ensures that the idea contributes to the brand's or firm's welfare.

For example, one of the major reasons that Apple's introductory ad for the Macintosh, "1984," had such an impact (see Chapter 1) was its difference from the standard advertising of the period. Apple used symbols and allegory, when the norm was to stress product attributes. Apple appealed to emotion, when the norm was to appeal to reason. Apple spliced its ad with humor and sarcasm, when the norm was to use arguments to persuade about product benefits. In addition, Apple used TV advertising, when other firms typically used print. Apple

advertised during the Super Bowl, an atypical time slot for computer products. In all of these ways, the "1984" ad was different from ads of its genre. Thus its impact was enormous.

In contrast, in the summer of 1995, Calvin Klein introduced an advertising campaign in which young models were interviewed, by an anonymous voice, about their clothes and bodies, in rough basement-type settings. The ads had strong sexual overtones, as do most Calvin Klein ads. But in their use and location of models, they were quite different, resembling the amateur shooting associated with pornographic movies of minors ("kiddy porn"). The ads created a public outcry against Calvin Klein, forcing the company to withdraw the campaign. Most advertising analysts felt that the campaign intentionally mimicked kiddy porn, demeaned youth, lacked taste, and hurt the brand. That campaign was surely different, but it earned the label "cheap" or "counterproductive" rather than creative.

Creativity requires foresight on the part of the artist to *see ahead* that the difference he or she designs is going to be productive. Yet most people judge whether an ad is creative in hindsight, after the results are in. These two facts are not self-contradictory. If everyone had the same foresight as the designer about the potential of the new design, then everyone would be using the design and it would not be different. The essence of creativity is to *foresee* that a difference will be productive. That is why authors of creative ideas are said to be "ahead of their time."

The key question for us is, what thought processes, activities, and organizational forms foster creativity? This section addresses these issues. It also explores the question of whether agencies have creative styles, and touches on an important debate in the industry—whether ads should appeal to consumers on the basis of message content or creative execution.

Processes of Thinking Creatively

We humans tend to develop routines in order to operate our daily lives efficiently. For example, we tend to brush our teeth in the same way every day, buy the same brands over and over again, and maintain the same set of friends for years. For the sake of efficiency, the human mind also tends to develop routine ways of perceiving and interpreting the world. Certain symbols and shapes mean certain things, while others trigger certain set responses. Most of our thoughts today are not different from those of yesterday. Prejudices and stereotypes are born of this mental effort to simplify the external environment and avoid new ways of visualizing the world. Psychologists refer to this mental approach to the external world as "precognitive commitment" or "perceptual bias." (Chapters 4 and 5 will probe this phenomenon in greater depth). This approach to thinking also permeates the education system, where we are taught to latch on to solutions discovered by experts before us, rather than to think out solutions for ourselves.

While precognitive commitment helps us to operate efficiently, it is the very opposite of creativity. Creativity thrives on difference. Precognitive commitment is bound to sameness. Researchers and practitioners in several fields have studied the problem of thinking creatively. Their conclusions provide us with insights about the thought processes that overcome precognitive commitment and foster creativity.[47]

Edward deBono describes creativity as lateral thinking rather than vertical thinking.[48] Vertical thinking proceeds linearly from one premise to the next. In contrast, lateral thinking proceeds in discontinuities, jumping around from idea to idea without structure. Vertical thinking is a closed process. Lateral thinking is an open exploratory process, working with different ideas in different ways and combinations. Vertical thinking sequences ideas in strict order, following the rules of logic. Lateral thinking is disorganized, welcomes chance intrusions and may even be chaotic. But such chaos may carry the seeds of a productive solution that no one has thought of before.

The psychologist J. P. Guilford suggests that creativity requires divergent rather than logical thinking.[49] In **logical thinking**, one reasons step by step to a conclusion that is indisputable. The steps may require intense thought, but since the conclusion derives from the sequence of steps, it generally does not involve originality. In **divergent thinking**, however, thoughts flow in all directions from one starting point, even if the path seems illogical. In the

latter mode of thinking, one is more likely to hit on an original idea.

James Young, a vice president of the J. Walter Thompson advertising agency, described creativity as associative thinking.[50] In **associative thinking** the individual puts together unrelated ideas. A novel idea is more likely to emerge from such novel associations.

Roger Von Oech, president of Creative Think, describes creative thinking as soft thinking.[51] **Soft thinking** includes metaphorical, paradoxical, ambiguous and fantasy thinking. **Hard thinking** includes exact, analytical, logical and focused thinking. Hard thinking implies that answers are black and white; soft thinking implies that answers come in shades of gray. All these views of creativity are similar in that they emphasize the openness, imprecision, or disorder involved in creative thinking.

Fostering Creative Thinking

The lack of rules or order in thoughts that we have attributed to creativity does not imply that creativity is the effortless fruit of an idle mind. On the contrary, concerted effort can increase the chance of producing creative ideas. Some activities that foster creative thinking are preparation, incubation, exchange, and verification.[52] These activities are not necessarily sequential stages through which every creative individual proceeds. Rather, they are activities in which an individual or organization should engage to enhance the chance of creative output.

Preparation involves the collection and analysis of all the facts relating to the current situation. Such an exhaustive search may be tedious, but can be very useful. In such a search, one fully describes the current situation, indicates the whole array of possible causes, and lists all solutions tried in the past, both successful and unsuccessful. Thus preparation allows the creative thinker to concentrate on improving on the past rather than on reinventing the wheel. Data collection provides the raw material on which an individual can dwell to find creative solutions. James Young uses the more expressive terms of **immersion** and *digestion* when referring to data collection and analysis, respectively.[53] David Ogilvy writes about preparation in this way:

". . .Set yourself to becoming the best informed man in the agency on the account to which you are assigned. If, for example, it is a gasoline account,

read textbooks on the chemistry, geology and distribution of petroleum products. Read all the trade journals in the field. Read all the research reports and marketing plans that your agency has ever written on the product. Spend Saturday mornings in service stations, pumping gasoline and talking to motorists. Visit your client's refineries and research laboratories. Study the advertising of his competitors. At the end of your second year, you will know more about gasoline than your boss."[54]

Preparation need not imply a rigid, rule-based handling of the data. There is room for creative insight even in preparation. For this purpose, the researcher should look at the data from different perspectives, incorporating lateral, divergent and associative thinking. For example, consider the data in Exhibit 3-9. A basic analysis would be to display the percentage of companies that use each method of compensation. A little deeper analysis would be to display the same distribution over time, to identify trends. Further insight can be obtained by cross-tabulating these trends by large or small agencies, large or small advertisers, and long-term or short-term relationships to identify possible causes for the trends. Thus thinking of nontraditional ways to collect and analyze data can reveal new insights and stimulate creative ideas.

Incubation involves setting aside the problem, to leave time for ideas to germinate. Many creatives find that they cannot force the pace of solutions. Forcing the mind to come up with solutions may actually confine it to the few paths that the individual is most conscious of at that time. Setting aside the problem for some time is more likely to allow for lateral, divergent and associative thinking. Once faced with a problem, the human mind will remain alert for solutions to it even without conscious effort. When involved with unrelated events, the individual is more likely to use lateral or divergent thinking with respect to the problem. Such thinking can be the source of original solutions not considered before. The classic stories of how Newton understood gravity on being hit by a falling apple, and how Archimedes understood specific gravity when soaking in his bathtub, indicate how serendipitous events can illuminate a solution to a problem.

Exchange refers to the give-and-take among individuals about the problem and its solutions. Exchange is an important source of creative solu-

tions. Each individual has a unique perspective born out of a unique set of experiences, knowledge and training accumulated over time. Each individual who immerses himself or herself in a problem brings a wide spectrum of new associations, from which a creative thought can emerge. Moreover, as one individual communicates a new perspective, the communication may set off new associations in the mind of the receiver, which can trigger a creative idea. As several individuals discuss the problem, this process feeds on itself, increasing the momentum toward a solution. When many individuals are involved with this process, their combined effort constitutes a rich set of associations from which a novel idea is more likely to merge. The history of many apparently revolutionary ideas can be traced to the small increments that many individuals added at different times.[55] The accumulation of these ideas over time appears as a "radical revolution" to the outsider not aware of the buildup of ideas over time.

Verification involves testing the idea on a small scale to determine whether it is feasible and productive. Chapter 14 covers the variety of ways in which ideas and ads can be tested. Verification is the moment of reality. Many ideas look good in the abstract; only in implementation can one see all the problems associated with them. Verification is the activity that sifts practical and productive ideas from impractical and unproductive ones. It also lets the artist fashion his or her idea into a form that promises to be most productive. Indeed the finished product might be better, even though different from the original idea. Verification is the point at which the free thinking involved in idea generation has to face the test of reality.

Organizing for Creativity

Are certain organizational structures more likely to sponsor creative ideas? Research over many decades in many fields indicates that the answer to this question is "yes." In particular, some organizational characteristics that foster creativity are freedom from rules, decentralization and risk tolerance.[56]

The simple truth about rules is that they promote conformity and suppress diversity. As a result, an organization that prescribes a large number of rules tends to restrain creativity. Rules and regulations make for an orderly functioning organization. However, rules also constrain individuals to certain acceptable behaviors and practices. Thus, rules suppress one of the prerequisites of creativity: diversity. To have bite, rules must also carry penalties for noncompliance. These penalties generate an atmosphere of fear, which further suppresses an individual's effort to think up different solutions to problems. For example, in 1995, a San Francisco agency, Goodby, Silverstein and Partners, won many awards. The creative director, Rich Silverstein, attributed his success to one cause: "We've got the magic because we allow people in the company freedom."[57]

As organizations get large they tend to add many levels of hierarchy. The problem with hierarchical organizations is that they require each idea to be approved by senior managers prior to implementation. Creative ideas are those that are not obvious to the majority of people. Each time an idea needs approval, it runs the risk of being disapproved by an individual who is not sympathetic to the difference, or who considers it risky. The more hierarchical the organization, the greater the scrutiny. The greater the scrutiny, the greater the probability that an outstanding idea will be screened out. Thus, in the long run, a large bureaucratic organization will screen out creative ideas and endorse similarity. Small agencies or autonomous units of large agencies may be more creative because they require fewer layers of approval. For example, the 1992 survey of the most notable print ads found that small and in-house agencies had 10 of the 17 best ads.[58] This number has been increasing in recent years, despite the increasing size and greater resources of large agencies.

An organization that tolerates risk is one that does not penalize executives for mistakes. A creative idea is one whose promise is not obvious to everyone. It thus involves risk. Novel ideas frequently bomb, because the authors of the idea overestimate the value of the benefits, or underestimate the difficulty of implementation. Thus, it may take many misses before one successful hit. An organization that wants creativity must be willing to take risks, and to accept bombs when novel ideas do not pan out. An organization that penalizes every failure also fosters an atmosphere of fear that minimizes experimentation, restrains lateral thinking, and kills creativity. A wide tolerance for errors can encourage managers to experiment with new ideas.

Tolerance for risk is especially important in an agency, which has to overcome the tendency to penalize errors within both its own organization and that of the client. As discussed earlier, Chiat/Day

developed a reputation for its creative ads. Its chief creative director, Lee Clow, had this to say of his agency's boldness which fostered that creativity:

"Most agencies don't have the balls to support a good idea. They might board it up once in a while, because there's lots of good creative people in this business. They might even take it out to the client every once in a while. But as soon as it gets killed by someone in authority, they don't have the rapport with their client to say, 'Now wait. We know this is risky, but here's why you should do it.' Most [account people] would go back to the office and say, 'Sorry guys. We gave it a try. Now this is what the client wants.'"[59]

Creative Styles

Do advertising creatives have distinctive styles? Do these styles work best for certain products or situations? Many people in the advertising profession think so. Consider the following examples:

- Benetton's advertising is often associated with provocative social themes. This advertising has helped to create tremendous awareness for the Benetton brand name, as well as to promote its style of clothing as bold and unconventional (see Exhibit 3-6).
- Calvin Klein has repeatedly used provocative sexual themes in its advertising. The style of advertising works well for Calvin Klein's products—clothing and cosmetics—which promise sexual attractiveness.
- Wieden and Kennedy's ads for Nike were quite different from anything done before. The ads used endorsers and aroused emotions in new and creative ways. They are especially famous for developing the Air Jordan athletic shoe brand around the image of Michael Jordan, and Nike's famous slogan of empowerment, "Just Do It." This style of advertising worked very well for Nike but failed for Subaru.
- Some small advertising agencies on the West Coast have become famous for a bold and irreverent style that pitches niche brands against industry leaders. For example, Chiat/Day's introductory campaign for the Apple Macintosh ridiculed IBM's dominance of the computer market, while its ad for the mid-sized Nissan car, Altima, parodied ads for Toyota's luxury car, Lexus.

▼ **EXHIBIT 3-10.** Leo Burnett Company, Inc.'s appealing ad personalities.

Source: © 1993 by Kellogg Company. Reprinted with permission of Kellogg Company.

Source: 9-Lives®Plus™ Cat Food.

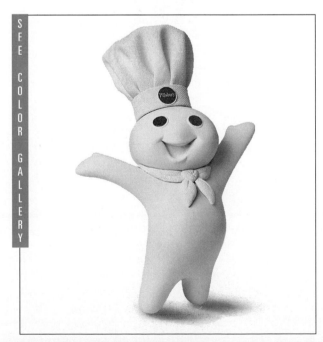

Source: Courtesy of The Pillsbury Company.

■ The Leo Burnett Company, Inc., following the philosophy of its founder, Leo Burnett, has become famous for a style of advertising that is warm, human and believable.[60] The ads defined a distinct image for the brand, often characterized by symbols and icons such as Kellogg's Tony the Tiger®, Morris the Cat, the Pillsbury Doughboy, the Marlboro Man, Charlie the Tuna, the Keebler Elves, and the Jolly Green Giant (see Exhibit 3-10).

Why do advertising creatives evolve these distinctive styles? One reason may be differences in tastes and personalities. Just as artists have styles of painting, and writers have styles of writing, advertising creatives have distinctive styles that permeate their work. Another reason may be the uncertainty of knowing what is going to work. While empirical knowledge about what type of advertising is effective has increased substantially over the last few decades, no one can assert with certainty which execution is *the best* in a situation. In the absence of certainty, creatives rely on their own beliefs about what they think is most effective. This belief influences their choice of executions, leading to the distinctive styles we observe. A third reason may be the competence of the creatives. Some creatives have a great facility at arousing deep emotions, others at kindling humor, still others at building strong logical arguments. Abilities lead to certain preferential modes of work, which we perceive as styles. Thus a combination of tastes, beliefs, and abilities leads creatives to certain distinctive styles of advertising.

While individuals have distinctive styles, we should not exaggerate the role of styles in agencies as a whole. Large agencies employ large numbers of creatives with many different styles. Thus one may be able to identify as many styles within an agency, as between agencies. Founders of particular agencies may have distinct styles that they foster within their own agency. However, as the agency grows, hires new personnel, and works for different advertisers with different needs, the style tends to get enriched, but also loses its sharpness. Perhaps the only clear distinction is whether the agency tends to emphasize bold creative executions or research-based content when creating ads. This choice between the two is the subject of an enduring debate in advertising to which we now turn.

Emphasizing Content or Execution

In 1968, the Martin and Woltz Agency, a three-year-old agency in Richmond, Virginia, had an opportunity to bid for the Virginia tourism account.[61] The agency started by collecting other states' tourism brochures. It then analyzed Virginia's assets relative to those of other states. It found that the state was endowed with magnificent mountain ranges, beautiful beaches and rich history. That inventory of attractions led to the proposition that Virginia was for mountain lovers, beach lovers and history lovers.

Based on that proposition, the creative team coined the theme, "Virginia is for lovers." (See Exhibit 3-11.) Besides hinting at Virginia's natural attractions, the theme capitalized on a popular word in the late sixties, "love." The Vietnam-war protesters' slogan "Make love, not war" was popular on campuses, and Erich Segal's novel *Love Story* was a bestseller. However, the theme clashed with the image of the state of Virginia, which had a reputation for being conservative. When the theme "Virginia is for lovers" was first presented to the client, everyone in the audience laughed. But the chairman of the state's tourism committee was impressed by the novelty and appeal of the theme. It was adopted as the slogan for the campaign.

The logo of the campaign was the slogan in white letters on a black background, followed by a red heart. One TV ad showed Debbie Shelton running on a beach in a "Virginia is for lovers" T-shirt. When she became Miss USA a little after, it further enhanced the appeal of the ad. To capitalize on the popularity of the slogan, the agency prepared T-shirts, sweatshirts and buttons featuring the slogan. These items were such a great hit that the agency made more profit on the T-shirts than on the advertising.

Was Martin and Woltz's success with the Virginia tourism account due to clever words and images, or to research that revealed Virginia's unique, undiscovered assets? More generally, was the campaign's success due to its execution or its content? This issue is one of perennial contention in advertising circles, and is the subject of this section.[62]

Content refers to the nature and form of the message that is communicated through the ad. It covers the merits of the brand, derived from research on consumers, the brand's competitors and the brand itself. In the ad for Virginia tourism, the content is Virginia's mountains, beaches and history. **Execution** refers to the form of communication that the ad adopts. Examples from the Virginia tourism ad are the choice of Debbie Shelton running on a beach in a T-shirt, or the four words "Virginia is for lovers." Most creatives assert their allegiance to creative execution, echoing the beliefs of William Bernbach, who may have fathered the creative revolution in advertising.[63] However, most clients, advertising researchers and account executives put their faith in content, following the philosophy espoused by advertising stalwarts such as David Ogilvy and Rosser Reeves.

The debate can be the source of much misunderstanding, conflict and tension during the development of the ad. For example, one agency vice president was supposed to have said, "There is a type of personality that becomes the brand manager. He ends up where he is because he has at some time in his life rejected the creative side of life."[64] On the other hand, a brand manager was supposed to have remarked, "One of the common perceptions of brand managers is that a creative person is a very funny type of guy. Like he has long hair. He wears pants that don't match his suit, and he comes to meetings in tennis shoes. Let me tell you, I've seen more than one idea shot down because brand men have the theory that this guy is some kind of East Village, Greenwich Village, Haight-Ashbury, Sunset Strip nut."[65] Bernbach and Ogilvy provide a stronger rationale for the execution versus content debate, respectively, than do the above caricatures.

▶ **EXHIBIT 3–11. "Virginia is for lovers" ad.**

WELCOME TO VIRGINIA—

A STATE OF EXTRAORDINARY NATURAL BEAUTY AND RICH HERITAGE

Virginia's appeals today are as broad and diverse as its geography and as abundant as its nearly four centuries of history. Stretching from the Atlantic Ocean to the Blue Ridge and Allegheny mountains, Virginia is a mixture of exciting cities, thrilling theme parks, historic homes and villages and as much recreational activity as you'd care to squeeze into your stay.

History comes alive throughout Virginia. Visitors to the commonwealth find much to enjoy. Experience the lives of those who founded the first permanent English settlement in the New World. Tour birthplaces and homes of seven of the eight Virginia-born U.S. presidents. Discover numerous Revolutionary and Civil War battlefields and sites on Virginia's soil.

The longest stretch of the Appalachian Trail runs along the western bend of Virginia. Barrier islands off the Eastern Shore offer some of the East Coast's most exciting saltwater fishing. The warm, sandy beaches of Hampton Roads and Tidewater and the stately elegance of James River plantations are close enough for a single day's visit. Giant limestone caverns extend under the serene Shenandoah Valley, and scenic highways like the 105-mile Skyline Drive and the 217-mile Virginia portion of the Blue Ridge Parkway allow travelers to take in scenic vistas.

Visitors enjoy a full range of recreational activities including camping, hiking, bicycling, skiing and golfing at its four-season resorts and at Virginia's more than 50 regional, state and national parks. Nearly 3,000 miles of freshwater streams, rivers and lakes, and more than 1,200 miles of tidal shoreline afford water activities galore.

Located mid-way between New York and Miami, the commonwealth boasts well-maintained major highways and scenic byways, service at 12 commercial airports-including Washington Dulles International and Washington National airports - and at 57 general aviation airports, and Amtrak rail service connecting Virginia cities to commuter and long-distance travel routes.

Virginia is for lovers of mountains and beaches, history and culture, theme parks and natural wonders, vibrant cities and postcard-perfect towns. Your first visit here might be as a visitor, but you will undoubtedly return as a lingering traveler.

VIRGINIA IS FOR LOVERS

Source: Courtesy of Virginia Tourism Corporation.

▼ **EXHIBIT 3-12.** Bernbach's provocative ad for Volkswagen.

Source: Courtesy of J.L. Jordan III, DDB Needham Worldwide.

William Bernbach was a believer in creative advertising. He said, "Finding out what to say is the beginning of the communication process. How you say it makes people look and listen and believe."[66] Consistent with this philosophy, Bernbach did not believe in research. He felt that research was too quantitative and led different people to the same conclusion and execution. He claimed, "The memo-rable never emerged from a formula."[67] To achieve his goal, Bernbach resorted to two-sided advertising that incorporated humor and paradox. His humor stopped viewers cold, and flattered them into think-ing they were sophisticated.[68] His memorable ads include the "We Try Harder" ad for Avis, the "Lemon" ad for Volkswagen and the "You don't have to be Jewish" ad for Levy's bread.[69] The creative punch in these ads is their admission of a weakness in the client's brand. However, the ad then comes back to emphasize the strength of the brand and undercut its weakness (see Exhibit 3-12). Chapter 6 discusses the logic of this communication strategy in greater depth.

Advertising stalwart David Ogilvy took the opposite position. Ogilvy believed strongly in communicating the merits of the brand rather than in colorful communication. He listed 11 commandments for building a great campaign, the first three of which emphasize the paramount importance of content:

1. What you say is more important than how you say it.
2. Unless your campaign is built around a great idea it will flop.
3. Give the facts.[70]

Ogilvy started with the premise that the consumer is intelligent and wants information to make better decisions. The advertiser therefore has to provide this information. He felt that the advertiser has no business selling the product if he or she does not believe it is better than the competition. Thus he had little patience for subtleties, euphemisms, or plain lies. He said of the advertising he saw: "Today, everybody is talking creativity, and frankly, that's got me worried. I fear all the sins we may commit in the name of creativity. I fear that we may be entering an age of phonies."[71] Ogilvy used extensive copy, no humor, and striking, colored pictures. Indeed, some of these pictures made him famous: the Hathaway man with his eyepatch, the Schweppes salesman's Vandyke and the quietly ticking clock in the Rolls Royce.[72] He used these pictures as a hook to gain consumers' attention and represent the merits of the brand described in the copy.

Ogilvy believed that good advertising must be rooted in research to identify the platform on which to sell the brand, and to determine the sales effectiveness of that platform. Following this line of reasoning, some authors have developed a model to guide creatives. The model uses a bank of research findings on advertising effectiveness to develop norms that suggest what ad appeal, copy strategy, execution or other aspects of an ad will be most effective in specific situations.[73]

Ogilvy's philosophy is consistent with that of another great advertiser, Rosser Reeves, who frowned on clever words and attention-getting ads. Reeves described the purpose of advertising as follows: "Let's say you are a manufacturer. Your advertising isn't working. Your sales are going down. Your future depends on it, your family's future depends on it, other people's future depends on it. What do you want out of me? Fine writing? Do you want masterpieces? Do you want glowing things that can be framed? Or do you want to see the . . . sales curve stop moving down and start moving up?"[74] Reeves coined the term *USP* or *Unique Selling Proposition*. The USP is a proposition that captures the most important attribute of a brand, distinguishes it from its competitors, and fills an unmet need of consumers (see Exhibit 3-13).

The content versus creative debate is not merely a historical event. It is very active today. Creatives today generally believe in the Bernbach philosophy of creative execution. On the other hand, researchers, account executives and especially clients believe in the Ogilvy philosophy of content-based advertising. The key question is, do these two approaches need to be mutually exclusive? Is there a middle ground?

One study that evaluated 1,000 ads concluded that the most important reason for an ad's effectiveness was the presence of a unique message that differentiated the brand from its competitors.[75] According to this study, content is more important than execution. On the other hand, a review of *Advertising Age*'s 50 best TV ads of 50 years[76] indicates that many of them achieved their excellence based on a novel execution. Thus, neither content nor execution is likely to be the sole basis for creating outstanding ads. Either of these two approaches may sometimes be sufficient for excellence in advertising. But can content and execution be combined for better advertising?

An important premise of this book is that the combination of research-based content with creative execution may constitute a powerful basis for effective advertising today. Moreover, even within the area of execution, decades of research in the social sciences indicate that some forms of communication are more appropriate in certain situations than other forms. That body of research provides the principles of effective communication which indicate what type of advertising is most effective in certain situations. For example, advertising can adopt reason, emotion or endorsement appeals.

▼ **EXHIBIT 3-13.** Ad for Lee Jeans based on its unique selling proposition, "The brand that fits!"

Tonight, all over America, women will be slipping into something a little more comfortable.

Ahhhhh. Relaxed Rider™ jeans. There's no better way to feel like yourself again. Off with your stuffy 9 to 5 work clothes and into your favorite jeans. Nobody fits your body...or the way you live...better than Lee.

R E L A X E D · R I D E R S

The brand that fits!

Source: Courtesy of Lee Apparel Co., Inc.

Appeals based on reason could adopt supportive, refutational, or inoculative arguments. Appeals based on emotions could arouse love, humor, fear, loyalty, and so forth. Part II of this book describes the principles of communication that tell us when each of these forms of communication is most effective. It would be foolish for advertising creatives to ignore this body of knowledge.

However, this knowledge still does not indicate which specific form of words, picture, sounds and actions is most effective in particular situations. For example, even if research suggests that the ad should use a particular argument, the copywriter must compose the creative combination of words that best achieves this goal. If a researcher suggests the use of fear, the art director must still choose the combination of images, color, sounds and words that arous-

es the right degree of fear to persuade the consumer to action. Thus, the reliance on research for selecting the content of the ad and the form of communication still leaves creatives with ample room for the execution of their art.

A good example of the effective combination of content and execution is the successful ad campaign for Virginia Tourism Corporation by the Martin and Woltz Agency. The agency began with research on the attractions of the state of Virginia and the advertising campaigns of other states. This research suggested that Virginia's unique assets were its natural attractions, mountains and beaches, and its rich history. The creatives then took over to fashion the attractions into captivating slogans, scenes and action. No doubt, the campaign also benefited from some fortuitous events. But the key to the success of this campaign was the combination of good research with clever execution.

Summary

Advertising agencies solicit clients, create ads, and place ads in the media. The single factor that most shapes the structure of the agency is its competitiveness. The market of advertising agencies is very competitive because of the lack of an enduring basis of competitive advantage, the easy entry of new agencies into the market and the increasing replacement of human skills by relatively inexpensive computers. The most important function of an agency which helps it win and retain clients is creative design. The other important functions of agencies are accounts management, media buying, and marketing research. Full-service agencies provide all of these functions, while specialized agencies provide one or a few of these functions. Full-service agencies can adopt one of three types of ownership structures: independent, integrated or holding company. Ownership structure affects the clients that agencies serve, their creative style, and their innovativeness. The two typical organizational forms that agencies adopt are the functional and accounts-based forms.

The first agency decision that the advertiser has to make is whether to use an external agency, or develop and operate one internally. If the advertiser uses an internal agency, it should operate as a stand-alone unit. But if the advertiser uses an external agency, it may be better off integrating the advertising department with the marketing department within the firm. The selection of the agency is an important dynamic decision that the advertiser revisits through its performance evaluation. Given the proliferation of advertising agencies, the advertiser rarely lacks choice. However, the advertiser should refrain from terminating an agency's contract except for compelling reasons. This practice ensures agency loyalty, while reducing the cost of formal reviews and prospective campaigns.

Four important methods of compensating agencies are commission, fee, cost and performance. Over the last few decades, the popularity of the commission method has declined. Each method has its advantages and disadvantages. A good approach may be a hybrid of two or more of the above methods that capitalizes on their advantages but avoids their limitations.

The most important function of an agency is designing creative ads. The mental processes that foster creativity are associative, lateral, divergent or soft thinking. The important activities that foster creative thinking are preparation, incubation, illumination, exchange and verification. The organizational characteristics that foster creativity are freedom from rules, decentralization and risk tolerance.

A major debate within the profession is whether advertising should emphasize the content of the message or the creativity of the execution. The thesis of this book is that superior advertising can result from a combination of good content and creative execution. Such an approach capitalizes on the wealth of knowledge obtained from research, but leaves ample room for novel executions by the creative staff.

Questions

1. By the end of 1994, Saatchi & Saatchi Co. was a huge holding company with enormous potential, but heavily laden with debt. Shareholders were pressing for the demotion of Maurice Saatchi. However, Maurice Saatchi had also recruited and held the trust of a number of important clients. What should the board have done?

2. Why is life in an agency so competitive, and fraught with so much uncertainty? What can agencies do to develop loyal clients?

3. An agency can carry out a number of functions for its clients. Which of these functions are more important? Which functions distinguish an agency from its competitors? Why?

4. Only a few major advertisers currently resort to an internal agency. Why? When should advertisers prefer an internal agency to an external one?

5. Advertisers frequently call for agency reviews followed by prospective campaigns, in order to ensure that they get the best service for their advertising budget. Evaluate the merits of these policies. What would you recommend?

6. What are the pros and cons of the various methods of compensating agencies? Develop a compensation method that is superior to the ones currently used.

7. Many advertisers currently treat agencies as a cost center, striving to get the most from their services for the lowest price. What alternative approaches are there to dealing with agencies? Compare these alternatives with advertisers' current treatment of agencies.

8. Creativity is a critical ingredient in developing ads today. But it is not easy to identify or foster. What actions should large agencies and corporations take to maintain the creative spark within their organizations? What are the costs of these actions?

9. Is content or execution more important in designing ads? Why? Which one, if any, of these two factors should agencies emphasize today?

10. Find ads that you believe are effective, and those you believe are ineffective. Now analyze these ads to see if their strengths and weaknesses are due to an emphasis (or overemphasis) on content alone, execution alone, or a good blend of the two.

NOTES

1. Based on Goldman, Kevin, Kyle Pope, and Tara Parker-Pope (1995), "Saatchi's Implosion: Tale of Power and Ego Across Two Continents," *The Wall Street Journal*, January 12, A1; Goldman, Kevin (1995), "At Saatchi, 3 Executives Quit Over Co-Founder's Ouster," *The Wall Street Journal*, January 10, B6; Wentz, Laurel (1995), "Maurice Flies," *Advertising Age*, May 8, 1; Collis, David J. (1989), "Saatchi and Saatchi Company PLC," Case 9-387-170, Boston, MA: Harvard Business School, Publishing Division; Wentz, Laurel (1995), "War Between Maurice, Cordiant Cools Off," *Advertising Age*, May 29, 38; Parker-Pope, Tara (1995), "Former Saatchi and Saatchi Settles Dispute With Founder," *The Wall Street Journal*, May 23, PB6; Wentz, Laurel (1995), "Saatchi Truce May End," *Advertising Age*, September 18, 8.

2. Actually a £25,000 investment.

3. Lipman, Joanne (1992), "Study Shows Clients Jump Ship Quickly," *The Wall Street Journal*, May 21, B8.

4. Fixed costs to run an agency are so low that one study estimates that economies of scale are virtually exhausted once gross incomes reach $3 to $4 million: Silk, Alvin J. (1994), "Economics of Advertising Agencies as Multiproduct Firms: Implications for Advertisers," *Marketing Science Institute Conference Summary*, Boston: The Marketing Science Institute.

5. Porter, Michael (1985), *Competitive Advantage: Creating and Sustaining Superior Performance*, New York: The Free Press.

6. Silk, Alvin J. (1995), "Economics of Advertising Agencies as Multiproduct Firms: Implications for Advertisers," *Marketing Science Institute Conference Summary*, Boston: The Marketing Science Institute.

7. Based on Prince, Greg W. (1993), "Annual Soft Drink All-Star Review: But The Brands Played On," *Beverage World*, March, 51–56; *USA Today* (1994), "Operating Systems Market Shares," May 9.

8. Based on King, Thomas R. (1995), "Creating Chaos: How A Hot Ad Agency, Undone By Arrogance, Lost Its Independence," *The Wall Street Journal*, April 17, A1, A5.

9. *Ibid.*

10. *Advertising Age* (1990), "Agency of the Decade; Chiat Proves Big Can Be Better," January 1, 10.

11. King, "Creating Chaos."

12. *Advertising Age* (1995), "50 Years of TV Advertising," Spring, 44.

13. Kover, Arthur J., and Stephen M. Goldberg (1995), "The Games Copywriters Play: Conflict, Quasi-Control, A New Proposal," *Journal of Advertising Research* 35, 4, 52–62.

14. *Ibid.*

15. Dalrymple, Goodrum (1990), *Advertising in America: The First Two Hundred Years*, New York: Harry N. Abrams, 21.

16. Based on Goldman, Kevin (1993), "Talent Firm's Ads Fill New Coke Campaign," *The Wall Street Journal*, February 11, B3; Elliott, Stuart (1993), "A Shake-Up of Agencies By Coca-Cola May Be Just The Beginning Of A Wider 'Ideas Wanted' Push," *New York Times*, October 11, C7, D7; Magiera, Marcy (1993), "CAA Asks Production Houses For Coke Ideas," *Advertising Age*, July 5, 8; Goldman, Kevin (1994), "Coke Blitz Keeps Successful '93 Strategy," *The Wall Street Journal*, February 8, B9; Wallenstein, Andrew (1995), "Coca-Cola's Sweet Return To Glory Days," *Advertising Age*, April 17, 4.

17. Based on Goldman, "Talent Firm's Ads Fill New Coke Campaign."

18. Elliott, "A Shake-Up of Agencies By Coca-Cola May Be Just The Beginning Of A Wider 'Ideas Wanted' Push."

19. Atler, Stewart (1995), *Truth Well Told, McCann-Erickson and the Pioneering of Global Advertising*, New York: McCann-Erickson Worldwide.

20. *Advertising Age* (1996), "World's Top 25 Agency Brands," April 15, S15.

21. Elliott, Stuart (1994), "IBM To Transfer Advertising Work To Single Agency," *New York Times*, April 24, D1.

22. Gleason and Pat Sloan (1995), "Up In The Ayer," *Advertising Age*, September 11, 1, 8.

23. *Ibid.*

24. Ogilvy, David (1963), *Confessions of an Advertising Man*, New York: Atheneum.

25. Teinowitz, Ira (1994), "Why A-B Bounced Bud," *Advertising Age*, November 21, 1.

26. Blasko, Vincent J., and Michael P. Mokwa (1988), "Paradox, Advertising and the Creative Process," *Current Issues and Research in Advertising* 2, 11, 351–364.

27. Rothenberg, Randall (1994), *Where The Suckers Moon*, New York: Vintage Books.

28. Flynn, Julia, Kathleen Kerwin, and Mark Landler (1992), "Days of Doubt for a Creator of Icons," *Business Week*, October 19, 75–76.

29. Kover and Goldberg, "The Games Copywriters Play."

30. Glover, John (1993), "Benetton Bucks The Trend," *International Management* 48, 7, 48.

31. Elliot, Stuart (1993), "A Survey Shows That The Industry's Davids are Stinging the Goliaths," *New York Times*, June 23, 18.

32. Ripley, M. Louise (1991), "What Kind of Companies Take Their Advertising In-House," *Journal of Advertising Research* (October/November), 73–78.

33. Vertical integration is the ownership of suppliers (or customers). The same principle applies to owning of such customers as wholesalers or distributors.

34. *Advertising Age* (1993), "Ad Follies," December 20, 17.

35. *Ibid.*

36. Ogilvy, David (1992), "We Sell. Or Else," *The Advertiser*, Summer, 23.

37. Flynn, Kerwin, and Landler, "Days of Doubt for a Creator of Icons."

38. Lazarus, George (1993), "Burnett Beats The Odds, Keeps Oldsmobile's Ad Account," *Chicago Tribune*, February 2, 1.

39. Ogilvy, "We Sell. Or Else."

40. Adapted from Bayor, Leslie (1993), "Home Depot's $40M Account On The Loose," *Advertising Age*, March 22, 1.

41. That is, $17.65 = (15/85,000) \times 100,000$.

42. The 17.65% is obtained by dividing 15% by $(100 - 15)$. In general, if r is the commission rate, then the rate for grossing up the bill is $r/(100 - r)$.

43. Ogilvy, "We Sell. Or Else," 21–24.

44. Liesse, Julie (1991), "Quaker 'Guarantees' Agency Pay," *Advertising Age*, October 28, 4.

45. Wells, Melanie, and Laurel Wentz (1994), "Coke Trims Commissions," *Advertising Age*, January 31, 2.

46. Smith, Dave (1994), "The Secret Life of Commercials," *New York Times*, April 24, C4.

47. Some ideas in this subsection are based on Moriarty, Sandra E. (1991), *Creative Advertising*, Englewood Cliffs, NJ: Prentice-Hall.

48. deBono, Edward (1971), *Lateral Thinking For Management*, Chicago: American Management Association.

49. Guilford, J. P. (1973), "Creativity—Retrospect and Prospect," *Journal of Creative Behavior* 7, 4, 247–252.

50. Young, James Webb (1975), *A Technique for Producing Ideas*, 3rd ed., Chicago: Crain Books.

51. Von Oech, Roger (1983), *A Whack On The Side Of The Head: How To Unlock Your Mind For Innovation*, New York: Warner Books.

52. Wallas, Graham (1926), *The Art of Thought*, New York: Harcourt, Brace and World.

53. Young, *A Technique for Producing Ideas.*

54. Ogilvy, *Confessions of an Advertising Man*, 142.

55. Kuhn, Thomas S. (1970), *The Structure of Scientific Revolution*, 2nd ed., Chicago: University of Chicago Press.

56. Chandy, Rajesh (1995), "Organizing For New Product Introduction," unpublished dissertation, University of Southern California; Nord, Walter R., and Sharon Tucker (1987), *Implementing Routine and Radical Innovations*, Lexington, MA: Lexington Books.

57. Cuneo, Alice Z. (1995), "Goodby Crafts Winning Ways," *Advertising Age*, June 19, 8.

58. Elliot, "A Survey Shows That The Industry's Davids are Stinging the Goliaths."

59. *Advertising Age*, "Agency of the Decade."

60. Fizdale, Rick (1995), "Seeking Creativity That Is 'Daring . . . Fresh . . . Human . . . Believable,'" *Advertising Age*, July 31, LB-8.

61. Adapted from Meyers, Janet (1995), "From Richmond, With Love," *Advertising Age*, September 25, M-2.

62. This section is based on Blasko and Mokwa, "Paradox, Advertising and the Creative Process."

63. *Advertising Age*, "50 Years of TV Advertising."

64. Blasko and Mokwa, "Paradox, Advertising and the Creative Process."

65. *Ibid.*

66. *Ibid.*

67. *Ibid.*

68. Dalrymple, *Advertising in America.*

69. Antin, Tony (1993), *Great Print Advertising*, New York: John Wiley & Sons.

70. Ogilvy, *Confessions of an Advertising Man*, 142.

71. Ogilvy, "We Sell. Or Else," 21.

72. Dalrymple, *Advertising in America.*

73. Burke, Raymond R., Arvind Rangaswamy, Jerry Wind, and Jehoshua Eliashberg (1990), "A Knowledge-Based System For Advertising Design," *Marketing Science* 9, 3 (Summer), 212–229.

74. Ogilvy, David, "We Sell. Or Else."

75. Stewart, David W. and David H. Furse (1986), *Effective Television Advertising: A Study of 1000 Commercials*, Lexington, MA: Lexington Books.

76. *Advertising Age*, "50 Years of TV Advertising."

Communication
Strategy

By the early 1990s, milk had suffered a two-decade decline in per capita consumption. The primary reason for the decline was that consumer misconception of milk as being high in fat and cholesterol, and a belief that only kids need milk. So in 1994, the National Fluid Milk Processor Promotion Board contracted with the advertising agency Bozell Worldwide for a $36 million campaign to address these issues. Based on consumer research, the agency decided to target women ages 25 to 44, who had

Introduction to Persuasion

the greatest need for the calcium in milk, were generally gatekeepers of the home and responsible for other family members, but were also part of the diet-conscious group that was avoiding the product. The overall message of the campaign was to communicate milk's broad nutritional benefits and correct some of the misconceptions that existed. To that end, the ads spread the messages that: skim milk had the same amount of nutrients as whole milk with no fat, that milk can help prevent osteoporosis, and that milk has an essential role in athletes' and other active people's diets.

The cornerstone of the campaign was the use of a print campaign with photos of celebrities sporting milk mustaches and the tagline "Milk. What a surprise!" Each celebrity expressed his or her own reasons for drinking milk, but every one appeared with the characteristic milk mustache (see Exhibit 4-1). They were photographed by a leading photographer to make portrait-like ads that embodied the personality of the celebrities. The campaign used 20 celebrities, including athletes (Pete Sampras), models (Kate Moss), actors (Lisa Kudrow), music stars (Tony Bennett), and TV stars (Vanna White).

The campaign was enormously popular and successful. Video Storyboards Tests conducted a survey among consumers which found it to be the Top Print Campaign of 1995. The agency's research found improvements in consumers' awareness of milk's nutritional benefits and positive attitude towards the product. With sales on the upswing and positive attitude shifts in all of the areas addressed by the program, the Milk Board decided to renew the campaign in 1996

▼ **EXHIBIT 4-1. The milk mustache.**

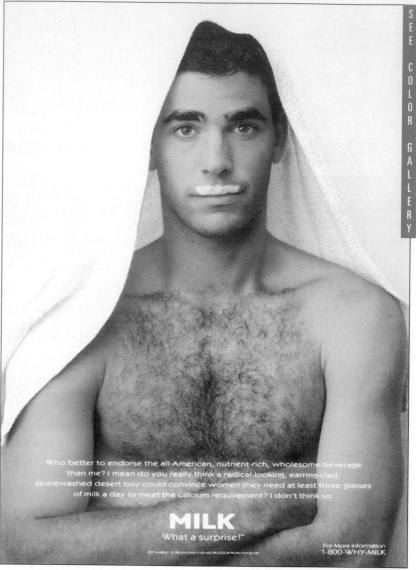

SEE COLOR GALLERY

Who better to endorse the all-American, nutrient-rich, wholesome beverage than me? I mean do you really think a radical-looking, earring-clad, stonewashed desert boy could convince women they need at least three glasses of milk a day to meet the calcium requirement? I don't think so.

MILK
What a surprise!™

For More Information
1-800-WHY-MILK

PETE SAMPRAS ©1995 NATIONAL FLUID MILK PROCESSOR PROMOTION BOARD

Source: Courtesy of Pistol Pete, Inc., the National Fluid Milk Processor Promotion Board, and Bozell Worldwide, Inc.

with a $110 million budget and additional target groups.[1]

Why was the milk mustache campaign so successful? How did it persuade consumers to drink more milk or to view it more favorably? What alternatives did the agency and the Milk Board have? These are central issues in persuasion, and questions that this chapter and others in Part II address. Persuasion is used in all walks of life. For example, lawyers, preachers, politicians, managers and military leaders need to persuade their audiences or subordinates. But persuasion is critical in advertising and is the core of any promotional effort.

This book defines **persuasion** as a change in opinion, attitude, or behavior caused by some communication. This definition is purposely broad, as it does not specify the type of communication by which the change is effected. Many people assume that persuasion involves the use of information and argument. Indeed, these are important means of persuasion, and this is the definition of *persuasion* that the dictionary adopts. Chapter 6 covers the use of information and argument, including supportive, two-sided, refutational and inoculative arguments. However, this book defines *persuasion* as change that is brought about either by reason or by other more subtle methods that do not involve reasoning. Examples of the latter include the use of cues, such as endorsers, and of emotion, such as fear or joy. This dichotomy between persuasion that involves reason and persuasion that does not is important because it distinguishes an entire category of persuasion methods that are heavily used in contemporary advertising. Among these methods, the use of emotion is probably the most important. Chapter 7 covers the use of emotion and means of arousing emotion such as drama, music and humor. Another common means of persuasion today is by endorsements. Advertisers use celebrities, experts or laypeople to endorse their brands for several reasons. Chapter 8 explains the different types of endorsers, the theory behind their effectiveness and how to use them effectively. A precondition for all communication is that the communicator hold the attention of the audience. Chapter 5 covers this important topic.

Because persuasion is such a pervasive and important phenomenon, researchers have proposed many theories to explain it. This chap-ter describes the general theories, concepts and principles of persuasion used in advertising and promotion today. It focuses on four concepts particularly relevant to advertising and promotion: classical conditioning, repetition, involvement and elaboration.

CLASSICAL CONDITIONING

In the late nineteenth century, the Russian physiologist Ivan Pavlov first discovered conditioned responses when studying the gastric secretions of digestion. His discovery led him to perform controlled experiments with dogs. In a typical experiment, the dogs were outfitted with a device to measure their salivation accurately. A tuning fork was sounded, and 7 or 8 seconds later, a plate containing a fixed type and amount of food was given to the dogs. After 10 repetitive associations of the tone and food stimuli, the tone alone evoked only a little salivation; but after 30 repetitions, the tone alone caused much salivation. After the first few repetitions, the tone had to be sounded for 18 seconds, to stimulate salivation; but after many repetitions, salivation began after just 1 or 2 seconds of the sounding.[2]

Pavlov's experiments are some of the best known in the psychology of learning. **Learning** is a relatively enduring change in behavior that results from exposure to stimuli. There are different types of learning (see Exhibit 4-2). The form of learning

▼ **EXHIBIT 4-2.** Types of learning.

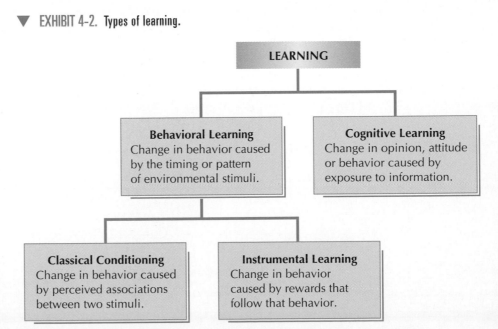

depicted by Pavlov's experiments is called **classical (or Pavlovian) conditioning**. Classical conditioning is the relatively enduring change in behavior that results from perceived associations between two stimuli, such as the tone and food in the case of Pavlov's dogs. This type of learning may explain why advertisers associate their brands with celebrity endorsers (see Chapter 8), popular jingles (see Chapter 7), or attractive pictures. How exactly does conditioning occur? What factors influence it? The next subsections address these questions.

The Process of Conditioning

Classical conditioning takes place through associations between a pair of stimuli: the unconditioned and conditioned. A *stimulus* is any object that an individual can sense. An **unconditioned stimulus** is one to which an individual already has a natural predisposition to respond. For Pavlov's dogs, food is the unconditioned stimulus. At the sight or smell of food, a dog's natural response is salivation. An **unconditioned response** is the natural response to the unconditioned stimulus, such as a dog's salivation at the smell of food. The **conditioned stimulus** is one which does not initially elicit the unconditioned response. For Pavlov's dogs, the bell was the conditioned stimulus. The conditioned stimulus may elicit some other natural response before conditioning takes place. For example, a dog may perk up its ears at the sound of a bell.

In Pavlov's experiments, the repetitive association of bell and food ultimately led the dogs to associate food with the sound of the bell and to salivate at the sound of the bell, even when it was not followed by food. This new response of salivation elicited by the conditioned stimulus, the bell, is called the **conditioned response**. Exhibit 4-3 presents a schematic

diagram of the classical conditioning process. The ultimate test of classical conditioning is the triggering of the conditioned response (salivation) by the conditioned stimulus (bell), even in the absence of the unconditioned stimulus (food). Inadequate association of the two stimuli may not lead to the desired (conditioned) response.

Once learned, a conditioned response does not require repetitive associations of the two stimuli to be sustained. However, if either of the two stimuli occurs alone, then the association between the two is weakened, and leads to the ultimate loss of conditioning. This process is called **extinction**. For example, suppose a dog that has been conditioned to salivate at the sound of a bell neither hears the bell nor receives food for a few days. Then the conditioning remains as strong as before, and the next occurrence of the bell would lead to salivation as intensely as before. However, if in the three days, either the bell rings without food or the food is served without the bell, then the conditioning between bell and food will be weakened.

Does classical conditioning occur in humans? Can it be used in advertising? Some controlled laboratory studies do support the effectiveness of conditioning in a marketing context.[3] One study showed that repeatedly exposing subjects to an ad for a new brand of toothpaste with attractive water scenes led them to like that brand more than did subjects in a control group who saw the ad without the water scenes.[4] This behavioral change is ultimately what many advertisers hope to achieve by associating their brands with attractive pictures and personalities. .

Another study argued that conditioning was the primary reason for the use of celebrities.[5] The meaning that celebrities acquire in their careers and lives transfers to brands when the two are repeatedly associated. In this case, the celebrity is the unconditioned stimulus, the brand is the conditioned stimulus, and the feeling of attraction is the response. One example is Bozell's use of celebrities to enhance the image of milk. By attractively portraying celebrities with milk, the campaign's director, Jay Schulberg, claimed to have "assigned glamour to a product that was, frankly, as plain as a glass of milk." Another example is Pepsi's

▼ EXHIBIT 4-3. The process of conditioning.

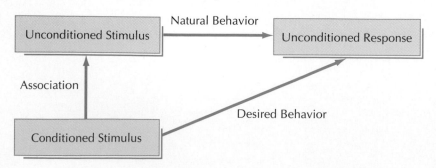

advertising campaign based on the theme, "Choice of a new generation." By using this theme, Pepsi repeatedly associates its brand with youthful, fun-loving celebrities having a good time with Pepsi. The campaign never gives a reason why Pepsi is a drink for young people, or a drink that brings joy. The advertiser hopes that association of Pepsi with youthful personalities and enjoyable occasions will lead to a transfer of feeling from the latter to the former.

Association can also encompass the other senses. An example is cinnamon. Real estate agents sometimes advise clients who wish to sell a house to boil some cinnamon before showing the house to prospective buyers. Many people associate the smell of cinnamon with home-baked confections, and the warmth of a caring parent and happy family life. Entering a house suffused with the smell of cinnamon may evoke in a buyer images of a warm and caring family home, making the house seem desirable. This example involves two stages of conditioning. In the first stage, the smell of cinnamon (the conditioned stimulus) evokes the feeling of warmth (conditioned response) from a loving parent baking confections (the conditioned stimulus) by repeated association during one's growing years. In the second stage, the homeowner hopes that the smell of cinnamon (the new unconditioned stimulus) imparts the feeling of warmth to the home (the new conditioned stimulus) when it is inspected by a prospective buyer.[6]

Factors Favoring Conditioning

When is conditioning most likely to occur? Extensive experiments have shown that four factors favor the success of conditioning: the predictiveness, distinctiveness, appeal and link of the unconditioned stimulus.

First, the conditioned stimulus should *predict* the unconditioned one.[7] In other words, the occurrence of the conditioned stimulus should be a good indicator of the occurrence of the unconditioned stimulus. For example, if every ring of the bell is followed by food, and food never arrives without the bell, then the bell would be a perfect predictor of food. On the other hand, if sometimes food arrived without the bell, or the bell rang alone, then the bell would not be a good predictor of food. The effectiveness of conditioning depends on how accurately the conditioned stimulus predicts the unconditioned

one. Many people incorrectly believe that the timing of the stimuli is critical, so that the conditioned stimulus must precede the unconditioned one (the bell before the food). This order of stimuli is called **forward conditioning**. However, research indicates that, while timing is important, predictiveness is more important.

Second, the unconditioned stimulus should be *distinct*. A distinct stimulus is one that has rarely or never been used before. For example, when selecting an endorser as a stimulus, an advertiser should choose a candidate who has not endorsed other brands before. The candidate should also arouse a clear feeling with which the advertiser wishes to associate the brand to be advertised. Thus, a beautiful model in an ad would be more effective to the extent that she represents a unique message that has not been associated with some other brand. (Chapter 8 discusses this issue in greater detail.) Note that distinctiveness is positively correlated to predictiveness. In other words, an unconditioned stimulus that frequently occurs with other brands will not be distinct and will not be a good predictor of the target brand. However, Bozell devised a creative way to overcome this problem. While its campaign for milk did not use unique celebrities, it used them in a consistently unique way—sporting a milk mustache.

Third, the unconditioned stimulus should have a *strong appeal* for the recipient. This third factor tends to be negatively correlated with the first two, especially in the context of celebrity endorsers. The reason is that celebrities with strong appeal tend to be in high demand among advertisers and may, as a result, be overused. In general, a distinct stimulus with a moderate appeal is better than an overused stimulus with a strong appeal.

Fourth, there should be a good *link* between the two stimuli. For example, water scenes would be a good stimulus for boating equipment, while a well-dressed celebrity, for elegant clothing. Chapter 5 discusses the importance of a good link.

Conditioning is an important learning mechanism in humans and animals. It may also explain a very pervasive phenomenon in advertising and promotion—marketers trying to promote their brands by association with attractive stimuli. Yet consumers do not approach ads as passive, nonthinking observers. They may reflect on, argue against or even discuss with others the material in ads. For example, a viewer of a perfume ad with a female model could reason that many perfume ads show attractive models, but that perfume will never make her as attractive as the models. Such reasoning could weaken the effect of conditioning. The other three concepts covered in this chapter address the role of reason in persuasion.

REPETITION

Repetition is the exposure of an ad (or some other stimulus) to a subject two or more times in succession. Repetition is a major factor in advertising today. It is studied extensively in the fields of psychology, marketing, advertising and consumer behavior. This section examines two types of repetition, mere exposure and message repetition. It also discusses one related concept that continually fascinates people: subliminal advertising.

Mere Exposure[8]

A mysterious student attended a class at the University of Oregon for two months enveloped in a big black bag. Only his bare feet showed. Each Monday, Wednesday and Friday at 11:00 A.M. the Black Bag sat on a small table near the back of the classroom. The class was Speech 113, Basic Persuasion. Charles Goetzinger, professor of the class, knew the identity of the person inside. None of the 20 students in the class did. Goetzinger said the students' attitude toward the Black Bag changed from hostility to curiosity and finally to friendship.[9]

In July 1975 a New Hampshire man named John Adams won the Republican primary in the state's First Congressional District, defeating his closest competitor, Edward Hewson, by 4,000 votes. What was interesting about the campaign was that Adams made no speeches, issued no press releases, and spent no money. "I did absolutely no campaigning," he said. "With a name like mine I didn't figure I had to." The New Hampshire GOP chairman explained the victory thus, "When people went to the polls, they saw four names they didn't recognize. I guess they picked the one that sounded familiar."[10]

Mere exposure means making a stimulus available to an individual's perception without encouraging further thought about it. The *mere exposure effect* refers to the increased liking that subjects develop for certain previously perceived stimuli, even

though they do not recall having been exposed to them. A psychologist, Robert Zajonc, stimulated much research in this area with his claims of the existence of a mere exposure effect. In one experiment, Zajonc exposed subjects to nonsense syllables a varying number of times. He then measured their recall of and preference for the syllables. Subjects preferred syllables they had seen more often to those they had seen less often, even though they neither understood nor recalled the familiar syllables better than the other syllables. A vast number of studies tried to replicate the findings of Zajonc under different conditions and with different stimuli. While the results are not identical, the cumulative evidence suggests that increasing repetition leads to increased liking for the stimuli. However, beyond some point of saturation, increasing repetition leads to decreased liking for the stimuli.[11]

The two earlier anecdotes demonstrate the basic principles of the phenomenon of mere exposure: that repetition leads to familiarity and liking (as with the Black Bag) and that familiarity leads to preference and choice (as with John Adams). Note that in both cases the processes work even in the absence of information about the stimuli. Is mere exposure just another term for classical conditioning? Not really. In contrast to classical conditioning, mere exposure suggests that the mere act of the repetitive exposure of a stimulus can lead to preference for the stimulus, without the need for a conditioned stimulus. For example, frequent listening to a melody may lead to preference for it over an unfamiliar melody. The repetitive exposure of jingles, slogans and logos in ads is probably grounded in this belief about the effect of repetition.

Why does repetition lead to liking in this way? A combination of two factors, habituation and tedium, provides the most plausible explanation. This explanation has come to be called the **two-factor theory**. When subjects first see novel stimuli, the novelty leads to uncertainty and tension. Repeated exposure reduces this uncertainty and tension, leading to familiarity and liking. This process is called **habituation**. At the same time, repetitive exposure to the same stimuli leads to growing boredom and decreased liking. This process is called **tedium**. Habituation is strong early on, while tedium is strong later in the sequence of repetitions. The two factors together create a bell-shaped response to repetition (see Exhibit 4-4).

▼ **EXHIBIT 4-4.** The two-factor theory.

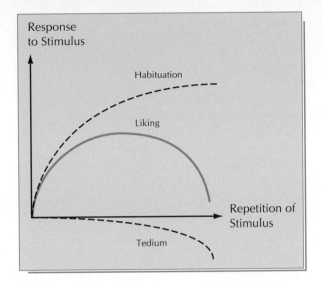

The cycles in sales of new records is a good example of this explanation. At first hearing, a new recording may be ignored or, at best, may arouse curiosity. Repetitive playing of the record may lead to consumer familiarity and liking, and to increased sales for the record. Indeed, record companies go to great lengths to get radio stations to play their new recordings frequently. In the highly competitive world of recording, lack of familiarity with a piece is likely to be its doom. Once a piece becomes a hit, it receives extensive play on radio stations, in private homes and in public places. Extensive repetition leads to tedium and sometimes displeasure, even with the best-selling record. The music world is then ready for the next hit.

Subliminal Advertising

Is mere exposure the same as subliminal advertising? **Subliminal advertising** refers to persuasive ad messages that are just below the threshold of perception, and are embedded in material that can be perceived. Examples include messages flashed between images of a video ad so quickly that they cannot be seen, or messages that can be heard only when a tune is played backward. Proponents claim that subliminal messages work because these messages are perceived subconsciously, making recipients unable to resist their influence. Subliminal advertising is radically different from mere exposure. Mere exposure assumes that stimuli are perceptible even if not intel-

ligible, gaining effectiveness from repetition. Subliminal advertising assumes that stimuli are intelligible even though they are not perceived normally.

The controversy about subliminal advertising started in the 1950s based on an experiment described in Vance Packard's best-seller, *The Hidden Persuaders*.[12] In the experiment, conducted by James McDonald Vicary, the words "*eat popcorn*" and "*drink Coca-Cola*" were flashed on a movie screen for 1/3000th of a second. Sales of Coke increased 58 percent and of popcorn, 18 percent. If advertising could persuade people against their will and knowledge, it would be a powerful force. The current thinking among professional psychologists and advertisers is that subliminal advertising is not effective, for three reasons.

First, many attempts were made to replicate Vicary's study. Most failed to find any significant support for subliminal advertising. Among these were Vicary's own efforts at replication, which were unsuccessful.

Second, the original study did not include strong control groups. A **control group** is an independent sample comparable in every way to the experimental sample, except that it is not subjected to the treatment. Control groups ensure that the observed effects are due to advertising only and not to other factors, such as the environment or the movie. For example, environmental factors, such as hot weather, or stimuli in the movie, such as food scenes, could have boosted purchases of food and soft drinks. As a result, some researchers suggest that the original study was seriously flawed, if not actually fabricated. One recent review suggests that Vicary used his claims of the effectiveness of subliminal advertising to collect retainer and consulting fees from advertisers. Then, in June 1958, he disappeared without a trace.[13]

The third and major argument against subliminal advertising is that it is difficult for something to be effective if it is not even perceived by the human senses. If a subliminal message such as "eat popcorn" could reach the human mind *imperceptibly*, why would it mean "eat popcorn" and not "do not eat popcorn" or just "eat more vegetables"? A more practical argument is that if subliminal messages were all that effective, advertising researchers and all other communicators would be better off using that approach rather than laboring with more difficult modes of persuasion. Government agencies could use subliminal advertising to persuade people to stop taking illicit drugs, stealing cars, abusing children, driving while drunk and cheating on their income taxes.[14]

Although a few researchers still believe subliminal advertising is effective, the majority do not. Moreover, the effects are so debatable that even some proponents of the theory question its commercial viability.[15] Further, those who believe in it have failed to develop a market for what would be a potent means of persuasion. Nevertheless, the public continues to believe in subliminal advertising. Surveys have found that 40 to 50 percent of the public have heard of the term and a majority (70 to 80 percent) believe that advertisers use it.[16] This belief may reflect the public's general skepticism about advertisers and may be fueled by uncritical accounts of the efficacy of subliminal advertising by some journalists. Alternatively, people may mistake mere exposure effects for subliminal advertising. They may be affected by stimuli they do not recall, mistaking that mere exposure effect to be subliminal advertising.

Advertisers generally communicate with messages that are overt and that stimulate consumer thought and reflection. Thus, recent research has focused more on message repetition than on subliminal messages or mere exposure.

Message Repetition

In contrast to mere exposure, **message repetition** refers to the repetition of stimuli that stimulate consumer thought. A large number of studies on message repetition have led to some consistent findings about its effects.[17]

First, repetition leads to higher persuasion, measured by variables such as recognition, recall, attitude, preference, behavioral intention and behavior. This may be the reason why candidates in minor city and county elections will often run a massive poster campaign that maximizes exposure of their faces and names, but gives little other information. They hope that such advertising will lead to increased awareness, familiarity, liking, and, eventually, votes—even in the absence of substantive information.

Second, the positive effect of repetition on recognition, recall, attitude, preference, behavioral intention and behavior declines roughly in the order listed. The strongest effect is on recognition and the least strong on behavior. In other words, repetitive exposure to a candidate's picture is likely to increase the awareness of the candidate among voters, but the level of familiarity will be less than that of awareness, the level of liking less than that of familiarity, and the level of favorable voting, less than that of liking.

Third, the response to repetition is generally nonlinear, first increasing and then leveling off or declining. This pattern is similar to that for mere exposure (Exhibit 4-4) and can be explained similarly by the two-factor theory.

Fourth, the effects of repetition vary by a number of conditions. Three particularly important factors will be discussed at greater length: the frequency, familiarity and complexity of the message.

Message Frequency **Frequency** means the number and pattern of repetitions in a given time period. An issue in message frequency that has puzzled advertisers for decades is, how many exposures are enough for a desired response.

One view in advertising circles is that three exposures to an ad are enough for persuasion to occur. Beyond that, tedium sets in and makes further repetition counterproductive. The rationale for three exposures was first proposed by advertising manager and theoretician Herbert Krugman.[18] He argued that the first exposure elicited interest in the topic, the second elicited interest in the message and the third worked as a reminder or closure. Some studies in laboratory settings have supported the hypothesis of three exposures.[19] In natural settings, however, three exposures may be inadequate. In such settings, the uneven exposure of consumers to ads, their inattention even when exposed and the pressure from competing ads may all work to increase the optimal number of exposures required.[20]

A related question is what is the best pattern of exposures, or how far apart should they occur? Research has shown that some delay in the delivery of exposures can increase the probability of positive effects of repetition.[21] For example, a pattern of five exposures, each a day apart, is better than one of five exposures, all on the same day. A reason for this effect is that immediate repetition does not stimulate interest and attention to later exposures.[22] Another reason is that the delay in repetition of exposures postpones the onset of tedium and facilitates the positive effect of habituation, as explained by the two-factor theory. A third reason is that the delay allows for better absorption, appreciation and retention of the message.

Message Familiarity Research by the author has shown that familiarity with the brand featured in an ad is an important factor that mediates the effects of message repetition.[23] Exhibit 4-5 shows the brand purchases of a sample of households that resulted from television exposures to ads for a familiar and unfamiliar brand.[24] The study defined *familiarity* as the extent to which households had purchased the brand in the past. Sales response to the ads for the familiar brand reached a peak and then declined at a fairly low level of ad exposures per week. In contrast, the unfamiliar brand required many more ad exposures to achieve a positive response. However, the positive response kept increasing, and did not decline within the range of ad exposures measured in the study.

The difference in response to advertising of the familiar and unfamiliar brand may be due to a number of causes. First, because consumers attend to ads selectively, ads for the familiar brand may receive greater attention at lower repetitions than do those for the unfamiliar brands. Second, consumers may also identify more with ads for the familiar brand, because of their experience with the brand. Third, to maintain consistency between their actions and beliefs, they may interpret ads for the

▼ **EXHIBIT 4-6.** A two-sided ad.

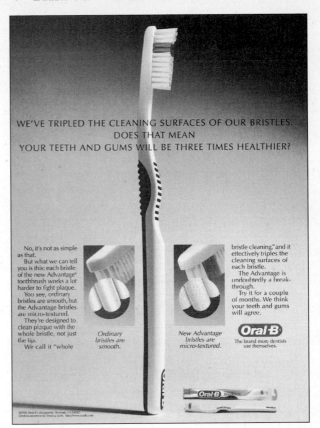

Source: Courtesy of Oral-B Laboratories.

▼ **EXHIBIT 4-5.** Household purchases in response to TV ads.

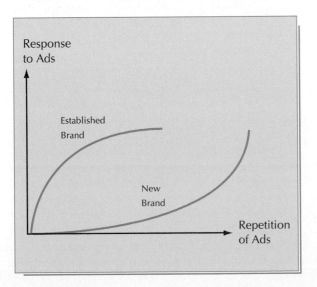

familiar brands more favorably. For the same reasons, however, higher repetitions of the ad for the familiar brand may lead to tedium and decreased effectiveness. In contrast, because of the novelty of the unfamiliar brand, higher repetitions of its ad may not lead to tedium and decreased effectiveness.

An important implication of the role of familiarity is that brands with a large market share enjoy a double advantage. They have a larger following of consumers and are more familiar to them, than are brands that are new or have a small market share. So large-share brands need less advertising than small-share brands. One solution for new or small-share brands is to induce brand trial as a means to increase familiarity among consumers who are unaware of the brand. Such trial can be stimulated by samples, price discounts or other sales promotions. Chapters 9 and 17 discuss this problem and its solution in greater detail.

▼ **EXHIBIT 4-7. A refutational ad.**

MCI's savings plans may sound great over the phone.

Unfortunately, it's how they look on your bill that counts.

Maybe that's why over half the people who switch from AT&T to MCI switch back to AT&T within 6 months.

When you first get your MCI bill, you may find yourself looking at numbers that are higher than you expected. That's because when you hear MCI's sales pitch over the phone, you could miss some important details. Like anytime you call a number you didn't give MCI in advance, you don't save anything at all. Or how MCI's monthly fees can decrease your savings.

So it's no wonder most people switch back to AT&T.

With AT&T **True USA**℠ Savings, all you have to do is spend $25 a month on long distance, and we'll subtract 20% off your AT&T bill.* That's 20% off on calls to anyone, anywhere in the USA, anytime. Guaranteed. With no calling circles, and no fee.

So when MCI comes a-calling, why not save yourself some trouble? Just say politely, "No, thanks". And stick with AT&T. For information, call 1 800-673-3770.

AT&T. Your True Voice.℠

AT&T

*Available in most areas. Discount off AT&T basic residential rates. Certain exclusions apply.

© 1994 AT&T

Source: Courtesy of AT&T.

Message Complexity A **complex message** is one that is so difficult, rich or ambiguous that the receiver cannot absorb all the information it contains in a single exposure. Studies have shown that repetition will enhance the persuasive effect of ads containing complex messages.[25] These results can also be explained by the two-factor theory. Each repetition of an ad with a complex message allows the receiver to gain new insights about the message. This maintains the receiver's interest in the ad and delays the onset of tedium. Complex messages can take several forms.

The most commonly used in advertising are complex arguments, soft-sell messages, hard-sell messages, ad campaigns and compressed messages.

A **complex argument** is one that uses several reasons or pieces of evidence, some in favor of and others against the advocated position. Good examples of a complex message are two-sided and refutational appeals. A **two-sided appeal** couples some weak or irrelevant cons with the strong pros of an advocated position. An example is Oral-B's ad for a new toothbrush, which claims a triple increase in cleaning surfaces of its bristles while admitting that benefits do not increase proportionally (see Exhibit 4-6). A **refutational appeal** first presents the counterarguments to a position being advanced, then destroys them. An example is AT&T's claim that MCI's promotional plans do not deliver as great savings as they promise (see Exhibit 4-7). Chapter 6 discusses these strategies in greater detail.

A **soft-sell message** is a subtle one that allows for different interpretations, persuades by suggestion and makes no direct request for action or change. The ad for Guess apparel in Exhibit 4-8 is an example. Because of the expressiveness of the picture and the ambiguity of the message, repetition is likely to increase recall of the brand and positive feelings toward it but unlikely to lead to tedium soon. Moreover, in the presence of favorable brand experience, a soft-sell message may induce a viewer to develop his or her own positive interpretation of the message, enhancing the effectiveness of the ad.[26] In Bozell's campaign for milk, the milk mustache itself can be interpreted as a soft sell that is subject to different interpretations. For example, most consumers would find the ad funny; for some it might evoke warm memories of drinking milk as a kid; others might find their favorite celebrity cute with a milk mustache; still others might infer that milk is cool.

Hard-sell messages are direct requests to act accompanied with some pressure or urgency. One example is the type of ad some auto retailers run: "*Every car in the showroom on sale. Unbelievable*

▼   **EXHIBIT 4-8.** An ad that was a soft sell.

Source: Courtesy of Guess, Inc.

discounts! Hurry! Visit our showroom while super deals last." While repetition of the soft-sell message may lead to greater acceptance, repetition of the hard-sell message may cause greater tedium and irritation.

An **ad campaign** consists of a series of ads linked by a single theme. The multiple executions maintain interest in and promote a better understanding of the message, while repetition of the theme ensures greater persuasion. One example is Bozell's first-year campaign for milk, which had 20 celebrities appear in a common format using the same tagline, "Milk. What a surprise!" Another example is the print campaign for Absolut vodka, which has been running since the early 1980s. Each ad in the campaign presented a scene that took on the image of the Absolut bottle, with no copy save for a two-word tagline consisting of the name of the brand and the scene. The novelty of

the picture and tagline drew consumers' attention. At the same time, repetition of the bottle and brand name in these novel executions increased awareness of and familiarity with the brand without tedium. The campaign was enormously successful, making Absolut one of the leading vodkas in the United States.

A **compressed ad** is one that drops less essential portions of a longer version of the ad. A compressed ad is a form of a complex message. Strictly speaking, compressing an ad tends to simplify it. However, dropping some of the less salient aspects already familiar to the subjects stimulates them to fill in the missing portions by themselves, increasing thinking and recall of the ad. For example, during the 1991 Super Bowl, Pepsi introduced a humorous 2-minute ad starring Michael J. Fox. An attractive young female neighbor knocks on Fox's door, requesting a can of Pepsi. Overwhelmed, Fox answers positively, only to find his refrigerator bare. He then scrambles out his back window, over a railing and across a street to a neighboring apartment to get the can of Pepsi for his neighbor. While relishing the woman's satisfaction with the Pepsi, Fox is surprised by her roommate who also requests a Pepsi. In subsequent screenings of the ad, Pepsi reduced the length to 1 minute and, later, to 30 seconds, each time showing only the key elements of the drama. Because the initial ad had obtained wide exposure, the subsequent compressed ads stimulated interest, humor and satisfaction without causing tedium.

How many exposures are enough? We return to the question with which we started this subsection. Advertisers need a simple, numerical answer to the question when scheduling an ad campaign or deciding how often to run an ad. However, as the above discussion indicates, there may be no simple, numerical answer. The effectiveness of repetition depends on many factors that change substantially from ad to ad. The variety of nuances involved in message complexity make any rules simplistic for the exact number of repetitions. In addition, other factors such as the level of thinking, emotion and involvement may further qualify the role of repetition. The principles discussed here can serve as broad guidelines for designing ads or scheduling a campaign. A specific answer for a particular ad would depend on ad testing as explained in Chapter 14.

INVOLVEMENT

A mother watches a television program while her baby plays on the carpet nearby. When an ad (for Heinz ketchup) appears, she turns to play with her baby. She hears some bits and pieces of the ad and the phrase "thick and rich." She is too engrossed with her baby to think about it closely. However, after many repetitions of the ad, an association forms in her mind: that Heinz ketchup is the thickest and richest available.

Much television advertising today contains numerous repetitions of short commercials that offer limited information and seem trivial or sometimes, plain silly. Journalists comment on the emptiness of these ads, while social critics decry their shallowness. Many critics of advertising suggest that the low level of attention consumers pay to television ads may render the ads ineffective. Yet advertisers affirm their faith in such ads by spending billions of dollars on them each year. Herbert Krugman was one of the first to make a convincing case for the effectiveness of the apparently simplistic ad.[27] He suggested that communication through TV ads is different from that through ads in newspapers or magazines, which tend to have extensive copy and strong arguments. The difference is due to the *involvement* of the audience. Krugman claimed that much television advertising receives **low-involvement processing**, in which consumers notice the ads but do not think about them extensively. He argued that repetition of such ads can persuade as effectively, if not more so, than repetition of ads with strong arguments. Indeed, the distracted state in which many of these ads are received by consumers may lead to a lowering of the consumers' defenses and an easier acceptance of the message.

Krugman's ideas have spawned a whole stream of research on the role of low-involvement processing.[28] This research has expanded the concept and enriched the explanation of the phenomenon. There are at least two types of involvement: **cognitive involvement** (thought) and **emotional involvement** (feeling).[29] The term *involvement* as used here primarily refers to cognitive involvement, in which the receiver of a message more or less actively processes the message. An individual's level of involvement may arise from several factors. The more common factors are the context, message, individual or brand

itself. The *context* of an ad is the program with which, or the people with whom it is viewed. Contextual involvement could be triggered when a question in the ad leads to a discussion with others watching the ad. Message involvement arises from an individual's immersion in the issues, symbols or images that the ad raises. Individual involvement arises from an individual's natural interest in the advertised product category. Brand involvement arises from the individual's knowledge about the brand. Low-involvement processing results when none of these factors leads the consumer to be involved in an ad.

Recent research supports Krugman's intuition about low-involvement processing and provides a rationale for the effect. For example, one study found that subjects were more likely to believe trivial statements when they were less involved in evaluating them.[30] An example of a trivial statement was, "Nature Valley Vitamins are especially formulated for quick absorption." In the high-involvement condition, subjects had to evaluate the truth of the statement, while in the low-involvement condition, they had to rate its readability. The study argued that if subjects were involved in the statements, they were more likely to evaluate the truth of the statements based on their knowledge and reasoning. But if they were distracted, they were more likely to respond based on their familiarity with the statements, formed from repetition. Indeed, less-involved subjects judged the information to be more true when they experienced an "it rings a bell" reaction. These results show that persuasion by low involvement does take place, and it is enhanced by the subject's lack of involvement in the message.

Low involvement can also explain the effectiveness of the milk mustache campaign. Note that celebrities who appeared in the ads provided reasons for drinking milk. However, their milk mustache provided a humorous digression from the message, lowering resistance to it. This approach may have been more effective than a hard sell with strong arguments. In the face of strong arguments, consumers could always come up with counterarguments, such as milk still contains cholesterol or skim milk is not that tasty.

The theory of low-involvement processing has important implications. First, advertising that occurs in a low-involvement situation with little or no direct processing of the ad is neither trivial nor ineffective. Indeed, distractions that commonly occur in the television viewing environment may enhance the effectiveness of such ads. In a low-involvement context, distractions can decrease attention and resistance to the message but increase recognition, believability and compliance. Second, a critical issue for advertisers is to know when consumers are likely to adopt high- versus low-involvement processing. Advertisers can then design suitable ads and place them in the appropriate context. Third, distraction during advertising can be a strategic asset if it reduces resistance to a message without lowering exposure to it. Advertisers need to identify what factors distract consumers in this way. The theory of elaboration provides insight into the latter two issues.

▼ EXHIBIT 4-9. The elaboration likelihood model.

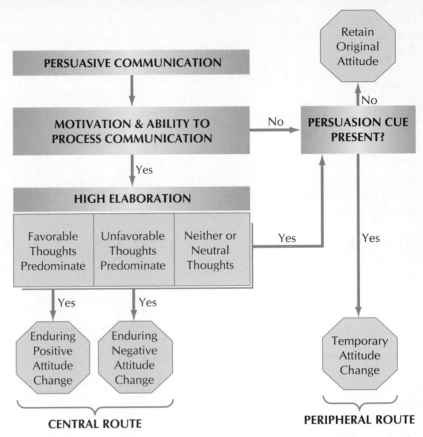

Source: Adapted with permission from Cacioppo, John T., and Richard E. Petty (1985), "Central and Peripheral Routes to Persuasion: The Role of Message Repetition," in *Psychological Processes and Advertising Effects: Theory, Research and Applications*, Linda F. Alwitt and Andrew A. Mitchell, eds. Mahwah, NJ: Erlbaum, 91–111.

ELABORATION

When a stimulus gains the attention of a subject, he or she may evaluate it or reason about it to varying degrees. This evaluation or reasoning is called **elaboration.** Psychologists John Cacioppo and Richard Petty suggest that the extent of elaboration is a critical feature in persuasion.[31] They propose the **elaboration likelihood model (ELM)** to explain this process. The model's name comes from the fact that it predicts the probability (likelihood) that individuals will be persuaded by a message by reasoning about (elaborating on) the message.

The Elaboration Likelihood Model

The basic premise of the elaboration likelihood model is that when people have both, the motivation and the ability to evaluate a message, their likelihood of elaboration will be high; in that state they look for and respond to good reasons in favor of the message. This form of persuasion is called the **central route.** If they lack either the motivation or the ability, they are more likely to respond to cues associated with the message. This form of persuasion is called the **peripheral route** (see Exhibit 4-9). Thus people are "neither always thoughtful nor always mindless" in forming their opinions and decisions, but are likely to adopt a central or peripheral route depending on their motivation and ability.[32]

Persuasion via the central route implies that receivers of a message carry out the following activities:

- Attend to the message.
- Recall relevant information from their memory.
- Evaluate the merits of the argument against their own prior information.
- Draw inferences about the issues at hand.
- Arrive at an overall conclusion, attitude change or decision.

In this mode, the strength of the argument is the key to persuasion. If the process leads to a predominance of favorable thoughts about the message, a positive change in attitude results and the message is accepted. A predominance of negative thoughts leads to a negative change in attitude and a rejection of the message. If negative and positive are about equal, or if neutral thoughts dominate, the attitude does not change.

In contrast, in the peripheral route these activities and thoughts are less likely; instead individuals are likely to arrive at conclusions based on the persuasion cues present with the message. Examples of persuasion cues are the fame of the endorser, the cost of the ad, or the *number* of arguments (as opposed to the *strength* of the arguments). The ad campaign for milk used celebrity endorsers as a persuasion cue. There was only a little copy on the merits of milk. In contrast, Exhibit 4-10 shows an ad for an IBM laptop computer that relies on information and argument to make its point.

▼ EXHIBIT 4-10. The central route of persuasion.

Source: Courtesy of IBM Corp.

The approaches of students taking a multiple-choice test illustrate how the two routes are used to reach conclusions. Motivated students who have studied and are informed are capable of thinking through a question. They are most likely to answer multiple-choice questions using thoughtful evaluation of the alternatives (central route). But students who are not prepared either because they lack the motivation or ability might not be able to evaluate the alternatives. Such students would resort to guessing based on the order of alternatives, the position of the right answer on the previous question, and so on (peripheral route).

Note that both motivation and ability are required for the central route. **Motivation** is the willingness of the individual to evaluate a message. In advertising, the most common motive is consumers' involvement with the advertised product,

▼ **EXHIBIT 4-11.** Motivating message processing by asking a question.

▼ **EXHIBIT 4-11.** Motivating message processing by asking a question.

Source: © InterIKEA Systems B.V. 1996.

either because they bought it in the past or they intend to buy it in the future. Advertisers can also motivate receivers to evaluate a message by asking a question or riddle at the start of the ad. For example, a British ad for the Swedish company IKEA has a clever headline that questions how pot sells for £2 (see Exhibit 4-11). Punning on the word "pot," IKEA reminds viewers that it sells inexpensive though classy housewares, such as potted plants. **Ability** is the competence of the individual to engage in the required mental effort. Many factors affect the ability of a receiver to elaborate on a message. Ability requires adequate language skills, proper training in logical thinking, adequate knowledge about the issues and quiet time to carefully think through the issues. Because persuasion by the central route requires both motivation and ability, each of which may not occur easily, this form of persuasion must be used selectively.

Cacioppo and Petty cite a large number of studies that support the elaboration likelihood model.[33] In one study, they tested subjects' responses

to alternative ads for a fictitious "Edge" brand of disposable razors.[34] The ads used either strong arguments or weak arguments (see Exhibit 4-12) and were endorsed either by famous athletes or laypeople. In addition, the researchers manipulated subjects to fall into two conditions of involvement with the message of the ad. To induce high involvement, they told subjects that they could buy Edge, which would soon be introduced in their city, right after exposure to the ad for it. To induce low involvement, they told subjects that they could buy some other product right after exposure to the ad, for Edge would be introduced in some other city. The results of the study demonstrate that when subjects are involved with the message, they adopt a central route of processing, in which the strength of the arguments is important (see bottom panel of Exhibit 4-13). But when subjects are not involved with the message, they adopt a peripheral route of processing, in which cues

▼ **EXHIBIT 4-12.** Alternative copy for ads for fictitious "Edge" disposable razor.

Copy From Ad Using Strong Argument	Copy from Ad Using Weak Argument
■ Scientifically designed ■ New advanced honing method creates unsurpassed sharpness ■ Special chemically formulated coating eliminates nicks and cuts and prevents rusting ■ Handle is tapered and ribbed to prevent slipping ■ In direct comparison tests, the Edge blade gave twice as many close shaves as its nearest competitor ■ Unique angle placement of the blade provides the smoothest shave possible	■ Designed for beauty ■ Floats in water with a minimum of rust ■ Comes in various sizes, shapes and colors ■ Designed with the bathroom in mind ■ Can only be used once but will be memorable

Source: Petty, Richard E., John T. Cacioppo and David Schumann (1983), "Central and Peripheral Routes to Advertising Effectiveness: The Moderating Role of Involvement," *Journal of Consumer Research* 10 (September), 135–146, 1983. Copyright 1983 The University of Chicago Press.

▼ EXHIBIT 4-13. **Effect of endorser type and argument strength on persuasion.**

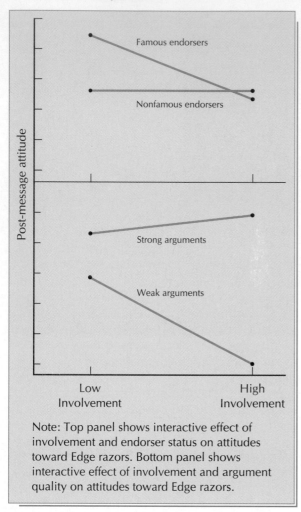

Note: Top panel shows interactive effect of involvement and endorser status on attitudes toward Edge razors. Bottom panel shows interactive effect of involvement and argument quality on attitudes toward Edge razors.

Source: Petty, Richard E., John T. Cacioppo, and David Schumann (1983), "Central and Peripheral Routes to Advertising Effectiveness: The Moderating Role of Involvement, " *Journal of Consumer Research* 10, September, 1983, 135–146. Copyright 1983 The University of Chicago Press.

such as the type of endorser are important (see top panel of Exhibit 4-13).

Stability of Persuasion by Processing Route

How stable are changes in opinions or attitudes brought about by the central and peripheral routes? To answer this question, we need to consider two key aspects of the stability of changes in persuasion: permanence and resistance.

Permanence is the extent to which the change caused by persuasion endures. Changes that occur via the central route are generally thought to be more permanent than those that occur via the peripheral route. The reason is that individuals who use the central route engage in careful and detailed analysis of the arguments, comparing them against their own prior views and arriving at a well-thought-out conclusion. These individuals are likely to remember the issues or at least the conclusion because of the effort involved, and to hold to the changed opinion or attitude. On the other hand, because the peripheral route involves simple inferences based on persuasion cues, the issues and conclusions are unlikely to be remembered for long. Repetition, however, is more likely to be effective for the peripheral route. For the central route, the repetition of strong arguments may lead to tedium and irritation unless the arguments are suitably complex.

Resistance is the extent to which the changes due to persuasion survive attacks based on new information. Although permanence is likely to occur with resistance, the two are independent, as can be seen from cultural truisms.[35] Belief in a truism, such as "Brush your teeth every morning after waking up," is generally instilled more by repetition during childhood (reinforced by the authority of adults) than by careful arguments. Individuals who do not develop these beliefs by argument have a hard time defending them. When presented with strong counterarguments, they can break down. A counterargument would be, "Brushing after a meal is crucial for dental health because it clears food particles and kills bacteria; brushing as soon as you wake up has little value if you eat breakfast soon after." Cultural truisms unsupported by arguments may be permanent, but they are not resistant.

Persuasion by the central route is usually permanent and resistant. Persuasion by the peripheral route is neither permanent nor resistant. However, it can be made more enduring by repetition and more resistant by the provision of supporting arguments. For example, until two decades ago, the dominance of Coca-Cola in the United States may have been due to consumers' loyalty to the brand developed over generations, passed on through family behavior and reinforced by ads that use the peripheral route of persuasion. Beginning in the mid-1970s, Pepsi attacked the position of Coca-Cola using central-route ads that argued comparability in blind taste tests. Drinkers of Coca-Cola had weak defenses against this frontal attack. The advertising strategy has been effective, leading to parity in the market shares of the two brands.

While the elaboration likelihood model principally contrasts the role of arguments versus cues in persuasion, Cacioppo and Petty suggest that the framework can also explain the roles of some other variables involved in persuasion, particularly emotion, humor, mood and music.[36] These variables are important primarily in the peripheral route to persuasion, although they could play a supporting role to central-route arguments. For instance, while the use of emotion could enhance the effect of strong arguments in the central route, emotion can be the sole means of persuasion in the peripheral route. Similarly, while humor can ease resistance to a strong argument in the central route, in the peripheral route it may persuade by merely generating goodwill toward the brand. The same can be said for the other two variables, music and mood.

Some authors have suggested that the role of emotion may be more complex than just described because emotions can propel message receivers into a state of higher involvement. Emotions can also lead to immediate action more effectively than can reason. Graphic images of the killing of baby seals to harvest their coats served both to raise the public's involvement in this environmental issue as well as to motivate an immediate change in the public's demand for clothes made of seals' coats. Chapters 6, 7, and 8 detail the issues involved in persuasion through reason (central route), emotion (central or peripheral route) and endorsement (peripheral route), respectively.

INTEGRATION

This chapter has presented four key concepts of persuasion: conditioning, repetition, involvement and elaboration. These concepts arise from different fields of research, but each makes a distinct contribution to explaining persuasion. Classical conditioning describes the roots of persuasion by laying out the psycho-physiological processes by which individuals learn from associations. Studies of repetition describe the number and nature of repetitions required to make exposures persuasive. Research on involvement explores the extent to which persua-

sion differs under low and high involvement, and the role experience plays in each. The elaboration likelihood model describes two routes of persuasion and the variables effective in each.

Besides being complementary, the four concepts share an important trait: each acknowledges a dichotomy in the routes to persuasion.[37] Thus we have behavioral and cognitive learning, mere exposure and message repetition, high and low involvement, and central and peripheral routes to persuasion. The reason for the dichotomy is best described by the elaboration likelihood model. The model suggests that if an individual has motivation and ability he or she will adopt a central route of persuasion; in the absence of either, the individual will adopt a peripheral route of persuasion.

However, the four concepts vary in the amount of mental effort required of message recipients, even in the noncognitive or peripheral route of persuasion. Mere repetition is probably the most primitive, in that minimal cognitive effort is expected of the receiver; indeed, the stimuli need not even provoke thought. The next level of effort is low-involvement processing, where recipients attend to the ads but do not think about them extensively. In conditioning, recipients may not also think about the stimuli, but they may notice associations among stimuli pairs and are often involved with the stimuli (as when subjects are exposed to food and drink). Finally, in the peripheral route of persuasion, while elaboration is low, recipients do make inferences based on cues, suggesting some cognitive effort.

Another distinction between these concepts is that the factors that lead to the peripheral route of persuasion are not the same ones that lead to low-involvement processing. Low-involvement processing occurs when receivers of a message *lack the motivation* to evaluate the message even though they may have the ability to do so. Because persuasion by the peripheral route may occur when *either* motivation or ability is absent, it encompasses a broader set of conditions than low-involvement processing. Consider, for example, a consumer choosing an expensive wine to present as a dinner gift. Suppose this consumer is not an expert on wines and chooses by the glossiness of the ads or the presence of French names. This consumer's decision process is a high-involvement one, but one that follows the peripheral route of persuasion.

SUMMARY

Persuasion is a change in opinion, attitude, or behavior brought about by some communication. Researchers have proposed numerous theories to explain persuasion. From those theories, four concepts are particularly relevant to advertising and promotion: classical conditioning, repetition, involvement and elaboration.

Classical conditioning is the transfer of a response naturally elicited by an unconditioned stimulus, to a conditioned stimulus due to the association among those two stimuli. A conditioned response is enduring and becomes extinct only if either of the two stimuli occurs alone. Conditioning is affected by the predictiveness, distinctiveness, response strength and link of the unconditioned stimulus.

The mere exposure effect refers to the increased liking that subjects develop for certain stimuli, even though they may not recall having been exposed to them. Message repetition refers to the repetition of stimuli that stimulate consumer thought. The response to repetition is generally nonlinear, first increasing and then leveling off or declining. It can be explained by the habituation that results from exposure to novel stimuli, and the tedium that results from excessive exposure to the same stimuli. The effectiveness of message repetition depends on the frequency, familiarity and complexity of the message.

Subliminal advertising refers to persuasive ad messages that are just below the threshold of perception, yet embedded in material that can be perceived. While mere exposure involves stimuli that are perceptible but not necessarily intelligible, subliminal advertising involves stimuli that are intelligible but not perceived. No consistent scientific research has emerged to support the effectiveness of subliminal advertising.

Low-involvement processing is a state in which consumers notice ads but do not process or think about them extensively. Persuasion in low-involvement processing can occur as effectively as persuasion through message repetition. The reason may be that individuals who are not involved in an ad are less resistant to messages in the ad, and do not generate arguments against them.

The elaboration likelihood model (ELM) predicts the probability (likelihood) that individuals would be persuaded by a message by reasoning about (elaborating on) the message. The basic premise of the model is that when individuals have *both* the motivation and the ability to evaluate a message, their likelihood of elaboration will be high. In that state they look for and respond positively to strong arguments in favor of the message. This form of persuasion is called the central route. If they lack *either* the motivation or the ability, they are more likely to respond to cues associated with the message. This form of persuasion is called the peripheral route. Persuasion by the central route is generally permanent and resistant. Persuasion by the peripheral route is generally neither permanent nor resistant.

QUESTIONS

1. How exactly does conditioning occur? What factors influence it?
2. Does classical conditioning occur in humans? How can it be used in advertising?
3. What is the mere exposure effect? Is it just another term for classical conditioning?
4. Why does repetition lead to liking and to familiarity?
5. What is subliminal advertising? Is it the same as mere exposure? Why or why not?
6. What factors influence the effectiveness of message exposure?
7. How many repetitions of an ad are best for persuasion? What is the best pattern of those repetitions?
8. Can ads for alcohol or tobacco ever successfully use the central route of persuasion, given the public's current interest in healthy habits and its concern with drug abuse?
9. Can distraction during exposure to ads enhance ad effectiveness? Discuss.
10. What is the elaboration likelihood model? How does it relate to the other key concepts in persuasion?
11. How stable are changes in opinions or attitudes brought about by the central and peripheral routes?
12. Why was the milk mustache campaign so successful? How did it persuade consumers to drink more milk or view it more favorably? What alternatives did the agency and the Milk Board have?

NOTES

1. Beatty, Sally Goll (1996), "Milk-Mustache Ads: Cream of the Crop," *The Wall Street Journal*, May 20, B6; Elliot, Stuart (1996), "Milk Mustaches Are Sticking Around, But Can They Stay Fresh?" *New York Times*, July 10, D6; Rubel, Chad (1996), "Mustache Ads Change Toward Milk," *Marketing News*, August 26, 2; Gleason, Mark (1996), "Men Are Newest Target For 'Milk Mustache' Ads; Travolta and Schwarzenegger," *Advertising Age*, July 1, 10.

2. Kimble, Gregory A. (1961), *Hilgard and Marquis' Conditioning and Learning*, New York: Appleton-Century-Crofts, Inc.

3. Shimp, Terrence A. (1991),"Neo-Pavlovian Conditioning and its Implications for Consumer Theory and Research," in *Handbook of Consumer Behavior*, Thomas S. Robertson and Harold H. Kassarjian, eds. Englewood Cliffs, NJ: Prentice Hall, 12–187.

4. Stuart, Elnora W., Terrence A. Shimp, and Randall W. Engle (1987), "Classical Conditioning of Consumer Attitudes: Four Experiments in an Advertising Context," *Journal of Consumer Research* 14 (December), 334–349.

5. McCracken, Grant (1989), "Who is the Celebrity Endorser? Cultural Foundations of the Endorsement Process," *Journal of Consumer Research* 16, December, 310–321.

6. Note that the response to cinnamon itself is not natural. It is probably learned by repeated association between the smell of cinnamon-flavored baked foods and the warmth of a caring parent.

7. McSweeney, Frances K., and Calvin Bierley (1984), "Recent Developments In Classical Conditioning," *Journal of Consumer Research* 11, September, 619–631; Janiszewski, Chris, and Luk Warlop (1993), "The Influence of Classical Conditioning Procedures on Subsequent Attention to the Conditioned Brand," *Journal of Consumer Research* 20, September, 171–189.

8. Examples and ideas in this subsection have been inspired by Sawyer, Alan (1981), "Repetition, Cognitive Responses and Persuasion," in *Cognitive Responses in Persuasion*, Richard E. Petty, Thomas M. Ostrom, and Timothy C. Brock, eds. Hillsdale, NJ: Lawrence Erlbaum Associates, 237–261.

9. *Ibid.*

10. *Newsweek*, September 27, 1976, 36.

11. Sawyer, "Repetition, Cognitive Responses and Persuasion."

12. Packard, Vance (1981), *Hidden Persuaders*, New York: Pocket Books.

13. Rogers, Stuart (1994), "Subliminal Advertising: Grand Scam of the 20th Century," in *Proceedings of the 1994 Conference of The Academy of Advertising*, Karen Whitehall King, ed., Athens, GA: AAA, 61.

14. *Ibid.*

15. Synodinos, Nicolaos (1988), "Subliminal Stimulation: What Does the Public Think About It?" *Current Issues and Research in Advertising*, 11, 1, 157–187.

16. *Ibid.*

17. Sawyer, Alan (1981), "Repetition, Cognitive Responses and Persuasion"; Tellis, Gerard J. (1988), "Advertising Exposure, Loyalty and Brand Purchase: A Two Stage Model of Choice," *Journal of Marketing Research* 25 (May), 134–144.

18. Krugman, Herbert E. (1972), "Why Three Exposures May be Enough," *Journal of Advertising Research* 12 (December), 11–28.

19. Sawyer, "Repetition, Cognitive Responses and Persuasion"; Pechmann, Cornelia, and David Stewart (1988), "Advertising Repetition: A Critical Review of Wearin and Wearout," *Current Issues and Research in Advertising*, 11, 2, 285–330.

20. Cacioppo, John T., and Richard E. Petty (1985), "Central and Peripheral Routes to Persuasion: The Role of Message Repetition," in *Psychological Processes and Advertising Effects: Theory, Research and Applications*, Linda F. Alwitt and Andrew A. Mitchell, eds. Hillsdale, NJ: Erlbaum, 91–111.

21. Sawyer, "Repetition, Cognitive Responses and Persuasion."

22. Craig, C. Samuel, Brian Sternthal, and Clark Leavitt (1976), "Advertising Wearout: An Experimental Analysis," *Journal of Marketing Research* 13 (November), 356–372.

23. Pechmann and Stewart, "Advertising Repetition: A Critical Review of Wearin and Wearout"; Tellis, "Advertising Exposure, Loyalty and Brand Purchase"; Hoch, Stephen J., and John Deighton (1989), "Managing What Consumers Learn from Experience," *Journal of Marketing* 53 (April), 1–20.

24. Tellis, "Advertising Exposure, Loyalty and Brand Purchase."

25. Sawyer, "Repetition, Cognitive Responses and Persuasion."

26. Ha, Young-Won, and Stephen J. Hoch (1989), "Ambiguity, Processing, and Advertising-Evidence Interactions," *Journal of Consumer Research* 16 (December), 354–360.

27. Krugman, Herbert E. (1965), "The Impact of Television Advertising: Learning Without Involvement," *Publication Opinion Quarterly* 29 (Fall), 349–356; Schumann, David W., Richard E. Petty, and D. Scott Clemons (1990), "Predicting the Effectiveness of Different Strategies of Advertising Variation: A Test of the Repetition-Variation Hypotheses," *Journal of Consumer Research* 17 (September), 192–202.

28. Muehling, Darrel D., Russell N. Laczniak, and J. Craig Andrews (1993), "Defining, Operationalizing and Using Involvement in Advertising Research: A Review," *Current Issues and Research in Advertising* 15, 1 (Spring), 21–57.

29. Celsi, Richard L., and Jerry C. Olson (1988), "The Role of Involvement in Attention and Comprehension Processes," *Journal of Consumer Research* (September 15), 210–224.

30. Hawkins, Scott A., and Steve J. Hoch (1992), "Low-Involvement Learning: Memory Without Evaluation," *Journal of Consumer Research* 19 (September), 212–225.

31. Petty, Richard E., and John T. Cacioppo (1986), *Communication and Persuasion*, New York: Springer-Verlag. See also MacInnis, Deborah, and Bernard J. Jaworski (1990), "Two Routes to Persuasion Models in Advertising: Review, Critique, and Research Direction," *Review of Marketing* 4, 3–42.

32. Petty and Cacioppo, *Communication and Persuasion*.

33. Cacioppo, John T., and Richard E. Petty (1985), "Central and Peripheral Routes to Persuasion: The Role of Message Repetition," in *Psychological Processes and Advertising Effects: Theory, Research and Applications*, Linda F. Alwitt and Andrew A. Mitchell, eds. Hillsdale, NJ: Erlbaum, 90–111.

34. Petty, Richard E., John T. Cacioppo, and David Schumann (1983), "Central and Peripheral Routes to Advertising Effectiveness: The Moderating Role of Involvement," *Journal of Consumer Research* 10 (September), 135–146.

35. Petty, Richard E., Rao H. Unnava, and Alan J. Strathman (1991), "Theories of Attitude Change," in *Handbook of Consumer Behavior*, Thomas S. Robertson and Harold H. Kassarjian, eds. Englewood Cliffs, NJ: Prentice Hall, 241–280; McGuire, W. J. (1964), "Inducing Resistance to Persuasion: Some Contemporary Approaches," in *Advances in Experimental Social Psychology*, 1. New York: Academic Press.

36. Petty and Cacioppo, *Communication and Persuasion*.

37. For generalizability of this dichotomy, see MacInnis and Jaworski, "Two Routes to Persuasion Models in Advertising."

During the 1989 Super Bowl, Anheuser-Busch introduced a new ad for its Budweiser brands of beer, in which bottles of Bud and Bud Light played football against each other in a competition called the Bud Bowl. The bowl took a further humorous twist as the personified bottles parodied well-known players and coaches. The concept seemed simple, even trivial. Indeed, some critics thought the ads insulted consumers' intelligence.

Yet the Bud Bowl was a great hit with consumers and was on all the lists of the

5

How to Win and Hold Consumers' Attention

top ten ads of 1989. Sales of the Budweiser brands for the first quarter increased greatly over sales from the same quarter of the previous year. Anheuser-Busch attributed the increase primarily to the Bud Bowl campaign. The campaign itself was not as simple to develop as it looked. It took 130 designers, builders and animators to create. It cost about $1 million to produce and $4 million to air.

The firm extended the concept with a summer promotion of a Bud game at the beach, called Bud Bowl II. These ads were not as successful. Journalists criticized the campaign, and consumers rated it among the ten worst of the year. Anheuser-Busch continued the Bud Bowl series for a few more years, but subsequent ads never seemed to recapture the initial enthusiasm and response.

Why was the Bud Bowl campaign so effective initially? Why did it lose effectiveness later on? At face value, the ads were low on information, and their relationship to the advertised product was weak. However, the ads were a great attention getter, due primarily to their novelty and close link with the program (the Super Bowl) within which they were placed. They drew attention to the Budweiser brand against stiff competition from a number of big advertisers vying for consumers' attention during the Super Bowl. As the company repeated the ads in various new forms, they lost their novelty and thus their main strength—the ability to draw attention.

Attention is the act of focusing one's senses to receive external messages or stimuli. Gaining the consumer's attention is the first of the tactical goals of advertising (see Chapter 1). The other tactical goals—to inform, remind, persuade and generate loyalty—are the subject of the remaining chapters in Part 2 of this text. Advertisers must have the attention of the consumer before they can achieve any of the other goals. This chapter first examines the dynamics of consumer attention. It then describes some important methods by which advertisers can gain the attention of consumers. Finally, it explains how to design components of the ad to gain and retain consumers' attention.

THE DYNAMICS OF CONSUMER ATTENTION

We first discuss the principle of selective attention and then the different states of consumer receptivity to the message.

The Principle of Selective Attention

Most consumers are bombarded by a large number of messages or stimuli that clamor for their attention each day. The messages include information from books and magazines; communications from friends, relatives or business associates; interactions with store clerks or bus drivers; and commercials on the various media such as TV, newspapers, or billboards. Some studies estimate that consumers are exposed to hundreds of commercials and thousands of messages each day. Several of these messages require simultaneous attention. How do people cope with all these messages?

The principle of **selective attention** holds that consumers simply ignore most messages that reach them and focus on only a few, usually one at a time.

Explanations for Selective Attention Why do consumers have a systematic pattern of preference for some stimuli? There are at least three explanations for consumers' selective attention: pragmatism, consumer preference and cognitive consistency.

At the most basic level, we can explain selective attention by *pragmatism*. An individual cannot focus on two or more things at the same time, much less pay attention to the numerous messages clamoring for attention every day. An individual's efficient performance and even survival may require that he or she attend selectively to the most relevant stimuli. For example, a driver must focus on the traffic ahead, especially when zipping down a freeway at 65 miles per hour. This principle of selective attention works as much for commercial messages as for noncommercial communications. Car buyers are likely to attend to car ads and cereal buyers to cereal ads to glean the information relevant to their decision.

A second explanation for selective attention is *preference*. Consumers are more likely to pay attention to subjects that they like, are familiar with, or have experienced. A consumer in a doctor's waiting room, for example, would be most likely to pick up a magazine that deals with topics he or she enjoys. Thus a sports enthusiast is likely to pick up an issue of *Sports Illustrated* and see ads for sporting goods or sporting events. An investor is likely to pick up *The Wall Street Journal* and notice ads for new stock issues.

A third explanation is that individuals are selective in attention to maintain *cognitive consistency*, or harmony between their knowledge and behavior.[1] For example, consider the problem of a smoker. Over the years, scientific evidence that smoking is injurious to health has mounted. As a result, the current social environment is becoming increasingly hostile to smoking. Giving up smoking might seem the most practical way to come to terms with the evidence and the environment, but that is very hard to do. How then, can a smoker relieve the tension? One way would be to question the validity of the scientific evidence, and to dismiss the laws against smoking in public places as an overreaction. To maintain such beliefs, the smoker might screen out messages suggesting that smoking is harmful and attend to messages supporting an individual's right to smoke.

Or consider a consumer who just bought a Honda Accord, a midsize car. Such a consumer is likely to be very attentive to ads about midsize cars, and less attentive to ads for other classes of cars or products. Among ads for midsize cars, the consumer is likely to be more receptive to ads for Honda Accords than to those for its rival, the Toyota Camry. This behavior ensures that the consumer receives messages that support the choice of the Accord over the Camry or some other midsize car.

Implications for Advertisers The principle of selective attention has some important implications for advertisers. It can be a great asset because pragmatic self-selection makes it likely that those consumers who need a product are likely to attend to the ad for that product. The advertiser can enhance the odds of this happening by carefully choosing media that are most likely to reach the target consumer.

Conversely, selectivity can work against advertisers who are interested in expanding the market share of their product to new users. People who are unfamiliar with a product might just screen out all ads for the product as a matter of routine, even though it would be useful for them. For example, performance analyses of alternative investments over the long term show that stock mutual funds are one of the best means of saving, outperforming most other investments, especially bank savings accounts. Yet consumers who have all their savings in bank savings accounts and are unfamiliar with mutual funds are unlikely to attend to ads for mutual funds, even though such investments could be of great advantage to them. Thus, selectivity could work against the advertisers of mutual funds.

Similarly, selectivity may give established brands an edge over newer brands. Cognitive consistency suggests that consumers who are loyal users of a brand are more likely to pay attention to ads for their favorite brand and screen out ads for newer brands, even when the latter are superior. Since established brands have more buyers with a higher degree of loyalty, their ads are likely to enjoy a selective advantage.[2]

What should advertisers of newer, less established brands do? How should advertisers get the attention of nonusers of their product? More generally, how can advertisers turn consumers' selective attention to their advantage? The sections that follow discuss the methods to gain consumer attention in these and other circumstances.

Consumers' States of Receptivity

Although most consumers consider advertising essential for businesses, most do not yearn for ads.[3] A few consumers search the media for ads. Some are amused by ads and others are bored by them. Many consumers dislike ads, while a few try to avoid them. Researchers identify four distinct states of consumer receptivity to ads: search, active processing, passive processing and avoidance.

Search The term **search** refers to consumers' explicit effort to collect information about various brands of a product they plan to purchase. Generally, consumers are more likely to search for information for goods that are expensive, infrequently purchased, or complex, such as automobiles, appliances or vacations. A consumer planning to buy a stereo system, for example, may be on the lookout for ads about stereo systems, may look up evaluations of specific systems in *Consumer Reports*, or may even go from dealer to dealer, collecting promotional brochures on each brand.

One survey found that consumers' checking of ads for information increased from 14 percent for the purchases of low-priced ($5 to $9) products to 46 percent for the purchases of high-priced (over $50) products.[4] Clearly, drawing the attention of consumers searching for information should not be a major problem for advertisers. The key challenge for the advertiser is to provide these consumers with credible information and to persuade them that its brand is superior to the competition.

Contrary to popular perception, many consumers do not resort to active search, even for expensive and infrequently purchased products. Note that the flip side of the results of the study just cited is that consumers do not check ads from 54 to 86 percent of the time, depending on the cost of the item.

Active Processing **Active processing** is a state in which consumers think about messages they receive, although they do not make an effort to get this information on their own. For example, buyers of health foods may not make a study of products before they buy them, because they do not cost much and are purchased frequently. However, these buyers may actively think about information on specific brands that happens to come their way. Here again, the advertiser is in an advantageous position because consumers are motivated to follow ads for these products. The major concerns for advertisers are the proper placement of the ads and the provision of persuasive information. For example, Nature Valley does not have to make an extra effort to draw the attention of health-conscious consumers to its ads for fat-free granola bars. It does need to make sure the ads properly communicate the health value of the ingredients and are placed in appropriate media.

Passive Processing Until about the mid-1960s, the dominant assumption of advertising researchers was that most consumers were active processors, so that advertising achieved its goal of persuasion through information and argument. More recently, advertisers have come to realize that, at best, consumers may be passive processors of their ads. **Passive processing** is a state in which consumers receive messages but do not actively process them. They also neither seek out nor avoid such messages. Passive processing is also called **low-involvement processing.** The vast majority of ads for low-cost, frequently purchased products, such as beer, soap, cereals and tissues, typically win this level of receptivity from consumers.

Consumers may engage in passive processing for several reasons. They may not see the benefit of searching for information about low-priced products; they may feel they already have enough information about such frequently purchased products; or they may just be disinclined to follow such ads. The challenge to advertisers is to gain and retain the attention of consumers who are in this state.

The passivity of consumers does not imply that ads targeted to them are ineffective. Rather, low-involvement processing can be quite effective and has become an important focus of advertising research[5] (see Chapter 5).

Avoidance **Avoidance** is the state in which consumers consciously attempt to avoid stimuli. Consumers avoid ads for several reasons. First, the ads may be for low-priced, frequently purchased products about which the consumers may not want any more information. Second, consumers may be heavily involved in the TV show or article in which the ads appear and may find the ads a distraction or nuisance. Third, consumers may be loyal to a competing brand and may not want opposing information. Fourth, consumers may find the ads boring, stale or offensive. Advertisers face their greatest challenge in gaining the attention of consumers who avoid ads.

Advertisers have always had a problem dealing with consumers who try to avoid ads. For a long time, the broadcast media had an advantage over print media in that consumers could not avoid their ads without some effort, such as leaving the room. For example, studies estimate that 20 to 33 percent of a TV audience leave the room during commercial breaks.[6] One study estimates that even when present in the room, only 31 percent of viewers pay full attention to the TV.[7]

The problem of avoidance has become acute now because consumers have many alternate opportunities for recreation besides the major media. In addition the number of media outlets (competing TV and cable networks, for example) has exploded. Moreover, new technologies enable consumers to follow the regular programming without the ads. Two mechanisms, the videocassette recorder and the remote control, have made it easier to avoid TV ads through zipping and zapping, respectively.

Zipping is the process of fast-forwarding through ads that have been taped along with the programs with which they were aired. Zipping has been facilitated by the wide availability of video recorders and remote control gadgets and may be prevalent among 50 to 70 percent of viewers.[8] **Zapping** is the process of avoiding ads by switching among channels. Zapping has been facilitated by remote controls and the large number of channels available, especially to cable subscribers. Zapping may cut the prime-time TV audience for ads by at least 10 percent.[9] Zipping avoids the audio portion of the ad and speeds the visuals, whereas zapping cuts out both channels of communication. Another avoidance method is muting, by which consumers cut off only the audio portion of the commercial. The prevalence of zipping and zapping increases the pressure on advertisers to attract consumers' attention in the first few seconds of the ad.

Conclusion This discussion of consumer receptivity to advertising should not imply that product categories alone define consumer states. Differences among consumers themselves may also be a factor. For example, one study found that one-third of all car shoppers buy a car from the first dealer they visit.[10] Some consumers prefer to buy even big-ticket items on impulse or without much search. Other studies have shown that some consumers clip and file coupons and follow prices closely to get the best deal even on routine purchases;[11] so other consumers are information gatherers and careful shoppers. Advertisers need to determine which states consumers are in with suitable research prior to deciding how to gain and keep their attention.

GAINING THE CONSUMER'S ATTENTION

In 1987, Nestlé introduced an ad for its Gold Blend brand of instant coffee that initiated an 11-part serial campaign and ran in the United Kingdom for six years. The series was a slow-moving romance about a couple that gets to know each other and falls in love around the sampling of Gold Blend. The series was not planned. It evolved based on the success of earlier parts and the continuing public interest in the fictional story. Indeed, the public became so involved in the story that when the male character finally professed love for the female character, the event made headlines in the United Kingdom, and even sidelined Princess Anne's wedding announcement. A book about the characters promised to be a best-seller. The ads had only a short line about the brand itself, but the series of events gave wide exposure to the brand name and suggested an image of sophistication for the brand. The campaign was very successful, leading to a 40 percent increase in U.K. sales of Gold Blend since 1987. A similar series for Nestlé's Taster's Choice began in the United States in 1990. It generated considerable enthusiasm among the public and helped increase sales of Taster's Choice by 10 percent.[12]

Why was the campaign for Gold Blend so captivating? Are there other effective methods of drawing attention? How should an advertiser choose the right method? This section attempts to answer these questions. It first describes methods of gaining attention, then highlights the attributes of attention-getting ads, and finally describes which methods an advertiser should choose in particular situations.

Methods of Gaining the Consumer's Attention

The Gold Blend advertising campaign relied on drama to arouse the emotions of consumers. We can identify four broad methods by which ads draw the attention of consumers: manipulating physical stimuli, providing information, arousing emotions and offering value. While any one of these methods is best suited for certain situations, an effective integration of all four can greatly enhance the attention-getting ability of an ad.

Manipulating Physical Stimuli Manipulating physical stimuli is a powerful means to gain or repel consumers' attention. **Physical stimuli** are all the things that can impact the five senses (sight, hearing, smell, taste and touch). Sight and hearing are particularly important in advertising. For sight, the key stimuli are color, size, shape, brightness and motion. For hearing, the key stimuli are pitch, timing and texture; these stimuli, when combined to produce music, play an important role in setting the mood of an ad. Physical stimuli can be combined in a variety of ways to produce numerous patterns. Which patterns are most likely to arouse interest? Two theories that address this issue are Weber's law and Helson's adaptation-level theory.

Weber's Law **Weber's law** is a theory about human perception of stimuli that is based on the work of a nineteenth-century physicist, Ernst Weber. In simple words, Weber's law states that a *perceivable* change in a stimulus depends on the initial level of that stimulus. For example, when the background noise is high, one has to yell to be heard. But in dead silence, even a whisper can draw attention. As the initial intensity of the stimulus increases, the change in intensity must be proportionally larger to be perceived. Therefore, to draw attention, ads must use levels of stimuli substantially different than the level to which the consumer is accustomed. For example, consider Exhibit 5-1. The colors, shapes and brightness combine to produce a striking ad for Hewlett-Packard's DeskJet printer.

Formally, Weber's law states that the ratio of the smallest perceivable change in a stimulus relative to the current level of that stimulus is a constant.[13] This constant is not universal but varies for each sense. Note that Weber's law deals with relative intensity. Ads normally appear in conjunction with

▶ **EXHIBIT 5-1.** Use of stimulus intensity to gain attention.

Source: Courtesy of Hewlett-Packard Company.

other material, such as television programs, magazine articles or other ads. If this material contains intense stimuli, an ad would need to have even more intense stimuli to gain attention. An alternate strategy would be to greatly decrease the intensity of one or more stimuli in the ad. For example, in a magazine containing many glossy color photographs, a simple ad containing large white text on a black background can draw attention. In television, where programs are characterized by the intensive use of sound, silence can be an effective means of drawing attention. One survey found that 30 of 53 creative directors of advertising agencies considered silence to be very effective in drawing general attention to an ad.[14]

One can also use motion, such as rapid changes in the pattern of stimuli within an ad, to attract and keep attention. Ads for TV and video sometimes contain a series of short, quickly changing scenes that draw viewers to the screen and keep their attention through the sheer rapidity of change. This type of ad is called the *quick cut*. An example is the Roman era ad by Diet Coke. The ad consists of several quick shots of athletes engaged in varying sports, interspersed with printed lines about Diet Coke. It creates a sense of high energy and great performance that rivets the viewer's attention.

Adaptation-Level Theory The physical stimuli of the ad combine to form various intelligible patterns or meanings in consumers' minds. A psychologist, Harry Helson, proposed **adaptation-level theory** to explain how individuals perceive and react to these patterns of stimuli.[15] He identified three important stimuli that influence this process: the **focal stimuli**, or objects of attention; the **contextual stimuli**, or background to the objects; and the **residual stimuli**, or past experiences of individuals that form a standard of evaluation. For example, consider a consumer viewing the colored shapes in Exhibit 5-1. Here, the shapes are the focal stimuli, the other elements in the ad and the magazine in which it appears are the contextual stimuli, and the prior experiences the consumer has had with these shapes and such ads are the residual stimuli.

The central premise of Helson's theory is that individuals adapt to the stimuli they have experienced in the past to form certain standards of comparison or *adaptation levels*. New focal stimuli are evaluated to the extent that they relate to the residual stimuli or the consumer's adaptation level. Thus, focal stimuli do not have absolute meaning in themselves but acquire meaning only in the context in which they are embedded and relative to an individual's past experience. For example, a bowl of warm water would feel cold to a hand that has been immersed in hot water. A room in which one has slept all night may smell normal when one wakes up but bad when one returns to it from the outside. Similarly, a funny ad may seem hilarious after a drama but fall flat after a comedy.

One major implication of adaptation-level theory is the importance of **stimulus novelty**. A stimulus is *novel* when it differs from its surroundings and the consumer's reference point or adaptation level. The more it differs, the greater the novelty; the greater the novelty, the more likely the stimulus is to attract the consumer's attention. As the opening vignette of the chapter shows, the first Bud Bowl ad was a great hit with consumers because it used such a novel format. The second Bud Bowl ad, however, run just a few months later, was rated by consumers among the ten worst ads of the year because it used the same unsurprising format.

A consumer can have several reference points with regard to a particular ad: the preceding ads, the regular programming within which the ad appears, the other ads in the product category, and the scenes or sounds within the ad itself. For example, a catchy jingle may appear tame if cast in a very appealing musical program. An ad with much warmth may not be effective when screened within an emotionally draining drama. On the other hand, if all competing ads use celebrity endorsers, then one that uses drama may be very effective. The Diet Coke Roman era ad, for example, cleverly used drama and promoted athletic shoes at a time when the industry was using humor and endorsers.

Although novelty is a key to gaining attention, advertisers need to be careful not to deviate too far from the mood of the regular program in which an ad is to appear. For example, in a serious newscast describing some tragedy, a humorous ad may draw attention, but it may also offend. The difficulty of appropriately drawing attention to a commercial may be why advertisers pulled all ads off the air on the first day of the 1992 Gulf War between Iraq and the U.S.-led allies. They were also reluctant to advertise during coverage of the war. The Gulf War may have cost NBC alone $55 million.[16]

Advertisers also have to be careful that the stimuli are not so novel as to cause consumers to focus on them to the detriment of the message. For example, an ad with grotesque images or brilliant colors may rivet consumers' attention to the stimulus, leading them to ignore the message. To avoid this problem, the attention-getting stimuli need to be closely linked to the message.[17] Some of the ads reviewed earlier are appealing because the stimulus that draws attention is also well linked to the brand or the message. For example, the use of color to draw attention for the DeskJet is especially appropriate for a product whose distinguishing feature is color printing (Exhibit 5-1).

Providing Information Another method to gain consumers' attention is to satisfy their thirst for knowledge with interesting information. What do consumers consider newsworthy? What is interesting to them?

Sociologist Murray Davis suggests that what people consider interesting is what contradicts their underlying beliefs or assumptions.[18] Up to a point, the stronger the subject's beliefs, the more interesting will the subject find information that contradicts those beliefs. However, if the information contradicts some very strongly held beliefs, the consumer may consider the new information ridiculous, and reject it. Thus interest can have an inverted-U relation with the degree that the information challenges consumer assumptions (see Exhibit 5-2).

▼ **EXHIBIT 5-2.** The attention-getting power of information.

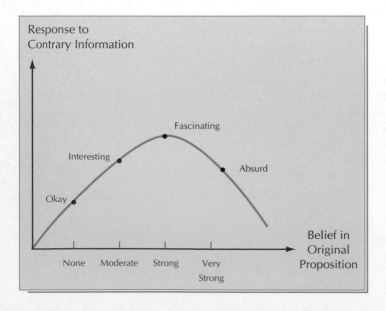

Consider the following claims for vitamin E:

- "Vitamin E is essential for good health."
- "High doses of vitamin E slow arteriosclerosis."
- "High doses of vitamin E enable you to live 120 years."

The first statement is well known and would elicit a yawn from many audiences. The second statement is a relatively new finding that would interest many audiences. The third statement is certainly new information. But is it credible? Most people are aware that modern medicine can provide a fuller and longer life than was possible decades ago. But most would immediately reject a claim that an elixir can help them live 120 years.

A Duxiana ad provides an example of drawing consumers' attention with information. The ad opens with a catchy headline that promises to provide the bed your back has been aching for (see Exhibit 5-3). It then argues that a good bed should have flexibility and support, information consumers may not have known. The ad then offers Duxiana as the only brand that provides those benefits.

Another way to offer information is to provide details about product attributes, product use or product purchase in long ads. Such ads describe which attributes are important, what role they play in the product's use, and how the consumer should go about choosing products based on these attributes. Such broadcast ads are called **infomercials,** while their print counterparts are called **advertorials.** Although the ads tend to adopt the format and tone of the regular programming of the medium to enhance credibility, they can be distinguished by announcements (in broadcast media) or a special typeface (in print media). The attention-getting power of infomercials and advertorials resides in their promise of providing relevant and reasonably objective information to consumers. Chapter 15 covers this form of advertising in greater detail.

Arousing Emotions A third method for gaining consumer attention is by stimulating emotions. We can define **emotion** as a state of arousal indicated by specific types and levels of biochemical activity in the brain and the body. For example, anger, pride,

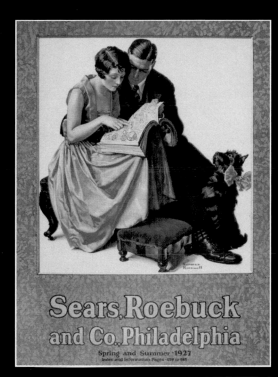

Source: Courtesy of Sears, Roebuck and Co.

▲ EXHIBIT 1-10

Companies can inform their customers about the availability of their products through direct mail. This was the route taken by the founders of Sears, Roebuck and Co. in the late 19th century.

Source: 9-Lives ® Plus™ CatFood

 EXHIBIT 3-10
Leo Burnett Company, Inc.'s appealing ad personalities.

Source: Courtesy of The Pillsbury Company.

Source: Courtesy of Virginia Tourism Corporation.

WELCOME TO VIRGINIA—

A STATE OF EXTRAORDINARY NATURAL BEAUTY AND RICH HERITAGE

Virginia's appeals today are as broad and diverse as its geography and as abundant as its nearly four centuries of history. Stretching from the Atlantic Ocean to the Blue Ridge and Allegheny mountains, Virginia is a mixture of exciting cities, thrilling theme parks, historic homes and villages and as much recreational activity as you'd care to squeeze into your stay.

History comes alive throughout Virginia. Visitors to the commonwealth find much to enjoy. Experience the lives of those who founded the first permanent English settlement in the New World. Tour birthplaces and homes of seven of the eight Virginia-born U.S. presidents. Discover numerous Revolutionary and Civil War battlefields and sites on Virginia's soil.

The longest stretch of the Appalachian Trail runs along the western bend of Virginia. Barrier islands off the Eastern Shore offer some of the East Coast's most exciting saltwater fishing. The warm, sandy beaches of Hampton Roads and Tidewater and the stately elegance of James River plantations are close enough for a single day's visit. Giant limestone caverns extend under the serene Shenandoah Valley, and scenic highways like the 105-mile Skyline Drive and the 217-mile Virginia

portion of the Blue Ridge Parkway allow travelers to take in scenic vistas.

Visitors enjoy a full range of recreational activities including camping, hiking, bicycling, skiing and golfing at its four-season resorts and at Virginia's more than 50 regional, state and national parks. Nearly 3,000 miles of freshwater streams, rivers and lakes, and more than 1,200 miles of tidal shoreline afford water activities galore.

Located mid-way between New York and Miami, the commonwealth boasts well-maintained major highways and scenic byways, service at 12 commercial airports-including Washington Dulles International and Washington National airports -

and at 57 general aviation airports, and Amtrak rail service connecting Virginia cities to commuter and long-distance travel routes.

Virginia is for lovers of mountains and beaches, history and culture, theme parks and natural wonders, vibrant cities and postcard-perfect towns. Your first visit here might be as a visitor, but you will undoubtedly return as a lingering traveler.

VIRGINIA IS FOR LOVERS

▲ EXHIBIT 3-11
An ad that matches good creative with relevant content.

Tonight, all over America, women will be
slipping into something a little more comfortable.

*Ahhhhh. Relaxed Rider™ jeans. There's no better way to feel like yourself again. Off with your stuffy 9 to
5 work clothes and into your favorite jeans. Nobody fits your body...or the way you live...better than Lee.*

R E L A X E D · R I D E R S

The brand that fits.

▲ EXHIBIT 3-13
The unique selling proposition: "The Brand that Fits".

▲ EXHIBIT 4-1 Pete Sampras was among the many celebrities to participate in the milk mustache ads.

▲ **EXHIBIT 5-1**

The use of stimulus to attract attention. The color, shapes
and brightness combine to produce a striking ad for
Hewlett-Packard's DeskJet printer.

Your team won't be taken seriously if it's not wearing adidas.

Liverpool. Germany. Bayern Munich. Glasgow Rangers. If anyone knows how to make a bunch of guys look like pros, we do. Introducing the adidas Team Soccer Program.

Now we can outfit your team with the same high-quality kit the pros wear. From jerseys to shoes, everything has the look and feel of Professional Club equipment. After all, 16 of the last World Cup teams were outfitted from head to toe by adidas. So if you'd like to see what your team could be wearing, call 1-800-665-KICK for

a free adidas Team Soccer catalogue and the name of your local Team Soccer retailer. Don't be seen in anything less.

adidas team soccer uniforms.

The gentleman pictured in last month's ad was Adi Dassler, founder of adidas. Congratulations, if you guessed correctly.
And many thanks to The Kick of the Canadian National Soccer League for being so immodest on our behalf.

▲ **EXHIBIT 5-5**
<u>Sports Illustrated</u> found this ad too provocative to run, although it publishes a controversial swimsuit edition each year.

▲ EXHIBIT 5-4

The use of animals to gain attention in a DuPont ad.

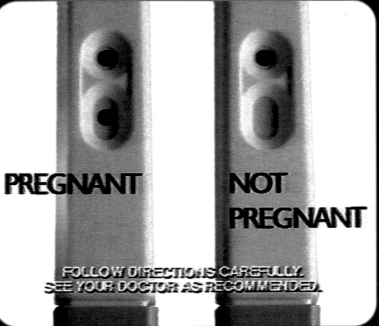

 EXHIBIT 7-1

Scenes from a TV ad that uses drama to arouse emotion.

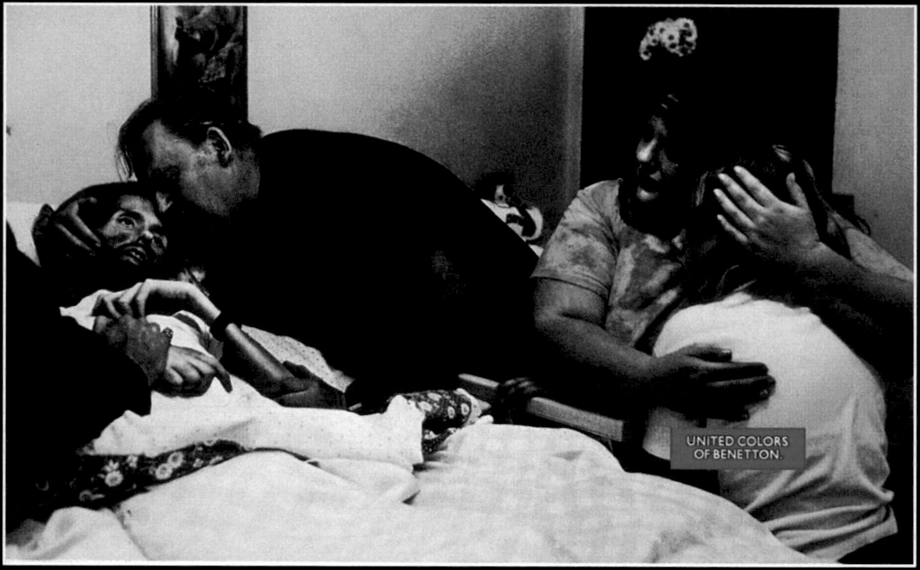

Source: Courtesy of United Colors of Benetton.

▲ EXHIBIT 7-6

A controversial Benetton ad that uses highly emotive themes of tragedy and compassion to advertise clothing.

Burn the cookbooks. Make it up as you go along.

There is something about the look of stainless steel that compels you to create, to experiment, to discover the chef inside you. Now you can have that professional look, uniquely accented with white or black. And it's very affordable: standard suite of refrigerator, range and dishwasher accented with black costs less than $4000*. They're also available with exclusive features: the range has a separate warming drawer

below the large self-cleaning oven. The refrigerator has an ice and water filter to remove impurities. And the dishwasher's wash system can handle even a dinner party's worth of dishes without prerinsing. The Frigidaire Gallery Professional Series™ freestanding and built-in appliances. You will not simply leave this kitchen; you will emerge triumphant. Call 1-800-FRIGIDAIRE or http://www.frigidaire.com

FRIGIDAIRE GALLERY PROFESSIONAL SERIES

THE LOOK OF BETTER PERFORMANCE　　■FRIGIDAIRE

COLOR GALLERY

▲ EXHIBIT 7-9
An emotional appeal for a kitchen appliance.

Our training for flight attendants is extremely rigorous. Maybe that's why our flights are so relaxing.

Simply to qualify for the Korean Air training program is an accomplishment. Of every thousand who apply, only a few possess just the right blend of grace and poise.

Then, nine hours a day, six days a week for a month or even more, their natural abilities are refined. They study world-class service. And hospitality. And a number of different languages.

By the time our flight attendants graduate, they're skilled in all the arts of comfort. Which leaves our passengers nothing to do but relax.

KOREAN AIR
Fly the spirit of dedication.™

Source: Courtesy of Korean Air.

▲ EXHIBIT 7-18
An ad that arouses warmth solely with the picture.

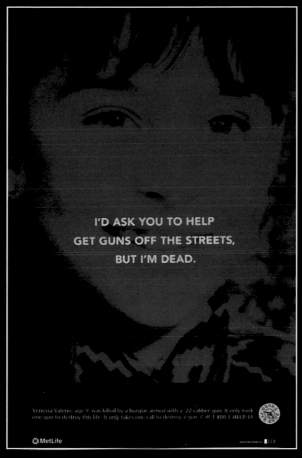

COLOR GALLERY

▲ EXHIBIT 7-20
An ad that arouses feelings of sadness instead of fear.

▲ EXHIBIT 9-4
An O'Doul's promotion that offers coupons and
reinforces the message.

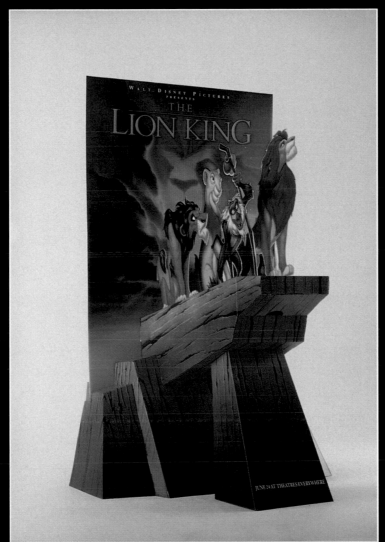

▲ EXHIBIT 10-3

Disney's "The Lion King" lobby display is an example
of an attention getting store display.

▲ EXHIBIT 12-12

Sweepstakes are drawings in which winners are determined purely by chance. Because of this, sweepstakes like this Philadelphia Cream Cheese offer cannot be limited to buyers of the brand.

▼ **EXHIBIT 5-3.** Providing information to gain attention.

The DUX® bed
The bed your back has been aching for℠

In Sweden, the people who make the DUX® bed have proven that a firm bed is not necessarily a better bed.

They've proven that a firm bed resists, rather than conforms to, the position of the body. So the body must constantly adjust in order to get

Lying on a firm bed, the spine is curved.

Lying on a sagging bed, the spine is curved.

In a DUX bed, the spine is straight.

comfortable — sometimes as much as 60 to 80 times a night.

Small wonder so many people wake up tired. And with a backache.

The DUX bed is designed to help eliminate back problems and give you a more restful night's sleep. It's the best made bed in the world.

It has two layers of innersprings instead of the usual one.

The upper layer moulds itself to the contours of the body, allowing the spine to lie straight.

The bottom layer acts as a buffer against harsh movement and provides firm support.

Made of the finest Swedish steel, the inner spring unit is so superior it should last a lifetime. So in the long run the cost of owning a DUX

bed is only a few pennies more per night than the cost of an ordinary bed.

This remarkable bed is available only in our DUXIANA® Shops in a wide range of sizes. You'll find a beautiful collection of fine European linens, Down comforters and pillows, not to mention our adjustable headboards and beds.

A bed is one of the most important purchases you'll ever make. After all, you spend about 8 hours a night in bed — that's one third of your life.

So come in and try the DUX bed. Lie in it; take a nap. You're going to love it. Your back will too.

DUXIANA®
ADVANCED TECHNOLOGY IN SLEEPING

Bellevue, 818 102nd Ave. N.E.
(206) 637-9725

For an instant FAX brochure call (800) 205-4003 with your fax number

For more information send for our FREE booklet "Advanced Technology in Sleeping"

Name _____
Address _____
City _____ State _____ Zip _____

Source: Courtesy of Dux Interiors Inc., New York.

---

affection and sadness are emotions that imply certain levels and qualities of arousal. The arousal may be observed as alertness, sweating or a faster pulse rate. Emotion involves mental activity but is distinct from thought and can exist independently of rational thinking. For example, a person can be afraid at the thought of some childhood monsters even though he or she knows that this fear is irrational. Yet emotions are typically aroused or dissipated through a sequence of thoughts triggered by stimuli. Chapter 7 explains the use of emotion in persuasive advertising using drama, humor and music. Here we consider only its attention-getting ability.

Even though advertisers can arouse a variety of emotions to draw attention, they have resorted to

some more than others: the nurturing instinct, love for animals, fear, sexual arousal and curiosity. The presence of infants in ads arouses the nurturing instinct and is also a strong attention-getting mechanism for parents. Children and many adults have a spontaneous love of animals, so the use of animals is a good attention-getting mechanism (see Exhibit 5-4). Fear is also a powerful means of gaining attention, and its use is covered in Chapter 7.

The use of sexy models, activities and episodes is a sure attention getter for some teen and adult market segments. One of the early users of this means of drawing attention was Elliott Springs, president of Spring (textile) Mills and other businesses.[19] Springs identified four guidelines for the use of sex as an attention getter. All warn against rampant sexual images:

- Treat the reader as intelligent.
- Use sex images as a tease—make them suggestive but not explicit.
- Use sex images with humor and respect.
- Link the images to clear product benefits.

Another useful emotion for drawing attention is curiosity. Advertisers can arouse curiosity by building anticipation about a real or fictitious event. An example of the first is introduction of a new car by announcing first only the date of introduction, then later the product category (but with the car in wraps), and finally the details about the car. The 1994 introduction of Chrysler's Neon followed this approach. An excellent example of the fictitious event is the 11-part serial ad campaign for Nestlé's Gold Blend, described earlier. Nestlé created an entire drama to captivate the imagination of consumers and direct their attention to the brand and message.

One of the biggest risks with using an emotional appeal to draw attention is using too strong a stimulus. Consumers then get so riveted to the stimulus that they don't absorb the message. For example, one study showed that sexy illustrations in ads gained slightly better readership and immediate recall of a brand name than similar, nonsexy ads.[20] However, recall after a week was much lower for the ads with the sexy illustrations. Apparently subjects noted the ad because of its sexiness but did not focus enough on the brand and message to recall it later on. At the other extreme, ads can arouse so much fear or discomfort that viewers tune them out to spare themselves the pain of exposure.

One factor that can counteract the distracting effect of a stimulus is its link to the brand or message. The attention-drawing power of a stimulus will be more productive if its link with the message is strong and natural. Nestlé's campaign for Gold Blend was so effective because the riveting drama was closely related to the positioning of the brand as a sophisticated choice for entertaining guests. Note that truly sophisticated viewers may find the series affected, slow moving or trivial, while connoisseurs of coffee may find any instant coffee quite unsophisticated. However, these segments are not the target for instant coffee. DuPont's use of animals to get attention (Exhibit 5-4) is similarly appropriate because the ad announces measures it has taken to protect the environment. On the other hand, one ad for Oneida silver showed a large picture of a white bunny next to a fork holding a

piece of lettuce. The ad had no copy. The cute bunny draws attention and the arrangement of the fork and bunny heightens attention to the ad. However, the link with the product is not apparent and may leave viewers puzzled.

Strong emotional appeals, especially if unconnected with the brand, run the additional risk of not being acceptable to the media. For example, one ad from Adidas featured the Canadian soccer team nude except for their Adidas cleats. See Exhibit 5-5. The ad, targeted for *Sports Illustrated*'s May 1993 issue, described the ability of Adidas (better known as a shoe company) to fully outfit a sports team. The ad was funny and attention-getting. However,

▼ **EXHIBIT 5-4.** Use of animals to gain attention.

Source: Courtesy of DuPont.

▼   **EXHIBIT 5-5.** Use of explicit sex appeal to gain attention.

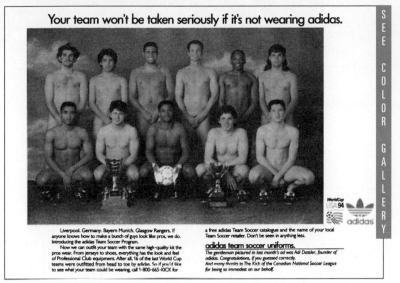

Source: Courtesy of Adidas.

the magazine found the ad so provocative that it refused to print it.

Ads that arouse emotions without a clear or strong link to the message also appear to be exploitative. For example, Benetton is often accused of exploiting important, emotional issues to sell mundane items of clothing (see Exhibit 5-6). These scenes have only a weak connection to the brand or message.

Offering Value One of the most effective means to gain attention is to offer consumers something of value. Often, the value is associated with the brand itself. For instance, if the advertiser has a new product that meets a real need not currently met by any other competitor, stating that fact simply and directly should be a good attention getter. In 1993, UltrAir introduced new airline service on the East Coast of the United States for $99. A key feature of the service was that it "freed the airline ticket" from the restrictions that most other airlines had, such as a designated class of seating, limited travel times or restricted destinations. The ad draws attention by offering the superior value to consumers simply and directly.

The value offered in an ad may also be in the form of a sales promotion, such as a discount, sample, sweepstakes, or the like. A good ad in this category is one that offers something of value that is

related to the product and that requires consumers to read the copy to obtain the item (see Exhibit 5-7). In the same spirit, David Ogilvy once suggested that two key words to draw a consumer's attention were "free" and "new." However, extensive use and misuse of these two words have dulled their appeal. Many ads with offers of "free" goods have some catch written in small print or discovered later, when the consumer purchases the item. Indeed, some experienced consumers have come to see these words as signs of a misleading ad and may screen them out immediately.

Aside from this problem with simplistic promises of value, sales promotions are a rich set of techniques for motivating sales. Chapters 9–12 cover them in more detail.

Summary The previous discussion describes four methods to draw attention: manipulating stimuli, providing information, arousing emotions and offering value. Although these methods are substantially different, they incorporate similar principles. Three of these principles are particularly important: the novelty and strength of the attention-getting stimulus and its link with the brand or message. Novelty is the starting point for drawing attention. Novelty attracts, while a routine appeal leads to a nondistinctive ad that gets lost in the noise. At the same time, the stimulus should not be so novel that viewers focus on the stimulus to the exclusion of the message. The best way to ensure that an attention-getting ad is effective is to adequately link the stimulus with the message. Indeed, a strong link between the stimulus and the brand or message is the most important principle of drawing attention.

Choosing a Method to Gain Attention

How should an advertiser choose among these different methods of gaining consumers' attention? At least three factors affect which method an advertiser should use: the consumers' state of receptivity, the type of product and the creative approach.

The most important factor is the consumers' state of receptivity to advertising. Although no method of drawing attention would be totally unsuitable to any

▼ EXHIBIT 5-6. Attention-getting ads unconnected to the brand or message.

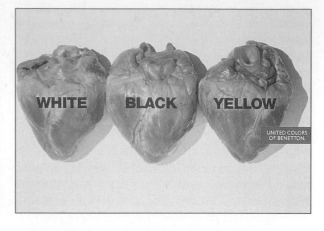

Source: United Colors of Benetton.

particular consumer state, some methods are better suited to one state than another. When consumers are searching for or actively processing ad information, arousing their curiosity is likely to be the best means of gaining their attention. Offering something of value would also be a good means of drawing attention. Each of these two methods would directly tie in with what is uppermost in such consumers' minds: collecting information to make a decision. If consumers are passively processing information, an emotional appeal may be suitable because it draws them into the ad without much effort on their part.

When consumers are actively avoiding ads, manipulating stimuli to gain attention may be the most appropriate. Advertisers have only a few seconds to draw the attention of these consumers before they turn off the ad. Novel, intense stimuli may be the only ones that can draw attention in that short a time. A genuine offer of value may be effective if it is

succinct and credible to such consumers who are probably also skeptical of advertising.

There is some support for the hypothesis that the appropriate method of getting a consumer's attention depends on the consumer's attention state. One study divided subjects into two conditions: one in which they were involved in their task and likely to process information actively, the other in which they were not involved and so likely to process information passively. [21] Subjects in each condition were further split into two groups, each of which saw either a distinctive or a nondistinctive ad. The distinctive ad had striking color pictures. The study found that when subjects were involved, they were indifferent to the two ads. However, when they were not involved, they had more favorable thoughts when exposed to the distinctive ad than when exposed to the nondistinctive one (Exhibit 5-8). Thus, creating a distinctive ad with striking and attractive stimuli is probably more critical when consumers are in a state of passive processing.

The nature of the product is another factor that determines the choice of method for gaining attention. An ad for a new product with a distinct advantage can attract attention by offering consumers unique value. An ad for a complex product can draw attention by offering an intelligent scheme to simplify the choice process. A style or fashion product can draw attention through stimulus intensity or appeal to sex.

The creative approach is a third factor that determines the choice of method for gaining attention. Depending on the theme (see Chapter 1) or the creative platform (see Chapter 4), one or the other method would be most suited. For example, an ad

▼ **EXHIBIT 5-7.** A promotional offer that gains attention by emphasizing the message.

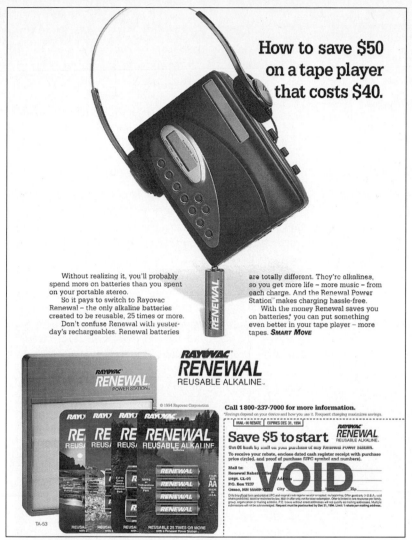

How to save $50 on a tape player that costs $40.

Without realizing it, you'll probably spend more on batteries than you spent on your portable stereo.

So it pays to switch to Rayovac Renewal – the only alkaline batteries created to be reusable, 25 times or more.

Don't confuse Renewal with yesterday's rechargeables. Renewal batteries are totally different. They're alkalines, so you get more life – more music – from each charge. And the Renewal Power Station™ makes charging hassle-free.

With the money Renewal saves you on batteries, you can put something even better in your tape player – more tapes. *SMART MOVE*

RAYOVAC®
RENEWAL.
REUSABLE ALKALINE.

© 1994 Rayovac Corporation

Call 1 800-237-7000 for more information.

*Savings depend on your device and how you use it. Frequent charging maximizes savings.

Save $5 to start

VOID

Source: Courtesy of Rayovac Corp.

that uses a rational platform would do best to arouse curiosity, while an ad that uses drama would do best to appeal to emotions early on.

DESIGNING COMPONENTS OF AN AD TO GAIN ATTENTION

The previous discussion leads us to an important strategic issue in applying what we have just learned:

how to design and place an ad to gain consumers' attention. While we will cover some of this topic in greater depth in subsequent chapters, here we focus on the design and placement aspects of an ad that affect its attention-getting ability.

The Components of the Ad

Different parts of the ad play different roles in gaining consumer attention. An ad consists of two broad sets of components: verbal and nonverbal. The verbal components are the headline, the copy, and the tagline. The nonverbal components are pictures and sound. For an ad to be effective, it must first draw the consumer's attention. The nonverbal components and headline can be crucial in this regard. Of these components, the tagline has more to do with memory than with drawing attention, so it will be discussed in Chapter 6.

Headline The **headline** is the first or most prominent line of a printed ad or statement of a video or audio ad. The headline has two important roles: to draw the attention of the audience and to introduce a message. A good headline meets these two goals efficiently. What are characteristics of attention-getting headlines?

An extensive study of headlines in a sample of over 2,000 U.S. magazine ads describes current practice among advertisers.[22] Exhibit 5-9 provides a selection of headlines from this survey. It suggests characteristics of headlines that may be effective. Most importantly, the sampled headlines on average had eight words. A short headline is easier to read and more likely to be read by busy consumers. It can be crucial to the success of the ad.

The study also found that 74 percent of the sampled headlines used at least one figure of speech. A

▼ EXHIBIT 5-8. **Effectiveness of distinctive ads by consumer involvement.**

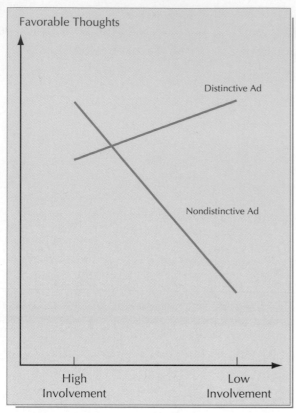

Source: Andrews, Craig J., Syed H. Akhter, Srinivas Durvusula, and Darrel D. Muehling (1992), "The Effects of Advertising Distinctiveness and Message Content Involvement on Cognitive and Affective Responses to Advertising," *Journal of Current Issues and Research in Advertising* 14, 1 (Spring), 46–58. Reprinted with permission of CTC Press, 1997. All rights reserved.

figure of speech is an artful variation from common usage of words. It has something catchy that attracts attention. The most common figures of speech were puns (17 percent) and alliteration (17 percent).

The study found that 84 percent of the sampled ads contained both a headline and a picture. Of these, 88 percent linked the headline and picture in a synergistic way so that the headline led to the picture or the picture built on the headline. These findings suggest that a short, well-crafted headline linked to the picture may make for an effective ad.

The headline is not the only means of drawing attention, as we will discuss shortly. Copy, pictures and sounds can also serve this purpose and can enhance the effectiveness of the headline or replace it in certain circumstances.

Copy The **copy** is the main verbal component of the ad. The primary purpose of the copy is to inform and persuade the consumer. Well-written copy can also enhance attention and aid recall. One of the most common misconceptions about copy is that it must be short to retain attention. Many readers come to this conclusion because they skip over the copy of most ads. However, long copy by itself has no negative effect, provided it is well integrated with other ad components. Moreover, consumers who are in a state of search or active processing will be looking for relevant information in the copy. For example, the copy in Exhibit 5-3 ties in well with the picture and headline and gives details of why the Dux bed is a good choice.

The copy itself should be attractively written to retain the interest of the consumer. Writing expert William Zinsser suggests a principle of good writing for journalists that is equally relevant for copywriters: *the copy should be so interesting that each line pulls the reader or listener on to the next.*[23] Research has shown that to retain the interest of consumers, copy should be detailed rather than ambiguous, using images and concrete words rather than abstractions.[24]

Pictures and Sound Pictures and sound are the nonverbal components of an ad. Their use depends on the medium: still pictures for print ads, sound for audio ads, and moving pictures and sound for video ads. Sound effects and especially pictures are important components of any ad because they can serve many goals. They help draw attention, facilitate communication, enhance persuasion and aid recall. Of these, perhaps their most important role is to draw attention.

Pictures and sounds can instantly draw attention, as with a stunning picture, an unusual sound, or some dramatic action. Overwhelming evidence from field studies indicates that the inclusion of a picture in an ad increases attention. In general, the larger the picture, the greater its attention-getting ability.[25] However, there is a trade-off between the benefit of a large picture to attract attention and the benefit of communicating the message with copy. The type of picture also affects its ability to draw attention.

▼ **EXHIBIT 5-9.** Figures of speech used in magazine ad headlines.

	Advertiser	Headline	Type of Figure of Speech
			I. Pun
A: The Tropes	British Airways	Our frequent fliers can frequent other fliers.	Antanaclasis
	Panasonic copiers	If you want to get read, use red.	Paronomasia
	Good Seasons salad dressings	Some people really know how to dress.	Syllepsis
	BMW 535I	A power plant that recharges human batteries	Other
			II. Associations
	Land-O-Lakes Country Morning Blend	40% Sin, 60% Forgiveness	Allusion
	Fabrilock Film for jeans	We make it tough for kids.	Irony
	Tilt-Wheel	If people . . . had adjustable bodies, they wouldn't need Tilt-Wheel.	Metaphor
	Max Factor	2000 Calorie Mascara. The only thing you gain is fat lashes.	Paradox
	Extra gum	Introducing the sugar-free gum recommended by 2 out of 3 patients	Parody
	Tampax	For 50 years, more women have trusted the special moments of their lives to Tampax.	Euphemism
B: Grammar Structure	Sundown sunblock	Sundown vs. Sun damage	Antithesis
	Turismo de Mexico	Come. Feel the warmth of Mexico.	Asyndeton
	Edge shaving gel	A shave this close used to take guts. Today it takes gel. Gel makes a difference.	Anadiplosis
	General Electric	Get your money's worth. Or your money back.	Polyptoton
	KitchenAid	KitchenAid. For the way it's made.	End rhyme

Source: Leigh, James H. (1994), "The Use of Figures of Speech in Print Ad Headlines," *Journal of Advertising* 23, 2 (June), 17–33. Reprinted with permission of the American Academy of Advertising.

Pictures showing humans or human faces are more appealing than those showing inanimate objects. For example, a brochure for an MBA program is more interesting if it shows students and faculty, preferably close up, than if it shows only beautiful grounds and elegant buildings. Part of the reason may be instinctive. Humans, being social, are drawn more to images of other humans than to those of animals or objects. Infants have been found to follow and respond to drawings of the human face more than to those of geometrical shapes.

Ad Placement

The physical placement of an ad in a medium can itself affect the attention it gets. Two important aspects of such placement are size and position.

As intuition suggests, the larger an ad, the more attention it gets. However, the relationship is not linear. One study suggests that attention increases as the square root of the increase in space for print ads.[26] So a 36-square-inch ad would be only twice as attention getting as one that covers 6 square inches (since 6 is the square root of 36). Another study confirms what many readers suspect, that 30-second TV ads are more effective than 15-second ads. However, contrary to expectations, 15-second ads are only 20 percent less effective than 30-second ads.[27] Thus, for print and TV ads, attention increases with the size or length of an ad, but at a declining rate.

The position of an ad affects attention. An ad in the first 10 percent of the pages of a printed medium gains more attention than a later ad.[28] The reasons are that probable reading declines with increasing pages or readers believe later material is less important so they do not read it as closely. An ad in the upper half of a printed page also gets more attention, but attention does not vary due to left or right placement.[29] The reason is that English-speaking consumers normally read from top to bottom and left to right, but they probably attend equally to both sides of an open magazine.

Thus, in addition to choosing an appropriate method to draw attention, the advertiser can also design various components of the ad and appropriately place the ad to attract and retain the attention of consumers.

Summary

Drawing and retaining a consumer's attention is the first step in communication. In order to draw attention and communicate their message effectively, advertisers must understand the state of their audiences. Audiences can be in one of four states of receptivity: search, active processing, passive processing and avoidance. The latter state has become more widespread with the growth of zipping and zapping. Within these states, consumers selectively attend to stimuli. They are more likely to attend to those stimuli and messages they find necessary, familiar or consistent with their behavior.

Advertisers can use one of four means to draw consumers' attention: manipulating stimuli, arousing emotions, providing information and offering value. Four characteristics determine the effectiveness of each of these methods: the novelty and strength of the stimuli, its link with the message and its relevance to the audience. The choice of these methods depends primarily on the state of the target consumers. Thus providing information is most useful when consumers are in a state of search or active processing. Arousing emotions is most effective when consumers are in a state of passive processing or avoidance, and manipulating stimuli is most effective when consumers are in a state of avoidance. The choice of method also depends on the type of product being advertised and the creative strategy the advertiser adopts.

The ad itself has four important parts: headline, copy, picture and sound and tagline. Each of these components has different goals. The primary purpose of the headline is to draw the consumer's attention. It also serves as a link between the picture and the copy. The copy provides information and persuades the consumer. The picture and sound serve to draw attention, enhance the argument, and persuade in their own right. The tagline serves to wrap up the argument, provide a memorable line and link the ad with other ads in the campaign.

Questions

1. Are all consumers equally indifferent to all advertising? Explain.
2. Why do consumers have a systematic pattern of preference for some stimuli? Which stimuli do they prefer? How does this happen?
3. How can advertisers take advantage of consumers' selective attention to gain their attention?
4. Most consumers are loyal to a few brands. Does this loyalty affect their attention to ads for different brands? Discuss.
5. What should advertisers of newer, less established brands do to draw the attention of consumers? In general, how should advertisers get the attention of nonusers of their product?
6. What are the different methods of drawing attention? Which one is the best? Discuss.
7. Which patterns are most likely to arouse interest?
8. What do consumers consider newsworthy? What is interesting to them? How can those principles be used to design attention-getting ads?
9. Advertisers' extensive use of sex appeal to gain attention has been variously criticized as ineffective, self-serving, and exploitative. Is that true? Discuss.
10. What are the characteristics of attention-getting headlines?
11. Review all the ads in the exhibits of this chapter. Which have the best headlines? Why?
12. How should advertisers place their ads to most effectively draw consumers' attention?
13. Why was the Bud Bowl campaign so effective initially? Why did it lose effectiveness later on?
14. Why was the campaign for Gold Blend so captivating?
15. Was *Sports Illustrated* fair in rejecting the Adidas ad, given that they also put out the "Swimsuit Edition" each year?

NOTES

1. Abelson, Robert P., et al. (1968), *Theories of Cognitive Consistency: A Sourcebook*, Chicago: Rand McNally and Company.

2. Amit, Ghosh, V. Kumar, and Gerard J. Tellis (1992), "A Decomposition of Repetitive Response Behavior," *Marketing Letters* 3, 4 (October), 407–417.

3. Mittal, Banwari (1994), "Public Assessment of TV Advertising," *Journal of Advertising Research* (January/February), 35–53.

4. Bucklin, Louis P. (1965), "The Informative Role of Advertising," *Journal of Advertising Research* 5 (September), 11–15.

5. Krugman, Herbert (1965), "The Impact of Television Advertising," *Public Opinion Quarterly* 29 (Fall), 349–356.

6. Soley, Lawrence C. (1984), "Factors Affecting Television Attentiveness: A Research Note," *Current Issues and Research in Advertising* 1, 141–148.

7. Clancey, Maura (1994), "The Television Audience Examined," *Journal of Advertising Research* 34, 4 (July/August), 38–39.

8. Kaatz, Ronald B. (1987), "The Zapping Problem and Suggestion for Solutions," *Journal of Media Planning* (Spring), 29–34; Gilmore, Robert F., and Eugene Secunda (1994), "Zipped TV Commercials Boost Prior Learning," *Journal of Advertising Research* (November-December), 28–38.

9. Kneale, Dennis (1988), "Zapping of TV Ads Appears Pervasive," *The Wall Street Journal*, April 4, 29.

10. Newman, Joseph W. (1977), "Consumer External Search: Amount and Determinants," in *Consumer and Industrial Buying Behavior*, Arch Woodside, Jagdish Sheth, and Peter Bennett, eds. New York: North Holland.

11. Narasimhan, Chakravarthi (1984), "A Price Discrimination Theory of Coupons," *Marketing Science* 3, 2 (Spring), 128–146.

12. Bowes, Elena (1992), "Coffee Couple's Story To Percolate In Book," *Advertising Age*, December 14, 6; Garfield, Bob (1993), "One More Cup Of Coffee For That Perky Couple," *Advertising Age*, July 26, 40.

13. The law can be described formally as:

$$dI/I = K, \text{ where}$$

dI = smallest perceivable change in stimuli
I = current intensity of stimulus
K = a constant for a particular stimulus.

14. Olsen, Douglas (1994), "Observations: The Sounds of Silence: Functions and Use of Silence In Television Advertising," *Journal of Advertising Research* 34, 5, 89–95.

15. Helson, Harry (1964), *Adaptation Level Theory*, New York: Harper & Row.

16. Lipman, Joanne (1992), "Networks Try to Persuade Firms Not To Flee When Crisis Strikes," *The Wall Street Journal*, January 27, B10; to understand the interaction between media and attention devices, see Lord, Kenneth R., and Robert E. Burnkrant (1993), "Attention Versus Distraction: The Interactive Effect of Program Involvement and Attentional Devices on Commercial Processing," *Journal of Advertising* 22, 1 (March), 47–60.

17. Percy, Larry, and John R. Rossiter (1992), "Advertising Stimulus Effects: A Review," *Current Issues and Research in Advertising* 14, 1 (Spring), 75–90.

18. Davis, Murray (1971), "That's Interesting . . ." *Philosophy of Social Science*, 309–344.

19. Dalrymple, Goodrum (1990), *Advertising in America: The First Two Hundred Years*, New York: Harry N. Abrams, Inc., 80.

20. Steadman, Major (1969), "How Sexy Illustrations Affect Brand Recall," *Journal of Advertising Research* 9 (March), 15–19.

21. Andrews, Craig J., Syed H. Akhter, Srinivas Durvusula, and Darrel D. Muehling (1992), "The Effects of Advertising Distinctiveness and Message Content Involvement on Cognitive and Affective Responses to Advertising," *Journal of Current Issues and Research in Advertising* 14, 1 (Spring), 46–58; see also Myers-Levy, Joan, and Laura A. Peracchio (1995), "Understanding The Effects of Color: How The Correspondence Between Available And Required Resources Affects Attitudes," *Journal of Consumer Research* 22 (September), 121–138.

22. Leigh, James H. (1994), *Journal of Advertising* 23, 2 (June), 17–33.

23. Zinsser, William (1990), *On Writing Well*, 4th ed., New York: Harper Perennial.

24. Percy and Rossiter, "Advertising Stimulus Effects: A Review"; McGill, Ann L., and Punam Anand (1989), "The Effect of Vivid Attributes on the Evaluation of Alternatives," *Journal of Consumer Research* 16 (September), 188–196.

25. Percy and Rossiter, "Advertising Stimulus Effects: A Review."

26. Barton, R. (1964), *Advertising Media*, New York: McGraw-Hill.

27. Patzer, Gordon L. (1991), "Multiple Dimensions of Performance for 30-second and 15-second Commercials," *Journal of Advertising Research* 18 (August/September), 18–25.

28. "Position in Media Advertising," *Media Scope*, March, 76–82.

29. *Ibid.*

CHAPTER

6

Persuasion with Information and Argument

In the late 1970s a rumor erupted in the Chicago area that McDonald's Corporation makes its hamburgers out of red worm meat. As with other such stories, there was no basis to the rumor. To combat the rumor McDonald's carried out several activities. Store managers posted a letter from the Secretary of Agriculture endorsing the quality of their meat. Television and print advertisements emphasized the use of 100 percent pure beef. And public relations personnel explained that using worm meat which

cost $8 to $10 a pound did not make financial sense. The strategy for combating the rumor was ineffective. The company continued to receive calls while sales did not return to their normal level and continued to decline in some areas.[1] Indeed, denial of the rumor may have helped to spread it. There was no rumor in Cleveland, Ohio. But after denial of the rumor in Cincinnati, Dayton and Columbus, word got out to Cleveland.

Why did the worm rumor spread despite McDonald's denials? What type of strategy did McDonald's use? What alternatives did the corporation have? This chapter explains the use of information and argument for persuasion. By the end of this chapter you should be able to identify the relevant principles needed to answer these questions. The most explicit means of persuasion is through argument. For a good argument, information is essential. Indeed, arguments are just means of crafting information to serve a communicator's goals. This chapter describes persuasion through argument in two parts: the consumer's processing of information; and the communicator's use of that information in various argument strategies. **Information processing** is how the mind receives, deals with and stores information. **Argument strategy** describes what forms of reasoning the communicator can use to persuade consumers.

HOW CONSUMERS PROCESS INFORMATION

The processing of information by the human mind involves three distinct activities: perception, cognition and memory. **Perception** is the process of forming mental patterns and drawing meaning from external stimuli.[3] **Cognition** is a term for the thought processes stimulated by the perception of external stimuli. **Memory** refers to people's mental coding of information for future use.

Perception: Making Sense of External Stimuli

Charles King is a 33-year-old Canadian immigrant from England who suffered a head injury in a car accident in 1988. Since that time he has had difficulty seeing pictures. For example, when shown a drawing of an asparagus, King calls it "a rose twig with thorns." Yet he can easily draw a recognizable picture of an asparagus. When shown a hand-drawn map of his native England, King cannot recognize the place. Yet he himself drew the map of his country. He can write a letter, but he cannot read it![2]

Why does King have difficulty seeing and recognizing, even though he can reproduce *the very same images* without any difficulty? This section helps you answer that question. It first describes the nature of perception and then the level of comprehension of contemporary ads.

The Process of Perception *Perception* occurs through the senses. Our five sense organs (eyes, ears, nose, mouth and skin) serve as gates that channel external stimuli to our mind as nerve signals. But the organs themselves do not make meaning of these stimuli— the mind does. In neurological terms, various electrochemical processes within the nerve cells of the brain form patterns that provide meaning.

Stages of Perception Perception consists of two stages: *analysis* and *synthesis*. **Analysis** involves comparing external stimuli with images stored in memory to identify patterns. Whole items (a word, an animal) or their components (letters of a word, features of the animal) may be compared. **Synthesis** is the process of drawing appropriate meaning from patterns based on the context of their occurrence. For example, we would recognize a cougar-looking object prancing on the sidelines of a football field as a mascot but a similar object in a zoo as a real cougar. Humor and puns involve placing familiar objects in incongruent contexts so that a second incongruent or funny meaning can be drawn. This is why Tony the Tiger's saying that Sugar Frosted Flakes are "Grrreat!" is funny.

The presence of these two processes of perception suggests that memory is essential for perception: memory provides the images with which to compare the external stimuli and the reference contexts from which to draw meaning. That is why a newborn with five active senses perceives very little—it has so few images and contexts with which to compare the new stimuli. For the same reason, although we can see the words or letters of a foreign language, we perceive little meaning from them. However, repeated exposure—especially if accompanied with education—can lead to familiarity, recognition of patterns and ultimately, perception of meaningful stimuli. *But the meaning is in the mind, not in the stimuli!*

The importance of memory in perception and the distinction between perception and memory can be further seen from the example of Charles King cited at the beginning of this section. King's accident severed a link in his brain between the part that receives external stimuli and the part that stores images of those stimuli. As a result, he can still *see* well, and he can *remember* well enough to write and draw images stored before his accident. But he cannot *perceive* those very same objects today.

Strategic Implication: Perception Is Selective Perception is a selective process. Because the mind must compare external stimuli with internally stored ones to draw meaning, it is strongly influenced by prior images stored in memory. This process is so strong that two different individuals can see different meanings in the same stimulus, depending on their training and expectations. The difference depends on what images they call up in their minds to compare with the external stimulus. For example, a photographer may look at an X ray and "see" various shades of gray at certain levels of resolution. An orthopedist may look at the same picture and "see" swollen tissue surrounding fractured bones.

The major implication of this discussion for advertisers is that they must consider the prior experiences of consumers when designing a message. Consumers' internal images drive the unique meaning they perceive in a message. This fact is particularly important when an ad criticizes a brand or disparages a position dear to a consumer. For example, negative references to a competitor the consumer likes may be perceived as positive. This reversal of meaning occurs most strongly when a consumer is not motivated to carefully monitor the ad. For example, a comparative ad campaign by Crown Cola against Coca-Cola may lead ironically to an increase in the latter's market share. Thus negative statements about rivals should be simple and very clear.

More generally, unless they are well crafted, communications may be misunderstood because of the varied backgrounds of individuals who receive them. Each receiver adds a slightly different meaning, depending on his or her background, while some may perceive a substantially different meaning. Thus communications rarely go through to the receiver *exactly* as intended by the communicator. What is the level of comprehension of contemporary ads? The next section addresses this issue.

Level of Comprehension A common assumption among advertisers is that most viewers follow the contents of an ad fairly well, once the advertiser gains their attention. Attention and persuasion are considered the major hurdles in successful advertising—not

proper comprehension of the message. However, managers, public relations specialists, journalists and others involved in day-to-day communication have more realistic appraisals of the effectiveness of communication.

Miscomprehension of TV Messages An innovative study evaluated the level of comprehension for regular TV and print ads and TV programming.[4] The study's sample of 2,700 respondents aged 13 and over was reasonably representative of the U.S. population. The study tested respondents' comprehension of 60 different TV communications (including 25 ads) with a six-item true-false quiz. The major findings?

- The vast majority (97 percent) of the respondents misunderstood at least some portion of the two communications each respondent saw.
- On average, respondents misunderstood about 30 percent of the content of each communication.
- Every one of the 60 communications was misunderstood by at least some viewers at some time.
- On average, miscomprehension of communications ranged from 23 to 36 percent.
- Miscomprehension related only slightly to demographic characteristics of viewers, such as their age or education.

Miscomprehension of Print Messages The authors of the previous study replicated their research with print communications.[5] In this case they used 108 communications, consisting of 54 ads and 54 editorial excerpts. They sampled 1,347 readers who were broadly representative of the U.S. population, each of whom read two ads and two editorials. The testing format was similar to the previous one with one change being the inclusion of a "don't know" alternative. The main findings from this second study were as follows:

1. A single reading resulted in 63 percent correct answers to the questions based on the content of the communications.
2. The correct rates were a little higher for ad content (65 percent) than for editorials (61 percent).
3. At least 21 percent of the meanings of the communications were misunderstood. This figure is

in addition to a 16 percent "don't know" response.

4. With the exception of education and income, most other sociodemographic variables were not related to the miscomprehension rates.

5. Regular readers misunderstood the communications just as much as regular nonreaders.

Strategic Implication: Designing Effective Copy Many authors have questioned the level of miscomprehension of these two studies.[6] Some have pointed out that the single exposure the respondents received may have been less than ads normally receive in real settings. On the other hand, respondents had as much time as they wanted, while ads in real settings may have limited time. Also, real ads are often received with much distraction. Others have suggested that guessing on the part of respondents may have led to a 10 percent increase in estimated miscomprehension. Even then the net level of miscomprehension is fairly high. These findings show that besides attention and persuasion, advertisers must also consider simple and clear communication of a message to an audience. Note that these findings relate to both regular and commercial programming, and to print and TV media. Thus the rules of good writing taught in writing classes and emphasized by journalists need to be followed as assiduously by advertising copywriters, who face a busy, uninterested or hostile audience:

■ Be brief and to the point.
■ Write simply, clearly and directly.
■ Choose appropriate words and images to suit the receiver's mind-set.
■ Use short, simple sentences rather than long, convoluted ones.
■ Use small, simple, commonly used words rather than big, compound or technical words.
■ Use concrete, clear words rather than abstract or ambiguous words.
■ Draw conclusions rather than leave the audience with subtle suggestions.[7]
■ Minimize negatives, and avoid double negatives.

Successful communication does not stop at perception. What an individual *thinks* about a message is as important as what he or she perceived. The next section discusses this topic.

Cognition: Thinking about Incoming Messages

The Cognitive Process The word *cognition* is used here to mean the process of thinking. For example, what happens when an involved audience listens to a message from a communicator? Listeners do not immediately accept the message or try to memorize it. The incoming message from a communicator merely prompts listeners to think. These thoughts are called *cognitive responses*. They can be brief or extensive, in depth or shallow, positive or negative.

Consider again the elaboration likelihood model discussed in Chapter 4. The peripheral route adopted by consumers when they lack the motivation or ability to think about the message implies brief or minimal elaboration (thinking). Further, such elaboration is shallow, relying on cues about the message and messenger, rather than deeply focusing on the arguments. On the other hand, when consumers adopt the central route they are likely to think about the message. In that case the number, intensity and direction of their thoughts are critical to the final opinion or attitude formed. Positive thoughts in response to a communication are called **support arguments,** while negative thoughts are called **counterarguments.** For example, consider the AT&T slogan, "Reach out and touch someone." This line could prompt the following support arguments on the part of a listener:

■ My aunt would be so happy to hear from me.
■ Phone calls cost very little these days.
■ I ought to call more often.

Alternatively, the message could also generate the following counterarguments on the part of the listener:

■ AT&T is just out to exploit emotional ties.
■ It's okay for them to make these suggestions but I have to pay the bills.
■ Phone calls are fun, but I hate the answering machine.
■ I wish AT&T would sell gift certificates that I could send my grandma so she could call more often.

An advertiser can gain insight into the effectiveness of a communication by collecting such thoughts through interviews or surveys. Gauging the type, intensity and direction of the thoughts helps an advertiser unravel the process of persuasion, and make suitable changes in copy. In the AT&T example, if the first counterargument came up often, AT&T would need to address the issue of costs in its ads. If the latter two counterarguments arose often, the firm would need to provide suitable services, make them appealing or advertise their availability. On the other hand if support arguments predominate, the ad has the potential to be effective.

Strategic Implications: Manipulating Factors to Influence Cognition

Making specific changes in the copy is not the only means by which advertisers can reduce consumers' counterarguments. They can control or avoid them by considering individuals' desire for cognitive consistency or manipulating key factors of the message: argument strength, repetition and mood.

Cognitive Consistency Cognitive consistency refers to individuals' desire to have consistency between information they receive and their beliefs, preferences and behavior. Inconsistency between new information and a recipient's prior experience leads to one of two effects: either the new message will be counterargued against and rejected or it will be reinterpreted and accepted. If an inconsistent message is clear and threatening, the recipient is likely to argue against the message and reject it. For example, cigarette smokers tend to reject the ample, clear evidence that cigarette smoke causes lung cancer and other diseases. On the other hand, if the message is ambiguous, recipients are likely to reinterpret it to be consistent with their own beliefs and behavior. They may even use such messages to further support those beliefs and behavior. For example, economists with radically different views often interpret the same economic data as supporting their own school of thought.

There are many explanations for cognitive consistency.[8] The

basic premise underlying these explanations is that individuals maintain consistency among their knowledge, attitudes, preferences and behaviors, because inconsistency creates stress. Since behavior is the most difficult of these attributes to change and knowledge (in the form of incoming information) the easiest, individuals are likely to adjust their acceptance or interpretation of incoming information to fit their beliefs, preferences and behaviors. Note that the end outcome of this process is *selectivity in message acceptance*, similar to the selectivity in perception discussed earlier.

For example, consider the trial of O. J. Simpson, who was accused of murdering his ex-wife and a friend of hers. The case won international notoriety because of O. J.'s celebrity, the gruesome nature of the murders and the racial differences among the parties involved.[9] O. J. is African-American while the victims were both white. Details about the murder, the actual trial and the verdict were widely disseminated by all the media. However, note how people's judgment of that information differed strongly by race (see Exhibit 6-1). Here, race may be considered a surrogate variable for people's prior experiences and beliefs, especially in terms of their liking for and identification with the experiences of the defendant or the victims.

The jury in the criminal trial found O. J. Simpson not guilty. A poll immediately after the verdict showed a dramatic split in agreement with the verdict by race. A large proportion of African-Americans agreed with the verdict. On the other hand, a similarly large proportion of whites disagreed with the verdict. The differences in opinions between these two groups are equally dramatic about the work of the Los Angeles Police Department (LAPD). Ironically, interviews with respondents during the trial showed that as new evidence emerged about O. J.'s guilt, those who were sympathetic to him dismissed it with various counterargu-

▼ **EXHIBIT 6-1.** Preference and perception.

Percentage of Los Angeles County residents expressing reactions to evidence and verdict in O. J. Simpson's trial		
	RESIDENTS' RACE	
Residents' Responses	**African-American**	**White**
Agree with verdict	77%	28%
Disagree with verdict	12%	65%
Don't know	11%	7%
Total	100%	100%
Police planted evidence	75%	21%
Police did not plant evidence	7%	62%
Don't know	18%	17%
Total	100%	100%

Source: Decker, Cathleen (1995), "Faith In Justice System Drops," *Los Angeles Times*, October 8, S2.

▼ EXHIBIT 6-2. **Use of flanking attacks in the soft-drink market.**

Time	Incumbent	Attacker's Strategy	Ad Theme	Result
1930s	Pioneer Coca-Cola dominated cola market with unique formula and an attractive 6.5-ounce bottle.	Pepsi-Cola offered a 12-ounce bottle for a nickel. Coca-Cola had an inventory of a billion 6.5-ounce bottles and hundreds of thousands of nickel soft-drink machines.	"Pepsi-Cola hits the spot. Twelve full ounces, that's a lot. Twice as much for a nickel too. Pepsi-Cola is the drink for you."	Pepsi-Cola passed Royal Crown and Dr. Pepper to become the number two brand in the market.
1960s	Coca-Cola still market leader with loyal consumers.	Pepsi-Cola presents itself as a drink of the young, repositioning Coca-Cola as dated.	"Come alive, you're in the Pepsi generation." "Choice of a new generation."	Pepsi-Cola grew in size from 40% to 87% of Coke's market share.
1968	Strong consumer recognition of leading soft-drink brands Coca-Cola and Pepsi-Cola.	7-Up positions itself as an alternative drink to the colas.	"Uncola."	Sales went up 15% the first year.
1980s	Coca-Cola and Pepsi-Cola still dominate the soft-drink market.	7-Up emphasizes that it has no caffeine.	"Never had it, never will."	7-Up became the leading caffeine-free drink till entry of caffeine-free Pepsi-Cola and Coca-Cola.

Source: Adapted from data in Al Ries and Jack Trout (1986), *Marketing Warfare,* New York: New American Library.

ments. Similarly, as new evidence about the shoddy and suspicious police work on the case emerged, those sympathetic to the victims dismissed it with counterarguments. Thus subjects' prior experiences and beliefs colored their assimilation and judgment of new information.

Consumers' desire for consistency creates a major problem for advertisers trying to overcome entrenched loyalty to a dominant brand. A **head-on attack** of an audience's position is unlikely to be effective. A better approach is a **flanking attack,** in which an advertiser redefines the key strengths of the dominant brand or emphasizes a new strength of the advertised brand.[10] Some classic examples of the effectiveness of flanking come from the soft-drink market, where the less popular brands won market share against entrenched leader Coca-Cola without directly attacking the latter's unique and much-liked flavor (see Exhibit 6-2).

Argument Strength Advertisers need to adjust the strength of their arguments depending on the motivation and ability of audiences to process information. As Chapter 4 explained, if the audience is motivated and able to process information, advertisers

need to use strong arguments; or else the audience will rip through weak arguments with counterarguments. For example, in the earlier AT&T example, a weak argument in the ad could be, "Now that you have better phones, do not hesitate to call." Not all consumers have updated their phones with new technology, nor are they likely to feel that that is a good reason to make more calls. On the other hand, a strong argument would be: "The cost per minute of a weekend long-distance call has dropped by 25 percent in one year. No other means of travel or communication has become cheaper as fast." Consumers unaware of this fact are likely to be surprised by the size of the decline, and most are likely to think that is a good reason to call more often. When consumers do not have either the motivation or the ability to process information, advertisers need to use cues such as endorsers or a large number of arguments.

Repetition As Chapter 4 explained, repetition of a message leads first to a positive response due to habituation, then to saturation and finally to a negative response due to tedium. This inverted U-shaped pattern also holds for the number of support arguments that an audience generates. However, the number of counterarguments in response to an ad follows a U-shaped curve, first declining, then leveling off and finally increasing (see Exhibit 6-3). So, the optimum or best number of repetitions is at that point where the spread between support arguments and counterarguments is the greatest. For example, the optimum number of repetitions for simple, strong messages is likely to be small, while that for complex messages is likely to be high.

Mood Receivers of a message are likely to generate support arguments rather than counterarguments if they are in a good mood. For example, they may be more likely to agree with the message of an ad that humors them than with one that irritates them. Many factors of an ad can put the audience in a good mood. Music, humor and stimuli that arouse positive emotions are some of the more obvious factors. More subtle factors include the overall tone of the ad, its aesthetic appeal and its sensitivity to the audience's feelings. Chapter 7 explores some of these factors in greater depth.

Memorizing and Retrieving Information

In 1953 a surgeon removed the hippocampus and nearby brain tissue of Harry Field, a Connecticut resident, to stop his seizures. The seizures ended, but so did

▼ **EXHIBIT 6-3.** Pattern of support arguments and counterarguments in response to message repetition.

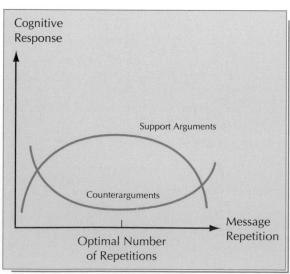

a part of his ability to remember events. Field can recall very well numerous events of his life before 1953, but can remember absolutely nothing that has happened after 1953, except for a few minutes. He tells stories, solves crosswords and remembers facts for a short period of time by repeating them to himself, over and over. However, he does not know where he lives, how old he is or anyone whom he has met anew since his surgery. Most sadly, each time he hears that his parents have died, he cries afresh with grief, even though they died several years ago.[11]

The brain is a complex and fascinating organ. It has enormous potential that we have barely begun to understand. It is also the location of memory. What is memory? What factors affect it? The above examples provide some clues to our understanding. This section describes both the structure of memory and the organization of information in memory. It then draws implications for advertising and promotion.

Structure of Memory Memory is the ability to remember information to which an individual has been exposed in the past. Researchers generally classify memory into two types, short-term and long-term memory. **Short-term memory** is the ability to remember information for about 20 seconds after receiving it. For example, remembering a toll-free phone number from an ad for a few seconds before dialing, relies on short-term memory. Short-term memory helps us to function from moment to moment, enabling us to complete tasks we have begun. **Long-term memory** is the ability to remember information for long time periods after receiving it. An example is parents' recall of positive information and experiences about the name Fisher Price when choosing toys for their kids.

Storage is the mental function that retains information in long-term memory, while **retrieval** is the function that brings information from long-term memory to our consciousness (short-term memory). All memory resides in the brain. The storage function probably resides within one part of the brain, the hippocampus. Proof that storage, retrieval, short-term and long-term memory are separate comes from the functioning of Harry Field and others like him. Field has short-term memory, he has long-term memory, and he can retrieve information from long-term memory, but having lost the hippocampus, he lacks the ability to form new long-term memories.

How does the brain store information? Research from a number of fields has converged on the understanding that memory is the result of electrochemical and cellular changes in the brain. Specifically, memory involves a system of nodes that are linked to other nodes via paths. The nodes contain the information, while the paths to other nodes serve as tracers that allow one to recall that information. In this sense, the brain is like a library, where the books are the information and the catalogue is the tracer to reach the books. For example, off the cuff we may not be able to remember an ad for Taster's Choice that we saw on TV the previous evening. But when given a cue such as "a coffee ad," or "a romantic couple," we are more likely to remember it. The ad has been stored with a path to coffee or romance, which then work as tracers to the ad. These tracers are called **retrieval cues.**

The linking of one piece of information with another is called **association.** In general, the more associations, the easier the recall of information, while loss of associations leads to poorer recall, even though the code for the information itself may remain in the brain. At the prompting of the brand name loyal buyers of some brands (e.g., Corvette) can recall a whole series of ads about and experiences with the brand. Their feelings for the brand have led them to identify with the ads and make a large number of links among the ads, the brand and aspects of their life.

Rehearsal is the mental strengthening of the paths linking the node that stores information with other nodes. It occurs in response to the repetition of a stimulus that first triggered that information or to a new stimulus that relates to that information. This strengthening ensures that pieces of information are more easily retrieved and less likely to be lost with time. For example, we are more likely to forget the name of a new brand of toothpaste we bought three months ago than one we used regularly when we were growing up, even if we have not used the latter for a few months. The latter name has been rehearsed so many times that retrieval is almost instantaneous.

How do people forget information? Researchers now believe that we forget a piece of information because its retrieval cues are involved in new associations, rather than because that information is lost from a node.[12] In the absence of rehearsal, a link between a piece of information and its retrieval cue does not get stronger. If the retrieval cue is associated with new information, then it will not lead distinctly to the first piece of information with which it was associated. An individual may then be unable to recall that information, saying he or she has forgotten it. For example, if only two or three firms advertise during the Super Bowl, consumers may be able to remember all the ads. However, when 60 ads appear during the Super Bowl, consumers have difficulty remembering even a few. Ironically, the absolute number of ads remembered may even decline as the number of ads aired increases sharply. The reason is that consumers make so many links between the Super Bowl and the ads that aired, that the links are not distinct, and may even get confusing.

Organization of Memory Different parts of the brain specialize in different functions. Most well known is the distinction between the left brain which processes verbal information and controls the muscles of the right half of the body, and the right brain which processes pictorial information and controls muscles of the left side of the body. Less well known is the fact that different parts of the left or right brain also process different components of language, such as verbs (that describe action) and nouns (that describe things). Evidence in support of the specialization of brain tissue comes from victims of strokes. Depending on which part of the brain is damaged, some can use one part of the body, and not another. Others can move well but not hear well. Still others can deal well with some parts of language such as nouns, but fumble with other parts such as verbs.[13]

Storage of information tends to occur in integrated units, called **chunks.** A brand name is a good example of a chunk. For example, a name such as Mercedes could signify to an individual cars, quality, reliability, prestige, luxury or exclusivity. Another name such as Kmart may indicate convenience goods, value, low prices, etc. Names for similar objects (such as brand names of cars) are stored together, leading to potential confusion among names if they are not distinct.

The mental process that organizes information in chunks is called **categorization.** A new piece of information—say about an encyclopedia on a compact disk—would first be classified as an encyclopedia, then as a compact disk, and then the two would be linked to form a new category, such as an "encyclo-disk." A brand that first creates this category, or dominates a category, may come to symbolize the category for the individual. This brand then becomes a prototype, and is the first recalled when the category is triggered.

In terms of depth or detail remembered, memory may be of two types: explicit and implicit memory.[14] **Explicit memory** is retrieval of information to which an individual has been previously exposed, plus retrieval of the context in which that exposure took place. For example, consider two individuals exposed to an ad for "In-and-Out Burger." When asked the next day about names of commercially available burgers both list "In-and-Out Burger" among other names. However, one subject remembers the ad while the other does not. The one who remembers the name and the ad that reinforced the name exhibits explicit memory for the name. The other who remembers the name but not the ad exhibits implicit memory for the name.[15]

Implicit memory is retrieval of information received during an event without retrieving the event. Another example of implicit memory is when an individual who knows *how to tie* her shoes cannot remember the *sequence of actions* she takes without actually carrying out the task physically or mentally. An individual who can recall both how to tie her shoes and each of the steps she takes has explicit memory for it. Implicit memory may account for a large fraction of what we have learned. The reason is that over time we remember information that we use but tend to forget the exact context in which we learned that information.

A form of implicit memory called **perceptual priming** may involve retrieval of no information, but could still facilitate behavior. An example of perceptual priming occurs when a man buys a Michelob beer after seeing an ad for the beer, even though he cannot recall any information from the ad, or the ad itself. Perceptual priming may explain the mere exposure effect discussed in Chapter 4. The prevalence of perceptual priming has been well established in nonadvertising situations. It has great significance for advertising especially of the type that enhances exposure to brand names without providing any other information. However, the effect of perceptual priming does not last long.

Strategic Implications This exposition of memory has many important implications for advertising and promotion.

Maximize Links The American Express advertising campaign, "Don't leave home without it" has appeared for many years with different executions, relating to different experiences of travelers. The same tagline has come to be associated with numerous episodes when the card came in handy. This strategy increases the number of associations with the tagline and the name, increasing the chance that the consumer will evoke the brand when the need to make a choice arises.

Increase Rehearsal Nike's slogan "Just do it" has been associated with its brand name and logo ("the swoosh") numerous times in many ads and ad campaigns over the years. Such repetition increases rehearsal of the link between the name, Nike, the swoosh and the theme. As a result, Nike sometimes uses its slogan as a tagline without the name or logo. The appearance of the tagline itself probably reminds audiences of the brand and helps to reinforce both the message and the name.

Use Distinct Retrieval Cues One reason firms use endorsers is to help consumers better remember their brands. However, if several brands use the same endorser, then consumers make multiple links between the endorser and brand name, and will not be able to remember any one brand distinctly. So a unique endorser may be more valuable if he or she is not that popular.

Be the Prototype The term **prototypical brand** suggests that a brand is the best example or is typical of a category. In an age where brands are similar and innovation is quickly copied, brands need to establish identities that set them as prototypes of categories or subcategories. The Ford slogan "Quality is Job 1" may serve this purpose. By suggesting that its foremost task is to produce top-quality cars, Ford wants consumers to know that when it comes to *quality cars* Ford is the prototypical brand. Similarly, Lee Jeans' consistent use of the slogan "The brand that fits" has placed it as the premier manufacturer of good-fitting jeans.

Maximize Exposure Because of the large number of ads and other stimuli competing for the consumer's attention today advertisers cannot hope that every message will be fully processed. So they should try to take advantage of implicit memory and perceptual priming by creating ads that also enhance exposure to the brand name. Firms that sponsor sporting events probably do so to get short but extensive brand name exposure.

Increase Recency Because perceptual priming is effective in the short rather than the long term, simple ads that increase exposure to the brand name or slogan should be placed close to the point of purchase. Such placement may also enhance recall and recognition of previously stored information. So ads for fast foods and hotels are often seen on billboards on the freeway; coupons offering some discount from the price of a brand often carry information about the brand to increase the probability of the consumer's evoking the brand and its attributes at the time of purchase. In-store displays not only allow consumers to sample some products, but they also serve as critical reminders at the point of purchase.

Keep Messages Simple Because of the number and complexity of messages that bombard an individual every day, the probability of any one being memorized is low. Simple, briefly worded themes and catchy, practical slogans serve to increase memorability. For example, the slogan of Maxwell House Coffee, "Good to the last drop," uses simple, one-syllable words. These words conjure up practical images of relishing the very last drop of coffee. Indeed, most of the slogans we have cited fit this pattern of word usage.

We have explained how individuals process information, and the implications of that process for advertising strategy. An important purpose of using information in advertising is to persuade individuals. An advertiser can persuade by crafting the information in one of several types of arguments. That is the subject of the next section of this chapter.

ARGUMENT STRATEGY

With the deregulation of the telephone industry in the 1970s, and the breakup of AT&T in the early 1980s, MCI started a persistent advertising and promotion campaign to chip away at AT&T's market share by stressing MCI's lower price. MCI's increase in market share over the years indicates that its efforts met with success. However, AT&T responded with various ads, some of which blunted MCI's attack. Then in the early 1990s, MCI introduced Friends & Family, which offered 20 percent discounts for calls to members in a calling circle if those members also subscribed to MCI. The program was successful, with MCI reaching a market share of about 20 percent, while AT&T dropped to around 60 percent. AT&T began to take note by offering figures of its own claiming to provide more reliable and better quality service. MCI challenged those claims with humorous and critical ads of its own. By early 1993, the AT&T and MCI advertising battle had become so bitter that it promised to burn both companies without providing either with any distinct advantage.

Then in late 1994, AT&T undertook a major change in strategy due to new managers and a new advertising agency. The new strategy involved a direct attack on MCI's claim of being less expensive: the offer of a 20 percent discount if a customer's monthly bill exceeded $25. To introduce the new service AT&T came out with a stinging ad campaign based on the theme "true." For example one ad refuted the extent of MCI's savings with the headline "MCI Math? 20 percent = 6 percent." The ad argued that because only one-third of an average customer's calls were to members in the calling circle, the true savings from the plan were only one-third of 20 percent or 6 percent. In contrast, the company's new offer amounted to "AT&T True Math. 20 percent = 20 percent." The AT&T ads claimed that the true savings from MCI were not as dramatic as MCI claimed (see Exhibit 6-4). MCI refuted those claims with strident ads that questioned AT&T's credibility. But the campaign offered consumers no hard evidence to support its own claims, and no positive reasons to stick with MCI. By early 1995, AT&T declared (to the press) that its new campaign had been effective, winning one million new subscribers. MCI countered with its own claim that AT&T "bought" new customers with discounts of $75 for merely switching to AT&T. The truth probably lay somewhere in between the rivals' claims.[16]

Why are AT&T and MCI involved in negative advertising? What other alternatives do advertisers have for stating their case? When should advertisers use each of them? These are some of the questions addressed in this section.

Firms can use many strategies to persuade consumers with information and argument. These strategies can be classified into five main types: comparative, refutational, inoculative, framing and supportive arguments.[17] The section explains each of these strategies paying special attention to when and why they are effective.

Comparative Argument

Comparative argument refers to a message comparing the target brand to some competitive standard.

▼ EXHIBIT 6-4. AT&T's ad refuting perceived savings from MCI.

MCI Math?

20% = 6%

20% = The discount on calls to MCI customers in your Friends & Family calling circle.

6% = The average discount that shows up on your MCI Friends & Family Basic bill.

Huh? MCI advertises a 20% discount off your long distance calls, as long as you call other MCI users who are also in your calling circle.

Well, truth is, when the bill comes, the average discount MCI Friends & Family Basic callers really see is only about 6%.* Not 20%.

Because about two-thirds of their calls aren't to MCI users on their calling circle list. They're to other people, maybe even other MCI customers, and they don't count.

And if people are in your circle and then leave MCI—for their

own reasons—then your calls to these people don't count any more. Although MCI allows calling circles of up to 20 people, most people really call only 1 or 2 people in their circle.

So that discount that started out with a big number can turn out a lot smaller when you check the math for yourself. In fact, 2 out of 3 Friends & Family users on Basic will save more with AT&T *True USA*℠ Savings.

So if MCI Math doesn't add up for you, please read the other page, and you'll see...

AT&T True Math.

20% = 20%

20% = The discount you get on calls to everyone.

20% = The discount you see on your AT&T bill with True USA℠ Savings.

Introducing AT&T *True USA*℠ Savings. Spend $25 a month on AT&T long distance and save 20% off your calls to anyone, anywhere in the USA, anytime.* Guaranteed. **Just call 1 800-TRUE-USA**℠ and enroll.

Call 1 800-TRUE-USA

AT&T. Your True Voice.™

AT&T

Source: Courtesy of AT&T.

▼ EXHIBIT 6-5. Comparative ad for a named competing brand.

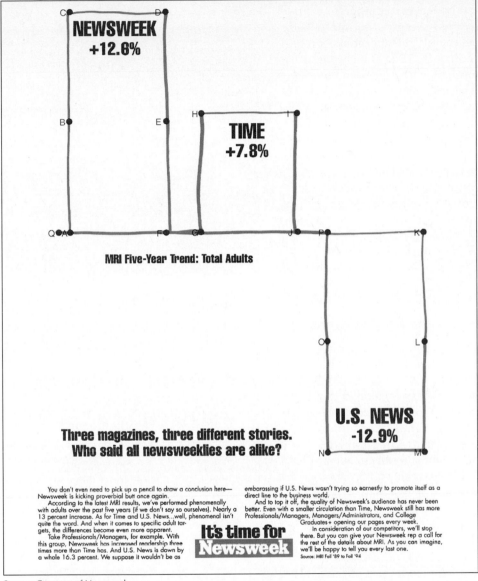

Source: Courtesy of Newsweek.

For a standard, advertisers may use a named competing brand (see Exhibit 6-5), an unnamed competing brand or the general industry performance (see Exhibit 6-6).[18]

Before 1970, comparative ads were rare. Discouraged by the Federal Trade Commission, they were avoided by firms and their agencies. The FTC was concerned that comparative advertising would confuse or mislead consumers and that larger firms would take undue advantage of smaller firms. Major firms opposed the strategy for fear it would help small firms or new entrants compare their brands to those of the major firms. Advertisers and their agencies feared that such advertising would create legal problems for the advertised brands, while giving free exposure to the rival brand used as the standard for comparison. However, under pressure from consumer advocates, the Federal Trade Commission changed its policy in 1971 and began actively encouraging firms to use comparative advertising. The new thinking was motivated by a belief that specific information about brands, especially of the comparative kind would help consumers make more informed decisions.[19] In addition, to the extent that such information was truthful and substantiated, it could help superior brands to advertise that fact, improving consumer choices and increasing market efficiency.

Since that time comparative advertising has increased steadily (see Exhibit 6-7). These statistics indicate that advertisers and their agencies now seem to place much faith in comparative advertising. They believe that it helps establish a brand position, gain credibility and initiate trial. These benefits are plausible because a comparison of a target brand with a better-known brand would clarify its competitive position and increase consumer belief in its claims. Consumers may then be willing to try the lesser known brand. On the other hand, advertisers and ad agencies believe that comparative advertising is not effective in creating positive feelings, positive attitudes or loyalty to the advertised brand. Here again the reason might be that a comparative ad tends to be critical of a rival and may offend loyal users of the rival brand.

Empirical studies do not support the universal superiority of comparative advertising or of these beliefs of advertisers and ad agencies.[20] The empirical studies vary in their findings with some being contradictory. However, a few tentative conclusions have emerged, especially regarding two factors that influence the effectiveness of comparative advertising: two-sided appeals and competitive position.

Two-Sided Appeals Message sidedness refers to whether a message contains a one-sided or two-sided appeal. A **one-sided appeal** involves only positive statements about an advertised brand and only negative statements about a rival brand, if it is men-

▼ **EXHIBIT 6-6.** Comparative ad for an unnamed competing brand.

MALAYSIA AIRLINES SERVES *more* PEOPLE THAN ANY OTHER AIRLINE FROM SOUTHEAST ASIA.

Imagine the future for one of the world's fastest growing airlines. In 1992, we flew over 12 million passengers, more than any other airline from Southeast Asia. On a fleet of the latest 747-400s and 737-400s, some of today's most advanced aircraft. Spanning a truly international network of 90 destinations. Across 5 continents, graced with service from the heart which says, you mean the world to us. Imagine. Fly Malaysia Airlines.

A member airline of Continental Airlines **OnePass** program.

Source: Courtesy of Malaysia Airlines.

tioned. A **two-sided appeal** contains both pros and cons about an advertised brand or a rival. A two-sided appeal is likely to be more effective than a one-sided appeal for several reasons.

First, consumers do not normally expect an advertiser to speak ill of its own brand. Thus, a two-sided appeal that acknowledges a limitation is likely to arouse interest and draw attention. Second, no brand is likely to be entirely free from defects; similarly, no rival brand is likely to be entirely flawed. A two-sided appeal is more credible because it suggests that the advertiser is sufficiently objective about its brand to acknowledge some of its cons, or some pros of a rival.[21] Third, comparative advertis-

▼ **EXHIBIT 6-7.** Trend in use of comparative ads over time.

Year	Percentage Using Comparative Ads
1973	7%
1977	5 to 10%
1980	14%
1982	23%
1984	35%
1986	> 50% of NBC TV spots

Source: Based on review of Rogers, John C., and Terrell G. Williams (1989), "Comparative Advertising Effectiveness: Practitioners Perceptions versus Academic Research Findings," *Journal of Advertising Research* (October/November), 22–37.

ing tends to motivate counterarguing by the audience.[22] Two-sided appeals have the potential to reduce such counterarguing by addressing some of these opposing arguments.[23] To do so, a two-sided ad should start by acknowledging a brand's known or unimportant weaknesses but then emphasize its important strengths.[24] For example, a claim such as "we cost more but are worth it," acknowledges a brand's high price but makes a virtue of it.

Similarly, two-sided ads that acknowledge some unimportant strength of a rival can be effective. This is especially true if the rival is the pioneer, the market-share leader, or a strongly liked brand.

The city of Los Angeles ran an ad for locating businesses in the city. It showed that LA far outstripped New York, Chicago, Dallas and Houston in number of small businesses. This is a comparative ad with named competing cities. It involves a one-sided appeal that presents only the advantages of Los Angeles. It appeared in 1996 after Los Angeles faced several years of businesses closing because of the recession, shrinking defense budget and other problems. A skeptical reader is likely to wonder whether Los Angeles is unquestionably superior to the other cities listed. A two-sided appeal that acknowledged some strengths of the other cities, or some weaknesses of Los Angeles may have been more credible. One possible theme may have been: "While some big firms leave, many small ones thrive."

One study provides direct support for the effectiveness of comparative two-sided appeals[25] (see Exhibit 6-8). Note from the exhibit that a comparative claim is inferior to a noncomparative claim in winning acceptance when a one-sided appeal is used. However, a comparative claim with a two-sided appeal fares much better. Notice also that of the four

combinations of appeals, a two-sided comparative appeal is the best, while a one-sided comparative ad is the worst.

Competitive Position *Competitive position* is the strength of a target brand relative to the rival named in the ad. Important aspects of relative strength include the market share (small or large), the order of entry (early or late) and consumer loyalty (strong or weak). A **dominant brand** is one that has a large share and strong loyalty; a **subordinate brand** is one that has the opposite qualifications. In which position should a brand compare itself to its rival, when it is dominant or subordinate? The answer is fairly intuitive: when the brand is subordinate rather than dominant. For example, Pepsi first started comparative advertising against Coke; similarly, MCI first started comparative advertising against AT&T. Several reasons justify this strategy.

First, comparative advertising between two brands leads consumers to view them as similar. Such an effect is better for a small-share, new or less-liked brand.[26] Second, comparative advertising gives a rival brand free exposure.[27] A dominant brand already well known to a population is unlikely to benefit much from the free exposure, especial-

▼ **EXHIBIT 6-8.** Effectiveness of appeal by comparativeness and message sidedness.

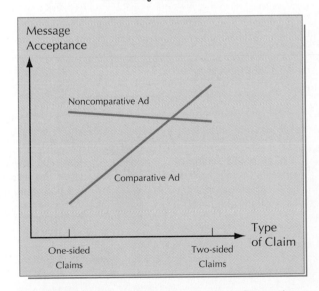

Source: Swinyard, William R., "The Interaction Between Comparative Advertising and Copy Claims Variation," *Journal of Marketing Research* 18 (May) 1981, 175–186. Reprinted with permission of the American Marketing Association.

ly if associated with mention of its negatives. However, a subordinate brand can benefit from comparison with a market leader, even if the comparison states some of its negatives. Third, comparative advertising leads to an ad war, prompts counterarguing by consumers, and increases their dislike for both brands. In all of these cases, a dominant brand has more to lose than a subordinate one.

Refutational Argument

Among the general public, Mercedes-Benz probably has had the reputation for having the highest resale value among luxury cars. In mid-1994, BMW ran a campaign that questioned the validity of this belief using facts and figures from the N.A.D.A. Official Used Car Guide (see Exhibit 6-9). BMW's ad strategy is called a **refutational argument**. It first presents a counterargument against the advertised brand, then destroys that argument. Refutational ads can be used for several purposes. First, they can refute a widely held negative belief about a brand. An example would be Chrysler's Lee Iacocca ad campaign of the early and mid-1980s refuting the idea that a Chrysler purchase would be risky. Second, refutational ads can refute a belief about or claim of a rival. Examples include the BMW ad in Exhibit 6-9 and the AT&T ad in Exhibit 6-4. Third, they can refute negative implications about a brand stemming from some recent event. Why and when is refutational advertising effective?

Research indicates that refutational advertising is effective because it directly addresses the concerns of the audience.[28] As stated before, persuasive messages tend to trigger some counterarguing on the part of message recipients. This counterarguing is more severe if an ad doesn't address some widely held negative belief about the advertised brand. In such circumstances, braving the facts, bringing up the negatives, and then destroying them is more satisfying to the audience and more effective. Of course, for this strategy to be effective, the brand must have some new, unambiguous information that can refute its existing negatives. Also, if the refutation involves comparative advertising, these facts should not be so narrow that a rival brand can easily refute them, leading to an ad war that renders both brands in a poorer light. For example, the AT&T ad in Exhibit 6-4 could also have been criticized and refuted by MCI if a majority of AT&T's customers do not ring up more than $25 in monthly long-distance calls. Indeed, at

▼ EXHIBIT 6-9. Ad refuting a rival brand's reputation.

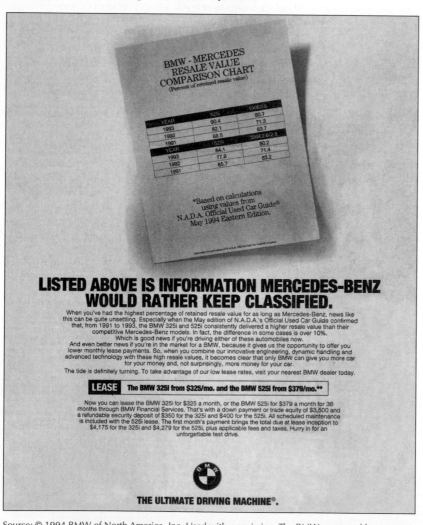

Source: © 1994 BMW of North America, Inc. Used with permission. The BMW name and logo are registered trademarks.

one point, the AT&T-MCI advertising war had reached a point where neither side had a clear advantage, and further refutational advertising only led to a poorer image of each. On the other hand, BMW's ad is based on information from a neutral source and is less susceptible to criticism.

The prior example suggests that refutational advertising is not a strategy to be used indiscriminately, but one that may be effective in certain conditions. These conditions are a widely held and enduring negative belief about the brand, no ambiguity about the issues involved, or attack by a rival.

Widely Held Negative Most importantly, the claim or belief to be refuted must be held by a large proportion of the audience. For example, Chrysler's bankruptcy in the early 1980s was widely covered in the press, so that any strategy of renewal had to address the viability of the company and the reliability of its cars. However, not every reader of *The Wall Street Journal* was aware of Reebok's firing of Chiat/Day. So if Chiat/Day wanted to stress its contribution to Reebok, running a refutational ad in *The Wall Street Journal* may not have been appropriate (unless Chiat/Day's intent was to remind investors, who knew of the firing, about its past achievements). Alternatively, if Chiat/Day wanted to reassure major advertisers, then running the same ad in *Advertising Age* may have been effective, because Chiat/Day's firing would have been well covered in that magazine and known to major advertisers.

Enduring Negative The claim or belief that is to be refuted must be of an enduring nature, not temporary. Often during a crisis, a firm or brand gets a great deal of negative publicity. However, if the crisis is carefully handled through public relations, with apologies for wrongdoing, promises of remedial work, or strong defenses of the firm's integrity, it is likely to subside. A refutational campaign may not only be unnecessary but may reinforce the negative publicity. For example, in mid-1993 reports surfaced of needles and syringes in Pepsi and Diet Pepsi cans. Pepsi responded through its public relations department with strong defenses of its manufacturing integrity. At the same time the company ran a massive TV ad campaign for Diet Pepsi featuring the popular trio, the "Uh-huh Girls," and no mention of the crisis. The reports were found to be false and the crisis passed.[29] In contrast, the superior resale value of Mercedes-Benz cars is a fairly enduring belief among the public, so BMW's ad has the potential to be very effective.

Unambiguous Issues The issues surrounding the claims and counterclaims of the refutational ad should be unambiguous. In 1982, Johnson & Johnson was hit by a cyanide poisoning disaster. Seven people died after ingesting cyanide-laced Tylenol capsules. The disaster was due to the pure malice of one or more perpetrators, possibly store customers who tampered with the capsules. At that time, all pharmaceutical products had simple packages that were easily amenable to tampering. Johnson & Johnson had made no error and had done no wrong. So, there was ambiguity about the blame. In such a situation, a refutational campaign justifying Johnson & Johnson's position or denying wrongdoing would have been counterproductive and appeared unnecessarily defensive. A supportive campaign emphasizing consumers' and doctors' longtime trust in Tylenol would have been more appropriate. That is the strategy that Johnson & Johnson successfully adopted for its subsequent advertising. Similarly, a rumor involves ambiguity about the facts, and should be countered with supportive arguments rather than refutation.[30]

Attack by Rival A **rebuttal** is an argument in which an advertiser immediately refutes a rival's critical ad. Research indicates that a target brand's failure to rebut a rival's attack leads consumers to believe the rival's criticism.[31] The 1988 U.S. presidential campaign is a good example. Democratic candidate Michael Dukakis had a 51 percent to 34 percent lead over George Bush in opinion polls right after the Democratic convention.[32] At that point, Bush started a blistering attack on Dukakis especially targeting his policy on prison furloughs and the pledge of allegiance to the flag. Against the advice of his managers, Dukakis neither criticized Bush nor responded to the latter's critical ad campaign. Dukakis assumed that criticizing a rival was demeaning, disliked by the public and ineffective. In the three months that followed, the unquestioned Bush ad campaign had the desired effect, reversing Bush's position in the polls to a 55 percent to 34 percent advantage. While other factors may also have contributed to Dukakis's decline, the failure to rebut Bush's attack is supposed to be the major factor.

Dukakis, though, may have been right about his first two assumptions. Rebuttal and counterrebuttal lead to increasingly negative ads, which turn off consumers and cause a decline in ratings for both parties. Indeed, negative advertising has become one of the hallmarks of political advertising. What is the solution to this problem? President Bill Clinton probably hit the right note with his 1992 election strategy. He had a rejoinder for every one of Bush's attacks, but these rejoinders were often given by his assistants and mostly to the press. His ads, however, kept stressing his strengths. The need for immediate response may have been one of the reasons that MCI immediately rebutted AT&T's "true" campaign. However, MCI did not have enough good evidence to drive home the rebuttal effectively.

Inoculative Argument

Prior to the U.S. presidential elections, each political party holds a convention to nominate its candidate for the election. These conventions are a great opportunity for free favorable publicity that greatly builds up the party's candidate. During the 1992 Republican convention Bill Clinton ran an ad that sniped at President Bush's record. The ad was cleverly timed and distributed. By raising doubts about President Bush's credentials at a time when Bush would get his greatest boost in the polls, Clinton reduced the one-sided attention that Bush would receive during the convention, and protected himself from the serious drop in the polls that normally follows a rival's party convention. Also, by releasing the ad only in Houston, Clinton's strategists made sure they captured some airtime even beyond Houston, but for free: a number of newspapers and TV newscasts across the nation reported the ad alongside reports of the Republican convention.[33]

An **inoculative ad** is one that protects a brand's position with current consumers by alerting them about and helping defend against an impending attack by a rival. One example of inoculative advertising is the ad run by Bill Clinton during the 1992 Republican convention in Houston. How does inoculative advertising work?

In medicine, inoculating individuals involves infecting them with a weakened dose of a disease, which their immune system can easily withstand. The immune system is then sensitized and can deal effectively with the more virulent form of the real disease if it comes along. A similar principle applies in this strategy. We have discussed how consumers' attention and perception are selective processes that lead them to resist change and hold to their current beliefs and practices. However, when faced with strong arguments to change to a rival brand, they may accept the new position if they are motivated and able to process the new information. Inoculative advertising presents the rival's position with weak supporting arguments, followed by strong counterarguments refuting that position. Consumers can use the counterarguments against the actual ads of the rival brand when they see or hear them. Thus inoculative advertising enables a consumer to develop a position strongly favorable to the target brand *before* the consumer can develop such a position toward the rival brand.

Some evidence does support inoculative advertising.[34] In general, *defensive marketing* (giving consumers good arguments to withstand an attack by a rival) is more effective and less costly than *offensive marketing* (trying to win consumers back after they have switched to the rival's brand). Inoculative advertising can be an effective means to defend against new brand entry, price cuts by rivals, or rivals' major promotional events. This strategy is especially useful if the defending firm cannot or will not match the rival's specific efforts in products, features or price.

Framing

Dr. Joycelyn Elders was President Clinton's first appointee for U.S. Surgeon General. She had strong views on a number of issues, and she did not hesitate to express these views. Frequently, these views were not consistent with those of the administration and may have been more liberal than positions held by the majority of the population. However, Dr. Elders expressed her views in a context in which they had some merit. The American Renewal, a group opposed to her and to President Clinton's policies, ran an ad that put together in one place a number of Dr. Elder's statements, out of the context in which they were originally expressed (see Exhibit 6-10). The ad created a picture of Dr. Elders as opinionated, extreme, and insensitive to the views and values of mainstream Americans. Because Dr. Elders was President Clinton's appointee, the ad went on to question his judgment about his other programs. (Dr. Elders finally resigned when another of her statements about educating children about masturbation became controversial.)[35]

▼ EXHIBIT 6-10. **Example of framing.**

Bill Clinton Chose This Doctor

Elders on why we should spend more on AIDS research (#9 killer) than on heart disease and cancer (#1 and #2):

"Most of the people who die with heart disease and cancer are our elderly population...we all will probably die with something sooner or later."

Washington Post
June 25, 1994, p. A 29

Elders on the Boy Scouts:

"Q: Did you say you believe the Boy Scouts should admit homosexuals?

A: Yes. I also think girls who are lesbians should be allowed to join the Girl Scouts"

USA Weekend
June 3-5, 1994, p. 5

Elders on sex and drugs:

On CNBC's "Talk Live" program on June 19, 1993, Dr. Elders said: *"I would hope that we would provide them [drug-abusing prostitutes] Norplant, so they could still use sex if they must to buy their drugs."*

The Washington Times
June 27, 1993

Elders on free drugs for addicts:

"When we say 'legalize,' I'm really talking about control. We [could] have doctors or clinics set up where addicts can get their drugs free or pay one dollar."

The Washington Times
June 2, 1994, p. A3

Elders on abortion:

"Abortion has an important and positive public health effect."

The Washington Times
August 14, 1993

Elders on fighting crime:

"...we would markedly reduce our crime rate if drugs were legalized."

Washington Post
December 8, 1993, p. 3

Elders on gay adoption:

"Elders says gays and lesbians can play an important role by adopting children..."

The Advocate
March 22, 1994, p. 36

Dr. Joycelyn Elders
Surgeon General of the United States

Now He Wants To Choose Yours

The Clinton health plan would permit Big Government to control who enters medical school, who enters which medical specialties and where they can practice. *You will lose* your choice of doctors.

"Americans don't want a Big Government-run health plan. Nor do we want a Surgeon General with such extreme views."

Gary Bauer
Former White House Domestic Policy Advisor

I want to stop the Clinton Plan now.
Write or call Gary Bauer toll-free 1-800-225-4008

I'll help run this ad all over America. I am enclosing a gift of:
$25___ $50___ $75___ $100___ $250___ $500___ Other___

Name _____

Address _____

City _____ State _____ Zip _____

Please make check payable to American Renewal. Clip this form and send it along with your gift to the address below. American Renewal is registered as a 501C(4) corporation. Gifts are not tax-deductible.

ARAS 4

Paid for by American Renewal 700 Thirteenth Street NW, Suite 500 Washington, D.C. 20005

Photo Credit: U.S. Department of Health and Human Services

Source: Robert G. Morrision (American Renewal).

Framing is the presentation of information in a context that provides it with new meaning. Framing involves changing the reference point of viewers. It plays a very important part in the perception and evaluation of prices, and is discussed in depth in Chapter 10. Framing is also relevant in the area of argument strategy. It can be a subtle means of making a damning statement about another party. The ad in Exhibit 6-10 makes a strong attack on Dr. Elders by merely presenting in one place some of her statements. Note that the chosen statements are direct quotes, with full references and without any refutations. However, they have been chosen because they are all at variance with the views of the population to which the ad is targeted. Moreover, the statements have been selected out of their context, where they may have appeared less extreme.

Although the word *framed* is sometimes used casually to mean someone was wrongly accused, here it does not necessarily imply deception or impropriety. Framing involves presenting information that the opponent normally offers about herself or himself, but doing so with a slight to moderate change in the reference point, so that the opponent appears less desirable to the target segment. The power of framing is that it does not involve explicit criticisms that raise the defenses of the viewers. Other forms of framing include hyperbole (exaggeration) and sarcasm. Framing is effective when the target segment does not have all the information about a brand or person targeted for attack, and has a different reference point than the brand or person. While this form of argument lends itself better to political ads, it may also be used effectively for products and services.

Supportive Argument

A **supportive argument** involves an affirmation of the positive attributes of a brand without any comparison, refutation, inoculation or framing. It is by far the simplest and most common strategy. Supportive arguments can use a hard-sell or soft-sell approach, issues covered in greater detail in Chapter 4. Supportive argument is appropriate when there is no advantage to any of the other argument strategies already discussed.

SUMMARY

The processing of information by the human mind involves three distinct activities: perception, cognition and memory. Perception involves forming mental patterns from external stimuli, and drawing meaning from them. Memory is essential for perception, and is the key reason that perception is biased. This bias leads to misperception of communications, and a relatively high level of misperception of contemporary ads. Such misperception can be avoided by using simple, crisp and clear copy.

Perception stimulates thinking. However, because of cognitive consistency individuals reinterpret incoming information to match their current beliefs and behavior. As a result, advertisers cannot change entrenched attitudes and behaviors easily. They can do so only indirectly by emphasizing new bases for brand comparisons.

Memory occurs through the linking of pieces of information with other pieces. Memory can be short term or long term, implicit or explicit. The structure of memory suggests that advertisers should link their brands or brand message with many distinct cues. They should strive to frequently rehearse these links with maximum exposure for their brands, especially close to the time or place of purchase. They should also strive to make their brands prototypical of categories.

To persuade consumers, advertisers can craft information into different types of arguments. Five argument strategies are particularly relevant to advertising: comparative, refutational, inoculative, framing and supportive arguments. The effective use of these strategies depends on consumers' perception of the issues, the advertised brand and its rivals.

QUESTIONS

1. Is perception selective? Why?
2. Can communicators pass on their message to audiences easily and clearly? How and why?
3. What is the approximate level of comprehension of contemporary ads? Is it high or low? What implications does miscomprehension have for advertisers?

4. New entrants face a formidable task to convert loyal users of established brands to their products. Discuss fully why this happens. What strategies can they use to overcome this problem?

5. What is memory? What factors affect it? What implications do the structure and organization of memory have for advertising?

6. Much political advertising today is negative advertising. Is this an advantage to the candidates and voters? When should politicians break the cycle of negative advertising? How can they do so?

7. What strategies can advertisers adopt to make persuasive arguments? Explain when each of these is most relevant.

8. When should advertisers resort to comparative arguments versus supportive arguments?

9. Explain the logic of the use of inoculative and framing arguments in advertising.

10. Why did McDonald's sales decline or not return to previous levels in the late 1970s? What type of strategy did McDonald's use? What alternatives did it have?

NOTES

1. Tybout, Alice M., Bobby J. Calder, and Brian Sternthal (1981), "Using Information Processing Theory to Design Marketing Strategies," *Journal of Marketing Research*, 73–79; Greene, Bob (1978), "Worms? McDonald's isn't laughing," *Chicago Tribune*, November 11.

2. Charles King is a pseudonym. The case is based on Bishop, Jerry E. (1993), "One Man's Accident Is Shedding New Light On Human Perception," *The Wall Street Journal*, September 30, 1, 8.

3. Some authors may define perception as the process of drawing patterns from external stimuli, and comprehension as that of drawing meaning from the patterns.

4. Jacoby, Jacob, and Wayne D. Hoyer (1982), "Viewer Miscomprehension of Televised Communication: Selected Findings," *Journal of Marketing* 46 (Fall), 12–26; Jacoby, Jacob, and Wayne D. Hoyer (1990), "The Miscomprehension of Mass-Media Advertising Claims: A Re-Analysis of Benchmark Data," *Journal of Advertising Research* (June/July), 9–16.

5. Jacoby, Jacob, and Wayne D. Hoyer (1989), "The Comprehension/Miscomprehension of Print Communication: Selected Findings," *Journal of Consumer Research* 15 (March), 434–443.

6. Scott, Linda M. (1994), "Images in Advertising: The Need for a Theory of Visual Rhetoric," *Journal of Consumer Research* 21, 2 (September), 252–274.

7. Percy, Larry, and John R. Rossiter (1992), "Advertising Stimulus Effects: A Review," *Journal of Current Issues and Research in Advertising* 14, 1 (Spring), 75–90. However, there is some evidence to indicate that when subjects are involved, ample evidence is provided, and the advertiser uses a complex format such as two-sided arguments, not having a conclusion may be more effective. The reason is that the consumer processes the information himself or herself, arriving at more firmly held and enduring beliefs. See Sawyer, Alan G. and Daniel J. Howard (1991), "Effects of Omitting Conclusions in Advertisement to Involved and Uninvolved Audiences," *Journal of Marketing Research* 28 (November), 467–474.

8. Abelson, Robert P., et al. (1968), *Theories of Cognitive Consistency: A Sourcebook*, Chicago: Rand McNally.

9. Decker, Cathleen (1995), "Faith in Justice System Drops," *Los Angeles Times*, October 8, S2.

10. Ries, Al, and Jack Trout (1986), *Marketing Warfare*, New York: New American Library.

11. Stipp, David H. (1993), "Amnesia Studies Show Brain Can Be Taught at Subconscious Level," *The Wall Street Journal*, October 5, A1, A4.

12. Keller, Kevin Lane (1989), "Memory Retrieval Factors and Advertising Effectiveness," in *Memory in Advertising: The Effect of Advertising Retrieval Cues on Brand Evaluation*, Cambridge, MA: Marketing Science Institute.

13. Bishop, Jerry E. (1993), "Stroke Patients Yield Clues to Brain's Ability to Create Language," *The Wall Street Journal*, October 12, A1, A18; Stipp, "Amnesia Studies Show Brain Can Be Taught at Subconscious Level."

14. Lee, Angela (1994), "Effects of Stimulus Exposure on Information Processing: An Implicit Memory Perspective," working paper, The University of Toronto.

15. Researchers establish that recall of the name is due to the ad by comparing the spontaneous mention of a brand name in one group that has been exposed to the ad against another group that has not been exposed to the ad. Typically, ads for less common brand names may be used in such tasks.

16. Goldman, Kevin (1993), "AT&T-MCI Negative Ad Volleys Are Long-distance Risk For Both," *The Wall Street Journal*, April 14, B8; Goldman, Kevin (1993), "MCI Ad Rebukes AT&T Tactics In Bid For Market Share," *The Wall Street Journal*, December 20, B5; Fitzgerald, Kate (1995), "How AT&T Finally Found Its True Calling," *Advertising Age*, January 1, 3, 6; "AT&T's 'True'-ly Effective Campaign," *Advertising Age*, January 2, 10.

17. McGuire, William J. (1964), "Inducing Resistance to Persuasion, Some Contemporary Approaches," in *Advances in Experimental Social Psychology*, Vol. 1, L. Berkowitz, ed. New York: Academic Press.

18. Wilkie, William L., and Paul W. Farris (1975), "Comparison Advertising: Problems and Potential," *Journal of Marketing* 39 (October), 7–15; Muehling, Darrel D., Donald E. Stem, Jr., and Peter Raven (1989), "Comparative Advertising: Views from Advertisers, Agencies, Media and Policy Makers," *Journal of Advertising Research* (October/November), 38–48.

19. Petty, Ross D. (1992), *The Impact of Advertising Law on Business and Public Policy*, Westport, CT: Quorum Books.

20. Pechmann, Cornelia, and David W. Stewart (1992), "The Development of a Contingency Model of Comparative Advertising," working paper no. 90-108, Cambridge, MA: Marketing Science Institute.

21. Pechmann, Cornelia (1992), "Predicting When Two-Sided Ads Will Be More Effective than One-Sided Ads: The Role of Correlational and Correspondent Inferences," *Journal of Marketing Research* 29 (November), 441–453.

22. Gorn, Gerald J., and Charles B. Weinberg (1984), "The Impact of Comparative Advertising on Perception and Attitude: Some Positive Findings," *Journal of Consumer Research* 11 (September), 719–727.

23. Kamins, Michael A., and Henry Assael (1987), "Two-Sided versus One-Sided Appeals: A Cognitive Perspective on Argumentation, Source Derogation, and the Effect of Discomforting Trial on Belief Change," *Journal of Marketing Research* 24 (February), 29–39; Crowley, Ayn E., and Wayne D. Hoyer (1994), "An Integrative Framework for Understanding Two-sided Persuasion," *Journal of Consumer Research* 20 (March), 561–574; Gorn and Weinberg, "The Impact of Comparative Advertising on Perception and Attitude."

24. Pechmann, Cornelia (1992), "Predicting When Two-Sided Ads Will Be More Effective Than One-Sided Ads," *Journal of Marketing Research* 19, November, 441–453; Crowley, Ayn E., and Wayne D. Hoyer (1994), "An Integrating Framework."

25. Swinyard, William R. (1981), "The Interaction between Comparative Advertising and Copy Claim Variation," *Journal of Marketing Research* 18 (May), 175–186.

26. Pechmann, Cornelia, and David W. Stewart (1990), "How Direct Comparative Ads and Market Share Affect Brand Choice," *Journal of Advertising Research* (December), 47–55; Pechmann, Cornelia, and David W. Stewart (1990), "The Effects of Comparative Advertising on Attention, Memory, and Purchase Intention," *Journal of Consumer Research* 17 (September), 180–191; Gorn and Weinberg, "The Impact of Comparative Advertising on Perception and Attitude."

27. Pechmann and Stewart, "The Development of a Contigency Model of Comparative Advertising."

28. Kamins and Assael, "Two-Sided versus One-Sided Appeals."

29. Horovitz, Bruce (1993), "Pepsi Takes Offensive Against Image Fizz," *Los Angeles Times*, June 17, D1.

30. Tybout et al., "Using Information Processing Theory to Design Marketing Strategies."

31. Weigold (1993), "Negative Political Ads: Effects of Target Response and Party-Based Expectations on Candidate Evaluations," American Academy of Advertising, Montreal Conference Proceedings.

32. Shriman, David (1988), "Self-inflicted Injury: Dukakis Missed Opportunities during His Campaign; Reprieve at Polls Today?" *The Wall Street Journal*, November 8, A8.

33. Colford, Steven W. (1992), "Clinton's Forces Score with 'Tactical' Use of Ads," *Advertising Age*, August 4, 3.

34. Bither, Stewart W., Ira J. Dolich, and Elaine B. Nell (1971), "The Application of Attitude Immunization Technique in Marketing," *Journal of Marketing Research* 8 (February), 56–61; Kamins and Assael, "Two-Sided versus One-Sided Appeals."

35. Johnson, Richard D. (1987), "Making Judgment When Information Is Missing: Inferences, Biases and Framing Effects," *Acta Psychologica* 66 (October), 69–82; Durairaj, Maheshwaran, and Joan Myers-Levy (1990), "The Inference of Message Framing and Issues Involvement," *Journal of Marketing Research* 27, (August) 361–367.

7

In 1992 Warner-Lambert introduced a new campaign for e.p.t., a home pregnancy kit. The campaign consisted of three spots, in each of which a couple is shown discovering the results of a home pregnancy test they just carried out with e.p.t.[1] For example, one spot shows the experience of Helen and Nick, who are desperate for a family.

HELEN: "My body tells me I might be, but then, you know, a woman's body is kind of—you never know."

Persuasion with Emotion:
Use of Drama, Humor and Music

SUBTITLE: These are real people—not actors—about to find out if they're having a baby.

NICK: "And we're at a very nice stage to start having them. Thirty-four. I'm 34. I'm ready."

SUBTITLE: They just used new one-step e.p.t.

HELEN: "I've always been ready." (Laughter.)

(The product shows how easy it is to read the results: two red spots for pregnant, one for not.)

NICK: "The most important thing is my family and that is having a child."

HELEN: (Reading the results.) "It's negative." (See Exhibit 7-1.)

NICK: "Don't get worried, man. We're going to keep trying." (Hugging his wife as she chokes back tears.)

Source: Courtesy of Warner-Lambert Company.

In this spot, Helen and Nick want a baby but are pained to find they are not pregnant. The uncertainty of the outcome and the live enactment of this intensely personal event makes for high drama and rivets viewers' attention. While the drama proceeds, the ad emphasizes the convenience of the home pregnancy test. In another spot, Jennifer and Scott also want a baby. The ad vividly portrays their joy on reading a positive result. In a third spot, Erin and David are not ready for a baby. They are relieved to get a negative result.

▼ **EXHIBIT 7-1. Scenes from a TV ad using drama.**

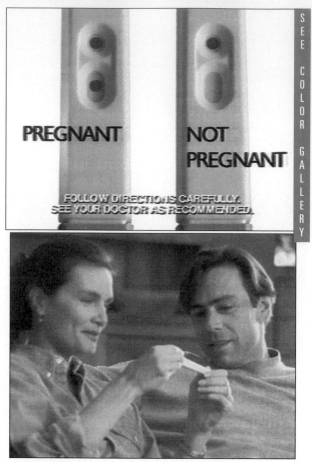

Source: Courtesy of Warner-Lambert Company.

Is the ad for e.p.t. a good one? Why? The unique feature of the ad is that most of it plays out a drama between two characters, with little explicit description of the product. The ad works by arousing emotion. What is emotion? How does it persuade? When do emotions work? The first section of the chapter answers these questions. The next two sections of the chapter then describe the major methods for arousing emotions and the major emotions that advertisers arouse in ads.

EMOTION

What Is Emotion?

Emotion is probably one of the least understood of mental activities. Indeed, until recently, advertising researchers did not focus much on emotions. Over the last decade that has begun to change, though our understanding of emotions is still fairly elementary. We can define **emotion** as a state of arousal. For example, anger, pride, affection, and sadness all imply certain levels and qualities of arousal. This arousal can be measured as specific types and levels of biochemical activity in the brain and the body; for example, alertness, sweating, pulse rate changes, or energy. Emotion is distinct from thoughts and can exist independently of rational thinking, as the example of the irrational fears of the Vietnam veteran indicates (see Exhibit 7-2). Yet, emotions are typically aroused or dissipated through a sequence of thoughts triggered by stimuli, as when a sad story causes sadness. The association of stimuli, (such as thunder and lightning) with a certain emotion (fear) takes place through conditioning. Once the link has

▼ EXHIBIT 7-2. The irrationality of emotions.

An explosion of thunder awakens the Vietnam veteran, flooding him with panic and dispatching his mind back 27 years from the safety of his Connecticut bedroom to the harrowing jungle of wartime Southeast Asia. "I am right back in Vietnam, in the middle of the monsoon season at my guard post," the man explains to his doctor. "I am sure I'll get hit in the next volley and convinced I will die. My hands are freezing, yet sweat pours from my entire body. I can't catch my breath and my heart is pounding. Suddenly I see what's left of my buddy Troy, his head on a bamboo platter, sent back to our camp by the Viet Cong. Propaganda messages are stuffed between his clenched teeth." The next bolt of lightning and clap of thunder make him jump so much that he falls to the floor.

Source: Waldholz, Michael (1993), "Study of Fear Shows Emotions Can Alter 'Wiring' of the Brain," *The Wall Street Journal*, September 29, 1.

been established, the emotion can be triggered even without thinking, and even when rational thought suggests the emotion is unwarranted. Thus emotions are powerful human energies that exist independently of reasoning.

Humans are capable of a vast array of emotions with many subtle variations. Yet a good way to understand emotions and to use them effectively is to classify them. Many researchers have tried to classify the range of emotions,[2] but as yet no classification is compelling. Exhibit 7-3 presents a simple classification based on two dimensions: **intensity of emotions** on a positive to negative continuum and the target of emotions: either object- or event-oriented.

For advertisers, the simplest and most important dimension is that between negative and positive emotions, such as joy-sadness, love-hate. Each of these emotions ranges on a continuum from very positive to very negative. For example, a person's feelings toward another individual can go from rage-anger-irritation to liking-love-passion. Tracking the intensity and direction of emotions is important because, as emotions aroused by an ad are transferred onto a brand, positive emotions may lead to favorable behavior, but negative emotions may lead to unfavorable behavior. We shall discuss this process in the next sections. Further, strong positive emotions may lead to a strong positive response, while strong negative emotions could boomerang. For example, ads that arouse excessive fear of the consequences of AIDS may lead to denial of the risk of contracting AIDS and a rejection of the advertised message.

The second dimension of the classification is the target of the emotions: what or who arouses the emotion, or to whom or to what the emotion is directed. The target can range from an object (such as a person or thing) to an event. For example, one is angry with the dog, one loves a friend; so anger and hate are targeted at objects. But one is sad about some current mishap, one hopes for some future visit; so sadness and hope are aroused by events. Based on these two dimensions, Exhibit 7-3 classifies

▼ EXHIBIT 7-3. A classification of human emotions.

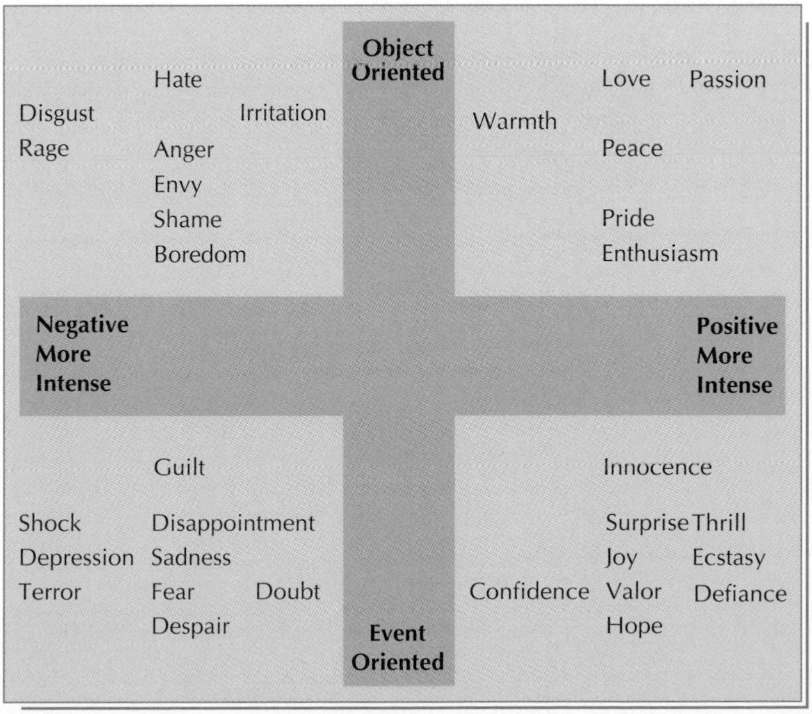

many of the common emotions in our daily lives. Note that one may not always have a precise antonym for some emotions. For example, hate is the opposite of love, but what is the opposite of anger?

How Does Emotion Persuade?

We first discuss how emotion works relative to logic and then present the advantages and disadvantages of emotion.

Emotion versus Logic A good way to understand the persuasive role of emotion is to contrast it with logic, which is the core of argument. Logic relies on the existence of some objective evidence. **Objective evidence** is data about which two or more people would come to the same conclusion. In actual fact, no piece of evidence would be strictly objective, because each person who collects, presents or receives that evidence would put his or her unique slant on it. This is due to the problem of selective attention, perception and retention of stimuli, which we discussed in prior chapters. But logic proceeds on the assumption that there is objective evidence. It then seeks to convince a viewer of this reality with the use of arguments and evidence. Viewers, especially if they do not hold that opinion, are likely to respond with counterarguments. The effort required of viewers to think through the message and the message's stimulation of counterarguments are the major problems with the use of logic.

The arousal of emotions also persuades viewers, but in a different way. The communicator uses various stimuli that are likely to stimulate emotions. These stimuli may be pictures, sounds, sequences of events and actions, or various cues. The stimuli are more interesting, easier to follow, and easier to recall than arguments. The aroused emotion then persuades the recipient to action in one of three modes: implicit, explicit or associative.[3]

In the **implicit mode,** the advertiser arouses emotions while showing rather than arguing about various features of the product. The drama of Nick and Helen trying out e.p.t. works in this way. The emotion aroused from the e.p.t. ad works implicitly. The drama enacted is so real and compelling for the viewers, that it immerses them in the action and gets viewers to empathize or *feel with* the characters.[4] At the same time the drama acquaints the viewers with the product (e.p.t.) and persuades them of the

message (convenience). Note that the persuasion is implicit: there is no direct claim of convenience. The emotion captivates the viewers and may even lower their defenses against the message.

In the **explicit mode**, the advertiser arouses emotions using stimuli to drive home a point of view. In contrast to the implicit mode, the advertiser explicitly makes the claim and may support it with arguments. However, the persuasion occurs primarily through the arousal of emotion rather than through argument. The emotions raised are of sympathy (*feeling for* or *against events or actors*) rather than of empathy as in the implicit mode.[5] An example is an antismoking ad that graphically shows the destruction of lungs by cancer, and the ultimate death of the smoker. The ad does make an explicit argument against smoking. But it achieves its goal with stimuli that arouse great fear and loathing for the consequences of smoking. The strong emotion of fear also gives the viewer impetus to make the decision to stop smoking, and the courage to sustain that resolution in the face of the discomfort from not smoking. The explicit mode can also be used with more subtle arguments and less dramatic stimuli. For example, Michelin's ads work by arousing parental attraction and caring for children, while still offering reasons to buy its tires: "A lot of tires cost less than a Michelin . . ." and "because so much is riding on your tires" (see Exhibit 7-4). Here the reasons help viewers rationalize their actions that flow from the emotion.

The **associative mode** arouses emotions with stimuli that are only tangentially related to the product. For example, a McDonald's ad shows a basketball shootout between Michael Jordan and Larry Bird, for the reward of a Big Mac. There is no explicit claim of any product benefit, while the implied theme, that basketball stars would compete for a Big Mac, is more of a spoof than a claim. In this case, the drama draws the audience into the action, allowing the pleasant emotions to be passed on to the audience. The purpose of the ad is to capture the audience's attention and to associate the McDonald's name with happy times. Thus persuasion occurs through better recall of the brand name and its association with happy times, rather than through any explicit or implicit brand attribute.

Thus emotion can be an independent means of persuasion as in the implicit mode, or it can work with argument and endorsements as in the other two

▼ **EXHIBIT 7-4.** Emotional appeal that offers a reason for action.

Source: Courtesy of J.L. Jordan III, DDB Needham Worldwide.

modes. The advantages of emotion can be best achieved when it is used alone. When combined with argument or endorsement, the advantages of emotion are not as strong, but some of its limitations are lessened. We now consider these advantages and disadvantages in detail.

Advantages of Emotion Emotion has several advantages over logic. First, emotion, especially if it relies on the implicit or associative route, does not raise the viewers' natural defenses. The emotion-arousing stimuli draw the viewers into the action and distract them from the advertiser's intention to persuade.

Second, emotion requires less effort from the viewer. When following logic, a viewer has to carefully attend to and evaluate the argument. Pictures, music or actions that arouse emotion require far less cognitive effort on the part of a viewer.

Third, emotion-arousing stimuli are generally more interesting. A plot, especially one that arises from conflict among characters, tends to be captivating. An argument that has a number of facts bound together by logic is not intrinsically or universally as interesting.

Fourth, emotion-arousing stimuli such as pictures and music are easier to recall than is factual evidence.[6] Moreover, emotions themselves may endure in memory far longer than arguments. For example, the fear of the Vietnam veteran is so strong that the stimuli of thunder and lightning immediately evoke the initial experience of 27 years back (see Exhibit 7-2).

Fifth, emotion may lead to behavior change more immediately than logic would. Consider the following examples:

▼ EXHIBIT 7-5. A battle between emotion and reason.

As ideological wars go, the dull, dry letters full of regulatory language that Gillette sends out in an effort to defend its stance aren't nearly as captivating to students as the colorful MTV-like magazines published by Peta. Based in Washington, Peta is an activist group that considers Gillette its main target. It relies heavily on teachers and students to push its ideological points.

Gillette letters invoke such rubrics as "Sections 1500.40, 1500.41, 1550.42 and 1500.135 of Volume 16 of the Code of Federal Regulations." By contrast, Peta's publications feature everything from Hollywood actress Candice Bergen's recipe for veggie burgers to "cool mystery prizes" like T-shirts and music CDs that children can win by spreading the word about Gillette's "nasty" tests on animals.

Assault by Numbers

Peta distributes maudlin pictures of sad-eyed bunnies. Gillette dispenses facts—that 98% of test animals are rodents, that between 1990 and 1994 the number of rodents used per year declined 0.3% from 2.320. Says Elizabeth Millington, a seventh-grade science teacher at the Walker Grant Middle School in Fredericksburg, Va., of her students' reactions: "That was

not interesting to them at all, all those numbers."

Peta gives youths eye-catching "Gillette Kills" stickers. Some 500 anti-Gillette "kits" are mailed to students each month. Those who ask—and about 200 do each year—can also get Peta videos of disfigured laboratory animals, including one allegedly filmed in a Gillette facility. Gillette says the shots are misleading and, in some cases, faked. Peta responds that the animals were filmed by an undercover investigator at Gillette.

Often, it is the students' teachers who first put them on to the animal-testing issue, frequently during a social-studies discussion of civil rights, or an English class on letter writing.

At the Jack Gordon Elementary School in Miami, third-grade teacher and Peta member Jean Hewitt says she wondered about exposing her eight-year-olds to photos of disfigured laboratory animals, but did anyway. "I got nervous," she confides. "I thought, 'I hope this isn't too much for them,' but they handled it."

In Petaluma, Calif., Heidi Doughty, a sixth-grade teacher, showed her class pictures of mutilated animals from a Peta magazine, telling stu-

dents, "It's kind of hard to look at these—you don't have to, but if you want to, they're here." Ms. Doughty, a vegetarian, objects to most animal killing. "Sometimes, I think it's OK if you're hunting in the woods and you're hungry, or if you respect the spirit of the animal, like the Native Americans did," she says. Her students, she adds, should "know what the animals are going through."

Gillette wrote Ms. Doughty, asking her about objective inquiry and learning. She replies, "Everything's subjective. If you look at our history book in the sixth grade, ancient history, there are only about four women in the book; it's not objective, so in everything we teach, we have to interpret." When Gillette accused Terry Brodsky, a teacher at the Hannah School in Beverly, Mass., of not presenting both sides, she shot back a terse letter: "I have no intention of teaching them 'your side.'"

Words like "vivisection" fire the students—and parents—up. In Bellefonte, Pa., Jonathan Olssen, 11, a fourth-grader, wrote Mr. Zeien, "Take the heat, or else deadmeat." His mother, Susan Straley, says she was impressed by her son's clever phrasing.

Source: Excerpted from Barbara Carton, "Gillette Faces Wrath of Children in Testing on Rats and Rabbits," *The Wall Street Journal,* September 5, 1995, A1, A6. Reprinted by permission of *The Wall Street Journal,* © 1995 Dow Jones & Company, Inc. All rights reserved worldwide.

■ PETA, an animal rights group, prepares promotional material that depicts cute animals that are subjected to ghastly experiments in Gillette's laboratories. The graphic pictures and horror stories immediately prompt children and adults to boycott Gillette's products, write to Gillette and even threaten Gillette's employees with violence. Gillette responds with figures that show that its laboratory tests are in conformation with all federal regulations, declining in number, essential for human safety and the only evidence acceptable in court. However, Peta's use of emotion is far

more effective than Gillette's resort to reason (see Exhibit 7-5).

■ Pro-life activists argue their cause by showing graphic scenes of singing children interspersed with pictures of dead fetuses. The images arouse such strong feelings of horror and guilt among viewers as to win immediate converts to the cause of opposing abortions.

■ During the 1970s, various reports and promotional material from consumer groups described how Nestlé's promotions for infant formula in developing countries led to unnecessary illness and death of infants. The (debatable) conclusion from these stories that "Nestlé's kills babies" created such an outrage in the United States that it pressured Nestlé into revamping its strategy.

Disadvantages of Emotion   Emotion also has some disadvantages relative to logic. First, the arousal of emotions, especially indirectly with a story, generally requires more time than the communication of a message through argument. As a result, there is not as much space or time to communicate the product benefits in detail as when using argument. Second, viewers could get so involved in the emotions that they may miss the central message. This situation is likely if the emotion aroused is not closely linked with the message. Third, negative emotions (fear, sorrow) may be so unpleasant that viewers may just screen out the stimuli and the message. Fourth, the arousal of strong emotions may lead some or all of the audience to feel that the communicator is exploiting a situation. Consider the following examples:

■ Benetton has often used highly emotive themes of love and compassion to advertise its clothing. One dramatic ad shows a father caring for his son dying of AIDS (see Exhibit 7-6). An AIDS service organization criticized the ad for using controversial and arresting images "to sell clothing."[7] Other ads which have similarly antagonized audiences include a bloody newborn child with an intact umbilical cord, a black woman breast-feeding a white baby and a poor child clinging to its doll.

■ Nike has adopted a theme of empowerment with the tagline "Just Do It" in an indirect campaign for its athletic shoes. One ad shows a gripping dialogue in which inner-city youth discuss the lack of attention from their fathers. Some commentators criticized the ad for perpetuating myths about the problems of inner-city youth, while urging the same youth to spend scarce dollars on expensive fashionable shoes.

■ Most laundry products are sold using logic and evidence. However, an ad for Stain Stick from Spray 'n Wash shows a very touching scene of a mother talking about her Down's syndrome child, who is shown at play in a picture of innocence. The ad was criticized for exploiting the helplessness and innocence of the child to communicate an unrelated message.[8]

What makes an ad appear to exploit people's emotions? The absence of a link between the emotion-arousing stimulus and the message is probably the cause of the appearance of exploitation. There is no apparent link between Benetton's clothes and the themes in its ad. The same can be said for Stain Stick and Down's syndrome. A child character with Down's syndrome may have been appropriate to raise funds for or increase people's sensitivity to special children. The execution of Nike's ad seems better linked to its message. However, Nike has a problem because some social workers believe inner-city youth already tend to invest too much in athletic shoes designed in the latest

▼ **EXHIBIT 7-6.** A controversial Benetton ad.

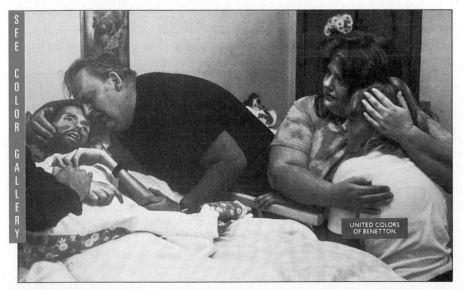

Source: Courtesy of United Colors of Benetton.

▼ EXHIBIT 7-7. Foote Cone and Belding (FCB) classification of products.

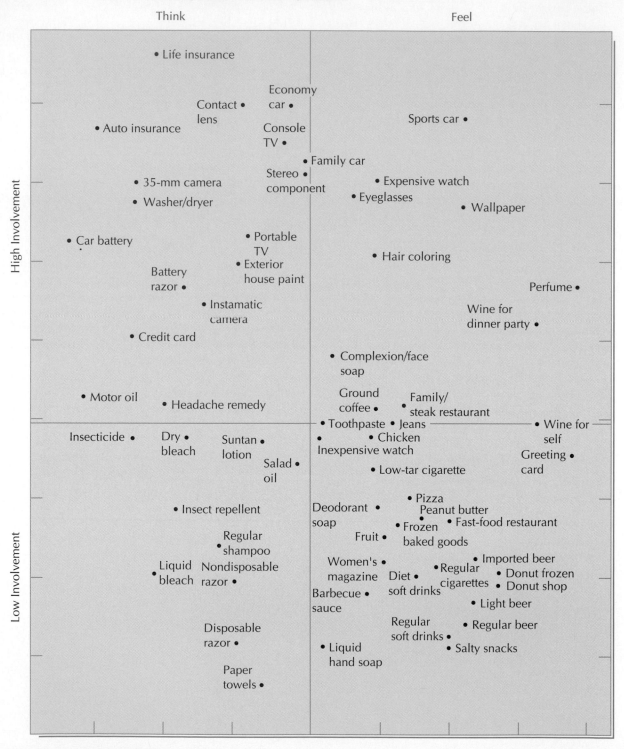

Source: Ratchford, Brian T. (1987), "New Insights About the FCB Grid," *Journal of Advertising Research* 27, 4 (August/September), 31. © 1987 by the Advertising Research Foundation.

fashion. The e.p.t. ad may also prompt some people to feel that the firm is invading the privacy of the couple and the child who may have been conceived. For that reason Warner-Lambert may not have shown a fourth combination in which a couple who do not want a baby find they are pregnant; the latter may have raised too many sensitive issues and detracted from e.p.t.

In contrast, the Michelin ads are so appealing because the link between stimulus and message is clear and strong. In general, ads that have a better link with the brand or the message are likely to be more effective.[9] Emotion that uses the implicit or explicit mode tends to have a stronger and more explicit link than that which uses the associative mode.

When Do Emotions Work?

The prior discussion suggests that neither logic nor emotion is universally superior. Each has advantages and disadvantages that indicate times when each may preferably be used. When should one use emotion rather than logic? Three factors can be used to answer this question in the context of purchase behavior: the audience's involvement in the purchase decision, the attributes of the product being purchased and the mood of the audience.

Audience Involvement and Product Attributes When an audience is *involved* in a purchase decision, it has the motivation and the ability to process messages about that decision. The elaboration likelihood model (see Chapter 4) suggests that arguments should be used when an audience has the motivation and the ability to process them. In such a situation the audience is looking for relevant information (motivation) and has the intelligence, time and expertise (ability) to process it. The logical use of arguments and evidence is likely to be effective. On the other hand, emotion may be effective when an audience lacks the motivation or the ability to process the message.

Product attributes may be classified as either feeling or thinking. **Feeling attributes** are those that are preference-based, not reason-based, on which two or more individuals could reasonably differ. Examples of such attributes are taste, flavor, style or design. Examples of products purchased primarily on these criteria are perfumes, wines, greeting cards or sports cars. In contrast, **thinking attributes** are those that are based on reason, on which consumers are likely to agree. Examples of such attributes are perfor-

mance, reliability, quality or fit. Products where these attributes are important are laundry detergent, insect repellent, a 35-mm camera or a car battery.

Using these criteria, audience involvement and product attributes, one study classifies products on a two-by-two matrix (see Exhibit 7-7).[10] Emotional appeals are preferable in the right-hand side of the matrix, especially in the top right quadrant. Rational appeals seem preferable in the left-hand side of the matrix, especially in the top left quadrant. Many ads support this classification (see Exhibit 7-8).

However, these two criteria are not necessarily absolute; the strategy of competitors may also affect the decision of a rational versus an emotional appeal. If all the competition uses emotional appeals, then a rational appeal may stand out, grab attention and be especially effective. Conversely, if the competition is using primarily a cerebral approach of argument and logic, then an emotional appeal may be effective. The ad in Exhibit 7-9 tries to make an emotional appeal for an appliance, in which category rational appeals are the norm.

Mood of the Audience **Mood** can be defined as a transitory, generalized emotional state that is not directed at any particular object or activity. Moods can be individual based or context based. The former are unique to each individual based on the experiences and personality of that individual prior to the advertising. Context-based moods are those that are stimulated by the environment of the ad and can be common to all individuals facing that environment. For example, horror when viewing a news report about the bombing of the federal building in Oklahoma would be context induced, which could then affect all individuals who view an ad that follows that news item.

Several studies indicate that, in general, positive moods are associated with more persuasion and positive attitudes toward the ad and the brand. On the other hand, negative moods are associated with less persuasion and more negative attitudes toward the brand.[11] Thus the mood of the subject, whether pre-existing or aroused by the ad or the program, can affect the response to the ad. A more important question is whether a subject's mood *moderates* the effectiveness of positive and negative appeals. Studies have found support for some moderating effect.

For example, one study explored whether positive or negative moods interact with positive or negative

▼ EXHIBIT 7-8. **Rational and emotional appeals.**

Rational appeal for a low-involvement "thinking" product

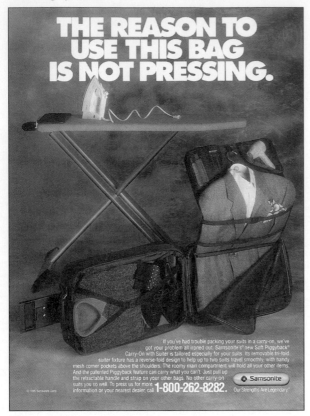

Source: Courtesy of Samsonite ® Corp.

Emotional appeal for a high-involvement "feeling" product

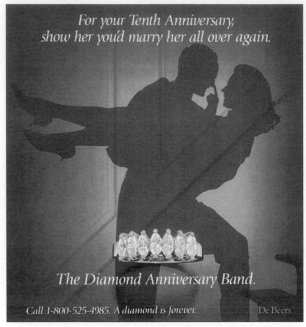

Source: Courtesy of DeBeers Consolidated Mines, Ltd.

appeals. The study argued that if an ad arouses positive emotions and the viewer is in a positive mood, then response to the message will be positive. The reason is that the harmony of positive states would enable the viewer to better empathize with the ad and accept the message. Similarly, a negative effect would probably occur for negative moods and emotions. In contrast, if the viewer is in a negative mood and the ad arouses a positive mood, then a viewer is unlikely to respond positively. For example, a viewer saddened by a news report of starvation in battle-scarred Bosnia is unlikely to identify with a playful set of characters espousing the merits of a beer.

Another study found support for a similar effect.[12] The study manipulated moods by having subjects find a dime (positive mood of a happy feeling) or break the experimenter's camera (negative mood of a guilty feeling). The study found that a positive mood increased donating to a charity (positive action) but only when the message suggested a positive reason such as the desirability of helping. On the other hand, the negative mood increased donating to a charity only when the message stressed a relative negative, such as the obligation to help. Thus compliance depends on the matching of message content (desirability of helping or obligation) to context-induced mood (joy or guilt).

These results indicate the importance of considering the emotional state of the recipient and the environment when choosing the appeal or content of an ad.

METHODS OF AROUSING EMOTIONS

How can advertisers arouse emotions? The following subsections describe three methods of arousing emotions that are particularly relevant to advertisers: drama, humor and music. Drama itself is closely related to two other forms of communication, story and demonstration, which will also be covered.

▶ **EXHIBIT 7-9.** Emotional appeal for a kitchen appliance.

*B*urn the cookbooks. Make it up as you go along.

There is something about the look of stainless steel that compels you to create, to experiment, to discover the chef inside you. Now you can have that professional look, uniquely accented with white or black. And it's very affordable: standard suite of refrigerator, range and dishwasher accented with black costs less than $4000.* They're also available with exclusive features: the range has a separate warming drawer below the large self-cleaning oven. The refrigerator has an ice and water filter to remove impurities. And the dishwasher's wash system can handle even a dinner party's worth of dishes without prerinsing. The Frigidaire Gallery Professional Series™ freestanding and built-in appliances. You will not simply leave this kitchen; you will emerge triumphant. Call 1-800-FRIGIDAIRE or http://www.frigidaire.com

FRIGIDAIRE GALLERY PROFESSIONAL SERIES

THE LOOK OF BETTER PERFORMANCE

FRIGIDAIRE

Source: Courtesy of Frigidaire Company.

167

Drama

Consider the previous ad for e.p.t. and one for a rival brand QTest which simply explains the product's attributes. Which of these two ads would be more appealing? The e.p.t. ad is a lot more dramatic, and by that measure, more interesting and captivating. Indeed, one of the most effective ways of arousing emotions is by drama. What exactly is drama? One way to understand the role of drama is to relate it to argument, demonstration and story.[13] Consider the following examples, which show how the same benefit can be communicated differently by each of these forms of communication:

- *Argument:* An ad in which a narrator states: "Determining if you are pregnant is an intensely personal matter. With e.p.t. testing kit you can determine if you are pregnant quickly and conveniently in the privacy of your home."
- *Demonstration:* An ad in which a nurse shows how you can use the inexpensive e.p.t. testing kit to determine if you are pregnant, conveniently and privately at home.
- *Story:* The story of the e.p.t. ad told by a narrator, who also highlights the product benefits.
- *Drama:* The e.p.t. ad already described.

These examples highlight the similarities and differences between these four forms of communication. Argument relies primarily on logic. Drama is the most captivating form and relies primarily on emotion and little on logic. Argument holds the viewer apart, and presents him or her with the evidence. Drama draws the viewer into the action with the characters who are locked in a plot. When successful, argument persuades a viewer by the force of the logic and the weight of the evidence; feeling is not necessary and may even be perceived as tainting the "objectivity" of the evidence. In contrast, when a drama is successful, a viewer gets lost in the plot and identifies with the feelings of the characters. Story and demonstration lie in between. This distinction between argument and drama explains the different mechanisms by which each is effective. Across these four forms of persuasion, there is a trade-off between evidence and emotion. As a communicator goes from argument, to story, to demonstration and to drama, he or she relies less on logic and more on emotions.

Further analysis reveals that the structure of these four forms of communication depends on their use of three components: narrative, plot and characters (see Exhibit 7-10).[14] At one extreme, argument has narrative but no plot or character. At the other extreme, drama has plot and character but no narrative. Story and demonstration lie in between. What exactly is meant by narrative, character and plot in a promotion context?

Character implies the presence of people whom the viewers observe in the scene (such as Nick and Helen in the e.p.t. ad). To be effective characters do not need to be real; but they need to be distinct, consistent and plausible. Distinct characters stand out from the background. Consistent characters behave in a similar way through all the events, both big ones and small ones. Plausible characters are those who resemble persons that the audience would have experienced at one time or another in the real world. The appeal of Nick and Helen is that they are ordinary people whom viewers feel they "know." Characters need not only be people. Animals and objects can also be construed as characters. In the e.p.t. ad, the brand itself serves as a silent key character. The power of drama and story over demonstration and argument is that they make viewers identify with the characters and share their feelings. So why do advertisers use demonstration? Demonstration is less time consuming than story or drama because it does not develop characters. It can be an effective form of communication, when an advertiser wants to show some unique characteristic of the product.

Plot implies a sequence in the action that leads to increasing tension due to some unknown outcome,

▼ **EXHIBIT 7-10.** Use of components by forms of communication.

	COMPONENTS		
Communication Forms	Narrative	Plot	Character
Argument	Yes	No	No
Demonstration	Yes	Yes	No
Story	Yes	Yes	Yes
Drama	No	Yes	Yes

Source: Deighton, John, Daniel Romer, and Josh McQueen (1989), "Using Drama to Persuade," *Journal of Consumer Research* 16 (December), 1989, 335–343. Copyright 1989 The University of Chicago Press.

which is finally resolved. The strength of a plot depends on how much tension builds up, how surprising the solution is, and whether the solution comes from the nature of the characters, rather than from some external unrelated event. In the e.p.t. ad, the tension comes from the uncertainty of knowing if the couple is pregnant given they so much want a baby. The solution comes from the technological advance of the third character, e.p.t. The surprise comes from the quick, clear and instantaneous result. The power of drama, story and demonstration over argument is that they contain a plot that captures the attention of the viewers and draws them to experience the emotions of the events or characters. The nature of the outcome itself is by no means neutral. A pleasant outcome leaves an audience happy, while an unpleasant outcome leaves an audience sad. These feelings can transfer to the brand and affect the acceptance of the message as we will discuss shortly. So, choosing an appropriate outcome is also important. But far more important is the plausibility of the outcome. The home pregnancy kit can indeed tell pregnancy more reliably than a woman's feeling at that early stage. And more important than our sadness at the outcome is our gratitude for the product that can give such a solution so easily and privately.

Narrative, or storytelling, implies the presence of some spokesperson who describes or interprets the action. The subtitles in the e.p.t. ad serve as the narrative. Thus narrative may exist along with characters. However, the narrator is a third party who prevents the viewer from becoming fully involved in the plot. The narrator may also limit the emotional impact by doing some of the thinking for the viewer. When not restricted by the narrative, viewers may better connect the plot with their own experiences, and draw more implications, enhancing the impact of the ad. Why then do ads contain a narrator? One reason is efficiency. A narrator can, in a few seconds, provide the background for the plot and bring the viewers up to speed with the situation. Having characters detail the background of the plot would take much longer than the time most ads command. Another reason is precision. The narrator can succinctly provide the link between the plot or characters and the product being advertised, precisely defining the message that the advertiser wants to communicate.

If an advertiser wants to arouse strong emotions, then drama, story and demonstration may be the most effective means, in that order. However, humor and music are two other means of arousing less strong emotions.

Humor

In his 1993 world tour, Michael Jackson, at that time a Pepsi spokesman, was hit by allegations of child molestation. During the controversy, Jackson excused himself from some performances in Thailand, saying that he was dehydrated. Shortly thereafter, Coke came up with an ad in English-language newspapers in Bangkok with a simple question and answer: "Dehydrated? There's always Coke."[15]

Cereal boxes frequently carry promotions. In late 1993, Kellogg's Crispix ran a joint promotion with the NBC *Tonight Show* featuring Jay Leno. The promotion offered an autographed T-shirt of Jay Leno for $8.99 and two proofs of purchase of Crispix. The package also carried some of Leno's jokes, including: "You know it's cold in Los Angeles when people in Beverly Hills are seen wearing two sweaters tied around their neck."

Consider the above two promotions as well as the ad in Exhibit 7-11. Are they appealing? Why?

Elements of Humor Humor is an elusive entity. It is easy to spot and enjoy, often triggering instantaneous laughter. But it is difficult to analyze, and may evaporate on analysis. **Humor** may be defined as painless incongruity. The essential element of humor is the incongruity between two elements that the communicator brings together. The response from the audience is first one of surprise because the unison of the two elements is unexpected and unusual. The incongruity in humor can arise from incongruous events (cold weather in Los Angeles, Jackson's dehydration and endorsement of Pepsi), incongruous images (Beverly Hills residents wearing two sweaters around their necks), a **pun** or word with two meanings (". . . anyone can *see* that" in the tagline in Exhibit 7-11) or an incongruous word and picture. The term **resonance** refers to this last form of humor; it is used because the play of word and picture creates an echo or multiplication of meaning.[16] Resonance is a form of humor that probably occurs more often in advertising than in literature. Indeed,

▼ EXHIBIT 7-11. Ad that uses humor and resonance.

"Before I'll ride with a drunk, I'll drive myself." —Stevie Wonder

Driving after drinking, or riding with a driver who's been drinking, is a big mistake. Anyone can see that.

Source: Permission granted by Reader's Digest Foundation.

some authors consider resonance to be advertising's unique contribution to literary form.[17]

However, the issue of painlessness is also critical in humor, because what is painless to one group is painful to another. Coke's ad can offend Jackson fans, loyal Pepsi drinkers or athletes who often suffer from dehydration. That is why Coke withdrew the ad after complaints of insensitivity from Pepsi. Ethnic jokes, which at one time were common in advertising, are another case. They poke fun at a minority by exaggerating the latter's known idiosyncrasies. The jokes may entertain a majority but are painful to that ethnic group, and to those who empathize with the group. For advertisers, the incongruity has to be painless not only to the majority, but

to viewers nationally and internationally. This is a communication challenge. The Leno joke on Beverly Hills dress style may offend, but only a very small minority and that too only mildly. So Kellogg could adopt it in its promotion without much risk.

If the incongruity causes no pain to the audience, then the surprise leads to entertainment. Consider the Coke ad in the previous example. Many commentators doubted that Jackson's excuse of dehydration was genuine. (Indeed some weeks later he canceled his tour, citing drug addiction.) Coke's ad has humor and bite. It brings out the incongruity in the excuse by suggesting that an endorser of Pepsi should not suffer from dehydration, unless Pepsi is not a good thirst quencher—in which case, there's always Coke.

We need to differentiate slapstick humor from sophisticated humor. **Slapstick humor** uses a simple means to incongruity, typically by putting together two incongruous images. This approach creates little tension and requires minimal thought to appreciate. So it appeals to the less sophisticated. Sophisticated humor first builds an expectation of a certain meaning, then surprises by providing an unexpected meaning that fits equally well. The incongruity in meanings requires mental effort to resolve while the surprise and mental effort increase the pleasure. For example, an ad for visiting England opens with the headline: "ENGLAND, known for its rock groups" but shows a picture of Stonehenge. The phrase "rock groups" leads the reader to expect the popular meaning of music group. England has had some famous rock music groups, but they are no longer popular, and certainly not on exhibition. But then the picture surprises by presenting the image of the Stonehenge rocks, a tourist attraction for which England is more famous. Leno builds anticipation by suggesting two sweaters to protect against the cold in what is known to be a warm climate, then surprises by suggesting that they are worn around the neck; this image is plausible and also mocks the fashion-conscious Beverly Hills lifestyle.

Two marketing professors, Edward McQuarrie and David Mick, studied 1,286 full-page print ads in the 20 best-selling magazines, sampling one issue per magazine in a 6-month period of 1990–1991.[18] Exhibit 7-12 lists examples of resonant ads that they found. What are the key elements in each ad that are humorous? How effective would they have been with and without the humor?

▼ **EXHIBIT 7-12.** Examples of resonance in magazine ads.

Magazine	Advertiser	Headline	Visual
Family Circle	Sorel boots	It's Haute as Hell in Aspen	Boots in snow
Business Week	Boeing	This Man's Looking for Trouble	Manager beside AWAC's plane
Forbes	Embassy Suites	This Year, We're Unwrapping Suites by the Dozen	Chocolate kisses with hotel names/locations underneath each
Cosmopolitan	Equalizer driving gloves	The Right Stuffers	Gloves in a Christmas stocking
Better Homes and Gardens	Corelle tableware	Fashion Plates	Dinner plates' different designs
Money	Toyota auto parts	Our Lifetime Guarantee May Come as a Shock	Man holding a shock absorber
U.S. News & World Report	FTD Florists	Avoid the Holiday Whirlwind— Send a Hurricane	Candle in a hurricane lamp enclosure with bouquet
GQ	Daniel Craig Fine	Forget-Me-Knots	Men's ties arranged as a knot
Good Housekeeping	Huggies disposable training pants	Start Toilet Training on the Right Foot	Child standing on right foot putting on training pants
Car and Driver	Bucks filter cigarettes	Heard of These?	Cigarette pack with picture of stag
Golf Digest	Mitsubishi Diamond Tel Cellular	Invest in Diamonds	Picture of Diamond Tel portable cellular phone
Time	AT&T National Pro Am Tournament	Come See the Shooting Stars	Picture of golfer in midswing
Woman's Day	Bounce fabric softener	Is There Something Creeping Up Behind You?	Woman's dress bunched up in back of legs because of static cling
Inc.	Westin Resorts	We Also Have Resorts for Those Who Don't Want to Lie in the Sand	Picture of golf green with sand traps
People	ASICS athletic shoes	We Believe Women Should Be Running the Country	Woman jogging in rural surroundings
Playboy	J&B Scotch	Meet Over a J&B	Beef cattle standing on top of letters "J&B"
Sports Illustrated	Pepsi	This Year, Hit the Beach Topless	Crumpled cap to a Pepsi bottle lying on sand
Newsweek	Isuzu	Dirt, Cheap	Picture of four-wheel-drive vehicle on a dirt road
Fortune	Hitachi Metals	How We Control What You See On Television	Rays of light passing through shadow mask of a TV monitor
Glamour	Estée Lauder makeup pencils	Get the Point, Automatically	Makeup pencils with points exposed

Source: McQuarrie, Edward F., and David Glen Mick (1992), "On Resonance: A Critical Pluralistic Inquiry into Advertising Rhetoric," *Journal of Consumer Research* 19 (September), 1992, 180–197. Copyright 1992 The University of Chicago Press.

Role of Humor Some advertising experts have cautioned against humor. For example, Claude Hopkins, a "grandfather" of modern advertising, asserted that "frivolity has no place in advertising."[19] At one time authors advised against humor in ads. However, advertisers continue to use humor in advertising. Reports indicate that humor was used in 36 percent of TV ads in the United Kingdom, and in 24 percent of TV ads, 31 percent of radio ads and 15 percent of magazine ads in the United States.[20] Why do advertisers use humor? How does humor work?

Many factors contribute to humor's effectiveness. First, humor relaxes an audience. Public speakers often start their talks with a joke. At the start, tension is high as the audience and speakers do not know what to expect of each other. Humor tends to break the ice and establish a bond between communicator and audience.

Second, by arousing feelings of surprise and entertainment, humor puts the audience in a pleasant mood, which can transfer to the brand, or ease the acceptance of the message.

Third, humor may also help to attract or retain attention. In the midst of many hard-sell argumentative ads, or others with routine appeals, humor can provide a welcome diversion. For example, the line in a Pepsi ad, "This summer hit the beaches topless," conjures up a reckless suggestion of abandonment and pleasure. The viewer is prompted to read further to figure out the reason for such a wild suggestion. A capless Pepsi bottle provides a surprising but pleasing resolution to the tension. Further, if the humor is memorable, it may be repeated to others who had not seen the ad, increasing repetition, exposure and recall of the message and the brand.

Fourth, as with drama and story, humor may also serve as a digression that distracts the viewer's attention and reduces his or her resistance to the central message. The resistance arises from counterarguments to any direct appeal by argument. For example, a (hypothetical) headline for a strawberry shortcake that reads "rich and tasty," besides being bland, may immediately raise an objection about its bad health effects. However, the actual headline "berried treasure" (Exhibit 7-13) prompts the reader to resolve the incongruity between the apparently misspelled headline and the picture of the strawberry cake.[21] The viewer may then decode the pun on the word *berry* for bury, and go further and substitute the meaning of the cake being a rare, rich reward, as in a treasure hunt.

Fifth, various forms of humor provide a small intellectual puzzle. The audience has to make an effort to solve the tension created by the double meaning as in the two examples above. The solution leads to satisfaction, which may transfer to the brand. Also, the mental effort, albeit small, is likely to help assimilation and recall of the message, or at least the brand name. In a laboratory and field experiment, the McQuarrie and Mick study found support for this proposition.[22]

Thus, humor has several factors in its favor. However, indiscriminate use of humor may do more to hinder than help the acceptance of the message. Three factors need to be kept in mind to use humor

▼ **EXHIBIT 7-13.** Ad that uses resonance.

Source: ® Reddi-wip is a registered trademark of Beatrice Cheese, Inc.

▼ **EXHIBIT 7-14.** Emotions aroused by musical elements.

| Musical Element | EMOTIONAL EXPRESSION | | | | | | | | |
	Serious	Sad	Sentimental	Serene	Humorous	Happy	Excited	Majestic	Frightened
Mode	Major	Minor	Minor	Major	Major	Major	Major	Major	Minor
Tempo	Slow	Slow	Slow	Slow	Fast	Fast	Fast	Medium	Slow
Pitch	Low	Low	Medium	Medium	High	High	Medium	Medium	Low
Rhythm	Firm	Firm	Flowing	Flowing	Flowing	Flowing	Uneven	Firm	Uneven
Harmony	Consonant	Dissonant	Consonant	Consonant	Consonant	Consonant	Dissonant	Dissonant	Dissonant
Volume	Medium	Soft	Soft	Soft	Medium	Medium	Loud	Loud	Varied

Source: Developed primarily from Hevner (1937), Kinnear (1959), and Vinovich (1975) with additional information from Gundlach (1935), Sherer and Oshinsky (1977), Watson (1942), and Wedlin (1972). Bruner, Gordon C. II (1990), "Music, Mood and Marketing," *Journal of Marketing* 54, 4 (October), 94–104.

effectively. First, humor has to be developed fairly precisely to be appropriate. While it may be difficult to think of an excessively funny ad, what is more likely is one in which the humor is obscure, too simple (slapstick), unbelievable, unrelated to the message or offensive to one group in the audience.[23] Second, advertisers need to take into account the emotional context of the audience. In a very serious or tense moment, a mild form of humor may provoke much joy; on a sad or sorrowful occasion, the same humor may be offensive. Third, the social context of humor can affect its enjoyment. Research indicates that humor is more funny when it occurs in a string of humorous episodes than when it occurs alone. Also, the sight or sound of a social group enjoying jokes increases an individual's enjoyment of the same.[24] Thus humor during programs such as major sporting events, which are generally viewed in groups, is likely to be specially enjoyed, and probably more effective than at other times.

Music

"A Diet Coke spot opens with a Radio City premiere with a cast of hundreds of celebrities. The Rockettes dance around a gargantuan Diet Coke while waiters serve samples on silver trays. There is no audio message, except the jingle. The lyrics themselves are the kind of advertising message that has meaning only for a brand manager:

'Introducing Diet Coke!

You're gonna love it just for the taste of it.

. . .

. . .

Just for the taste of it,

Diet Coke.'

What is persuasive in this commercial is not the self-congratulatory verbals. What is persuasive is the crowd of celebrities and the rhythmic movement of the repeated rising tones in the jingle."[25]

Music can grab attention, as a sudden burst of harmony; it can linger in memory as a catchy jingle. But the most important and common use of music is to establish mood or arouse emotions. Examples include music played at important life occasions, at religious and spiritual events, during various forms of entertainment and for numerous forms of promotion. The use of music for the latter purpose is pervasive. One study of 1,000 TV commercials found that music was present in 42 percent of the ads. It explicitly carried the message in 12 percent, as in the Diet Coke ad just described.[26]

The Effects of Music on Emotions and Behavior What is music? How does it affect our emotions? There is a vast variety of music originating in different countries, cultures, epochs and styles. Yet all of these different forms of music are formed by permutations and combinations of three important elements: pitch, timing and texture.[27] **Pitch** is the organization of notes in a musical piece. **Timing** is the temporal organization of the components of the piece. **Texture** describes the qualitative richness of the musical piece. These components are important because research has shown that each of them impacts mood and emotions in different ways.

What Emotions Does Music Arouse? Research in music, anthropology and other disciplines has tried to calibrate the precise emotions aroused by the different components of music. Some results may be commonly known. For example, a sentimental piece tends to be slow, flowing and soft; a triumphant piece tends to be loud and fast. What is less well known is that the elements of music may be associated with specific emotions. Exhibit 7-14 and Exhibit 7-15 summarize some findings from a review of past research.[28] For example, a promoter wishing to amplify the serenity of a scene should choose music that is slow, flowing and soft as one may intuitively suggest, but also has medium pitch, consonant harmony and a major mode.[29] Such music would differ from sentimental music in only one important way; sentimental music would preferably be in minor mode, while serene music would be in major mode. Musicians who create music for a promoter probably do so on the basis of aesthetics and fit with the context of the ad. However, Exhibits 7-14 and 7-15 can be a valuable guide for managers to ensure that the music meets their goals. In addition, the exhibits list precise emotional expressions that go with various musical components.

What Behaviors Does Music Affect?

Music at the point of purchase is very common, and is often chosen to establish special moods. However, the effects of music on behavior have not been as well researched as those on emotions. One study found that slow background music in a restaurant increased the average time spent in the restaurant to 56 minutes relative to 45 minutes when fast music was played. The patrons also spent 36 percent more on drinks with slow music rather than fast music ($30 instead of $22).[30] The authors argued that slow music was more relaxing and encouraged a more leisurely pace. But because the amount of food that can be consumed is lim-ited by physical and etiquette constraints, the patrons spent more on drinks. This study indicates that one component of music, tempo, can affect behavior. It would be interesting to find out if the other components of music also affect behavior.

Are The Effects of Music in Humans Instinctive or Learned?

Research on this issue has not come to a consensus. The answer is probably both, with some very basic aspects being instinctive and subtle aspects learned within the context of a culture or subculture. For example, sudden, loud sounds tend to frighten newborn animals and humans even if they have no prior experience of them.[31] This

▼ **EXHIBIT 7-15.** Emotional expressions in music.

Time-related Expressions

1. Duple rhythms produce a rigid and controlled expression in comparison with triple rhythms, which are more relaxed or abandoned.
2. The faster the tempo, the more animation and happiness is expressed.
3. Even, rhythmic movement can represent the unimpeded flow of some feeling; dotted, jerky, uneven rhythms produce more complex expressions.
4. Firm rhythms suggest a serious mood whereas smooth-flowing rhythms are more playful.
5. Staccato (sharp, broken) rhythm gives more emphasis to a passage than legato (smooth) rhythm.

Pitch-related Expressions

1. "Up" and "down" in pitch not only correspond to up and down in the physical world, but can also imply "out-and-in" as well as "away-and-back," respectively.
2. Rising and falling pitch can convey a growing or diminishing intensity in a given emotional context.
3. Songs in higher keys are generally considered to be happier than songs in lower keys.
4. Music in the major mode expresses more animated and positive feelings than music in the minor mode.
5. Complex harmonies are more agitated and sad than simple harmonies, which are more serene and happy.

Texture-related Expressions

1. Loudness can suggest animation or proximity whereas low volume implies tranquillity or distance.
2. Crescendo (soft to loud) expresses an increase in force whereas diminuendo (loud to soft) suggests a decrease in power.
3. The timbre of brass instruments conveys a feeling of cold, hard force whereas reed instruments produce a lonely, melancholy expression.

Source: Bruner, Gordon C. II (1990), "Music, Mood and Marketing," *Journal of Marketing* 54, 4 (October), 94–104. Reprinted with permission of the American Marketing Association.

response may be one that evolved to protect the species. Also, the findings listed in Exhibits 7-14 and 7-15 may hold across cultures, suggesting some universal human responses to music.[32] At the same time some researchers argue strongly that music is a rich and complex form of human expression that derives its meaning only from a culture. According to this view, one has to "learn" to appreciate music and to associate various meanings and emotions with it.[33] Further, because familiar forms of music tend to be associated with specific stories, events and emotions (as with pop songs, the national anthem), they may each evoke a set of unique meanings and emotions. For example, Christmas carols put us in a Christmas mood, which people may associate with happy holidays, joyful gifts, relaxing winter activities, and warm family time.

The cultural interpretation of music has two important implications for promoters. First, the findings of Exhibits 7-14 and 7-15 must be applied carefully in an international context, because most of them have been derived with studies in Western culture. Second, a new piece may be better than a well-known piece for specific ads. A well-known piece may arouse instant recognition, liking and emotions, but some of these emotions may not be consistent with the promoter's goals. An original composition may not have instant appeal or recall, but careful design and repetition in a campaign may render it an effective means to arouse strong emotions and loyalty to a brand. For example, the rhythm of the Diet Coke ad builds an audience's involvement and expectation, while the repetition of lyrics and melody over many exposures builds familiarity and liking for ad and brand. On the other hand, using popular music may be ideal in some circumstances. For example, what better music can a store play during the pre-Christmas shopping season than carols? At other times, stores may use lighter versions of old songs to provide a familiar, relaxed atmosphere for shopping.

When Are the Effects of Music Likely to Be Most Important? As suggested by the elaboration likelihood model the effect of music is likely to be strongest when viewers are using a peripheral route of persuasion based on cues. Music could still help when a central route is being used, but in the latter situation the information and the strength of the argument are likely to be the more important influences.

HARNESSING SPECIFIC EMOTIONS

Advertisers arouse some emotions more often than others, either intentionally as part of their strategy, or unintentionally due to the product, execution or timing of the ad. These emotions include irritation, warmth, fear and inspiration. We need to understand the potential energy in these common and important emotions.

Irritation

A Stayfree ad opens with two professional models running to catch a taxi. The taxi driver turns out to be an attractive female. Once in the taxi, the established model tells the younger model and the taxi driver in detail about Stayfree maxi pads. She then pulls out a package to demonstrate the product attributes.

A Tylenol ad shows a mother in obvious discomfort describing the onset of a headache. She points to where it starts and where it moves. She claims that her two boys are usually the headache cause and she was mean to them. She then takes Tylenol and enjoys quick relief from her symptoms.[34]

Many viewers may find these ads irritating. That is a common emotion aroused by advertising today. One cause for irritation may be that much advertising today is intrusive. People receive ads through their TV, radio, newspapers, magazines, mail and phone often when they do not expect, need or want them. But even then advertising need not be irritating; it could be stimulating, entertaining and enjoyable. The key questions we need to address are: Why are ads like the ones above irritating? Is irritating advertising less effective? How common is irritation?

Level of Irritation At least two studies, one around 1964 and the other around 1985, examined the issue of irritation in advertising.[35] The results from both studies are similar. The latter study surveyed the response of 1,000 households to 524 prime-time TV commercials. The study found that on average 6 percent of the respondents rated as irritating the commercials that they recognized. In comparison, the rating for silly was 7 percent, for amusing 13 percent and for informative 18 percent. Thus overall, irritation does not seem to be a dominant emotion aroused by ads. However, the cause for irritation was not random, and came from certain distinct features of the ad.

Causes of Irritation Exhibit 7-16 shows the mean rating of irritation by type of ad and product category. Two points are evident in this exhibit. First, irritation is strongly influenced by product category. Notice especially that ads for products for feminine hygiene, hemorrhoids and laxatives score consistently higher on irritation. Second, there is a difference within categories by brand and by execution of the same brand. For example, Massengill scores 36 (the percentage of respondents that find the ad irritating), Stayfree scores 33, while New Freedom scores 22. Thus proper execution can mitigate the irritation that would normally be aroused by a product, while poor execution may increase it.

The authors of the study analyzed the ads' content to find out what specific execution factors were responsible for irritation. They identified nine factors that are organized into three groups: illustration, plot and characterization.

- *Illustration:* The ad explicitly shows the picture, use or effect of a sensitive product (such as the absorptive power of Stayfree). The ad shows a graphic detailed demonstration of discomfort (such as pain from hemorrhoids or headaches).
- *Plot:* The situation in the ad is contrived, phony, unbelievable or overdramatized (the quick response with Tylenol). The tension from the plot is uncomfortable (as from two professional women discussing Stayfree). The ad includes a suggestive scene.

- *Characterization:* The ad "puts down" a character in terms of appearance, knowledge or sophistication (mother berates a child for choosing a toothpaste on a wrong criterion, taste). The ad involves a threat to an important relationship such as parent-child, husband-wife or close friend (as when a wife threatens to quit a husband's bed

▼ **EXHIBIT 7-16.** Degree of consumer irritation with commercials.

Category	Brand	Sample Size	Consumers Finding Ads Irritating
Feminine hygiene	Massengill	278	36%
	Stayfree	367	33
	Kotex	305	30
	Kotex	294	29
	Stayfree	353	29
	OB tampons	348	27
	Tampax	330	26
	New Freedom	339	<u>22</u>
	Average		29%
Hemorrhoid & laxative	Preparation H	323	20%
	Phillips	326	19
	Phillips	279	17
	Preparation H	356	<u>15</u>
	Average		18%
Women's undergarments	Playtex bra	255	18%
	Playtex bra	409	15
	Playtex briefs	351	<u>15</u>
	Average		16%
Soap/bleach	Clorox	373	16%
	All	258	16
	Palmolive	441	<u>15</u>
	Average		16%
Misc. drug products	Pepto-Bismol	323	18%
	Colgate	325	17
	Scope	416	17
	Rolaids	489	16
	Arthritis Pain	324	16
	Aim	370	16
	Listerine	367	16
	Fabergé	325	15
	Right Guard	407	16
	Tums	437	<u>15</u>
	Average		16%
	Global Average		19%

Source: Aaker, David A., and Donald E. Bruzzone (1985), "Causes of Irritation in Advertising," *Journal of Marketing* 49 (Spring), 47–57. Reprinted with permission of the American Marketing Association.

if he sneezes once more). The casting of a character is poor.

Relative to product and execution, demographics do not appear to be a major factor influencing irritation. Nonusers tend to be more irritated by ads for the product than users of a product. But surprisingly, for feminine hygiene, the levels of irritation do not vary by user group. Thus product sensitivity and execution are critical factors for this category. There were small differences by gender and socioeconomic group. Irritation was higher among white-collar, more highly educated and upper income consumers. It was a little higher among men than among women.

Effectiveness of Irritating Ads Two theories address the issue of how irritation aroused by an ad affects response to the ad. One theory suggests a simple monotonic response: higher irritation leads to increasing dislike of the ad and the brand advertised. The reason could be conditioning, whereby repeated association causes irritation with the ad to transfer to the brand, or selectivity, whereby viewers pay less attention to ads they find irritating.

Another theory suggests a "check-mark-shaped" curve between ad response and the emotional appeal of the ad[36] (see Exhibit 7-17). The left arm of the check mark shows that irritating ads are more effective than neutral ones. The higher positive response of irritating ads relative to neutral ones may be because irritation heightens attention and recall of the message, while distracting from counterarguments. As a result, the respondent is more likely to remember the brand and its attributes and choose it over its rivals. The right arm of the check mark shows that ads that arouse a positive emotion, such as warmth, are more effective than both neutral ones and irritating ones. Warm ads probably have all the attention-gaining and recall benefits of irritating ads, while they also transfer a positive emotion to the product.

Which of these two theories is correct is still an open matter. Some studies using print ads in laboratory experiments seem to support the first theory, while others support the second. In either case, advertisers need to consider arousing warmth as frequently if not more often than arousing irritation.

Warmth

In 1984, Ronald Reagan ran a reelection campaign against the Democratic candidacy of Walter Mondale, who was behind Reagan in all the polls. In that context, Reagan ran an advertising campaign called "Morning in America" with seven different TV spots. Each spot depicted scenes of beauty and serenity and happy, productive people. The copy was simple but strong emphasizing that people were at work, inflation was down and the future was bright. The general theme was that the country was on the right track and life in America was beautiful. The spots provided little information about Reagan's plans for the next four years but aroused feelings of warmth, pride and confidence.[37] The campaign was successful, or at least did little damage, since Reagan was reelected in a landslide.

While irritating ads may still be effective, intentionally developing irritating ads may be risky. A better strategy may be to use warmth in advertising because of the check-mark-shaped response discussed earlier. Warmth may have the same attention and recall advantages of irritation, but may be even more effective in persuasion for the brand and message.[38] The reason is that warmth relaxes viewers and puts them in a positive frame of mind. Through adequate repetitions this feeling can transfer to the brand and message, enhancing persuasion.

Warmth may be a background feeling that is the by-product of a carefully crafted ad, or it may be a primary purpose of an ad, as in Reagan's reelection ad campaign. It can be stimulated by pictures or stories of love, friendship, caring, tenderness among humans or animals. For example, the Korean Air

▼ **EXHIBIT 7-17. Consumers' response to irritating ads.**

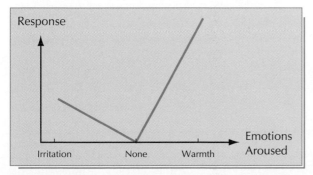

Source: Aaker, David A., and Donald E. Bruzzone (1985), "Causes of Irritation in Advertising," *Journal of Marketing* 49 (Spring), 47–57. Reprinted with permission of the American Marketing Association.

ad in Exhibit 7-18 creates an atmosphere of warmth solely with the picture. The strength of the ad is the close link between the feeling of warmth and the message of the airline—the warm care of flight attendants ensures a comfortable trip. Warmth can also be stimulated by scenes of peace, tranquillity, harmony among people, animals and nature. Besides positive relations and nature, humor and music can also promote an atmosphere of warmth to aid the persuasiveness of the ad.

Fear

A TV ad for First Alert, a carbon monoxide detector, shows pictures of real people enjoying life. Each of their loved ones then tells how they died of carbon monoxide poisoning. Besides the fear of death, the ad evokes the guilt of the survivor who could have prevented the accident with First Alert.

A print ad for Volvo pictures people who were in terrible auto accidents. A headline on the next page then announces (in capital and reverse type), "The people on the preceding pages all share a common belief: that a car saved their lives." The tagline has the logo, "VOLVO," with "Drive Safely" below it.[39]

▼ **EXHIBIT 7-18.** Ad that arouses warmth.

Our training for flight attendants is extremely rigorous. Maybe that's why our flights are so relaxing.

Simply to qualify for the Korean Air training program is an accomplishment. Of every thousand who apply, only a few possess just the right blend of grace and poise.

Then, nine hours a day, six days a week for a month or even more, their natural abilities are refined. They study world-class service. And hospitality. And a number of different languages.

By the time our flight attendants graduate, they're skilled in all the arts of comfort. Which leaves our passengers nothing to do but relax.

KOREAN AIR
Fly the spirit of dedication.

Source: Courtesy of Korean Air.

Fear is a common emotion that ads arouse today, and its use may be on the rise.[40] Fear seems more relevant to a particular class of products—those dealing with health and safety. Thus it seems natural to develop fear appeals against drug abuse, alcoholism, smoking, unsafe driving, unsafe sex, unsafe houses or lack of insurance, to name some examples. A layperson unfamiliar with the problems of addiction is likely to suggest a strong advertising campaign that vividly portrays the dangers of the unhealthy or unsafe practice. He or she believes that arousing intense fear is likely to generate immediate and sustained compliance with the desired behavior.

Nature of Response to Fear However, the response to fear is not necessarily linear. In simple words, greater fear does not necessarily mean greater compliance. A large number of studies tried to determine how consumers respond to fear. While the results of these studies are not completely in agreement, there is a strong rationale for an

▼ **EXHIBIT 7-19.** Consumers' response to fear.

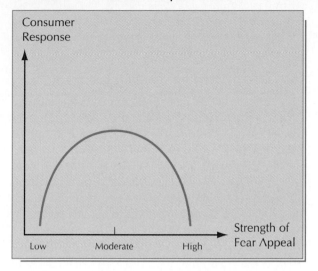

parents of the importance of good safe tires (see Exhibit 7-4).

Another subtle use of fear is to build a story or drama where the message is not clear until the last line, by which time the viewer is unable to build a defense mechanism. For example, consider the radio public service announcement against unsafe sex in Exhibit 7-21. As in real life, there is a suddenness in which one of the characters realizes death is a possibility from AIDS. The earlier part of the ad is fairly subdued with no dramatization of the dangers of unsafe sex.

A clever use of fear is to mix it with humor. Instead of emphasizing the dangers of noncompliance, the ad can joke about it. Consider the two ads in Exhibit 7-22 on page 181. The first ad explicitly arouses fear by listing all the disadvantages of not flossing in a fairly uninteresting manner. A hypochondriac might

inverted U-shaped response to fear (see Exhibit 7-19).[41] That is, moderate-level fear is more effective than little fear or extreme fear. The reason is that a little fear may be ignored, while extreme fear may prompt a **defense reaction**. In the latter situation, viewers may dismiss the stimulus as exaggerated, or dismiss the evidence as unscientific, or just screen out the entire ad to protect themselves from the pain of viewing it. As a result, the fear appeal may boomerang promoting no response to the message or even a hardening of the original position. Besides preventing defense reactions, moderate fear may also be more effective, because some understatement may prompt the viewer to do more of the thinking on the issue. Thus a clever fear appeal is to suggest the danger of noncompliance as mildly as possible while stressing the advantage of compliance. Mixing warmth, surprise or humor with or instead of fear can be quite effective, as the next four examples illustrate.

Graphic descriptions of auto accidents caused by poor tires or drunk driving can arouse fear and loathing among viewers. Two advertisers try to persuade by arousing alternate feelings. The Goods for Guns Foundation uses the warm smiling faces of victims of handgun accidents to arouse sorrow at this avoidable loss (see Exhibit 7-20). Michelin uses the smiling faces of cuddly babies to remind

▼ **EXHIBIT 7-20.** Ad that arouses feelings of sadness instead of fear.

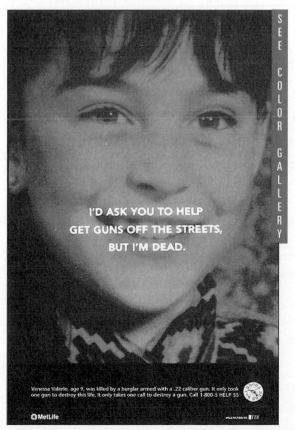

Source: Courtesy of Andrew Morris.

▼ EXHIBIT 7-21. Ad using drama to arouse moderate fear.

SFX:	BAR SOUNDS WITH MUSIC UNDER.
1ST WOMAN:	Hmmm, you're right—this place is pretty nice.
2ND WOMAN:	Yeah, this where I met that guy Brian I was tellin' you about.
1ST WOMAN:	Oh yeah, I remember.
2ND WOMAN:	It was only one night, but this guy was so unbelievable! So sexy!
1ST WOMAN:	I'm dying to see him.
2ND WOMAN:	Well, he says he comes here all the time.
1ST WOMAN:	Let's ask the bartender.
2ND WOMAN:	Excuse me, you know that guy Brian?
BARTENDER:	You a friend of his?
2ND WOMAN:	You might say that.
BARTENDER:	He doesn't come around any more.
2ND WOMAN:	Really! What's the matter?
BARTENDER:	I heard he has the AIDS virus.
2ND WOMAN:	No way...he looked fine.
1ST WOMAN:	And you slept with him?
ANNCR:	You just can't be sure who has the AIDS virus. That's why you've got to protect yourself. If you choose to have sex, use a condom. It's your best protection. AIDS. If you think you can't get it, you're dead wrong.

For more information on AIDS call 1-718-485-8111. That's 1-718-485-8111. This message was brought to you by the New York City Department of Health.

Source: New York City Department of Health, AIDS Public Service Announcement, "Two Women," 60 seconds.

relish reading the whole litany of illnesses that can arise from not flossing, but the average reader may not. The second ad arouses fear with the use of resonance. The headline promises what the reader thinks might be an easier alternative to flossing. Then it surprises with a picture of dentures.

Ennobling Emotions

Ennobling emotions are those that inspire audiences to difficult action with feelings such as pride, courage or dedication. Ads that most often arouse these emotions are for professions where the salary is low while the apparent costs are high. The mili-

tary, public service, teaching or religious life are examples. What motivates people to adopt these professions? One important factor may be affinity for the work involved in these professions. A more important factor may be the intangible satisfaction derived from performing a service even though, or precisely because it is not rewarded adequately in monetary terms. For example, what price can one put on getting maimed in defense of one's country? How can one measure the joy of reading to the blind, teaching a child or giving someone peace of mind? The deeper rewards of these professions are thus intangible, subjective and not based on price.

Promotions for these professions then can adopt one of the two routes to persuasion discussed earlier, argument or emotion. They can use argument to emphasize the tangible merits of adopting the professions. For example, the army's campaign "Be all that you can be" stresses the training in the army that lets you attain your fullest potential at its cost. However, the use of emotions may be the more powerful route to fire the minds of those who adopt these professions. Story and drama seem to be the best methods to adequately tap such emotions. For example, an ad for the army shows dramatic and heroic scenes of soldiers working and battling under severe conditions. Would such an execution be better than the "Be all that you can be" campaign? Why? To what audiences?

These examples show how the lives and motives of members of the profession can be used to develop inspirational ads for new recruits. However, the Nike Company showed that the arousal of ennobling emotions need not be restricted to professions. It could also be aroused for athletic goods, where the cost of training can also be steep, and the benefits are not always immediate or tangible. For these campaigns, Nike adopted several approaches.

One approach imbued the drama and intensity of athletic activity into the personality of the shoes. For example in one spot, quick cuts of athletes in various dramatic episodes gripped viewers' attention, while a final shot of "Nike" associated these feelings with the brand name. Another approach was less explicit. It emphasized self-actualization with the theme "Just do it." Various stories or mini-dramas portrayed the challenges of daily life and the need for consumers to take a stand and make the tough choices. A shot of the Nike logo appeared in

▼ **EXHIBIT 7-22.** Use of fear and resonance in ads for dental floss.

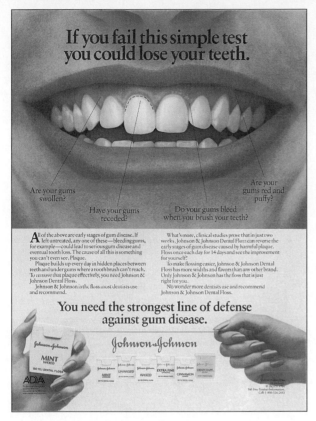

Source: © Johnson & Johnson Corporation.

the ad, without any explicit connection to the shoes. Would the second strategy be effective without any explicit copy on the shoes? Why?

A third approach lay in between these two strategies. It consisted of a series of four two-page ads for women's shoes. The power of these ads is in the copy, which is part story, part deep empathy with a woman's athletic problems, part inspirational homily. This campaign of Nike's was very successful. One ad jammed Nike's switchboard. Women called up to indicate how the ad changed their lives, or convinced them that Nike really understood a woman's feelings. Overall, the campaign generated 110,000 phone calls in six months, and fueled a 24-percent growth in sales of women's shoes.[42]

Summary

Emotion is a state of arousal indicated by specific types and levels of biochemical activity in the brain and the body. There is a vast array of human emotions including love, warmth, joy, excitement, curiosity, patriotism or sexual arousal, all of which can be effectively harnessed for persuasion. The use of emotion for persuasion is independent from the use of logic, and has several advantages over it. From the perspective of the viewer, the arousal of emotion is more interesting, requires less effort, does not raise the viewer's defenses, and can lead to more immediate action, and more enduring recall of the message. However, the use of emotion for persuasion also has some disadvantages relative to that of logic. The arousal of emotion takes more time and can distract the viewer from the message. The arousal of strong negative emotions such as fear, guilt, disgust and anger may cause the viewer to reject the emotion-arousing stimuli and the message to avoid the discomfort of the emotion. The arousal of emotion may also appear exploitative and be ineffective, if the means of arousing the emotion is not well connected to the message.

Drama, story, demonstration, humor and music are the important methods of arousing emotions. Of these methods, drama is probably the strongest because it involves the viewer most completely; but it is also the most time consuming. In contrast, while humor and music may not be as captivating as drama, they require much less time and can be easily combined with other methods of persuasion such as logic. Music in particular can easily accompany most other forms of communication, establishing a mood and enhancing persuasion. In general, the arousal of emotion does not preclude the simultaneous use of logic or other means of persuasion. However, the arousal of emotions is especially important for products that can be characterized as "feeling" products and when the viewer does not have the motivation or ability to evaluate the product attributes. Effective use of emotions also requires harmony between the audience's mood and the emotion being aroused. The most important consideration for the use of emotions is the link between the stimulus used to arouse emotions and the message. The stronger and more natural the link, the more effective the ad will be.

QUESTIONS

1. Explain the role of emotion in developing persuasive advertising.
2. What are the pros and cons of using emotion for persuasion?
3. When does the use of emotions work well? Explain fully.
4. Many critics of advertising believe that ads today are trivial because they lack good arguments and meaningful information. They suggest that drama, music and humor are gimmicks to draw attention but generally ineffective. How valid are such criticisms? Discuss.
5. Some ads are all drama and no message. Critics dismiss these ads as pure hype. What do you think? How and why does advertising dramatic events help a message?
6. Compare and contrast the use of drama, story, demonstration and argument for persuasion.
7. What is humor and resonance? Why are they effective in ad persuasion? How would you use them?

8. At one time advertising theorists and practitioners advised against the use of humor. What are the dangers of using humor in advertising?
9. Music entertains, creates atmosphere, evokes feelings and reflects moods. Can music persuade? Discuss.
10. Give examples of specific types of music and the corresponding emotions they raise.
11. What are the causes of irritation in advertising? Why would advertisers use ads that have the potential to irritate?
12. Explain fully when and how arousing fear helps persuasion.

NOTES

1. Garfield, Bob (1992), "Ads For E.P.T. Pregnant with Feeling and Honesty," *Advertising Age* 63, 33, August 17, 46.
2. Batra, Rajeev, and Michael L. Ray (1986), "Affective Responses Mediating Acceptance of Advertising," *Journal of Consumer Research* 13, 2 (September), 234–249.
3. For a slightly different typology see Deighton, John, and Stephen J. Hoch (1993), "Teaching Emotion With Drama Advertising," in *Advertising Exposure, Memory and Choice,* Andrew A. Mitchell, ed. Hillsdale, NJ: Erlbaum.
4. Stern, Barbara B. (1994), "Classical and Vignette Television Advertising Dramas: Structural Models, Formal Analysis and Consumer Effects," *Journal of Consumer Research* 20 (March), 601–615.
5. *Ibid.*
6. Stewart, David W., Kenneth M. Farmer, and Charles I. Stannard (1990), "Music as a Recognition Cue in Advertising-Tracking Studies," *Journal of Advertising Research* (August-September), 39–48.
7. Smith, Martin J. (1992), "Designing a Dispute," *The Orange County Register,* February 14, 1.
8. Garfield, Bob (1993), "This Heavy-Handed Ad Exploits Someone New," *Advertising Age,* May 10, 50.
9. Kamp, Edward, and Deborah J. MacInnis (1995), "Characteristics of Portrayed Emotions in Commercials," *Journal of Consumer Research* (November/December), 19–26.
10. Ratchford, Brian (1987), "New Insights about the FCB Grid," *Journal of Advertising Research* 27, 4 (August/September), 31. FCB is an acronym for Foote, Cone and Belding.
11. Gardner, Meryl P. (1993), "Responses to Emotional and Informational Appeals: The Moderating Role of Context-Induced Mood States," in *Attention, Attitude and Affect in Response to Advertising,* Eddie M. Clark, Timothy C. Brock, and David W. Stewart, eds. Hillsdale, NJ: Lawrence Erlbaum Associates; Goldberg, Marvin E., and Gerald J. Gorn (1987), "Happy and Sad TV Programs: How They Affect Reactions

to Commercials," *Journal of Consumer Research* 14 (December), 387–403.

12. Cunningham, Michael, Jeff Steinberg, and Rita Grev (1980), "Wanting to and Having to Help: Separate Motivation for Positive Mood and Guilt-Induced Helping," *Journal of Personality and Social Psychology* 38 (2), 181–192.

13. Deighton, John, Daniel Romer and Josh McQueen (1989), "Using Drama to Persuade," *Journal of Consumer Research* 16 (December), 335–343. The subsequent subsection draws ideas and propositions from this paper.

14. *Ibid.*

15. Horovitz, Bruce (1993), "Coke's Jab at Jackson May Pop the Top on Cola Wars," *Los Angeles Times,* August 28, D1.

16. McQuarrie, Edward F., and David Glen Mick (1992), "On Resonance: A Critical Pluralistic Inquiry into Advertising Rhetoric," *Journal of Consumer Research* 19 (September), 180–197. Some examples and ideas in this section are also drawn from this article.

17. Sheldon, Esther K. (1956), "Some Pun Among the Hucksters," *American Speech* 31, 13–20.

18. McQuarrie and Mick, "On Resonance."

19. *Ibid.*

20. Weinberger, Marc G., Harlan Spotts, Leland Campbell, and May L. Parsons (1995), "The Use and Effect of Humor in Different Advertising Media," *Journal of Advertising Research* (May/June), 44–56; Weinberger, Marc, and Harlan Spotts (1989), "Humor in U.S. versus U.K. TV Advertising," *Journal of Advertising* 18, 2, 39–44; Weinberger, Marc G., and Leland Campbell (1991), "The Use and Impact of Humor in Radio Advertising," *Journal of Advertising Research* (December 1990–January 1991), 44–51; McQuarrie and Mick, "On Resonance."

21. McQuarrie and Mick, "On Resonance."

22. *Ibid.*

23. Scott, Cliff, David M. Klein, and Jennings Bryant (1990), "Consumer Response to Humor in Advertising: A Series of Field Studies Using Behavioral Observation," *Journal of Consumer Research* 16, (March), 498–501; Alden, Dana L., and Wayne D. Hoyer (1993), "An Examination of Cognitive Factors Related to Humorousness in Television Advertising," *Journal of Advertising* 22, 2 (June), 29–37.

24. Zinkhan, George, and Yong Zhang (1991), "Television Advertising: The Effects of Repetition on Social Setting," *Advances in Consumer Research* 18, 813–818.

25. Scott, Linda M. (1990), "Understanding Jingles and Needle Drop: A Rhetorical Approach to Music in Advertising," *Journal of Consumer Research* 17 (September), 223–236.

26. Stewart, David W., and David H. Furse (1986), *Effective Television Advertising: A Study of 1000 Commercials,* Lexington, MA: Lexington Books.

27. Bruner, Gordon C. II (1990), "Music, Mood and Marketing," *Journal of Marketing* 54, 4 (October), 94–104. The subsequent definitions are adapted from this review of the literature on the topic.

28. *Ibid.*

29. *Harmony* is the simultaneous occurrence of two or more notes. Harmony that is pleasing is called *concordant* while that which is displeasing is called *discordant. Mode* is a fixed set of notes in which a song, or parts of a song, are played. Western music uses one of two modes: *major* or *minor.*

30. Milliman, Ronald E. (1986), "The Effect of Background Music on the Behavior of Restaurant Patrons," *Journal of Consumer Research* 13 (September), 286–289.

31. Waldholz, Michael (1993), "Study of Fear Shows Emotions Can Alter 'Wiring' of the Brain," *The Wall Street Journal,* September 29, 1.

32. Bruner, "Music, Mood, and Marketing."

33. Scott, "Understanding Jingles and Needle Drop."

34. Aaker, David A., and Donald E. Bruzzone (1985), "Causes of Irritation in Advertising," *Journal of Marketing* 49 (Spring), 47–57.

35. Bauer, Raymond A., and Stephen A. Greyser (1968), *Advertising in America: The Consumer View,* Boston, MA: Harvard University Press; *Ibid.*

36. Aaker and Bruzzone, "Causes Of Irritation in Advertising."

37. "MacNeil/Lehrer News Hour," Educational Broadcasting and GWETA, May 21, 1984.

38. Aaker, David A., Douglas M. Stayman, and Michael R. Hagerty (1986), "Warmth in Advertising: Measurement, Impact and Sequence Effects," *Journal of Consumer Research* 12 (March), 365–381.

39. Deveney, Kathleen (1993), "Marketers Exploit People's Fears of Everything," *The Wall Street Journal,* November 11, B1, B5.

40. *Ibid.*

41. The appropriate level of fear that gets the most positive response is likely to vary across contexts. For this reason, studies done in different contexts may not always have consistent findings. Rotfeld, Herbert J. (1988), "Fear Appeals and Persuasion: Assumptions and Errors in Advertising Research," *Journal of Current Issues and Research in Advertising* 11 (1 & 2), 21–40; Henthorne, Tony L., Michael S. LaTour, and Rajan Natarajan (1993), "Fear Appeals in Print Advertising: An Analysis of Arousal and Ad Response," *Journal of Advertising* 22, 2, (June), 59–69.

42. Nike's 1992 Annual Report.

CHAPTER

8

On March 2, 1989, Pepsi aired a 2-minute ad called "Make a Wish" featuring pop singer Madonna, who was paid $6 million for this her first endorsement. At that time one testing agency estimated that Madonna was recognized by 88 percent of the population but liked by only 25 percent. Yet many of Pepsi's target segment, the younger generation, may have fallen in that 25 percent. To those consumers Madonna represented sexual freedom, expression, bold rebellion and youthful attraction. As a result, the choice

Persuasion Using Endorsers

of endorser and the execution of the ad were widely praised. The ad was apparently also successful, earning a top rating by *Advertising Age* and the highest score in an unaided recall test by the Gallup poll.[1]

A day after the airing of the ad, Madonna released a video that was aired on MTV. The video featured a new song, "Like a Prayer," which was also the theme song of the ad. The video had controversial images of burning crosses, a rape scene and Madonna receiving the stigmata of Christ. Stigmata of Christ are marks resembling the wounds of the crucified Jesus Christ, which Christians believe appear on deeply spiritual individuals through religious ecstasy. Madonna herself wore a low-cut dress and a gold cross. Some Christian leaders were outraged and demanded that Pepsi immediately scrap the ad and disassociate themselves from Madonna or risk a boycott of their products. Pepsi was in a dilemma. Should the company ignore the threatened boycott, or should it scrap a very costly and apparently successful ad?

Madonna, Bill Cosby, Michael Jordan. These names have become symbols of the role of endorsers in advertising. Firms spend millions of dollars to sign up celebrities to endorse their products. Some popular endorsers such as Michael Jordan earn as much as $40 million a year from endorsements alone.[2] Endorsement contracts are now so lucrative that many professionals in sports and entertainment direct their careers to this end. In some sports, such as track and field events, winning at the Olympics has pretty much become a means to subsequent endorsement contracts.

Firms spend all this money on endorsements because finding the right celebrity endorser for their products can pay tremendous dividends. For example, some brands such as Nike's Air Jordan have been built around the image of a star. Nike earned over $200 million from its Air Jordan lines of shoes and clothes in 1991 alone.[3] Yet as the example of Madonna suggests, celebrity endorsers can be a powerful means of communicating a distinct image for a brand to a target segment, as well as a source of problems for the advertiser. Other types of endorsers can be equally effective but cost much less.

What are the different types of endorsers? What role do they play in the communication of a firm's message? When and how should firms use endorsers? This chapter addresses these questions.

TYPES OF ENDORSERS

An **endorser** is a person, character or organization that speaks or appears in an ad in support of the advertiser or its claim. The term *endorser* includes the terms **spokesperson** or **model**. The latter term is used for a person who is chosen primarily for his or her physical attractiveness. The **endorsement process** is the identification, selection and use of endorsers to communicate with a target segment.

Endorsers can be grouped into three broad classes: experts, celebrities and lay endorsers. Each has special characteristics and roles in the communication process. We will first consider a definition of the three types of endorser and then describe their roles.

Experts

In January 1956, Procter & Gamble launched Crest toothpaste with the theme of cavity prevention. Despite heavy advertising over four and a half years, Crest achieved only a 12 percent market share versus Colgate's 35 percent. Colgate had been the leading brand of toothpaste in the U.S. market for many decades. Then in August 1960, Crest won an endorsement by the American Dental Association as the only toothpaste that prevented dental cavities, and one of only three means of fighting dental cavities. A massive advertising campaign announcing that endorsement catapulted Crest into the leadership of the toothpaste market, a position it still retains.[4]

Experts are individuals or organizations that the target population perceives as having substantial knowledge in a particular area. Examples include one of the most successful managers of mutual funds, Peter Lynch, for choosing stocks, or former U.S. Surgeon General C. Everett Koop for dental care (see Exhibit 8-1). Typically experts are chosen because of the knowledge they have accumulated through experience, training or study. The FTC has strict guidelines about who may appear as experts, for what products, and under what conditions (see Chapter 2). The purpose is to protect consumers from misleading endorsements.

Various organizations such as the American Medical Association, the American Dental Association, *Good Housekeeping* and the U.S. Department of Agriculture will certify the quality of products, sometimes through awarding seals of

▼ **EXHIBIT 8-1.** Endorsement by an expert.

Just filling cavities is leaving a hole in your oral health.

"You're not healthy without good oral health."

C. Everett Koop, MD
Former Surgeon General
National Honorary Chairman
of Oral Health 2000

Millions of Americans only visit a dentist when they're in pain and want the pain to go away. But there's a lot more to good oral health than just filling cavities.

That's why 3M is a corporate sponsor of Oral Health 2000...uniting corporations, government agencies, foundations, dental health professionals, and the public in the largest preventive oral health initiative ever undertaken. Oral Health 2000 centers around making Americans aware that oral health is a vital part of overall health, and preventive care may eliminate future pain from unattended dental problems.

Take care of your family and yourself. See your dentist. Your dental health professional can share Oral Health 2000 information that will protect everyone from the youngest baby to the great-grandparents.

Oral Health 2000 is an initiative of Oral Health America, America's Fund for Dental Health. For more information write to us at 410 N. Michigan Avenue, Suite 352, Chicago, Illinois 60611-4211.

3M Dental

Source: Oral Health America, America's Fund for Dental Health.

approval. A **seal of approval** is a logo of the certifying organization that appears on the product's package or ad and states that the certifying organization vouches for the merits of the product. In some cases the organizations are paid by the manufacturer of the products, while in other cases the endorsement is made in the public interest. Since the American Dental Association's effective endorsement of Crest, organizational endorsements in ads have become so common that their use may now exceed their benefits.[5] Indeed, the U.S. Environmental Protection Agency found it necessary to run a Public Service campaign to explain its own new seal of approval for energy efficiency: the ENERGY STAR® (see Exhibit 8-2).

Celebrities

Celebrities are individuals or characters who are known to a large portion of the general population, primarily because of the publicity associated with their lives. Most celebrity endorsers come from the entertainment world (Whitney Houston in AT&T's "True Voice" campaign) or the sports world (tennis legends Jimmy Connors and Chris Evert Lloyd for Nuprin). Talk show hosts (Rush Limbaugh for orange juice), business personalities (Lee Iacocca for Chrysler cars) and politicians (Bill Clinton for a public service campaign against violence) are also used. Reporters (Dan Rather), educators (Carl Sagan), consumer advocates (Ralph Nader) and religious leaders (Billy Graham) could also serve as effective endorsers, though they may be unwilling to tarnish their images by appearing in paid commercial endorsements. The term *celebrity* itself need not exclude individuals who may be controversial or disliked by the general population (Madonna for Pepsi, Dan Quayle for Frito Lay), as long as they are used carefully to convey a certain image. For example, Pepsi has always promoted its drink as the choice of a younger generation. Madonna probably personified many characteristics that generation valued, such as sexual freedom, self-expression and rebellion against strictures.

Advertisers often develop and use fictitious characters to serve as spokespersons for their brand. Fictitious characters could be actors, actresses, animal personifications or fantasy creations. To introduce its brand of wine coolers, Bartles and Jaymes developed the lovable characters Ed and Frank who appeared in a humorous miniseries of their own. Other fictitious characters include Federal Express's fast-talking executive in a hurry, Minnesota Valley Canning Company's Jolly Green Giant, Isuzu

▼ **EXHIBIT 8-2.** Ad for a seal of approval.

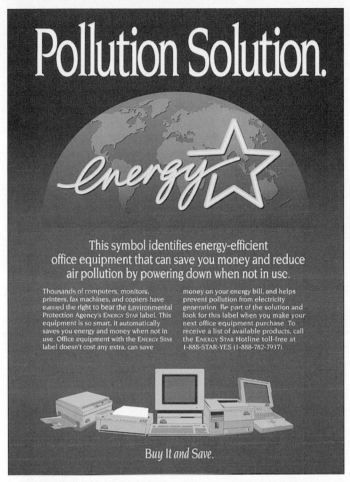

Source: Public Service Announcement Developed by U.S. EPA ENERGY STAR® Program.

Motors' scheming Joe Isuzu and General Mills' reassuring Betty Crocker. Friendly personifications of animals or fantasy characters can have wide appeal across ages, ethnic groups and even nationalities. Examples include Disney's Mickey Mouse, Kellogg's Tony the Tiger, the Energizer Bunny and Little Caesar's Pizza! Pizza! Character. We can classify fictitious characters as celebrities because their use involves an essential element of celebrity endorsement that we discuss later in the chapter: they have a distinct personality that communicates unique meaning to the target segment.

Celebrities may not always be explicitly identified by name, especially if they are well known to the target audience. For example, the actor Jimmy

Stewart did an uncredited voice-over for Campbell's Home Cooking brand of soups. Advertisers may use celebrities as a voice-over without identification either because they are so well known or because of the special appeal of their voice. In most cases, however, the voice-over is that of an anonymous lay endorser.

Lay Endorsers

One of the major proposals launched by U.S. President Clinton early in his tenure as president was a revamping of the U.S. health care system. Many groups were staunchly opposed to this intrusion of government into a sphere of private choice. The Health Insurance Association of America launched a TV advertising campaign in opposition. The ads portrayed a middle-class married couple named Harry and Louise, with occasional visits from a neighbor, Libby. The characters discuss in simple terms at the kitchen table their concern about the costs of the proposed health care system. The ads were a great success because the couple connected with common people. Some analysts attributed the shift in public opinion against the proposed health care system to the effectiveness of the ad campaign, which ran for about six months in 1993–1994.[6]

Lay endorsers are unknown individuals or characters who appear in ads, just like Harry, Louise and Libby. They are selected to closely resemble the target segment, enabling the target segment to identify with the endorser and the message. However, for some products such as perfume or clothing, and services such as insurance and health care, these lay endorsers may be chosen because they personify the aspirations of the target segment. Lay endorsers may be real or fictitious, and are (initially at least) unknown. The anonymous voice-over in audio and video ads is generally that of a lay endorser. In such cases, the target segment may not visualize an explicit person as endorser, but may treat the speaker as the voice of the advertiser announcing the advertiser's position. So, advertisers need to take care in selecting speakers for this role, though the selection may not be as critical as with an endorser who is visible.

The three categories of endorsers are not mutually exclusive. As explained above, sustained and effective use of lay endorsers over time may make them celebrities in their own right. Also, some individuals could belong to more than one category depending on the product they endorse. For example, Joe Montana's appearance for LA Gear could be considered an expert's endorsement of shoes but his appearance for Hanes hosiery would be that of a celebrity. Because sports celebrities frequently endorse sporting goods as well as other products, there may be an especially large overlap in classifying endorsers from the world of sports as experts or celebrities. So, while this classification of endorsers is a good starting point, the more important issue for us is to understand what role they play in the endorsement process.

ROLE OF ENDORSERS

What role or purpose do endorsers serve in advertising today? Researchers have proposed three major models to explain the role of endorsers in the communication process: source credibility model, source attractiveness model, and meaning transfer model. The term **source** includes the endorser who appears on behalf of the advertiser, or the advertiser itself, who is the source of the message.

The Source Credibility Model

The **source credibility model** is based on the central premise that consumers are more likely to accept a message if they find it credible. Consumers' **credibility** in a message depends on two qualities of the source, expertise and trustworthiness.

Expertise is the ability of the source to make valid claims, as perceived by the audience. Audiences are likely to perceive a source as an expert to the extent they perceive the source as knowledgeable about the issue. Several studies have shown that an audience will accept the claims of a source that it perceives as more knowledgeable than itself on the issue.

Trustworthiness is the willingness of the source to make honest claims. A source is likely to make an honest claim if it has no vested interest in the outcome or is not under pressure to slant the evidence. Buyers would consider most advertisers to have a vested interest in stating the claims of their products. Thus, choosing an independent spokesperson in an ad helps to reduce this perceived bias. However,

audiences generally know that spokespersons are paid.[7] The effectiveness of the endorsement then depends on whether the audience's prior perception of the endorser as trustworthy overcomes any perceived bias that arises from the audience's knowledge of the payment.

Chrysler ads featuring Lee Iacocca are a good example of the role of expertise in the source credibility model. As an executive of Chrysler Motors, Iacocca was a biased party. However, his knowledge of the auto industry, his reputation as a vigorous competitor, his record for putting Chrysler back on track and his forceful communication style combined to make him a credible guarantor of Chrysler products. For these reasons, Chrysler's ad agency used Iacocca as the mainstay of its ads through the 1980s (see Exhibit 8-3). In these ads Iacocca probably appeared as an expert in the auto industry vouching for the quality of Chrysler's product. On the other hand Nick and Helen of Warner-Lambert's e.p.t. ad (see Chapter 7) are not experts, but they are very trustworthy. This trust is triggered by their honest looks and their appearance without rehearsal or knowledge of the outcome. Thus either expertise or trustworthiness could enhance the credibility of an endorser.

According to the source credibility model, if the receivers of an ad's message find the source of the ad sufficiently credible, they will adopt the opinion or attitude presented by the ad as the objectively correct position in that particular context. They will then integrate the new opinion or message with their belief system. This process is called **internalization**. The receivers are said to have internalized the opinion or attitude and are likely to retain it even if they forget about the endorser. Consider, for example, new car buyers who decide primarily on reliability and are convinced by Lee Iacocca's 5-year or 50,000-mile guarantee. These buyers are likely to internalize the message that Chrysler makes reliable cars. So they would attribute their purchase to the warranty (the message) and not to their trust in Iacocca (the endorser).

The Source Attractiveness Model

The **source attractiveness model** posits that the acceptance of a message depends on the attractiveness of the source, which in turn depends on three central attributes: familiarity, likability and similarity.[8] **Familiarity** is the audience's knowledge of the source because of prior exposure to it, **likabili-**

▼ **EXHIBIT 8-3.** Endorsement demonstrating expertise.

Source: Courtesy of Chrysler Corporation.

opinion or attitude lasts only as long as the receiver finds the source attractive. The changes due to identification are not as permanent as those caused by internalization. For example, a gang member probably adopts a gang's dress code through identification with other members or the gang leader. But if that member is rejected from the gang, he or she is likely to reject the dress code and other symbols of the gang.

Another explanation for the effects of source attractiveness is conditioning (see Chapter 4). By this explanation, the endorser would be the unconditioned stimulus, and the brand or product would be the conditioned stimulus. When the endorser is repeatedly associated with the brand, the attractiveness of the endorser is supposed to pass to the brand. Conditioning typically leads to greater permanence in the effect of source attractiveness than identification. The reason is that the attraction for the source stimulus, which transfers to the target stimulus, can persist even if the audience has forgotten the ads that made the association.

Relevance of the Source Attractiveness Model Many laboratory studies support the effectiveness of source attractiveness in eliciting positive reactions from respondents. However, the evidence from studies carried out in the field is not as conclusive.[9] A major reason may be that the attractiveness of an endorser may not be the sole or main criterion for his or her effectiveness. The meanings associated with the endorser may be more important. Consider the following two examples.

A good example of an ad that may work via the source attractiveness model is the well-known Calvin Klein ad starring Brooke Shields, who asks "You know what gets between me and my Calvins? Nothing." The innocent seductiveness and contemporary appeal of Brooke Shields is cleverly used to portray Calvin Klein jeans as sexy and fashionable. The wordplay on "nothing" further heightens the processing of the ad message.

In another ad, Brooke Shields endorses Toshiba's laptop computer. The ad coincided with Brooke Shields' university days. Was it a good endorsement? If one went purely by the source attractiveness model, Brooke Shields is a beautiful model who may have attracted many college students. However, there is a serious mismatch between the meanings associated with her image and those associated with a Toshiba computer, which even the headline

ty is the audience's positive regard for the source because of its physical appearance and behavior, and **similarity** is the resemblance between the source and receiver. The higher a source rates on each of these attributes, the more attractive it would be, and the more acceptable its message. How does attractiveness affect message acceptance? At least two explanations are available: identification and conditioning.

Identification means that the receiver of the message begins to see himself or herself as similar to the source because of the latter's attractiveness. In so doing, the receiver becomes more willing to accept the opinions, beliefs, attitudes or behavior of the source. For example, teens may adopt the dress style of a model they like very much. In contrast to the source credibility model, the adoption of the new

▼ EXHIBIT 8-4. The meaning transfer model.

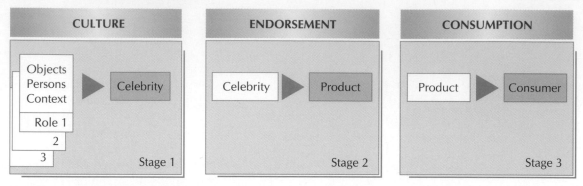

Key: ▶ = path of meaning movement
 ▢ = stage of meaning movement

Source: McCracken, Grant (1989), "Who is the Celebrity Endorser? Cultural Foundations of the Endorsement Process," *Journal of Consumer Research* 16 (December), 1989, 310–321. Copyright 1989 The University of Chicago Press.

"Beautifully intelligent" may be unable to link. Brooke Shields was best known for her appearance in the Calvin Klein ad. That image of Brooke Shields as hip, innocent and seductive is inconsistent with that of intelligence and advanced technology that Toshiba claims for its computer. Moreover, one study found that beauty itself had many images, such as "girl next door," "sex kitten," "cute," "exotic," "trendy" or "classic." Each of these may be exemplified by a particular model.[10]

A marketing professor, Grant McCracken,[11] claims many mismatches between endorsers and brands may be the reason they failed: Bill Cosby for E. F. Hutton, John Houseman for McDonald's, George C. Scott for Renault, Ringo Starr for Sun Country Classic. In these cases, the endorsers may have been chosen on the basis of credibility, attractiveness or popularity as the models described above suggest. However, both endorsers and brands had well-developed, distinct images or meanings that may not have been compatible with each other. The next model describes this aspect of the endorsement process.

The Meaning Transfer Model

McCracken proposes the meaning transfer model as a richer, more complete description of the endorsement process than that offered by the source credibility or source attractiveness models. The central premise of the **meaning transfer model** is that a celebrity encodes a unique set of meanings that can, if the celebrity is well used, be transferred to the endorsed product. This transfer is supposed to occur in three stages (see Exhibit 8-4).

In the first stage, culture, each celebrity develops an image that encodes a unique set of meanings. These meanings arise by the types of people they are, the roles they have played, the things they have done and the stories that have developed around them. The set of meanings encoded by a celebrity's image can be described in terms of dimensions such as age, gender, race, wealth, professional status, personality or lifestyle. However, the image of the celebrity itself represents this set of meanings more fully, efficiently and effectively than any verbal listing. Exhibit 8-5 presents key images evoked by some celebrities. A complete, valid profile of the entire set of meanings encoded in a celebrity's image requires a survey of consumer perceptions of the celebrity. This type of survey is described later in the chapter.

In the second stage, endorsement, the celebrity's skillful endorsement of a product in an ad transfers the meanings encoded in his or her image to the product. The advantage of celebrities over lay endorsers is that the celebrity encodes an image that cannot be found anywhere else, nor can it be described precisely and efficiently in the confines of an ad. When skillfully portrayed, celebrities can communicate this image more powerfully than lay endorsers or other forms of communication. For example, McCracken claims that John Houseman lent time-tested integrity to the Smith Barney name with his line, "We make money the old fashioned

▼ **EXHIBIT 8-5.** Celebrity images.

Category	Image	Celebrity
Social status	Patrician man	Peter Jennings
Social status	New wealth	Diane Sawyer
Gender	Rugged male	Sylvester Stallone
Gender	Tough male	Paul Newman
Gender	Sexy female	Loni Anderson
Gender	Tough female	Sigourney Weaver
Age	Prematurely ancient	Danny DeVito
Personality	Irascible	David Letterman
Personality	Agreeable	Gary Collins
Lifestyle	Perfect dad	Bill Cosby
Lifestyle	Wisdom	Charles Kuralt

Source: McCracken, Grant (1989), "Who is the Celebrity Endorser? Cultural Foundations of the Endorsement Process," *Journal of Consumer Research* 16 (December), 1989, 310–321. Copyright 1989 The University of Chicago Press.

way, we earn it."[12] The advertiser needs to evaluate all the meanings encoded in the celebrity's image, determine which if any of those meanings are desired by its target segments and fashion an ad that transfers all the desired meanings and only the desired meanings, from the celebrity to the product.

In the third stage, consumption, consumers buy the endorsed product with the intention of capturing some of the desirable meanings with which the celebrity has imbued the product. The meaning transfer model assumes that consumers purchase products not merely for their functional value but also for their cultural and symbolic value. The consumer's purchase for symbolic value could be through explicit reasoning (such as "if I buy the perfume, Sophia, I will capture some of Sophia Loren's mystique") or through affect (as when an ad with Sophia Loren endorsing Sophia makes the perfume more appealing to a consumer). Typically, socially visible products would fit this category. For example, designer clothes, perfumes, premium cars, exclusive mansions or club memberships are often chosen more for their social rather than their functional value. Perfume designers often design a perfume on the image of a celebrity. Examples include Passion and White Diamonds by Elizabeth Taylor, Moments by Priscilla Presley and Magnetic by Gabriela Sabatini.

While the source attractiveness and credibility models rely on only a few key characteristics of the source, the meaning transfer model is richer because it focuses on a wide spectrum of meanings that can be transferred. However, the task of transferring the key meanings is challenging and requires creativity in identifying, profiling and selecting celebrities, and skillfully using them to exploit their useful meanings for the brand.

Application of the Models

Which of these three endorsement models is the most accurate or appropriate? None of the three endorsement models describes a complete picture of the endorsement process involving different types of endorsers. Each model is more relevant for explaining the use of some types of endorsers rather than others (see Exhibit 8-6). The source credibility model is most relevant for explaining the role of experts as endorsers; indeed, the central concepts of the model, expertise and trustworthiness, are defining characteristics of experts. The source attractiveness model is most relevant in the case of lay endorsers; the familiarity and likability of these endorsers and their similarity to the target audience are key to their effectiveness. The meaning transfer model best explains the use of celebrities as endorsers; it provides an insightful framework for using the complexity of meanings associated with celebrities.

The above discussion should not suggest that only one model applies to each ad; more than one type of model can explain the effectiveness of any particular ad. For example, consider the Chrysler ad in Exhibit 8-3. The source credibility model provides the key explanation for the effectiveness of this ad. However, following the source attractiveness model, Lee

▼ **EXHIBIT 8-6.** Types and models of endorsers.

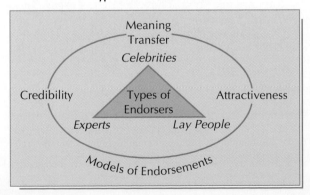

Iacocca needed to be positively appealing to the target segment or else he would have turned off customers for the car. Also, following the meaning transfer model, the no-nonsense image that Lee Iacocca portrayed may have been a good match for Chrysler, which needed to reassure buyers that the company could survive and tide over its problems.

Advertisers also use endorsers for two reasons that are not covered by the three models: attention and recall. The appearance of a celebrity in an ad can help to draw an audience's attention to the ad and to its message. The association of a celebrity with a message or a brand may help consumers to recall the brand or message at the time of purchase. These advantages of a celebrity may hold even for lay endorsers. For example, one study found that subjects could recall visual aspects of a print ad better if the ad were endorsed by a model.[13]

Given the multiple roles of an endorser, advertisers need to evaluate a potential endorser on more than just one or two dimensions. For example, one survey using a standardized rating scale found that some top brands like Kodak received a rating of 84 on the scale; this score was higher than that obtained by some top celebrities like Bill Cosby, who received a rating of 75.[14] Why would an advertiser use a celebrity who rated lower that its brand? The answer lies in considering the different roles of endorsers as described by the three models above. Standardized ratings of brands and celebrities typically use a few dimensions such as awareness, attractiveness and credibility. Well-known endorsers may draw attention to the ad. Attractive endorsers may increase the likability of the brand. Endorsers who are experts may increase the credibility of the message. But any one endorser brings a whole package of meanings to a brand that goes beyond individual characteristics such as attention, attractiveness or trust as measured by standardized tests. These meanings may help to efficiently communicate the message of the brand and uniquely position it relative to competitors.

THE USE OF ENDORSERS

When should advertisers use each type of endorser? What mode of communication should the endorser use? How cost effective is the use of endorsers? These are pertinent questions that are covered under three headings: audience characteristics, communication modes and cost effectiveness.

Audience Characteristics

Which of these three types of endorsers an advertiser should use, if any at all, itself depends on the underlying characteristics of the audience. The elaboration likelihood model (covered in Chapter 4) suggests that persuasion with endorsers occurs by the peripheral route of persuasion. This route is effective when the audience is not motivated or able to process a message. Using these two criteria of motivation and ability, Exhibit 8-7 shows the combination of audience characteristics for which each type of endorser is particularly appropriate. When the consumer is both motivated to process an ad and has the ability to do so, reason is the best route of persuasion. For example, consider a consumer in the market for a new personal computer. If that consumer is a programmer (high motivation and ability), he or she would probably decide which computer to buy based on reason; he or she may even be offended by an endorser in an ad for computers as in Brooke Shields' Toshiba ad. If the consumer is an amateur (high motivation, low ability) he or she may be responsive to the endorsement of an expert. If the product is soap (low motivation, high ability) then a lay endorser would probably be appropriate. If the product is cologne (low motivation, low ability) then a celebrity would probably be in order.

Some tests of the elaboration likelihood model provide partial support for this explanation. For example, one study found that the attitude of sub-

▼ EXHIBIT 8-7. Use of endorsers, by audience characteristics.

		Motivation to Process Information	
		High	Low
Ability to Process Information	High	Reason	Lay Endorsers
	Low	Experts	Celebrities

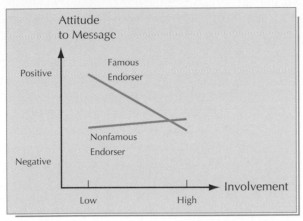

Source: Petty, Richard E., John T. Cacioppo and David Schumann (1983), "Central and Peripheral Routes to Advertising Effectiveness: The Moderating Role of Involvement," *Journal of Consumer Research* 10 (September), 1983, 142. Copyright 1983 The University of Chicago Press.

jects after exposure to an ad in a low-involvement condition was much more positive if the ad used a famous endorser rather than a nonfamous endorser (see Exhibit 8-8). However, the attitude of subjects in a high-involvement condition after exposure to the same message did not differ by type of endorser. In contrast, strong arguments were more effective than weak arguments in enhancing attitude to the message in the high-involvement condition. The results suggest that the use of celebrities is probably more effective in low-involvement conditions, and that of strong arguments in high-involvement conditions.

Communication Modes

Ads can use endorsers in different **modes** or presentation styles. The most commonly used modes are:[15]

Imperative: "You use this product."

Explicit: "I endorse this product."

Implicit: "I use this product."

Passive: Mere appearance with the product.

The type of endorser and the role he or she plays in the ad are key factors that determine the mode of endorsement. The imperative mode needs to be used carefully because it requires a measure of submission or receptivity from the audience that one rarely finds. One possible use of this mode is with an

endorser acting as a caring parent or as a firm counselor. Experts can easily adopt the explicit mode because of the authority vested in their knowledge or experience. Celebrities can adopt the passive mode because their visibility and appeal is so strong that they only need to be associated with the brand.

Lay endorsers generally use the implicit mode, because they have neither the credibility of experts for an explicit endorsement, nor the appeal of the celebrity for a passive endorsement. The **testimonial** is a type of implicit endorsement in which the endorser describes his or her experience with the product (see Exhibit 8-9). The primary appeal of these ads lies in the audience's identification with the spokesperson. For this reason, advertisers should choose a spokesperson who is reasonably attractive but with whom the average person can identify in terms of demographics and lifestyle. Further, the plot or scene depicting the lay endorser should appear natural or be unrehearsed. Examples would be the use of a candid interview of the lay endorser, or a hidden camera observing the lay

▼ **EXHIBIT 8-9.** Implicit endorsement by testimonials.

The best ads for Dove are the women who use it.

Lauren Chase
Costa Mesa, California

25 Years of Dove

Dove® contains ¼ moisturizing cream.   It won't dry your face like soap.

Source: Courtesy of Lever Brothers Company.

endorser's pleasant surprise with using a particular product. However, the overuse of testimonials often in phony plots coupled with the audience's knowledge that all spokespersons are carefully screened and paid has diminished the efficacy of this type of endorsement.

Cost Effectiveness

At some point in the decision to use endorsers, advertisers have to consider the cost effectiveness of their choice. In doing so they have to consider several issues.

First, the endorsers who appear to have the most potential, tend to be the most popular and charge the highest fees. The demand for sports and entertainment celebrities has grown so much that advertisers may have to pay thousands of dollars for a few seconds of endorsement time for the most popular endorsers. Rather than pursuing a popular endorser, advertisers can do well by looking for a lesser known person who nicely matches the message of the brand and appeals to the target segment. In this sense, picking endorsers may be like picking stocks. Much is gained by discovering a new personality that brings value to one's brand or message.

Second, the use of celebrities is a high-risk decision. A good choice can pay off handsomely. But celebrities have feet of clay and sometimes lose favor with the public because of some public gaffe, embarrassing secret or scandal. The list of celebrities whose careers were rocked by scandal or tarnished by mishaps is long and includes Tonya Harding, Michael Jackson, Michael Jordan, Magic Johnson, O. J. Simpson, Burt Reynolds and Mike Tyson. Even the most revered are vulnerable. The high cost associated with some celebrity endorsements increases the risk of the contract. At the same time, celebrities as a class remain popular and their endorsements may still be effective. One study found that the credibility of celebrity endorsers, measured by their approval rating, went up from 20 percent in 1986 to 28 percent in 1993.[16] Thus advertisers need to carefully evaluate whether the payoff from using celebrity endorsers is worth the risk.

Third, many celebrities endorse multiple brands, switch brands, and compete with other celebrities, sometimes in the same product category. As a result, one study found that although consumers could correctly identify the endorsers, they were less accurate in matching the brands that they endorsed (see Exhibit 8-10). Thus the payoff from any one endorsement contract is uncertain.

Fourth, while lay endorsers do not have instantaneous name recognition, they can bring freshness and sincerity to an advertising campaign, as did Harry and Louise of the anti–health care system ads. To the extent that consumers can identify with them, their performance may be quite effective. Lay endorsers do not charge a high rate, although their fees may increase if their spots become popular and air frequently. For example, lay endorsers such as Nick and Helen of the e.p.t. ad were paid little for their appearance, but came across as sincere and appealing.

A good starting point for determining the cost effectiveness of an endorsement strategy is the evaluation of endorser, to which topic we now turn.

THE EVALUATION OF ENDORSERS

Because of the growing use of celebrities in advertising, researchers have developed standardized tests and research models to gauge their public standing or suitability for endorsements. The standardized tests

▼ **EXHIBIT 8-10.** Celebrity and brand recognition during Super Bowl XXIV.

Celebrity	PERCENT OF RESPONDENTS CORRECTLY RECOGNIZING OR MATCHING	
	Celebrity Recognition	Brand-Celebrity Match
Joe Montana	70%	18%
Jay Leno	66	53
Michael J. Fox	64	35
Bo Jackson	54	42
Lee Iacocca	29	25
Fred Savage	27	17

Source: Reprinted with permission from *Marketing News,* published by the American Marketing Association, "Celebrity Alone Isn't a Sure Hit" by David Shani and Dennis Sandler, August 5, 1991, 8.

are based on surveys of consumers' perceptions of celebrities. These tests are carried out periodically by research companies in response to demand by advertisers and publishers. Each research company uses its own survey design the same way over the years for consistency. The three better known standardized tests are Q-ratings, Video Storyboard Tests and Total Research Corporation's ratings. In addition, advertisers can carry out their own customized research to evaluate the effectiveness or performance of specific endorsers.

This section describes one standardized test, Q-ratings, and one customized approach to evaluating endorsers.

Q-Ratings

Q-ratings are prepared by Marketing Evaluations Inc. of Port Washington, New York. The ratings are widely used by marketers and agencies to select celebrity endorsers, and also by TV networks and Hollywood producers to cast characters.[17] Marketing Evaluations Inc. evaluates the familiarity and likability of about 1,500 public personalities, drawn from lists of names provided by subscribers to the report. Each subscriber can nominate about 50 names for the annual study. In 1993, subscribers had to pay from $9,000 to $20,000 for a copy of the report, depending on their subscriber status and their planned use of the report.

Marketing Evaluations Inc. surveys a sample of about 1,500 respondents by mail. It draws the sample from The People Panel, a nationally representative cooperating panel. All members over 6 years of age within a selected household are required to answer the questionnaire. Because the firm evaluates a large number of personalities, the sample of respondents is broken down into four demographically matched and balanced subsamples, each of which evaluates approximately a quarter of the personalities. The data from the respondents is pooled across the four samples and analyzed by demographic groups.

Each respondent evaluates each personality on a six-point scale, shown in Exhibit 8-11. The **total familiar score** is the percentage of the respondents who rate a candidate on a scale that ranges from "one of my favorites" to "never seen or heard of before." The candidate's **Q-rating** is the percentage of those familiar with the performer who rate the candidate as "one of my favorites." The letter "Q"

▼ **EXHIBIT 8-11.** Marketing Evaluations, Inc., ratings framework.

Scale

One of my favorites
Very good
Good
Fair
Poor
Never seen or heard of before

Categorization of Respondents

Age (7 levels)
Age of males (6 levels)
Age of females (7 levels)
Income (4 levels)
Occupation (2 levels)
Education (2 levels)
Nielsen county size (3 levels)
Geographic region (4 levels)
Race (2 levels)
View prime time (3 levels)

Classification of Public Personalities

TV performers (4 categories)
Actors/actresses (4 categories)
Comedians (2 categories)
Musicians (3 categories)
Hosts and news reporters (4 categories)
Athletes and sports figures
Producers
Models
Miscellaneous

Data source: Marketing Evaluations, Inc.

stands for this quotient or ratio, which gives the rating. The results are available in the aggregate as well as by type of personality and demographic group of the respondent. Personalities are classified into 21 categories, while respondents may be classified into groups on each of ten demographic characteristics (see Exhibit 8-11).

To use the Q-ratings appropriately, advertisers need to keep track of the key features of the score: the familiarity and liking of the personality, and the target demographic group being surveyed. For example, in Exhibit 8-12A, Jack Lemmon has almost the same Q-rating as Robert J. Woods, because each of them is the favorite of about a third of the respondents familiar with them. However, Jack Lemmon is much better known, with a total

▼ EXHIBIT 8-12. Marketing Evaluations, Inc., ranking of celebrities from standard ratings.

A. Q-Ratings among Adults 35–49 Years Old for 1992

Performer	Category	% Favorite	Total Familiar	Q-Rating
Jack Lemmon	Non-TV actor	29%	96%	31
Robert Woods	Daytime TV actor	5	17	29

B. Q-Ratings for Bob Hope for 1992

Segment	% Favorite	Total Familiar	Q-Rating
Males ≥ 50 years	55%	98%	56
Females 18–34 years	28	96	29
Males 18–34 years	35	98	36
Youth 6–11 years	22	61	35

familiarity of 96 percent while Robert J. Woods has a total familiarity of only 17 percent. They have equally strong appeals (Q-ratings), but Woods's appeal is much narrower than Lemmon's. Now consider Exhibit 8-12B. Bob Hope is equally well known among males over 50 years and females 18 to 34 years. But he is much better liked among the former, leading to a Q-rating of 56 for males over 50 versus 29 for females 18 to 34 years old.

Q-ratings provide a fairly simple measure of a celebrity's appeal to various segments. Because of this simplicity, they are easily available for a large number of personalities by a number of demographic segments. To retain simplicity, Q-ratings evaluate celebrities on only two key dimensions: familiarity and likability. These two dimensions are key constructs of the source attractiveness model, which provides the theoretical foundation for Q-ratings. The limitation of this framework for evaluating celebrities is that it ignores the distinct meanings that may be associated with each celebrity. This aspect is captured by the next research approach.

Customized Research

In contrast to standardized tests, an advertiser has the option of carrying out customized research to evaluate one or more candidate endorsers. Customized research has three advantages over standardized tests. First, the advertiser can choose the candidates it would like to evaluate, including names that may not appear on any of the standardized

tests. These candidates could be endorsers it has used in the past or others it intends to use in the future. Second, the advertiser could specify the criteria on which it would like to evaluate these candidates. These criteria could go beyond the few dimensions such as familiarity and likability used in the standardized tests. In particular, the customized research could try to capture the complexity of meanings encompassed by each of the candidate endorsers, as suggested by the meaning transfer model. Third, the customized research could study the effectiveness of matching up specific brand names with specific candidates. The main disadvantages of this approach are the higher cost, trouble and greater time it takes to customize research for the individual needs of the advertiser.

A marketing professor, Wayne DeSarbo, and his associate Richard Harshman developed one model to carry out customized research in the context of the automobile market.[18] They surveyed target consumers' agreement or disagreement with a large number of characteristics that described candidate celebrities and brands. Consumers' responses were measured on a seven-point bipolar scale with agreement coded +3 and disagreement coded -3. Sample characteristics included how formal, aggressive or strong the consumers rated the images of the brand or the celebrity.

The authors analyzed their data using multidimensional scaling, described in Chapter 1. The resulting maps show how consumers perceived various brands and celebrities. For the advertiser, a good candidate for endorser would be one whose image is close to that of the brand, or who has an image that the company would like the brand to develop.

STRATEGIC IMPLICATIONS

The prior discussion of the endorsement process has some important strategic implications for advertisers today. These implications will be discussed under the following headings: matching celebrities to consumer segments, and the overuse, screening and management of endorsers.

Matching Celebrities to Consumer Segments

A critical issue in choosing endorsers is matching them to the target audience. For this reason, advertisers should first avoid judging candidate endorsers by broad *overall* ratings of a celebrity's appeal. Such indicators may mask the appeal of celebrities to special segments. For example, Madonna may have had a low overall liking of only 25 percent in the survey referenced in the opening vignette of this chapter, but her appeal in the target group of teenagers who identified with her may have been much higher. Fortunately, syndicated agencies also publish ratings for specific target segments, which may differ even for well-known celebrities (see Exhibit 8-12B). Second, advertisers need to consider the unique meaning encoded in a celebrity's image, in addition to the available ratings on familiarity and liking. They should then carefully use endorsers for specific brands and market segments so as to match the images of brand and endorser with the needs of the target segment. Nike follows this policy assiduously, even down to matching different endorsers for different brands within the same subcategory of athletic shoes, to target different market segments.

For example, Nike initially selected John McEnroe to endorse the Challenge Court line of tennis shoes because he projected the "bold and irreverent" image the firm wanted for the brand. In the words of Ian Hamilton, the director of sports tennis marketing, McEnroe "epitomized the type of player Nike wanted for its shoes—talented, dedicated and loud. He broke racquets, drew fines and most of all won matches. His success and behavior drew attention on and off the courts and put a lot of people in Nikes."[19]

McEnroe calmed down as he grew older, which caused his image to change. At the same time, Nike wanted to appeal to the 75 percent of the market for regular tennis shoes, which did not favor the Challenge Court image. They then discovered Andre Agassi, who Hamilton describes as follows: "He had long hair on one side of his face and no hair on the other side. His approach to the game was as it is today, 'hit the ball as loud as you can.' And he was the best player around. From a marketing perspec-

tive, Andre was the perfect vehicle for Nike. He was anti–tennis establishment and he was different."[20]

To use McEnroe's more mature image effectively, Nike launched Supreme Court, a "tuxedo tennis" brand of shoes endorsed by John McEnroe. Andre Agassi was then the perfect choice to inherit the endorsement of Challenge Court.

Similarly, in basketball, Nike also has three different brands of shoes. Air Jordan is a high-performance shoe built around the personality of Michael Jordan. Force, endorsed by David Robinson and Charles Barkley, has a more aggressive, muscular image like that of the endorsers. Flight shoes are lighter and more flexible, reflecting the high-flying style of Scottie Pippin, who endorses this brand.

Overuse of Celebrity Endorsers

One study of endorsements found that in 1989, Coke and Diet Coke used 27 celebrities plus 31 NFL players while Pepsi and Diet Pepsi used 5.[21] Some of the names used during that year and the following year include Billy Crystal, Fred Savage, Kirk Cameron, Randy Travis, Jerry Hall, Chris Evert, Phylicia Rashad, Vanna White, Joe Montana, Sugar Ray Leonard, Paula Abdul and Elton John. These stars also endorsed other products, while numerous other celebrities were associated with other brands.

All of these endorsements may be difficult to keep straight even for ardent stargazers. Why did Coke resort to so many endorsers? What are the disadvantages of using multiple endorsers?

Several factors may be responsible for Coke's policy. First, the 1980s witnessed a splintering of the mass market by the proliferation of brands (for example, diet and caffeine-free colas) and media (for example, many new magazines, newspapers and TV channels). Advertisers may use different celebrities to appeal to different market segments through different media and programs. Second, competition for celebrities could heat up just like competition for other resources. In that case, a firm may sign up a celebrity to preempt another firm from using that person. Alternatively, a firm may sign up celebrities to match any real or perceived advantage from the celebrities signed up by a rival.

However, a firm's use of multiple endorsers could have some undesired results. First, consumers' trust in endorsers declines as they endorse multiple products, especially if consumers are aware of the multiple endorsements.[22] The reason is that consumers may question whether the endorser really believes in and uses all the products he or she endorses. Second, as endorsers take on multiple brands, consumers may be unable to correctly recall which brands they stand for (see Exhibit 8-10). Third, since each endorser has a unique image, a multiplicity of endorsers might blur the image of the brand. Even if these endorsers were used in different media or programs, because of segment overlap across media, multiple endorsers could still blur the brand image. Fourth, the use of many endorsers may lead to the reduced effectiveness of this means of persuasion. This is true of endorsers as of any other means of persuasion. The overuse of celebrities may be one reason for their declining popularity. Video Storyboard Tests Inc. surveys several thousand people each year to rank the best-liked ads. In 1981, celebrity ads were much liked, claiming 7 of the top-scoring ads. But by 1989 only 2 celebrity ads made the top 20. Cartoons, animations and fantasy ads were much more popular.[23] In 1994, celebrities featured in only 1 of the top 10 ads.[24]

Fifth, multiple endorsements for each brand are likely to aggravate the related problem of individual celebrities endorsing multiple brands. This effect may occur either because of the increasing demand for celebrities or the smaller available budget to tie them to exclusive contracts. Some celebrities endorse so many brands that the unique qualities of their image might well be lost. For example, at one time Bill Cosby appeared in ads for Coca-Cola, Jell-O, E. F. Hutton, Kodak and Texas Instruments,[25] while Michael Jordan endorsed products for 14 companies.[26] The meaning transfer model suggests that Bill Cosby's image would be affected by the roles he plays in each of those ads. Multiple roles lead to a blurring of his unique image and contribution to any one brand. Further, subjects' liking, trust and perception of the expertise of a celebrity can decline with the number of endorsements.[27] It was probably for these reasons that Wendy's dropped Clara Peller ("Where's The Beef?") as an endorser when she also appeared for a spot for Prego.[28]

Firms have the option of selecting only those endorsers who have few or no brands associated with their names, or binding a celebrity to an exclusive contract that prohibits him or her from endorsing other brands. However, the celebrities with the most appeal are also most in demand; the exclusive contract could well cost the firm the equivalent of what the endorser could have earned from other contracts. Not even Nike, which had a profitable, long-term relationship with Michael Jordan, limited him to an exclusive contract. It may have been too expensive for Nike, as Jordan earned over $30 million from endorsements of brands such as Gatorade, McDonald's and Hanes.

Instead of an undisciplined quest for multiple endorsers, advertisers should strive to develop long-term relationships with one celebrity, to ensure a single, clear, consistent brand strategy over time. Nike, for example, takes care in developing brands around key celebrities and maintaining the relation over time. Its relationship with Michael Jordan was so strong that he stood for Nike even against the wishes of the U.S. Olympic Committee. The 1992 U.S. Olympic basketball team, the Dream Team, was sponsored by Reebok. As part of the deal, members of the team had to wear Reeboks at the award ceremony when the team won its gold medal. Even though Nike had no objection, Jordan refused to use Reebok's shoes at any time. "It's like saying you're going to pick someone over your father," Jordan explained. "I won't do that."[29]

Screening of Candidates for Endorsers

In November 1991, Earvin "Magic" Johnson announced to a stunned news audience that he had tested positive for the AIDS virus and was resigning from the Los Angeles Lakers. At that time Johnson was a spokesman for a number of brands, including Nestlé, Converse, Nintendo, Pepsi's Slice, Spalding and Kentucky Fried Chicken.[30] The firms that had contracted with Johnson faced a dilemma: Should they continue using him in ads and risk displeasing consumers who were critical of a lifestyle that led him to contract the AIDS virus? Or should they immediately drop him from their ads and risk displeasing his ardent followers? Pepsi postponed screening a new TV spot, apparently at Johnson's request. Most other firms decreased or delayed using Johnson as their spokesman. Johnson returned to basketball as anchor for the U.S. Olympic "dream team" and guard for the LA Lakers, only to resign from the Lakers after a small accident on court that alarmed his teammates. He again joined the Lakers in 1996, and resigned one more time after he could not recapture his previous form.

Since the early 1980s, Michael Jackson was well known and loved for an image that one commentator described as: "a kind of child-man, asexual and eternally pre-adolescent, with his childish contralto and his different manner. He is also weird, living with a menagerie of animals in a sprawling retreat, but he is otherwordly weird, like E.T., not threatening weird."[31] For over a decade Pepsi had a mutually lucrative endorsement contract with Michael Jackson. Then in late 1993, while on a worldwide concert tour sponsored by Pepsi, Jackson was hit with allegations of child molestation. Shortly thereafter, he canceled his tour and sought treatment for an addiction to prescription pain killers. Pepsi dropped its sponsorship of the tour and stopped using Jackson as an endorser.

These examples like that of Pepsi and Madonna show how past or current actions of celebrities can harm or alter their images. Such changes can negatively affect the meanings that advertisers wish to transfer to their brands through the endorsement. Advertisers can reduce the damage from such incidents by carefully screening endorsers before signing a contract. For example, exploratory research or discussions with Madonna might have revealed her plans for the video. Alternatively, a detailed contract would have prevented her from releasing a video with overlapping material. Some may argue that the video was not necessarily bad for Pepsi and the company may well have seen it as a means to gain added publicity for the ad campaign. Even then knowledge of Madonna's intentions would have helped Pepsi's planning.

Could the problems associated with Magic Johnson and Michael Jackson have been uncovered by background checks on their lifestyle and behavior? And if they could, would they not have been good endorsers for the duration of their contracts? Celebrities by their very nature are public figures whose moves are carefully watched by the media and whose achievements and failings are quickly publicized. No celebrity is perfect, and everyone carries the risk of some damaging incident or revelation. Even Michael Jordan, who was probably the most liked and successful endorser in recent history, was rumored to have problems with gambling. The media may exacerbate the ups and downs in a celebrity's life. When a star is on the rise, the media will glorify him or her; when he or she is in a slump, the media seem to gloat over it. Firms can ensure against some surprises by properly screening candi-date celebrities to ensure that they are buying the right image, and that the risks with the celebrity contract are worth the potential for damage.

Careful screening is especially important because many companies probably choose celebrities with a short-term orientation. In contrast, Nike's approach to recruiting celebrity athletes is designed for success over the long term.[32] According to Ian Hamilton, Nike's director of tennis sports marketing, he begins by scouting the tennis courts looking for athletes with talent, character and style. In talent, Nike looks for players who are at the top of their category to reinforce the image of Nike as a superior performance brand. In character, Nike looks for athletes who are committed to the sport, have a sense of humor, and have an attitude that will be popular with the public. In style, Nike looks for athletes who are distinctive, draw attention to the sport, and make a statement. Hamilton meets with the players and their parents, coaches and agents to see if a contract will work for everyone.

To protect against embarrassments, advertisers could also use a morals clause in the contract with the endorser. A **morals clause** is a legal statement that gives an advertiser the option of terminating a contract with a partial fee or no fee at all. A general form of the clause would run as follows: "Company (advertiser) shall have the right to terminate this agreement if Talent (endorser) becomes involved in any situation or occurrence which, in the Company's reasonable opinion, subjects Talent or Company to ridicule, contempt or scandal."[33] However, the precise wording would have to be negotiated, and would depend on the relative bargaining power of the advertiser and endorser.

Managing Endorsers

"Magic" Johnson and Converse had a dispute over the failure of the Magic shoe line. Johnson criticized Converse for not involving him in the design of the shoe and not promoting him or the shoe adequately. Converse claimed that it involved Johnson at every stage.

LA Gear and Michael Jackson had a conflict over a failed shoe line. The shoe company sued Jackson for breach of contract and fraud, claiming that the singer did not support a line of high-top sneakers despite a $7.5 million two-year contract beginning in September 1989. Jackson disagreed with the charge.[34]

These examples show that managing celebrities is almost as important as their screening and selection. In particular, advertisers need to ensure that celebrities are involved in planning, are used appropriately, and use the products they endorse.

Advertisers can benefit from involving celebrities in the planning of both the product and the advertising campaign. The involvement motivates celebrities to be more loyal to the advertiser and the brand. They can also provide advertisers with new perspectives or ideas. In contrast to the example of Converse cited above, Nike shows great skill and consistency in its management of celebrities. It involves them in designing the products. It has named buildings after them. It stands by them even when they are sidelined by injuries. Tinker Hatfield, Nike's creative director, describes how he used Bo Jackson in designing the Stability Outrigger, a cross-training shoe.[35] He started by studying Bo. Bo is big, with big muscles and a big face that make him appear larger-than-life. He reminded Hatfield of Mighty Mouse, who has bulging muscles and seems to be always moving forward with a slant to his body. He designed the Stability Outrigger to be larger-than-life, brightly colored with an inflated-looking rubber tongue top. The effectiveness of Nike's endorsement strategy has translated into high sales and potential profits on some popular lines.[36]

Advertisers should ensure that celebrities are used fully for all the exposure and meanings they can effectively deliver to the brand. At the same time they need to ensure that celebrities are not overused in frequency or misused in context so that their appearances have an undesired effect on the brand. Most importantly, in planning celebrity ads, advertisers need to consider other appearances and commitments of the celebrity. For example, the problems LA Gear had with Michael Jackson can be attributed to the many other commitments including endorsements that Jackson had, and the small part that LA Gear played in his life.

Advertisers should ensure that celebrities use the products they endorse. A discovery that the endorser is not a genuine user of the brand can damage the celebrity's image and the effectiveness of the endorsement. Also, the FTC requires that the endorser continue to use the product if he or she claims familiarity with it in the ad. The stature of the celebrity is frequently a major impediment in this regard. Often, celebrities believe that they live in a world of their own with their own rules, and endorsements are an external means of earning income, not intrinsic to their lifestyles. One of the reasons that people respond to celebrities in ads is that they hope to capture some of the aura of the celebrity. If a celebrity does not really use the product he or she endorses, the magic is gone and the meaning is lost.

STEREOTYPING OF ENDORSERS

An important consideration in the selection and use of models and endorsers is the issue of stereotyping. **Stereotypes** are perceptions or depictions of individuals based on a simplistic, biased image of the group to which they belong, rather than on their own individual characteristics. The stereotyping of endorsers may occur in **casting** (the selection of individuals for characters), or **characterization** (the portrayal of those characters). In advertising, stereotyping in casting involves the heavier selection of individuals for a task from one particular group, although individuals of other groups may also perform such a task. Examples would be choosing only white males for airline ads, females for detergent ads, or teens for jean ads. Stereotyping in characterization involves designing roles that conform to a stereotype rather than to reality. Examples would include portraying women as homemakers, Asians as math freaks, the Irish as beer guzzlers, or the elderly as physically limited.

Stereotyping is almost as old as advertising. Consider this description of the problem as it prevailed in the 1920s:

> "The women shown in the ads were always bright and eager typists making a good impression in the office, or capable mothers running a neat and caring home. The men in the ads of the time were invariably businessmen. No laboring man seems to have bought anything. If the businessman was ever shown away from his desk, he was either playing golf or tennis and dressed accordingly. Any ills were shown threatening his chance of promotion; halitosis, constipation, pink toothbrush, foot odor, and dropping socks could all hold back his climb up the ladder of prosperity."[37]

The growing consciousness over the last three decades of the equality of all people, as well as the efforts by various civil-rights groups, have heightened the public's sensitivity to stereotyping. This sensitivity has also spilled over into advertising. Stereotyping is not as common or obnoxious as in the 1920s. Nevertheless, it is still prevalent in advertising today, especially in the areas of gender, race and age.

Gender Stereotypes

In Fall 1991, Stroh's Brewery poured millions of dollars into a campaign featuring the buxom blonde "Swedish bikini team" to promote its Old Milwaukee brand of beer. The ad was supposed to be a spoof of the pervasive sexism in beer advertising. It showed the bikini-clad derrieres of three platinum blondes, with a headline that asked, "Why the average beer commercial has more cans than bottles." The copy read, "At some breweries, the selling of beer is a more highly developed art than the brewing of it. And pretty girls, we are told, sell beer. That's why beer commercials focus tightly on them." But the ad went on to say that this company prefers "to spend money on the brewing time, not TV time."

The ad created bad publicity for Stroh's. In addition, the models who posed in the ad appeared on the cover of the January 1993 issue of *Playboy* and in sexually explicit poses inside the issue. The models also got their own 900 number. For $3 a call, one could hear the models' sexually explicit talk. Stroh's said it did not initiate the *Playboy* spread and did not authorize or even know about the 900 number. But it conceded it did not try to stop the nude layout, which was organized by one of the models.[38]

Even as it claimed to spoof the sexism prevalent in beer advertising, the ad benefited from it. Moreover, when the models went on to appear in *Playboy*, they endorsed the sexism of the ad. Advertising commentators were highly critical of the ad, and women's groups were furious. Initially, Stroh's stood by its ad and refused to back down. However, when five female employees sued Stroh's for sexual harassment, citing the bikini-team ad as evidence of Stroh's sexist mentality, Stroh's finally agreed to stop the ad.

One of the most common criticisms of advertising is the gender stereotyping that is prevalent in contemporary ads. While stereotyping in casting has declined in the last decade,[39] that in characterization is still widespread. Endorsers (lay or celebrities) are typically presented as young, beautiful and sexually attractive. For example, Singapore Airlines developed a reputation for excellent service with its ad campaign begun in 1972 that featured the "Singapore Girl," a pretty young female, draped in a

form-fitting sarong and a gracious smile. Some ads go further in their stereotypical characterization of women models. Beer ads have a long history of portraying women as sex objects that reward macho males for buying the advertised brand. Indeed, the macho image of beer is one of the strongest for low- to medium-priced beers. The stereotyping of characters may be one reason why in one study consumers, especially women, found beer ads to be the most distasteful.[40] The controversy about the Swedish bikini team apparently did not send a message to other advertisers. In the aftermath of the controversy, Bugle Boy aired three 30-second spots on MTV of pouty and partially clad or undressing women with provocative captions. It also justified the ad as a spoof on the use of sex in advertising.

Advertisers resort to stereotypes for many reasons. First, advertisers assume that sexy models draw attention to the ad or that provocative images keep the brand name in the news. Calvin Klein and Benetton may have used controversial sex appeals for the latter purpose. Second, advertisers assume that the feelings aroused by the model would pass on to the product with which the model appears, especially for products that have sexual overtones. Third, advertisers hope to better appeal to target segments with stereotypical portrayals. For example, they may assume that more women than men do the laundry (as in the past), so a female model would be more appropriate. How valid are these assumptions? Research indicates that the use of sexy appeals is effective only if there is a close link between the brand and the appeal.[41] For example, sexy appeals may work better with lingerie than with computers.

Many studies have examined the portrayal of women in stereotypical roles. One study tested three such portrayals: traditional, modern superwoman, and modern egalitarian.[42] The traditional one showed a woman as a housewife; the modern superwoman showed a woman holding an outside job and doing the housework; and the modern egalitarian showed a woman sharing housework with her husband (see Exhibit 8-13). The study found that women responded much better to either of the modern portrayals than to the traditional one. In addition, the egalitarian scored a little better than the superwoman in preference and effectiveness. However, there were differences by type of woman subject. Women who earned a higher income and had a more contemporary gender ideology favored

▼ **EXHIBIT 8-13.** Copy depicting three portrayals of women.

Portrayal	Copy
Traditional	I enjoy spending time in the kitchen. And I like to have my husband's dinner ready for him when he comes home from work. But when I have a hectic day around the house I rely on Rice-A-Roni to help me out.
Modern Superwoman	Working all day in the office and doing most of the housework myself is tough. When I get home from work my second job begins. And when I'm tired from a hectic day at work, it's nice to have Rice-A-Roni to help me out at home.
Modern Egalitarian	In our home my husband and I decided to share the household chores. Since we both have full-time jobs, we're often too tired to cook when we get home. That's when we rely on Rice-A-Roni to help us out.

Source: Richins, Marsha L. (1991), "Social Comparison and the Idealized Images of Advertising," *Journal of Consumer Research* 18 (June), 71–83. Copyright 1991 The University of Chicago Press.

the egalitarian portrayal over the other two to a larger extent than did women who earned lower incomes and had a more traditional gender ideology. Other studies have also shown that women differ in their receptivity to various portrayals of women in ads. Thus advertisers need to be conscious of their target market, but when in doubt, a modern portrayal is likely to be better liked and more effective.

Besides the issue of effectiveness, stereotyping can have unfavorable effects that the advertiser never intended. One unintended effect may be that certain audiences are so captivated by attractive models that they miss the message, as explained in Chapter 5. A second effect may be that viewers compare themselves to the models, and respond with feelings of inadequacy, disbelief or disgust[43] (see Exhibit 8-14). If such feelings are mild some consumers may go out and buy the product in the hope that it will imbue them with the same virtues as the models. However, if such feelings are strong, consumers may find the models unbelievable, and reject the message and the brand. For example, the physically perfect, sexually irresistible models that frequently appear for automobiles, soft drinks, clothes, diet medications and health clubs may lead a viewer to consider the model's figure to be artificial. That in turn would lead to a feeling of disgust for the ad and a rejection of the message.

A third effect is that some market segments who are exposed to the ad may be offended by the stereotyping and may avoid the product or generate negative publicity about the advertiser. For example, Stroh's Brewery's casting of the Swedish bikini team led Stroh's own employees to sue the company. The negative publicity that the event generated may have turned off a number of consumers. Indeed some consumer groups are critical of any ads that use sex appeal, which they interpret as sexist. For example, Coca-Cola was criticized for "reverse sexism" because a Diet Coke ad showed a group of women ogling a beefy construction worker as he stripped off his T-shirt.[44] Advertisers face a difficult situation, trying to balance an effective use of sex appeal with the desire not to offend such segments.

A fourth effect is that problems of bulimia and anorexia may be aggravated by the appearance of unrealistically beautiful, slim models in ads. Impressionable teens and young adults may begin associating slimness with beauty and attractiveness, aggravating any tendencies they have to these disorders. For example, when Kate Moss appeared as a waiflike model for Calvin Klein's jeans, Boycott Anorexic Marketing, a special-interest group in Boston, called for a Klein boycott.[45] The United Kingdom's Advertising Standards Authority asked for the ads to be yanked because of Moss's nude "child-like" form.[46]

However, advertising is not solely responsible for all problems with stereotyping. To begin with, the appeals used in ads are as much the result of audience expectations as the cause of audience behavior. Advertisers persist in using such appeals because audiences continue to respond to them. In addition, stereotyping occurs in the regular programming of all media, especially magazines, music videos and movies. For example, the problems of bulimia and anorexia may be the result of learned values and

▼ **EXHIBIT 8-14.** Audience responses to attractive models in ads.

A. Selected Free Responses

General comparison	"God! I wish I looked like that." (Written comment about a cosmetics ad before discussion began.) "There's certain [ads] that I look at and say, 'Wow! I'd sure like to look like that.'" "In high school, you want to think that you could look like that if you try. Then in college, you realize, 'Oh, forget it!'"
Ads generating specific body comparisons	"When I see ads, I always look at the chest. I like it when she has no chest. Because, you know, I don't either." "I have wide hips. I always look at the hips. I guess I'm just jealous." "When I look at a model I look at the arms, because my arms are awful."
Negative self-feelings from viewing ads	"You look at these ads and you feel inadequate, like you can't measure up." "It's frustrating when you start to realize you should look that way—I mean—I can't." "I used to go through these magazines every day and look at [models in the ads] and wish I looked like them. I used to go running every day, and I really thought maybe I could look like them. I remember, I even picked one model in particular and cut out ads with her in them. I was pretty obsessed. And I finally realized this wasn't realistic. But I sometimes still look and think, 'Well, maybe.'"

B. Responses to Survey Statements

Survey		Percent True*
Comparison Act	"When I see models in clothing ads, I think about how well or how badly I look compared to the models."	71.3%
	"When I see ads for personal care/cosmetics items, I think about how well or how badly I look compared to the models."	53.8
Dissatisfaction	"Ads for clothing items make me feel dissatisfied with the way I look."	33.8
	"Ads for personal care/cosmetics products make me feel dissatisfied with the way I look."	35.0
	"I have wished I looked more like the models in personal care/cosmetics advertisements."	48.8
Comparison Standard	"When dressing for a special occasion or buying clothes, I look at ads to give me ideas about how I should look."	46.3
	"When dressing for a special occasion or buying personal care/cosmetics items, I look at the ads to give me ideas about how I should look."	36.3

*Note: Percent true refers to the percentage of female college students who said the statement was often true, usually true, almost always true, or true about half the time.

Source: Richins, Marsha L. (1991), "Social Comparison and the Idealized Images of Advertising," *Journal of Consumer Research* 18 (June), 1991, 71–83. Copyright 1991 The University of Chicago Press.

social pressures that patients undergo in their homes and peer groups and not necessarily related to the appearance of attractive models in advertising.

In recent years, advertisers have been more sensitive, especially to gender stereotyping, which has resulted in a broader casting and characterization of models.[47] Women have been portrayed as executives and buyers or users of typically "male" products such as cars and beer, while men have been cast as nurturing parents. Anheuser-Busch said it would be abandoning the traditional portrayal of women as sex objects. Instead, the Bud ads would feature a broader spectrum of characters, including older adults and women in more realistic roles.[48] This particular change by Anheuser-Busch may be motivated as much by demographics as by ethics, because the profile of beer drinkers has changed to include more women and older men. However, a study confirms that while there is a trend toward more equal representation among male and female models relative to the past, the gap is still quite wide.[49]

Race Stereotypes

While racial stereotypes occur across all races, the issue has been most heavily researched in the context of African-American stereotypes. An analysis of the data in this area would be instructive of the issues involved.

A 1989 study found that African-Americans appeared in 19 percent and Hispanics in 6 percent of television commercials containing endorsers.[50] The percentage for African-Americans shows a substantial increase from 1967–1970, when the incidence of African-American endorsers was found to range from 5 percent to 11 percent. Also, the 1989 study found a very high percentage of integration, with African-Americans and Hispanics appearing in ads with multiracial endorsers. Yet African-Americans and Hispanics continue to appear primarily in minor and background roles and shorter time periods than do whites. These facts prompt the following question, why do advertisers not use more African-American endorsers for major roles? Are advertisers and their agencies biased in their selection and portrayal of African-American endorsers? Or are African-American endorsers less effective than white endorsers?

To begin with, race is no longer automatic grounds for rejection of a good candidate for an endorsement. One author claims that in the 1930s and 1940s "stereotyping was acceptable as long as it presented African-Americans as gleeful 'Sambos' or reassuring mammies."[51] Today, personality and image may play a much more important role. Bill Cosby and "Magic" Johnson are African-Americans who have had a wide appeal and have earned millions for their endorsements without hiding their ethnicity.[52] And Michael Jordan may have earned more for his endorsements than any other celebrity endorser of any race. Differences within race show the greater importance of personality and image. For example, while "Magic" Johnson, the humble, endearing athlete, is universally appealing, the heavyweight champion Larry Holmes, a successful but unexciting boxer, was not.

Yet advertisers may not use African-American candidates as endorsers in proportion to their popularity because they suspect that such endorsers may not be as effective as white endorsers. Many studies have tried to test the effectiveness of endorsers by race. Typically, these studies have done so by surveying college students or using them in experiments. However, college students tend to be more educated, cosmopolitan and racially tolerant than the general population, so that the results of such studies may not generalize to the population at large. One study sought to answer this question by recruiting 160 paid white volunteers from a southeastern city for an experiment that compared their response to black versus white endorsers.[53] Racial prejudice toward endorsers, if any, would be more apparent among these subjects than among college students. Prior to the experiment the authors measured the racial prejudice of the subjects, if any, by a standardized test that measured their agreement with 10 statements that contained a subtle racially derogatory belief.

The study found that high-prejudiced white subjects perceived themselves as more similar to the white than the black endorsers. In contrast, low-prejudiced white subjects perceived no differences in their similarity to white or black endorsers. In addition, high-prejudiced white subjects found it more difficult to identify with the black than the white endorsers. Low-prejudiced white subjects showed no such differences. Overall, regardless of the measured attitudes of the white subjects to blacks, white subjects were less likely to purchase the products and had less favorable attitudes toward the products when they were endorsed by black rather than white endorsers. It is not clear how these results would generalize to other samples in this and other cities, or to the general U.S. population. Nevertheless advertisers and their agencies may have similar information, or may suspect that such preferences exist in the general population.

In conclusion, while racism may not be currently rampant in the choice of endorsers, it may still exert a subtle influence in the selection process. The reason may be the personal prejudices of advertisers and their agencies or their beliefs about how receptive the general population is to endorsers of different races.

Age Stereotypes

The stereotypical characterization of the elderly is less topical and less controversial than that of gender or race. However, it is no less offensive. The elderly are normally stereotyped in one of two ways.[54] One is a negative stereotype of the elderly, who are portrayed as weak, senile, bumbling, incompetent or suffering from deafness, irregularity, dentures or insomnia. The other is a positive stereotype of the elderly as grandfatherly, authoritarian, wealthy, learned or working in prestigious jobs. Neither portrayal is valid, though the former is likely to be more offensive. One study found that the elderly are sensitive to their inaccurate portrayal in ads and are likely to boycott some products that use them.[55]

The stereotypical casting of the elderly has been addressed by an extensive study of magazine ads.[56] The study analyzed a sample of 5,195 ads from four issues of each of nine magazines covering distinct topics over a 30-year period (1950–1980). Two raters, each over 60, judged whether each of the 5,195 ads contained an elderly endorser, defined as one over 60 years of age. Of these ads, the two raters judged 469 ads to portray an elderly endorser. One finding was that between 1950 and 1980, the appearance of elderly in ads increased from 6.8 percent to 11 percent, while the population of elderly increased from 12 percent to 16 percent. The trend probably reflects the increasing buying power of the elderly and greater consciousness about the need to be age neutral.

A second finding is a dramatic difference in the casting of endorsers across product categories, from a low of .7 percent elderly in cosmetics to a high of 21 percent elderly in liquor (see Exhibit 8-15). Advertisers may argue that these differences are due to the age differences of the buyers of the products. However, that explanation may not account for the sharp differences in the percentage of elderly across product categories. For example, food (soft drinks), hygiene (shampoo), clothing and cosmetics ads tend to cast their spokespersons as young and beautiful, although consumers of all ages use these products. A third finding is that among elderly spokespersons, males exceed females by about 8 to 1 (see Exhibit 8-16).

The reader may question the relevance of the study given that it extended only up to 1980. Ideally, an update of the study for the 1990s would be informative. In the absence of such an update, the question can be partly addressed by noting the changes over time. For example, the first finding suggests that the number of elderly in ads has increased from 6.8 percent to 11 percent over the three decades. Assuming a linear trend, the figures for the 1990s would have to be adjusted by that ratio.

▼ EXHIBIT 8-15. Distribution by product class of ads incorporating elderly persons.

Product Class	Percent of 469 Ads Containing Elderly Persons
Liquor	20.9%
Cars and trucks	17.2
Banks	17.2
Cameras	16.4
Magazines and newspapers	15.2
Electronics and communications	15.0
Hotels	14.3
Music	14.3
Institutional	14.1
Jewelry	13.5
Machinery	13.5
Sporting goods	13.0
Travel and vacations	12.5
Health and medicine	10.8
Society (ideological crusades, charities, etc.)	9.0
Food	7.3
Hygiene (diet ads, shampoo, etc.)	6.5
Tobacco	6.3
Household (appliances, tools, etc.)	4.1
Clothing	2.7
Cosmetics	.7

Source: Ursic, Anthony C., Michael L. Ursic and Virginia L. Ursic (1986), "A Longitudinal Study of the Use of the Elderly in Magazine Advertising," *Journal of Consumer Research* 13, 1 (June).

SUMMARY

Endorsers may be broadly classified into three groups: experts, celebrities or lay endorsers. This classification is not rigid, because some celebrities also endorse products based on their expertise, while some lay endorsers are so effective and popular that they become celebrities. The more important issue in the endorsement process is understanding what role endorsers play.

Three theories explain the role of endorsers: the source attrac-

▼ **EXHIBIT 8-16.** Casting and characterization of elderly persons in 370 ads, by time and activities.

CASTING (USE) OF ELDERLY PERSONS OVER TIME

Year	Males (%)	Females (%)	Both (%)
1950	72.2%	11.1%	16.7%
1955	80.6	6.4	12.9
1960	86.1	1.4	12.5
1965	74.2	6.1	19.7
1970	76.5	15.6	7.8
1975	80.0	13.3	6.6
1980	80.2	9.9	9.9

CHARACTERIZATION (PORTRAYAL) OF ELDERLY PERSONS BY ACTIVITIES

Activities	Males (%)	Females (%)	Both (%)
Recreational or social interaction	66.7%	13.3%	20.0%
Interaction with family members	35.3	13.8	50.8
White-collar occupation	96.7	2.7	.5
Blue-collar occupation	91.0	6.0	3.0
Miscellaneous	87.5	12.5	0.0
No portrayal	71.0	19.3	9.7

Source: Ursic, Anthony C., Michael L. Ursic and Virginia L. Ursic (1986), "A Longitudinal Study of the Use of the Elderly in Magazine Advertising," *Journal of Consumer Research* 13, 1 (June).

tiveness model, the source credibility model and the meaning transfer model. These three models are complementary and provide different rationales for the use of endorsers. Each model is most suited to explaining the role of one of the three types of endorsers. The meaning transfer model is most relevant for celebrities, the source attractiveness model is particularly relevant for lay endorsers and the source credibility model is most relevant for experts. The choice of experts, celebrities or lay endorsers depends on the characteristics of the brand, the message, and especially the target audience for the ad.

The effectiveness of endorsers can be evaluated by standardized or customized research. Standardized research consists of tests that are regularly conducted by certain research agencies. These tests evaluate public personalities on a limited set of criteria and the results are sold for a fee. In contrast, customized research is tailored to the specific candidates being considered for endorsers and is carried out on any dimensions that the advertisers may desire.

In using endorsers, advertisers need to keep in mind four principles. First, they should try to match the endorser to the image of the brand and the aspirations of the target segments. Second, they need to be cautious about overusing a particular endorser or relying too much on endorsers relative to the other methods of persuasion. Third, they need to screen candidates for endorsers to ensure that the association may not embarrass them in the future. Fourth, they need to manage their relationship with the endorser so that the endorser feels honored and likely to support the endorsed brand in and away from the ad.

Despite considerable progress in the last few years, the stereotyping of endorsers is still prevalent, especially in the areas of gender, race and age. Such stereotyping may reveal itself in either the casting or the characterization of endorsers. Stereotyping in any form is abhorrent and may also be counterproductive.

QUESTIONS

1. Who is an endorser? How would you classify and describe the different types of endorsers?
2. Describe the source credibility and source attractiveness models of endorsements.
3. Explain the meaning transfer model of the endorsement process. What is its special appeal?
4. Compare and contrast the three models that explain the endorsement process. When or how does each model apply?
5. How should one go about evaluating and choosing endorsers?
6. Some brands today have a higher reputation among consumers than any single endorser. Why then do advertisers of such brands need the help of endorsers?
7. Popular celebrities earn millions of dollars as endorsers. Yet all of them have feet of clay, and many fall from their popularity at some time or another. Why do advertisers associate their valuable brands with the fallible names of celebrities?

8. Do advertisers overuse endorsers? Explain.

9. How should advertisers screen and manage celebrity endorsers?

10. Some critics claim that advertisers perpetuate social stereotypes by their casting and characterization of endorsers. Explain.

11. Has stereotyping in ads declined over time? Why?

NOTES

1. "PepsiCo and Madonna" (1990), Harvard Business School Case N9-590-038.

2. Associated Press (1995), "Jordan Scores Again—As A Top Earner," *Los Angeles Times*, December 4, D3; Jensen, Jeff (1993), "Bowe is Endorsement Heavyweight, Too," *Advertising Age,* June 14.

3. Lipman, Joanne (1992), "Pairing Stars with Sneakers is Reassessed," *The Wall Street Journal,* September 9, B6.

4. *Advertising Age* (1960), "Dentists' Okay of Crest As Bar to Decay Elates P&G," August 1, 1, 5.

5. Beltramini and Edwin R. Stafford (1993), "Comprehension and Perceived Believability of Seals of Approval Information in Advertising," *Journal of Advertising* 22 (September 3), 3–13.

6. Colford, Steven W. (1994), "Harry & Louise vs. Billary," *Advertising Age*, February 14, 1, 40.

7. Tripp, Carolyn, Thomas D. Jensen, and Les Carlson (1994), "The Effects of Multiple Product Endorsements by Celebrities on Consumers' Attitudes and Intentions," *Journal of Consumer Research* 20 (March), 535–547.

8. McCracken, Grant (1989), "Who is the Celebrity Endorser? Cultural Foundations of the Endorsement Process," *Journal of Consumer Research* 16 (December), 310–321.

9. Caballero, Marjorie, James R. Lumpkin, and Charles S. Madden (1989), "Using Physical Attractiveness as An Advertising Tool," *Journal of Advertising Research* 29, 4.

10. Englis, Basil G., Michael R. Solomon, and Richard D. Ashmore (1994), "Beauty *Before* The Eyes of Beholders: The Cultural Encoding of Beauty Types in Magazine Advertising and Music Television," *Journal of Consumer Research*, 49–64.

11. McCracken, "Who is the Celebrity Endorser?"

12. *Ibid.*

13. Reid, Leonard N., and Lawrence C. Soley (1981), "Another Look at the 'Decorative Female Model,'" *Current Issues and Research in Advertising,* 123–133.

14. Colford, Steven W. (1991), "How To Find the Right Spokesman," *Advertising Age*, October 28, 17.

15. McCracken, "Who is the Celebrity Endorser?"

16. Study by Video Storyboard Tests, as reported by Miller, Cyndee (1994), "Celebrities Hot Despite Scandals," *Marketing News*, March 28, 1.

17. Mandese, Joe (1992), "Stewart, Cosby top Q Ratings; Where's Mike?" *Advertising Age*, August 31, 3.

18. DeSarbo, Wayne, and Richard Harshman (1985), "Celebrity-Brand Congruence Analysis," *Current Issues and Research in Advertising* 1, 17–51.

19. Willigan, Geraldine E. (1992), "High Performance Marketing," *Harvard Business Review* (July-August), 95.

20. *Ibid.*

21. King, Thomas R. (1989), "More Pros Find Celebrity Ads Unpersuasive," *The Wall Street Journal*, July 5, B1.

22. Tripp, Jensen, and Carlson, "The Effects of Multiple Product Endorsement by Celebrities."

23. Lipman, Joanne (1990), "When It's Commercial Time, TV Viewers Prefer Cartoons to Celebrities Any Day," *The Wall Street Journal,* B10.

24. Goldman, Kevin (1994), "Polar Bears And A Pizza Man Star in Most Popular Ads of 1994," *The Wall Street Journal*, March 16, B1, B8.

25. *Forbes* (1987), "It Seemed Like A Good Idea At The Time," February 28, 98.

26. Tripp, Jensen, and Carlson, "The Effects of Multiple Product Endorsements by Celebrities."

27. *Ibid.*

28. Goldman, Kevin (1995), "Ad Industry Pitches Old 'Stars,' Recycling Them Anew," *The Wall Street Journal*, August 15, B8.

29. Levin, Gary (1992), "Endorsements Cause Dilemma for Dream Team," *Advertising Age*, August 3, 1–2.

30. Miller, Cyndee (1991), "Advertisers Forced to Rethink 'Magic' as Their Spokesman," *Marketing News*, December 25.

31. Gabler, Neal (1993), "Trapped in the Amber of Public Image," *Los Angeles Times*, September 12, M1, M6.

32. Willigan, "High Performance Marketing."

33. Rabinowitz, David, and Helene Godin (1994), "What to Do With a Fallen Star," *Advertising Age*, November 4, 30.

34. Lipman, "Pairing Stars With Sneakers is Reassessed."

35. Willigan, "High Performance Marketing."

36. For example, Nike earned $200 million on all Air Jordan shoes and clothes in 1991 alone. If Nike's margin on sales were 40% and the cost of advertising (including endorsement fees) were as high as $30 million then its profits would be $50 million ($200 × .4 − 30).

37. Dalrymple, Goodrum (1990), *Advertising in America: The First Two Hundred Years,* New York: Harry N. Abrams, 38.

38. Lipman, Joanne (1991), "Stroh Ad Campaign Spins Out of Control," *The Wall Street Journal,* December 12.

39. Jaffe, Lynn J., and Paul D. Berger (1994), "The Effect of Modern Female Sex Role Portrayals on Advertising Effectiveness," *Journal of Advertising* (July-August), 32–42.

40. Rickard, Leah (1994), "Consumers Would Rather Skip Feminine Hygiene Ads," *Advertising Age*, March 14, 29.

41. See Chapter 6.

42. Jaffe, and Berger, "The Effect of Modern Female Sex Role Portrayals."

43. Richins, Marsha L. (1991), "Social Comparison and the Idealized Images of Advertising," *Journal of Consumer Research* 18 (June), 71–83.

44. Goldman, Kevin (1994), "From Witches to Anorexics, Critical Eyes Scrutinize Ads for Political Correctness," *The Wall Street Journal*, May 19, B1.

45. *Ibid.*

46. *Advertising Age* (1994), "Objection, Your Honor," December 19, 19.

47. Pomice, Eva (1993), "A Few Good Women," *Lear's,* March, 100–130; Sharkey, Betsy (1993), "You've Come A Long Way Madison Avenue," *Lear's,* March, 92–99; Serafin, Raymond (1994), "I Am Woman, Hear Me Roar . . . In My Car," *Advertising Age*, November 7, 1, 8.

48. Teinowitz, Ira (1991), "This Bud's For Her," *Advertising Age*, October 28, 1, 49.

49. Bellizzi, Joseph A., and Laura Milner (1991), "Gender Positioning Of A Traditionally Male-Dominated Product," *Journal of Advertising Research* (June/July), 72–79.

50. Wilkes, Robert E. and Humberto Valencia (1989), "Hispanics and Blacks in Television Commercials," *Journal of Advertising* 18, 1 (Winter), 19–25.

51. Quote by Jackson Lears, author of *Fable of Abundance,* as reported in Hirsch, James S. (1995), "Offensive Advertising—Racist, Sexist or Ageist—Is An American Tradition," *The Wall Street Journal*, October 19, B1.

52. Lipman, Joanne (1988), "Sports Marketers See Evidence of Racism," *The Wall Street Journal*, October 18, B1.

53. Whittler, Tommy E., and Joan Dimeo (1991), "Viewers' Reactions to Racial Cues in Advertising Stimuli," *Journal of Advertising Research* (December), 37–46.

54. Langmeyer, Lynn (1984), "Senior Citizens and Television Advertisements: A Research Note," *Current Issues and Research in Advertising* 1, 167–178; Festervand, Troy A., and James R. Lumpkin (1985), "Response of Elderly Consumers to Their Portrayal by Advertisers," *Current Issues and Research in Advertising* 2, 203–209.

55. *Ibid.*

56. Ursic, Anthony C., Michael L. Ursic, and Virginia L. Ursic (1986), "A Longitudinal Study of the Use of the Elderly in Magazine Advertising," *Journal of Consumer Research* (June).

Sales
Promotion
Strategy

9

In Winter 1994, Northwest Airlines ran a promotion that encouraged consumers to book Northwest flights to the Twin Cities' giant shopping and entertainment complex, the Mall of America. The promotion offered round-trip fares ranging from $38 to $98 for travel from 42 midwestern cities to Minneapolis, on eight Saturdays between November 1993 and January 1994. The discounted fares made air travel a convenient, inexpensive alternative to bus travel, the primary transportation mode for Mall of America shoppers.

Overview of Sales Promotions

Northwest supported the promotion with press releases but no advertising. The promotion had a tremendous impact on sales. Northwest had projected sales of only a few thousand promotional tickets, but sold 14,000 promotional tickets during the eight-week period.[1]

Sales promotions are all around us. We are constantly faced with coupons, sweepstakes and price-cuts that try to make products ever more appealing and induce us to make a purchase. These promotions can have dramatic effects. They can catapult the brand

▼ EXHIBIT 9-1. Software promotion showing expiration date.

Source: Courtesy of Microsoft Corporation.

a brand's image among consumers even though it may not trigger a dramatic, short-term sales increase. Sales promotion agencies counter that the shift in expenditures is because firms have realized that sales promotions are more effective than advertising.

What are sales promotions? What role do they play? What characteristics of consumers render promotions effective or ineffective? This chapter addresses these questions.

A **sales promotion** is any *time-bound* program of a seller that tries to make an offer more attractive to buyers and requires their *participation* in the form of an immediate purchase or some other action. Examples include coupons, sweepstakes, rebates, sampling, or price-cuts like the Northwest Airlines offer. One key term in the definition is *time-bound*. Sales promotions generally hold for a well-defined time period that is announced to consumers. For example, the Northwest Airlines promotion ran for eight weeks between November 1993 and January 1994. Similarly, coupons have an expiration date, sweepstakes have a drawing date, and rebates have a last date for mailing. A permanent price-cut is not a sales promotion, nor is a continuous sweepstakes, such as a state lottery. For example, in August 1996, Microsoft offered an attractive promotion for its new Microsoft® Internet Explorer, which included a free version of the product and free subscription to some leading Internet sites (see Exhibit 9-1). Note the expiration date of the offer (in small print at the bottom). A second key word in the definition of promotion is *participation*. Sales promotions generally require consumers to participate by using a coupon, entering a sweepstakes, using a sample or buying the product by a specific date.

Many people, including some professionals, have serious misconceptions about sales promotions. One misconception is that sales promotions constitute

into market leadership or buy the brand a bunch of headaches. Firms' sales promotions have been on a steady increase over the last decade, while advertising expenditures have shrunk by almost half. This shift in marketing expenditures has triggered a major controversy. Advertising agencies have routinely described the shift as shortsighted. They claim that sales promotions cause short-term increases in sales while eroding a brand's long-term image; in contrast, they claim that advertising builds or reinforces

▼ EXHIBIT 9-2. Definition of sales promotions.

Trade Promotions

Price-based trade deals, temporary reductions in price of a product that a manufacturer offers a retailer for a preannounced period of time, called the deal period (e.g., off-invoice and quantity discounts).

Nonprice trade deals, incentives from manufacturer to retailer for a preannounced period of time, called the deal period (e.g., slotting allowances).

Cooperative advertising, offer by manufacturer to pay some fraction of retailer's advertising costs, and sometimes to design a retail advertisement.

Display support, manufacturer's supply and allowance for various setups within or near a retail store to draw attention to a product or demonstrate its features.

Exhibits, displays that manufacturers set up at conventions to show their products to the trade.

Conventions, meetings (generally annual events) at which members of association meet to exchange views, plan events or examine new products.

Consumer Promotions

Manufacturer coupons, certificates from firms offering consumers some fixed saving off retail price of the product if they meet some conditions.

Rebates, guarantee by firms to reimburse consumers by mail for purchase of a product subject to certain conditions. Technically, the term has the same meaning as a *refund,* except that *rebates* is used for durables and *refund* is used for nondurables.

Refund, see Rebates.

Price packs (also called *cents-off packs*), packages on which firm offers a temporary lower price to consumers.

Premiums, gifts that a single firm provides to consumers free or at a reduced price, and without any special benefit to the producer of the gift.

Tie-ins, joint promotions for two or more items by one or more firms.

Bonus plans, programs in which a buyer can accumulate points towards free purchases of same or some other product(s).

Sweepstakes, drawings in which winners are determined purely by chance. Because of the latter criterion, sweepstakes cannot be limited to buyers of the brands.

Contests, games or a combination of games and sweepstakes in which winners are at least partly determined by rules of the games.

Sampling, free or subsidized availability of a product for consumers' trial.

Retail Promotions

Price discounts, reductions in list price that generally hold for a week. Retailers and the public refer to this price cut as a sale.

Double coupons, retailer's offer to double the value of a manufacturer's coupon.

Retail coupons, same as manufacturer coupons except that they are offered by retailers to consumers.

Displays, in-store arrangements that give greater visibility to a brand relative to competing brands.

Features, mostly controlled by retailers and serve the latter's goals.

unnecessary incentives that inevitably erode a brand's value. Actually, sales promotions span a wide spectrum of activities (see Exhibit 9-2), many of which have a long-term positive effect on a brand's appeal. For example, sales conferences generate great enthusiasm among a manufacturer's retailers, trade conventions help suppliers contact their clients, consumer sampling generates trial for new brands, and coupons can contain vital information on brand features.

A second misconception is that sales promotions are ad hoc attempts to shore up a declining brand. Although promotions may constitute a weapon of last resort that firms can use to remedy some problems with a marketing plan, promotions require advance planning to be effective. For example, P&G's annual promotional plan for detergents follows a two-month cycle, during which promotions across brands and cycles complement each other (see Exhibit 9-3). Thus while Tide offers a deal to the trade (retailers) in one cycle, Cheer offers coupons to consumers, and Oxydol offers specially priced packs. Such planning minimizes internal competition among brands and appeals to consumers who differ in shopping patterns. In addition, good planning

▼ **EXHIBIT 9-3.** Illustrative promotion schedule for Procter & Gamble detergents.

Brand	Jan–Feb	Mar–Apr	May–Jun	Jul–Aug	Sep–Oct	Nov–Dec
Tide	Trade deal	Coupon		Price pack		Trade deal
Cheer	Coupon		Price pack	Trade deal		Price pack
Oxydol	Price pack		Trade deal		Coupon	

Source: Adapted from data in Alice MacDonald and John Quelch, "Procter & Gamble (B)," 1983, Harvard Business School Publishing, Cambridge, MA.

ensures that at least one of the firm's brands is always on some type of promotion, competing with promotional offers by rival firms. An even more important strategic role of sales promotion is to price discriminate among segments of consumers who differ in information, loyalty or price sensitivity to the brand. A section on price discrimination later in the chapter discusses this important issue.

A third misconception is that sales promotions constitute short-term tactics while advertising constitutes long-term strategy. Although some firms may adopt this approach to advertising and promotion, it is a poor strategy. Sales promotions are most effective when they constitute an intrinsic part of the marketing strategy and are closely linked with advertising. For example, the mail-in ad on O'Doul's brew (Exhibit 9-4) emphasizes the brand's positioning, "America's favorite non-alcohol brew," while the $1 coupon elicits ad readership and brand trial. Another example is the budgeting of advertising and promotion over the life cycle of a durable product. One effective strategy is to use heavy advertising with sampling in the introductory stages and light advertising with price discounting during brand maturity. Exhibit 9-5 summarizes the variety of goals of sales promotions using the general framework of goals for all types of promotions explained in Chapter 1.

Some companies do use sales promotions as an ad hoc measure to boost sales with little long-range planning. This use of promotions is more likely to lead to a disaster. For example, in spring 1993, the British subsidiary of Hoover Vacuum Cleaners, under pressure from declining sales, ran an attractive promotion. The company offered all buyers two free round-trips to the United States if they purchased vacuum cleaners and other Hoover appliances worth more than $375. To minimize the number of claimants, the company set up stringent conditions for the offer, such as early expiration dates and flights with unpopular timings and departure cities. However, with the value of the promotion at over $600, the deal attracted thousands of buyers who went to great pains to meet the conditions. Some even ran ads for unopened boxes (with appropriately dated sales receipts) of Hoover appliances. Hoover's vacuum sales exceeded all expectations, but it also received 200,000 claims for the free trip, more than it was willing to or could handle, creating a public relations disaster. The company compounded the disaster by initially making it very dif-

▼ **EXHIBIT 9-4.** Promotion that offers coupon and reinforces message.

Source: Courtesy of Anheuser-Busch.

▼ EXHIBIT 9-5. **Goals of sales promotions.**

Following the framework given in Chapter 1, we can classify the goals of promotions as short-term tactical goals, intermediate strategic goals, or ultimate long-term goals. Sales promotions serve a number of subordinate goals within each of these three groups.

Tactical Goals

To combat promotional efforts, or increase in market share of competitors.

To move goods that are no longer needed damaged or overstocked or not selling fast enough.

Strategic Goals

To motivate consumers to switch from a rival brand to the promoted brand.

To increase consumers' consumption of a product.

To build downstream inventories of the product either at the distributor, retailer or consumer level.

To motivate brand repurchasing and loyalty.

To motivate dealers lower down in the distribution channel to promote the brand to customers.

Ultimate Goals

To increase sales.

To increase market share.

To increase profits.

ficult for claimants to receive their rewards. Finally, the parent company in the United States, Maytag Corporation, set aside $30 million to meet the rightful demands of claimants and fired the senior managers responsible for the debacle.[2]

Thus managers need to fully understand the potential of sales promotions, and know how to use them well. The rest of the chapter provides an overview for this purpose. The first section discusses the principal dimensions of sales promotions, in order to understand their scope and classify them conveniently. The next four sections discuss the principles of price changes, which are a major component of promotions.

KEY DIMENSIONS OF SALES PROMOTIONS

This book covers over 20 types of sales promotions (see Exhibit 9-2). Managers may develop numerous permutations and combinations of these 20. In addition, creative managers frequently develop new types of sales promotions. So a complete enumeration of all promotions is not easy. However, a good way to describe and explain the variety of promotions is to classify them on their principal dimensions. Two important dimensions of sales promotions are channel characteristics and promotion characteristics.

Channel Characteristics

The channel characteristics of the promotion refer to whether it is a trade, retail or consumer promotion. The term **channel** here refers to the path in the distribution system that the promotion takes (see Exhibit 9-6). **Trade promotions** are promotions that the manufacturer offers a distributor, wholesaler or retailer. **Retail promotions** are promotions that the retailer offers the consumer. **Consumer promotions** are promotions that the manufacturer offers the consumer directly. Each of these types of promotions has distinct goals and methods and merits a separate treatment. So the next three chapters of the text discuss each of these types of promotions in detail. Ultimately the goal of all sales promotions is to elicit a positive consumer response. However, consumer promotions do so directly, while trade promotions, and the retail promotions they trigger, do so indirectly. Manufacturers offer trade promotions at least partly to motivate retailers to promote their brand to consumers with retail promotions. This form of promotion is also called a **push strategy**, because it helps a manufacturer push the product through the distribution system. On the other hand, consumer promotions are also called a **pull strategy**, because they create primary demand for the product that pulls it through the distribution system.

The fraction of the trade deal that retailers pass on to consumers is called the **pass-through**. Pass-through is typically low, and has become one of the major problems of trade promotions. Chapter 11 details the causes of this problem and its potential solutions. To compensate for low pass-through, manufacturers can always resort to consumer promotions. Consumer promotions reach the consumer directly and elicit a good response. However, they incur high distribution costs as the manufacturer must pay to send them to consumers, who may be scattered all over the country or even the world. Trade promotions do not have such distribution costs, but they typically have low pass-through. Thus, the essential trade-off in promotions for the manufacturer is between using a push strategy, which entails low pass-through, or a pull strategy, which entails high distribution cost. Chapters 11 and 12 explain how the manufacturer must make this trade-off.

Manufacturers and retailers are currently involved in a major effort to reduce the costs of sales promotions. One strategy would be for manufacturers to use accounting practices that encourage retailers to pass through more of the trade deal. For example, a manufacturer might structure a trade deal so that the discount applies only on the incremental sales that exceed the regular level, and that occur from the price-cut that the retailer offers to consumers. Another strategy would be for manufacturers to reduce distribution costs by more precise targeting of promotions only to those consumers who would use them. For example, the manufacturer could use a computerized data bank to develop a list of likely rebate users based on past behavior.

Promotion Characteristics

Sales promotions can be broadly classified as being primarily communicative or incentive. The term **communication** is used in its broadest sense to mean any form of persuasion or information transfer, as explained in Part II of the text. For purposes of sales promotion, we can summarize the role of communication as serving one of the following specific goals:

- *To provide information* on product characteristics. An example is a quiz whose answers are based on product attributes.
- *To build awareness* or *help recall* of a product at the time of purchase. An example is an in-store display.
- *To reduce risk* of buying a new product. An example is a sample of a product to induce consumer trial.
- *To create excitement* about a product. An example is an exhibit at a conference, or sweepstakes.

▼ EXHIBIT 9-6. **Channels of sales promotions.**

- *To create goodwill* toward a product. An example is a tie-in with a charity.

The first two of these goals are more informative in nature, while the latter two are more motivational or affective in nature. The target of communication is not only the final consumer, but all agents in the distribution system. For example, an attractive sweepstakes run by a manufacturer may motivate the sales staff, wholesalers and dealers as well as the ultimate consumer. Some promotions of manufacturers may be targeted entirely to the channel members (wholesalers and retailers) to induce them to run their own promotions for consumers. Any particular promotion may incorporate more than one of the goals of communication described here.

An **incentive** is a practical motive to buy a brand, either because of net reduction in price or an increase in benefit. A net decrease in price may take place directly by a price-cut or a discount for the same quantity as before, or indirectly by a coupon or a rebate. These types of sales promotions are called **price promotions**. An increase in benefit may take place directly by an increase in quantity offered at the same price as before, or by an offer of a supplementary gift or service. These sales promotions are called **non-price promotions**.

Subsequent sections on price discrimination and price response show how these changes in value, especially in price, can be used effectively by firms to maximize long-term growth and profitability. The characteristics of promotion provide another basis for classifying promotions. However, promotions do not have to be solely either informative or incentive; they could serve as both: an incentive to buy the brand as well as a means to disseminate information about the brand. For example, Exhibit 9-4 shows how a direct-mail flyer can offer coupons and emphasize key benefits of a brand through picture and copy. Exhibit 9-7 classifies the most common sales promotions by channel, characteristic and goal.

▼ **EXHIBIT 9-7.** **Classification of promotions.**

Type of Promotion	PRIMARILY INCENTIVE		PRIMARILY COMMUNICATIVE	
	Price	Nonprice	Informative	Motivational
Trade	Price-based trade deals (e.g., discounts off invoice)	Nonprice trade deals (e.g., slotting allowances)	Exhibits, cooperative advertising, display support	Conferences, dealer contests
Retail	Price discounts, retail coupons, double coupons	Premiums, tie-ins, bonus plans, financing	Features, displays, sampling	Games, sweepstakes
Consumer	Manufacturer coupons, rebates, price packs, trial coupons	Premiums, tie-ins, bonus plans	Samples, trials	Games, sweepstakes

PRINCIPLES OF PRICE PROMOTION

John, age 10, accompanies his mother on a shopping trip to some department stores. He notices the numerous sales and discounts across each of the stores. He asks his mother, "Why do stores offer all these discounts? Wouldn't they be better off keeping the same high price?" Mary, age 10, frequently accompanies her dad on grocery shopping trips. She notices how prices change regularly on hundreds of products. She asks, "Why do retailers change the prices on hundreds of items each week? Wouldn't they be better off finding one price for each item and sticking to it?" Indeed, wouldn't everyday high prices make for higher profit, greater efficiency and easier management?

A change in price is one of the central activities associated with sales promotions. This change in price may be direct and immediate as with a price discount, immediate but conditional as with a coupon, delayed and conditional as with a rebate, or indirect as with a gift or service attached to the sale. A thorough understanding of the principles that determine why, when and how prices change, and how consumers respond to these changes, is essential to analyzing and planning sales promotions.

A number of important principles guide the appropriate strategy for making changes in price. Traditionally, strategists derived these principles solely from economic theory. Economic theory assumes agents are fully informed, and make rational choices irrespective of human contexts.

However, recent research from consumer behavior, managerial decision making and social psychology suggests that these three assumptions of economics may not be fully valid. We call this new field of research **behavioral research**, because it describes the *actual* behavior of consumers rather than the *assumed* behavior posited in economic theory. Behavioral research leads to key insights about consumer response to price changes and about pricing strategy. We cover the relevant insights under four headings: knowledge of prices, price discrimination, price response and perception of fair price.

Knowledge of Prices and Discounts

Consumers respond only to stimuli they perceive. In the case of prices, consumers need to observe, interpret and process changes in prices to respond to them. Traditional economic theory assumed that consumers made purchases based on perfect information. However, prices for most consumer products are constantly varying. This variation occurs across competing brands and stores, and especially over time for the same brand and store. The variation is primarily due to price discounts by stores to attract price-sensitive consumers. This practice raises a natural question: how well do consumers follow price changes, or how well do they know prices in stores? Recent behavioral research has found some surprising answers to these questions.

Before proceeding, try to answer the following specific questions:

- What percentage of shoppers will correctly state the price of a grocery product *immediately* after a purchase?
- Do buyers of discounted brands differ in their knowledge of prices and in their shopping behavior from those who buy brands at the regular price?
- When do consumers consider a price increase fair? Do the same principles for price increases apply for price decreases?

Many behavioral studies found that consumers' knowledge of prices and promotions was not very good.[3] One problem with those studies was that researchers asked consumers about prices outside of the shopping environment, many hours after a purchase. Consumers may not memorize specific prices of products, given the vast amount of other more important information they need to keep in mind.

A novel study sought to determine the extent of consumers' knowledge of price and promotions by surveying consumers *in the store, immediately after a purchase.*[4] The study was restricted to only four grocery stores in one city, but the main results of the study are informative:

- Forty-two percent of shoppers spent 5 seconds or less making a purchase; 85 percent handled only the chosen brand.
- When asked about the price of the product *they had just bought,* only 47 percent of the shoppers stated the correct price.
- Those who bought a brand on promotion (at a discount) claimed to have undertaken more search and price seeking. However, the most intriguing result is that these shoppers did not actually spend any more time than other shoppers, and were not more accurate in their price estimates.
- Only 50 percent of shoppers correctly noted whether the item they had just selected was on promotion.

Another study surveyed consumers who lived near a supermarket by mail. It asked about certain characteristics of promotions run in that supermarket during a 12-week period.[5] The main findings are as follows:

- On average, only 16 percent of respondents were correct about the frequency of promotions during the period.
- On average, only 20 percent of respondents were correct about the sale price of the promoted items.
- Only 15 percent of respondents were correct about the regular price of the promoted items.

The results of these two studies are similar to prior studies in finding that shoppers are not well informed about prices and promotions. The amazing difference is that this knowledge is so poor *immediately after* a purchase. Indeed, only 50 percent of consumers could correctly state that an item they had just purchased was on promotion. Note that this poor knowledge of prices and promotions is about frequently purchased products in grocery stores. Thus consumers' knowledge of these variables for infrequently purchased products is likely to be much inferior.

At the same time, a number of studies find that on the aggregate, consumer markets are very sensitive to price. On average a 1 percent decrease in prices could lead to as much as a 2 percent increase in sales.[6] This increase is even higher if the price reduction is promoted with ads in the store or in the local newspapers.[7] If price knowledge is low, how can price sensitivity be high? Two reasons may account for the difference.

First, *all* consumers do not need to be informed for an entire market to be price-sensitive. Markets are generally segmented, with some consumers being very sensitive to prices, others paying some attention to prices, and still others ignoring prices. Assume that the segment of very price-sensitive consumers is small (say 2 percent). But if these consumers regularly choose the lowest price, then a firm with a little higher price (say 1 percent) could lose this entire segment. Thus even a small group of price-sensitive consumers could lead to a highly price-sensitive market. Moreover, because firms typically compete for small gains in market shares, a small group of price-sensitive consumers could greatly impact their price strategies.

Second, consumers may not labor to memorize prices to conserve mental effort for more important tasks. However, *they may compare the prices of products on the store's shelf.* Thus they might use the prices of competing brands on the shelf as reference prices, and buy the one with acceptable quality that has the lowest price.[8] Since consumers make on-the-shelf comparisons, they may not memorize these prices long enough to correctly answer survey questions.

These results suggest some important implications for managers.

- Because consumers differ in their knowledge about prices and promotions, firms could vary their offers to consumers. In particular, they could offer lower prices to price-sensitive consumers with discounts, without having to lower the list price to all consumers. This strategy is called price discrimination, and is covered in the next section.
- Because consumers do not commit prices to memory, the actual size of a discount may not be as important as *advertising* the discount.[9] Indeed, an advertised discount can be a powerful means of promotion, as Chapter 11 explains.
- The *absolute value* of prices or price discounts may not be as important as their *value relative* to competing brands on the store's shelf. Thus keeping pace with competitors becomes an important goal of promotions.

Price Discrimination

Price discrimination means charging different prices to different consumers. The purpose is to earn as much revenue from each consumer as he or she is willing to pay. It is one of the most important principles in promotion. Such a strategy involves issues of fairness (discussed later in the chapter) and deception discussed in Chapter 2. Thus these strategies have to be used discreetly.

There are a large number of price discrimination strategies, many of which go well beyond the scope of this chapter.[10] Here we focus on only those strategies that are offered as promotional discounts. Such discounting strategies are not merely ad hoc short-term tactics as many people assume, but may involve deliberate, long-term strategies of firms to maximize profits. How can price discounting be a profit-maximizing strategy over the long term? A well-designed strategy of price discrimination gives one method.

Ideally, a firm that wants to maximize profits should charge every consumer the most he or she is willing to pay. However, in mass markets, the vast number of consumers makes such a strategy cumbersome, or even unnecessary because segments of consumers have similar preferences. The next best alternative is to charge each segment of consumers what it is willing to pay. While few would dispute this general principle, it does raise three questions: How can one identify these groups? How does one retain the goodwill of consumers who end up paying the high price? How does one keep these groups separate and prevent leakage or arbitrage?

Leakage is the phenomenon of consumers who would have paid the higher price, adjusting their behavior to get the lower price. For example, a Los Angeles–New York airfare may cost $300 with a Saturday night stay-over, instead of $1,500 for weekday travel. To save $1,200, travelers who would have bought the regular ticket may prefer to buy the one with a Saturday night stay-over. Discount sales to such travelers are called leakage. **Arbitrage** is the phenomenon of middle agents who buy at the lower price and sell to consumers who would have bought at the higher price. For example, some wholesalers buy goods at discount in one state, and sell them to retailers in another state in which the discount is not offered. Marketers of sporting events sometimes give free or subsidized tickets to longtime patrons. Some ticket agents buy these tickets from patrons and sell them to regular buyers at discount prices.

Successful price discrimination involves maximizing profits by identifying consumer segments with different demand, retaining the goodwill of all consumers and preventing leakage and arbitrage. These goals can be achieved by a number of strategies depending on the circumstances. We can identify three bases for price discrimination that lead to three types of discounting strategies: periodic discounting, random discounting and qualifying discounts (see Exhibit 9-8). The next sections consider each of these in detail.

Periodic Discounting

Consider a store that faces the following pricing problem for a particular style of fall skirts for women. It can buy the skirts at $45 apiece for 20 units and $30 apiece for at least 40 units. There are over 100 consumers who may buy the skirt during the season. However, 20 of them are *time-sensitive* consumers and will buy it only at the start of the season even if they have to pay $50 apiece. Another 20 are *price-sensitive* and would buy the product at any time during the season but will pay no more than $30 apiece. The rest will pay no more than $20 apiece for the skirt and can be ignored. For convenience, assume that the retailer must get $10 apiece for profit and overhead. At what price should the retailer sell its product?

▼ **EXHIBIT 9-8.** Types of price discrimination and price discounting.

Bases of Price Discrimination	Discounting Strategy	Examples
1. By time	Periodic discounting	After-Christmas sales
2. By information costs	Random discounting	Sporadic sales on selective items
3. By demographics; or by regions	Qualifying discounts; second market discounts	Seniors' discounts; discounts for foreign markets

winter coats), seasonal goods (barbecue grills, Christmas cards), perishable goods (fish, flowers), perishable services (theater seats, restaurant tables, haircuts), cyclical services (telephone, hotel and air transportation services), and annual models (auto models). For each of these products, some segments are value conscious and want the product at a set time; others are price conscious and will have the product at any time. By discriminating between them a firm can charge the (high) regular price when demand is strong, and the (low) promotional price when demand is weak.

The above examples bring into focus a number of important principles that make such a strategy feasible.

Initially it seems that the store cannot market the skirt because the cost plus the overhead exceeds demand. Note that if it targets only the 20 time-sensitive consumers, the skirts will have to sell at $55 ($45 + $10), which is more than the $50 they are willing to pay. If it tries for economies of scale, buys 40 units and prices them at $30 apiece, it will sell all 40, but at a loss. (Its selling price would fall below its costs of $30 + $10.)

However, by discriminating between the two segments the retailer can market the product profitably. It should order 40 units for $30 apiece. With overhead and profit these would cost $40 apiece. At the start of the season it could then sell the skirts for $50 each, and through the season it could discount them for $30. On average, the store would earn $40 apiece, which would cover its costs, overhead and profits.

This strategy is called **periodic discounting**. It involves charging different segments of consumers different prices at different times depending on their price sensitivity. The underlying factor in periodic discounting is price discrimination over time. In general, such discrimination applies to products whose value changes systematically with time, because consumers' demand for the product varies with time. Discrimination by time drives the periodic promotions for a vast number of products and services. Examples include fashion goods (dresses, swimwear,

- The discounting strategy is known to most consumers. Any consumer who learns about the difference in rates can take advantage of it if he or she so chooses. Thus there is no loss of goodwill.
- Consumers are differentiated by their preferences. So there is little leakage between segments. However, the firm should not drop prices too early in the season so that the time-sensitive consumers take advantage of the lower price, nor too late so that price-sensitive consumers spend their money on other items or at other stores.
- Both segments are necessary for the strategy to succeed, even though one pays more of the costs than the other. The time-sensitive consumers are generally too few to enable the firm to buy the product at a low cost or price. The price-sensitive consumers pay a low price but they provide economies of scale.

Random Discounting

A department store is considering the pricing strategy for a charcoal grill. For convenience, assume the firm can buy the grill for $30 and has a profit plus overhead charge of $10 per unit. Assume that all consumers who want the grill are willing to pay $50 for it. However, because of competition, prices range in the market from $30 to $50. Because of this variation, consumers have to search for the lowest price. Assume it takes an average consumer 1 hour to search for such a price. It takes longer for an uneducated consumer, and less for one who is educated. If they do not search and buy randomly, consumers may get the low price of $30 if they are lucky, and the high price of $50 if they are unlucky. Assume that on average consumers who buy randomly pay $40 for the product. What would consumers do and how should the store price the product?

Consumers should compare the benefits of search with their cost of time. The benefits of search are $40 minus $30, that is, the expected price of a random buy minus that of an informed buy. If consumers earn more than $10 an hour, they should not search and should buy randomly; if they earn less than that, they should search and buy at the lowest price of $30. Let's call the former segment **uninformed consumers,** and the latter, **informed consumers.**

The best strategy for the firm is to discriminate among consumers by their costs of search. The firm can do this by keeping a high list price of $50 to meet the demand of the uninformed, and *infrequently* and *randomly* discounting the price to $30 to attract the informed. The infrequent discounting minimizes leakage: the informed consumers' getting the low price by luck without searching. The random discounting makes it difficult for consumers to figure out the pattern of discounts, and thus keeps the costs of search high.[11] This strategy is called **random discounting.**

Most discounting today in specialty stores, department stores and especially grocery stores is of this type. Many services such as restaurants, clubs, hotels, and auto shops also have random discounts to discriminate among informed and uninformed consumers. Random discounting can also be used to discriminate between loyals and switchers. *Loyals* are consumers who like a brand so much that they are quite willing to buy it at the regular price. *Switchers* like a brand, but will buy it only at its discounted price. Recently, some manufacturers and retailers have initiated a strategy of "everyday-low price." This strategy is designed to appeal to switchers who are sensitive to lower prices, but who are too busy to take advantage of the random discounts. Thus the size of consumer segments is a critical factor that determines when each of these discount strategies would be profitable. Chapter 11 discusses this issue in greater detail.

Coupons and rebates are also a form of random discounts. However, coupons and rebates require greater effort on the part of consumers to clip, save and redeem than does taking advantage of a price discount; thus coupons and rebates have higher costs of search than do price discounts. Also, because the savings from coupons and rebates are valid only for those who use them, they reduce the number of lucky uninformed consumers. Further, while retailers may honor a price discount if consumers complain that they paid the high price just the previous day, retailers are less likely to honor a price valid only with a coupon or a rebate if consumers do not meet the conditions. Thus coupons and rebates are even more powerful means of price discrimination than is the price discount.

In general, consumers who are more price sensitive and have more time are more likely to search for low prices and thus be informed.[12] However, two characteristics further differentiate the informed from the uninformed consumers. First, some consumers love to compare prices and get the best deal in town, either because they love shopping or they just like to beat retailers and get a bargain. Others buy a product at the first place they find it without price comparison. These consumers hate shopping or cannot be bothered with price comparison.

Second, many wealthy consumers also take advantage of discounts, not because they need them, but because they are educated and are better able to comparison shop. The wealthy also subscribe to more publications and are on more mailing lists, so they receive more coupons. In addition, wealthier consumers are more likely to have cars to drive to the stores with the lowest prices, and have bigger houses with more storage to stockpile goods that are on sale. These factors may suggest that richer consumers get lower prices, and the poor pay more, though the evidence on this latter fact is conflicting.[13]

This discussion underscores the principles of price discrimination that we alluded to in periodic discounting:

- Any consumer who learns about the difference in prices can take advantage of it if he or she so chooses. So there is no loss of goodwill.
- The frequency and duration of the discount are critical to making the strategy work and minimizing leakage between segments. Thus the firms should not hold the discount so long, or so often that many uninformed shoppers get the discount.

On the other hand they should not have the discount so infrequently that informed shoppers start buying the product at other stores. Firms should also keep random the pattern of discounts, to raise the costs of search.

■ As in the previous case, both segments are necessary for the firms to get economies of scale and for the strategy to succeed.

Qualifying and Second Market Discounting

A producer of sofas has a capacity of 200,000 units a year but currently operates at 50 percent capacity. It makes each piece for a variable cost of $100, and sells it at $200. At its current level of operation, its fixed costs work out to $60 per unit. The producer gets an order from an entirely new retailer. What is the minimum price at which it should sell the item?

In the example above, some readers might think that the minimum selling price should be $160, which covers the firm's current and fixed costs. Actually, the right answer is anything over $100. Because the firm's fixed costs are incurred anyway, and in this case are even covered by the selling price on the current demand, the firm need not consider these fixed costs when setting its price for the entirely new demand. This method of setting a lower price for an independent new segment is called **second market discounting.** When the new segment needs to meet certain conditions to qualify, the price discounts are called **qualifying discounts.**

The essential requirement of second market discounting is that a firm face a new, independent market for its product. Examples include sales in foreign markets (exports), sales to demographically determined segments (qualifying discounts), and sales under private labels or generics (dual branding). For example, marketers of magazines can greatly increase sales and profits by offering a discount to demographic segments, such as seniors and students, who do not generally subscribe to the magazine at regular price.

Note the principles that render this type of discrimination effective:

■ The new segment is separated by large geographic distances or clear demographics from the primary one, so that the latter would not hear of or object to the discount. Thus there would not be loss of goodwill.

■ The geographic and demographic criteria that separate segments are so defined that they minimize leakage and arbitrage between segments. For example, in the case of magazine subscriptions, the difference in rates should not be big enough to tempt a regular subscriber to switch the subscription to the name of a student relative (minimize leakage). Similarly, the rates across countries should not tempt intermediaries to buy in the country that is cheap and sell in the country where the price is high (minimize arbitrage).

■ Unlike the previous two cases, the second market is generally *entirely external* to the first. That is, the firm may succeed even by marketing only to the first segment. The second market is merely an incremental market that increases sales and profits. For example, the sofa producer is doing well even without the new business.

Consumer Response to Price Promotions

Mary Lee makes a trip to the drugstore for some purchases. She does not notice the 13¢ increase to $1.22 for a bottle of Pepsi; she is quite upset by the second recent increase of $1 in the $6 price of a bottle of Nature Valley Vitamin E tablets, and switches to the store brand. She notices and barely takes advantage of a $1 retailer coupon for the $8 pack of disposable diapers she was going to buy. Certainly the $1 coupon does not seem to redress her irritation at the $1 price increase.

Andy Gray gets a 3 percent raise in his $90,000 annual salary, equal to $2,700. He is unhappy with the raise, especially as his peer got a 5 percent raise. He has no plans to spend the extra money. He comes home to find that he won $100 in his local church lottery. He and his wife go out and spend all the money, plus some more on dinner that night.

Economic theory assumes that consumers respond to the absolute value of a change in price in the same way, whatever the context. For example, it assumes that for consumers a $1 coupon compensates for a $1 increase in price. However, the above examples show that consumers' response to price is neither simple nor symmetric. Consumers treat different prices differently, depending on their context. Indeed, consumers' real response to price is not necessarily a smooth negatively sloped curve as taught in economics (see Exhibit 9-9). According to that curve, consumers' perceived value of and demand

▼ **EXHIBIT 9-9.** Economic price response curve.

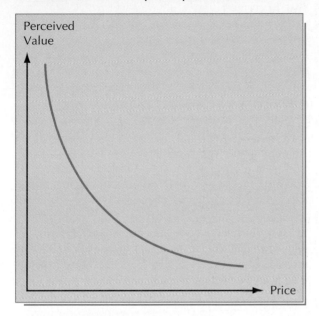

for a product decline monotonically, at a diminishing rate, as price increases. However, behavioral research suggests that consumers' response to price is probably a richer, asymmetric curve with many kinks (see Exhibit 9-10). We refer to this curve as a *behavioral price response curve*. This curve is the fruit of behavioral research that has discovered some

▼ **EXHIBIT 9-10.** Behavioral price response curve.

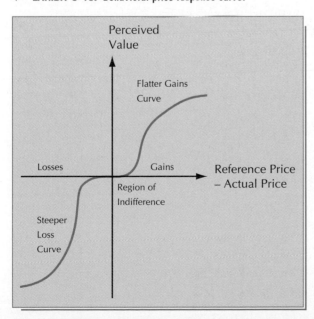

important principles of consumer response to price.[14] Four of these principles are especially relevant to promotion: reference prices, relativity, inertia and asymmetry.[15]

Reference Prices

In November 1990 Margaret Thatcher resigned the leadership of the Conservative party and the prime ministership of Britain after she "lost" a vote in a meeting of the members of her party. John Major was subsequently elected leader of the party in her stead, and thus became prime minister. Later, after reflecting on the events of the week, Thatcher regretted her resignation. In a two-way confidence vote she had won 55 percent of her party's vote, against a challenger's 41 percent.[16] At that point Major had not even stood against her, and would not have won had he done so. How then is her vote of 55 percent considered a loss?

In 1994 the Buffalo Bills suffered their fourth loss in the Super Bowl. The team players were dejected and humiliated. People considered them losers, and talk show hosts ridiculed them as perennial losers. Yet they were the second best team in the country, and with a record of four appearances in the Super Bowl, they were probably the best over that four-year period.

Sara Smith is excited about her new purchase. She just bought a stereo system for $399 from The Good Guys after the salesman reluctantly gave her a $60 discount from the list price of $459. She gets ready to enjoy her CDs on the new system, when her roommate, Anne Pollack, punctures her buoyant mood. Anne says that the specialty discounter Circuit City has the same system at an everyday low price of $299. Sara's excitement quickly turns to surprise, dejection and anger.

Each of these examples indicates the importance of reference points, which in the case of price becomes a reference price. A **reference price** is a standard price that consumers use for comparing the prices offered by marketers. Reference price is a key concept in understanding the behavioral response to price changes.[17]

Consider the examples above. Why did Prime Minister Thatcher resign her job when she polled 55 percent of the votes of her party? Only because party rules, the press and the public expected her to crush her opponent.[18] Why should the Buffalo Bills be humiliated and dejected when they placed second in the league? Because their sights and those of all their fans were on the number 1 spot, not on the majority of teams below them, or on their strong performance four years in a row. Why should Sara's excitement with her purchase so quickly turn to dejection? Because her $399 purchase is a good deal relative to the seller's $459 list price, but a bad deal relative to the competitor's $299 everyday low price.

Nature of Reference Prices These examples show that the absolute values of election results, sports victories or prices are irrelevant. They have meaning only with regard to certain reference points. Reference prices are not observed and cannot be directly measured. Asking consumers if they are aware of reference prices or if they use them would lead to affirmative answers because respondents to a survey like to please the questioner. Reference prices can only be affirmed implicitly by noticing the changes in consumers' behavior as these prices are manipulated. For example, consider the two hypothetical ads, A and B, for a KBC digital antenna system in Exhibit 9-11. The price of a comparable Pony system serves as a reference price. The only difference in the two ads is the advertised value of the Pony system, $699 in A and $499 in B. If the first ad elicits better sales, that implies that consumers probably use the price of a rival brand as the reference price. Using this indirect approach, behavioral research has confirmed the existence and important role of reference prices in consumer purchases.[19]

A key question is, what factors drive reference prices? Research suggests that the three most important factors are recall of past prices, awareness of competitive prices, and expectations of future prices. For example, a price of $250,000 for a home would be considered excessive to a middle-class homeowner who has lived all his life in Des Moines, Iowa; it would be a great deal to another who earns the same salary but grew up in Pasadena, California. Thus past experience plays an important role in determining reference price. For another example, consider that a $4 Big Mac would be cheap in Tokyo, fair in London and a rip-off in downtown Chicago, given the prevailing prices in those cities. Thus the competitive environment also determines reference prices. For a third example, consider how some consumers *wait* to buy Christmas cards till after Christmas, while they *rush* to buy airline tickets for Christmas before September. The reason is that consumers have opposite expectations of the future prices of these two items. Also, stock prices sometimes *decrease* on news of a strong economy, even though that should indicate stronger earnings per share. The reason is that investors *expect* the stronger economy to lead to higher inflation, with lower business growth and income. Thus expectations also determine reference prices.

The curve in Exhibit 9-10 shows the important role of reference price, in that consumers' perception of actual price revolves around the reference price. The horizontal axis plots the difference of reference price minus actual price. A positive value is perceived as a **gain** because the consumer gets a price lower than his or her reference price. A negative value is perceived as a **loss** because the consumer pays a price higher than his or her reference price. A price equal to the reference price yields a value of 0. The vertical axis plots the perceived value of the item. The subsequent discussion elucidates other characteristics of response to reference prices.

Relativity The **principle of relativity** suggests that consumers evaluate a gain or loss in purchase with respect to the price of the item purchased.[20] For example, a $1 rebate on a $3 video rental would draw more attention than a $1 rebate on a $30 cable subscription; while a $1 coupon on a $300 video recorder would arouse a smile if any response at all. In real terms the savings of $1 is the same in each of these instances. So why is there a different reaction? The reason is that the consumer evaluates the gain or loss relative to the price of the item. The same coupon represents a price reduction of 33 percent for the video rental, 3.3 percent for the cable subscription and only .33 percent for the video recorder.

▼ EXHIBIT 9-11. Comparable ads with different reference prices.

| KBC's Digital Antenna System Now Only

$399

Compare versus $699 Pony System | KBC's Digital Antenna System Now Only

$399

Compare versus $499 Pony System |

A similar phenomenon of relativity occurs (but in the opposite direction) for losses. Thus a price increase of $1 on a TV set may well be ignored, but the same increase on a gallon of milk may stimulate a strong negative reaction.

This relativity in response to prices is similar to that for physical stimuli described by Weber's law (see Chapter 5). The relativity of response is represented by the "increasing response" and then "diminishing response" of the price curve in the first and third quadrants of Exhibit 9-10. Thus, positive response to gains first increases rapidly and then more slowly with increases in gains. Negative response to losses first increases rapidly and then slowly with increases in losses. For example, a price drop providing a gain of $2 (see Exhibit 9-12) elicits an increase in purchase probability of .35; but twice that benefit, a $4 gain, leads to a relatively smaller increase in purchase probability of .45.

Inertia **Inertia** refers to the lack of response by consumers to some stimuli because of inadequate motivation. For example, small changes around the reference point are unlikely to trigger a response. Such changes may be too small to be noticed, or to justify the effort required to process the change and switch brands. Indeed, one study shows that retail managers of grocery products could increase their profits by gradually increasing the prices of frequently purchased products.[21] Consumers would not

notice the small price increases, and would adjust to the higher prices. This response is reflected by the flatter portion of the curve around the center of Exhibit 9-10, reflecting a region of indifference to small changes in price. Small gains or losses yield a relatively much smaller increase or decrease in response, respectively.

Asymmetry in Response

After completing his day's work, Jose Garcia goes to his office parking lot. He is furious when he finds out that he has a $5 ticket for parking across a yellow line. When he gets home he peruses his mail. He notices a $5 coupon on his next oil change at the auto distributor who normally services his car. He barely notices the coupon, and that coupon neither negates his irritation at the parking ticket, nor brings much joy.

Asymmetry in response refers to opposite but unequal reactions of consumers to positive and negative stimuli. In the context of reference prices, asymmetry in response reveals itself in the finding that consumers' reaction to losses is more negative than their reaction to gains is positive. Examples include Jose Garcia's experience in the example above or Mary Lee's in an earlier example. The phrase "losses loom larger than gains" is used to describe this phenomenon. Besides the two examples cited here, this phenomenon has been noticed in several different experiments.[22] The reason may be that consumers perceive a loss as the removal of part of their rightful endowment, yet they perceive a gain as an opportunity to earn something that is not yet part of their entitlement. In the case of prices, consumers may perceive price decreases as gains, but price increases as losses. The price response curve in Exhibit 9-10 captures this phenomenon, in that the loss curve has a steeper slope than the gain curve.

Strategic Implications The above discussion of reference prices suggests the following promotional strategies. We will refer back to these strategies when discussing specific promotions in subsequent chapters.

Keep List Prices High Manufacturers should keep list prices relatively high, subject to considerations of consumer demand and competitive supply. The listing can take the form of "Price should not exceed $—" or "Manufacturer's suggested list price." This strategy has many benefits. First, by

▼ **EXHIBIT 9-12.** Hypothetical price response curve for $50 software.

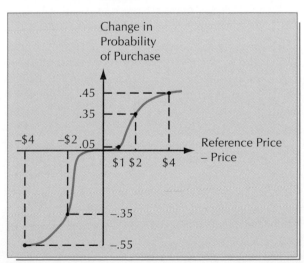

keeping the list price high, the firm raises the consumer's reference price. Second, to the extent that consumers infer quality from price, a high list price may lead consumers to infer the brand has higher quality than if it had a lower price. Third, with a high list price punctuated with periodic discounts, the firm can exploit any revenues from consumers who are willing to pay the high price. Fourth, while a regular low price may be more appealing to price-sensitive consumers, a discount, coupon or rebate is more likely to generate the interest, excitement and attention of consumers, while having the same appeal as a low price.[23]

Fifth, if costs rise, manufacturers can, within limits, pass these increases on without any explicit change in price. Manufacturers can raise the price to the retailer without raising the suggested list price. Retailers in turn will then set a selling price higher than their former price but still lower than the suggested list price. For example, grand pianos are often listed at twice the selling price. The selling price is negotiated by buyer and seller and is never listed anyway. As manufacturing costs increase, the manufacturer can, within certain boundaries, reduce retail margins, forcing the retailer to negotiate a higher selling price. But the list price can still be kept at the exaggerated level.

Sixth, temporary increases in costs due to fluctuations in supply may not necessitate increases in price. For example, in spring 1994, the wholesale price of coffee beans in the world market doubled. Retailers of low-priced coffee brands such as Maxwell House and Folgers had to increase their prices immediately or suffer lower margins. Sellers of premium coffees worked with a higher margin and were under much less pressure to raise prices.[24]

However, there are limits to how high the list price can be set. First, the price cannot be set so high as to discourage all sales. Second, the price cannot be set much higher than that of competing brands, without good reasons such as superior quality. Chapter 14 discusses this issue in further detail. Third, there must be some minimum sales at the list price to ensure that the strategy is not deceptive (see Chapter 2).

Avoid Dropping List Prices

When a price reduction is required, it is better to offer it as a temporary price discount, a coupon or a rebate, rather than as a one-time reduction in list price. Such a policy has all the benefits of maintaining high list prices cited earlier.

Segregate Gains

Consumers may treat various reductions in price as gains. When a firm offers a reduction in price, it is better to do so with several separate discounts, each large enough to appeal to consumers without causing diminishing returns. This strategy is called **segregating gains**.[25] For example, a $10 discount on a $50 software package could be broken up into two $5 "double coupons," or a $5 rebate plus $5 premium, or a $5 rebate and a 10 percent price discount. Offering consumers two smaller discounts instead of one large one is better because of the relativity of consumer response to gains and losses. It can be visualized in Exhibit 9-12. Beyond the steepest portion of the curve (at $4), price decreases lead to smaller increases in purchase probability. Thus an $8 price decrease on a $50 software package would gain much more sales if broken up into two $4 decreases. However, because of the S-shaped curve it would be less effective if broken up into four $2 decreases.

Landlords often segregate gains when advertising apartments in a soft market. Suppose a glut in vacant apartments persists despite the market rent for a two-bedroom apartment dropping to $499. Rather than drop the rent further, some owners offer a number of freebies. For example, they may offer a free newspaper subscription, free cable service for a year, a new VCR, tickets to a local sports attraction, or an expensive dinner at a local restaurant. Note that a combination of these or even any one of them, is likely to be much more effective than lowering the price of the apartment by the cost of the freebie. For example, the offer of a $240 VCR on a two-year lease would be equivalent to dropping the monthly rent from $499 to $489, a barely noticeable amount.

Integrate Losses

For a price increase, a firm should do just the opposite of that recommended above—that is, **integrate** price increases, which are perceived as *losses* by consumers.[26] Note from Exhibit 9-12 that two separate increases of $2 lead to a change in purchase probability of twice −.35, which is −.70. However, one increase of $4 leads to a change in purchase probability of only −.55, which is not as bad as −.70. Also, the flattening portion of the loss curve indicates that very steep increases may not elicit as negative a response. So a viable strategy would even be to exaggerate the price increase, and then offer back some of the loss as a gain to consumers in the form of various discounts. Note that, while many small increases below the threshold of observation would not elicit any big negative response, such a strategy can be deceptive, because the consumer would not realize there had been any increase at all.

Frame High Prices or Price Increases When a price is high, or a price increase is necessary, a firm should describe it in such a way as to minimize the apparent loss to consumers. A less unfavorable perception of a price increase can be achieved by raising the consumer's reference price. This strategy is referred to as **framing price increases.** There are several ways to implement this strategy:

- Pass on only a portion of the increase to consumers, and inform them how costs have increased even more than the amount by which their price has.
- Compare the new prices to a still higher price that consumers in some other markets pay for the equivalent product.
- Offer some higher value that does not cost much more, so that the price increase appears justified.

For example, Chivas Regal markets a premium scotch in the United States, which at one time sold for $20. Some lower priced brands of scotch, such as Scoresby, sold for as little as $13. To frame its high price as a good deal, Chivas ran a one-page ad that prominently displayed an elegant picture of the bottle with the bold tagline, "$45 in Japan."

Perception of Fairness in Pricing and Promotion

The preceding discussion rests on the premise that managers want to maximize the profits of their firms. This raises several questions. What justification exists for such a premise? Do consumers consider prices and promotions fair when firms try to meet the profit goal alone? This subsection tries to answer these questions.

A basic economic assumption is that all managers are profit maximizers. The approach taken in this book, as in most marketing books, is that managers should serve consumer interests at a profit. Thus profit maximization is a major, albeit not the sole goal of the manager. There is a simple strong argument in favor of profit maximization that dates back to Adam Smith's articulation of the *invisible hand*.[27] The argument is that when firms compete, even though each seeks its own profit, they strive to offer lower prices or higher quality to achieve higher sales and profits. Thus competition, like an invisible hand, works for consumer welfare at large. A good example is the retailing industry in the United States. In this industry, easy entry of new firms and intense competition lead to better retailing systems, each with successively lower prices at the same or better quality. Nobel Laureate Milton Friedman, in a statement in the *New York Times Magazine,* once derived what some might consider an extreme principle from this logic.[28] He argued that managers should be totally concerned about maximizing the profits of a firm, and not devote the firm's resources to charities or social causes. If shareholders subsequently wanted to indulge in charity they could do so with their returns from the dividends paid out by the firm's profits. In practical terms, this principle implies that managers should "price as high as the trade will bear."

What do people think about such a policy? Behavioral research in the last two decades has revealed that consumers are neither entirely against profit maximization nor fully in favor of it. Researchers have found three peculiarities of consumers' perception of fairness and sellers' response: dual entitlements, asymmetric perceptions and self-enforcement.

Dual Entitlements

Example A. In January 1995 a massive earthquake struck the city of Northridge, 10 miles north of Los Angeles, California. After the earthquake, consumers began to stock up on bottled water for fear that the piped water might be contaminated. Some retailers responded by raising the price of bottled water. Even as they bought the water at the higher prices, consumers were furious with the retailers' opportunistic behavior. The media criticized the practice, while local governments passed regulations against it and increased monitoring of prices of such commodities.[29]

Example B. Due to a delivery problem a local grocer has to pay 30¢ per head above the normal price for lettuce. The grocer sells the lettuce to customers for 30¢ per head above the previous price. In a survey of 101 customers, 79 percent found it acceptable, while 21 percent found it unfair.[30]

Note that, in both examples above, a retailer raises the price of goods, and consumers buy those goods. However, Example A suggests that consumers consider price increases to be unfair if the increases take advantage of their difficulties and raise retailers' profits, even though demand justifies the price increase. On the other hand, Example B shows that consumers consider price increases to be fair if they can be justified by sellers' costs. The two examples show that consumers' perceptions of the fairness of prices are not driven by market demand at those prices. Rather, their perception of fairness can be explained by the principle of dual entitlement. **Dual entitlements** mean that sellers are entitled to ongoing profits (Example B) provided they are not at consumers' duress (Example A), while consumers are entitled to ongoing prices (Example A), provided they are not at sellers' duress (Example B). In other words, consumers believe that sellers are entitled to ongoing profits, even if they pass on increases in costs to consumers. Similarly, consumers believe that they are entitled to ongoing prices, even if increases in demand justify higher prices, as long as sellers earn their ongoing profits. In both cases, perceptions of fairness are independent of market demand.

Asymmetry of Perceptions for Increases and Decreases The term *symmetry* means a mirror image or a movement in the same direction, while the term *asymmetry* means not symmetrical. Consumers' perceptions of fairness are not symmetric for cost increases and decreases, nor are they symmetric for price increases and price discounts.

First, to understand the asymmetry of perception for cost increases versus cost decreases, contrast Example B with the following example:

Example C. A small factory produces tables and sells all that it can make at $200 each. Because of changes in the price of materials, the cost of making each table has recently decreased by $40. The factory reduces its price for the tables, but only by $20. In a survey of 102 consumers, 79 percent found the strategy acceptable while 21 percent found it unfair.[31]

Note that, in strictly economic terms, any change in a seller's costs has the same monetary value irrespective of whether it is an increase or decrease. So in economic terms, changes in costs of a seller should be passed on to buyers, if the buyers are willing to buy at the new price. Yet, consumers think that a seller may pass on to consumers increases in

costs (Example B), but a seller need not pass on to consumers savings in costs (Example C). We refer to this characteristic as the *asymmetry in consumer perceptions for* price *increases and decreases.*

Second, to understand the asymmetry in perceptions for price increases versus price discounts, consider the following examples:

Example D. A shortage of a popular model of car has developed and customers must wait two months for delivery. A dealer has been selling these cars at list price. Now the dealer prices this model at $200 above list price. In a survey of 130 consumers, 29 percent found this behavior acceptable while 71 percent found it unfair.

Example E. This example is similar to the case above, except that this dealer has been selling these cars at a discount of $200 below list price. Now the dealer sells this model only at list price. In a survey of consumers, 58 percent found the behavior acceptable while 43 percent found it unfair.[32]

Note that, in strictly economic terms, whether $200 comes from a dealer's price increase, or from a dealer's cancellation of a discount, the monetary value is the same. Yet, that is not how consumers perceive the increase in price versus the cancellation of a discount. While consumers consider unfair a seller's price increase that takes advantage of consumers (Example D), consumers consider fair the cancellation of a discount under the same condition (Example E). We refer to this characteristic as the *asymmetry in consumer perceptions for* cost *increases and decreases.* The reason may be that consumers consider a seller's price increase an infringement on the ongoing price to which consumers are entitled, while the price discount is considered a concession from the seller's profits, which the seller has a right to withdraw.

Self-Enforcement Are firms aware of these norms? Do firms follow them? Consider the following example:

Example F. In 1994, Barbra Streisand decided to perform live in concert after a gap of 27 years. She faced strong demand for the shows despite prices of $50 to $350. For example, her initial 12 shows sold out in 1 hour, and she added an additional 6 shows. Such strong demand typically triggers a big black market for the tickets. Streisand was faced with a dilemma. If she raised the price of the tickets, she would appear as a price gouger, and be criticized as were the retailers in Example A. If she kept the price low, scalpers would profit at her expense, and that of her fans. Streisand developed a creative promotion. She set aside 4,000 prime tickets for select nonprofit organizations to sell at $1,000 each. She herself sold the tickets to these organizations at a price of $350 each. These organizations were able to sell most of their tickets for profits of $390,000 to $500,000, after expenses. Streisand herself grossed $16.6 million. This deal enabled Streisand to capture more of the market value of each ticket without appearing like a price gouger, while also gaining the goodwill of the public.[33]

Example F shows that marketers are probably aware of consumers' perceptions of fairness, and adjust their price and promotion strategies accordingly. This behavior is called **self-enforcement.** Casual observation suggests other similar examples. For example, sellers of tickets to popular games that are in heavy demand do not raise the price for these events, even though they know that scalpers would resell tickets at much higher prices. Instead, they offer tickets to longtime benefactors of their shows at prices below the market price. Benefactors perceive such tickets as a perk. Similarly, many retailers will run out of stock rather than raise prices for routine household items that come under heavy demand (such as snow shovels after a snowstorm).

Still another example is the pricing and promotion of automobiles and other expensive durables such as grand pianos, stereo equipment or mattresses. These products often have suggested list prices that are high relative to prices at which sales occur. When demand is weak, dealers can offer discounts from list prices to motivate sales. However, when demand is strong they can reduce the frequency or depth of discounts. The federal government and many state governments have regulations to ensure that some minimum sales do occur at these list prices to justify their name (see Chapter 2).

Strategic Implications These results suggest several practical norms that managers need to follow when making changes in price:

- Managers should not raise price by imposing an additional cost on consumers, and they should especially not do so by taking advantage of consumers' hardship. However, managers may profit fairly by reducing their own costs, whether by luck or ingenuity.
- Managers need not always follow a cost-plus pricing rule. For example, if costs go up, the seller can raise price following a cost-plus rule. But if costs go down, the seller does not have to cut price, violating a cost-plus rule.
- If a manager foresees changes in prices, then maintaining high prices and offering discounts has an advantage over everyday low prices. The former strategy allows for leverage should costs increase, enabling a manager to reduce or cancel discounts without offending consumers.
- Framing cost changes is vital. Whenever possible, the price increase should be justified by increases in costs rather than by market demand. The latter explanation may be perceived as unfair exploitation of demand.

SUMMARY

There are over 20 different types of sales promotions. These can be conveniently classified on two dimensions: the channel of distribution (either trade, retail or consumer promotion) and the characteristic of the promotion (either communicative or incentive promotion).

A promotion involving a change in price is called a price promotion, and is one of the most common and important types of promotions. Consumers' awareness of price promotions is not very high, possibly because of the large number of brands available, the constant changes in price promotions, and the amount of other information consumers may need or prefer to keep in mind. Markets, however, are quite sensitive to price promotions, possibly because even a small group of consumers who are informed and respond to the low price is enough to cause a serious loss in a seller's sales.

Price discrimination is a strategy of promotional discounting by which firms charge different consumers different prices that better match their willingness to pay. Firms can discriminate between consumers by time, information, location, or demographics of the consumers leading to strategies that are called random discounting, periodic discounting, second market discounting, or qualifying discounts. The most important and difficult task is to cleverly identify segments of consumers who will buy only with the incentive of a discount. Next, firms need to design promotions to avoid leakage or arbitrage between consumer segments that pay different prices, and maintain the goodwill of segments paying the higher price.

Consumers respond not to an absolute price, but to the price relative to some reference price. The reference price may be based on past prices a consumer has paid, current prices in the market or future prices the consumer expects to pay. Very small differences in prices relative to the reference price may not be observed. An observed price above the reference price is perceived as a loss, while an observed price below the reference price is perceived as a gain. Consumers' response to price is more negative for losses than it is positive for gains. For both losses and gains, consumers show initially increasing and then declining responsiveness as the size of the loss or gain increases.

Economists assume and shareholders expect that managers set prices to maximize the profits of a firm. In practice, this means they set prices in response to consumer demand. However, consumers do not think prices based on demand are fair. Rather, their concept of fairness in prices can be summarized by two principles: dual entitlement and asymmetry of perception. Sellers are aware of these perceptions and design strategies to price without seeming to be unfair (self-enforcement).

QUESTIONS

1. What are sales promotions? How can they be classified?
2. Manufacturers have to make a major trade-off when choosing between trade promotions and consumer promotions. Discuss.
3. Why do stores frequently offer price discounts? Would they not be better off keeping the same high price?
4. What percentage of shoppers can correctly state the price of a grocery product immediately after a purchase? Do buyers of discounted brands differ in their knowledge of prices and in their shopping behavior from those who buy brands at the regular price?
5. Markets are very sensitive to price-cuts. Does that mean that consumers are very well informed about prices and promotions? Explain in detail.
6. How can price discounting be a profit-maximizing strategy over the long term?
7. What is the logic of random discounting? Compare and contrast it with periodic discounting.
8. Explain how firms can price discriminate among consumers, yet retain their goodwill.
9. Explain the concepts of leakage and arbitrage. How do they apply in price promotions?
10. Why do retailers change prices on hundreds of items each week? Would they not be better off finding one price at which to sell each item and sticking to it? In particular, would an everyday high price not make for higher profit, greater efficiency and easier management?
11. Does the absolute price of a product ever matter in consumer choice? Explain.
12. What is reference price? How does it affect consumer choice? What factors drive reference prices?
13. How does the price response curve based on economic theory differ from that based on behavioral theory?
14. When do consumers consider a price increase fair? Do the same principles apply for price increases and decreases?
15. Most consumers in the United States are comfortable with the idea of free markets, and of sellers trying to maximize profits. Yet, they are quite offended when sellers try to price as high as the trade will bear. Similarly, consumers are comfortable with sellers canceling a discount, but are uncomfortable with sellers raising a price, even when both activities are driven by the same cost situations. Describe and explain the idiosyncrasies in consumers' perceptions of what is a fair change in price.
16. Are firms aware of consumers' perceptions of fair prices? How do those perceptions affect their pricing and promotion strategies?
17. What characteristics of consumers render price promotions effective or ineffective?

NOTES

1. *Promo* (1994), "Northwest Goes to the Mall" (April), R4; Creno, Glen (1994), "Northwest, America West Airlines

Offer Bargain Fares to Minneapolis Mega-Mall," *The Phoenix Gazetter,"* September 21.

2. *The Financial Post* (1993), "Hoover books seats on 1100 flights," April 28.

3. Zeithaml, Valerie (1988), "Consumer Perceptions of Price, Quality and Value: A Means-End Model and Synthesis of Evidence," *Journal of Marketing* 52, 3 (July), 2–22.

4. Dickson, Peter R., and Alan G. Sawyer (1990), "The Price Knowledge and Search of Supermarket Shoppers," *Journal of Marketing* 54 (July), 42–53.

5. Krishna, Aradhna, Imran S. Currim, and Robert Shoemaker (1991), "Consumer Perceptions of Promotional Activity," *Journal of Marketing* 55 (April), 4–16.

6. Tellis, Gerard J. (1988), "The Price Sensitivity of Selective Demand: A Meta-Analysis of Econometric Models of Sales," *Journal of Marketing Research* 25 (November), 231–241.

7. Blattberg, Robert C., and Scott A. Neslin (1989), "Sales Promotion: The Long And The Short Of It," *Marketing Letters* 1, 1, 81–97.

8. Rajendran, K. N., and Gerard J. Tellis (1994), "Contextual and Temporal Components of Reference Price," *Journal of Marketing* 58 (January), 22–34.

9. Inman, Jeffrey J., Leigh McAlister, and Wayne D. Hoyer, "Promotion Signal: Proxy For A Price Cut," *Journal of Consumer Research* 17 (June), 74–81.

10. These strategies are called type I, II and III discrimination in the economics literature. One article that provides a comprehensive and integrative review of these strategies is Tellis, Gerard J. (1986), "Beyond the Many Faces of Price: An Integration of Pricing Strategies," *Journal of Marketing* 50 (October), 146–160.

11. Krishna, Aradhna (1991), "Effect of Dealing Patterns on Consumer Perceptions of Deal Frequency and Willingness to Pay," *Journal of Marketing Research* 28 (November), 441–451.

12. Urbany, Joel E., Peter R. Dickson, and Rosemary Kalapurakal (1996), "Price Search In The Retail Grocery Market," *Journal of Marketing* 60 (April), 91–104.

13. Poorer neighborhoods also have fewer retail choices and more expensive outlets than wealthier neighborhoods. The reason may be that the larger chains do not wish to serve such neighborhoods because of the higher incidence of crime and higher insurance costs. Thus such neighborhoods are served by smaller retailers who have higher costs or charge higher prices. For references see Goodman, Charles S. (1975), "Do The Poor Pay More?," *Journal of Marketing* 32, 1 (January), 18–24; Feldman, Paul (1993), "Low-Income Consumers Pay More for Poorer Services, Study Finds," *Los Angeles Times*, October 6, B1, B8. Also, one study found that the poor are more price sensitive than the rich: Hoch, Stephen J., Byung-Do Kim, Alan L. Montgomery, and Peter E. Rossi (1995), "Determinants of Store-Level Price Elasticity," *Journal of Marketing* 32 (February), 17–29.

14. A similar curve was first proposed by Gurumurthy, K., and John D. C. Little (1986), "A Pricing Model Based On Perception Theories And Its Testing On Scanner Panel Data," working paper, MIT.

15. Some of these ideas are based on Thaler, Richard (1985), "Mental Accounting and Consumer Choice," *Marketing Science* 4, 3 (Summer), 199–214.

16. Ridley, Matt (1990), "Et Tu Heseltine? Unpopularity Was A Grievous Fault, and Thatcher Hath Answered For It," *Washington Post,* November 25, C2; Whitney, Craig R. (1990), "Back Home, Thatcher Vows to Fight," November 22, A3.

17. Kahneman, Tversky, and Amos Tversky (1979), "Prospect Theory: An Analysis of Decision Under Risk," *Econometrica* 47, 2 (March), 263–291; Thaler, "Mental Accounting and Consumer Choice."

18. Party rules required that she win over her challenger by 15% of the poll or face a second poll in which she needed to win by a simple majority. In the first vote she beat her challenger by 14% instead of the required 15%, forcing a second vote. This "fall" from her onetime dominant position discouraged her from going for the second poll.

19. Rajendran and Tellis, "Contextual and Temporal Components of Reference Price"; Kalwani, Manohar U., Chi Kin Yim, Heikki J. Rinne, and Yoshi Sugita (1990), "A Price Expectations Model of Customer Brand Choice," *Journal of Marketing Research* 26 (August), 251–262;. Winer, Russell S. (1986), " A Reference Price Model of Brand Choice for Frequently Purchased Products," *Journal of Consumer Research* 13 (September), 250–256.

20. Grewal, Dhruv, and Howard Marmorstein (1994), "Market Price Variation, Perceived Price Variation, and Consumers' Price Search Decisions For Durable Goods," *Journal of Consumer Research* 21 (December), 453–460; Thaler, "Mental Accounting and Consumer Choice."

21. Hoch, Stephen J., Xavier Dèrze, and Mary E. Purk (1994), "EDLP, Hi-Lo and Margin Arithmetic," *Journal of Marketing* 58, 4, 16–27.

22. Kahneman and Tversky, "Prospect Theory: An Analysis of Decision Under Risk."

23. Hoch, Stephen J., Byung-Do Kim, Alan L. Montgomery, and Peter E. Rossi (1995), "Determinants of Store-Level Price Elasticity," *Journal of Marketing Research* 32 (February), 17–29.

24. *Forbes* (1994), "No Break for Coffee Prices," June 13.

25. Thaler, "Mental Accounting and Consumer Choice."

26. *Ibid.*

27. Smith, Adam (1936), *An Inquiry Into The Nature and Causes of the Wealth of Nations,* Oxford, England: Oxford University Press.

28. Friedman, Milton (1970), "The Social Responsibility of Business," *The New York Times*, September 13, 122–126.

29. For experimental examples, see Kahneman, Tversky, Jack L. Knetsch, and Richard Thaler (1986), "Fairness as Constraint on Profit Seeking: Entitlement in the Market," *The American Economic Review* 76, 4 (September), 728–741.

30. Kahneman, Knetsch, and Thaler, "Fairness as Constraint on Profit Seeking."

31. *Ibid.*

32. *Ibid.*

33. Strauss, Neil (1994), "Streisand Tickets Prove Mixed Blessing for Charities," *New York Times*, June 29, C15, C17; *Chicago Sun-Times* (1994), "18 U.S. Shows Not Enough For Streisand Fans," March 29, 24.

Retail Promotions

Kmart and Wal-Mart are retail chains that have many similarities.[1] The two chain stores look alike, have similar products and appeal to similar customers. They have similar names and even started in the same year, 1962. Most importantly, they both are discount stores that promise consumers lower prices than the big department stores that were popular at the time they started: Sears, J C Penney and Montgomery Ward. The low-price strategy attracted shoppers and fueled the rapid growth of these chains, at the

expense of the department stores. By 1987, they had become the largest retail chains in the United States, having displaced Sears to the number three position. Kmart led with 35 percent market share and $26 billion in sales, while Wal-Mart was second with 23 percent market share and $16 billion in sales. Kmart seemed to have an edge over Wal-Mart with better, more expensive locations and 2,223 stores to Wal-Mart's 1,198.

After 1987, the two chains took on different strategies with dramatically different results. Kmart came under the leadership of Joseph Antonini, while Wal-Mart retained the leadership of founder Sam Walton until his death in 1992. To begin with, Kmart owned expensive real estate in urban areas, had greater visibility and a better record of competing with the large department stores. With this background, Antonini tried to spruce up Kmart's image. He invested heavily in national advertising, a more upscale line of clothes and glamorous endorsers for its clothes, like actress Jaclyn Smith. Antonini also diversified into related retail businesses, such as OfficeMax, Borders books and Pace Membership Warehouse clubs, expecting these stores to fuel growth and profits. In contrast, Sam Walton relentlessly pursued his low-price strategy. To back up his strategy he continued his drive to lower costs. In particular, he invested heavily in a sophisticated computerized inventory system, and conveniently located distribution centers and larger, more economic stores. With the help of computers that monitored sales at checkout scanners and convenient distribution centers, Walton was able to have efficient ordering, inventory and supplies.

By early 1995, Wal-Mart seemed to have won the battle between the two giant retailers. Wal-Mart was number one with 42 percent market share, while Kmart had dropped to 23 percent. The critical difference between the two stores seemed to be Wal-Mart's lower prices. It continued to grow and attract customers while Kmart seemed to have lost some of its original appeal. Kmart was also wracked with inefficiencies as products were frequently out of stock, warehouses were overstocked

with inappropriate inventory, and customers had to wait in line when checkout prices did not match shelf prices. The lack of a computerized inventory system was telling. Kmart's diversification also turned out to be distracting, contributing to a large proportion of sales, but much less of the firm's profits. The focus and efficiency of Wal-Mart's strategy were evident in the fact that it had achieved leadership with 500 fewer stores.

On March 21, 1995, Joseph Antonini was forced to resign as president and chief operating officer of Kmart Corporation for the poor performance of his company, especially against archrival Wal-Mart.

Because retailers offer consumers similar products, competition between stores hinges primarily on price. The opening example of Wal-Mart and Kmart shows the intensity of this competition, and the importance of having low prices. However, offering lower prices than a rival would soon lead to a price war with serious losses for all retailers. Sales promotions are a means by which retailers can creatively offer better value or lower prices than their rivals. For example, in southern California, grocery stores are locked in intense competition. To differentiate their offerings from each other, stores have developed various price-related promotion strategies. Luckys lays claim to the lowest-price full-service grocery store. Vons and Ralphs follow a strategy of high-low pricing, injecting some excitement with a strategy of random discounts and double coupons. Warehouse clubs offer everyday-low prices to consumers who are willing to pay for membership and buy in bulk.[2]

There are many more promotional strategies besides these few. What are the different types of retail promotions? What goals do they serve? How do consumers respond to them? How can retailers use them profitably? This chapter answers these questions. The introductory section provides an overview of the characteristics of retail promotions.

The second section details the major types of retail promotions. The third section analyzes the effectiveness of retail promotions. The last section shows how to evaluate the profitability of retail promotions.

Retail promotions are sales promotions that the retailer offers consumers. Three forces drive retail promotions. First, retailers may offer sales promotions on their own initiative based on their analysis of the retail environment. Thus retailers could offer retail coupons or temporary price-cuts without any action from manufacturers or other retailers, because they estimate that such promotions will enhance their sales or profits. Second, retail promotions may be influenced by manufacturers through trade promotions. Actually, a major goal of trade promotions is to motivate the retailer to promote the manufacturer's products to the consumers (see Chapter 11).

Third and most important, as the opening example suggests, retail promotions are heavily influenced by competition. Retailing competition is intense due to relatively easy entry of firms, a large number of competitors and constant innovation in retail format. It is to the advantage of each retailer to retain as much of the manufacturer's trade deal and pass on to consumers as little as possible. Retailers could also implicitly agree to do so by signaling each other. (Any explicit agreement among retailers on price-cuts or promotions is illegal.) However, due to intense competition, one or another retailer may break the implicit understanding, if any exists, and run a sales promotion or cut the price to consumers. Thus competition among retailers induces them to pass on trade promotions to consumers to the benefit of manufacturers and consumers. Indeed, some retail chains and retail malls in the United States have become famous the world over as attractive shopping grounds for good-quality manufactured goods at low prices.[3]

Retailers have a wide choice of promotions. For a better understanding of the scope of these promotions, Exhibit 10-1 classifies them using simple criteria discussed in Chapter 9. Retail promotions can be classified as primarily either incentive or communicative. Incentives can be further classified as either price or nonprice promotions, while communicative promotions can be further classified as either infor-

▼ **EXHIBIT 10-1.** Classification of retail promotions.

PRIMARILY INCENTIVE		PRIMARILY COMMUNICATIVE	
Price	Nonprice	Informative	Motivational
Price-cuts, retail coupons, double coupons	Premiums, tie-ins, bonus plans, financing	Features, displays, sampling	Games, sweepstakes

mative or motivational promotions. The promotions listed within each cell of the table are close substitutes. The rest of the chapter describes each of these promotions in greater detail.

Four types of retail promotions are unique to retailing, in the sense that they are typically not offered by manufacturers: displays, features, price-cuts and double coupons. One study on grocery products found that across all categories the percentage of sales due to retail promotions was as follows: price-cut = 17 percent, feature = 14 percent, display = 11 percent and store coupon = 1 percent.[4] In comparison, about 9 percent of sales involved manufacturer coupons. These promotions were not necessarily used in isolation; actually, they were more often combined in two frequently occurring combinations: feature with price-cut, and feature with display. In addition, many product categories sold with manufacturer coupons alone, while 44 percent of categories sold without any promotions. Another large-scale study found that over 40 percent of price-cuts were either displayed or featured.[5]

Because price-cuts, features, displays and double coupons are unique to retail promotions, they will be discussed at length in this chapter. Other types of sales promotions used by retailers are used more frequently in consumer or trade promotions and will be discussed in subsequent chapters.

DESCRIPTION OF RETAIL PROMOTIONS

Displays

Eye-catching displays of many low-cost products can boost sales dramatically. For example, Exhibit 10-2 shows the dramatic impact of displays on sales of four products. What are displays? What types of displays can retailers choose? What role do they play in sales promotions?

Displays are in-store arrangements that give greater visibility to a brand relative to competing

▼ EXHIBIT 10-2. Sales performance of brands on display.

Brand Sales for the 13 Weeks Ending September 13, 1992		
Product Category	Weeks on Display	Short-term Increase in Sales
Frozen dinners	5.8	245%
Laundry detergents	6.7	207
Salty snacks	12.5	172
Carbonated soft drinks	12.9	138

Source: Deveny, Kathleen (1992), "Displays Pay Off For Grocery Marketer," *The Wall Street Journal*, October 15, B1.

brands (see Exhibit 10-3). The costs of displays vary widely, from pennies per unit for a corrugated cardboard bin to over $2,000 per unit for an interactive electronic display.[6] Manufacturers provide the retailers with the materials necessary for the display and cover all or part of the costs of the display. Retailers can cover any additional costs of displays from their own promotional budget or the trade deal. One study estimates that the total spending on displays equaled $17 billion in 1994.[7] That was little more than the total advertising in magazines, but half of the total advertising in newspapers. There are a large variety of in-store displays. They can be classified by their location and their construction.

Location of Displays Displays can be classified by their location in a store. The price for a location is determined by its cost to the retailer who owns the store and the price that manufacturers are willing to pay. The more attractive the location, the higher its price. Typically, locations fall into four groups: front-of-store, end-of-aisle, in-aisle and shelf-talker.

Front-of-store displays are located in the lobby space near the store's entrance. They are the premier locations because almost all consumers who enter the store notice them. Also, consumers are the freshest and thus most impressionable at that point. In addition, consumers have empty carts and full wallets and are most susceptible to impulse purchases at that point.

End-of-aisle displays are in the next most attractive locations. These locations are visible to consumers within that aisle and within other aisles that lead to that spot. Another attractive feature of end-of-aisle displays is

that consumers may pass them more than once while traversing aisles.

In-aisle displays are less attractive locations as they are visible primarily to consumers within the aisle, and to a much lesser extent to those who pass by the aisle.

Shelf-talkers are signs or displays fixed onto the shelf, typically close to the product. They are visible only to shoppers in that aisle, mostly only while they are actually scanning that portion of the shelf. In 1994, shelf-talkers were the fastest growing

▼ EXHIBIT 10-3. Disney's "The Lion King" lobby display. An attention getting store display.

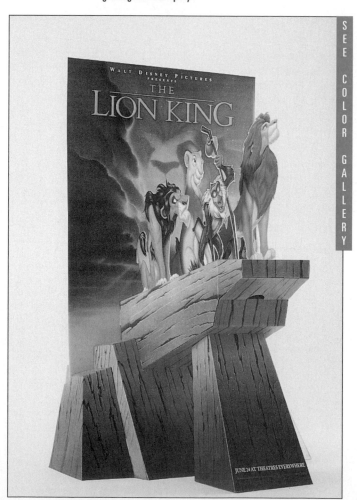

SEE COLOR GALLERY

Source: © Disney Enterprises, Inc.

display medium, probably because manufacturers found them to be less expensive than other media, while relatively quite effective.[8]

Types of Displays Displays can also be classified by their construction. They can be of three types: physical displays, electronic and interactive displays, and centers.

Physical displays are assortments of the product and signs, flyers or gadgets that better explain the product. These displays are the most popular types currently in use. In grocery stores, some displays are held in conjunction with a salesperson providing a sample of the product. In department stores, salespersons sometimes explain the nature or use of new products.

Electronic and **interactive displays** involve one or more of the new media, such as a TV monitor, video player, computer and various manipulatives for obtaining or providing information (see Exhibit 10-4). The advantage of the TV monitor is that it can show the benefits and uses of the product more effectively than can physical handling of the product. The interactive display enables information to be tailored to the particular needs and concerns of individual consumers.

Centers are *large* areas of a store dedicated to one or more products. The center attracts attention to, enhances the appeal of and above all provides infor-

mation on the product. The centers typically contain extended literature on or instructive displays of the product. Some centers may also have staff to answer consumers' questions.

Goals of Displays The primary purpose of displays is to draw attention to some new product, new feature or price-cut, or to remind consumers of a known product or feature. A large number of displays and other stimuli vie for the consumer's attention in the store. So the mere stacking of the product in the aisle of a store need not make for an effective display. Promoters need to be creative in designing displays to draw attention. In particular, two methods of drawing attention discussed in Chapter 5 are particularly relevant to displays: organizing stimuli and offering value. Exhibit 10-3 shows an attention-getting display that won a *PROMO* magazine award for best display in 1994.

A secondary purpose of displays is to let consumers try, taste, or sample the product. For example, drugstores may let consumers try out new gadgets. Grocery stores let consumers taste new packaged food products. Along these lines, displays should also let consumers easily pick up items for purchase. Displays need to provide easy access to the product to meet these goals. Easy access implies that the consumer can easily examine an item, choose from available alternatives, or pick up an item, without destabilizing the rest of the items on display.

Displays have their greatest appeal to buyers who are impulsive or who do not preplan purchases. While a discreet use of displays can enhance the overall marketing plan of the brand, promoters need to be wary of too much dependence on displays, as has happened for some brands (see Exhibit 10-5). For example, the exhibit shows that a majority of Pepsi sales (62 percent) occur with a display while only a quarter of rival Coca-Cola's sales do so. Because all consumers who visit the store can take advantage of the price-cut advertised in a display, its price discriminatory power is not high.

Features

Features are retail ads announcing a product's availability or low price, or a temporary price-cut. Features may be distributed through the mail, door to door, in the local newspaper or in a magazine. Certain categories of retail outlets generally feature their prod-

▼ **EXHIBIT 10-4.** Electronic interactive display that provides product information.

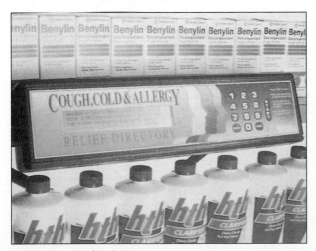

Source: Warner-Lambert Company.

▼ **EXHIBIT 10-5.** Proportion of total sales of popular brands attributable to display.

Brand	Percent of Annual Sales Due to Displays
Pepsi-Cola	62%
Dr. Pepper	49
Frito-Lay	37
Eagle Snacks	34
Nabisco Biscuit	30
Miller Brewing	27
Coca-Cola	25
Mars	25

Source: Adapted from Gibson, Richard (1992), "The Fine Art of Stocking A Supermarket's Shelves," *The Wall Street Journal*, October 15, B1, B6.

ucts in the same section of the newspaper, and sometimes on the same day of the week. For example, suppliers of car tires normally feature products in the sports section of the daily newspaper, while computer retailers normally feature products in the business section on Fridays. Grocery stores feature their products typically on Thursdays in the food section, while department and discount stores feature their products typically on Saturdays and Sundays.

Features may be classified into three groups based on their size: major ads, medium-sized ads and line ads. **Major ads** are large ads that cover a half or full page. They are typically used for products that move fast, are expensive or carry a large price-cut. Price-cuts on such items are likely to draw consumers to the stores. **Medium-size ads** use a smaller portion of a page and advertise the next most popular set of items. **Line ads,** as their name indicates, are just one or two lines and inform consumers about a price-cut.

Features are primarily controlled by retailers and serve their goals. Yet, many manufacturers gladly share the cost of features with the retailer. What purpose do features serve? Why would manufacturers share in their costs? Because most stores carry comparable merchandise, competition between stores frequently takes the form of offering a good assortment of brands, or offering specific brands at the lowest price. However, consumers who are price-sensitive cannot afford to shop from store to store for the lowest price. Features attract these consumers because they direct them to the store that has the brand they want at the lowest price. Thus features have become the principal means by which retail stores compete against other stores in the same cat-

egory (an appliance store against other appliance stores), and against stores across categories (a discount store against a drugstore).

Manufacturers generally promote features by agreeing to pay part of the costs of the features. There are several arrangements by which the exact support is calculated. Manufacturers may pay for a percentage of the retailers' sales of the product, or a fraction of the costs of the feature, or by offering a fixed amount provided the retailer agrees to a certain level of feature activity. Currently, appliance retailers cover 50 percent to 75 percent of their feature costs from trade deals and allowances, while food retailers cover almost all their costs of features from such sources.[9] We can estimate the total expenditures on features from the level of newspaper advertising. Most features appear as regional ads in newspapers. Regional ads constitute about 88 percent of all newspaper ads, which totaled $34 million in 1994.[10] Thus features constituted about $30 million in that year.

Most stores that carry products from several manufacturers prepare their own ads with limited input from the manufacturers. But manufacturers may prepare ads for retailers who feature only that manufacturer's brands. A good example of the latter is car dealers.

Price-Cuts

Most retail stores vary the prices of their products, offering periodic discounts at fixed times (preseason or end-of-season) or random discounts (the week of the discount is chosen at random). A few stores pride themselves on the fact that they offer an everyday-low price. Why do retailers adopt these different strategies? Which one of these is most effective?

Price-cuts are temporary reductions from the list price of the product. Retailers and the public refer to this price-cut as a **price discount**, a *discount* or a **sale**. This chapter uses the terms *discount* and *price-cut* interchangeably. Sometimes the price-cut may be for only one day, and at other times stores may run one-hour specials for selected items, for example, Kmart's "blue light specials."

Presenting a Price-Cut Price-cuts can be presented to consumers in at least four ways:

- Comparison of regular and special price ($200,000 home dropped to $180,000).
- Statement of the absolute price-cut value ($5 off the price of an Alaskan King Salmon).
- Statement of the price-cut percentage (25 percent off a facial).
- Offering a number of items for the price of one ("get two Hawaiian cruises for the price of one").

These ways of presenting a price-cut have the potential of being deceptive. The FTC has ruled they are indeed deceptive if the strategies imply a list, regular or market price that is not true (see Chapter 2). For example, stating 25 percent of list price, when few or no sales take place at the list price would be deceptive. While specific regulations may differ by states, a list, regular or market price is true if a majority of sales take place at that price instead of the discounted price.

In general, the latter three ways of presenting the price-cut are better than the first one, which requires the consumer to calculate the size of the price-cut. The only benefit in the first method of presenting the price-cut is that it provides consumers with the regular price. Of the second and third ways of stating the price-cut, the one which suggests a bigger numerical saving is likely to elicit a higher response. For example, when the item's price is low (say, $2), then stating the absolute price-cut ("save 50¢") is not as effective as stating the percentage price-cut ("save 25 percent"). However, when the item is costly (say, $1,000), then stating the absolute value of the cut ("save $100") is better than stating the percentage price-cut ("save 10 percent"). Research indicates that the fourth way of stating the price-cut (two-for-one, three-for-$1) may lead to the biggest increase in sales.[11] The reason is that many consumers assume that the price-cut applies only if they buy the total quantity stated in the offer, and not on each item as is strictly the case. Thus, consumers assume that three for $10 implies they must buy all three items to get the special price.

Aside from the issue of deception, the FTC has no regulation mandating use of any one form of price-cut over the other three. However, from an ethical perspective, a firm may prefer to choose one that does not unfairly exploit consumers' perceptions. For example, a firm may subtitle a three-for-$1 promotion with the phrase "prorated to purchased quantity."

Goals of Price-Cuts The major strategic goal of price-cuts is to price discriminate between informed and uninformed consumers, or between loyals and switchers (see Chapter 9). A second strategic goal of price-cuts is to build consumer inventories, which can have two benefits. One, as consumers stock up on a brand, retailers reduce their own inventories and thus their inventory carrying costs. Two, when consumers stock up on a brand, they are less likely to buy competing products. This is the reason for pre-season sales of goods, often weeks or months before the time consumers are likely to use the product. Retailers also offer price-cuts to move damaged or overstocked goods. This goal of price-cuts is a tactical and not strategic one as explained in Chapter 9.

Double Coupons

Manufacturer coupons are certificates from manufacturers offering consumers some fixed saving off the retail price of the product if they meet some conditions. The savings is called the **face value** of the coupon. **Retail coupons** are similar to manufacturer coupons except that they are from retailers to consumers. **Double coupons** are offers by retailers to double the face value of a manufacturer coupon. The retailer has to pay only the incremental cost of doubling the face value of the coupon, while the manufacturer reimburses the retailer for the initial face value of the coupon plus the processing cost. The manufacturer pays these two costs in addition to the costs of distribution, because the retailer's doubling of the face value of the coupon does not change any of these costs.

Double coupons have evolved as an important means of competition in some markets. Why has this happened? What are the benefits of this strategy? The main attraction of the double coupon for retailers is that it offers a consumer double the savings of retail coupons of the same face value, while costing retailers only the face value of the coupon. Because of their higher savings for consumers and the higher visibility and excitement with which they are generally promoted, double coupons have a higher sales response relative to retail coupons of the same face value. At the same time, because they take the form of coupons, double coupons have a higher price discrimination effect relative to price-cuts of the same total value. Thus *double coupons have a higher response than retail coupons and a higher price discrimination effect than price-cuts.*

Moreover, retailers who adopt a double coupon strategy can still maintain higher overall prices than retailers that do not adopt such a strategy, without consumers realizing the difference.[12] Because of these benefits to the retailer, double coupons have evolved as a very attractive means of promotion for the retailer, and an important means by which stores compete against each other.[13]

ANALYZING THE EFFECTS OF RETAIL PROMOTIONS

The early growth of Kmart and Wal-Mart described in the opening example, and the subsequent victory of Wal-Mart, emphasize the importance of price in retail competition. Consumers are very sensitive to low prices. However, the strategic use of promotions can enable retailers to offer low prices to price-sensitive consumers while still selling at higher regular prices to less sensitive consumers. To do so, firms need to understand how and to what extent consumers respond to price changes and promotions. This section explains this response in two subsections. The first one describes how sales respond to promotions, and the second one describes what causes the response in sales.

Response to Retail Promotions

Retail promotions elicit an immediate and sharp increase in sales, especially if they are linked to a price-cut. For example, a 20 percent price-cut may lead to a 200 percent increase in sales. To understand this increase we define two terms, the *main* and *interactive effect*.

Definitions The **main effect of a variable** is the change that it alone induces in some other variable. For example, if a store changes only the price of a brand from one week to another, and the sales of that brand change in response, then that change is called the main effect of price on sales. The **interactive effect of two or more variables** on some other variable is the incremental change caused by those two variables beyond what either of them causes individually. The **total effect of two or more variables** is the sum of their main and interactive effects.

For example, consider the following scenarios (shown in Exhibit 10-6):

- Let (a) = a 77% sales increase caused by a 10% price-cut *alone*.
- Let (b) = an 85% sales increase caused by a feature *alone*.
- Let (c) = a 227% sales increase caused by a 10% price-cut *and* a feature *together*.
- Let (d) = (c) − {(a) + (b)} = 65%.

Then, (a) and (b) are the main effects of the price-cut and store display respectively, (c) is the total effect of the price-cut and the feature together and (d) is the interactive effect of the price-cut and store display when they occur together. In other words, featuring the price-cut leads to a further increase in sales of 65 percent, over and above what would have occurred with the sum of the increases from a price-cut and a feature *alone* on separate occasions. These definitions are important because research has shown that the major boost from retail promotions comes not from the main effect of the individual promotion, but from the interactive effect of certain combinations of promotions.

▼ EXHIBIT 10-6. Main and interactive effects of retail promotions.

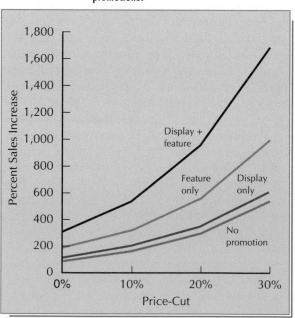

Source: Adapted from Blattberg and Neslin (1989), "Sales Promotions: The Long and the Short of It," *Marketing Letters*, 1, 1, 81–97, with kind permission of Kluwer Academic Publishers.

When referring to interactive effects, the terms *two-way, three-way,* etc., are used when two or three variables are involved. The total effect of two or more variables is the sum of their main and interactive effects.

Pattern of Response Exhibit 10-7 shows the response of sales to promotional activity for one brand in one store over time. This exhibit presents a dramatic picture of what goes on during a sales promotion. Such analyses are possible with the advent of scanner data that allow for detailed analyses of sales by store, brand, and week for every promotion (see Chapter 14). We need to identify several important aspects of this picture.

First, focus on the sales curve. Note that sales are neither smooth nor curvilinear, but jagged, with sharp peaks and valleys. Analysis over many brands and weeks indicates that these peaks and valleys are not due to any periodicity in sales, but due to retail promotions.

▼ **EXHIBIT 10-7.** Hypothetical retail sales of a brand in response to promotions.

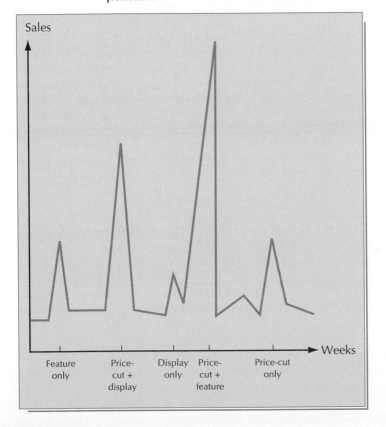

Second, almost every retail promotion leads to an immediate and sharp increase in sales. In this particular graph, the key promotions are price-cuts, features and displays. The height of each peak corresponds to the extent of response to the promotion. If more than one promotion occurs in the same week, then the height of the peak represents (c) the total effect of the promotion.

Third, each of the retail promotions could have a certain main and interactive effect on sales. However, the time series picture does not reveal that point clearly. The reason is that there are not enough occasions when each of the promotions occurs individually, in pairs and all together. In statistical terms this problem of contemporaneous occurrences of causes is called *multicollinearity*.

Fourth, there is no distinct increase or decrease in the height of peaks over time. Using terms from Chapter 17, there is no apparent buildup or wearout of the effects of these promotions on sales. However, this issue is hotly debated. Many critics of sales promotions assert that price-cuts increase price-sensitiveness and therefore lead to a wearout of their effectiveness over time. Perhaps such changes occur over long time periods, and are thus not visible in a snapshot of a few weeks' sales as in Exhibit 10-7.

What would happen if one were to aggregate sales over either brand, time or store? If the promotions for different brands or different stores did not occur in unison, then the sales curve would smooth out and we would not get this sharp a picture. Thus **disaggregate data,** or an analysis that breaks up sales into the smallest reasonable components (for example, by brand, store and week) gives a better picture of sales response to promotions than one that aggregates data over these dimensions.

Degree of Response Exhibit 10-7 still leaves one important unanswered question: what are the main and interactive effects on sales of a price-cut, feature and display? Field experiments, as well as many statistical analyses of data such as that presented here, have given us a better feel for the degree of response to sales promotions in terms of the main and interactive effects. One study found very strong interactive effects of displaying or featuring a price-cut (see Exhibit 10-6).

That figure charts the response (vertical axis) to various price-cuts (horizontal axis) for different combinations of display and features (the four curves). The first (lowest) curve gives the main effect on sales for each percentage cut in price without feature or display. Each subsequent curve corresponds to a certain type of promotional support: display, feature, or display and feature. The base level of sales, which is scaled to 100 units and occurs with no price-cut (0% on the horizontal axis) and no display or feature, is the first point on the bottom curve. The main effects for display and feature relative to this base level can be obtained by looking at the values of the second and third curves respectively along the y-axis, corresponding to this point (0% on the x-axis). All the other points on the curves show total effects (including main and interactive effects) of displaying a price-cut (second curve), featuring a price-cut (third curve), or displaying and featuring a price-cut (fourth curve). Note that the figure shows a strong two-way interactive effect of displaying a price-cut or featuring a price-cut, and a dramatic three-way interactive effect of displaying *and* featuring a price-cut. For example, a combination of a 30 percent price-cut with a display and a feature leads to a phenomenal level of sales of 1,719 units over the base of 100 units, or a 1,619 percent increase in sales!

Decomposing the Promotional Bump

What is the cause of the increase in sales following a retail promotion? The obvious answer is that it results from consumers buying more of the product. However, managers want to know exactly why and how consumers buy more of the product. Analysts have identified four sources for the sales increase: incremental consumption, brand switching, stockpiling and store switching. The increase in sales in response to a promotion is popularly called the **promotional bump**, while its breakdown into these four components is called **decomposing the promotional bump**.[14] In the subsequent discussion, the term *sales increase* refers to an increase in response to a promotion, while the term **incremental sales** means the increase over and above the normal or regular level

in the absence of a promotion. We now discuss each of these effects.

Incremental Consumption **Incremental consumption** is the consumer's higher use of a product relative to the normal level. In general, for many products incremental consumption is low. Consumption of many routine grocery items such as toilet tissue, milk, or pickles is unlikely to increase much because the items are on discount. Also, for many higher priced durable products, such as TVs or mattresses, which are necessities or have household penetration near 100 percent, consumption generally does not increase much due to normal price-cuts. The reason is that even consumers who are price-sensitive are likely to buy based on need. Incremental consumption for basic services such as dry cleaning or gardening is unlikely to be high in response to price-cuts. However, consumption for all these categories may increase substantially for discounts that are very steep, atypical, or unexpected.

Brand Switching **Brand switching** is the consumer's purchase of a rival brand rather than one he or she regularly buys. In each category of consumer goods, retailers generally offer many brands made by competing manufacturers, which are quite similar to each other. Frequently, the prices are also comparable. In such a scenario, consumers may have a weak preference for particular brands. However, when any one brand is on discount, it often becomes preferable to its rivals. Thus the biggest component of incremental sales for most consumer products and services comes from brand switching.[15]

One recent study found a plausible asymmetric pattern to brand switching for grocery products.[16] To understand this issue we need to consider the types of brands in stores. Brands can be broadly grouped into three classes based on price. The **national brands** are those that have established national names and reputations. They claim superior quality, advertise regularly and initiate product improvements or introduce new products. Examples are Levi's jeans, Whirlpool's appliances, or Kellogg's Corn Flakes. A second class consists of lower priced **private labels,** or brands owned by and labeled after the store in which they are sold. Examples are Sears appliances, Gap jeans, or Kroger's cornflakes. A third group consists of **generic brands,** which are even lower priced brands with no specific name and very simple packaging.

The study found that when a national brand goes on sale, it draws primarily from sales of private labels and to a lesser extent from sales of the generic brand (see Exhibit 10-8). When a private label goes on sale, it draws primarily from the sales of other private labels and the generic brands, but not from those of the national brands. When a generic brand goes on sale, it draws from sales of generics in other stores, but not from the sales of the other two classes of brands. The reason may be that each of

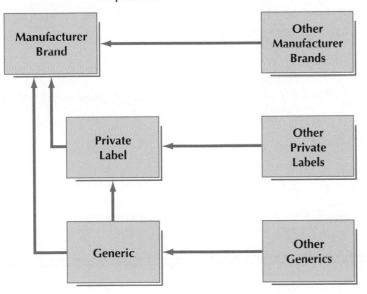

▼ EXHIBIT 10-8. Asymmetric draw of promotions: Direction of sales flow due to a price-cut.

these classes of brands has a group of consumers who patronize it at the regular prices. The buyers of the less expensive brands find the more expensive brand a better deal when it is on sale. However, the buyers of the more expensive brand have already made a choice of the higher priced brand (either rightly or wrongly in expectation of higher quality) and so are less sensitive to price-cuts from the lower priced brand. Thus, while brand switching is the major component of sales in response to a price-cut, it tends to be asymmetric across these three groups of brands.

Forward Buying and Stockpiling **Forward buying** means buying future requirements in the current period to

take advantage of a current trade deal. **Stockpiling** refers to holding a higher inventory of goods than needed to meet current demand. The terms refer to different aspects of consumer response to retail promotions. Analyses of consumer response to sales indicate that forward buying and stockpiling in response to promotions are not a major component of incremental sales. Indeed, an analysis of sales curves indicates that dips in sales before or after a promotion are not very big. There are two reasons for this finding, which have different implications for the retailer.

One reason for the lack of observed forward buying and stockpiling may be the hassle of stockpiling, the lack of storage space, the tie-up of capital or the danger of spoilage or obsolescence. This is especially true of durables, which are expensive, bulky, require infrequent replacement and become obsolete. Stockpiling of services is even more difficult. For example, one could stock up dirty clothes for an occasion when a dry cleaner offers a discount; but the task is neither easy nor convenient. One can accelerate one's periodic phone calls to loved ones when companies offer specials; but can one really "stock up" on phone conversations? The situation is a little different for some grocery products. For example, in response to price-cuts consumers do stock up on canned goods, which are frequently used, inexpensive, easy to store and do not spoil. Some families do resort to stockpiling groceries and may allocate rooms or freezers just for this purpose. Even for grocery products, the examples are exceptions rather than the rule.

Another reason for low stockpiling by consumers may be that retailers offer an abundance of promotions, so that consumers can always buy one or another brand on promotion. For example, without even accelerating their purchases, consumers can always get a brand on discount, if they are willing to switch among brands. Further, for some infrequently purchased products such as car wax, small appliances and especially large appliances discounts occur at much greater frequency than the time between a consumer's purchases. For example, TVs frequently go on sale before major holidays. Yet consumers buy a new TV once in three to ten years. In these cases, consumers could get their favorite brand on discount without having to adjust their time of purchase. Thus retailers need to be careful if they do not observe much stockpiling or forward buying. The low level of these activities may be due to too frequent discounting in the category, rather than any aversion to stockpiling itself.

Store Switching **Store switching** refers to a change in the store that a consumer frequents because of a promotion. The store switching on a consumer's purchase occasion depends on the price of a brand and the savings during a retail promotion relative to the basket of items that a consumer purchases on that occasion. If the brand is an expensive item, such as an appliance, *and* the consumer plans to buy only one or a few items on the purchase occasion, then store switching in response to discounts is likely. Indeed, if a set of competing retailers each stocks only one unique brand, then store switching is identical to brand switching, and is likely to comprise a major component of incremental sales. In contrast, for grocery products, which are generally low priced and for which a consumer is likely to buy several items on a purchase occasion, discounts on one brand may not stimulate store switching.

However, retailers sometimes use heavily advertised national brands as **loss leaders,** selling them at a steep discount and below cost in order to attract consumers to their stores. In these cases, store switching may comprise a major component of incremental sales, and the price-cut on that brand alone may not be profitable. However, the decision rule in these cases is not whether that brand's price-cut is profitable, but whether the loss incurred in the sales of that brand at a steep discount is compensated by the incremental profits from sales of other products in the store generated by the higher store traffic.

Of these four components of the sales bump, incremental consumption and store switching constitute real incremental sales to the retailer. Brand switching and stockpiling merely cause a change in the object or timing of the purchase and lead to no major benefits for the retailer. Thus the retailer needs to choose the type and combination of promotions that maximize higher consumption and store switching, while minimizing stockpiling and brand switching by consumers. When is a retail promotion profitable? The decomposition of the sales bump in

response to sales promotions is a key to answering these questions.

THE PROFITABILITY OF A PRICE PROMOTION

On March 1, 1989, the giant retailer Sears, Roebuck & Co. instituted a new strategy of everyday-low pricing. Previously the company followed a strategy of high-low pricing. The latter strategy involved regular prices interspersed with short, random or periodic discounts. The everyday-low price would probably lie between the high of the regular price and the low of the discount price. However, Sears advertised its everyday-low price as the same as a discount price. In a letter to customers describing the new price policy, Sears said, "Think of it as a sale that never ends." The company considered the new strategy "the biggest change in our 102-year history,"[17] and spent $200 million to advertise it to consumers.[18] However, as quickly as a month later, Sears continued to run "sales" with reduced prices on certain merchandise, albeit more selectively and less frequently. Then a year later Sears switched back to its former strategy of high-low pricing.[19]

Why did Sears initially have a strategy of high-low prices? Why did it adopt a strategy of everyday-low pricing? Why did it revert to high-low pricing subsequently? This section should provide you with the theory to answer these questions and determine whether Sears acted wisely. The section first shows how to analyze the profitability of a price promotion, then discusses some strategic implications of price-cuts, and finally applies the theory to the story of Sears's reversals in promotion strategy. Recall from Chapter 9 that a price promotion is a promotion involving a price-cut, and is the most common type of retail promotion.

Analysis of Profitability

The starting point in the analysis of the profitability of a price promotion is the sales response to that promotion, as shown in Exhibit 10-7. Based on that information, Exhibit 10-9 shows an idealized curve of weekly sales of one brand in one store. Weekly sales are steady except for a sharp increase during week 2 due to a price promotion.

The profitability of the retailer's price promotion depends on the trade-off between the profits from the incremental sales and the costs of the promotion.

▼ EXHIBIT 10-9. **Idealized sales response to a price promotion.**

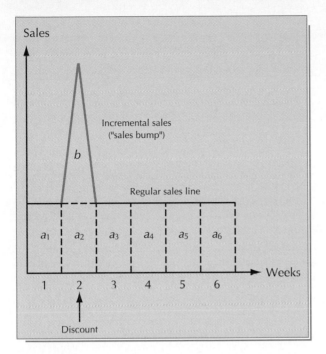

The costs are of two types: fixed costs that do not vary by unit sold, such as the cost of the feature, and opportunity costs.[20] Recall from Chapter 9 that an **opportunity cost** is a loss incurred by not taking advantage of an occasion to earn a profit. When the retailer offers a price promotion, it incurs an opportunity cost of some consumers who would have bought at the regular price, buying at the discounted price.

We analyze profitability and costs in three increasingly complex cases. Case 1 makes two assumptions: all incremental sales are beneficial to the retailer, and there are no fixed costs of the promotion. Case 2 relaxes the first of these two assumptions, and Case 3 relaxes both of them.

Case 1 In Exhibit 10-9, let the solid line reflect the unit sales curve. Let the area a reflect **regular sales** that take place in the absence of a promotion. Further, let a_1, where 1 is a subscript for week, represent the regular weekly sales of the brand. We can label the buyers responsible for these sales as loyals. Recall from Chapter 9 that loyals are consumers who buy their favorite brand at a regular time even if it is not on discount. Further, the portion of sales in week 2, a_2, can be attributed to **lucky loyals** who

get the benefit of a price-cut during a promotion even though they would have bought at the high price. The remaining weekly sales can be attributed to **unlucky loyals** who buy the product at the regular price. Let the area b reflect the incremental unit sales over regular sales, due to a price promotion. We can label the buyers responsible for these sales as switchers. Let m be the retailer's margin per unit sold before the price-cut, and let d be the price-cut per unit offered by the retailer. Given these values, do we have enough information to determine if the price promotion is profitable? If yes, can you derive the condition for it?

We do have enough information to determine profitability. The price promotion is profitable if the incremental profits from additional sales due to the price promotion exceed the total costs of the price promotion. In this case, because there are no fixed costs of the price promotion, all the costs are opportunity loss from regular buyers taking advantage of the price promotion. So, the price promotion is profitable if:

Equation 1: $b\,(m - d) > a_2 d$

By way of explanation, note that the profit per unit that the retailer gets from each additional consumer is the margin less price-cut $(m - d)$. Because there are b consumers who buy when the price is cut, $b \times (m - d)$ gives the **incremental profits**. The opportunity loss is due to the loyals receiving a price-cut when they would have bought at the regular price. There are a_2 lucky loyals who get the price-cut, d. Thus the total opportunity loss is $a_2 \times d$. Given the above information, the price of the product, the fixed costs of manufacture and the sales during the other weeks are irrelevant to determining the profitability of the promotion.

Case 2 In real markets, sales response to promotions is never as simple as that depicted in Exhibit 10-9. The bump in sales in that exhibit is merely the observed and not the real incremental sales. The **real incremental sales** is the increase in sales that *would not have taken place at all* in the absence of the price-cut. As explained earlier, four simultaneous events make the sales response more complex than what is observed: incremental consumption, brand switching, stockpiling, and store switching. Let us call the

▼ **EXHIBIT 10-10. Decomposing the sales bump.**

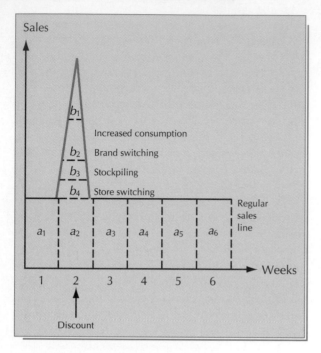

fraction of sales due to each of these factors b_1, b_2, b_3 and b_4 respectively (see Exhibit 10-10).

What is the profitability of the price promotion given this decomposition of the sales bump?

The decision rule is still the same. The price promotion is profitable if the incremental profits from the price promotion are higher than the cost of price promotion. However, note that the opportunity loss in this case is not merely a_2, but also b_2—the fraction of sales of other brands that would have occurred at their regular price, plus b_3—the fraction of sales that result from consumers who buy during the price promotion to stockpile. (For simplicity, assume that the other brands have a margin similar to the promoted brand's.) The real incremental sales are just b_1, the increase in consumption, and b_4, the store switching. Thus, following the logic of Equation 1, the price promotion is profitable if:

Equation 2: $(b_1 + b_4)\,(m - d) > (a_2 + b_2 + b_3)\,d$

Case 3 The retailer's decision to price-promote also involves some **fixed costs** of promotion that do not change per unit. The most obvious ones are those for displays and features. Both of these promotions can greatly increase the response to promotions, as shown in Exhibit 10-6. Retailers also incur some fixed costs of managing the promotion. One cost is that for retagging items or shelves with the new price. Another cost is that of managing higher inventory to accommodate increased sales. A third cost is that of planning the promotional strategy. Planning can be quite time consuming, given the large number of items a retailer carries, the constant variation in promotions for those items, and the need to take into account the variety of strategies that competitors adopt. At the same time, manufacturers do provide retailers with allowances to cover some of these costs, especially the costs of display and feature (see Chapter 11). All these costs and benefits must ultimately be allocated to the price promotion. Let f_1 represent the costs of features and displays less manufacturer's allowance; and f_2 represent the costs of managing the promotion. Then a price promotion is profitable if:

(Margin − Discount) × (Higher consumption + Store switching)

Equation 3: $(b_1 + b_4)\,(m - d) > (a_2 + b_2 + b_3)\,d + f_1 + f_2$

Relative to Equation 2, all that we have done is added the costs f_1 and f_2 to the costs of the promotion, or the righthand side of Equation 3.

Strategic Implications

The strategic relevance of Equation 3 depends on the values of the variables in the equation, especially of the components of incremental sales, b_1, b_2, b_3 and b_4. Our earlier review of research in this area suggests the following generalizations:

■ Incremental consumption (b_1) is low.
■ Brand switching (b_2) is the biggest component of incremental sales for most consumer products and services.[21]
■ Stockpiling in response to price promotions (b_3) is not a major component of incremental sales.
■ Store switching is high for high-priced items (such as appliances). For low-priced items store switching is low, except in the case of loss leaders.

These findings lead to three important strategic phenomena associated with price promotions:

timing of discounts, everyday-low-price stores and low pass-through.

Timing of Price Promotions

For most stores, price promotions are typically offered infrequently, for a short period of time, followed by a resumption of the high price. What is the reason for this pattern of discounts? The reason is that when price-cuts are offered frequently or for several weeks together, the increase in sales for each subsequent week tends to be lower than for the first week.[22] That first week of sales is when most of the consumers responsible for the incremental sales take advantage of the discount. At the same time, the cumulative number of lucky loyals and thus the opportunity costs or leakage keep increasing (see Chapter 9 for further discussion of this issue).

Everyday-Low-Priced (EDLP) Stores

Everyday-low price (EDLP) is a strategy by which a retailer routinely sells a product at a price that is generally as low as or lower than a promoted price offered by other retailers. In contrast, a **high-low pricing strategy** involves maintaining a high regular price, and intermittently offering price promotions. Recent years have witnessed a great increase in EDLP stores, such as Costco, Sam's Warehouse, and Price Club. What is the motivation for such stores? In some cities and localities, EDLP stores coexist with regular retailers who offer traditional discount pricing interspersed with regular high prices. The emergence of EDLP stores may be due to any one of these reasons: high costs of promotion, special segments of buyers and regulation.

High Costs of Promotion While a retailer's policy of price promotions leads to incremental sales from price-sensitive consumers, it also involves several costs such as retagging prices, managing inventories and planning strategy. An everyday-low price would avoid many of these costs and may sometimes be profitable. For example, at one time in its high-low pricing strategy, Sears, Roebuck & Co. was putting as many as 8,000 items on weekly special. The strategy cost the company $200 million annually.[23] EDLP stores may also keep their costs low by not stocking too many brands, not honoring coupons, and making their own purchases only when brands are on trade deal. What would be the rule that would render an EDLP strategy profitable? An EDLP is profitable if promotional costs are too high to offer promotions (Equation 3 is not satisfied), but the lower price draws enough people even when maintained permanently without promotional support (Equation 2 is satisfied).

The recent change to EDLP may be an overreaction by retailers to the high costs of promotion. Retailers may not have realized that when a low price is offered daily, it does not generate enough excitement to draw consumers into the stores. Alternatively, retailers may not have realized that with a high-low price strategy, high prices paid by consumers do contribute to profits. For example, a study at the University of Chicago manipulated prices in 19 categories in a supermarket chain, with some stores using EDLP and others using high-low pricing.[24] Stores with EDLP had slightly higher sales but much lower profits (17 percent) than those stores that had high-low pricing. Some retailers may also use EDLP as a sales gimmick to attract consumers, without a strategy of maintaining a low price for every product all the time.[25]

Special Segments of Buyers Price-sensitive consumers can be segmented into two groups, searchers and nonsearchers. Price-sensitive searchers are those who have the time and are willing to search for low prices, clip coupons or time their purchases to buy their preferred brands on promotion. Price-sensitive nonsearchers are those who want the low prices but have neither the time nor the willingness to shop for low prices. EDLP stores appeal to these price-sensitive nonsearchers. By guaranteeing low prices every day, they greatly simplify the shopping experience for these consumers without increasing the costs too much.

Regulation As explained in Chapter 2, the federal government and many state governments have restrictions on references to list or regular prices. The basic principle is that firms should not call a price a list or regular price unless adequate numbers of units sell at that price. Because of these restrictions, retailers that resort to high-low pricing may have to lower the high price if inadequate sales occur at that price. As a result, the difference between the high and low price may not be enough to make the low price an attractive discount, or to justify the costs of changing prices back and forth between the high and low price. In such cases, retailers may resort to an everyday-low price.

Low Pass-Through The major component of price promotions by stores is brand switching. As the above discussion suggests, brand switching does not necessarily help the profits of a retailer, especially if the retailer gets the same margin from the target brand (whose price is cut) and the substituted brand that the consumer would have bought in the absence of the price promotion. High brand switching reduces a retailer's motivation to offer promotions on a particular brand, even when the brand's manufacturer offers a trade deal to motivate retailers to do so. As a result, the retailer tends not to pass-through the trade deal to consumers. Chapter 11 discusses this problem in greater detail. The root cause of low pass-through is consumers' high brand switching (rather than higher consumption or store switching), in response to retail promotions.

The Story Behind Sears's Pricing Strategy

We are now in a position to answer the questions at the start of this section on Sears's promotion strategy.

Why did Sears initially have a strategy of high-low prices? The primary reason was to discriminate between price-sensitive and -insensitive consumers. In particular, during the 1980s discount stores such as Wal-Mart, Target and Kmart began attracting an increasing number of shoppers with prices that were generally lower than those at Sears for comparative products. By offering periodic or random discounts, Sears tried to match the low prices of these competitors without lowering the regular prices of its products.

Why did Sears adopt a strategy of everyday-low pricing? By the end of the 1980s Sears's discounts were so popular that most of its products were being sold at the discounted price. For example, a study by New York State's office of the attorney general found that in one period the vacuum cleaner listed in Exhibit 10-11 was sold at the discount price 4,301 times, while at the regular price 56 times.[26] The smaller number of items sold at the regular price probably did not justify the cost of maintaining a high-low pricing strategy. More importantly, in 1986, New York State's attorney general charged

▼ **EXHIBIT 10-11.** Regular and promotional prices at Sears.

Item	Regular Price	Promotional Price	Everyday-Low Price
Kenmore canister vacuum	$299.99 or $319.99	$199.99	$219.99
Dearborn three-piece living room sectional	$1,749.97	$899.94	$979.00
Saratoga sofa and chair combinations	$1,149.98	$699.96	$699.00

Source: Richter, Paul (1989), "NY Sues Sears, Alleging Pricing Policy Deceptions," *Los Angeles Times,* December 22, D3–D4.

Sears with deceptive pricing for advertising big discounts from the regular price, because sales rarely occurred at the regular price. Sears paid a fine of $75,000 to settle that charge.[27] Thus the pressure from regulators against and the costs of running the high-low pricing strategy led Sears to adopt an everyday-low pricing strategy.

Why did Sears revert to high-low pricing? Sears advertised its everyday-low pricing strategy with a $200 million budget. It claimed that the new pricing strategy (with the ad campaign) led to a 56 percent increase in profits relative to a comparable period. However, it still could not compete with discount retailers such as Kmart, Wal-Mart and Target.[28] Not only were the prices of those stores lower than those of Sears, but those stores ran frequent promotions. In the absence of such promotions, Sears found it difficult to generate consumer enthusiasm and store traffic. Only 36 percent of Sears shoppers said that they were very satisfied with the new format.[29] Moreover, investigators from New York State's attorney general's office found that the everyday-low prices were not as low as the prior discount prices. This difference would not have been critical if Sears had not run such a big advertising campaign claiming to have everyday-low prices equivalent to its former discount prices. Thus under further pressure from New York State's attorney general and under pressure from competitors, Sears reverted to its former strategy of high-low prices.

These changes indicate how companies must carefully note the key issues involved in choosing a pricing strategy: the relative proportion of price-sensitive to loyal consumers, the excitement generated by discounts, the costs of running those discounts, and the honesty in advertising regular and discount prices.

SUMMARY

Retail promotions are sales promotions that the retailer offers consumers. They are triggered by trade promotions, competition among retailers or specific goals of the retailer. While some retail promotions are similar to consumer and trade promotions, four types of retail promotions are unique to the retailer and constitute important means of retail competition: displays, features, price-cuts and double coupons.

There are a variety of displays, which may be classified by their location in the store or their physical construction. The primary purpose of displays is to draw attention to some new product or feature, to remind consumers of a known product or to announce a price-cut. Displays do not have high discriminatory power, but appeal strongly to impulsive shoppers.

Features may be placed in newspapers and magazines, mailed to households, or distributed door to door. Because most stores carry comparable merchandise, competition between stores frequently takes the form of offering a good assortment of brands, or offering specific brands at the lowest price. Features have become the principal means by which retail stores compete with other stores in the same category by announcing the availability and low prices of their products.

Price-cuts can be stated in at least four ways: comparison of regular and special price, statement of the absolute price-cut, statement of the percentage price-cut and the offer of a number of items for the price of one (for example, two for one). Retailers offer price-cuts to discriminate among loyals and switchers, to build consumer inventories or to sell damaged goods or reduce overstocking of inventories.

Double coupons offer consumers twice the face value of the coupons, although the retailer has to pay only for doubling the face value, and not for the initial face value nor for the distribution costs. Thus double coupons are more appealing to consumers than retail coupons of the same face value, while also having more discriminatory power than price-cuts of the same total value.

Price-cuts lead to an immediate boost in sales, which increase with the value of the price-cut. Displays and features also lead to a small increase in sales when used alone, but to a big increase in sales when combined with price-cuts. The sales increase from retail promotions consists primarily of brand switching, and secondarily of incremental consumption, store switching and stockpiling. Decomposing the promotional bump into these four components is important to determining profitability.

A price promotion is profitable if its total profits exceed total costs. The total profits are the real number of incremental units sold times the margin. When computing the real incremental units, retailers need to factor out increases in sales from buyers who stockpile or merely switch brands. The incremental costs are the sum of the fixed costs of running the promotion and the opportunity costs of regular buyers getting the price-cut without actually needing it. To enhance profits, retailers need to offer price promotions infrequently and for a short duration. Retailers are reluctant to offer (pass through) promotions sponsored by manufacturers because the brand switching that results from their own promotions does not really help their sales and profits. The high fixed cost of promotions and low sales at regular prices are reasons that retailers have started offering everyday-low prices.

QUESTIONS

1. What are the different types of retail promotions? What goals do they serve?
2. How effective are sales promotions in achieving their goals?
3. What purpose do features serve? Why would manufacturers share in their costs with retailers?
4. What strategies can retailers adopt to present a price-cut? What is the purpose of each of them? How effective is each?
5. What are double coupons? Why are they popular with retailers and consumers?
6. How can one observe the effect of retail promotions on retail sales? What is the best level of data to observe these effects? Explain.
7. What are the main and interactive effects on sales of a price-cut, feature and display?
8. What is the promotional bump? How does one decompose it?

9. Sales just before and after a price-cut do not show a dip, despite the promotional bump. Explain.

10. What is the minimum information you need to determine if the price promotion is profitable? Given this information can you derive the condition for it?

11. What is the profitability of a simple price-cut without promotional support?

12. What is the profitability of a price promotion given that an analyst can decompose the sales bump?

13. Price-cuts should be given infrequently and for a short duration. Why?

14. Recent years have witnessed a great increase in EDLP stores, such as Costco, Sam's Warehouse, and Price Club. What is the motivation for such stores?

15. What would be the rule that would render an EDLP strategy profitable?

16. Why did Sears initially have a strategy of high-low prices? Why did it adopt a strategy of everyday-low pricing? Why did it revert to high-low pricing subsequently?

NOTES

1. Adapted from Duff, Christina, and Bob Ortega (1995), "How Wal-Mart Outdid A Once Touted Kmart In Discount-Store Race," *The Wall Street Journal*, March 24, A1, A3.

2. Johnson, Bradley (1993), "Food Chains Stock Up On Promos: Recession Continues to Plague Southern California Supermarkets," *Advertising Age*, April 12, 26.

3. Carlton, Jim (1995), "Japanese Skip Waikiki, Head For Kmart," *The Wall Street Journal*, June 29, B1.

4. Fader, Peter S., and Leonard M. Lodish (1990), "A Cross-Category Analysis of Category Structure and Promotional Activity For Grocery Products," *Journal of Marketing* 54 (October), 52–65.

5. *Infoscan Report on Trade Promotions*, Chicago, Information Resources Inc.

6. Point of Purchase Advertising (1994), "Technology Gives P-O-P A New Look," *Advertising Age*, September 26, P6.

7. Haran, Leah (1995), "Marketer Getting With The Program," *Advertising Age*, October 23, 33.

8. The Editors (1995), "Still Bullish On Promotion," *PROMO Magazine's Source Book 95*, Wilton, CT: PROMO, 13.

9. Blattberg, Robert C., and Scott A. Neslin (1990), *Sales Promotion: Concepts, Methods and Strategies*, Englewood Cliffs, NJ: Prentice-Hall.

10. Haran, "Marketer Getting With The Program."

11. Blattberg and Neslin, *Sales Promotion: Concepts, Methods and Strategies*.

12. Hess, James D., and Eitan Gerstner (1991), "Who's Afraid Of Double Coupons," working paper 91-03, North Carolina State University, Department of Business Management, December.

13. Krishnan, Trichy V., and Ram C. Rao (1995), "Double Couponing and Retail Pricing in A Couponed Category," *Journal of Marketing Research* 32 (November), 419–432.

14. McAlister, Leigh (1983), "Decomposing the Promotional Bump," working paper, Massachusetts Institute of Technology.

15. Gupta, Sunil (1988), "Impact of Sales Promotions on When, What and How Much to Buy," *Journal of Marketing Research* 25 (November), 342–355.

16. Blattberg, Robert C., and Kenneth J. Wisniewski (1989), "Price Induced Patterns of Competition," *Marketing Science* 8, 4 (Fall), 291–309.

17. Schwadel, Francine (1989), "What Looks Like a Sale, But Isn't A Sale?" *The Wall Street Journal*, April 27, B1.

18. Fitzgerald, Kate (1992), "Brennan Will Have to Answer to Upset Sears Shareholders," *Advertising Age*, April 20, 3, 42.

19. *Ibid.*; Schwadel, Francine (1988), "Sears Switches Pricing Strategy to Combat Discounters," *The Wall Street Journal*, November 1, B1.

20. There is also a direct cost of the promotion such as the size of the price-cut, which varies per unit sold, and which is deducted from the margin in this analysis.

21. Gupta, "Impact of Sales Promotions on When, What and How Much to Buy."

22. Aradhna, Krishna (1994), "The Impact of Dealing Patterns On Purchase Behavior," *Marketing Science* 13, 4 (Fall), 351–373.

23. Schwadel, Francine (1989), "The 'Sale' Is Fading As A Retailing Tactic," *The Wall Street Journal*, March 1, B1.

24. Hoch, Steve, Xavier Dreze, and Mary Purk (1993), "Data Driven Micro-Marketing: An Analysis of EDLP and Hi-Lo Pricing Strategies," Working Paper, Graduate School of Business, University of Chicago.

25. *Progressive Grocer* (1994), "Is EDLP For Everyday?" (April), 30.

26. Richter, Paul (1989), "NY Sues Sears, Alleging Pricing Policy Deceptions," *Los Angeles Times*, December 22, D3–D4.

27. *Ibid.*

28. Fitzgerald, "Brennan Will Have to Answer to Upset Sears Shareholders."

29. Fitzgerald, Kate (1990), "Sears' Plan on the Ropes," *Advertising Age*, January 8, 1, 42.

Late in 1991, Procter & Gamble shocked its dealers by announcing a new **value pricing** strategy. The strategy involved a lower price to dealers on Procter & Gamble's products in exchange for its greatly reducing trade promotions. In a way, value pricing was akin to the every-day-low pricing that Sears and other retailers were adopting toward consumers. Large warehouse clubs such as Costco or Sam's Club and discount chains such as Wal-Mart welcomed the new strategy. However, most retailers that

Trade Promotions

use a high-low pricing strategy supported by retail promotions were opposed to it. Moreover, leading competitors such as Lever Brothers and General Mills did not follow immediately with value pricing strategies of their own. As a result, in 1992, Procter & Gamble suffered share losses of as much as 4 percent in almost every category in which it introduced value pricing. One report indicated that Procter & Gamble's national volume for 1992 fell 7 percent with wholesalers and 16 percent with drug chains. Many experts doubted whether Procter & Gamble would continue with its strategy in the face of such losses. However, Procter & Gamble was happy with its evaluation of the strategy, and stuck to it.[1]

In 1994 Quaker Oats moved to its own version of value pricing. The first important step of this strategy was to change the timing of its trade promotions to better match consumer demand. Initially, the change caused Quaker Oats to incur the displeasure of its dealers, just as it did for Procter & Gamble. The firm's revenues declined by $100 million as retailers ran down their inventories and switched to other brands. However, Quaker Oats stuck to the strategy, convinced that it would lower costs by $10 million to $15 million annually. Given that retailers would ultimately have to restock its products, the company estimated that within 6 months these savings could cover any losses from lower sales.[2]

W hy did Procter & Gamble and Quaker Oats reduce trade promotions and move to a value pricing strategy? What other alternatives did they have? In particular, what are the different types of trade promotions? What are their costs and benefits? How can one analyze the profitability of trade promotions? This chapter addresses these questions.

CHARACTERISTICS OF TRADE PROMOTIONS

Trade promotions are sales promotions that a manufacturer offers to dealers. The term **dealer** includes wholesalers, distributors and retailers. However, trade promotions tend to focus on the retailer, because that is the ultimate party through whom the promotion can be passed on to consumers. In addi-

tion, the growth of major retail chains that buy directly from manufacturers emphasizes the importance of the manufacturer-retailer relationship in trade promotions. To simplify our discussion, we describe trade promotions in the context of the manufacturer and retailer. However, these terms can refer to any two agents in a distribution channel that has more than two parties, such as the manufacturer and wholesaler, or the wholesaler and retailer.

Goals of Trade Promotions

The goals of trade promotions follow from the general discussion of goals in Chapters 1 and 9. In offering trade promotions manufacturers have three broad classes of goals: to win adequate distribution, control inventory or stimulate retail promotions for their brands (see Exhibit 11-1).

The most important goal of trade promotions is to win adequate distribution for the brand, in terms of both the number of retailers who carry the brand and the shelf space each retailer affords the brand. This goal is especially true for new brands, or those that do not have strong consumer demand. However, this goal is almost as important for mature brands. In mature markets, brands tend to be very similar. Consumers may easily switch among rival

▼ **EXHIBIT 11-1. Goals of trade promotions.**

Extend Distribution
- Gain distribution or shelf space for a new brand.
- Increase distribution or shelf space for an ongoing brand.

Control Inventory
- Build retailer inventory to avoid stockouts, especially when a new introduction or a consumer promotion is planned.
- Transfer inventory carrying costs from manufacturer to retailer.
- Build retailer inventory to preempt response to competing promotions.

Induce Retail Promotions
- Induce a reduction in retail price.
- Induce a retail advertisement.
- Induce a retail in-store display.
- Induce other retail promotions.

▼ **EXHIBIT 11-2.** Trends in manufacturers' expenditures on promotions.

	1981	1982	1983	1984	1985	1986	1987	1988	1989	1990	1991	1992	1993	1994	1995
	PERCENT OF TOTAL ANNUAL PROMOTIONAL BUDGET														
Trade Promotions	34%	36%	37%	37%	38%	40%	41%	43%	46%	47%	50%	45%	49%	51%	51%
Media Advertising	43	39	37	36	35	34	34	34	29	28	25	27	24	23	25
Consumer Promotions	23	25	26	27	27	26	25	24	25	25	25	28	27	26	24

Source: Donnelley Marketing Annual Survey of Promotion Practices, as reported in Hume, Scott (1992), "Trade Promotion $ Share Dips in '92," *Advertising Age,* April 5, 3; Carol Wright Promotions, Inc. (1996), *18th Annual Survey of Promotional Practices,* Naperville, IL.

brands in a store because their favorite brand is not in stock or easily found on the shelf. Consumers may even switch brands on impulse when passing by aisles. Thus, maintaining adequate distribution, shelf space and visibility is important to a manufacturer for both new and mature brands. As we will see later in this chapter, certain trade promotions, such as push money, are open-ended allowances that the manufacturer gives retailers just to win shelf space. Others, such as an off-invoice discount, are incentives that prompt a retailer to stock up and promote the manufacturer's brand.

A second goal of trade promotions is to control the inventory of their brands. Manufacturers need to ensure that retailers have more than enough stock of their brands. This goal is critical for new products that do have strong demand. It is also important for any products for which the manufacturer runs an ad campaign or consumer promotion. The effectiveness of consumer promotions is greatly enhanced if retailers have adequate stock when consumer response to the promotion peaks. This goal of trade promotions is achieved primarily by various time-bound incentives, such as the bill-back.

A third goal of trade promotions is to induce retailers to promote the brand to consumers. For example, when Kellogg's offers a 15 percent discount off the list price of cornflakes to retailers, it hopes that retailers in turn will offer a 15 percent price-cut to consumers. Chapter 10 shows the great impact of retail promotions on sales of a product. Currently, the level of retail promotions is very high. Thus, many manufacturers may see their brands lose share to rivals if they do not maintain some minimum level of retail promotions.

Growth of Trade Promotions

Trade promotions form a major component of the total promotion budget. They grew steadily between 1981 and 1995, to amount to half the promotion budget (see Exhibit 11-2). The increase has been primarily at the cost of media advertising, which has triggered an intense debate about the causes and effects of this shift in resources. Why have trade promotions increased so consistently and dramatically in the last decade? Several factors may be responsible, including brand similarity, brand proliferation, splintering of the mass market, growth of retailer power, changes in consumer shopping patterns and slow growth in population.[3]

Brand Similarity The rapid growth and diffusion of technology have enabled manufacturers to quickly imitate successful products of rivals. In addition, each year manufacturers introduce more than 20,000 new products, many with minor or no differences from competing brands.[4] The net result is that consumers have a choice among alternatives that differ only marginally from each other. The similarity of brands has put pressure on manufacturers to offer sales promotions. A creative sales promotion can emphasize a brand's unique features or can itself be a basis for differentiation. The use of sales promotions is especially important for brands that are new, have small market shares, do not have loyal consumers or are doing poorly.

Brand Proliferation The rapid diffusion of technology in industry today makes it easy for firms to enter markets with new brands and products. As a result, there are a large number of items on sale in any single category. For example, in the automobile industry, General Motors alone had 53 brands in 1994. The laundry detergent category may have hundreds of items on sale. Consider that there are 15 to 20 brands, most available in solid and liquid (and perhaps also sachet form), with three to six sizes of each form, and numerous new formulations for greater efficiency or cleaning power. In addition, manufacturers regularly introduce temporary new variants that differ only in price, size or promotional status. The multiplicity of brands reduces the attention and the market share that any one brand commands in the marketplace. Manufacturers resort to sales promotions to create some excitement for their brands and boost sales, even if only temporarily.

Splintering of Mass Market The proliferation of brands has also motivated manufacturers to appeal to more specific consumer markets or market niches. The growth of numerous alternate media channels in TV, radio, newspapers and magazines has similarly enabled manufacturers to reach these smaller niches. The two processes together have led to a splintering of the mass market, with fewer large-share, dominant brands that cater to it and more small-share, niche brands. The latter brands cannot afford costly media and are more prone to use sales promotions to compete with their larger rivals for market share.

Growth of Retailer Power The proliferation of brands and the splintering of the mass market have reduced the power of manufacturers relative to retailers. In particular, numerous similar brands compete for limited retail shelf space. As a result, retailers can demand certain terms and benefits from manufacturers. These demands take the form of costly trade promotions. Sometimes manufacturers offer promotions not so much to benefit consumers as to earn the goodwill of retailers or meet trade promotions of rival manufacturers.

Changes in Consumer Shopping With the increase in dual-income households, consumers spend more time working and less time shopping. As a result they may be more susceptible to promotions at the point of purchase, rather than to media advertising viewed in the home.

Slow Growth in Population Growth in the U.S. population has recently slowed to 0.8 percent per year, with only a modest growth in the sales of most mature product categories.[5] Thus manufacturers have little opportunity for growth in sales, intensifying the rivalry for market share. Because many sales promotions lead to an immediate increase in sales, manufacturers may use them in their quest for market share.

Dynamics of Trade Promotions

As stated earlier, one of the goals of trade promotions, especially trade deals, is to motivate retailers to offer promotions to consumers. Does this happen? Often, it does not, because of the peculiar dynamics of trade promotions. The trade deal triggers a major "game" between manufacturer and retailer. Manufacturers compete with each other by offering deals to retailers in the hope of stimulating retail promotions and increasing consumer sales. On the other hand, retailers try to maximize profits from trade deals, while passing on as little of the benefit as possible to consumers. The term **pass-through** refers to the fraction of the trade deal that retailers pass on to consumers. One study indicates that on average, retailers pass through only 30 percent of the deal to consumers.[6] The low pass-through is one of the major reasons that Procter & Gamble, Quaker Oats and other manufacturers reduced trade promotions in favor of a value pricing strategy. How exactly do retailers limit pass-through? They do so by at least four activities: pocketing the deal, forward buying and stockpiling, delaying purchases before a deal or diverting the product.

Pocketing the Deal Retailers **pocket the deal** amount when they buy the product at the lower deal price, but sell it to consumers at the regular list price. While some deals from manufacturers may explicitly require compliance (pass-through) by retailers, the large number of stores, brands and simultaneous promotions make it difficult for manufacturers to enforce compliance. Even if manufacturers did discover retailers who consistently failed to pass through promotions, manufacturers are probably better off trying to win the goodwill of retailers rather than antagonizing them with pressure to comply. Actually, the real pressure on retailers for pass-through is from competing retailers, any one of whom may promote certain brands in order to increase store traffic.

Which trade deals are most likely to be passed through to consumers? Retailers are more likely to pass through deals on brands that are most popular with consumers. Because popular brands easily draw the attention of consumers, retailers tend to promote such brands, sometimes even at a loss, to attract store traffic. Small retail stores also tend to pass through more trade deals than do large retailers, in order to compete more effectively with their larger, more popular rivals. Large manufacturers are likely to win higher pass-through for their brands because of their greater bargaining power.

Forward Buying, Stockpiling and Delaying Purchases Forward buying, stockpiling and delaying purchases are three responses by retailers to trade deals. **Forward buying** means buying future requirements in the current period to take advantage of a current trade deal. **Stockpiling** refers to holding a higher inventory of goods than needed to meet current demand. The terms refer to different aspects of the same phenomenon in which retailers buy on deal larger quantities than they need, to sell them at a higher list price after the deal. Such practices of course are not without costs, as retailers have to change their purchasing quantity and also have to bear the costs of carrying the higher inventory, which one analyst estimated at 6 percent of sales.[7] However, even at that cost, forward buying and stockpiling would be worthwhile given that trade deals often range from 10 percent to 20 percent of sales. If retailers know of an impending trade deal, they may also **delay purchases** just prior to the deal, so that they can run down their inventories, and then restock them at the lower deal price.

Diverting the Product Manufacturers often offer or limit a deal to a certain geographic area. Chain stores or wholesalers may bypass this restriction by diverting sales. **Diverting** involves buying the product in the region with the lower deal price, and then selling at the regular price in another region without the deal. This practice is legal. As trade dealing increased in the 1980s, diverting became widespread, spurring the rise of wholesalers whose only business was to divert sales. Large wholesalers such as SuperValue, Wetterau and Fleming were probably the first to capitalize on this opportunity because of their geographically dispersed buying and warehousing opportunities.[8] A good indicator of the enormity of diverting is a quote by Pat Collins, the now-retired vice chairman of Ralphs, "When I was first apprised of diverting, I said 'No way,' . . . until someone explained that I was missing out on $100,000 or more per week in profits."[9] Because of the enormous savings diverters could offer retailers, their numbers and clients grew, so that today, theirs is a well-accepted business that uses sophisticated buying, warehousing and shipping practices (see Exhibit 11-3 for a list of major diverters and their clients). However, such firms prefer to be called "in-house brokers" rather than "diverters."

Summary One analyst estimates that the low pass-through of trade deals costs manufacturers $100 billion a year, and contributes to 50 percent of retail profits.[10] Why do manufacturers still offer the deals to retailers if the latter behave so opportunistically? One reason is to earn the goodwill of retailers and

▼ **EXHIBIT 11-3.** Major diverters and their main clients.

In-House Broker (Diverter)	Major Clients
Damon Associates, New York, NY	Big Y, Delchamps, Dillon Cos., Fred Meyer, Fry's, Furr's, Giant Eagle, Haggen, Hy-Vee, Jewel, Key Food, Kash n' Karry, Ralphs, Price Co., Randall's, Red Food Stores, Riser Foods, Stater Bros., X-tra
Marketing Management, Ft. Worth, TX	Allied Grocer's, Bozzuto's, Bruno's, Camelia, Cardinal Foods, Fairway Foods of Michigan, First National, Fleming Cos., Harris-Teeter, Nash-Finch, Seaway FoodTown, Shurfine Central, United AG
Cal Growers, San Jose, CA	Big Bear, C&S Wholesale, Super Value, West Coast
Federated Foods, Arlington Heights, IL	Almac's, Albertson's
Ross Chamberlin, Kirkland, WA	Costco Wholesale
PLM Sales, Cincinnati, OH	Kroger
Pivotal Sales, Pleasanton, CA	Safeway Stores

Data Source: Schlossberg, Howard (1994), "Secret," *PROMO* (April), 51–56.

motivate them to display the manufacturers' products prominently. Another purpose of deals is to get retailers to stock up on a brand to ensure good product availability, especially for new products. A third reason is to get retailers to bear some of the inventory carrying costs, especially if the manufacturer's inventory carrying costs are high relative to the cost of the deal. Beyond these reasons, manufacturers probably resort to trade deals just to counter the deals of competitors, even if they do not find the deals profitable.

Manufacturers can encourage pass-through in three ways. First, they can sign a contract with retailers stating that the retailers will conduct certain promotions when they accept a trade deal. The difficulty with contracts is enforcement, especially as there are numerous retailers scattered all over the country. However, large manufacturers probably have the clout to enforce contracts with large retail chains that constitute a big proportion of sales. Second, manufacturers can schedule advertising and consumer promotions simultaneously with trade deals, to appeal directly to consumers. These activities increase the visibility of and demand for the brand. As a result, retailers compete among themselves to promote the brand and increase store traffic (see Chapter 10). In doing so they pass through more of the trade deal. Third, manufacturers can structure the trade deal so that it motivates retailers to pass through the discount to consumers. Such structures lead to the different types of trade deals being offered today (see Exhibit 11-4).

DESCRIPTION OF TRADE PROMOTIONS

Trade promotions vary a lot. Following the criteria laid out in the previous chapter, we can classify these promotions depending on whether they are primarily incentive (price or nonprice) or communicative (informative or motivational). Exhibit 11-4 classifies the various types of trade promotions using these criteria. A **trade deal** is any manufacturer promotion that offers the retailer a price reduction, more favorable terms or cash to more easily buy, stock or sell the product. The term *trade deal* includes all incentive-based promotions, including both price and nonprice. We now describe each of these trade promotions in detail.

Price-Based Trade Deals

Price-based trade deals are temporary reductions in the price of the product that the manufacturer offers the retailer for a limited time, called the *deal period*. These discounts can be offered in a number of ways, depending on the goals of the manufacturer and the nature of the product and market. The different ways in which a manufacturer can offer a deal to retailers lead to a variety of price-based trade deals, which are described next.

Off-Invoice Discounts **Off-invoice discounts** involve a direct reduction in the manufacturer's invoice or list price per unit of the product to retailers. The discount typically ranges from 10 to 25 percent for periods ranging from 2 to 12 weeks. The retailer may be allowed just one or multiple purchases during this period, and such purchases may require that the retailer pass on this discount to consumers. Sometimes the discount may be offered in terms of greater quantities of the product for the same price; for example, buy two, get one free. In effect, this form of the promotion amounts to a 33 percent discount to the retailer.[11]

The immediate effect of an off-invoice discount is to motivate retailers to buy more of the product. Manufacturers hope that the retailer's increase in purchases represents incremental sales over the retailer's regular level of purchases in the absence of any promotion. If the retailer passes through the savings from the deal to consumers, these incremen-

▼ EXHIBIT 11-4. Classification of trade promotions.

PRIMARILY INCENTIVE		PRIMARILY COMMUNICATIVE	
Price	Nonprice	Informative	Motivational
Off-invoice discounts, quantity discounts, quota incentives, bill-backs, count-recount	Slotting allowances, street money, trade contests, spiffs, financing	Cooperative advertising, display materials and allowances, exhibits	Conferences, trade games, trade sweepstakes

tal sales at the retail level would probably also translate into incremental sales at the consumer level. However, retailers pocket much of these discounts by forward buying or delaying purchases as explained above. Manufacturers still offer the discounts to win retailers' goodwill, increase retailers' inventory, or to combat competition. However, manufacturers have recently tried to structure trade deals to ensure a greater pass-through of the benefits to consumers. The following trade deals use various formats to achieve this goal.

Quantity Discounts Quantity discounts are similar to off-invoice discounts except that the discount has a sliding rate that is specifically tied to the quantity purchased. For example, one format could be 10 percent off for the first 100 units, 15 percent off for the next 100 units, 20 percent off for the third 100 units, etc. The advantage of quantity discounts over off-invoice discounts is that the quantity discounts can be designed to motivate retailers to pass through more of the discount to consumers.[12] How can the manufacturer exploit this advantage? The manufacturer does so by calculating a sliding scale that allows the retailer to use the discounts only for incremental sales and not for its regular sales.

For example, suppose a retailer's monthly sales to consumers are 100 units of a product, and its incremental sales to consumers are 50 percent on a 10 percent discount during a month. Its costs of inventory are 6 percent per month, for holding *additional units* over its regular sales level. If a manufacturer offers the retailer 10 percent off invoice for a month, how should the retailer respond?

The retailer would buy 250 units: 100 units for current regular sales, 50 units for incremental sales and 100 units to stockpile for future sales. It needs to offer consumers a discount of 10 percent for the first month only. Note that even with high inventory costs of 6 percent, the retailer earns 4 percent by stockpiling 100 units during a deal to sell at regular price the following month when the deal is off. How can the manufacturer structure a discount that prevents the retailer from stockpiling?

The manufacturer can do so by offering the following quantity discount: no discount on the first 100 units, 6 percent on the next 100 units and 12 percent on additional units. How should the retailer respond now? To avail of the discount, the retailer has to buy more than 100 units, which is the regular quantity it sells in a month. However, the second 100 units come at a discount that just covers its costs of inventory. The retailer must buy more than 200 units to get the full discount. But it cannot stockpile extra units for more than two months because its higher inventory costs would offset the discount. Thus it is best off buying and selling just 50 units (over the 200) by offering consumers a 10 percent discount.

The above example shows how a manufacturer can structure a quantity discount to discourage stockpiling and encourage pass-through. The problem with such quantity discounts is that it is difficult to arrive at a uniform discount schedule across retailers with different sizes of operations. By law, manufacturers may not explicitly discriminate in prices offered to different retailers unless justified by costs, such as economies of scale in transportation (see Chapter 2).

Quota Incentives **Quota incentives** are cash rewards or percentage rebates offered to retailers if they meet certain targets. Typically, these targets are tied to percentage increases over the previous year's sales. Quota incentives are more typical of exclusive dealerships, such as car dealerships, where each dealer handles the products of only one or two manufacturers.

Quota incentives are similar to quantity discounts except that the quantity that merits the reward varies by retailer, and the discount is stated as a reward. The quota incentive has two advantages over the quantity discount. First, the manufacturer can adjust the quantity that qualifies for the discount to ensure that the retailer sells more than its regular volume. To meet this additional volume, the retailer is motivated to offer its consumers some of the reward in the way of lower prices, thus ensuring a higher pass-through of the trade deal. Second, the incentive can also be framed as a competition among retailers, in which pride or competitive spirit itself may motivate retailers to meet their target, often by offering their own promotions to consumers.

Pay-for-Performance Incentives **Pay-for-performance** is a general term which applies to discounts the manufacturer pays only for units that the retailer actually sells to consumers on discount. It includes the bill-back, count-recount and scan-down forms of trade deals. **Count-recount** is similar to the off-invoice discount except that the manufacturer computes and pays the retailer the discount based only on the number of units sold during the trade deal.[13] In this method the manufacturer determines the sales by adding a retailer's purchases to its beginning inventory at the start of the deal period (count), and subtracting the retailer's inventory at the end of the deal period (recount). Thus the manufacturer gives the discount not on the retailer's purchases but on the retailer's sales. Retailers do not like the count-recount because it gives them less leverage than does the off-invoice discount, and forces them to pass the discount through to consumers.

A **bill-back** is similar to the count-recount except that the retailer computes and bills the manufacturer for the discount on the units sold during the trade deal.[14] Retailers like the bill-back even less than the count-recount, because it requires more accounting on their part. The term **scan-down** is applied to a bill-back or a count-recount, when the retailer's sales are recorded electronically by the checkout scanner. This form of recorded sales is called scanner data, and is discussed in detail in Chapter 14. Scanner data is often processed by a market research firm, such as Information Resources Inc. Manufacturers can reap substantial benefits by replacing off-invoice discounts with one of these performance-based incentive promotions. For example, Ocean Spray's scan-down replacement of a national off-invoice offer moved nine times more incremental volume out of stores.

Nonprice Trade Deals
Slotting Allowances

In 1994, beer makers were up in arms over a federal proposal that would allow retailers to charge alcoholic beverage makers for shelf space for their products. Such charges, called *slotting fees* or *allowances,* had been banned since Prohibition to avoid the revival of tied-houses. *Tied-houses* were retailers who were beholden to alcohol manufacturers due to the payments they received from them. The ban was issued by the U.S. Treasury Department's Bureau of Alcohol, Tobacco and Firearms. While tied-houses are unlikely in today's environment, characterized by powerful retail chains, brewers complain that slotting allowances may still restrict competition. Large brewers may easily afford the allowances, while small manufacturers would be hard-pressed to afford the same, and would be edged out of the market. Brewers argue that the boom in micro-breweries and import brands may not have occurred with slotting allowances. The federal bureau wanted to relax the rules against slotting allowances for alcoholic beverages because it had lost three court cases against brewers who had tried to get around the ban. The relaxation of the ban would also bring the brewing industry in line with other manufacturing industries that do have to pay slotting allowances. However, under pressure from the manufacturers, the bureau finally retained the ban on slotting fees.[15]

Slotting allowances are offered especially for new products that have not yet generated consumer demand, and for the best locations in the store, such as eye-level shelves. This practice raises some obvious questions: why should manufacturers offer such payments? Are the allowances not illegal bribes? Are the allowances too high?

Manufacturers offer slotting allowances partly in deference to retailers' bargaining power and partly to compensate them for their services. As stated earlier, each year firms introduce thousands of new products. Most of these are me-too products that are either only marginally different or not different at all from products of competitors. Shelf space in retail stores is too small to accommodate all these products. Thus, retailers are in a strong bargaining position, having a large number of brands competing for the limited shelf space they offer. They are thus able to charge a high price for their shelf space in the form of slotting allowances.

Retailers also incur costs for stocking products, especially if they are new. Such costs include informing stores within a chain about the new product, incorporating orders, storing and shipping for the new product within the current inventory system, rearranging shelf space for the new product and including a new entry for the product in the computer system. Slotting allowances compensate the retailer for these costs. However, the allowances may be much higher than the retailers' costs, reflecting the power of the retailers to command a premium for the space they offer.

Slotting allowances are not illegal bribes even though they may appear as such, because the money is offered to an organization, the retailer, for its use or profits, and not to any individual person within the organization. If such money were offered to individuals for their own use, it would constitute an illegal bribe.

The arguments that slotting allowances are too high or hinder free entry of new brands (as brewers claim) are not quite valid. The reason is that retailing is a very competitive industry. If slotting allowances were too high, then competition among retailers would drive that rate down to a fair market rate. Moreover, the current retail environment is characterized by too many rather than too few new products. Thus, slotting allowances are unlikely to be discouraging new product entry, and if they were, that may well be a service to consumers.

Push Money or Street Money   **Push money** or **street money** is a manufacturer's cash payment to a retailer to encourage it to promote the manufacturer's brands to consumers, or just to earn the retailer's goodwill. Push money is similar to slotting allowances except that it is offered for ongoing products and is meant to cover a retail promotion. Push money is opposite in spirit to the bill-back or the count-recount, because it is so open ended. Given that retailers have so much discretion in the shelf space and promotions with which they support manufacturers' brands, earning their goodwill may be a better strategy than pressuring them to conduct certain practices. Here again, push money is not illegal and not a bribe because the money is given to a business concern and not an individual.

Trade Contests   **Trade contests** are manufacturer-organized competitions among retailers, who are rewarded if they meet certain sales targets. Trade contests are similar to quota incentives, except that the reward is not cash or free samples, and so is not directly related to the price of the product.

The sales targets for the contest may be the same for all retailers within or across regions, or the targets may be percentage increases from each retailer's previous performance. While a common target puts all retailers on the same footing, the chosen target may be too hard for some retailers to meet, and too easy for others. Targets based on a percentage increase encourage improvement from all retailers, but they may be easier to meet for a retailer who performs badly during the previous period and harder for another who had an outstanding performance the previous year. Thus the target must be low enough to be fair yet high enough to be motivating.

The reward for the contest should be something retailers might not normally give themselves, as well as provide the manufacturer an opportunity to motivate and educate the retailers about the product. A good example is a free trip to Hawaii. In addition, the contest can be intensely advertised among retailers. The winners can be rewarded with attractive plaques, announced in trade bulletins or honored in public. The honor associated with such acknowledgments and the competition generated among retailers may well motivate retailers more than the monetary value of the reward.

Spiffs   **Spiffs** are incentives offered by a manufacturer to the retailers' sales force to motivate them to sell more of the product. Thus Whirlpool could offer a retailer's salespersons $25 for each Whirlpool refrigerator they sell during a certain promotion period.[16] Spiffs are especially useful when sales are sensitive to the promotional efforts of a retailer's sales staff, but the retailer is not motivated to promote any one particular brand. As with trade contests, spiffs can also be publicized to increase their motivational appeal.

The manufacturer needs to win the agreement of the retailer to offer such a promotion, and even more to publicize it. Retailers are likely to resist spiffs, especially aggressive ones that are publicized. The reason is that spiffs establish a relationship between the manufacturer and the retailer's sales force that has the potential of undercutting the power and control that a retailer has over its own sales force.

Financing   As is true of consumer purchases, financing involves terms provided by manufacturers to help retailers pay for their goods. These terms may involve part or full coverage of the cost of purchasing the goods. However, manufacturers may limit the time during which retailers may take advantage of this offer to a few weeks or months. Retailers then have a corresponding incentive to sell the goods within that time period, thus ensuring a rapid turnover of goods. Retailers may use the terms of financing for their own benefit, or they may pass the terms on to consumers to motivate the latter to buy the goods.

Informative Trade Promotions

Under informative trade promotions we classify promotional activities of manufacturers that provide information directly to retailers (such as conventions, trade shows, and exhibits), as well as those that enable retailers to provide information to consumers (such as cooperative advertising and display support).

Conventions, Trade Shows and Exhibits **Conventions** are periodic meetings (generally annual events) at which members of an association exchange views, plan events or examine new products. Conventions are most often sponsored by trade or professional associations, although of late independent organizers have begun to run such meetings. Conventions organized primarily to display products can be classified into three groups depending on who may attend: **trade shows** are open only to the trade, **consumer shows** are open to the general public, while **mixed shows** are open to both. In the United States, in 1994, 4,316 trade shows with 1.3 million exhibiting companies were attended by 85 million people. The three largest trade shows by exhibit area were the Computer Manufacturers and Dealers' Show (COMDEX), the International Manufacturer Technology Show and the International Winter Consumer Electronics Show.[17]

Exhibits are displays that manufacturers set up at conventions to show their products. For example, Intel's exhibit at the Fall 1993 COMDEX, which displayed a mock-up of a computer chip factory and a 30-foot-square model of a chip board, drew tens of thousands of viewers (see Exhibit 11-5).[18] Manufacturers typically pay rent for the exhibit space, although they may also have to share the costs of shows organized by associations of which they are a member.

Exhibits serve a number of goals. The primary goals of the exhibit are to generate awareness for the manufacturer's products, establish new contacts and renew old contacts. Other goals of the exhibits are similar to those for conferences. Manufacturers try to translate these goals into immediate sales by providing a mechanism to take and even fill orders for their products at the exhibit. The sales generated from exhibits may more than justify their costs. For example, one estimate is that a sale at a convention costs almost one-third as much as that from a field call.[19] The main reason for the greater efficiency of conventions is that they reach a far greater number of clients in a much shorter time with much lower personnel costs. In particular, firms that are smaller, newer or have better deals have much to gain from

▼ **EXHIBIT 11-5.** The Intel exhibit at COMDEX.

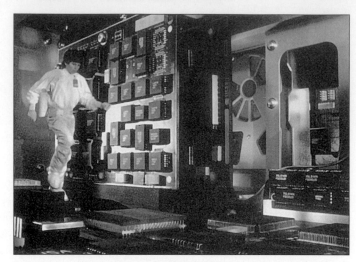

Source: Reprinted with permission from the November 23, 1997, issue of *Advertising Age*, "Vegas chips, $: It must be Comdex." Copyright, Crain Communications, Inc., 1997.

exhibits. The exhibits allow consumers to directly compare offers of different manufacturers, instead of relying solely on past relationships.

Cooperative Advertising **Cooperative advertising** is an offer by the manufacturer to pay for some fraction of the retailer's advertising, called features (see Chapter 10). This includes the costs of designing the ad and placing it in local media such as newspapers, local TV or a direct-mail flyer. Why would manufacturers offer to cover part or all of the costs of features in the form of cooperative advertising?

To begin with, any form of advertising by the retailer gets added exposure for the manufacturer's brand. Second, sales to consumers of the manufacturer's brand are generally much higher when retailers advertise the price-cut with a feature, rather than if they offer it alone (see Chapter 10). Third, retail advertising draws consumers into stores, and prompts other retailers to also increase their advertising. This process can trigger inter-retailer price competition and ensure that more of the manufacturer's trade deal is passed on to consumers. Fourth, local retailers can find better media outlets at possibly lower costs than can manufacturers residing in other areas. Thus manufacturers can get more for their advertising dollars, if they channel some of them through retailers. For all these reasons, the manufacturer's willingness to pay some of the costs of features with cooperative advertising is not only fair but also in its own interest. Moreover, if the manufacturer pays some of the costs, the retailer is more likely to advertise the product for their mutual benefit. Indeed, the increase in retail sales with an advertised discount is sometimes so much greater that a retailer can be better off passing on a trade deal with a feature paid for with cooperative advertising, than pocketing the trade deal. Thus a preferred promotional strategy for the manufacturer is to split its promotional support into a trade deal and cooperative advertising, rather than using all of it for a trade deal alone.

Exhibit 11-6 contains a numerical example to support this point. The second column describes the base case of a product of which a retailer sells 100 units, at $5 per unit. In this base case, the retailer enjoys a 10 percent margin and makes a profit of $50. When the manufacturer offers the retailer a 20 percent trade deal, the retailer earns a profit of $150 by not passing through the discount compared to a profit of $56 by passing through all of it. So the retailer is better off not passing through the trade deal. However, the picture changes when the manufacturer changes the offer to a 10 percent discount with a $50 cooperative advertising allowance. In this case the retailer is better off passing through the discount ($158 profit) than not doing so ($100 profit). Assuming there is no diverting and stockpiling, the manufacturer is also better off from offering a trade deal with a cooperative advertising allowance (profit $300) than from any of the other alternatives. The key factor in this situation is the interaction of discount and feature (see Chapter 10): sales to consumers of the product promoted with a feature reach a high of 350 units. This big increase provides adequate incentive for the manufacturer to offer cooperative advertising albeit with a slightly smaller trade deal, and for the retailer to pass through the trade deal to consumers with a discount and feature.

The disadvantage of cooperative advertising is that for slow-moving categories like trash compactors or hot cereals, the volume of sales is limited so that the cost of advertising for either the retailer or manufacturer is too high to be covered by the incremental sales.

Display Support As described in Chapter 10, displays are in-store arrangements that give greater visibility to a

▼ **EXHIBIT 11-6.** Manufacturer's payoff from a cooperative ad allowance.*

Condition	Base: No Trade Deal	Trade Deal, No Pass-through	Trade Deal, Pass-through	Trade Deal + Co-op Allowance, No Pass-through	Trade Deal + Co-op Allowance, Pass-through
Trade Deal					
(a) –% off retail list price	None	20%	20%	10%	10%
(b) – co-op allowance	None	None	None	$50	$50
(c) Retail response: % discount to consumer	None	None	20%	None	10%
(d) Net retail price per unit: $(100 - c) \times \$5$	$5	$5	$4	$5	$4.50
(e) Retail units sold	100	100	140	100	350
(f) Retail revenues: $d \times e$	$500	$500	$560	$500	$1,575
(g) Net retail margin: $10\% + a - c$	10%	30%	10%	20%	10%
(h) Net retail profit: $f \times g$	$50	$150	$56	$100	$158
(i) Net manufacturer margin per unit: $(30\% - a) \times \$5$	$1.50	$0.50	$0.50	$1.00	$1.00
(j) Net manufacturer profit: $(i \times e) - b$	$150	$50	$70	$50	$300

*Assume manufacturer sells to 1 retailer and suggests retail price of $5. Manufacturer keeps 30% margin and allows retailer only 10% margin when product not on deal.

brand relative to competing brands. Displays have been found to be very effective in increasing the sales of a brand, probably because of their immediacy to the consumer's purchase decision, and their ability to conveniently show off the product's features (see Chapter 10). The latter benefit is particularly important for new products. Thus manufacturers have a strong reason to support displays. They can do so by providing a display allowance, providing creative display materials, or setting up a display in the store. Professional agencies offer their services for the latter two functions (see Exhibit 11-7).

What is the purpose of the display allowance? The immediate purpose of the allowance is to pay for the store space and the expenses of setting up the display. But another purpose is to ensure greater pass-through of the trade deal, just as cooperative advertising does. Displays greatly enhance the response to retail discounts. Because of that effect, a retailer gains a much higher payback when displaying a price-cut, compared to offering a price-cut alone. This effect is so high that a retailer can gain more from the higher sales that result from offering consumers a price-cut and displaying it in the store with the manufacturer's allowance, than by pocketing the discount, not gaining the sales increase and not gaining the display allowance. Thus a manufacturer can trigger a higher pass-through by splitting its promotional support into an off-invoice discount and a display allowance. Exhibit 11-8 shows an ad by Land O'Lakes encouraging retailers to use its displays.

Motivational Trade Promotions

The main forms of motivational trade promotion are sales conferences, games and sweepstakes.

Sales Conferences   **Sales conferences** are manufacturer-sponsored private

meetings held for all retailers in a region at a planned time and place. The primary purpose of these meetings is to motivate the retailers to sell the manufacturer's brands. The motivation results from the mere fact of the manufacturer's sponsorship of the event, especially if it is at an attractive location or involves entertainment. For example, pharmaceutical companies may pay for physicians to attend a free four-day conference in the Cayman Islands. In this case, the physicians who prescribe drugs to their patients may be the key intermediaries between

▼ **EXHIBIT 11-7.** Agency ad to help manufacturers set up in-store displays.

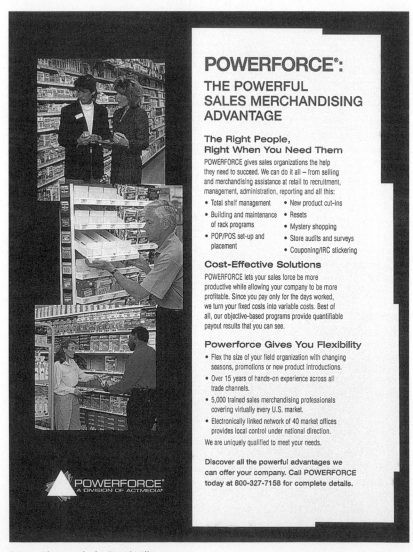

Source: Photography by David Hiller.

▼ **EXHIBIT 11-8.** Manufacturer's ad that encourages retailers to use its displays.

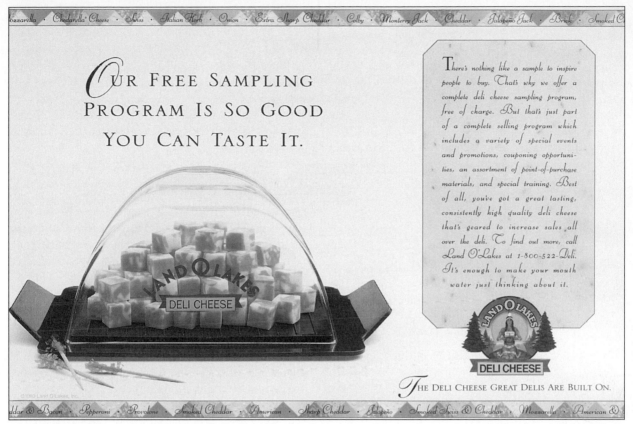

Source: © 1993 Land O'Lakes Inc.

pharmaceutical companies and their consumers. To make the trip more attractive, companies may have an educational session in the daytime followed by free entertainment in the evening. Alternatively, companies may allow physicians to bring family members for a nominal charge. While such incentives do generate goodwill and motivate retailers, recounting of product histories, talks by keynote speakers and guided discussion can provide a more powerful and enduring level of motivation.

A second purpose of the conference is to educate retailers about the brand. For example, in a conference session a manufacturer could provide new information about the brand or highlight important attributes. Manufacturers could also provide product literature to the retailers for their own consumption or to pass on to consumers. These educational materials and sessions are also important so that the conference does not become a free holiday to retailers, which is taxable by governments or dis-

couraged by professional associations. For example, the American Medical Association discourages or forbids its members from accepting gifts or bonuses from pharmaceutical companies, that do not have appropriate educational value.

A third goal of conferences is to prepare retailers for the introduction of new products. Especially in innovative product categories such as electronics, computers and automobiles, retailers look forward to the launch of new products each year. The conference is an ideal occasion for manufacturers to showcase the new product.

Manufacturers incur costs for transport, board, lodging and entertainment of the attendees, which they must weigh against these potential benefits of conferences.

Trade Games and Sweepstakes **Trade sweepstakes** are manufacturer-organized drawings for retailers in which the winner is determined purely by chance. In **trade**

games, contestants have to meet certain conditions, with or without a drawing. For example, in February 1994 SmithKline launched a "Sucrets Secret Sweepstakes" for its Sucrets Throat Lozenges, targeting 65,000 pharmacists nationwide. Pharmacists received brochures with brand information, and had to answer five questions relating to Sucrets and its active "secret" ingredient, Dyclonine. Pharmacists who correctly completed and returned their entries entered a sweepstakes with prizes that ranged from fifty $100 prizes to one $25,000 grand prize. Games and sweepstakes are more commonly run for consumers, and are covered in greater detail in Chapter 12.

PROBLEMS OF TRADE PROMOTIONS

Automobile retailing is characterized by numerous promotions, such as rebates, special financing, bundling of options and especially personal discounting of list price to buyers. Buyers often have to haggle with dealers to get the biggest discount in price. One of the hallmarks of General Motors' introduction of the Saturn was its relatively low fixed price without the typical promotions. Consumers loved this haggle free environment that provided good value for the dollar investment. The Saturn was very successful. In the early 1990s General Motors sought to extend this value pricing strategy to other brands. This strategy meant pricing each car fairly so it would sell at the list price and not require promotions. It also meant a great reduction in the number of options being offered. For example, the Pontiac Grand Am SE came with an air bag, a stereo, air conditioning and other options for a fixed price of $13,995. A comparably equipped Toyota Camry listed at $20,822. The Pontiac's sales shot up 20 percent over the previous year's. However, dealers were unhappy because they had less leverage on price, and on average could lose $200 per car due to the low fixed retail price. Their margins were sufficiently low that the increases in sales did not compensate them for these lower profits. However, for General Motors the new strategy represented a net gain. General Motors offered fewer options for each brand, had lower inventory costs, ran less costly promotions and ended up with higher sales and profits.

To evaluate the role of trade promotions in markets today, we need to consider their costs and benefits to manufacturers, retailers and consumers. We also need to consider how these various parties view trade promotions and what efforts are afoot to improve the existing situation.

Costs of Trade Promotions

Trade promotions involve a number of costs. Some of these costs go beyond the direct costs of the promotion, while others are hidden costs that may not be apparent when planning the promotion. Many of these costs have increased substantially in recent years with the growth in trade promotions. Indeed, some critics argue that trade promotions are too costly to be profitable for manufacturers. However, a proper understanding and management of the costs of trade promotions can help managers use this powerful means of sales promotion. A study at the Harvard Business School identified the following major costs: channel conflict, management distraction, inventory buildup, production dislocation, forward buying and diverting.[20] We discuss each of these costs.

Channel Conflict **Channel conflict** is the friction, mistrust and open conflict among members of a distribution network. Trade promotions can be a major cause of channel conflict. The most common type of conflict arises when retailers demand more allowances, or manufacturers attempt to make allowances cover real expenses. For example, in 1989 two of the largest U.S. grocery chains, Winn Dixie and Kroger, boycotted some products of Pillsbury, Procter & Gamble, Quaker Oats and other manufacturers when those companies refused to charge uniform prices throughout the chains' trading areas. Winn Dixie initiated the confrontation by demanding that everything it bought should be at the lowest price offered anywhere in its trading area. The manufacturers refused to comply with this demand, which they perceived as clearly infringing on their pricing prerogative. The chains responded by deleting hundreds of brands of these companies from their shelves, until negotiations ended the confrontation.[21]

Management Distraction Planning promotions can consume a vast amount of managers' time, distracting them from more productive activities. To appreciate this fact, one has only to consider the time it takes to work out the simple example in Exhibit 11-6. At any given time, managers can choose from a variety of individual promotions, and an even greater number of permutations and combinations of these promotions. To further complicate the picture, most managers have to contend with promoting multiple brands over multiple promotion periods. The biggest complicating factor is the difference in promotions over different regions of country, the pressures from different retail chains in each of these areas, and the even greater pressure from promotions of rival manufacturers. Consider, for example, the huge cost of planning and designing trade promotions at General Motors, which has multiple divisions, each having numerous brands of cars. Procter & Gamble estimates that designing, implementing and monitoring promotions consume 25 percent of salespersons' time and 30 percent of managers' time.[22] That is one of the reasons it adopted its value pricing strategy in 1991.

Costs of Inventory Trade promotions frequently cause a short-term spurt in sales. This response leads to higher inventory at all levels of the distribution system: manufacturer, distributor, retailer and even consumer. With the multiplicity of regional promotions for numerous brands manufacturers cannot easily predict the increase in response to their trade promotions. So manufacturers have to carry higher inventory to fully meet this irregular increase in demand. Wholesalers and retailers carry higher inventory to capitalize on trade promotions by stockpiling. The Harvard study estimates that this increase in inventory carrying costs for the grocery industry alone amounts to about $1 billion a year in higher inventory costs. While any individual wholesaler or retailer may find this cost less than the benefit from stockpiling, in the aggregate analysis, such costs are unnecessary and raise the overall costs of doing business.

Production Dislocations Trade promotions by definition are temporary. Manufacturers have to increase production in advance of a planned promotion to build inventory and ensure that the increase in retail purchases can be fully met. The irregularities in purchases caused by promotions increase the difficulty of optimally scheduling production. In general, manufacturers would either have to produce at a regular, higher level and incur higher inventory costs, or produce at irregular intervals to match sales spikes induced by promotion and incur higher production scheduling costs.

Costs of Forward Buying and Diverting As the first section of the chapter explains, the total costs of forward buying and diverting could amount to $100 billion and contribute to 50 percent of retailers' profits. Manufacturers tend to blame retailers for creating these costs. On the other hand, retailers blame manufacturers for providing the opportunity to profit from diverting. As such, the practice continued for years with neither party taking corrective action.[23]

Conclusion Procter & Gamble was content with its value pricing strategy, because the reduction in costs that it generated more than compensated for any loss in market share. However, note that *not all* the five costs listed above are universal costs in the sense that they are costs to *both* manufacturers and dealers. In particular, the first four costs discussed are real costs, so that retailers and manufacturers would both be better off eliminating them. However, the fifth item, forward buying and diverting, represents a competition for resources between manufacturers and retailers. It is a cost to manufacturers but a boon to retailers. So both parties would not agree on the best course to eliminate it. Moreover, forward buying and diverting may account for as much as 50 percent of retailers' profits.

The key question is whether the profits from forward buying and diverting are excess profits enjoyed by retailers, or intrinsic profits without which retailers would not be able to survive. Evidence indicates that retailing is a dynamic and competitive industry, with regular entry of new firms and the introduction of new retailing formats. As a result the benefits of forward buying and diverting now probably constitute an intrinsic portion of retailers' profits or have been translated into lower prices to consumers. A reasonable solution would be for manufacturers to set an everyday-low price that falls between the list and discount price. This price could be chosen so that manufacturers gain some savings over a high-low pricing strategy, retailers retain some portion of the profits they now obtain from forward buying and diverting, and consumers gain the rest of the benefit in the form of lower prices. GM probably set the pricing of Saturn along these lines.

Given these enormous costs and the potential for savings, readers might well ask why the various parties involved have not worked together to reduce or eliminate the problems. Such an effort,

Efficient consumer response (ECR), is indeed under way.

Efficient Consumer Response

Efficient consumer response (ECR) is a management system that tries to eliminate inefficiencies in the distribution and promotion of goods. The key components of efficient consumer response are efficient store assortment, product replenishment, product introduction and promotion. We first define the four key components and then describe the technology that may make possible their implementation.[24]

Efficient store assortment deals with the efficient production, stocking, storage and withdrawal of goods to eliminate waste, speed up transactions and give more space to fast-moving or high-margin brands. For example, in June 1996, Nabisco planned to eliminate some 300 items in its product line.[25]

Efficient product replenishment is the timely movement of goods from manufacturers through distributors to retailers. **Just-in-time inventory**, a component of efficient product replenishment, requires that a manufacturer or retailer retain an inventory level that is just enough to meet current demand, by communicating efficiently with buyers or suppliers. For example, Procter & Gamble ships more than 40 percent of its orders automatically, based on reported withdrawals from customers' warehouses.[26]

Efficient product introduction requires manufacturers to coordinate with retailers to introduce products that consumers want and that are likely to succeed, instead of introducing me-too products. For example, Nabisco Inc. is cutting new product launches by 20 percent and retiring about 15 percent of existing products.[27]

Efficient promotion is a program that eliminates forward buying and diverting by offering trade deals only on goods that pass through the deal to consumers. This is probably the most important component of ECR and the one that has the most potential for savings, yet is the most contentious. The reason is that no party agrees whether the savings should go to manufacturers, retailers, or consumers. For example, by streamlining trade promotions Procter & Gamble reduced the error rate on invoices from 33 percent to 6 percent.[28]

Reactions to ECR have ranged from complete disbelief to rave reviews. The major concern of some of the parties is that too many agents are involved to ever achieve the coordination for this system to work. Indeed, some manufacturers, such as Quaker Oats and Procter & Gamble, have already attempted to eliminate forward buying and diverting with a value pricing strategy. However, those attempts were probably unilateral decisions by manufacturers, and they may have reaped most of the benefits of the new policy.

ECR is different in that it involves cooperation among retailers and manufacturers. In particular, ECR may still involve trade promotions, but these would be joint promotions among all parties concerned and would apply only to goods that are actually promoted to consumers. For example, Tylenol got four times more market share with half its normal promotion spending, by using scan-down as a replacement for a freestanding-insert coupon. Apparently 60 percent of what the company spent on coupons went to printers and clearinghouses instead of to consumers. Hellmann's doubled its market share in Chicago, replacing a local marketing fund with a simplified pay-for-performance promotion. Even though ECR is a collaborative effort between all parties, because manufacturers have more to gain and better resources, they tend to take the initiative in implementing ECR.

ECR may also be facilitated by the advent of computerized data collection, storage and analysis such as scanner data. Scanner data has the advantages of being more detailed, timely and accurate than manually recorded or survey-based data (see Chapter 14). The two major suppliers of scanner data, Information Resources Incorporated and Nielsen Marketing Research, have already initiated ECR systems of their own. Firms can use their standard package for a fee, or order one to their own specifications.

Benefits of Trade Promotions

Despite their costs, trade promotions are likely to remain an enduring phenomenon, with or without ECR. The reason is that trade promotions serve some important goals of manufacturers as explained in the beginning of the chapter. In addition, trade promotions provide the following important benefits to manufacturers:

- Trade promotions draw the attention of sales staff, retailers and consumers to one particular brand that needs such attention. The brand may be new, overlooked, under attack or just under-exploited.

- Trade promotions and the retail promotions that they motivate lend variety and excitement to the retail environment. This excitement draws consumers into stores and motivates them to buy certain brands. The time limits associated with promotions lend an element of urgency that would otherwise not be there.

- Trade promotions are an important means for manufacturers to price discriminate among retailers, and for retailers to price discriminate among consumers. Through price discrimination, a firm can offer benefits to only those customer segments who need it.

- Trade promotions enable a manufacturer to compete with the lower prices of rivals, without having to permanently drop list prices. This benefit is especially true with respect to generics and private labels, which have made steady inroads into the shares of national brands. Indeed, some research shows that discounts of national brands stimulate switching from private labels and generics, but not vice versa.[29]

EVALUATING THE PROFITABILITY OF A TRADE PROMOTION

The evaluation of a trade promotion involves the same principles as that of the retailer's, discussed in Chapter 10, with one major difference. The decomposition of the promotional bump has a slightly different meaning for the manufacturer than for the retailer. In other words, the components b_1, b_2, b_3 and b_4 refer to slightly different factors. These differences lead to a slightly different condition of profitability for the manufacturer than for the retailer. Also, because of the differences between Exhibit 11-9 and Exhibit 10-9, the strategic relevance of the trade promotion is moderately different from that of the retail promotion. The subsequent discussion highlights the differences between the manufacturer's case and the retailer's. (Before proceeding, you should review the analysis of the profitability of a retailer's price promotion in Chapter 10.)

The starting point for evaluating a trade promotion is the sales response curve. Exhibit 11-9 shows

retailers' response to a trade promotion. As for the retailer, the manufacturer's sales or **shipments** increase sharply in response to a price promotion, especially one that has an incentive such as a discount. The pattern of response is similar to that of a retail promotion, with two critical differences (see Chapter 10). The manufacturer's sales show a modest dip prior to the promotion and a substantial dip after the promotion. These dips can be observed relative to the baseline. (The **baseline** is the estimated sales that would have occurred in the absence of a promotion.) The reason is that unlike consumers, retailers delay purchases before a trade deal, and stockpile for future periods. Also, if the promotion is announced for a period that lasts longer than the period between a retailer's orders, then the sales increase has at least two peaks, one at the start and the other at the end of the promotion period (see Exhibit 11-10). We discuss the reasons for these differences later.

Analysis of Profitability

For the retailer, the increase in manufacturer sales in response to a promotion can also be decomposed into four components, b_1, b_2, b_3 and b_4 (see Exhibit 11-10). The four components take on the following meaning for the manufacturer:

b_1 = *incremental consumption* by retailers; that is, buying more of the promoted brand to meet expected increases in consumer consumption.

▼ **EXHIBIT 11-9.** Sales to retailers in response to a manufacturer's trade deals.

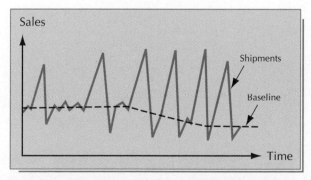

Source: Reprinted by permission Abraham, Magid M., and Leonard M. Lodish, "PROMOTER: An Automated Promotion Evaluation System," *Marketing Science* Vol. 6, No. 2 (Spring), 1987, 101–123, figure 4, p. 110. © 1987 The Institute of Management Sciences and the Operations Research Society of America (currently INFORMS), 2 Charles St., Suite 300, Providence, RI 02904 USA.

b_2 = *brand switching* by retailers; that is, buying more of the promoted brand of the manufacturer in lieu of brands of other manufacturers, to meet expected brand switching by consumers.

b_3 = *stockpiling* by retailers; that is, buying more of the promoted brand, to sell to consumers at the regular price later on, as well as to cover stockpiling by consumers.

b_4 = *incremental purchasing* by retailers on discount to accommodate consumers' store switching.

In this case, b_1 and b_2 represent real gains for the manufacturer, as the retailer buys and passes on to consumers more of the manufacturer's brand instead of other brands it would have bought. Components b_3 and b_4 represent opportunity costs; b_3 is the quantity that the retailer buys on discount instead of at the regular price, and b_4 is the quantity that other retailers would have bought at regular prices to accommodate sales to consumers who would not have switched stores in the absence of the retail promotion. As for the retailer, a trade promotion may involve some discount per unit, plus some promotional support such as display allowances. Following Chapter 10, we can define the following terms:

m = the margin per unit before the discount;

d = the discount per unit (if any);

f_1 = the fixed costs (if any) of the promotion, such as allowances and materials supplied;

f_2 = the fixed costs (if any) of the promotion, such as managerial time and inventory costs.

Given these definitions, the decision rule for a promotion being profitable in this case is:

Equation 1: $(b_1 + b_2)(m - d) > (a_2 + b_3 + b_4)d + f_1 + f_2$

In words, a promotion is profitable if the incremental profits from the deal are greater than the fixed and opportunity costs of the promotion.

Strategic Relevance

Stockpiling The major component of incremental sales in response to a trade promotion, especially one involving a discount, is stockpiling by retailers. This effect can be seen in Exhibit 11-9, where sales are lower just before and just after a promotion. Why do retailers stockpile so much more than consumers? There are at least three reasons for this behavior.

First, consumers normally buy only a few units of a product, but retailers buy in large quantities. In the case of a retail chain that buys for several stores, such quantities can be very large. What is a small savings for an individual consumer can amount to a major savings when aggregated over the large number of units purchased by a chain. Thus stockpiling during promotions can mean major savings for retailers.

Second, retailers normally carry some excess inventory because the cost of doing so generally exceeds the *stockout cost,* the cost of not having a product that the consumer wants. Given that they already have a system for ordering and storing inventory, retailers can increase margins and profits by stockpiling during a promotion.

Third, when retailers offer discounts they tend to keep the duration and frequency of the discounts low to minimize the number of lucky loyals. When manufacturers offer price discounts, they tend to keep the deal open for a longer period of time. Thus they do not discriminate effectively between segments of retailers who

▼ **EXHIBIT 11-10.** Decomposing retail response to trade promotions.

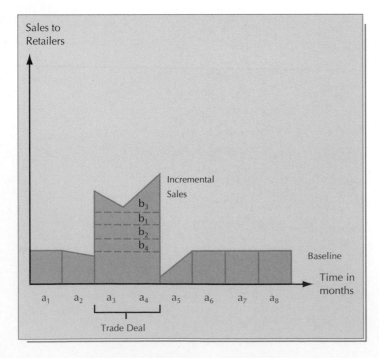

buy on deal to pass it on to consumers, and those who buy merely to stockpile.

Why do the retailer's purchases peak at the start and just before the announced end of the promotion? (See Exhibit 11-10.) The first peak in sales is the retailer's ordering in expectation of any increase in sales in response to the discount it would offer consumers. The peak just before the end is to stockpile the brand, which can then be sold at regular price after the promotion, and also for any sales increase in response to a price-cut. The retailers' stockpiling on deal for sales at regular price after the deal is what accounts for the low pass-through of promotions. Note that if manufacturers offer promotions randomly, and do not announce the end of the deal, the peak just before the end is unlikely to materialize.

Brand Switching While brand switching is a major component of consumers' response to a retailer's discount, it is not as big a factor in retailers' response to a trade promotion. The reason is that retailers pass through only about a third of the discount to consumers.[30] So only about a third of the retailer's incremental purchases from the manufacturer is passed on to consumers through a price discount; the rest represents the retailer's stockpiling. Thus retailers would need to switch purchases to the brand on promotion only to the extent of one-third of the expected brand switching from consumers. In other words, only a third of the brand switching at the retail level translates into brand switching at the manufacturer level.

Incremental Consumption and Store Switching Since incremental consumption and store switching are small at the retail level, they become even smaller at the manufacturer level. The reason is the same as that for brand switching. Since only a third of the sales increase in response to the promotion is passed on to consumers, only a third of the fractions attributed to store switching and incremental consumption at the retail level would translate into similar fractions at the manufacturer level.

Summary

Manufacturers offer trade promotions in order to obtain suitable distribution, control inventory and stimulate retail promotions for their brands. During the 1980s, trade promotions increased steadily at the cost of media advertising, to account for almost half of the promotion budget. The increase was due to at least five factors: brand proliferation, splintering of the mass market, growth of retailer power, changes in consumer shopping and slow growth in population.

Trade promotions can be classified as primarily incentive (price or nonprice) or communicative (informative or motivational). The term *trade deals* includes all incentive-based promotions, both price and nonprice. Price-based trade deals include off-invoice discounts, quantity discounts, quota incentives, bill-backs and count-recount discounts. Nonprice trade deals include slotting allowances, street money, trade contests, spiffs and financing. Informative trade promotions include cooperative advertising, display materials and allowances and exhibits. The major type of motivational trade promotion is conferences.

A trade deal triggers a major "game" between manufacturer and retailer. Manufacturers compete with each other by offering deals to retailers in the hope of stimulating retail promotions and increasing consumer sales. Retailers on the other hand buy to maximize profits from the trade deal, while passing on as little of the benefit as possible to consumers. The term *pass-through* refers to the fraction of the trade deal that retailers pass on to consumers. Retailers limit pass-through by pocketing the deal, forward buying, delaying purchases before a deal or diverting the product. The various types of price-based trade deals differ in how they restrict retailers from limiting pass-through.

Low pass-through is one of the major costs of trade promotions. In addition, trade promotions involve other costs, some of which are hidden. These costs include channel conflict, managerial time, production dislocations, and inventory buildup. All costs of trade promotions have increased substantially in recent years. Efficient consumer response (ECR) is a joint effort by manufacturers and retailers to control these costs. Its major component consists of trade deals that apply only to those items that retailers sell to consumers on discount. Its other components include efficient store assortment, efficient product replenishment, and efficient product introduction.

Trade promotions are likely to continue even if efficient consumer response is not successful and despite their costs, because they provide manufacturers with at least four benefits: they draw retailers' and consumers' attention to a particular brand; they lend excitement to the purchase environment; they help discriminate between price-sensitive and price-insensitive consumers; and they enable manufacturers to compete with low-priced generics.

A trade promotion is profitable if its total profits exceed total costs. The total profits are the real number of incremental units sold times the margin. When computing the real incremental units, manufacturers need to factor out increases in sales from retailers who stockpile or merely buy quantities that other retailers would have bought at regular price. The incremental costs are the sum of the fixed costs of running the promotion and the opportunity costs of retailers buying on discount what they would have at regular price. The high fixed cost of promotions and low sales at regular prices are reasons that manufacturers have started offering everyday-low prices.

QUESTIONS

1. Why did trade promotions increase so consistently and dramatically in the 1980s?
2. One of the goals of trade promotions, especially trade deals, is to motivate retailers to offer promotions to consumers. Does this happen?
3. What is pass-through? Why do retailers limit pass-through?
4. How exactly do retailers limit pass-through?
5. Which trade deals are least likely to be passed through to consumers? Why?
6. Why do manufacturers still offer deals to retailers if the latter limit pass-through?
7. How can manufacturers structure a trade deal to ensure a high pass-through? Explain fully.
8. What are slotting allowances? Are they illegal? Why do manufacturers offer such payments?
9. What is push money? Is the level of push money and slotting allowances too high?
10. What is cooperative advertising? Why would manufacturers take part in cooperative advertising, when the retailer benefits from it?
11. What is the purpose of the display allowance? Is offering a display allowance a good strategy for a manufacturer? Under what conditions?
12. Evaluate the major costs and benefits of trade promotions.
13. What is efficient consumer response? Is it a fair system for managing promotions? Why?
14. Explain the problem of diverting and forward buying. What are the obstacles in resolving this problem? What solution would you recommend?
15. Unlike retail sales, a manufacturer's sales show a dip just before and after a manufacturer's discount. Explain.
16. Analyze the profitability of a trade promotion.

NOTES

1. Lawrence, Jennifer (1993), "Supermarket Tug Of War: Will P&G's Pricing Policy Pull Retailers Over To Its Side?" *Advertising Age*, April 19, 1, 19; An *Advertising Age* Roundup (1992), "P&G Plays Pied Piper On Pricing," *Advertising Age*, March 9, 6.
2. "The High Cost of Value Pricing," (1995), *PROMO* (February), 4, 5.
3. For example, see Buzzell, Robert D., John A. Quelch, and Walter J. Salmon (1990), "The Costly Bargain of Trade Promotion," *Harvard Business Review* (March-April), 141–149.
4. Schiller, Zachary, Greg Burns, and Karen Lowry Miller (1996), "Make It Simple," *Business Week*, September 9, 96–104.
5. Buzzell, Quelch, and Salmon, "The Costly Bargain of Trade Promotion."
6. Cheavalier, Michel, and Ronald C. Curhan (1976), "Retail Promotions as a Function of Trade Promotions: A Descriptive Analysis," *Sloan Management Review* (Fall), 19–32.
7. Schlossberg, Howard (1994), "Secret," *PROMO* (April), 51–56.
8. *Ibid.*
9. *PROMO* (1995) "It's a Brand New Deal Out There," (February 3), 2.
10. Schlossberg, "Secret."
11. Some authors refer to this form of the promotions as *free goods* (e.g., Blattberg, Robert C., and Scott A. Neslin (1990), *Sales Promotion: Concepts, Methods and Strategies*, Englewood Cliffs, NJ: Prentice-Hall). If the free good belongs to another product category it is called a *premium*. For example, "buy two cases of soap, get one case of shampoo free." However, premiums are more common as a form of consumer promotions and will be discussed at that point.
12. For an analysis, see Gerstner, Eitan, and James D. Hess (1991), "To Deal Or Not To Deal? Motivating Middlemen To Price Promote," working paper, North Carolina State University.

13. Blattberg, Robert C., and Scott A. Neslin (1990), *Sales Promotion: Concepts, Methods and Strategies,* Englewood Cliffs, NJ: Prentice-Hall.

14. *Ibid.*

15. Adapted from Charles, Marj (1994), "Beer Makers Frothing Over Plan To Charge for Retail Shelf Space," *The Wall Street Journal*, April 22, B1, B3; Colford, Steven W., and Ira Teinowitz (1994), "Space Wars Heading to Taverns," *Advertising Age*, April 18, 1, 43; George Wells and Associates, Inc. (1995), "Slotting Fees Are Prohibited Under Federal Alcohol Trade Practices," *Washington Beverage*, October 25.

16. Blattberg and Neslin, *Sales Promotion.*

17. Trade Show Bureau (1994), *A Guide to the U.S. Exposition Industry*, Denver, CO: Trade Show Bureau.

18. Johnson, Bradley (1993), "Vegas, Chips, $: It Must Be COMDEX," *Advertising Age*, November 11, 3, 28.

19. Trade Show Bureau, *A Guide to the U.S. Exposition Industry.*

20. Buzzell, Quelch, and Salmon, "The Costly Bargain of Trade Promotion."

21. *Ibid.*

22. *Ibid.*

23. Schlossberg, "Secret."

24. Ball, Benjamin F. (1994), "For ECR to Work, Some Comfortable Practices Must Go," *Advertising Age*, June 6, 28.

25. Schiller, Burns, and Miller, "Make It Simple."

26. *Ibid.*

27. *Ibid.*

28. *Ibid.*

29. Blattberg, Robert C., and Kenneth J. Wisniewski (1989), "Price Induced Patterns of Competition," *Marketing Science*, 8, 4 (Fall), 291–309.

30. Chevalier and Curhan, "Retail Promotions as a Function of Trade Promotions."

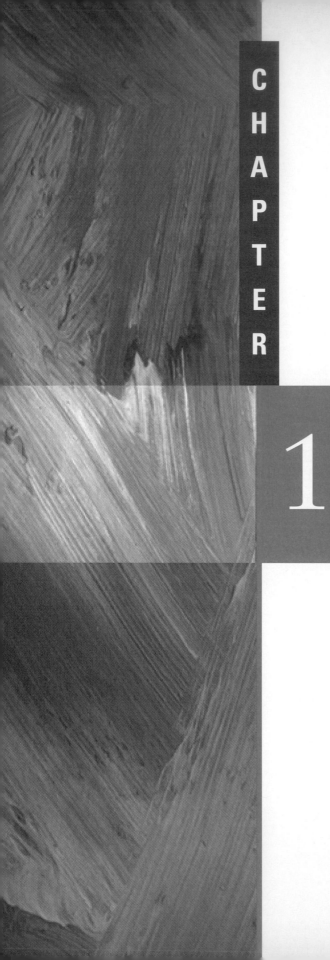

In April 1994, a Nestlé promotion for its Butterfinger candy bar won *PROMO* Magazine's Super Reggie award for the best promotion of 1993. The promotion was built around a mystery game, "Who Laid a Finger on Bart's Butterfinger?" The theme itself was a spin-off from the brand's ongoing relationship with Bart Simpson, the animated character who has warned TV viewers not to "lay a finger on my Butterfinger" in commercials since 1990. The game created five different wrappers for 65 million candy bars, each

12 Consumer Promotions

featuring Bart Simpson in a detective outfit and five suspect alibis. Consumers had to collect all five alibis to identify the culprit and then mail in their solutions for chances to win a $50,000 grand prize or one of 10,000 "Most Wanted" T-shirts. The contest was supported with display materials, 30-second TV spots, a toll-free hotline, print ads in *TV Guide,* "confidential police evidence" press kits and a joint Fox/Nestlé national radio contest offering 500 consumers chances to win prize packages, trips and concert tickets when they correctly guessed the culprit's name.

The brand received more than 59,000 entries, generated an average purchase of three bars per entry and increased sales by more than 51 percent during the two-month campaign.[1]

Nestlé's Butterfinger promotion is an example of a successful contest to generate excitement about a brand and increase its sales. Contests are only one of a variety of consumer promotions that a firm can choose (see Exhibit 12-1). **Consumer promotions** are sales promotions that a manufacturer offers consumers directly. The precise definition and measurement of consumer promotions is still evolving, so estimates of the relative expenditures on various promotions and their corresponding importance are not very reliable. The main advantage of sales promotions over trade promotions is their independence from dealers and retailers. As a result, manufacturers can design the promotion to pass through to consumers. However, consumer promotions are costly, risky and require considerable organization. For this reason, firms generally hire the services of a promotion agency to plan and execute various aspects of their promotions.

This chapter discusses the nature, goal and use of each of the different types of consumer promotions. The chapter begins with manufacturer coupons, for two reasons. First, coupons constitute the most popular type of retail promotions and the most widely researched. Thus, much knowledge has accumulated about this form of promotion. Second, couponing is a rich phenomenon that embodies both incentives and communications from manufacturers, and stimulates a complex pattern of response from con-

sumers. As such, it is a base against which other types of promotions can be compared.

MANUFACTURER COUPONS

In 1994, the Postal Inspection Service placed a coupon in local papers for a nonexistent product called "Durasoft" toilet tissue. Joseph A. Sorbara, owner, and Edward J. Martin, manager, of the Bridge Shop N Save in Philadelphia got caught when they redeemed 59 coupons for the brand. After further investigation and indictments the pair pleaded guilty to mail and wire fraud in connection with a 9-year scheme that defrauded firms of $1.1 million. They would purchase coupons from various sources and send them on to firms as validly redeemed by individual consumers.[2]

Despite misredemptions like this one, coupons have become a pervasive component of marketing. C. W. Post is the first known firm to have offered coupons, in 1895; the first coupon was a 1-cent offer that could be used to buy a new cereal called Grape Nuts.[3] Since that time coupons have permeated the entire spectrum of products and services, peaking at a massive volume of 310 billion coupons in 1992. That number was over $2\frac{1}{2}$ times that of 1981 (see Exhibit 12-2).[4] In recent years coupon distribution has decreased as manufacturers have sought to reduce promotional expenditures with everyday-low prices (see Chapters 10 and 11). Some consumers consider coupons to be a windfall and assiduously search for, clip, file and use them. Others consider coupons to be a bother and wish firms would just reduce the price. Retailers themselves find coupon handling a major administrative task.

What are coupons and why are they used? Is the high misredemption rate worth their benefits? Is the low redemption rate an advantage or disadvantage to firms? This section provides answers to these questions.

Types of Manufacturer Coupons

Manufacturer coupons are certificates from firms offering consumers some fixed savings off the retail price of the product if they meet some conditions. (The term *coupons* implies manufacturer coupons. This chapter does not discuss retail coupons.) The con-

---

▼ **EXHIBIT 12-1. Types of consumer promotions.**

| PRIMARILY INCENTIVE | | PRIMARILY COMMUNICATIVE | |
Price	Nonprice	Informative	Motivational
Manufacturer coupons, rebates, price packs, trial coupons	Premiums, tie-ins, bonus plans	Samples, trials	Games, sweepstakes

▼ **EXHIBIT 12-2.** Annual distribution of manufacturer coupons.

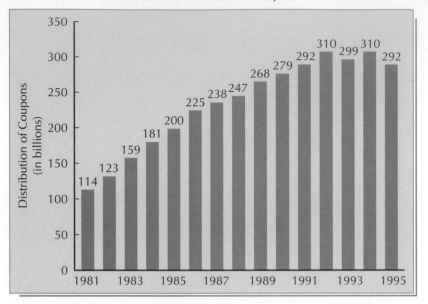

Source: Heitsmith, Glenn (1994), "Couponing. Sea Change Or Tidal Shift," *PROMO* Magazine, (April), 43–46; Schiller, Zachary, (1996), "First, Green Stamps, Now, Coupons?" *Business Week*, April 22, 68.

percent of the total value of coupons distributed (see Exhibit 12-3).[5] **Magazine coupons** appear in the pages of periodicals. **Run-of-press newspaper coupons** (**ROP newspapers**) are printed on the pages of newspapers. This is probably the main vehicle for coupon distribution in Canada, accounting for 83 percent of the coupons issued there in 1991.[6]

Direct-mail coupons are mailed directly to households based on general or specific mailing lists. These coupons have become increasingly important as they form a means of targeting specific consumer groups.

Package coupons appear on product packages. Package coupons are the most common means of coupon distribution in Spain and Italy. They may be further classified depending on where in the package they appear or how they may be used. **In-pack coupons** and **on-pack coupons** may be used only on subsequent purchases of the same product. **Instantly redeemable coupons** are found on the package but may be used for the current purchase of the product. **Cross-ruff coupons** may be found in or on the pack and may be used only for the purchase of another product of the same or a different firm.

Retailer-distributed coupons are manufacturer coupons distributed through retail stores. These coupons may be available through a retailer ad (called *in-ad coupons*), display, shelf handout,

ditions typically relate to a precise period of time for which the coupon is good. Other conditions may relate to the sizes or quantities of the product and the geographic region for which the coupon is good. The actual reduction in price is offered by the retailer, who is guaranteed reimbursement by the manufacturer for the face value of the coupon plus some processing costs. The **face value** of a coupon is the dollar amount clearly printed on the coupon, which a consumer can save by making a relevant purchase. **Coupon redemption** is the consumer's claiming of the cash value of a coupon at the time of purchase.

Manufacturer coupons are of four types based on the mode of distribution: media, direct mail, package and retailer-distributed coupons.

Media coupons are sent through the media, typically the print media. They take the name of the media through which they are available. **Freestanding inserts** (**FSIs**) are separate advertising sections of a newspaper, typically the Sunday newspaper. This is by far the most popular distribution vehicle, amounting to over 64

▼ **EXHIBIT 12-3.** Popularity of coupon vehicles.

Coupon Type	1993 Expenditures ($ million)	Percentage
Freestanding insert	$1,300	64.1%
ROP newspaper	33	1.6
Direct mail	520	25.7
In-store	154	7.6
Other	20	1.0
Total	$2,027	100.0%

Source: *PROMO* Magazine (1994), "Marketers Cut Distribution and Spending" (July), 36.

machine dispenser or electronic dispenser. Retailer coupons generally can be redeemed only at the retail outlet at which they were distributed. Retailers especially like in-ad coupons, because they attract attention and shoppers. Because of greater retailer support, manufacturers increased their use of in-ad coupons, which grew 700 percent in the early 1990s.[7] More recently, electronic coupons have been growing in importance because they enable firms to more precisely target consumers.

The Purpose of Coupons

In effect the coupon is a special type of price reduction by which a firm offers a discount directly to consumers without the retailer retaining any benefit. Yet, coupons can trigger support from retailers for the brand, typically in the form of double coupons (see Chapter 10). Coupons can also be used to draw the attention of consumers or to reinforce certain messages through an ad with which they appear. In addition, coupons serve many of the basic goals of incentive promotions covered in Chapter 9. Thus coupons prompt higher purchases of the brand due to switching, increased consumption or stockpiling by consumers.

However, many other promotional tools can achieve these goals, some more effectively than coupons. The unique advantage of coupons is that they can better discriminate among consumers than most other methods of promotion.[8] Because the coupon has to be clipped, stored, retrieved and used appropriately to be valid, it requires considerable planning by consumers. Only consumers motivated to get lower prices will make the effort. Typically consumers who are willing to buy the product anyway are less likely to redeem a coupon. The high effort required for redeeming a coupon relative to its benefit is the main reason why the redemption rate of coupons in the United States remains so low. Many critics bemoan the costs of couponing, especially given the low redemption rate. However, the low rate works to the advantage of firms, who can effectively offer the product at a lower price to one price-sensitive segment, without having to lower the price to all consumers.

Another important role of coupons is that they can be used to build a pattern of repurchasing that can lead to loyalty. For example, in-pack coupons good only on the next purchase motivate consumers to rebuy the product.[9] If subsequent packs also con-

tain coupons, consumers could get into a habit of buying the brand, and may continue to do so after the coupons have stopped. Alternatively, some theorists have reasoned that by slowly reducing the value of coupons firms could get consumers to continue using the brand while ultimately weaning them from the incentive.[10] Whether consumers who make the effort to redeem coupons can be weaned from coupons is a debatable point that has not been proven with hard data.

Coupon Redemptions

The extensive distribution of coupons raises some important questions: To what extent are coupons redeemed, or what is the rate of redemption? How are coupons used, or what is the pattern of sales and redemption? What are the characteristics of coupon users? Are there any long-term effects of redemptions? How and to what extent can coupons be misredeemed? We address these questions next.

Rate of Redemption The redemption rate of coupons has typically been low in the United States but high in other countries.[11] The main reason for this difference may be the differential novelty and benefit-to-cost ratio across these countries. Because of the intensive use of coupons in the United States, especially in the last decade, the cost to consumers of searching for, clipping, saving and using the right coupons has increased enormously. At the same time, in the United States the novelty or appeal of most coupons with standard face values is not very high relative to the value of time and disposable income. Indeed, the redemption rate of coupons has been steadily declining in the United States (see Exhibit 12-4). In contrast, in other countries, coupons have not reached the same level of intensity, complexity and commonness. Also, the value of coupons relative to the value of consumers' time and disposable income may be higher in other countries than in the United States. These factors may explain the higher incidence of redemption in other countries.

Pattern of Sales Response and Redemptions As one may expect, the **coupon drop**, or distribution of a coupon, leads to an increase in sales for the brand. How large is this increase? How long does it last? Is all of it due to redemptions?

Research indicates that a coupon drop leads to an immediate increase in sales and redemptions.

▼ EXHIBIT 12-4. Coupon redemption rate in the United States.

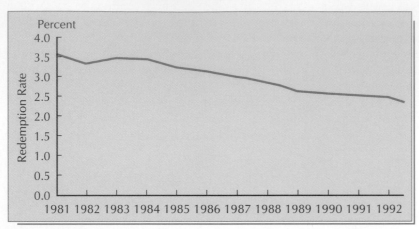

Source: Deveny, Kathleen (1994), "Awash in Coupons? Some Firms Try to Stem the Tide," *The Wall Street Journal*, May 10, B1, B6; *PROMO* Magazine (1995), "Coupon Redemption On The Slide" (March), 1, 11.

of the coupon is at an end and make a point of using it, rather than losing the opportunity of using the coupon. When no expiration date exists, lack of urgency may lead to procrastination, forgetting and lower redemption.

This phenomenon of expiration dates triggering redemptions may not be very large or widespread. Firms may or may not be aware of the phenomenon. But they have been including the expiration date on the coupon more often, while also shortening its life span (see Exhibit 12-6). One reason for this strategy may be to increase the discriminatory power of coupons. When coupons have a short life span, consumers who would have bought the brand anyway at their regular purchase occasion may not be able to use them. Only those consumers willing to advance their purchase timing to within the life span of the coupon are likely to use the coupon. Another reason for this strategy may be to decrease misredemptions, which have been

Studies found that sales increased as much as 50 percent, but the increase varied by the value of the coupon and the brand being promoted.[12] In general, sales increase with the value of a coupon, but at a diminishing rate.[13] Most but not all of this increase is due to consumers' redeeming coupons for the brand. Surprisingly, some of the increase may not be associated with coupon redemptions.[14] Two factors may account for the latter increase in sales. First, some consumers may plan to buy the brand with the coupon, but may end up forgetting to use the coupon, or using it on the wrong size so that it is not valid. Alternatively, because many coupons are placed in a print ad for the brand, the coupon may enhance the persuasion of the ad. Thus consumers may buy the brand even without redeeming the coupon. To the extent that a brand's sales increase without coupon redemptions, the increase forms an important source of "free" incremental sales for the brand.

For any particular coupon drop, the pattern of sales and coupon redemptions follows a standard exponential decay with a big peak at the time of the first drop and a subsequent downward-sloping curve (see Exhibit 12-5). One study suggests a small peak at the tail end of the curve due to higher redemptions just prior to the expiration of the coupon.[15] One possible explanation for this phenomenon may be **regret theory**—consumers note that the useful life

▼ EXHIBIT 12-5. Pattern of sales and coupon redemption over time (not drawn to scale).

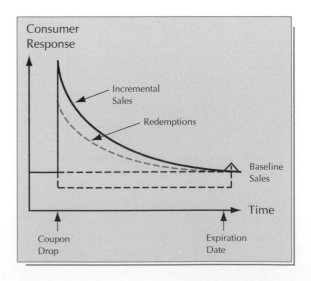

very high in recent years. Misredemptions typically require time and can be cut down by shortening the life spans of coupons.

Characteristics of Redeemers What type of consumers redeem coupons? Researchers have long suspected that coupon redemption is not a random process but is typical of a particular segment of consumers. That is, there may be a *coupon-prone segment*.[16] Indeed, descriptive analysis suggests that some households are more likely to redeem coupons than others. The key question is whether this segment can be accurately identified and described. Identifying redeemers means finding demographic variables associated with redemption. Describing redeemers means finding lifestyle or usage characteristics associated with redemption. Identification is more valuable than description, because the former helps the promoter to target coupons only to the consumers who use them, thus avoiding waste in distribution. The latter may help in positioning the brand and designing copy, but it still begs the question: who are the coupon redeemers?

Several researchers have tried to identify the coupon user, but with limited success. Some demographic variables are positively related to coupon usage, but only weakly. Four such variables are income, education, household size and media exposure, which are generally positively related to coupon usage.[17] Higher educated households may be better informed about the value of coupons, or receive more coupons through their wider subscription to newspapers and magazines. Thus they are more likely to use coupons. Larger households have broader preferences and buy more brands per category. They are more likely to be aware of and use many brands. Thus they are more likely to use a brand's coupons when available. The relationship of income to coupon usage is mixed.[18] The reason may be that to the extent that higher income households are better educated, they would redeem more

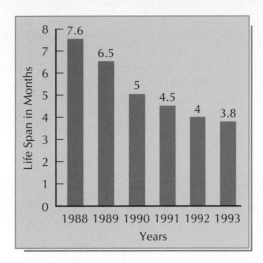

▼ **EXHIBIT 12-6.** **The shrinking life span of coupons.**

Data Source: *PROMO* Magazine (1994), "Marketers Cut Distribution and Spending" (July), 36.

coupons, but to the extent that they are less price sensitive, they may redeem fewer coupons. Households with wider exposure to the media, especially the Sunday newspaper, have more opportunities to see, clip and thus use coupons.[19]

Researchers have met with greater success when describing the characteristics of coupon usage. Brand loyalty is the single most important characteristic that affects coupon usage. In general, consumers who are more loyal to brands tend to use coupons less,[20] probably because their choice of brands is based on preference rather than on price. At the same time, consumers who use coupons tend to use them for the brands they favor.[21] The two findings together imply that coupon users are likely to switch to a brand if it can be purchased at a lower price with a coupon; however, if coupons are available on two or more brands, they will buy the brand they prefer with the coupon. To the extent that coupon redeemers would have bought the brand anyway in the absence of a coupon, the manufacturer incurs opportunity costs. As explained in Chapter 9, opportunity costs are unseen costs that the company incurs from certain opportunities that it foregoes. Other characteristics of coupon users are that they are price conscious, involved with shopping and venturesome.[22] These findings are not surprising in that consumers' search for, clipping, storage and usage of coupons require considerable effort and planning.

Long-Term Effects of Coupons Coupons have two types of effects on sales, short term and long term. The short-term effect is the change in the probability of buying the brand while the coupon is valid. This change has been covered already. The long-term effect is the change in the probability of repurchasing the brand later in the absence of coupons. The long-term effect of coupons has been a controversial topic, with three contrary positions.

One position is that coupons can reduce the probability of repurchasing the brand after the coupon expires. Two factors may support this claim. First, according to **attribution theory,** coupon redeemers may attribute or ascribe their purchase to the coupon and not to any innate preference for the brand.[23] When a coupon is no longer available they may not rebuy the brand. Second, redeemers may come to expect further coupons from the firm and may not buy the brand until the next coupon drop.

A second position based on **learning theory** posits that coupons can increase the probability of repurchasing the brand. This change could occur for two reasons. First, coupon redeemers could get used to buying the brand with a coupon, so that they continue to buy the brand even when the coupon is withdrawn. Second, coupon users learn new features of the brand and then repurchase it because they like such features. Either of these two reasons would imply specific circumstances for the brand (such as its being new or modified) and specific intent by the firm to induce learning on the part of consumers.

A third school of thought based on **price discriminatory theory** posits that coupons do not affect the probability of buying the brand. According to this view, coupon users form a distinct segment of consumers who will look for and use coupons whenever they are available. Sales increase when a coupon is available, as these consumers buy the brand; sales decline after a coupon drop, because these consumers cease to buy the brand. However, such purchases and coupon redemptions *cause neither an increase nor a decrease in the innate probability of repurchasing the brand among these consumers or among regular buyers.*[24] This position implies that firms use coupons to discriminate between loyals and switchers (see Chapter 9).

Which of these three positions is right? Careful analysis by at least one study on a *mature* brand and product category suggests that the first two viewpoints are not strongly supported. That is, the usage of coupons neither substantially increases nor decreases the probability of repurchasing the brand when it is not supported with coupons.[25] In other words, coupon usage does not induce attribution or learning on a substantial scale. The probable reason is that coupons have become such a pervasive phenomenon and are so extensively used (but by a relatively small group of consumers) that any change in preference due to coupons has already taken place

much earlier in the buying experience of these consumers. However, the situation is likely to be different for a *new* or *modified* brand. In this case, consumers have much to learn about the product, and a coupon could induce learning and higher repurchase. Thus for mature products, firms should use coupons to price discriminate among consumer segments. But for new or modified products, firms could use coupons to induce consumer learning about the brand.

Misredemptions   Either individual consumers, retailers or organized groups may misredeem coupons.[26] Individual consumers may intentionally or unintentionally redeem coupons at a store's checkout beyond the expiration date, for items that they have not purchased, or for sizes and quantities that do not apply. Because checkout cashiers process a large number of these requests under considerable time pressure they may not catch all the errors. Sometimes, retailers intentionally overlook such errors to maximize consumer purchases at their store. At other times, retailers themselves may misredeem coupons by including unredeemed coupons with those validly redeemed when they submit them for reimbursement. There is no published study of the extent of such misredemptions, though industry experts suspect it may not be very large.

A more serious problem is systematic misredemption by agents intent on defrauding firms. Typically such operations involve one or more retailers working in collusion with one or more **gang clipping operations.** The latter groups collect coupons, age them so they look used, sort them by firm and then sell them to cooperating retailers. The retailers in turn submit them to manufacturers as bona fide redemptions by consumers. The gang clippers may get their coupons by mass clipping them from print media, or they may obtain illegal diversions from some distribution houses, or they may recruit charitable organizations under false pretexts to send them coupons. One estimate is that gang clipping costs firms $500 million annually.[27] For example, for 10 years, Janet Lieber and her Canoga Park Women's Club mailed tens of thousands of coupons to a San Diego post office box. They thought they were helping to buy guide dogs for the blind. Then they realized the bitter truth: they had been duped by coupon racketeers.[28]

Federal, state and postal officers have tried to monitor and prosecute fraudulent redemptions of this type. One way to uncover such schemes is to distribute coupons for nonexisting brands and catch those retailers who try to redeem them. Another way is to monitor the number of redemptions by city, chain or store. A very high redemption rate from any one of these sources would point to fraudulent redemptions. While the efforts have uncovered some major fraudulent schemes, firms continue to lose millions to fraudulent redemptions.

Evaluating Coupon Strategy

In the summer of 1994, General Mills dropped a bomb on the promotion industry when it rolled back cereal prices and slashed coupons and other forms of price promotions by $175 million a year. "There's a tremendous cost associated with printing, distributing, handling and redeeming coupons," said the company's president, Steve Sanger. "Because of this inefficiency the 50 cents that the consumer saves with a coupon can cost the manufacturers as much as 75 cents." Apparently General Mills calculated that an everyday-low price was better than the costly route of high-low pricing with coupons.[29]

Why did General Mills slash coupons from its promotional mix? The answer depends on the analysis of the profitability of a couponing strategy. The principles involved in the evaluation of the profitability of a coupon promotion are similar to those in the evaluation of a retail or trade promotion (see Chapters 10 and 11). However, the analysis of profitability of coupons is a little simpler because with the act of redemption, manufacturers have a clear measure of who uses a coupon.

Analysis of Profitability The value of a couponing strategy to firms depends on the trade-off between the costs

▼ **EXHIBIT 12-7.** Coupon expenditures.

Item	Expenditures in 1993 ($ millions)
Redemption	$4,410
Distribution	2,024
Retailer fees	580
Processing	80
Total	$7,094

Source: The Editors (1995), "Still Bullish On Promotion," *PROMO Magazine's Source Book 95,* Wilton, CT: *PROMO* Magazine, 12.

and benefits of coupons. The benefit of offering coupons is the increase in sales that the distribution generates. The main costs of coupons are the distribution, redemption (including misredemption) and processing costs (see Exhibit 12-7). The starting point of the analysis is the response to a coupon drop described in Exhibit 12-5. Based on that exhibit, let us define the following terms:

b = the incremental unit sales following the coupon drop

r = the total redemptions of coupons, among both regular (loyal) buyers and switchers from other brands.

m = the firm's margin per unit sold

d = the value of the coupon

p = the processing cost per coupon

f = the cost of distribution of the coupon

Given these definitions, when would a coupon drop be profitable? A coupon drop is profitable *if the incremental profits following the coupon drop exceed the total costs of the drop.* The incremental profits are the number of incremental sales (in units) multiplied by the margin per unit (that is, $b \times m$). The total costs are the sum of the redemption costs, the processing costs, and the direct costs. The cost of redemptions is the number of coupons redeemed multiplied by the value of the coupon ($r \times d$). The cost of processing is the number of coupons redeemed multiplied by the cost of processing each coupon ($r \times p$). The fixed costs are the costs of distribution of the coupon, f. Note that f is treated as fixed costs because it occurs before the response to coupons.

Thus the coupon is profitable if:

$$\text{Equation 1: } bm > r\,(p + d) + f$$

Strategic Implications When analyzing the profitability of coupons, managers must consider many important issues.

First, all redemptions are not incremental sales. The reason is that some regular buyers also redeem coupons. Thus managers need to measure separately the regular and incremental sales and the redemptions. For this reason, the analyst must estimate the proper baseline sales in the absence of the coupon. This baseline should cor-

▼ EXHIBIT 12-8. Factors affecting cost per coupon redemption.

Coupon Vehicle	Number Distributed (millions)	Cost per 1,000 Distributed	Face Value	Processing Fee	Redemption Rate	Total Redemptions (millions)	Total Cost ($ millions)	Cost per Redemption
Freestanding insert	50.3	$7.06	$0.35	$0.11	3.6%	1.81	$1.18	$0.66
ROP (solo)	35.0	$12.92	$0.35	$0.11	2.1%	.76	$0.79	$1.08
Sunday supplement	20.6	$10.80	$0.35	$0.11	1.2%	.25	$0.34	$1.36
Magazine	38.0	$13.96	$0.35	$0.11	1.8%	.68	$0.85	$1.24
Direct mail	45.0	$16.47	$0.35	$0.11	5.8%	2.61	$1.94	$0.74

Source: Blattberg, Robert C., and Scott A. Neslin (1990), *Sales Promotion: Concepts, Methods and Strategies,* Englewood Cliffs, NJ: Prentice-Hall, Inc.

rect for seasonal and competitive effects. Most importantly, the baseline must include the sales that would have occurred anyway in the absence of coupons.

Second, all incremental sales are not made with a coupon. As discussed above, some portion of incremental sales may involve consumers who planned to use coupons but did not, or others who saw the ad bearing the coupon and decided to buy the brand. Failure to identify this portion of sales may lead to its inclusion as baseline sales and render the coupon less profitable than it is.

Third, the fixed costs of distribution need to be carefully monitored. The fixed costs of distribution vary depending on which vehicle is used (see Exhibit 12-8). Direct mail is probably the most expensive, while the freestanding insert is probably the cheapest. However, the redemption rate varies considerably among the vehicles. Because only a small fraction of coupons are redeemed, the costs incurred for all coupons must be borne by that small fraction. Thus the major determinant of the total costs per redeemed coupon is the redemption rate rather than the costs of distribution. Note from Exhibit 12-8 that the total direct costs per redemption are two to four times the face value of the coupon. Analysts must weigh whether the fixed costs of distribution and the number of redemptions are so high as to make the coupon strategy less profitable than an everyday-low-price. In summer 1994, General Mills had apparently come to that conclusion. Each coupon was costing an additional 50 percent in fixed costs, and 60 percent of all purchases were made with some coupon or discount.[30] In that situation, total costs of coupon-

ing probably exceeded profits, prompting General Mills to an everyday-low-price strategy.

Fourth, maximizing the redemption rate is not necessarily good. Even though the low redemption rate increases the costs per redemption, increasing the redemption rate is not necessarily beneficial to the firm. Increasing the redemption rate is useful only if the additional consumers redeeming the coupon would not have bought the brand in the absence of the coupon.

Fifth, managers need to consider the intangible benefits of coupons. The use of coupons may produce intangible benefits such as increasing consumer awareness or liking of the product and stimulating retail promotions such as double coupons. These intangible benefits must also be considered when evaluating the overall strategy. Such costs may not be easily quantified, and may lead to an incorrect conclusion that coupons are not profitable.

New Trends

Recent innovations have the potential to revolutionize the distribution and processing of coupons. The most radical changes have to do with electronic systems to distribute and process coupons.

Electronic distribution systems target coupons to specific groups to minimize wastage. For example, one system would target coupons only to groups who use coupons. Such a system would rely on profiles of coupon users developed from scanner data (see Chapter 14). It would then distribute coupons through media used by consumers with similar profiles. This system eliminates the costs of distributing coupons to nonusers, misredeemers and consumers who would have bought the brand anyway. Exhibit 12-9 describes one system, the Vons card, put in place by the Vons supermarket chain of southern California.

Another system consists of an interactive electronic coupon machine in the store that delivers coupons based on a short questionnaire. The questions determine what product categories the consumer plans to purchase, and what brands the consumer last bought. The machine then issues coupons from the categories the

▼ EXHIBIT 12-9. An electronic distribution system.

AT THE MANUFACTURER:
Brand managers select lifestyle and purchasing categories to pinpoint promotions. They can also target purchasers of competing brands. Vons then prepares monthly mailers with individually laser-printed coupons targeted to specific households.

MARKETING NUGGETS: THEY'RE IN THE CARDS
How the Vons card works for consumers and marketers

AT VONS HEADQUARTERS:
Customers are sorted into nearly 200 groups based on goods bought, ranging from antacids to wine, and into lifestyle groups—consumers of children's products, for instance.

AT THE CHECKOUT:
Customer swipes magnetic card and receives automatic deductions on selected items. Detailed purchase data is transmitted to a central computer.

Source: Courtesy of Laurel Daunis.

consumer is going to purchase but not for the brand he/she last bought. This system offers manufacturers the same benefits as the one above, but requires much less data analysis. However, smart consumers could learn and defeat such simplistic distribution systems by indicating they bought a different brand than they actually did, so that they could get coupons for their favorite brands.

While electronic coupons are still more expensive (per coupon distributed) than regular coupons, their redemption rate is four to five times higher. In 1993,

the number of electronic coupons distributed grew 50 percent.[31]

Electronic processing systems use the identification numbers on coupons, just as store scanners scan the universal product code on product packages. Such a system enables easy scanning, processing and perhaps even stamping of coupons to minimize costs of processing and misredemption.

While coupons will continue to be one of the most common promotional tools of firms in the next few years, all parties involved in the offer, distribution and processing of coupons are working hard to make the system more effective and less wasteful.

REBATES

Rock Valley, Iowa, is a small town of 2,540 residents with a deeply religious climate.[32] In 1992 the town had 11 churches, two religious schools and a strong Dutch Calvinist tradition. Yet for a decade in the 1980s, many citizens were drawn into a "Cash for Trash" program that raised money for two private schools by redeeming rebates. Residents would drop off at the two schools the sales receipts and used packages of products they had bought. Volunteers would then cut the universal product codes off the packages, fill in the rebate voucher, attach the appropriate receipts and mail in the packet.

The post office estimated that the city filed about 500 rebate redemptions a week, which went to firms like Eastman Kodak, Chesebrough-Pond's and Mobil Oil.

Promoters generally state that rebates are not transferable and that one household may not redeem more than one rebate. Companies became suspicious when they found that the city's zip code appeared frequently in the list of addresses for rebates: Rock Valley's redemption rate for rebates was 62 percent, compared with a national average of 5 percent of a city's residents. When the program participants were confronted with the scheme, they claimed that they were unaware that it was illegal. However, further investigation revealed that some addressees intentionally misspelled their names, altered their addresses, or provided fictitious sales receipts. One woman created sales receipts in her basement with a cash register she had bought for the purpose. In all, 56 percent of the rebate filings appeared suspicious. When addressees received the rebates, they endorsed the checks and turned them over to the schools. Investigators estimated that the program netted over $500,000 before it was discovered. The organizers of the program signed a cease-and-desist order, promising not to violate redemption rules in the future.

Rebates are a guarantee by firms to reimburse consumers directly for the purchase of a product, subject to certain conditions. Technically, the term has the same meaning as **refund**, except that *rebate* is used for durables and *refund* for nondurables. The typical conditions for a rebate are the mailing in of (1) the refund voucher, (2) a proof of purchase from the product container or package and (3) the sales receipt. The rebate is similar to the coupon. Thus much of our discussion about coupons would apply to rebates. However, rebates differ from coupons in one important way: they require much greater effort to redeem.

To redeem rebates, consumers need to collect all three pieces of information just listed. Consumers need to make a copy of the sales receipt if they need one for their records. Some rebates require original receipts, making redemption even more difficult if consumers also need the original for reimbursement. To get the proof of purchase, consumers must sometimes wait till the product is consumed. For example, getting the proof of purchase from a shampoo container requires the container to be empty. By that time, consumers may misplace the sales slip or the rebate voucher, or they may forget all about the rebate. These difficulties with redemption lead to

three characteristics that distinguish the use of rebates relative to coupons.

First, rebates require higher face values to motivate consumers to redeem them. Even then rebates have a lower redemption rate than coupons. Second, rebates are a more powerful means of price discriminating between consumer segments (see Chapter 9). Only consumers who are very price sensitive, well organized and have adequate time will redeem the rebate. Others will pay the list price. Third, rebates cause an increase in purchases without redemption, that may be higher than that for coupons. Compared with coupons, many more consumers decide to buy with the hope of redeeming the rebate, and do not actually do so.

Rebates also have the same problem of misredemption as do coupons. The story about Rock Valley is a good example. In that case, the church probably wanted to capitalize on its members' unwillingness to redeem the rebates by doing the hard work for them, and in exchange keeping the cash it redeemed. The problem with that scheme is that in effect it amounts to a group redemption with the proceeds from several rebates going to one party. Most rebates explicitly prohibit such redemptions. Also, any large-scale redemption program is prone to fraudulent redemptions by requiring fictitious receipts, names and addresses to avoid being discovered.

PRICE PACKS

Price packs (also called **cents-off packs**) are new packages on which the firm offers a temporary lower price to the consumer. The offer may involve a sign on the package showing the lower price (for example, "50¢ off"), multiple packs (for example, "two for the price of one"), or larger packs (for example, "contains 25% more"). We first consider the benefits of price packs and then the regulations that cover their use.

Differential Benefits of Price Packs

We can easily understand the role of price packs by comparing them to coupons. Here again, three differences in benefits are salient.

As an incentive, price packs have a higher response rate than coupons. The reason is that the price pack is visible to most shoppers who intend to make a purchase in the category, and it requires minimal effort to use. Although coupons are more widely distributed than price packs, consumers have to make an effort to find, clip, save and use the appropriate coupons.

On the other hand, price packs have a much lower discriminatory power than coupons. Price-sensitive consumers are unlikely to notice the price pack unless it is promoted, while all regular buyers of the product get its benefit even if they are not aware of it.

Third, price packs are primarily an incentive promotion. They have a minimal communicative role aside from the routine communication contained on any package.

A firm can use price packs if it wants an immediate increase in sales, especially among impulse buyers or those who make their decisions in the store by comparing prices. Manufacturers of national brands can also use price packs to combat market share losses to private labels and generics, which sell primarily as lower price imitations of national brands. Finally, retailers tend to synchronize their own promotions with price packs, especially if they are for a well-known brand. So manufacturers can use price packs to stimulate retail promotions.

Regulation of Price Packs

Like coupons, price packs also have the potential for misuse, though primarily by manufacturers and retailers. For example, retailers can raise the regular price of the price packs by the amount of the cents-off offered, or they can break twin packages to sell each separately at the regular price. Manufacturers may misuse price packs by suggesting that the price of the pack is a special, when in fact it is equivalent to the regular price of the brand. For this reason, the FTC has established some restrictions on the use of price packs (see Chapter 2).[33]

PREMIUMS

In the summer of 1994, Burger King offered a premium with its Kids Meals. Each meal contained one of seven plastic figurines modeled on the characters of the Disney film, *The Lion King*. Burger King budgeted for 30 million Kids Meals and figurines over the six weeks of the promotion. As with past movies, Burger King paid Disney for the license to use the movie characters. However, the popularity of the movie fueled a frenzy for the figurines. The company sold 17 million meals in just two weeks, and soon ran out of figurines. Because the figurines were too costly to produce again, the company substituted trading cards picturing the seven characters. "We used to sell 45 to 70 meals a day," said one store manager. "Now we're doing 220 to 300."[34]

Premiums are rewards or gifts that a single firm gives consumers free or at a reduced price. The manufacturer of the gift itself does not reap any special benefit aside from the sales.[35] Examples include a toothbrush with the purchase of toothpaste, a multimedia kit with a computer toy or the Lion King figurines that Burger King gave with its Kids Meals. Premiums can be broadly classified into three groups based on their mode of distribution:

- *In-pack* or *with-purchase premiums* are inside the pack or come with the purchase of the product. These premiums provide an instant incentive or reward for buying the brand.
- *Mail-in premiums* are premiums a consumer can claim by mailing proofs of purchase obtained from multiple purchases of the product. Consumers do not have to make any payment for the premium.
- *Self-liquidating premiums* are premiums a consumer can buy by mail for a price in addition to supplying proofs of purchase obtained from the product. The term *self-liquidating* means that the selling price to the consumer covers the firm's purchase price, packaging costs and mailing costs.

The Logic of Premiums

What is the logic of a premium? What makes for a great premium? The logic of a premium is similar to that of a gift: give consumers something of value that they would not normally have or buy for themselves. A good premium is one that is inessential, infrequently purchased and has a low turnover. As a result, it is not easily available, tends to be overpriced and may be of poor quality. For example, stationery marketers may give a uniquely designed letter opener to managers who purchase office stationery. Because the letter opener is a low-cost, slow-moving, low-volume durable, it is not widely available in good designs. The firm can get a good price and good quality by ordering it at one time on a large scale with minimal storage and handling costs.

In addition, because of its bulk purchase, the firm could also order a special design not generally available. Thus the premium could be of low cost to the firm but a good value to consumers.

For example, in Winter 1994, Pizza Hut sold one million Rawlings basketballs with special NCAA logos for $4.99 each, in a self-liquidating premium. Similar balls without the logos sold for $17 each in sports stores.[36] What was the reason for the phenomenal success of Burger King's Lion King figurines? The figurines were a unique embodiment of the movie's characters that was not available elsewhere. The choice of the figurines was clever and timely because at that time the movie was enormously popular. It was among the most popular movies of all time, grossing $150 million in two weeks.

However, demand and supply factors are not the only considerations in choosing premiums. A good premium should have a *natural match* with the product being promoted. In the Burger King case, the target segment for Kids Meals matched very well with that for the figurines. The upcoming discussion of tie-ins gives guidelines for potential matches that could apply equally well to premiums.

Goals of Premiums

Effective premiums serve several goals. First, these small gifts can earn the goodwill of consumers. For this purpose, premiums may be selected as are gifts—items to which consumers would not normally treat themselves.

A second goal of premiums is to provide an incentive to buy the product. For this purpose, premiums may be selected because the firm can obtain them at a much lower cost than can the buyer. For example, IBM-compatible personal computers are sold with the latest versions of DOS and Windows without a surcharge.

A third goal of premiums is to stimulate repurchasing, and possibly loyalty, by requiring buyers to turn in several proofs of purchase, as in the mail-in premium or the collector's set. For example, in 1920, Lion Brand condensed and evaporated milk offered retail store managers suitcases of coupons that could be redeemed for kitchen or bedroom furnishings when they got married. Loyalty to the Lion Brand was so strong that it carried the same stock of apple blossom dinnerware for 15 years, because so many families kept coming back to redeem their coupons

for more pieces with the same pattern.[37] For this purpose, the firm should choose premiums that have sufficient drawing power that consumers would make the effort to repurchase the brand, keep records and mail them in.

A fourth goal of premiums is to remind consumers of the product being promoted. For this purpose, the premium must be closely linked to the product so that at every use, the consumer is reminded of the product. For example, a specially designed toothbrush with the name of the advertised brand could be a great premium for a toothpaste; it would remind the consumer of the brand each time the consumer used it. The same holds for a letter opener offered as a premium for buying stationery. Alternatively, the premium could be designed to repeatedly present a brand's message. An example is the prepaid phone card that allows consumers to make long-distance phone calls worth about $10 when they initiate the calls with a special number. Promoters offering this premium can buy the time from long-distance carriers for a fraction of the value of the call. The card itself can have themes or logos that remind the consumer of the brand, while the special number can activate a short audiotape with a similar message. In contrast, offering candies as a premium in cereal boxes may motivate kids to demand a brand of cereal, but irritate parents who strive to foster good eating habits.

TIE-INS

In 1994 CoreStates Financial Corp. had a tie-in with Disney's Premier Cruise Lines. Customers who opened an account with the bank received free cruise tickets for two children when they booked a family cruise. Qualified customers also received jumbo CoreStates beach towels and Disney merchandise, catalogs worth $10, and CoreStates savings certificates. The bank advertised the promotion to three million credit card customers in brochures mailed with their monthly statements. The bank also used newspaper ads, radio spots and local print material. The promotion motivated 5,000 consumers to redeem their travel vouchers and yielded 42,000 new accounts, exceeding the target by 320 percent. It won *PROMO* Magazine's 1994 Reggie award.[38]

Tie-ins are joint promotions for two or more items by one or more firms, like the promotion between CoreStates Financial Corp. and Premier Cruise Lines. A tie-in is different from a premium in that both parties to the tie-in share in the costs and benefits of the promotion. In the CoreStates example, the free cruise ticket is like a premium for the bank's new account holders, but because the new customers must buy a family cruise ticket to earn the benefit, Premier Cruise Lines also benefits from the package. Thus the promotion is a tie-in with benefits to both parties. How do firms benefit from offering tie-ins? Why do tie-ins motivate sales?

Role of Tie-ins

A successful tie-in is one that creates an economy or a benefit for consumers and the firms in the tie-in. The economy can be used to increase profits to the firm or lower prices to consumers. The benefit increases the interest in and the visibility and sales of the promoted brand. In the above example, since many families with children do not take cruises because of the additional cost, the offer is a good incentive for them. But because the offer involves a benefit to Premier Cruise Lines, CoreStates did not have to bear the entire cost. The use of tie-ins has increased substantially in recent years.[39] One reason may be that the greater fragmentation of media and markets has made it more difficult for firms to reach consumers. Another reason may be that the smaller budgets during the recessionary years of the early 1990s increased the importance of economies in pro motion such as those available from tie-ins.

Bases for Tie-ins

While the items in a tie-in do not need to have any specific link (Exhibit 12-10), such a link can enhance the value of the promotion. Here are some bases for linking tie-ins:

Complementary Products. The two brands in the tie-in are complementary. An example is the offer of a bottle of white wine with the puchase of a Thanksgiving turkey.

Complementary Services. The two services in the tie-in complement each other. An example is a tie-in for a hotel room at a resort and an airline ticket to that destination.

Same Consumer Segment. Each party to the tie-in appeals to the same target segment. For example, cereal companies sometimes tie-in with video game marketers to offer children video games at reduced rates with multiple proofs of purchase of cereal boxes. For six weeks in summer 1994, Pizza Hut, in connection with Connector Set Toy Co., offered free "Air Extremes" (a series of four K'NEX construction set models) to children ages 6 to 12 who ordered a Kid's Pizza Pack.[40] Similarly, for mailing in six proofs of purchase of Kodak film, Kodak offered a free ticket to the movie *The Lion King*.[41]

Same Consumption Occasion. The two brands in the tie-in are consumed on the same occasion. In 1993, Busch theme parks (Busch Gardens and Sea World) had a tie-in with VISA in which each visitor got $3 off per entry into the gardens as well as the opportunity to win free family vacations to the parks if the purchase were made with VISA. The parks received a 5% increase in visitors, while VISA obtained a 25% increase in purchases of tickets with the card.

Same Purchase Location. The two brands in the tie-in are consumed at the same location. Many products and services are related in that they are

Source: Courtesy of Duracell International.

purchased at the same location. For example, grocers sometimes run promotions in which consumers who buy a certain amount at their store within a specified time period may obtain dinnerware at a low price.

Same Theme. The two brands in the tie-in have a common theme. Tie-ins with a common theme can enhance attention and memorability of the theme while generating excitement and sales. For example, to celebrate their common 30th anniversary, Philadelphia-based Wawa Food Markets and the Ford Motor Company had a tie-in sweepstakes called "The Great Mustang Give-away" in the summer of 1994.[42] Each day for a whole month Wawa Food Markets gave a free Ford Mustang to the winner of the sweepstakes. To add to the excitement and the history of the event, the award featured a different model year of the Mustang each day.

Same Cause. The two brands in the tie-in support the same cause. In one form of tie-ins that has increased substantially, companies promise to donate a certain fraction of their sales to a consumer's favorite cause or charity. Such tie-ins not only have the immediate benefit of increased sales but also increase the goodwill the firm enjoys with the target consumers. For example, during the 1994 Winter Olympics, VISA promised to double its donation to the 1994 Winter Olympics as consumers increased usage of its card. In 1994, Nabisco ran a "Go to Bat For Youth Baseball" promotion, in which teams won equipment by redeeming seals from certain Nabisco brands. Many grocers in southern California donate 6 percent of the purchases made with special certificates to the nonprofit organizations that sell these certificates.

This list of potential bases for tie-ins is not exhaustive. Indeed, the potential for novel and exciting tie-ins is limited only by the creativity of promoters.

Management of Tie-ins

Because more than one party is involved, tie-ins require more coordination than most other promotions. Here are some simple tips that make the management of tie-ins more effective:

- *Keep the promotions simple.* During the planning stage, tie-ins may get complicated as each party adds on what seem like creative variations. However, simplicity ensures smooth coordination of the promotion and easy adoption for consumers.
- *Share responsibility.* The responsibilities and costs of the promotion should be shared equally between the partners or made proportionate to the benefit.
- *Have similar images.* The images of the two brands or parties that are in a tie-in should not clash. A brand with a brash image should not associate with one with a classy image. One with a low-quality image should not associate with one with a premium image.
- *Have clear benefits and economies.* Perhaps the most important principle in a tie-in is that the economy to the firm should be easy to obtain and the benefit to consumers should be clear.

BONUS PLANS

Competition in the airline industry heated up after its deregulation in the late 1970s. Under pressure to retain consumer loyalty and reduce price shopping by consumers, American Airlines started a Frequent Flier program in 1981. Members received credit for each flight based on the miles traveled. These credits could accumulate toward a free ticket for the traveler's own benefit or that of his or her relatives. Because many tickets were paid for by businesses, but these benefits were not claimed by businesses or taxed by the government, the program was immediately popular with the public. Also, because miles would accumulate faster if consumers stuck to one airline, it stimulated loyalty. Other airlines soon followed American's lead. By summer 1993, consumers had earned billions of frequent flier miles from airlines, worth millions of dollars in free travel.[43] Thus, while the program has reduced price shopping to some extent, it has added to the airlines' debts.

Bonus plans are programs in which a buyer can accumulate points toward free purchases of the same or other products. Frequent flier plans are probably the best-known example. However, most hotels, car rental agencies, telephone services and credit card companies have their own system of bonus points, many of which also reward users with travel miles.

Many retailers and some manufacturers have had or tried to develop such plans jointly or individually. The primary purpose of bonuses is to attract and keep loyal consumers. Such plans become particularly relevant when the product is frequently purchased, competition is strong enough that product differentiation is hard to maintain, and consumers focus on price differentials. In that environment, bonuses are a means to attract loyalty and focus consumers' attention away from price. Bonuses are also a promotional tool that large firms with high overheads can better afford than small firms and new entrants. Thus large, established firms can use these programs to compete effectively against price competition from new or small firms.

Principles of Effective Bonus Plans

Four important principles can ensure that bonus plans achieve their goals and do not become just another cost for the firm: targeting promising consumers, instilling loyalty, creating value, and creating a profit center.[44]

Targeting Promising Consumers Since the purpose of bonus plans is to build loyalty, firms need to target customers who are likely to be loyal or heavy consumers of their product. For example, MCI designed a successful Friends and Family program by promising customers a discount on their long-distance phone bills if the people they call also subscribed to MCI. Customers who were most likely to be attracted to this program were those who made the most long-distance calls. These customers are also the heaviest users of long-distance service and thus the most profitable segment.

Building Loyalty The starting point of a good bonus plan is to reward customers for sticking to the brand. The reward structure should be designed so that the longer a customer stays with a program the better the benefits. This approach pays off especially over the long run, because loyal customers are easier to retain over time and pay higher prices. The bonus plan of the airlines is a good example. After a consumer earns miles for one free ticket, he or she is still motivated to stay with the airline in order to earn a second or third free ticket for family members. Further, as consumers join programs of other firms that also offer free miles on the same carrier, their commitment to the first airline increases.

Creating Value for Customers The bonus plan should create new value that a consumer could not just buy or get in the market. MCI's Friends and Family is a program that created value for consumers. Consumers had a sense of belonging to an MCI-sponsored club through which they could make calls less expensively. Burger King's premium offer of Lion King character figurines is another example of value creation. In contrast, Transmedia's restaurant discount card appears to be a bad bonus plan for restaurants. In exchange for up front cash from Transmedia, restaurants have to offer 25 percent off on meals for cardholders. The program is attractive to restaurants who are in current financial distress. However, the steep loss in margin hurts over the long run, without enhancing the image of the restaurant or its product offering.

Creating a Profit Rather than a Cost Center Bonus plans should be structured to become profit centers over the long run. For example, as each consumer enrolled more of his or her friends in MCI's Friends and Family program, MCI's circle of loyal consumers widened. Airlines' frequent flier programs could be classified either as profit or loss centers. Initially, as the airlines accumulated frequent flier miles, they had to give away seats they could otherwise have sold. However, the airlines minimized that loss by raising the number of miles to earn an award, charging for issuing or reissuing awards and limiting the number of available seats and dates for claiming awards. For example, by assigning awards only to undersold flights the airlines can limit the costs of the award to the marginal costs of each additional passenger, which may be very small. Moreover, airlines can profit substantially by bulk sales of frequent flier miles to other firms that participate in the programs, such as car rental, hotel, and telephone companies. Participating firms use these miles as their bonus plan to increase exposure for their own brands, widen their clientele base and retain loyal customers. For example, American Airlines currently has over 25 partners in its AAdvantage program (see Exhibit 12-11).

▼ EXHIBIT 12-11. Participants in the AAdvantage mileage program.

Hotels	Airlines
Conrad Hotels	Canadian Airlines International
Forte Hotels	Cathay Pacific Airlines
Forum Hotels	Hawaiian Airlines
Hilton Hotels and Resorts	Qantas Airways
Hilton International Hotels	Reno Air
Holiday Inns	Singapore Airlines
Inter-Continental Hotels	TWA
ITT Sheraton Hotels, Inns, Resorts and All-Suites	
Marriott Hotels, Resorts and Suites	**Other Businesses**
Vista Hotels	Citibank AAdvantage Visa or MasterCard
Wyndham Hotels and Resorts	MCI Long-Distance
	SNET MobileCom
Car Rental Agencies	American AAdvantage Money Market Fund
Avis Rent A Car	The American Traveler Catalog
Hertz	FTD/Florists' Transworld Delivery Association

Source: Lawrence, Jennifer (1994), "Yet Another Way to Peddle Frequent Flier Miles," *Advertising Age*, March 7, 8.

These principles are also relevant to other consumer promotions, especially those that seek to build consumer loyalty, such as mail-in premiums or in-pack coupons.

SWEEPSTAKES AND CONTESTS

In 1985, Cap'n Crunch, a presweetened cereal made by Quaker Oats, was losing market share in response to heavy competition from brands owned by Kellogg Co. and General Mills.[45] To revitalize the product and give the Cap'n a new image, Quaker Oats launched a "Where's the Cap'n?" contest. The company dropped the picture of Cap'n Horatio Crunch from the package, and challenged consumers to find his whereabouts. Consumers needed to buy three boxes of the cereal to get each of the three clues. Lucky drawings from the pool of correct entries received a reward of $100. Quaker promoted the contest with $6 million in TV advertising, print advertising, a music video, coupons and $1 million in prizes. The campaign was very popular, leading to a 25 percent increase in sales. The promotion was so strong that it led to the publication of a newsletter distributed at university campuses, the formation of Cap'n Crunch societies on some university campuses, and a follow-up contest by Quaker.

Sweepstakes are drawings in which winners are determined purely by chance (see Exhibit 12-12). Because of this, sweepstakes cannot be limited to buyers of the brands. **Contests** are games or combinations of games and sweepstakes in which winners are at least partly determined by rules, like the Cap'n Crunch or Butterfinger contest in the opening example. Compared to contests, sweepstakes are easier to execute and less likely to go wrong. For example, in May 1992, Pepsi ran a contest in the Philippines in which it promised a one-million-peso ($40,000) tax-free prize for anyone getting the lucky number 349 on a Pepsi bottle cap. Unfortunately, Pepsi found out that over 800,000 bottle caps had mistakenly gotten the number 349. When Pepsi refused to pay, people were outraged. They organized marches, boycotted Pepsi products, bombed or torched over 30 Pepsi trucks and threatened the lives of Pepsi executives. The contest ended in a debacle, an $11 million loss for the company and immense ill will.[46] A spell-your-name contest from Pepsi in the United States awarded prizes to names with very few vowels to minimize odds of winning. However, many members of ethnic groups had names with no vowels, which upset Pepsi's calculations and led to enormous costs for the company.[47]

The primary purpose of sweepstakes and contests is to boost sales by generating excitement about the product. For example, the "Where's the Cap'n?" contest by Quaker Oats propelled the brand into the leadership position for the segment. Contests can also serve as an occasion to educate or reeducate consumers about the product. Firms can achieve this goal by building clues or features of the game around attributes of the product. But the educational role of sweepstakes is limited to supplementary material included with the drawing.

Sweepstakes come under the jurisdiction of federal and state laws (see Chapter 2). Laws vary from

▼ **EXHIBIT 12-12.** Sweepstakes offer.

Source: Courtesy of Kraft USA.

state to state, which creates problems for firms in defining the legally correct terms for the offer. In addition, the huge payoffs that consumers can get lead them to resort to legal challenges if they believe they were misled, whether intentionally or unintentionally. Exhibit 12-13 gives some guidelines to minimize such problems and ensure successful sweepstakes.

SAMPLING

Prior to the Fall 1995 launch of Windows 95, general manager Bradley Chase supported a risky promotional strategy: putting one million copies of the test version of the software in the hands of computer specialists, software analysts, reporters and influential customers. The test versions had bugs, which could devalue the product and turn off these influential users of the program. But Chase gambled that the users would forgive the bugs because of the product benefits and would become a potent source of positive word-of-mouth for the product.

His gamble worked. Reviews by these early users created tremendous publicity and expectations of the product. Consumers were eager to have it. And when sales were authorized on August 24, 1995, shoppers were lining up well before 12:01 A.M. to get their hands on the product. Analysts estimate that worldwide, Microsoft may have sold three million copies in the first four days after launch, and four to six million copies in the first three weeks. Microsoft also launched a heavy advertising and promotional campaign for the launch, spending as much as $200 million. But the advertising was lackluster. Analysts credited the publicity arising from the test versions as the major reason Windows 95 became the most widely known and successful new product in the history of business.[48]

Sampling is the free or subsidized availability of the product for consumers' trial. It is the most effective means of disseminating knowledge about and generating trial of a new product. Because a sample offers direct experience of the product, it reduces much of the risk to consumers of buying a product they have never experienced. If the product also serves an unmet need of consumers, and if the price is right, sampling is a method of choice for generating quick trial and sales. The huge success of the introduction of Windows 95 in August 1995 can be attributed primarily to the free distribution of test versions of the product to important reporters, reviewers and users.

In 1993, firms spent about $587 million on sampling, making it one of the fastest growing of consumer promotions.[49] The main reason for the rapid growth of sampling is the recent shift in firms' expenditures from incentives to value pricing, for fear that incentives could devalue a brand in the eyes of consumers. **Value pricing** is a strategy in which firms maintain a fixed price that reflects the fair value of the brand, while promoting the brand with advertising and informative, sales promotions. Sampling is one of the most effective, informative promotions. Another possible reason for the shift to sampling is the large number of new products and the proliferation of brands, both of which make it difficult for consumers to be familiar with all the alternatives in the market.

▼ **EXHIBIT 12-13.** Guidelines for developing successful sweepstakes.

Terms
- Clarify who is eligible.
- Indicate states where promotion is not valid.
- Make sure "No purchase necessary" is conspicuous.
- Declare termination date of promotion.
- Clarify random drawing procedures.

Entries
- Offer a facsimile entry.
- Put no limit on mail entries, but restrict submission to one per outer envelope.
- State that mutilated or illegible entries will be disqualified.
- State that mass entries will be disqualified.
- Declare deadline for entries.
- List addresses for sending entries, requesting more information and getting list of winners.
- Disclaim liability for lost entries, quality of merchandise and lost or stolen entries.

Prizes
- Detail prizes.
- Disclose odds of winning.
- Affirm that decision of judges is final.
- When applicable, state that prizes will be handed only to parents or guardians.

Winners
- Indicate that winners will be notified.
- State that winners will be required to sign an affidavit of eligibility.
- Reserve the right to use winners' names and photographs for publicity.

Source: Adapted from a list prepared by Wood, Douglas J. (1994), "Hands On: Playing by the Rules," *PROMO* Magazine (April), 49.

Types of Sampling

Sampling can take three basic forms: samples, trial coupons and trials.

First, firms can physically distribute the product to consumers. Items distributed in this way are called **samples.** For example, small boxes of cereals, soaps and shampoos are often mailed to consumers for them to try at leisure in the privacy of their homes.

Second, the firm may distribute a coupon with a much higher face value than regular coupons to subsidize the risk to the consumer of trying the product or service. Such coupons are called **sampling coupons** or **trial coupons**. If the coupon has the same value as the price of a product, the offer is equivalent to a free sample. For example, restaurants frequently offer coupons with high face values for new locations, menus, or serving times. Compared to sampling, trial coupons save the firm the cost of distributing samples while giving consumers the burden of redeeming the coupons or paying part of the cost of the product.

Third, firms may make the product or service available to consumers to try out in a specific location and time period. This form of promotion is called **trial**. For example, most automobile dealers let buyers test-drive a vehicle they are considering buying. Some grocery stores offer trials of new food items at specific locations in their aisles on weekends. Many magazine publishers will allow consumers to try out their publication for an entire month to reduce consumers' uncertainty about the product. Alternatively, they might hope that preference (or at least inertia) would inhibit cancellations. Mail-order book and compact disc clubs allow members the option of trying out a monthly selection and returning it if it does not meet with their satisfaction.

Costs of Sampling

Sampling is one of the most expensive types of sales promotions. Per delivered unit, sampling can cost several times more than coupons. For example, Exhibit 12-14 presents the costs of Procter & Gamble's launch of Dawn dishwashing detergent. The exhibit shows that the costs of sampling for a new product could dwarf the costs of all other types of promotions.

Several factors account for the higher costs of sampling. To begin with, the firm incurs the cost of producing and packing the sample. Even though the materials per se may not amount to much, the fixed costs of setting up the manufacturing system and processing the special-size units are substantial. Second, sampling involves distribution costs. These costs could be more than those of coupons, because the samples weigh more than the coupon and need special packages. Third, because of the bulkiness of

▼ **EXHIBIT 12-14.** *Procter & Gamble's promotion cost for launch of Dawn.*

Item	Cost ($ millions)	Cost (% of total)
Sampling	$30.3	85%
Price packs	3.7	10
Trade deals	1.8	5
Total	$35.8	100%

Source: Adapted from data in Alice MacDonald and John A. Quelch, *Procter & Gamble (B)*, 1983 Harvard Business School Publishing, Cambridge, MA.

samples, they cannot be easily delivered through newspapers and magazines, as coupons are. Firms resort to the more expensive route of mail distribution. Of course, the use of mail also provides the benefit of more accurate targeting of the samples, especially if an appropriate mailing list exists.

In addition, sampling involves hidden costs in the form of the risks of the product being misused. Such misuse occurs because the sample by design is targeted to new users who are unfamiliar with the brand or even the product category. In their eagerness to try the new item, consumers may not read the instructions carefully, leading to dissatisfaction with the product or, what could be worse, harm to themselves. Because of the high costs of sampling, it is still used sparingly, accounting for 11 percent of the consumer promotion budget in 1993.[50]

Conditions Favoring Sampling

When exactly should sampling be used, given its high costs? Sampling is most useful when the product has one or more distinct advantages over competing brands but the target consumer is unaware of or has forgotten about these advantages. The most urgent situation is the introduction of new products. Indeed, many experts consider sampling to be essential to the launch of new products. But sampling may not be restricted to that situation alone. A second situation for sampling is when a product has been modified and the firm would like consumers to give it another try. Yet another occurs when the product remains the same, but the firm would like to target a new segment of consumers who are not currently using the brand. A fourth situation favoring sampling is poor visibility of a small-share brand in a crowded market. Competing advertising and promotions may increase the level of noise to the point that a smaller brand's efforts are inadequate. In such cases, sampling can cut through the noise and provide a brand with unique exposure and trial.

▼ EXHIBIT 12-15. Comparison of effectiveness of incentive promotions.

Criteria of Promotion	TYPE OF PROMOTION					
	Rebates	Media Coupon	In-pack Coupon	On-pack Coupon	Price Pack, Peel-off Coupon	Trial Coupon
Sales increase	Medium	Low	Medium	Medium	High	Very high
Repurchasing	Low	Low	High	High	Low	Medium
Price discrimination	Very high	High	Low	Low	Very low	Medium
Brand switching	Medium	Medium	Low	Medium	Medium	High
Cost	Medium	Medium	Low	Low	Medium	High

COMPARING METHODS OF PRICE PROMOTIONS

The different types of consumer promotions can be classified into those that are primarily incentive and those that are primarily informative (see Exhibit 12-1). The former can be further classified into price-oriented incentives and nonprice incentives. By using price-oriented incentives, firms can give consumers an effective price-cut in a variety of ways. By way of recapturing some of the important aspects of this chapter, we compare five of these means: rebates, media coupons, in-pack coupons, on-pack coupons and trial coupons. The discussion in this chapter as well as that in Chapter 9 suggests five criteria by which these forms of promotion can be compared: sales increase, repurchase, price discrimination, brand switching and cost.

Exhibit 12-15 compares the effectiveness of consumer incentive promotions using these five criteria. Note especially the trade-off between price discrimination and sales increase. The reason is that price discrimination occurs when an incentive is targeted only to one segment, thus limiting sales response. On the other hand, sales increase most when the incentive is available to as many consumers as possible, resulting in little discrimination. The goals of a promotion determine which of these methods become more attractive.

SUMMARY

Consumer promotions are efforts by a manufacturer to appeal directly to consumers without having to depend on the retailer. A major benefit of this independence is that the firm avoids the low pass-through that occurs with trade deals. However, consumer promotions involve a number of costs, considerable organization and many risks. Firms generally hire the services of a promotion agency to plan and execute various aspects of their promotions.

There are a large variety of consumer promotions. Manufacturer coupons are certificates from firms offering consumers some fixed saving off the retail price of the product if they meet some conditions. These coupons can be distributed through print media, mail, the product package or the retailer. Coupons help manufacturers price discriminate among consumers better than other methods of price discounting. They can also help to build a pattern of repurchasing and persuade or remind consumers about the product's benefits.

Rebates or refunds are a guarantee by firms to reimburse consumers by mail for the purchase of a product subject to certain conditions. Rebates involve delayed consumer response and require far more effort to redeem than do coupons. As a result, rebates have higher discriminatory power, and require higher face values than do coupons, to motivate consumer redemption.

Price packs are special packages through which a firm offers a temporary lower price to consumers. Price packs are primarily an incentive promotion. They have a minimal communicative or price discriminatory role.

Premiums are gifts that a firm gives consumers free or at a reduced price, without any special benefit to the producer of the gift. Premiums can be of three types: in-pack or with-purchase premiums, mail-in premiums and self-liquidating premiums. Premiums earn the goodwill of consumers, provide an incentive to buy the product, can be designed to stimulate repurchases, and remind consumers of the benefits of the product.

Tie-ins are joint promotions for two or more items by one or more firms. A good tie-in creates an economy for the firms or new benefits for consumers. A link between the two items in a tie-in can enhance the value of the promotion.

Bonus plans are programs in which a buyer can accumulate points toward free purchases of the same or other products. The primary purpose of bonuses is to attract and keep loyal consumers. The loyalty from bonus plans arises primarily from the external incentive and not from intrinsic preference for the brand.

Sweepstakes are drawings in which winners are determined purely by chance. Contests are games in which winners are at least partly determined by rules. The primary purpose of sweepstakes and games is to boost sales by generating excitement about the product.

Sampling is the free or subsidized availability of a product for consumers' trial. It is the most effective means of disseminating knowledge about and generating trial of a new product. However, it is also one of the most expensive types of sales promotions. It is most useful when the product has one or more distinct advantages over competing brands, but the target consumer is unaware of or has forgotten about these advantages.

QUESTIONS

1. What are coupons? Why are they used?
2. Is the high misredemption rate of coupons worth their benefits? Is the low redemption rate an advantage or disadvantage to firms?
3. Coupons are supposed to lead to an increase in sales. How large is this increase? How long does it last? Is all of it due to redemptions?
4. What is the rate of coupon redemption?
5. How are coupons used, or what is the pattern of sales and redemption? How and to what extent can coupons be misredeemed?
6. Are there any long-term effects of redemptions?
7. What type of consumers redeem coupons?
8. Why did General Mills slash coupons from its promotional mix?

9. What theories are available to explain the long-term effects of coupons? Which of these theories is right? Why?
10. When is a coupon drop profitable?
11. What are rebates? How do they differ from coupons?
12. What is the reason for using price packs instead of a discount or a coupon?
13. What is the logic of a premium? What makes for great premiums?
14. What was the reason for the phenomenal success of Burger King's Lion King figurines?
15. How do tie-ins differ from premiums?
16. Should tie-ins have a link? Explain fully.
17. How do firms benefit from offering tie-ins? Why do tie-ins motivate sales?
18. When exactly should sampling be used, especially given its high costs?
19. How can manufacturers use bonus plans effectively?
20. Explain the difference between sweepstakes and contests.
21. What are the benefits of sweepstakes and contests? What care should manufacturers take in offering sweepstakes and contests?

NOTES

1. Adapted from *PROMO* (1994), "*PROMO* Salutes the 1994 'Reggie' Winners" (April), R1.

2. Blalock, Cecelia (1994), "Retailer Snared in Coupon Sting," *PROMO* (February), 14.

3. Blattberg, Robert C., and Scott A. Neslin (1990), *Sales Promotion: Concepts, Methods and Strategies*, Englewood Cliffs, NJ: Prentice-Hall.

4. The Editors (1995), "Still Bullish On Promotion," *PROMO Magazine's Source Book 95*, Wilton, CT: *PROMO*, 12; Wascoe, Dan Jr. (1994), "NY Woman Has Made Coupon Refunds Her Business," *Star Tribune*, February 20, 3D; Heitsmith, Glenn (1994), "Couponing. Sea Change Or Tidal Shift," *PROMO* (April), 43–46; Deveny, Kathleen (1994), "Awash in Coupons? Some Firms Try to Stem the Tide," *The Wall Street Journal*, May 10, B1, B6.

5. Some sources cite a higher figure, for example, see *PROMO* (1994), "Coupon Watch" (April), 114.

6. *Marketing News* (1991), "Global Coupon Use Up; U.K., Belgium Tops in Europe," August 5, 5.

7. Lawrence, Jennifer and Scott Hume (1992), "Supermarkets Flock to 'In-Ad' Coupons," *Advertising Age*, October 5, 29.

8. Narasimhan, Chakravarthi (1984), "A Price Discrimination Theory of Coupons," *Marketing Science* 3, 2 (Spring), 128–147.

9. Raju, Jagmohan S., Sanjay K. Dhar, and Donald G. Morrison (1994), "The Effect of Package Coupons on Brand Choice," *Management Science* 13, 2 (Spring), 145–164.

10. Rothschild, Michael, and William C. Gaidis (1981), "Behavioral Learning Theory: Its Relevance to Marketing and Promotions," *Journal of Marketing* 45, 70–78.

11. Deveny, Kathleen (1994), "Awash in Coupons? Some Firms Try to Stem the Tide," *The Wall Street Journal*, May 10, B1, B6; *Marketing News*, "Global Coupon Use Up."

12. Bawa, Kapil, and Robert W. Shoemaker (1987), "The Effects of A Direct Mail Coupon on Brand Choice Behavior," *Journal of Marketing Research* 24 (November), 370–376; Neslin, Scott A. (1990), "A Market Response Model For Coupon Promotions," *Marketing Science* 9, 2 (Spring), 125–145.

13. Cole, Catherine A. (1990), "Factors Influencing Coupon Redemption Rates, Repeat Purchase Rates and Coupon Profitability: A Review and Agenda for Future Research," *Review of Marketing*, Volume 4, Valarie A. Zeithaml, ed. Chicago: American Marketing Association.

14. Srinivasan, Srini S., Robert P. Leone, and Francis J. Mulhern (1995), "The Advertising Exposure Effect of Free Standing Inserts,"*Journal of Advertising* 24, 1 (Spring), 29–40.

15. Inman, Jeffrey J., and Leigh McAlister (1994), "Do Coupon Expiration Dates Affect Consumer Behavior?" *Journal of Marketing Research* 31 (August), 423–428.

16. Blattberg, Robert C., Thomas Buesing, Peter Peacock, and Subrata Sen (1978), "Identifying the Deal Prone Segment" *Journal of Marketing Research*, 15 (August), 369-377.

17. Mittal, Banwari (1994), "An Integrated Framework for Relating Diverse Consumer Characteristics to Supermarket Coupon Redemption," *Journal of Marketing Research* 31 (November), 533–544; Blattberg and Neslin, *Sales Promotion*.

18. Blattberg et al., "Identifying the Deal Prone Segment"; Blattberg and Neslin, *Sales Promotion*.

19. Green, Corliss L. (1995), "Media Exposure's Impact On Perceived Availability And Redemption Of Coupons By Ethnic Consumers," *Journal of Marketing* (March/April), 56–64.

20. Mittal, "An Integrated Framework for Relating Diverse Consumer Characteristics to Supermarket Coupon Redemption."

21. Bawa and Shoemaker, "The Effects of a Direct Mail Coupon on Brand Choice Behavior."

22. Blattberg and Neslin, *Sales Promotion*.

23. Dodson, Joe A., Alice Tybout, and Brian Sternthal (1978), "Impact of Deals and Deal Retraction on Brand Switching," *Journal of Marketing Research* 15 (February), 72–81.

24. For an in-depth discussion of these three viewpoints, see Tellis, Gerard J., "Do Deals Increase, Decrease or Have no Effect on Brand Repurchase," paper presented at the Marketing Science Conference, Duke University, Durham, NC, 1989. Working paper available from the author. See also Ehrenberg, A. S. C., Kathy Hammond, and G. J. Goodhardt (1994), "The After-Effects of Price-Related Consumer Promotions," *Journal of Advertising Research* (July/August), 12–20; Inman, McAlister, Scott D. Davis, Jeff J. Inman, and L. McAlister (1992), "Promotion Has a Negative Effect on Brand Evaluation—Or Does It? Additional Disconfirming Evidence," *Journal of Marketing Research* 24, 1, 143–148; Neslin, Scott A., and Robert W. Shoemaker (1989), "An Alternative Explanation for Lower Repeat Sales After Promotion Purchases," *Journal of Marketing Research* 26, 2, 205–213.

25. Actually the study found a very small increase in repurchase rate among buyers who were not users of the brand, and a very small decrease in repurchase rate among regular buyers of the brand. The authors expected these changes to erode over time. Bawa, Kapil, and Robert W. Shoemaker (1989), "Analyzing Incremental Sales From A Direct Mail Coupon Promotion," *Journal of Marketing* 53 (July), 66–78.

26. Blattberg and Neslin, *Sales Promotion*.

27. Glionna, John M. (1992), "Coupon Clubs Try Not To Get Clipped," *Los Angeles Times*, November 8, E1.

28. *Ibid.*

29. Heitsmith, Glenn (1994), "General Mills Cuts Prices, Promotion Spending," *PROMO* (May), 6.

30. *Ibid.*

31. Fitzgerald, Kate (1994), "Paper Coupons Losing Lure in High-Tech Store," *Advertising Age*, March 21, s-14.

32. Adapted from Richard, Gibson (1992), "Pious Town Finds Mighty Temptation in Coupon Clipping," *The Wall Street Journal*, February 21, A1.

33. Association of National Advertisers, *Consumer Promotion Seminar Fact Book*, 7.

34. Hofmeister, Sallie (1994), "In the Realm of Marketing, 'The Lion King' Rules," *New York Times*, July 12, D1, D17.

35. Thus a premium differs from a tie-in in which the manufacturer of the gift would be a party to the tie-in and share in the promotion.

36. *PROMO* (1994), "Hot Premium Promotions: Seven Sure Winners" (May), 27.

37. *PROMO* (1994), "Milking Loyalty With Premiums" (May), 120.

38. Smith, Amie (1994), "Value-Added Campaigns Shine in Annual Awards Program," *PROMO* (April), r1–r11.

39. Schlossberg, Howard (1993), "Tie-ins Take Off," *PROMO* (March), 59–62.

40. *PROMO* (1994),"Pizza Hut Delivers Toys To Families" (July), 48.

41. Hofmeister, "In the Realm of Marketing, 'The Lion King' Rules."

42. Fitzgerald, Kate (1994), "Pair of 30-year-olds Give Away Car a Day," *Advertising Age*, May 16, 38.

43. Reynolds, Christopher (1993), "Frequent Fliers Tempt Fate Number 2: Taxes," *Los Angeles Times,* June 6, L2.

44. O'Brien, Louise, and Charles Jones (1995), "Do Rewards Really Create Loyalty?" *Harvard Business Review* (May-June), 75–82.

45. Adapted from Franz, Julie (1986), "Quaker Oats Finds Cap'n Crunch Loot With Hide-and-Seek," *Advertising Age,* May 26, 53.

46. Drogin, Bob (1993), "Bottle Cap Flap Riles The Masses," *Los Angeles Times,* July 26, A1, A8; Reuters Report (1992), "Pepsi Caps the Damages On a Promotion Gone Flat," *New York Times,* August 18.

47. Baum, Laurie (1987), "How Beatrice Lost At Its Own Game," *Business Week* 3, 2, 66.

48. Based on Johnson, Bradley (1995), "Windows 95 Opens With Omnimedia Blast," *Advertising Age,* August 28, 1, 32; Johnson, Bradley (1995), "Microsoft's Chase Starting Up Windows 95," *Advertising Age,* August 28, 4; AAII Staff Roundup (1995), "Is Microsoft Getting Its Bang For Buck, Peso or Rand?" *Advertising Age,* September 18, I3; Jaben, Jan (1995), "Eighth Wonder of the World," *Advertising Age,* September 18, I3.

49. *PROMO* (1994),"Still Bullish on Promotion" (July), 35.

50. *Advertising Age* (1994), "Sampling Continues to be Popular Choice," May 16, 38.

PART

IV

Planning Advertising and Sales Promotion

13

Setting Goals for Advertising and Sales Promotion

In June 1990, Wieden & Kennedy, a hot agency from Oregon, won the $75 million Subaru account, triumphing over an original list of 150 agencies.[1] The amazing thing about the selection was that the agency had no experience with automobile advertising. Indeed, it had no major clients besides Nike, and was called by Subaru to the final round of 6 candidate agencies as a wild card. Further, Subaru was quite aware of the agency's inexperience, and was particularly concerned about its insensitivity to the pressures

dealers faced to sell cars *immediately.* However, Wieden & Kennedy had developed outstanding ads for Nike, which had won almost every major advertising award in the previous three years. Some of its campaigns had fashioned highly popular and profitable brands. Nike itself regained leadership of the athletic shoe market a few years after rehiring Wieden & Kennedy as its advertising agency in 1986.

Wieden & Kennedy was proud of its achievements and not apologetic about its inexperience. Its pitch for the Subaru account was not free of arrogance or self-interest. Dan Wieden opened by saying, "Subaru is an incredibly significant piece of business for this agency. It serves two important goals for Wieden & Kennedy. It brings us outside of Nike and gives us potential to stretch our wings creatively."[2] In the same spirit, David Luhr, director of account services, said, "Diversity has been our key objective for the year and you fit very nicely into that objective; you're a perfect match for us."[3] The agency personnel proceeded to spell out their view of the advertising Subaru needed. They claimed that car ads had become very similar, with all of them portraying glowing commentaries about their respective models. What Subaru needed was radically different advertising based on "truth." It would be free of the myth and fluff that permeated competitive ads, even mock their appeal to style and status. Subaru was sufficiently impressed by the boldness and originality of the presentations to award the agency the account despite its misgivings.

Subaru of America, a company founded by two Americans in 1968, imported cars from Fuji Heavy Industries of Japan and marketed them in the United States. In the early 1980s the cars were a hit with consumers. Sales soared due to Subaru's low price and good engineering, which included such unique features as front- and four-wheel drive. Subaru's ad slogan, "Inexpensive and Built to Stay That Way," captured the car's appeal with consumers. However, from a high of 183,000 cars in 1986, sales fell to a dismal 109,000 cars in 1990. Similarly, profits fell from a high of $94 million to a $30 million loss, and the stock price fell to one-sixth its peak. This dramatic decline was probably caused by a rise in the price of Subarus due to appreciation of the yen. The lack of a marketing strategy, weak advertising and a dated ad slogan probably aggravated the decline. To reverse its fortunes, Fuji Heavy Industries purchased Subaru of America in January 1990, triggering an account review that led to Subaru's hiring of Wieden & Kennedy.

Many of the ads that Wieden & Kennedy produced for Subaru were bold and original. They emphasized Subaru's simple value and mocked the status claims of rivals' ads. One Subaru ad, for example, stated, ". . . if it (the car) improves your standing with neighbors then you live among snobs with distorted values" (see Exhibit 13-1). Some advertising critics praised the ads for their originality and humor. Some advertisers copied Wieden & Kennedy's execution tactics, while some car companies used advertising themes similar to those Wieden & Kennedy developed and Subaru never adopted. Overall, the work of Wieden & Kennedy was true to its reputation as a hothouse for creative ads.

However, a major portion of automobile advertising involves designing displays, posters, and regional ads for the benefit of distributors. Such advertising material had to be approved by the regional sales executives and distributors. It was here that Wieden & Kennedy's inexperience hurt the agency. Many of the national and regional ads by Wieden & Kennedy were severely criticized by Subaru's regional sales executives and distributors for

Subaru would like to introduce a special new feature for '92. The truth.

THIS IS TOUGH TO ADMIT:

But a car is a car. And its sole reason for existence is to get you safely from point A to point B. And back again.

It won't make you prettier. Or younger. And if it improves your standing with the neighbors, then you live among snobs with distorted values.

Now, let's discuss the "Driving Experience": To feel the exhilaration. To experience a sense of power. To be master of the open road and everything before you.

Please. That may have been true in 1918. But it's not true anymore. Not with extended urban gridlock. And the escalating costs of operating an automobile in the 90's.

Still, cars are necessary and the question is, what type of car should one buy?

The answer: The best machine for you. Yes, machine. Let's get rid of all the marketing glamour about the automobile and see the car for what it really is. A machine, and in choosing a machine there are many things to keep in mind.

How long will it last? How well will it do the job? Does it fit my budget? Could I get a comparable one for less? Will I keep having to repair it? And do I like the way this machine feels and looks?

After comparing cars and subjecting them to your checklist, we think you'll find a brand that always makes the finals—Subaru.

Subaru cars are, in short, intelligently designed machines. In fact, we've often been accused of "over-engineering." That's bad? To engineer something so it lasts longer and works better? We don't think so.

For one, we believe cars should have a longer life expectancy. That's why we try to do everything we can to help make sure the Subaru you buy now will be around for years to come. Case in point: 93% of all Subaru cars registered in the last 10 years are still on the road and running today.[1]

Secondly, we think a car should also be engineered to handle whatever occurs—bad weather, busy drivers, crummy roads, etc. Which is why we offer All-Wheel Drive and why many of our vehicles come with the 4-Channel Anti-Lock Braking System which monitors each wheel to help prevent the car from locking-up during emergency stops.

Now which Subaru should you consider? Basically it depends on what you need. And how much you want to spend. To give you an idea of the breadth of our line, we'll briefly mention the cars that cover the gamut.

The Subaru Justy, the Subaru Loyale, the Subaru Legacy and the new Subaru SVX:

The Justy* is for the person who just wants simple, dependable transportation. The Justy offers excellent gas mileage. "On Demand"™ All-Wheel Drive. Rugged engineering. An Electronically Controlled Variable Transmission which provides the power of a 5-speed with the convenience of an automatic. And the Justy does everything in such a superior low-budget way that for two years in a row it was named *MotorWeek's* "Best Bargain Car of the Year."

The Loyale* is what's referred to as a subcompact. Which is misleading because every Loyale is designed to carry five comfortably and the Loyale wagon has more cargo space than the Corolla wagon (just one more reason why Subaru has become the #1 selling import wagon in America).[2] The Loyale also has the same basic engine design as a Ferrari Testarossa. Vented disc brakes. And rack and pinion steering.

The Legacy* is our luxury car. Starting at $12,999* (aren't luxury cars supposed to cost a lot more?) it offers the amenities you'd only expect from a much higher-priced automobile: over 90 cubic feet of passenger space. Air conditioning. 130 horsepower engine. Multi-point fuel injection. And the Legacy, too, has not gone unnoticed. When the Legacy was introduced, *Car and Driver* stated: "The Legacy looks and feels like a quality piece. It makes us think Subaru's leap into the mainstream is going to create some surprisingly large ripples."[2]

Lastly, the new SVX. With a 230 horsepower engine capable of producing over 220 pounds of torque, the SVX can do what you'd expect from a muscle car. Like travel from 0 to 60 in 7.3 seconds.[3] But it also has the features you'd only expect from an absurdly priced luxury sedan: Climate control. Driver's-side air bag. Room for four hefty adults. And priced around $25,000,** the All-Wheel Drive SVX is built in the Subaru tradition of durable, reliable transportation.

As *Car and Driver* put it: "The SVX dives out of the fog of car wars like a Zero...It will not only change what the word 'Subaru' means, it will raise the all-around performance ante for subsequent cars."[4]

Well, that covers about everything. And we'd just like to say and scream and shout again—That a car is nothing more than a machine. And may the best machine win.

Subaru. What to drive.™

[1] Based on R.L. Polk & Co. registration statistics. [2] June, 1989. [3] *Road & Track's* Guide to the New SVX, May 1991. [4] September, 1991.
*Suggested retail price new $500 Extra Value Discount. Does not include dealer preparation, inland transportation, taxes, license and title fees. Dealer's actual price may vary.
*Suggested retail price. Does not include dealer preparation, inland transportation, taxes, license and title fees. Dealer's actual price may vary.
**Suggested retail price may vary.
For additional information, 1-800-284-8584. © Subaru of America, 1991.

Subaru Justy
Subaru Loyale
Subaru Legacy
Subaru SVX

Source: Courtesy of Subaru of America, Inc.

being too image oriented, not sales oriented. The ads apparently did not have enough information on attributes, value and price relative to competing brands to bring customers into the stores. The criticisms of the distributors and sales executives were also fueled by their high sales quota in the face of the recession. Wieden & Kennedy's staff slowly and reluctantly came to understand this practical dimension of car advertising. The staff did not really believe in it, disdained such work, and struggled to integrate it with the agency's initial platform for Subaru.

With Wieden & Kennedy's advertising, Subaru managed to hold on to its market share of 1.3 percent in 1992, for sales of about 105,000 cars. It achieved this feat during a recession. But the company never came close to meeting the target of 150,000 cars set by its parent, Fuji. Many sales executives and distributors and at least one advertising reporter blamed the advertising for this failure. Early in 1993, Subaru launched a new model, the Impreza, with an advertising campaign aired during the Super Bowl (see Exhibit 13-2). The ads were barely noticed against the attention-getting ads of Pepsi, McDonald's and Lee Jeans. Impreza sales ran 50 percent below target.

In the face of these apparent failures, Fuji appointed a new sales and marketing manager for Subaru. One of the first acts of the new manager was to fire Wieden & Kennedy, Subaru's ad agency for two years.

Why did Wieden & Kennedy fail with the Subaru account, given its outstanding work for Nike? Why were its ads apparently so ineffective? The recession of 1991–1992 probably played a major role. However, not every agency is fired after a recession. This chapter argues that Wieden & Kennedy's loss of the Subaru account was due to its failure to articulate goals for the advertising campaign. Such goals would have given direction to the campaign, won agreement among the conflicting parties, and provided a clear basis on which to evaluate the campaign.

The definition of goals is the first and most critical step in any planned activity, such as an advertising campaign. A **goal** of advertising is a statement of a result that a firm desires from advertising. The fictitious dialogue between Alice and the Cheshire cat provides a classic lesson on the importance of goals:

> Alice said, "Would you tell me, please, which way I ought to go from here?"
>
> "That depends a good deal on where you want to get to," said the cat.
>
> "I don't much care where," said Alice.
>
> "Then it doesn't matter which way you go," said the cat.[4]

Advertising is a complex social phenomenon that can adopt a variety of communication strategies. Each strategy has different outcomes that vary over individuals and over time. The choice of communication strategy, media strategy, budget and schedule depends on the goal of the advertiser. If a firm does not have an advertising goal, then it does not matter how it advertises, or what outcomes flow from that advertising.

This chapter discusses the role of goals in planning an advertising campaign. It has two parts. The first part describes the characteristics of well-defined goals. The second part reviews the relationship among the effects of advertising, to ascertain how these effects serve as goals for the advertising campaign.

CHARACTERISTICS OF WELL-DEFINED GOALS

What are the key characteristics of goals? We can identify four important characteristics: goals should be explicit, precise, inspiring yet attainable, and set jointly by all parties involved in implementing them.

Goals Should Be Explicit

When faced with a crisis, firms often change advertising agencies, hoping for a reversal of fortunes.

▼ **EXHIBIT 13-2.** A Wieden & Kennedy ad for Impreza.

"HILL-HOLDER" :30
SBOB 4346
Wieden & Kennedy
3/93

ANNCR VO: Introducing the new Subaru

Impreza

hill-holder.

You'll find it

on all

our manual transmissions.

At the moment, the brake is on, so the wheel isn't moving. The brake is now being released.

The new Impreza

is out of gear,

and the wheel still

hasn't moved.

It's not often a car can impress you

simply by

standing still.

The new Subaru Impreza. It's not just another new car.

(MUSIC OUT)

The new Subaru Impreza.
What to drive.

Source: Courtesy of Subaru of America, Inc.

Once a new contract has been signed, both agency and client work under the enthusiasm of a new contract, full of hope about the future. The agency is motivated by the challenge that the previous agency failed to meet. The client congratulates itself on making a radical change of agencies. What is often overlooked is the explicit definition of goals of the relationship and the advertising campaign. Explicit goals facilitate communication between advertiser and agency, and provide the foundation of a successful relationship. Lack of explicit goals is a prescription for trouble, if not disaster, in such a formal relationship. Each party *assumes* the other has the same understanding of the problem, solution, and desired result. But as Chapter 5 indicates, perceptions can vary even among individuals, let alone between organizations.

In the case of Wieden & Kennedy, the agency never translated its early pitch for the account into a set of goals for the advertising campaign, the marketing strategy, or its relationship with Subaru.[5] For its part, Subaru had a small portfolio of subcompact and compact models in stiff competition with many Japanese, American and European brands, most with much greater experience, market share and resources. It did not communicate to Wieden & Kennedy its goal for each brand and model. The relationship, strategy and campaign proceeded in the absence of explicit goals.

Goals Should Be Precise

A precise goal is one that focuses on a measurable variable, states the desired change in that variable, and states the time period within which the change is desired.[6]

For example, the goal "Reverse the bad fortunes of Subaru" seems an appropriate response to Subaru's situation in 1990. But it is vague because it focuses on the term "bad fortunes," which has no accepted measures. A more precise statement of the goal could be "return Subaru to profitability," because it contains the variable "profitability," which has well-known measures such as return on sales, equity or assets. The statement of a goal in terms that are measurable forces agency and advertiser to think through the reason for advertising and state precisely what they would like it to achieve.

The definition of desired change states how much the advertised brand's sales or market share should improve. Advertising is rarely totally effective or ineffective. Given a sufficiently high level of adver-

tising, some change can always occur. The key issue is whether the change is the one desired by the advertiser, and one for which the advertiser is willing to spend the necessary resources. Unless advertiser and agency agree on the change, they would not know what they have to achieve, and what they must do to achieve it. For example, the goal "return Subaru to profitability" is still imprecise because it does not state the *degree of change* desired. Moreover, profitability can be affected by sales, prices or costs. The goal still does not state which of these three variables will be changed to improve profitability. A more precise goal would be "increase Subaru's annual sales from 100,000 to 150,000." Note that this change is a massive 50 percent increase, yet is still 24 percent below Subaru's peak sales in 1987. Thus the statement of change clearly spells out how big a task lies ahead.

A further refinement of the goal is the statement of the time period within which the change will be achieved. This aspect of goals is especially important for advertising, because changes wrought by advertising are neither instantaneous nor of infinite duration. Most advertising professionals are aware of this fact. But most agencies are reluctant to be pinned down to precision when stating goals, and would like to argue that advertising works in an undefined "long term." That long term may mean several months or years. Some old economic studies even claimed that the effects of advertising lasted for 10 years. However, solid research in marketing indicates that those estimates are wrong for technical reasons.[7] Moreover, recent research indicates that the response to advertising generally begins to occur either early on (in the first few weeks or a month), or never.[8] Most of the effect probably occurs in the first few months.

Including a time period in the statement of the goal ensures that the agency and advertiser do not work under contrary assumptions of the effects of advertising. It gives the agency adequate time to achieve the change. It also renders the agency accountable to the advertiser, requiring it to deliver results within a finite time period. Both advertiser and agency can then determine more realistically whether the change can be affected in the time limit specified, how much effort is required, and how that effort should be deployed.

Subaru chose Wieden & Kennedy because it was impressed by the agency's creative presentation and its past record for creative work. Subaru's greatest problem was that the agency was immersed in the task of developing outstanding creative but not sensitive to Subaru's need to sell cars. In particular, the agency did not sense the *urgency* to sell cars under which Subaru's sales executives and distributors operated. Unfortunately, Subaru did not spell out this urgency to Wieden & Kennedy in terms of precise goals.[9] In particular, it did not impress on the agency the sales target of 150,000 cars (a 50 percent increase) that Fuji had imposed on the company for 1992.

Goals Should Be Inspiring but Attainable

Small goals do not inspire people to action as much as big, challenging goals. Humans are always fired up by the tall order, the previously unattained target, the apparently unattainable task. Goals must challenge in order to inspire. However, a *physically* unattainable goal can trigger discouragement, frustration, despair and inactivity. Subaru's sales executives and distributors probably experienced some of these feelings in Spring 1992, because of sales targets set by Fuji.

The rise of Japanese automobile exports to the United States in the 1980s, and the recession of 1991, led to pressures on Japanese automobile manufacturers to restrict their U.S. exports and increase their imports of U.S. automobile parts. In response, Japan's Ministry of International Trade and Industry (MITI) decided to give Japanese automobile manufacturers "voluntary" export quotas. In April 1992, it decided that Subaru's quota for 1993 would be its 1992 sales level. In order to guarantee a high quota for future years, Fuji decided to unilaterally increase its export of cars to Subaru of America by an additional 30,000 to 40,000 units for 1992. Fuji imposed this increase even though 1992 was a recession year, distributors had huge stocks of unsold cars, and the company had not improved its sales position much from 1990.[10] Further, the increase was imposed without any discussion of the support that would be necessary to move so many more cars. The new, high sales target put a tremendous burden on Subaru's regional sales executives and distributors. It frustrated them and increased their criticism of the company and its advertising agency.

Goals Should Involve All Relevant Parties

Goals need to be decided among all parties involved with implementation. When goals are an outcome of a negotiated agreement among superiors and subordinates or client and agency, all parties are committed to them and will try to achieve them. Wieden & Kennedy's relationship with Subaru of America occurred at a time in the latter's organization when goals were rarely determined in agreement among relevant parties. This lack of communication contributed to the failure of the advertising campaign.

For example, Fuji had a good rationale for increasing its exports to Subaru of America, even though the latter's sales were flat. However, the way it went about imposing sales goals on its U.S. subsidiary was counterproductive. A better strategy would have been for Fuji to explain the problem of externally imposed quotas to Subaru's executives, ask for solutions, and negotiate with them a high but attainable sales target with concomitant marketing and advertising support. That was not the way events evolved.

However, a deeper conflict of goals kept thwarting Wieden & Kennedy's relationship with Subaru. Wieden & Kennedy wanted to develop a distinct image for Subaru. But its purpose in doing so was to win plaudits for itself and reduce its dependence on Nike. As Dan Wieden stated in his initial pitch to Subaru, the Subaru account would "bring us outside of Nike and give us the potential to stretch our wings creatively."[11] Wieden & Kennedy made little effort to understand the dynamics of the automobile business. Unlike athletic shoes, automobiles are sold by dealers working one-on-one with car buyers. Dealers are under tremendous pressure to sell cars, and use various techniques to convince buyers of the cars' merits. They want ads that are urgent and draw consumers into stores for specific advantages that their cars enjoy over competitors' cars. They want ads that move cars *immediately*.

Jerry Cronin, Wieden & Kennedy's creative director for the Subaru account, slowly came to understand the dealers' concerns. However, as he realized that their passion for sales clashed with his interest in creative image building, he disdained their values and grew disgusted with the account.[12] Senior Subaru executives stood between the agency and the distributors. While they were aware of the differences between the two parties, they failed to articulate goals of the advertising campaign that were acceptable to all parties. For example, Subaru never explicitly presented the target of 150,000 cars for 1992 as the goal of Wieden & Kennedy's advertising campaign. Nor did the two parties agree on alternative sales goals. Yet, in the absence of alternative goals, that target became the criterion by which the advertising was evaluated.

Wieden & Kennedy's failure with the Subaru account can be attributed to a failure to set goals for the advertising campaign. While each of the parties had its own goals, these goals were not explicit, precise, reasonable or mutually agreed upon. As a result, although the advertising campaign was creative and clever, it failed to please the distributors or sales executives, it failed to get customers into the stores as the latter expected, and it failed to meet Subaru's sales quotas.

How should Subaru have gone about setting goals for its advertising campaign? The best starting point would have been to identify the potential effects of its advertising and how they were related to each other. One framework of analysis, the hierarchy of effects, can help advertisers set goals appropriately. The next section of the chapter addresses this topic.

HIERARCHY OF EFFECTS

The chapters on persuasion in Part II of this book suggest that advertising can have a variety of effects. For decades, researchers have been interested in knowing whether these effects of advertising are related in a sequential chain so that the response to one variable leads to the response to another. Such a chain of sequential responses is called the **hierarchy of effects.** Under the assumption that such a relationship does in fact exist, some researchers have proposed models that describe the effects of advertising as intermediate stages in a hierarchy of events ranging from the first exposure to the ad to the ultimate purchase of the brand. This section first presents a classification of the different effects of advertising, then presents different models of the hierarchy of effects, and lastly discusses the use of these models.

Classification of Advertising Effects

From a managerial viewpoint, the various effects of advertising can be classified as outcome variables and process variables.

Outcome Variables An **outcome** is the change in consumer behavior desired by an advertiser, such as a consumer's trial of a brand or a brand's sales to all consumers. A vast number of behavioral variables exist. They can be conveniently classified into four groups: brand choices, purchase intensity, market outcomes and a firm's accounting variables (see Exhibit 13-3).

The term **brand choice** refers to a consumer's selection of a brand, which can be decomposed into trial, repurchase or switching. **Trial** is a consumer's first choice of the brand. Every subsequent choice of the same brand is called a **repurchase.** The choice of another brand is called a **switch.** The separation of choices into trial, repurchase and switching gives a good picture of a brand's appeal. Trial indicates the breadth of consumer experience of a brand, repurchase indicates the depth of consumer loyalty toward a brand, while switching indicates the brand's immediate pull relative to a rival brand's.

▼ EXHIBIT 13-3. Key measures of the effects of advertising.

Effects	Type	Key Measures
Processes	Cognitive	Recall, recognition
	Affective	Warmth, liking, attitude
	Conative	Persuasion, purchase intention
Outcomes	Brand choice	Trial, switching, repurchase
	Purchase intensity	Timing, frequency, quantity
	Market	Market share
	Accounting	Unit sales, revenues, profits

Purchase intensity refers to the extent that a consumer buys a brand over time. It can be decomposed into timing, frequency and quantity. *Timing* refers to when consumers buy a brand, *frequency* to how often they do so, and *quantity* to how much of it they buy each time. Information on timing, frequency and quantity can help to determine what precise effects promotions have on consumer behavior. As explained in Chapter 10, if promotions change only the timing of purchase, then consumers may be responding to them opportunistically; however, if promotions lead to increases in frequency or quantity bought, then they may be causing net gains for the promoter. Thus decomposing purchases into timing, frequency and quantity can provide an insightful analysis of consumer purchase.

When we sum up or aggregate the choices of individual consumers at the level of the firm, we get the *accounting variables* of a firm's performance, sales, revenues and profits. The sum of all quantities of a brand purchased by consumers within a particular time period and region gives **sales in units**. The product of unit sales and the price per unit gives **revenues. Profits** are revenues less costs. Firms often measure the effects of advertising in terms of sales or profits rather than consumer choices, because the former variables are easier to track and record. Among the accounting variables, sales is generally a more proximate measure of advertising effects than profits, because the latter is dependent on a host of other cost factors.

Market outcomes measure a firm's performance in relationship to that of other firms in the market. The variable most commonly used is a brand's market share. The market share of a brand is the sales of a brand divided by the sales of all competitors in the market. Tracking market share is particularly important when brands are very similar to each other and the overall market is not growing. In that case, any improvement in a brand's performance can only come at the cost of another brand. Changes in the market shares of the various brands track such performance.

Process Variables **Process variables** are measures of mental activities, if any, that occur between a subject's exposure to an ad and the outcome in his or her behavior. Examples of process variables are awareness, persuasion, and purchase intention. If advertisers ultimately desire some change in consumer behavior (the outcome variables) why should they measure the process variables? Indeed, some researchers suggest that knowledge of the intervening or process variables is unnecessary. This approach to understanding consumer behavior is called the "black box," because it views the process of consumer decision making as unknown.

Nevertheless, the process variables are very important for two reasons. First, outcome variables, such as sales or market share, are affected by a number of variables besides advertising, such as price or promotion. Moreover, sales are not very sensitive to advertising, but are very sensitive to price and promotion (see Chapters 10 and 14). Thus, sales alone may not be a good measure of advertising effectiveness. Second, the process variables indicate

why, how and where in the sequence of decisions that leads to consumer purchases, the advertising is effective or ineffective. Thus they provide an opportunity for advertisers to adjust their ads. Third and most important, the process variables can be measured more easily and quickly during various stages of producing the ad. To the extent the process variables are related to sales, change in the process variables caused by advertising may be used as an early predictor of sales change.

For example, some managers at Subaru thought Wieden & Kennedy's advertising was ineffective. However, they did not know why it was ineffective. Was it ineffective because consumers did not notice it, did not attend to it, did not recall it, or were not persuaded by it? Or was it ineffective because the price and promotional support for the cars was inadequate? Research on the process variables could have answered these questions, and enabled the advertisers to alter the campaign for greater effectiveness.

The various process variables can be classified as cognitive, affective or conative. The term **cognitive** refers to thought processes, and includes variables such as attention or awareness. The most commonly used measures of attention and awareness are recall and recognition, discussed in Chapter 14. The term **affective** refers to emotions and includes a very broad spectrum of emotions that can be aroused by advertising (see Chapter 7). However, advertising researchers tend to focus on a few affective variables such as warmth, liking and attitude. The term **attitude** refers to a consumer's underlying predisposition to act. Researchers sometimes use the term narrowly as an affective variable, and sometimes broadly to encompass all three dimensions of response: cognitive, affective and conative. The term **conative** covers variables that are proximate to behavior, such as persuasion and purchase intention. At times the term *conative* is also used to include behavior.

Exhibit 13-3 summarizes the classification of the process and outcome variables. The key question that has interested professionals in advertising is not the classification of advertising's effects per se, but the relationship, if any, that may exist among the process variables. In particular, the question has revolved around whether consumers pass through any fixed sequence of stages or effects from the moment of exposure to their final behavior in response to the ad. People who think so have designed various models of the hierarchy of effects that describe their beliefs.

Models of the Hierarchy of Effects

One of the first hierarchy of effects models proposed was AIDA, which was discussed as early as the 1920s.[13] **AIDA** is an acronym for the four variables involved in the hierarchy:

$$Attention \rightarrow Interest \rightarrow Desire \rightarrow Action$$

The rationale for this model was that a consumer was likely to pass though these stages when going from ad exposure to ultimate action such as purchase. Also, as the consumer passed through the hierarchy, he or she became more likely to take the desired action. Since then researchers have proposed a number of hierarchy models for different products, consumers or situations. In an attempt to put some order in this field of study, a Stanford marketing professor, Michael Ray, suggested that the various hierarchies could be classified into one of three types, which he described as follows:[14]

Learning hierarchy:
cognitive → affective → conative

Dissonance/attribution hierarchy:
conative → affective → cognitive

Low-involvement hierarchy:
cognitive → conative → affective

Note that Ray uses the broader classification of the cognitive, affective and conative variables to simplify the discussion of the various hierarchies.

Learning Hierarchy The **learning hierarchy** describes how a consumer buys a product only after learning about it. It applies to decisions that the consumer considers important and undertakes carefully. Examples include the purchase of a house, car, major appliance, insurance or education. The AIDA model is one type of learning hierarchy.

Dissonance/Attribution Hierarchy The **dissonance/attribution hierarchy** is so called because it can be explained either by dissonance theory or attribution theory. **Dissonance theory** suggests that consumers adjust their thoughts and feelings to be consistent with their behavior (see Chapter 6). **Attribution theory** suggests that consumers develop reasons for their observed behavior, even though such reasons may not have motivated the behavior. An example of the dissonance/attribution hierarchy is:

$$Purchase \rightarrow Liking \rightarrow Brand\ comparison$$

This hierarchy applies to products for which consumers choose a brand for the first time without searching or evaluating alternatives. They may do so because of the similarity of alternatives, or the unavailability of alternatives, their familiarity with one brand, or the low cost of the brand relative to the cost of shopping for alternatives. An example of such a brand choice is a freshman who first leaves home and lives in a dorm. Among the numerous purchases he has to make to live on his own is the choice of a laundry detergent. He is overwhelmed with the alternative brands available, and the number of choices he has to make. He purchases Tide because his parents bought that brand. He has no problems with the brand, keeps buying it on subsequent purchases and begins to like it. When comparing alternative brands on shopping occasions, he justifies his purchase of Tide by surmising that it is the most reliable or popular brand.

Low-Involvement Hierarchy The **low-involvement hierarchy,** based on Krugman's theory of low-involvement purchases by consumers (see Chapter 4), applies to products such as toothpaste, yogurt, fast food or TV programs. An example of the hierarchy is:

$$Purchase \rightarrow Recognition \rightarrow Recall \rightarrow Liking$$

In such situations a product category is so inexpensive that consumers prefer to learn about a brand by buying and using it rather than by an extensive prepurchase study of the alternatives. If consumers do not like their trial purchase they can just toss out the item, or not repurchase the brand. Consumers may not try out every brand in the category to determine the best. Rather they might just repurchase a brand that they find satisfactory. Their prior purchase leads them to recall the brand name, which helps in its repurchase. Repeated purchase of this brand ultimately leads to liking. An example of such a purchase would be a new or untried brand of cereal, or a new snack.

Use of Hierarchy of Effects

The hierarchy of effects was quite popular at one time, and has become an integral part of advertising research in some firms. Several factors account for its appeal.

First, the hierarchy provides a nice way to select and organize the vast number of variables that can be used to measure the effects of advertising.

Second, once an advertiser has identified the hierarchy that is relevant for a brand, it can estimate the **transition probabilities**, or fraction of consumers who pass from one stage to another. Suppose research or past experience with the model indicates that these fractions are as follows:

$$.6 \qquad .5 \qquad .4 \qquad .1$$
$$\textit{Awareness} \rightarrow \textit{Interest} \rightarrow \textit{Evaluation} \rightarrow \textit{Trial} \rightarrow$$
$$\textit{Repurchase}$$

In this case, each 500 consumers who became aware of the new product by advertising would lead to 6 adopters of the product.[15]

Third, the use of the hierarchy of effects with the transition probabilities provides the advertiser with a method to define a set of goals that are measurable, related to each other and clearly indicate the change desired.

However, the simple elegance of the hierarchy of effects models may mask an important problem. The models are not universal. This means that the models may not apply the same way to all product categories, or any one model may not apply to all consumer segments who purchase a product. For example, some impulsive buyers will not follow the learning hierarchy, even for an expensive product such as an automobile. As of yet, we do not have sufficient research to indicate the product categories to which each of the three hierarchy models apply.

So advertisers must first determine if the hierarchy of effects applies to their product category. Further, if the model does apply, they need to determine whether consumer segments follow one or several different hierarchies. Finally, if they find the appropriate model for the various segments, managers must still determine which particular variables best describe the stages of consumer response to advertising. Only then can they begin to calculate the transition probabilities that describe what proportion of consumers pass from one stage to another.

To use this framework effectively advertisers should carry out research to ascertain the following for their brand:

- Identify the key variables that measure consumer response to advertising.
- Postulate one or more hierarchies of effects that best describe how advertising affects consumer behavior.
- Test the alternate hierarchies to see which best fits their category.
- Calculate the transition probabilities that describe the fraction of consumers who pass from one stage of the hierarchy to another.

Understanding the hierarchy of effects for a particular brand is essential to setting goals for advertising, measuring the effects of advertising and evaluating that advertising. Consider again the example of Subaru. Fuji had given Subaru managers a clear sales target of 150,000 cars for 1992. Subaru had hired Wieden & Kennedy to help it better advertise its cars. Was that advertising supposed to *help* the company sell 150,000 cars? All parties probably implicitly believed the answer was yes.

The critical question was *how?* How would advertising lead to a 50 percent increase in sales over 1991, for a total of 150,000 cars in 1992? What changes in the intervening process variables would be required? What exact hierarchy of effects would consumers traverse between seeing an ad and buying the car?

Subaru had identified no such hierarchy. Wieden & Kennedy identified no such hierarchy. In the absence of any hierarchy, neither party knew how the advertising would help achieve the sales target. In the absence of any alternative goals, the only measure of the success of the advertising remained the target of 150,000 cars. Yet Subaru had not explicitly proposed that target as a goal of the advertising, and Wieden & Kennedy had not accepted it as one. Each party to the relationship had its own goals and expectations, which were not explicitly linked by a hierarchy of effects.

SUMMARY

The definition of goals is the first and most critical step in any planned activity, such as an advertising campaign. Goals should be explicit, precise, inspiring yet attainable, and determined by all parties involved in implementing them. The best starting point for setting advertising goals is an understanding of the effects of advertising.

The various effects of advertising can be classified as outcome variables and process variables. Outcome variables can further be classified as consumer choices, market outcomes and the accounting variables of performance, depending on the level of analysis. The process variables can be classified as cognitive, affective and conative, corresponding to the three different dimensions of mental activity.

The effects of advertising are probably related to each other by a hierarchy that is specific for each brand or product category. The transition probabilities describe the fraction of consumers who pass from one stage of the hierarchy to another. Identifying this hierarchy and its corresponding transition probabilities for a particular brand is essential to setting goals for advertising, measuring the effects of advertising and evaluating that advertising.

QUESTIONS

1. Are goals important for an advertising campaign? Why?
2. What does the term *hierarchy of effects* mean? What are the different types of hierarchies? How do they differ from each other?
3. Is knowing the hierarchy of effects of an advertising campaign important when setting goals for the advertising? Why?
4. What alternatives to the hierarchy of effects can a firm use when setting goals? Explain.
5. Why did Subaru hire Wieden & Kennedy? Was it a wise decision?
6. Evaluate Subaru's working relationship with its agency. Could it have done better? How?

7. Why did Subaru terminate its contract with Wieden & Kennedy? How could Wieden & Kennedy have fared better?

NOTES

1. Based on Rothenberg, Randall (1996), *Where the Suckers Moon: The Life and Death of an Advertising Campaign,* New York: Vintage Books; Armstrong, Scott (1996), "How Should Firms Select Advertising Agencies? Review of *Where the Suckers Moon, Journal of Marketing,* 60, 3, 131.
2. Rothenberg, *Where the Suckers Moon,* 157.
3. *Ibid.*
4. Carroll, Lewis (1966), *Alice's Adventures in Wonderland,* New York: Delacorte Press/Seymour Lawrence.
5. Rothenberg, *Where the Suckers Moon,* 334.
6. Colley, Russell H., *Defining Advertising Goals for Measured Advertising Results,* New York: Association of National Advertisers, Inc.
7. The data used for determining such long-term effects were annual data. Research has shown that the longer term the data (i.e., years' rather than months' or days' worth), the longer the estimated duration of advertising's effects. Using more appropriate data indicates that advertising's long-term effects are in the region of weeks or months: Tellis, Gerard J. (1994), "Modeling the Effects of Advertising in Contemporary Markets: Research Findings and Opportunities," in *Attention, Attitude and Affect in Response to Advertising,* Eddie M. Clark, Timothy C. Brock, and David W. Stewart, eds. Hillsdale, NJ: Lawrence Erlbaum Associates; Clarke, Darryl G. (1976), "Econometric Measurement of the Duration of Advertising Effect on Sales," *Journal of Marketing Research* 13 (November), 345–357; Tellis, Gerard J., Charles Whiteman, and Byung-Do Kim (1989), "What Data Interval for Econometric Models of Advertising," working paper, University of Southern California.
8. Abraham, Majid M., and Leonard M. Lodish (1990), "Getting the Most Out of Advertising and Promotion," *Harvard Business Review* (May-June), 50–58.
9. Rothenberg, *Where the Suckers Moon,* 177.
10. *Ibid.*
11. *Ibid.,* 157.
12. *Ibid.*
13. Lipstein, Benjamin (1985), "An Historical Retrospective of Copy Research," *Journal of Advertising Research* 24, 6 (December), 11–14.
14. Ray, Michael (1973), "Marketing Communication and the Hierarchy of Effects," working paper, Report No. P-53 C, Cambridge, MA: Marketing Science Institute.
15. This number comes from multiplying the fraction of consumers who pass from one stage to the other.

C
H
A
P
T
E
R

14

Testing the Effectiveness of Advertising

The December 1991 issue of the *Journal of the American Medical Association (JAMA)* published three articles indicating that R. J. Reynolds's ads that featured the cartoon character Joe Camel prompted youth to take up smoking. The publication triggered enormous media attention, widespread condemnation of RJR's advertising and legislative action against the Joe Camel brand. One analysis found 172 newspaper articles, 82 editorials, 23 syndicated columns and 71 wire service reports on the *JAMA* articles.[1] Many were critical of Joe Camel and 32 editorials called for the banning or stricter regulation of the campaign. In 1992, a search of the Dialog information service revealed over 540 related stories in major daily newspapers.

The three *JAMA* studies also prompted a harsh response from then–U.S. Surgeon General Antonia Novella, who called on Reynolds to voluntarily stop the campaign. She asked magazines and retailers to discard or reject any signage that featured the cartoon character's likeness. In

1994, Surgeon General Joycelyn Elders picked up where Novella left off. Elders too called for a ban of Joe Camel advertising and for strict controls on all cigarette marketing practices. While the surgeon general has no authority to enforce a ban, her position signals government backing of the opposition to Joe Camel. The strongest move against Joe Camel came when the attorneys general of 27 states asked the FTC to ban the advertising campaign, and the FTC's staff itself formally recommended that the FTC do the same.

The hue and cry against Joe Camel prompted some members of the advertising community to call on R. J. Reynolds to voluntarily withdraw the campaign. They believed that negative publicity would lead to a total ban of all cigarette advertising—something that would adversely affect the entire industry. An editorial in *Advertising Age* stated that Reynolds should kill the campaign before "the call for an advertising ban . . . boil(s) over."[2]

Who exactly was Joe Camel and why did the *JAMA* studies whip up such antagonism against him? Old Joe, a camel in a desert scene, was a long-standing character associated with the Camel brand. In 1974, British artist Nicholas Price created Joe Camel, an anthropomorphic camel with a large nose, for a French ad agency. In late 1987, R. J. Reynolds introduced a revised version of Joe Camel to the United States. This version of Joe Camel had a wise-guy smirk, sported trendy clothes (sometimes including shades or a hat), and often appeared in attractive social contexts to depict an image of a "smooth character." This image became the nonverbal theme of the new advertising campaign for the brand. Many analysts thought the campaign revitalized the brand and reversed the long-term decline in its market share. However, critics felt that the campaign appealed to youth and explicitly prompted them to take up smoking. The appearance of the three articles in the *Journal of the American Medical Association*, which had supported antismoking efforts, seemed to scientifically back up this suspicion.

One study by Fisher et al. surveyed brand logo recognition among 229 three- to six-year-old children.[3] The researchers asked children to match 22 logos with 14 brand names of children's, adults' and cigarette products. The study found that the Disney Channel logo and Joe Camel were the most highly recognized among children's products and cigarette products, respectively. Recognition of Joe Camel increased with the age of the children, and was as high as that of the Disney Channel logo among six-year-olds. The authors concluded that "very young children see, understand and remember advertising" and "R. J. Reynolds Tobacco Company is as effective as The Disney Channel in reaching 6-year-old children."[4]

A second study, by Pierce et al., tried to determine whether tobacco advertising was targeted to young people to get them to start smoking.[5] The authors surveyed 24,296 adults and 5,040 teens in 1990, to determine which cigarette brand they purchased, which were most heavily advertised and which they smoked. The study also compared the results of this survey with a similar 1986 U.S. survey. The authors found that from 1986 to 1990, market share among younger smokers had increased for Camel but not for Marlboro. The authors concluded that "perception of advertising is higher among young smokers," "tobacco advertising is causally related to young people becoming addicted to cigarettes," and "cigarette advertising encourages youth to smoke, and should be banned."[6]

A third study, by DiFranza et al., tried to determine if RJR's advertising is more effective in promoting Camel cigarettes to children or adults, and if children see, remember and are influenced by cigarette advertising.[7] The study compared the recognition and appeal of the Joe Camel advertising campaign among high school students to that among adult drivers aged 21 to 87 years. The study concluded that Joe Camel ads were better known and preferred among students, and appealed to them more than to adults. The study found that as a result, "Camel's share of the illegal children's cigarette market segment had increased from 0.5 percent to 32.8 percent, representing sales estimated at $475 million per year."[8] The authors concluded that "Old Joe Camel cartoon advertisements are far more successful at marketing Camel cigarettes to children than adults."[9]

R. J. Reynolds claimed that the *JAMA* studies were flawed. It held onto its long-standing position that advertising did not prompt youth to take up smoking. Indeed, the company claimed that advertising did not increase the consumption of cigarettes at all; it merely affected which brand smokers purchased. The company refused to stop or even cut back on advertising with Joe Camel. On the contrary, it

fought opposition to the campaign in four ways: it sponsored studies that criticized the *JAMA* studies; it sponsored research to show that advertising did not prompt youth to smoke; it carried out an advertising and publicity campaign to support the advertising of cigarettes as a free-speech issue in keeping with the First Amendment to the U.S. Constitution; and it created goodwill with a public-service campaign designed to discourage underage smoking.

By the end of 1995, R. J. Reynolds seemed to have won the war over Joe Camel. No government agency passed any resolution against Joe Camel, while the opposition to Joe Camel seemed to have waned in the face of contrary evidence, and the advertising and publicity of R. J. Reynolds.

Why did the JAMA articles have such an impact? Why were they ultimately ineffective in prompting controls over the Joe Camel campaign? More generally, how effective is advertising? What precisely are its effects? These are some of the questions that you should be able to answer after reading this chapter.

ADVERTISING EFFECTIVENESS: SOME BASIC DEFINITIONS

The terms **effects of advertising** or **advertising effectiveness** refer to the changes advertising causes in the mental or physical state or activities of the recipient of an ad. The controversy about Joe Camel was in essence a controversy about the effects of advertising. Indeed, the billion-dollar question in advertising is, *does advertising really work?* If it does work, what exactly are its effects? The question is as pertinent today as in 1926 when John Wanamaker, a Philadelphia department store tycoon, was supposed to have said, "I am certain that half of the money I spend on my advertising is completely wasted. The trouble is, I don't know which half."[10] The question is one that persists—in the research lab, the market research firm, among media sellers, within the advertising agency, in the brand manager's office, in the corporate boardroom, in the medical community and among social scientists. The reason the question does not fade away is that even though research tools and data on advertising effectiveness have improved substantially over the years, the evidence is not conclusive.

At the same time, numerous parties have an enormous stake in the decision about advertising effectiveness. Generally suspicious of business activity, social critics have at various times asserted that advertising has a stranglehold on the minds of consumers and is the root of rampant materialism in contemporary society. Media owners and ad agencies like to believe that advertising has a strong influence on consumer behavior. Some media, such as newspapers, are heavily dependent on advertising revenues, while others, such as network television, are entirely dependent on this source of income. Advertising agencies have grown from small operations to major corporations on the widely held premise that advertising is crucial to launching new products and establishing major brands.

On the other hand, some promotion agencies would like firms to believe that sales promotion, not advertising, increases sales, so firms would spend more of their fixed budgets on sales promotions. Firms themselves believe that the effects of advertising are grossly exaggerated. Firms that operate in an environment of tight budgets often take a hard look at advertising budgets in order to trim ineffective advertising expenditures.

Various interest groups also have strong opinions about specific types of advertising. As the opening example illustrates, many in the medical community believe that advertising motivates people to take up or maintain the habit of smoking, and would like it to be banned. Their belief is probably motivated by the evidence that smoking causes severe lung diseases, and the inference that people would not take up smoking unless urged by some force, such as advertising. However, although the evidence that smoking causes lung disease is conclusive and not disputed even by cigarette companies, the evidence that advertising increases smoking is not. Cigarette companies in particular assert that their advertising merely helps to maintain their share of the market, not to initiate or increase cigarette consumption.

The debate about advertising effectiveness remains intense because the evidence itself is ambiguous despite centuries of advertising and decades of research on it. Why? Advertising is a complex phenomenon that takes a variety of forms and acts in consonance with many other factors. For example, advertising can take the form of images or words, organized to be seen or heard, communicated directly by an endorser or indirectly by story and drama. Each of these individual forms can be combined in many ways and can be communicated through a variety of media. Each form of advertising can have different effects on consumers depending on the environment and the state of the consumer. Advertising's effectiveness depends on human response, which is a complex entity. Humans act in response to a number of stimuli, of which advertising is only one.

The difficulty of evaluating advertising does not mean that no progress has been made, or that the problem is not solvable. To begin with, most researchers agree on the principles for evaluating advertising effectiveness. These principles derive from the scientific method to test causality between an independent variable (in this case, advertising exposure) and its effect (recall, sales). Moreover, progress in statistics, psychology and the other social sciences during the last few decades, and new methods for collecting data in the last decade have enabled researchers to more accurately measure advertising and its effects. These advances have spurred enormous strides in solving this problem.

Where do we begin? The best approach to understanding this problem is to explore three important aspects of advertising: the scientific approaches, methods of data collection and variables for studying the effects of advertising. The first two sections of this chapter explain the scientific approaches and data collection methods for studying the effects of advertising. The variables for evaluating advertising effectiveness depend on the goals of advertising (see Chapter 13). The third section of this chapter explains the measures for the key variables for evaluating advertising effectiveness. The fourth section summarizes the main findings of the effects of advertising on sales.

APPROACHES TO RESEARCHING ADVERTISING EFFECTIVENESS

We can evaluate advertising effectiveness through a variety of methods, which can be broadly grouped into two approaches: the laboratory experiment and the field approach. Each of these approaches has roots in different disciplines and serves different goals. Neither is universally superior: each has its advantages and disadvantages. Ideally, using both approaches together, or developing a hybrid method that combines the strengths of each, is better than using either one alone. Either one or the other approach permeates most ad testing today, so that thoroughly understanding both approaches is essential to an understanding of ad effectiveness. We first describe each approach, discuss its strengths and weaknesses, and then show how new hybrid methods can solve some of the problems of these traditional approaches.

Laboratory Experiment

Diana's Diner, a one-year-old restaurant, hires Bruce Johnson, a researcher, to study how its print advertising affects patronage by its clients. In particular, the restaurant wants him to evaluate three types of advertising: a simple informative ad, a glossy image ad, or no ad at all. He begins by designing three booklets. All three booklets look the same and contain the same news items, but differ in the ads for the restaurant within their pages. Booklet A has no ads for the restaurant, booklet B has a simple informative ad for the restaurant, and booklet C has a glossy image ad for the same restaurant.

Bruce then recruits 90 shoppers from a nearby mall and asks them to evaluate the readability of news in print. He divides them into groups of 30. Each group is assigned one type of booklet. Every shopper in a group is given his or her own copy of the same booklet. Bruce asks the shoppers to read the booklets in the room and evaluate their readability. After giving them 10 minutes to peruse the booklet, Bruce tells them to set it aside. He then tests the shoppers' comprehension of the material, and also their recall of messages in the ads and their intentions of eating at Diana's Diner.

After that, he debriefs the shoppers about the real purpose of the experiment. Finally, to evaluate the effectiveness of the different types of advertising, he compares the shoppers' responses on recall and intentions across the three groups.

The diner example describes a simple laboratory experiment. What are the characteristics of this experiment? What purpose does it serve? What makes its results valid?

Designing Experiments An **experiment** is a setup that manipulates one or more independent variables to observe their effect on a dependent variable of interest. A **factor** or **independent variable** is a suspected cause of a particular phenomenon, such as the type of advertising in the diner example. A **dependent variable** is a measure of the phenomenon, such as recall of advertising or intent to visit the restaurant in the example. The relationship a researcher expects between the dependent and independent variables is called a **hypothesis**. A **laboratory experiment** is one that occurs in an artificial environment, such as the room in the diner example. Laboratory tests of a TV ad prior to release are sometimes called **theater tests** because of the location used for testing them. The participants recruited for the experiment are called **subjects**.

The task that the subjects are given when they are recruited so as not to alert them ahead of time to the purpose of the experiment is called the **disguise.** If subjects guessed the purpose of the experiment, they would pay much more attention to an ad than they would in real circumstances. The disguise can also prevent subjects from guessing the researcher's hypothesis, and altering their response to confirm that hypothesis.[11] As a result, the experiment would be less realistic. Is the disguise deceptive? The disguise is not deceptive if it gets information from the subjects that is not of material interest to them (such as whether an emotional ad is more effective than a persuasive ad), and if the researcher debriefs subjects about his or her true intent after the experiment. However, if the disguise gets information that the subject would rather not divulge (salary, sexual preferences), it would be deceptive.

Exhibit 14-1 depicts Bruce Johnson's experiment as a matrix or table. The independent variables appear as headings of the rows or columns of the matrix, while the dependent variables are the entries in the cells of the matrix. The arrangement of the experiment (one independent variable with three levels of advertising, each shown to three groups of participants) is called the **design.** The level of the independent variable is called the **treatment** (in this example, the three treatments are no ad, simple ad

▼ EXHIBIT 14-1. Experiment with one independent variable and three treatments.

INDEPENDENT VARIABLE		
No Ad	Simple Ad	Glossy Ad
Responses of 40 subjects	Responses of 40 subjects	Responses of 40 subjects

and glossy ad). When an experiment manipulates more than one factor (such as price and advertising, as in Exhibit 14-2) then subjects in each cell receive more than one treatment. A cell of a matrix in which subjects are exposed to multiple treatments is called the **condition**.

In a well designed experiment, the number of conditions increases rapidly with the number of levels of independent variables (see Exhibit 14-2). For example, suppose Bruce Johnson believes that price could also affect the consumer's decision, in the following way: a high price without advertising would turn consumers away; a low price with a simple ad would attract some consumers, but a high price with a glossy ad would attract the most consumers. What would be an appropriate design to test his beliefs?

Table 14-2A gives one solution. One group of subjects sees no ad and faces a low price, another sees the simple ad and faces a low price, and a third sees a glossy ad and faces the high price. Is this design valid? The answer is no. The reason is that both factors (price and advertising) keep changing as we go from condition to condition. So we are unable to tell whether the difference between any two conditions is due to price or advertising. What then would be a valid design?

Table 14-2B is an illustration of a valid design. Its strength is that it fully crosses the three levels of advertising and the two levels of price, resulting in a 2×3 matrix of 6 cells or conditions. Now any two adjacent conditions differ by only one factor, so differences in the responses of subjects between those two conditions can be attributed to the effect of that factor alone.

Evaluating Experiments We can evaluate an experiment by its ability to test causality and achieve relevance. The former criterion is called **internal validity**, while the latter is called **external validity**.

Testing Causality The primary purpose of an experiment is to test if the independent variable affects or causes the dependent variable. In our example, the purpose is to determine if different types of advertising increase intention to visit Diana's Diner. How can Bruce Johnson determine this fact? The researcher can do so by ensuring that *the only difference among the conditions or groups of subjects is the difference in the independent variables*. In the example, Bruce has to ensure that the three groups of shoppers have the same type of room, booklet and environment, and differ only in the ads they see. Then, if he finds any differences in recall or intentions among these groups, he can attribute them to the ads.

What about individual differences in subjects' knowledge of Diana's Diner? Could these differences

▼ EXHIBIT 14-2. Design of multifactor experiments.

A. An invalid design

INDEPENDENT VARIABLES		
No Ad, Low Price	Simple Ad, Low Price	Glossy Ad, High Price
Responses of 40 subjects	Responses of 40 subjects	Responses of 40 subjects

B. A valid design

	INDEPENDENT VARIABLES		
	No Ad	Simple Ad	Glossy Ad
Low price	Responses of 40 subjects	Responses of 40 subjects	Responses of 40 subjects
High price	Responses of 40 subjects	Responses of 40 subjects	Responses of 40 subjects

not vary across conditions and cause differences in intentions? To avoid this problem, the researcher has to assign subjects to the different conditions randomly. **Random** assignment means that each subject has an equal chance of being in any of the three conditions. Then, for a large number of subjects (over 30) in each condition, the chance that individuals on average would have different prior knowledge across the conditions is very small. So, the observed differences in recall or intentions across the conditions would result primarily from differences in advertising.

A laboratory experiment can become a strong test of causality because the researcher can control differences among the conditions or groups of subjects as explained above.

Relevance **Relevance** refers to the extent to which the subjects' behavior in the experiment reflects their behavior in real life. Most laboratory experiments are weak on relevance. The reason is that subjects are pulled out of their natural environment and asked to observe the ads in artificial situations. Even if the researcher uses a good disguise, subjects' viewing of ads is far more free of distractions than it is in their normal lives. In addition, the subjects represent only a small and often selective sample of the general population. The researcher does not know how well that sample relates to the general population.

Thus experiments are strong on testing causality, but weak on relevance. This trade-off is intrinsic. As one controls the experimental conditions to ensure a better test of causality, one makes those conditions less representative of the real world.

Evaluation of *JAMA*'s DiFranza Study

With this background we are now in a position to evaluate the study by DiFranza et al., one of the three *JAMA* studies that stirred up the Joe Camel controversy. The reason the three studies had such an impact was that they appeared to be well-designed experimental studies that proved that the Joe Camel advertising *caused* youth to take up smoking. Thus they seemed to answer one of the great puzzles about smoking—why youth took to the habit despite the severe diseases caused by long-term smoking.

DiFranza and his colleagues conducted an experiment in which they compared (among other things) preference for Camel cigarettes among students in seven surveys conducted in the period 1976–1988 (before the new Joe Camel campaign) to that among students surveyed in the period 1990–1991 (after the Joe Camel campaign began). The subjects in the 1990–1991 survey saw seven Joe Camel ads *immediately before* the survey, while those in the 1976–1988 surveys were not shown any such ads. [12] The authors found that preference for Joe Camel had gone up a great deal from 1976–1988 to 1990–1991. From that difference in preference among the two sets of surveys, they estimated that "Joe Camel's share of the illegal children's cigarette market segment had increased from 0.5% to 32.8%, representing sales estimated at $475 million per year." [13] They attributed the increase to the Joe Camel campaign.

The problem is that this experiment changes not one but two factors between the 1976–1988 and 1990–1991 surveys. First, the 1976–1988 surveys were conducted before the Joe Camel campaign started, while the 1990–1991 survey was done after the campaign started. Second, students in the 1976–1988 saw no ads for Joe Camel or for any other cigarette brand just prior to the survey; students in the 1990–1991 survey were shown seven ads with Joe Camel *just prior to the survey*. So we cannot tell whether the huge differences in preference for Joe Camel across the two survey periods were due to the start of the campaign, as the authors alleged, or to exposure to seven Joe Camel ads. In particular, after students saw seven ads for a brand in quick succession, they would have been more conscious of that brand, and more likely to express preference for it (see Chapter 4). Also, after seeing so many ads for only one brand, students may have guessed the purpose of the study and expressed higher preference for Joe Camel to please the researchers.

A more valid design would have been to survey the 1990–1991 sample of students with *exactly the same questionnaire and method* administered to the 1976–1988 sample. Differences in preference for Camel cigarettes could then be attributed to the campaign. Alternatively, the authors could have surveyed two groups of 1990–1991 students, one after exposure to a couple of Joe Camel ads, and the other after exposure to a couple of ads for another brand or category. They would need to have developed adequate disguises so the students could not guess the research goal. Differences in preference for Joe Camel could be attributed to the Joe Camel ads. With DiFranza's simple design we can never tell whether the true cause for the increase in preference was the campaign, the impact of the seven ads, or demand bias on the part of students.

A second major conclusion of DiFranza was that ". . . Joe Camel cartoon advertisements are far more successful at marketing Camel cigarettes to children than adults."[14] This conclusion was based on comparing preferences of students aged 12 to 19 years with those of adults aged 21 to 87 years, after both groups saw the seven Joe Camel ads. The problem with this part of the study was that it intentionally omitted the responses of young adults aged 19 to 21 years. This segment was the target of the Joe Camel ads. A reanalysis of the data by partitioning the respondents into groups under 19, 19–24 and over 24 years shows that the 19- to 24-year-olds had the highest preference for Joe Camel.[15] Many discovery documents emerged out of a subsequent court case filed against R. J. Reynolds. These documents showed that DiFranza *deliberately* omitted these data and reclassified his analysis to reach his conclusion, and to avoid disproving his own theory.[16]

The other two *JAMA* studies also had problems, though none as serious as those with the DiFranza study.[17] Overall, as a group, poor design, poor analysis or questionable manipulation of data compromised the findings of the important studies on Joe Camel published by *JAMA*. This is one of the primary reasons judicial and legislative bodies did not move against the campaign. However, well-designed laboratory studies could find that cigarette ads encourage youth to smoke. For example, one laboratory study found that cigarette ads prompted nonsmoking adolescents to have more favorable thoughts about smokers, while antismoking ads diminished their evaluations of smokers. In addition, the FTC may now have evidence that R.J. Reynolds targeted underage smokers, and even developed Joe Camel for that purpose.[18]

Field Approach

In the **field approach** a researcher analyzes the relationship between advertising and sales from records of their occurrence in real or natural markets, without manipulating either variable. For example, Bruce Johnson could determine if the advertising for Diana's Diner was effective by examining the variation in weekly advertising expenditures and sales over the last year. If sales are up when advertising expenditures are up, and down when advertising expenditures are down, then the two variables are probably related. Field tests of an ongoing TV ad are sometimes called **on-air tests.**

A number of statistical methods can analyze such relationships precisely, to determine how strong they are and how likely they are to differ from chance occurrences. One simple method is regression analysis. **Regression analysis** is a statistical procedure that attempts to determine the effects of independent variables, such as price and advertising, on a dependent variable such as sales. By including in the analysis other variables (prices, promotions, seasons, holidays) that could potentially affect sales, **multiple regression** analysis can rule out or control the effects of these other variables on sales, to determine the sole effect of advertising. If the relationship between advertising and sales is still strong, the researcher may then attribute the changes in sales to advertising. However, the researcher may not assert causality without reservations because of two problems associated with regression: multicollinearity and reverse causality. The next section discusses these problems.

Evaluation of the Field Approach We can evaluate the field approach on the same two key criteria that we used for experimental analysis: testing causality and achieving relevance. In contrast to the experimental approach, the field approach is strong on relevance but weak on testing causality.

The field approach relies on historical market data on sales, advertising, pricing or other relevant variables. The researcher does not manipulate the firms and consumers to obtain these data. Thus these records represent actual consumers responding to actual stimuli such as advertising or pricing. They are thus highly representative of the real conditions in which consumers make choices. Thus regression analysis of these data has high external validity.

At the same time, the method has low internal validity, for two reasons: multicollinearity and reverse causality. **Multicollinearity** means that two or more independent variables change in the same way, so it is unclear which particular one influences the dependent variable. For example, a marketer of beer could plan major promotions just prior to and during various holidays to capture the increased beer consumption that occurs during these periods. The promotions are characterized by higher advertising and coupons, and lower prices in the stores for the brand. Sales are typically higher during these holidays. Is the increase in sales due to the holiday season, the advertising, the coupons or the lower prices? The simultaneous occurrence or **covariation** in these variables is called multicollinearity. Because regression analysis suffers from such multicollinearity, it cannot determine the effect of each variable separately and unambiguously.

Reverse causality means that the dependent variable could itself cause the independent variable. In the beer marketing example, sales and advertising are likely to be positively related. This positive relation may be because advertising increases sales, or because managers vary advertising in expectation of sales. In the latter case, when they expect sales to be high, they advertise more, and when they expect them to be low they advertise less. So the sales pattern could cause the advertising level. This relationship is called reverse causality, because the relationship is opposite to what a naive researcher would assume.

Returning to the Joe Camel example, because of problems of multicollinearity and reverse causality, researchers cannot determine the effects of tobacco advertising on teens' consumption of cigarettes by simply regressing the historical records of the latter variable on the former. Other factors, such as changes in culture, fads initiated by movies and music, and antismoking education in school could also affect teens' smoking (multicollinearity). Cigarette companies could also change the level of advertising over months or years to better match smokers' consumption of cigarettes (reverse causality).

While statisticians have developed methods to mitigate the problems of multicollinearity and reverse causality, no solution is better than obtaining better data. If current data are seriously deficient, then the best solution is to go out and collect fresh data. In the final analysis, good data alone can reveal the true effects of advertising. The limitations of historical data probably prompted the authors of the *JAMA* studies to carry out their research to collect fresh data. Unfortunately, their studies were also not without problems.

Field Experiment

As the preceding discussion argues, laboratory experiments and field data have opposing strengths on internal and external validity. While laboratory experiments are strong on determining causes (they have high internal validity) they are not representative of real situations (they have low external validity). While the field approach is representative of real situations, it is weak on determining causality.

Can the two approaches complement each other? Can they be joined to produce a better hybrid method?

The answer is yes. One hybrid method is a **field experiment**, an experiment in which the different levels of an independent variable are varied across time in one or more real markets. The independent variable could be advertising, pricing or some other variable the experimenter can control. The markets could be cities or regions similar to each other but unrelated in the sense that one market does not affect another. The effects of the independent variables are measured primarily in terms of sales across the cities (in addition to any other dependent variables the researcher may measure such as recognition, recall, persuasion). For example, suppose the test period extends for two months, June and July. During the test period, the researcher may increase the level of advertising in one city, but keep it constant in another city that forms the control. The effects of advertising on sales can be observed in both cities during the test period, as well as for many periods before and after the test. In addition, the pattern of sales can be observed for the same two months of many previous years.

The field experiment is relevant because sales result from the choices of subjects in natural markets. To the extent that the two cities differ only by the level of advertising or some other independent variable that the researcher controls, the experiment provides a good test of causality. In addition, because sales during the test period can be compared with sales before and after the tests, as well as with sales during a similar period in preceding years, the field experiment allows for multiple comparisons. Thus the field experiment can have almost as strong controls as a laboratory experiment, with the relevance of a field study, without suffering too much from the limitations of the two approaches.

COLLECTING DATA ON ADVERTISING

Two sociologists from the University of Notre Dame, James Cavendish and Mark Chaves, studied Catholics' *actual attendance* at church. Their study covered 48 Catholic dioceses, representing 38 percent of the U.S. Catholic population in 1990. They divided head counts of people actually in church in those dioceses with the number of people in the dioceses who described themselves as Catholic. They estimated that only 27 percent of Catholics attend church in a given week.

The sociologists then compared their results with results of a 1991 Gallup Poll based on *self-reports* of Catholics' church attendance. The Gallup Poll suggested that 51 percent of Catholics attend church, almost double the percentage the sociologists obtained. Chaves said of the results, "I don't think people are liars. It's a well-known phenomenon in survey research that people over-report what they think is socially desirable behavior."[19]

The problem cited by Chaves is the bane of research that relies on self-reports. Self-report is one of two important methods by which researchers collect information on advertising. The other method is observation. This section first explains these two methods of collecting data, and then describes a variety of tools to do so.

Evaluating Methods for Collecting Data

Self-reports are statements made by respondents or subjects about the phenomenon or object under study. The respondents' statements are prompted by questions of a researcher as in a questionnaire, or by statements of another respondent as in a focus group. A study that obtains information through self-reports is sometimes called a **survey**. In **observation,** the researcher collects information on the phenomenon directly by inspection or indirectly with certain tools, such as cameras and scanners.

Note that either of these two methods of collecting data can be used for both the experiment or field study. For example, when running an experiment, the researcher can either observe the behavior of a subject or ask subjects about their reactions to the ads. Similarly, when analyzing historical data, the researcher may obtain the data by asking subjects about their purchases (self-report) or by obtaining the record of consumers' purchases at a store through the laser scanner (observation). We first evaluate the pros and cons of the two methods of collecting data, and then describe the tools for collecting data.

Which method of collecting data is better, self-reports or observation? Self-report is superior to observation in many ways. Self-report is more accessible, flexible, sensitive, convenient, fast, and inexpensive. However, self-reports can be more biased than observation. Each of these points is explained below.

Advantages of Self-Reported Data **Accessibility** refers to the depth of information that can be obtained on various topics. Self-report can access more remote information than can observation. For example, by relying on subjects' self-reports researchers can reach their innermost thoughts. These thoughts cannot be suitably observed even with modern brain-wave research. In addition, everything from the past is beyond the reach of observation but can still be accessed by self-report.

Flexibility refers to the ability to adapt to a respondent's needs. Self-reports are more flexible than observation, because self-reports allow a researcher to explain questions to the respondent. In observation, the researcher does not interact with the respondent.

Sensitivity refers to the willingness with which respondents provide information. Self-reports are more sensitive than observation. While all respondents are reluctant to give information on sensitive topics such as their income, susceptibility to ads or sex life, they are even more reluctant to let researchers observe such behavior.

Convenience refers to the ease with which information is obtained from respondents. Self-reports are more convenient than observation. Observation requires time—time to set up the experiment, time to wait for the appropriate behavior to occur and time to observe the behavior. For example, suppose researchers want to measure the effectiveness of Chrysler's ads during the Super Bowl. They have to wait for the next Super Bowl, set up observation points in a sample of stores, and observe sales for a suitable time. In contrast, using self-report, researchers can carry out a telephone interview of a sample of respondents about their purchases at a convenient time and place.

Speed refers to the time it takes to obtain data. For reasons cited above, self-report data are quicker to obtain than data from observation.

The expenses of collecting data arise due to the costs of equipment, space, time and training of personnel. Self-report data are less costly to obtain than observational data because they require less equipment, space and specialized staff, and because they are gathered faster and more conveniently.

Disadvantages of Self-Report Data A **bias** is an error of unknown size but in a known direction. For example, parents may underreport to a researcher how much TV their children watch, in order to appear good parents. Catholics may overreport their attendance at church either because they remember their attendance more than their nonattendance, or because they want to appear devout to researchers. Both these cases show biased responses. On the other hand, asking very little children their TV viewing habits may lead to quite inaccurate results because children have difficulty understanding and answering such questions. Such data are said to be noisy. **Noise** refers to the prevalence of errors of unknown size and direction. The bias of self-reports may be due to one of three sources: social desirability, demand or memory lapse. Each of these sources of bias is discussed below.

Social Desirability Bias **Social desirability bias** is the tendency of respondents to respond to questions in a manner that they think is desired by society. For example, most people think that being quality conscious is more respectable than being price conscious. The former characteristic may denote good taste while the latter characteristic may reflect stinginess. Thus when asked how important price and quality are in their decisions, consumers may overstate quality and understate price relative to their true behavior. Similarly, respondents tend to report greater honesty, intelligence or knowledge of facts than they actually possess; greater charity, religious activity or consumption of premium goods than they actually perform; or less consumption of undesirable goods than they actually indulge in. In the context of advertising, respondents may report less viewing of TV in general, and of violent or sexy programs in particular.

Social desirability bias may vary on the same question depending on who asks and answers the question. For example, teens may overreport smoking to a student reporter, and underreport smoking to an adult reporter. The bias may also vary over different segments of the population depending on their behavior. For example, TV addicts may underreport TV viewing, while people who do not watch TV at all may overreport TV viewing, so as not to appear different from the average person.[20] The researcher rarely has access to the true records to verify the scope or depth of social desirability bias. This is the greatest limitation of self-reports. However, two solutions can partly redress this problem.

First, researchers can develop indices of answers by asking the *same questions* repeatedly over the years. Chapter 15 explains how to develop indices. To the extent that social desirability bias does not change over the years, comparison of these indices can give bias-free information. For example, polls of voting intentions and attitudes toward the performance of public figures are generally compared to similar polls taken in the past. Surveys of consumers' recall or recognition of ads are compared with information obtained from similar surveys in the past. The limitation of this solution is that it is restricted to organizations that have a long history of survey research, such as the Gallup Poll or Nielsen.

Second, some researchers have developed a scale that determines to what extent individuals are prone to social desirability bias. This scale is based on first asking subjects how they agree with a set of selected questions on which people are known to bias their responses. Examples of these statements include, "I always tell the truth" or "I always apologize when I'm in the wrong." People high on social desirability bias are likely to strongly agree with these statements. By totaling the response to all these questions, researchers can determine to what extent an individual's responses are biased. The problem with this approach is that the questions are not generally related to the current study of the researcher, tend to be intrusive or even offensive and greatly add to the length of the questionnaire. Thus, this solution is more appropriate for in-depth studies with large budgets.

Demand Bias **Demand bias** or **demand artifact** is the tendency of respondents to guess the hypothesis of the researcher and adjust answers in a manner that would support the researcher's hypothesis to please him or her. Suppose a researcher asks a respondent a simple question such as, "Have you seen an ad for Folgers coffee recently?" The respondent may assume the researcher is looking for a positive answer and respond positively. So respondents may report greater awareness of and response to ads, messages or brands than they actually possess. A similar bias occurs from leading questions. A **leading question** is one that prompts a specific answer. An example is, "Didn't you see the American Airlines ad last night?"

Demand bias may have affected the responses of students in the DiFranza study, when students were asked their preference for Joe Camel after viewing seven ads portraying Joe Camel. Demand bias may have also led Catholics in the Notre Dame survey to report greater church attendance than they actually practiced. Demand bias can be controlled by not asking leading questions, and not developing designs or asking questions that reveal the identity of the client or the goal of the research.

Memory Lapse **Memory lapse** is the tendency of respondents to forget aspects of their past. By itself, a memory lapse would lead to an unanswered question and thus greater noise in the data. However, respondents tend to answer a question even if they do not know the answer. These answers are especially prone to demand bias and social desirability bias. In addition, many people tend to remember the good aspects of their life, and forget the bad aspects. Thus memory lapses can aggravate underlying biases in responses. Researchers can reduce the problem of memory lapses by not asking facts respondents find difficult to remember. For example, they should ask about behaviors in the last day, week or month, rather than in the last few months or year. Also, questions should allow for a "don't know" option, to let respondents who genuinely do not know, say so without feeling guilty.

In conclusion, on several criteria self-report is superior to observation. However, observation is superior to self-report in being more free from bias. Because bias is of unknown size, it may seriously compromise the value of self-reports. This one problem may more than outweigh the many advantages of self-report relative to observation.

For observation to be free from bias, researchers have to observe subjects without their knowledge, or observe behaviors that they cannot consciously change (such as brain waves). Researchers can observe subjects without their knowledge only in public. An example would be a researcher viewing subjects buying products in a store without their knowledge. To observe subjects' private acts, researchers would need to obtain their permission, which may alert them and bias their acts in the same way as self-reports. For example, say some subjects agree to being

in a panel, whose purchases are then recorded electronically by a checkout scanner. In such cases the subjects may not buy socially undesirable products at stores where their purchases are recorded. Overall, the bias from observation with subjects' permission is probably much less than that from self-report. Thus researchers prefer to go through the greater effort and cost of observing phenomena rather than relying on consumers' self-report of these phenomena.

Tools for Collecting Data on Advertising

A large number of tools can help researchers collect information on various aspects of advertising. We can classify these tools based on two criteria, the method they use to collect data and the aspect of advertising on which they focus. As regards data collection, the tools can be classified as either self-report or observation tools. As regards their focus, tools can be classified as focusing on input, process, or outcome variables associated with advertising. Chapter 13 discusses the process and outcome variables for measuring advertising's effects. The **input variables** are the various measures of advertising to which consumers are exposed, such as the advertising media, the frequency of the ads or the total level of advertising. Chapters 15 and 16 discuss these variables in depth. Exhibit 14-3 presents the classification of research tools using these two criteria, data collection method and focus. The subsequent discussion of research tools is organized according to whether they measure advertising input, processes in response to advertising, or outcomes in response to advertising.

Tools for Measuring Advertising Input Of the many tools available to research input variables, we discuss seven

▼ **EXHIBIT 14-3.** Classification of research tools.

Data Collection	On Inputs	FOCUS On Processes	On Outcomes
By Self-Report	Questionnaire, diary, people-meter, active meter	Focus group, interview, questionnaire, hand- (or foot-) meter	Questionnaire, diary, personal scanner
By Observation	Telemeter, audiometer, passive meter	Pupillometer, eye camera, brain waves	Checkout scanner

that are frequently used in advertising research: the one-shot questionnaire, the diary, the telemeter, the audiometer, the people-meter, the passive meter and the active meter.

Questionnaire The **questionnaire** is a list of questions asked of a respondent. The questions could be about past, current or future behavior, mental processes or plans. It is the simplest and oldest means of collecting information from respondents. A study consisting primarily of a short questionnaire is called a **poll,** while one consisting primarily of a long questionnaire is called a *survey*. The key advantages of the questionnaire are that it is quick, flexible, has high accessibility and is cheap. The main disadvantage of the questionnaire is that it is subject to social desirability bias, demand bias and memory lapse.

Diary The **diary** is a periodic record of an individual's activity. The researcher recruits a sample of respondents willing to keep the diary, and instructs them about the activities to record and the format in which to record them. The diary corrects one of the problems of the questionnaire. By sensitizing respondents about the activities, and motivating them to keep regular records, it ensures that memory lapses do not weaken the record. However, the diary does not overcome social desirability bias, and may accentuate it. If respondents suffer from such bias for a single questionnaire, the bias may be heightened when they keep a routine diary and observe the results. Moreover, by sensitizing respondents about the need for recording certain activities, the diary may bias these activities. For example, a consumer recording his or her exposure to ads may observe more ads than the normal or average consumer.

The diary was used extensively by Nielsen to record exposure to TV ads. However, in today's complex TV environment, the biggest limitation of the diary is the extreme inconvenience of promptly recording every change in TV channel, or the extreme difficulty of correctly remembering these changes if recorded later. For this reason, the diary is being replaced by the people-meter, a tool discussed later.

Telemeters and Audiometers **Telemeters** are devices that are hooked to a household's TV set to record when and to which channel it tunes in. The recordings of the telemeter are made by a small computer with a modem. At a fixed time each night, the computer dials a central computer and relays the infor-

mation. In a separate effort, shows on TV stations are continuously monitored for ads. The ads are then identified and converted into a digital "fingerprint." Matching the outcome from the telemeter with the ads aired on the various stations indicates which household was exposed to a commercial. **Audiometers** are devices that operate in a manner similar to the telemeter, but are used to record when a radio is turned on. Audiometers predate the telemeter, but have not been used since 1964 because the proliferation of channels and the extensive listening in cars or offices have reduced the value of in-home measurement of exposure to radio ads.

The telemeter can record data about households' exposure to TV programs and ads. These data have greater detail than that obtained from questionnaires and diaries. For example, the researcher can have access to channel viewing and ad-zapping at 5-second intervals. These data are also less biased than that obtained from a diary or questionnaire, because the telemeter records the data unobtrusively and without viewer input. However, telemeters suffer from two limitations.

First, some households leave the TV on even when no one is watching. Frequently this practice may occur only for short breaks between programs. However, these are the times when ads are normally screened. Other households may leave the TV on for extended periods of time, even when everyone leaves the house or is asleep. Although this problem does not bias the findings, it adds noise to the data. Second, the data from telemeters is at the household level and not at the level of individual members of the household. Most purchases are by individual members of the household, and such data are more useful. Moreover, advertisers require viewership demographics in order to plan their media buys. To overcome this problem, data from the telemeter is normally combined with that from diaries, or from the people-meter.

People-Meter The **people-meter** is a partly interactive electronic device connected to a TV set, which records who in the household is viewing a TV program (see Exhibit 14-4). Like a telemeter it can record when the TV set is on and to which show it is tuned. It has six buttons, each of which can be assigned to a member or guest of the household. Each member of the household must record the moment he or she starts or stops viewing a particular TV program. The people-meter also comes

▼ EXHIBIT 14-4. Nielsen's people-meter.

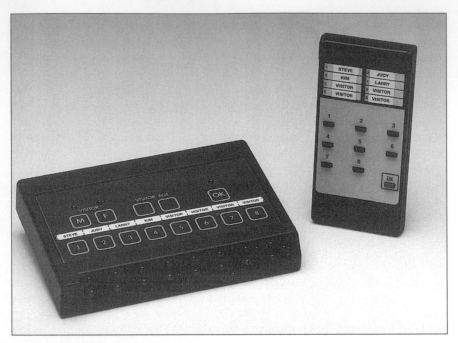

Source: Courtesy of Nielsen Media Research.

and who is in the room. It does this by silently scanning images of individuals in the room and then, with the help of pattern-matching hardware and software, matching these images with previously stored images of members of the household. The problem with the passive meter is that it creates a scenario of Big Brother watching over an individual's every move (see Exhibit 14-5). Panelists may not accept the gadget, or they may try to actively defeat it by choosing remote positions in the room.

The **active meter** is a gadget worn by the panelist or embedded under his or her skin. It transmits the individual's location to an adjunct unit attached to the TV set. The two units together can then record when the set is on, and who is in the room potentially watching the program. The active meter is even more intrusive than the passive meter, raises ethical and privacy issues and is even less likely to be accepted than the passive meter.

Tools to Measure Process Variables The tools to measure the process variables include the focus group, interview, questionnaire, hand-meter, eye camera, pupillometer, brain waves, skin galvanometer, electromyography (for voice pitch), and heart rate monitor. The section covers only the first five of these tools because they are more relevant to advertising research than the others.

Focus Group, Interview, Questionnaire The focus group, interview and questionnaire are the most commonly used tools for measuring the process variables. A **focus group** consists of a sample of respondents who are led through a group discussion by a facilitator who has an agenda of issues but no complete set of questions. The assumption of the focus group is that respondents would stimulate each other with their remarks, uncovering important issues of which the researcher was unaware. An

with a remote to facilitate respondent input. In addition, it has blinking lights that prompt viewers to record their presence at the start of and during the program. The people-meter was introduced to replace the combination of telemeter and diary for recording TV viewership. But it introduces two new problems prevalent with any method that relies on respondent input.

First, panelists might forget to record their entry into or exit from the room. Second, they might alter their viewing of shows due to social desirability bias. For example, panelists might not want to suggest that they watch too much TV or might not like to record that they view certain shows. However, the people-meter may be superior to the questionnaire and diary because it is easier to use and partly automated.

Passive and Active Meter The passive meter and active meter are fully observational tools that improve on the people-meter by not requiring any input from panelists. Both gadgets are in the prototype or testing stage, and have not yet been implemented.

The **passive meter** is located near a TV set and hooked to it so that it can record when the set is on

▼ **EXHIBIT 14-5.** Is Big Brother watching your every move?

Libraries, banks, medical institutions, and insurance companies obtain private information about individuals. The confidentiality of such information is protected by some government regulations, as well as by the policies of those companies. On the other hand, computers enable firms to record, analyze and disseminate a great deal of information about individuals that is not as well regulated. Consider the following examples:

- Credit card companies have records of purchases of their customers over long periods of time. These data allow for detailed analyses of the consumption and traveling behavior of their customers.
- Many stores encourage customers to use a store card when making purchases. Such cards allow stores to track the purchases of their customers, allowing detailed analysis of response to advertising, price and promotion.
- Using caller identification technology, firms can record the phone number of every customer who calls to ask for information, complain or buy a product. Such records can be analyzed to determine the type of customer, his or her broad interests, and his or her attitude to sellers and to products.
- Manufacturers of durables encourage buyers of new durables to register their purchase in case of changes in product specifications or product recalls. The registration card requests information on demographics and purchase behavior.
- Publishers of magazines and newspapers also get some information from their buyers. Telephone and cable TV companies get similar information from their subscribers.

Pooling the latter pieces of information can lead to a formidable database that can provide a detailed profile of individuals as potential consumers. For example, insurers may not want to insure certain people based on their eating habits, determined from grocery purchases or their eating record at restaurants. The level of detail in such data, and the ease and anonymity with which it can be collected raise the fear of Big Brother watching consumers' every move.

Several consumer groups have urged legislators to better regulate such data collection.[52] However, as yet, no comprehensive legislation protecting citizens against the collection, analysis and dissemination of personal data has emerged. Consumers proceed on the implicit trust that information they provide will be adequately protected. Many firms are also careful not to indiscriminately disseminate the information they have, so as to maintain this implicit trust.

interview consists of a structured dialogue in which a researcher probes the responses or knowledge of the respondent through a set of open-ended questions. The interview is suitable when the researcher is aware of the issues but not of the types of responses, and the researcher wants responses uncontaminated by those of other subjects. The questionnaire is suitable when the researcher is aware of the issues and the types of responses, but needs to know the precise number of respondents with each response. The interview is more structured than the focus group, but not as structured as the questionnaire.

The focus group and interview are especially used for soliciting consumers' mental responses to ads prior to their completion. For print ads, researchers could use rough drawings, or even finished versions if the latter do not involve costly photography or endorsers. However, for radio ads, and especially for TV ads, researchers normally use rough versions of the ad to stimulate consumer response, and make changes. Researchers use various forms of completed ads for this purpose (see Exhibit 14-6).

The focus group is a strong tool for refining the research problem, or for gauging consumer response to alternative ad concepts or ad themes. The limitation of the focus group is that it is slow and limited to small samples that may not be representative of the population. The interview and questionnaire are useful for obtaining more detailed information about mental responses of subjects, because these processes are not externally observed. However, the problems with these tools are even more relevant for process variables than for input variables. That is because consumers may not be fully aware of their mental processes, they may forget them easily or may not be able to report them accurately. The other problem with these tools is that because mental processes are so private, respondents may be very reluctant to reveal them to others that may bias their responses.

Hand-meter The hand- (or foot-) meter is an electric or electronic device that lets respondents move a lever with their hand (or foot) to express their response to an ad.[21] The meter can be of different types. In one type, respondents move the lever to

▼ EXHIBIT 14-6. Forms of TV ads used in pretests.

Form of Ad Stimulus	Explanation	Reported Use by Agencies	Reported Use by Advertisers
Animatic	Film or videotape of drawings of ad scenes with audio	80%	65%
Storyboard	Visual frames of ad scenes with script of audio	75	60
Finished Version		53	53
Photomatic	Film or videotape of photographs with audio	41	22
Ripamatic	Footage of existing ads spliced together	37	24
Liveamatic	Rough video involving live talent but not final actors or scenes	27	8
Other		11	4

Source: Whitehill King, Karen, John D. Pehrson, and Leonard N. Reid (1993), "Pretesting TV Commercials: Methods, Measures, and Changing Agency Roles," *Journal of Advertising* 22, 3 (September), 85–97.

one side if they like the stimulus and to the other side if they do not like the stimulus. For example, each year *USA Today* elicits responses of a sample of respondents to the TV ads aired during the Super Bowl using a hand-meter (see Exhibit 14-7). Another type lets respondents increase (or decrease) the intensity of the stimulus depending on how appealing it is. The hand-meter overcomes the questionnaire's problem of memory lapse because it obtains the response instantaneously with the screening of the ad. The changes in meter recordings as respondents watch an ad also indicate which part of the ad they like more. However, the response to the ad is limited to one variable, liking, and that response too could still suffer from bias.

Eye Camera The eye camera records how the eye moves in response to a visual stimulus. The camera may directly record the movement of the eye or of a light beam reflected off the eye. It can detect which portion of the stimulus drew the eye's attention, how many times and for how long. All three issues provide information on the response to the ad. For example, consider a respondent viewing an ad with a sexy model promoting an automobile. If the eye focuses first on the model and then on the copy, the model serves as an attention getter. But if the eye focuses on the model, then hovers around portions of the model's body with only momentary glances over the copy, then the model serves as a distraction. Active eye movements show attention and interest. Lack of movement, especially a fixed stare at some irrelevant portion of the stimulus, may imply lack of interest. Analyses of eye camera data can let advertisers know what aspects of the ad are drawing the most attention.

The eye camera is an observational technique that seems to overcome the problems of the questionnaire. But it has some limitations of its own. First, it provides information only on consumers' attention to certain aspects of the ad, not on other variables. Second, because respondents are asked to focus on the ad, leaving little room for disguising the researcher's true intent, the approach could suffer from social desirability bias. Respondents could adjust their behavior to focus on certain aspects of an ad that reflect well on themselves. For example, a respondent watching a sexy ad may focus on the copy rather than the model, even though

▼ EXHIBIT 14-7. An ad meter.

the latter may be more appealing. To minimize this problem, researchers should use the eye camera to analyze responses to ads that do not have a potential to arouse social desirability bias. Also, researchers should use disguises when recruiting respondents to avoid demand bias. In addition, researchers should encourage respondents to watch the ad exactly as they would in a normal situation.

Pupillometer The **pupillometer** records the dilation of the pupil. The human pupil dilates (or opens wider) in response to interesting, pleasant or mentally taxing stimuli, and constricts in response to uninteresting or unpleasant stimuli. Thus pupillometers can let the advertiser know if the ad is interesting, pleasing or intellectually stimulating. Combined with an eye camera it can show what portion of an ad elicits specific responses.

The pupillometer has advantages and disadvantages similar to the eye camera's. One difference is that while the eye camera provides information on the point of attention and processing, the pupillometer provides information on feelings about the ad. The dilation of the pupil is also supposed to be more of an autonomic response than are eye movements, and thus less prone to biases from self-report. The main limitation of this tool is that researchers are unsure about and still debate the precise feelings reflected by pupillometers.[22]

Brain-Wave Recordings and Functional MRI **Brain-wave recordings** measure the activity in various parts of the brain. Their use is based on the premise that specific mental activities occur in certain regions of the brain, and the intensity of the brain waves reflects the intensity of the mental activity. Research indicates that certain parts of the brain are responsible for certain activities, such as computation, verbal activity, or graphic activity. Thus the region of the brain that shows the most stimulus indicates what type of activity an ad stimulates. The intensity of the activity indicates how involved the subject is in that stimulus, and may predict memory of the stimulus.[23] Individual differences do exist, and the intensity of brain waves needs to be calibrated for each individual before determining response toward any particular advertising stimulus.

A number of tools are available for detecting brain waves, though functional magnetic resonance imaging (functional MRI) is probably one of the least expensive and most promising of the newer tools. Functional MRI works by subjecting a person's brain to a magnetic field. As a person acts or thinks, he or she uses different parts of the brain. These parts then use increasing amounts of blood in proportion to the activity involved. The oxygen in the blood causes a change in the magnetic field in that region. The change can then be measured to indicate mental activity. The method can identify fairly small changes in mental activity quite precisely. For example, consider the three activities of simply tapping a finger, tapping in a pattern that requires computation, and imagining tapping the finger. Each of these activities is controlled by different portions of the brain, which light up differently in a functional MRI.[24] Unlike previous imaging techniques, functional MRI does not require the injection of chemicals and does not subject the individual to harmful rays. It is thus safer, besides also being cheaper and more accurate than other brain imaging techniques. It is likely to be increasingly used for brain research.

The main advantage of brain-wave response is the precision with which it can detect the intensity and location of mental activity. However, the approach has several limitations in comparison to other methods for measuring ad response. First, the relationship of brain-waves to the various process variables has not been fully mapped. Second, the method is costly. Third, it is invasive, in the sense that subjects must be hooked up to the instrument in artificial conditions to process the ads. Thus their responses may not be representative of responses of consumers to real ads. Therefore brain-wave research is high on internal validity but low on external validity.

Tools for Measuring Outcome Variables The outcome variables refer to characteristics of consumer behavior such as brand choice or purchase intensity, or characteristics of the firm such as sales or market share (see Chapter 13). The four most commonly used tools for measuring outcome variables are the questionnaire, diary, checkout scanners and personal scanners.

Questionnaire and Diary The questionnaire and diary collect information on outcome variables too. Their advantages and disadvantages for this task are similar to those for collecting information on the input variables.

Checkout Scanners **Checkout scanners** are devices that record items purchased by reading a laser beam that bounces off the item's universal product code. The **universal product code** is a unique 10-digit number that firms assign to every manufactured product. A store's computer stores the prices and promotions in effect for every item in the store for that day. By drawing on those computer records, the checkout device can compute the price that the customer has to pay for the item. The checkout device then relays to the computer the quantity, value and time in minutes of the sale. If the customer uses a magnetic identification card provided by the store, the scanner can record his or her identity. Thus checkout scanners provide a very detailed description of the sale, in terms of quantity, price and promotional status of the product, by buyer, item bought, and the time it was bought.

Personal Scanners **Personal scanners** are similar to checkout scanners with the exception that a household keeps the scanner at home and members must scan their purchases each time they return from a shopping trip. How does the personal scanner differ from the checkout scanner? Despite their similarity, checkout and personal scanners have clear differences with major implications for the quality of the data.

Checkout scanners are typically installed by the store and the data belong to the store. In order to get meaningful data, the researcher must have access to data from all stores in a city. Thus hooking up a system based on checkout scanners can be time consuming and expensive. Even then, small stores or certain categories of stores (perhaps warehouse clubs, drugstores) may not have access to scanners and may not cooperate with the researcher. In contrast, personal scanners require the cooperation of only a sample of households. The disadvantage of this method is that households may forget to scan their purchases, especially those from a less comprehensive trip. Also, each time they scan their own purchases, they are conscious that they are reporting information and so may be subject to social desirability bias. Thus, they may systematically fail to scan certain purchases. In sum, checkout and personal scanners display all the pros and cons of observation versus self-report, respectively.

STANDARD MEASURES OF ADVERTISING EFFECTIVENESS

Advertisers' need for information on advertising effectiveness has spawned a vast industry of data suppliers or market research firms that produce such information. These firms collect information on many measures of advertising effectiveness, sometimes using standard measures, and at other times using their own unique measures (see Chapter 13). The various measures of advertising effectiveness are sometimes classified as pretest and posttest. Pretest measures are taken before an ad is aired, and posttest measures, after it is aired. The measures can also be classified as observational or self-report depending on how researchers collect data on them. Exhibit 14-8 classifies the main measures of advertising effectiveness using these two criteria.

Reviewing all these measures is beyond the scope of this chapter. Moreover, an earlier section of this chapter covered the physiological measures of ad response, while Chapters 4 to 8 already discussed many of the pretest measures of advertising response. On the other hand, three posttest measures have become important benchmarks for the performance of advertising: recall, recognition, and inquiries. The importance of these measures is due more to their historical impact than to their ability to predict the sales effectiveness of advertising. However, the most important indicators of advertising effectiveness are the outcome variables, such as brand choice, purchase intensity, market share, and

▼ **EXHIBIT 14-8.** Classification of measures of advertising effectiveness.

	Pretest	Posttest
Self-Report	Readability	Recognition
	Comprehension	Recall
	Warmth	Inquiries
	Endorsements	
	Preference	
	Attitude	
	Persuasion	
	Purchase intention	
Observation	Physiological response	Brand choice
		Purchase intensity
		Sales

especially sales. So, after reviewing the three bench-mark measures, the section focuses on measuring the sales effectiveness of advertising.

Recall

Recall of an ad is an individual's ability to bring to mind some aspect of a previously observed ad. One of the most popular measures of recall is day-after recall. **Day-after recall** measures the proportion of a sample of the audience that can correctly recall an ad one day after viewing it. The test was probably pioneered by George Gallup in the 1940s, popularized in the 1960s as Burke's day-after recall, and is used today in various forms by a number of agencies including Mapes and Ross and Gallup and Robinson.[25]

For a recall test, researchers contact about 150 to 300 subjects, one to three days following the airing of a commercial. Subjects are first asked if they can recall any ad from the previous day's viewing in the product category of interest (for example, refrigerators). If they cannot, they are given some clues, such as the brand name, or a picture of a scene from the ad with the brand name hidden. Subjects' recall without any clues is called **unaided recall,** while their recall with some help is called **aided recall.** Subjects who are able to recall the ad are then asked to recall specific information about the ad such as the endorsers, the scenes, the copy or the dialogue.

The audience of an ad is the subjects within the sample who view the ad and some portion of the program immediately before and after the airing of the ad. This definition of the audience of the ad ensures that the score measures the performance of the ad alone and not that of the program or medium. The **percentage proven recall** is the percentage of the sample audience who recall specific information about the ad. This measure is the typical day-after-recall score. The **percentage related recall** is the percentage of the audience who recall the ad but are unable to provide specific information.

Day-after recall has been used extensively in industry practice to determine how well an ad is doing with its target audience. The test was severely criticized in the 1980s, primarily because results were not consistent from test to test.[26] However, recent research suggests that more reliable results can be obtained with better controls over the selection of the sample.[27] These results, when observed over several decades and product categories, can provide norms against which any single ad can be compared. For example, scores from several testing services over several decades indicate that the mean recall is between 20 and 24. However, systematic differences exist by age, newness of the product, categories of products and even brands.[28] Thus any

▼ **EXHIBIT 14-9.** Average ad recall over time in a South African study.

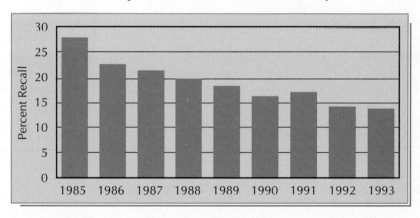

Source: Reprinted from Eric du Plessis, "Recognition versus Recall," *Journal of Advertising Research*, 34, 3, 1994, pp. 75–91. © 1994 by the Advertising Research Foundation.

particular ad should be compared with the norm for its target segment, category and brand. When using such norms, managers need to keep in mind that recall scores have been declining over time (see Exhibit 14-9), probably because of increasing clutter, shorter duration of ads, and lower attention to ads.

The major problem with the use of recall to measure advertising effectiveness is that researchers are not exactly sure what the score means. The argument for measuring recall is rooted in the assumption that a consumer needs to remember a brand before he or she can evaluate it, develop a preference for it and decide to buy it. So recall would be necessary, although not sufficient, for preference and brand purchase. However, this simple assumption may not be valid, while studies show that the score itself does not correlate well with persuasion and brand purchase.[29] A good example is Isuzu's ad campaign featuring the lying car salesman, Joe Isuzu. The ad was the most remembered of all television commercials during the two years it ran. Yet, during the same two years, the number of Isuzu cars actually sold sagged steadily downwards.[30] Recall may not be a good predictor of brand purchases for three reasons: different hierarchy of effects, the role of emotions and the role of implicit memory:

- Consumer purchase may not always follow a simple hierarchy of effects from awareness to liking and persuasion to purchase. Other hierarchies exist in which purchase may come first (see Chapter 13). In such cases, recall may not be a prior cause of behavior.
- Recall tries to ascertain an individual's verbal or numerical processing of information. Persuasion could result from such processing, but also from emotions, which exist independently of memory for information (see Chapter 7). So an individual may feel a strong attraction for a brand and buy it without recalling its merits.
- Even if an individual is persuaded by information and reason, over time that individual may forget the reasoning in an ad that led to that belief (explicit memory), while still holding the belief (implicit memory; see Chapter 6). To the extent that questions on recall tap explicit memory, current recall may not be necessary for persuasion and purchase.

Thus the ability of recall to predict sales or other changes in attitude is not clear. Perhaps the best interpretation is that recall measures the ability of the ad to hold attention long enough to increase awareness for the brand or the message. Indeed, some studies show that the recall score correlates to involvement and interest in the ad.[31] A conservative use of recall would compare an ad's current score with those of past ads for the same brand or product category to ascertain its relative effectiveness.

Recognition

Recognition is an individual's claim that he or she has been previously exposed to an ad. Tests of ad recognition were initiated by Starch in the early 1930s.[32] Recognition of an ad is primarily a measure of attention to it. A subject would not recognize an ad that never caught his or her attention. In recognition tests a subject is presented with a visual of the ad and asked if she or he has seen it before. Thus the test relies on self-report. As such it suffers from all the biases of self-reports. First, subjects may claim recognition because they wish to appear well informed or observant (social desirability bias). Second, subjects may claim recognition because they suspect the researcher wants a positive response, and they would like to please the researcher (demand bias). Third, subjects may claim recognition of an ad because they mistake it for a similar ad for the same or another brand to which they have been exposed (memory lapse).

One approach to correct for these biases is to present subjects with real and fictitious ads. An individual's false-positive responses on the fictitious ads can then be calculated and used as an index by which to adjust his or her scores on the real ads. Another approach to correct for recognition is to test a subject's recognition of the ad with the brand name hidden. If the answer is positive, the researcher can then ask the subject for the brand name. The latter correction may also be prone to guessing, as some subjects may be able to infer the brand name from the type of ad. The correction also tends to tap recall. A third approach is to present the recognition task as a multiple-choice test.[33] Typical recognition tests ask subjects whether or not they recognize an ad. A multiple-choice test, for example, can ask a subject which of five taglines of a brand he or she recognizes. Recognition can then be used even for verbal material.

A major debate in the field is the relationship and relative importance of recall and recognition. The debate is not yet fully resolved, but there may be support for the following tentative conclusions:[34]

- Recall and recognition scores of an ad are positively correlated, but only weakly so.
- Recognition and recall tap different aspects of memory. Recall measures verbal memory, while recognition measures visual memory.
- Because people have much better visual than verbal memory, scores of recognition are normally higher than those of recall.

- Emotional ads may be able to capture high scores on recognition, even though they may not do so on recall.
- Recognition scores for an ad decline slowly over time, and may not show any decay over the first few weeks after ad exposure. Recall scores tend to decline more rapidly over time.
- Recognition scores may show a floor effect: subjects can recall all ads to which they have been exposed in a particular test. In contrast, recall scores may show a ceiling effect: subjects may have no recall for all ads in a test.
- Younger people generally have better recognition and recall for ads than do older people.

The final result is one that authors of the DiFranza study on Joe Camel were not aware of, and which modifies the interpretation of their results. DiFranza et al. found that youth could recognize Joe Camel better than adults. They interpreted that to mean that Joe Camel appeals to youth, and that R. J. Reynolds targets youth. However, a comparison of their data with norms for recognition obtained by research agencies in numerous tests over time indicates that the better recognition of Joe Camel by youth relative to adults is similar to their better recognition of commercials in general (see Exhibit 14-10). This finding shows that recognition and recall should not be interpreted in absolute terms, but relative to norms. The norms serve as controls, akin to a control group in an experiment. The comparison of recognition scores against their norms prevents flawed interpretation of results.

Inquiries

Inquiries are efforts by consumers to contact an advertiser. Consumers most often inquire by mail or telephone. Typically, consumers contact advertisers to request information about some advertised brand. However, consumers also contact an advertiser to express pleasure or annoyance with ads. Inquiries may arrive spontaneously because of the content of an ad. Alternatively, the advertiser may solicit inquiries by not providing all information and explicitly offering a toll-free phone number, a mailing address or a web site for the consumer to get more information. So the number of inquiries by itself does not indicate either a positive or negative consumer response. The advertiser must also take into account the nature and spontaneity of the inquiry, and the intensity of feelings expressed.

The primary use of inquiries is as a measure of the attention the ad received. However, by comparing the number of inquiries from an ad to the inquiries triggered by previous ads, the advertiser can get an indication of the relative attention-drawing power of the current ad. Inquiries can also be used to predict sales. To do so, the advertiser needs to find a relationship between ad exposure and inquires, and between these two measures and sales. The advertiser can then use that relationship to predict future sales. Such a prediction can help it design the ad campaign, or make plans for big increases or decreases in sales.

▼ **EXHIBIT 14-10.** Comparison of DiFranza's recognition scores for Joe Camel with Bruzzone's recognition norms.

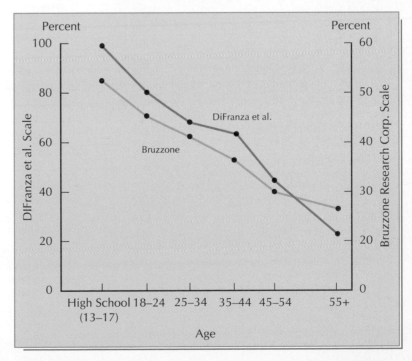

Source: Reprinted from Joel S. Dubow, "Advertising Recognition and Recall by age, Including Teens," *Journal of Advertising Research*, 35, 3, 1995, pp. 55–60. © 1995 by the Advertising Research Foundation.

For example, suppose an airline has found that three insertions a week of a full-page newspaper ad for a discount fare generate about 1,000 inquiries, and help it sell 100 percent of the seats for that fare. It has also found that if an ad triggers well over 1000 inquiries, demand exceeds supply and passengers get frustrated. Then, if the very first insertion of a new ad causes 1,000 inquiries, the airline knows it has a good response. It then must either stop running the ad or plan for more seats at that fare.

Firms sometimes use coupons, rebates, quizzes or contests to measure the extent to which an ad prompts consumers to contact the advertiser. However, rather than measuring attention to the ad, coupons and rebates may measure consumers' price sensitivity, while quizzes and contests may measure consumers' interest in such activities.

Sales

In the mid-1970s, four entrepreneurs developed a system to collect data from the checkout scanners of grocery stores, to provide a detailed, on-line method for tracking consumer response to stores' promotions. They approached Nielsen, a leading market research firm, with their innovation. Nielsen declined to implement the system. With the help of a venture capitalist, the researchers formed Information Resources Inc. (IRI) in 1978, to develop the data collection system and market its research output. A few years later, when they went public with the company, the stock price soared, and each of the entrepreneurs became a millionaire several times over. In the 1980s, scanner data came to revolutionize data collection on grocery purchases, while IRI became a leading supplier of scanner data and grew to become the second largest research firm in the United States in 1993.[35]

J. D. Power Associates became a well-known syndicated research company with its much-cited and popular Customer Satisfaction Index for automobiles. Early in 1994, the company initiated an effort to hook up the 18,000 automobile dealers in the United States in a system that can electronically record sales of automobiles. The database when complete will be able to provide detailed analyses of sales by dealer, region, brand and promotion effort. The company president describes the new effort as being "20 times more important than customer satisfaction."[36]

American Express Co.'s most cherished possession is its 500 billion bytes of data on how consumers have used its 35 million green, gold and platinum charge cards to spend $350 million since 1991.[37]

As these examples indicate, many companies have acquired large databases on consumer purchases that were never possible in the past. These data are an invaluable source of information on consumer response to advertising and other marketing variables (see Exhibit 14-11). In the past, firms had no good means to measure consumer response to their efforts. They relied on annual surveys of consumer purchases, quarterly sales, staff reports of orders, monthly factor shipments to wholesalers, or Nielsen's bimonthly audits of retail sales. The new data are far more accurate, timely and complete. The appeal of scanner data can be gauged by the speed of IRI's growth. By 1994, IRI's gross revenues had grown to $318 million in just 16 years of existence. In comparison, revenues of the leading market research firm, Nielsen, had grown to $750 million in 73 years of existence.[38] The tool most responsible for this development is the computer. But many associated tools such as scanners, telemeters, people-meters, and instantaneous electronic reporting of transactions have contributed to the availability of such data. Perhaps the single most important outcome of the new tools is the emergence of single-source data, because of the high quality of these data and the large number of firms that can use them.

Single-source data are a combination of precise data on individual sales and all of the marketing variables that influence sales, in one system or data bank. In particular, single-source data consist of scanner data and cable data. **Scanner data** are laser scanner records of consumer purchases at the checkout point of stores. These data are detailed records of individual households' purchases by item, promotional status and minute of occurrence. The promotional status includes the price, in-store displays, retail advertising and coupons redeemed at the time of purchase. **Cable data** record the same households' exposures to TV advertising at 5-second intervals. Who collects single-source data? Why are the data important? What purposes do such data serve?

Sources of Single-Source Data Information Resources Inc. (IRI) pioneered this data system, and in competition with Nielsen Marketing Research is the major supplier of single-source data. The data collection consists of three important components. First, the research firm chooses a sample of cities in which all major retail stores and drugstores agree to sell their laser-scanned sales records to IRI. Second, the firm selects a sample of thousands of households who

▼ **EXHIBIT 14-11.** Using computers to divine who might buy a gas grill.

At a secret location in Phoenix, security guards watch over one of American Express Co.'s most cherished possessions: 500 billion bytes of data on how customers have used its 35 million green, gold and platinum charge cards to spend $350 billion since 1991.

American Express wants to mine the data board for such marketing gems as how many people flew to Paris last year and might be eager for another international trip. But using big mainframe computers for such narrow queries is too expensive and time-consuming.

Now a new generation of technology that started in science labs is giving American Express and others—airlines, banks, insurers, Wall Street firms and consumer marketers—their first crack at the loosening the data gridlock. Techies call the new approach "data mining," and businesses hope it will allow them to boost sales and to reap millions of dollars in savings by improving distribution, narrowing direct-mail targets and developing a new view of customers.

Data mining uses "massively parallel" supercomputers that wire together dozens or hundreds of standard microchips from personal computers. The machines run sleek "relational" database programs that slice data into dozens of narrower, smaller pools of information.

The "parallel processors," once the purview of physicists trying to simulate atomic particle collisions, can do in minutes or hours the tasks that a mainframe needs weeks and a specially written program to perform.

A mainframe processes data one chunk at a time, drawing lists from a single, rigid database. A parallel machine's "engines" break down the question, split up the tasks among dozens of chips, and grab the answers from multiple pools, cross-referencing them.

"Companies want to take all this raw data and turn it into intelligence, but until now there just wasn't a feasible way to do it," says Katrina Garnett, vice president at software firm Sybase Inc.

At the American Express site in Phoenix, alongside the old IBM mainframes, analysts are testing two supercomputers from Thinking Machines Corp., that they hope will reveal how often card holders shop, how much they spend and which stores, restaurants and hotels they seem to prefer.

With the knowledge that a Mrs. Smith buys most of her dresses at Saks Fifth Avenue, American Express plans to offer her a discount on Saks shoes as a "reward" for using the card. It hopes that as a result, customers like Mrs. Smith will charge more purchases and the store will handle more American Express business. A dozen similar programs are in the works.

"It's a quantum leap, "says Frank Skillern, president of the U.S. consumer card group at American Express. It gives the marketing people an ability and speed we couldn't even consider before."

It also gives some consumers the creeps. Customers would benefit from new discounts, but the potential for abuse is huge if companies sell the new profiles to other businesses, not to mention the Internal Revenue Service. "The companies doing this have a big responsibility. Otherwise there will be an information Chernobyl," warns Mary Culnan, an associate professor of business at Georgetown University. She recently cut off a credit card after she got a telephone pitch for

dental insurance shortly after she had used the card to pay a dentist's bill.

Marketers have been collecting this sort of data for three decades. "Business is awash in data. It's an absolute gold mine," says Howard Richmond II, a vice president at the Gartner Group research firm, who says sales of parallel systems could expand tenfold to $5 billion by 1998.

AT&T Corp.'s Teradata line leads, with commercial customers, up threefold in five years. The market is especially critical for International Business Machines Corp., which just has introduced two new systems. Eventually supercomputers will supersede IBM's old mainframe mainstay, says Nicholas Donofrio, who heads IBM's large-scale computing business.

Using the parallel approach, auto maker Rover Group Ltd. wants to track which batches of parts went into which production runs of Land Rovers, narrowing any recalls when one batch has a flaw. Airlines are already targeting frequent fliers, mailing out incentives when customers travel less. Insurers are ferreting out fraud by matching multiple claims from the same doctor or patient.

Fingerhut Cos., a Minnetonka, Minn, catalog marketer, is using a Sun Microsystems machine, hoping to divine which of its 25 million customers bought outdoor patio furniture recently and thus might respond to a pitch for a gas grill. The answer lies somewhere amid six trillion characters of data. "We are taking weeks down to days and saving millions," says Glenn Habern, chief information officer at Fingerhut.

continued

▼ **EXHIBIT 14-11.** (Continued)

Data-mining technology isn't cheap, though. Advanced models can run more than $1 million a piece, and converting just one program from a mainframe can take a year of a programmer's time at $175,000 in salary and benefits.

Designing database that will serve up the right numbers also has been problematic. At CNA Insurance Cos., five programmers worked for nine months loading five years of claims data into a parallel system; only to discover the data had been miscoded on the old mainframe. The entire project had to be started over.

Some programs run well, but workers balk at using them. Buyers for big retailers sometimes shun the reports on what consumers are purchasing, continuing to order by "gut" instinct. Kmart Corp., a parallel pioneer, uses laser guns to scan items on the shelf and zap the

inventory count back to a supercomputer in Troy, Mich., which schedules new deliveries. Yet some Kmart store managers resist using the setup.

Even a supercomputer can't solve some problems. AMR Corp.'s American Airlines monitors the activity of frequent fliers, mailing out bonuses when someone starts traveling less. But the system can't tell when the slowdown is because of retirement and no amount of incentives would work. "That's one area we've been disappointed in," says John Jaynes, marketing director.

Mostly however, data miners cite rich rewards. Royal Caribbean Cruises Ltd. in Miami says its system offers special packages, filling berths up to the last minute and maximizing profits. Half of Royal's passengers have taken cruises before, and the parallel approach

lets it pinpoint which ones splurge on longer trips and might be primed for an expensive tour of Scandinavia and Russia.

First Bank System in Minneapolis was able to expand the pool of customers eligible for home-equity loans way beyond a credit bureau's recommendation. It analyzed five years of checking and savings account behavior, tracking overdrafts, bonuses, cash flows and whether paychecks went in by direct-deposit. That has helped First Bank increase the number of "relationships" each household has with the bank to 3.7 from 3.1 in 1990.

When the bank first considered parallel processing, "we thought it was completely nuts," says Philip Heasley, vice chairman. "But now we realize we have a lot more decision data on people than we could ever buy on the outside."

Source: Laurie Hays, "Using Computers to Divine Who Might Buy a Gas Grill," *The Wall Street Journal,* August 16, 1994, B1, B4. Reprinted by permission of *The Wall Street Journal,* © 1994 Dow Jones & Company, Inc. All rights reserved worldwide.

agree to make all their purchases from one of these stores with a card. A central computer records their purchases together with price, quantity and promotional status by minute of occurrence. Third, the firm supplies each household with a telemeter that records whether their TV set is on, and to which channel it is tuned at 5-second intervals. This tool is the basis for determining TV ad exposures.

A fourth component of the system, which is not essential for data collection but helps run field experiments, is the IAT. The **IAT** or **individually addressable tap** is a gadget that enables a central computer to send a cable TV signal directly to a specific household.[39] The IAT enables sample households to receive special test ads through cable TV. The system enables the research firm to run field experiments of TV ad effectiveness, called split cable tests. In a **split cable test**, matched samples of households are sent different levels or executions of an ad campaign, without their knowledge of the research design.

Their viewing behavior and purchase behavior can then be tracked to monitor the sales effectiveness of the ads.

Both Nielsen and IRI provide standardized research packages to clients. These packages consist of selected data, with analytical reports and software for managers to carry out their own analyses. The best known packages are probably Infoscan from IRI and Marketscan from Nielsen. The limitations of these data are due to the limitations of the laser scanners and telemeter used for data collection, which were discussed earlier.

Importance of Single-Source Data As discussed in the previous section, field studies try to determine the effect of advertising on sales after controlling for other causal variables such as price and promotions. In the past, firms used several sources for such data, including their own factory shipments for sales, media-supplied gross rating points for advertising, and retailer-supplied prices for price. Such multisourced data were crude, sometimes not quite compatible, and frequently suffered from multicollinearity and reverse causality. Single-source data represented a revolution in data collection for several reasons.

Firstly, the data are very detailed, giving information by market, store within market, and consumer household within the store. They also provide information by brand, size of brand, and promotional status of the brand. Further, this information can be broken down by week, days within weeks, and finer time periods if that is required.[40]

Second, the data contain records on all marketing variables likely to affect sales, such as advertising, price, coupons, in-store displays or retail ads in local newspapers. Indeed, scanner data contain records on almost 100 variables, versus only about 10 variables in previous data. Controlling for all these variables helps determine the effect of advertising on consumer purchases or sales more accurately.

Third, the data cover all major competitors in the market. Thus they give a complete picture of market activity, which was not easily available before.

Fourth, the data are available fairly soon after the records are made. To determine brand sales in the market, the best source was formerly Nielsen's bimonthly audits of retailers. Through single-source data, advertisers can now access data within a week of their occurrence, and even quicker if they need to.

Fifth, the data from a split cable test can be very relevant and provide a strong test of causality. The relevance follows from the natural setting in which households watch TV ads and make purchases with minimal intervention from the researcher. The strong test of causality follows from the fact that the researcher can select two similar sample households *in the same market*, which differ only by the type of ads shown to them through cable TV.

Uses of Single-Source Data Single-source data can be used for powerful field experiments in highly natural environments. For example, IRI can split the sample of households in a city into groups, each of which is shown a different execution of an ad, or subjected to a different level of advertising. Comparisons of sales across these groups enable the researcher to determine what type of ad or level of advertising provides the best returns in sales in a very natural environment.

Single-source data can also be used for sophisticated field studies and are less susceptible than traditional data to problems of multicollinearity and reverse causality. The reason is that the data can be analyzed at the level of individual households, whose ad exposures are recorded in seconds and whose purchases are recorded by minute of occurrence. Analyses of data at such a disaggregate level are less prone to multicollinearity because different households see ads, use coupons and respond to discounted prices at different times. Therefore, such analyses are also less susceptible to reverse causality, because managers are unlikely to target ads to match the precise purchase occasions of individual households. In contrast, when researchers correlate aggregate data, such as monthly sales and advertising at the national level, they could pick up the manager's scheduling of advertising to match sales cycles, rather than the effect of advertising on sales.

While single-source data were initially developed for grocery products, their use is rapidly spreading to other categories. Most retail firms now record sales electronically with scanners. It is merely a matter of time before research firms begin to offer single-source data systems for such retailers and the manufacturers who supply them. Credit card companies, telephone companies, banks, restaurants and other service organizations also have extensive records of sales by individuals. Some of this information is confidential and other portions are not. These organizations can link the nonconfidential information with records of their promotions to develop their own systems of single-source data. These data can serve to provide new, detailed and insightful analyses of the response of sales to advertising and promotion.

HOW ADVERTISING AFFECTS SALES

This section focuses on the effect of advertising on sales and profits.[41] We have already covered the effect of advertising on the process variables in Chapters 4 to 8. Sales and profits are two of the key variables by which advertisers determine whether advertising is working, and whether they should continue with a campaign. Because profit is the product of margin per unit and sales, the profitability of advertising is closely related to sales effectiveness. Margin can change from firm to firm, and also from day to day within a firm, as prices and costs change. Thus, it is difficult to develop any generalizable principles of the effects of advertising on profits. However, by using the research approaches, tools and variables described in this chapter, researchers have assembled a good though not complete picture of whether, when, and how advertising affects sales. This knowledge can be very useful for managers who do not have the time to carry out studies of their own advertising.

In the subsequent discussion, **advertising level** refers to the amount of advertising in terms of number of exposures, gross rating points or dollars spent. Practitioners and researchers also use the terms **ad-weight** and **ad-intensity**, respectively, for advertising level.

Major Studies on the Advertising-Sales Relationship

Studies of the relationship between advertising and sales can be classified into two groups depending on the primary approach of the research: field experiment or field analysis. In each group some important studies provide fairly consistent results about the effects of advertising.

Field Experiments Many field experiments have evaluated the effect of advertising on sales. Four of them are worthy of our attention because of their large scale and important discoveries.

1. **Anheuser-Busch Experiments:** Experiments at Anheuser-Busch, Inc., in the mid-1960s varied advertising levels, schedules, media and other promotional activity across different regions.[42] The most elaborate of these experiments involved changes in levels of advertising of −100%, −50%, −25%, 0%, +50%, +100%, and +200% relative to ongoing expenditures. Each level was tried over six geographic areas for more accurate results.

   The experiments showed that in the short term, decreasing the level of advertising had no negative impact on sales. However, a complete suspension of TV advertising for more than a year led to some deterioration in sales. In these situations, sales levels could be restored with just the previous (normal) advertising level.

2. **Campbell Soup Experiments:** Campbell Soup Company carried out 19 experiments in the mid-1970s to test the effects of advertising on the sales of six brands.[43] The experiments varied the levels of advertising from −50% to +50%, the ad schedules, the media mix, the ad copy and the target market. Each experiment was compared with each market's sales during a test period, with sales during an earlier nontest period, and also with sales in control markets.

   The experiments found that changes (including increases) in the level of advertising had little or no impact on sales. However, changes in copy, media, and target markets did result in sales increases in some situations. In particular, sales increased significantly in three of the five experiments, in which the media reach was extended to include new target markets. Sales also increased by over 11% in two of five experiments in which the creative copy was changed. Whenever sales increased significantly, the increase occurred early on rather than after prolonged repetition of the ad.

3. **AdTel Experiments:** AdTel was a marketing research firm that operated a 2,000-person diary panel in each of three test cities. One review summarized the results of 120 AdTel experiments.[44] Of these, 48 tests were on ad level, 36 were on ad copy and 24 were on ad schedules. Panel members had access to cable TV while AdTel controlled advertising by varying either ad level, ad copy or media schedules to split samples in each city.

   Six of the 48 ad-weight tests, including 2 that ran for over two years, involved lower levels of advertising. However, none of these tests showed any decline in sales even though some had the potential to detect long-term effects. Of the 42 remaining tests that involved increased advertising levels, only 30% showed sales changes different from those of the control groups. Most of the latter tests were for new products. In contrast, 47% of the copy tests showed significant differences in sales between test and control groups.

4. **Experiments at Information Resources Inc.:** One review summarized the results of 360 field experiments over 10 years at Information Resources Inc. (IRI).[45] These experiments were based on the BehaviorScan advertising tests. In each test market, IRI had established a panel of about 3,000 households. The panelists agreed to make all their grocery purchases with a card

and allowed their cable television viewing to be monitored by a telemeter. By subjecting various split samples to different levels, content and duration of TV advertising, IRI tested the effectiveness of the advertising on sales.

The IRI experiments found that increasing advertising levels was effective only half the time and profitable in the short term only about 20% of the time. However, the effects of advertising were stronger for new products, and persisted over time. Mature or established products did not get as much response from advertising as did the new products. However, mature products could enhance ad effectiveness with new creative copy. In general, the effects of advertising did not die out immediately after the campaigns stopped: about 76% of the initial increase persisted for one year and another 28% persisted for a second year.

Field Studies Numerous field studies estimated the elasticity, or responsiveness, of sales to changes in the level of advertising or price. The elasticity of sales to advertising (or price) is the percentage change in sales for a 1 percent change in the level of advertising (or price). We may now have 300 to 400 estimates of these two elasticities from studies done on different products, over different time periods, and in different countries. One review summarized the findings from all of these studies.[46] It found that, on average, the elasticity of sales to advertising is .1. In other words, a 1 percent increase in the level of advertising results in only a .1 percent increase in sales. The corresponding elasticity of sales to price is –2.5. Thus sales are about 25 times more elastic, or responsive, to changes in price than to changes in the level of advertising.

Summary of Findings A review of all these field experiments and studies suggests the following important conclusions about the effects of advertising on sales.[47]

1. **Decreases in the level of advertising do not lead to an immediate decrease in sales. An increase in the level of advertising by itself does not lead to an increase in sales.** These results are supported by experiments at Anheuser-Busch and Campbell Soup and the AdTel data. The results imply that many companies may be using ads that are ineffective, or for periods of time or at levels well beyond the point at which they are effective.

2. **On average, half of all ongoing ad campaigns are ineffective.** This finding was supported by the IRI experiments. The fact that companies may have kept advertising even when half of the ad campaigns were ineffective provides additional support for the previous result that much advertising may not be effective.

3. **Changes in the creative, medium, target segment or product itself sometimes lead to changes in sales, even though increases in the level of advertising alone do not.** This result was supported by the Campbell Soup, AdTel, IRI and other experiments. Together with the previous results, it suggests that *novelty*, either in media, target segment or, especially, in the product or the creative itself, is more likely to lead to increases in sales than is a mere increase in the level of advertising (see Exhibit 14-12). In the exhibit, each vertical bar represents one four-week period of ad repetition, and each type of shading represents a new ad. Note how market share gradually declines as the same ad is repeated, then increases as a new ad is introduced.

4. **When advertising is effective, it is effective either early on or never.** This result was supported by the Campbell Soup experiments. In the face of weak or no response to some ad campaigns, managers may believe that they need to give the campaign more time. They may reason that advertising works in the long term through repetition. However, this result suggests that repetition of an *ineffective* ad campaign does not make it effective. If one does not see results in the first few repetitions (for example, the first few weeks), the campaign will probably be ineffective in the long run too.

5. **Advertising may have long-term effects.** The IRI experiments found that the effect of advertising over the long term (two to three years) was as large as its effect in the first year. The Anheuser-Busch experiments found that complete suspension of an ad campaign for over a year caused some deterioration in sales. However, in these cases renewal of the campaign could revive sales. These results suggest that advertising does have certain long-term or carryover

▼ EXHIBIT 14-12. Effect on market share of repeating old and new ads.

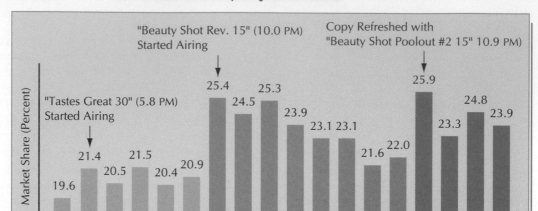

Source: Reprinted from Adams and Blair, 1992, using A. C. Nielsen SCANTRACK as reported in Margaret Henderson Blair and Karl E. Rosenberg, "Convergent Findings Increase Our Understanding of How Advertising Works," *Journal of Advertising Research* 34, 3, 1994, pp. 34–45. © 1994 by the Advertising Research Foundation.

effects. Because of these long-term effects, advertisers can stop advertising for brief periods of time without suffering immediate losses in sales. Indeed, when unaware of these long-term effects, advertisers may overuse an effective campaign. Scheduling of advertising in flights, with temporary suspension between flights, may be more effective and efficient than continuous advertising at an even rate year-round (see Chapter 17).

6. **When advertising does affect sales, its impact is not large and is much smaller than that of price.** A summary of hundreds of studies that estimated elasticities indicates that on average the advertising elasticity of sales is .1, while the price elasticity of sales is 2.5. So in general, sales are much more responsive to changes in price than they are to changes in advertising.

Why Do Advertisers Continue with Ineffective Ads?

The major findings of the effect of advertising on sales suggest that advertising is not the strong force many laypeople believe that it is. Indeed, advertisers do not and probably never will control the minds and behavior of U.S. citizens as some critics suggest. Actually, much advertising may be ineffective. If that

conclusion is true, one may well ask why firms resort to such advertising, or why they continue with ineffective ads. Several factors may be responsible for their behavior, including lack of testing, the role of the ad agency, competitive pressure to advertise, the budget process, and indirect effects on prices.

Lack of Testing Many advertisers do not adequately test ad campaigns that are already running. One study found that only a quarter of advertisers or their agencies evaluate ongoing advertising campaigns for effectiveness.[48] Lack of testing may occur for several reasons. First, many ads go through several rounds of evaluation, including various forms of testing, prior to being adopted. Advertisers may think that further testing is not necessary. Second, testing requires money, and advertisers may not be willing to spend the amounts necessary. Also, advertisers see the expenses of ad tests as out-of-pocket expenses. The savings from not spending on an ineffective campaign are opportunities that they may not perceive as sources of income. For example, assume an advertiser has planned a $1 million ad campaign. The $25,000 for an ad test may be perceived as an additional expense over the $1 million, rather than as a small cost that may save the whole

$1 million from being wasted. Third, many managers assume that ad testing takes much longer and costs much more than it really does.

Role of Ad Agency Two forces within an agency may work against ad testing—the incentive system and the creative talent. First, when running an ad campaign, agencies provide advertisers with a package of services, which includes carrying out preliminary research, developing the creative, buying media time and space for the campaign and evaluating the campaign. However, many agencies are primarily paid based on some fraction of the media budget for the ad campaign (see Chapter 3). They are generally not compensated on the basis of the sales or profit generated by the campaign, or the savings from not running the campaign. Given this incentive system, agencies are motivated to execute the campaign with purchases of media, rather than to determine whether the campaign is effective and profitable for the advertiser.

In addition, the creative talent within agencies thrives on being original. To a certain extent, the entire process of testing may lead to too much introspection and may therefore dampen creativity (see Chapter 3). Creatives may also be reluctant to subject their ads to testing, under the belief that testing will not do justice to their creativity or capture all its richness. Thus both of these forces—incentives and creativity—work against the testing of ads.

Competitive Pressure to Advertise Some firms advertise not to gain market share but simply not to lose market share to competitors (see Chapter 17). They fear that even if their advertising does not increase sales, it prevents competitors' advertising from gaining market share at their expense. In this sense, advertisers may be caught in a type of prisoner's dilemma, with all firms in a market advertising to compete with each other, and no firm willing to stop, although stopping may be beneficial to all.

Budget Process In some firms, brand managers compete for advertising dollars against other brand managers. The brand managers are evaluated not on the basis of profits generated, but on the basis of sales generated. It is therefore to their advantage to have big advertising budgets, even if the effectiveness of such advertising is unclear. In such an environment, brand managers strive to win the largest ad budgets

they can, and to spend them early in the year before any cutbacks arrive. They have less concern for the effectiveness and efficiency of their advertising.

In other firms, advertising budgets are determined by affordability or as a percentage of expected sales (see Chapter 17). In such cases, when sales or profits are high, firms spend generously on advertising, but when sales or profits are low, they cut back. Thus the effectiveness of advertising is often not an important factor when determining how much to spend on advertising.

Indirect Effects of Advertising on Prices Some authors have argued strongly that, for mature products, the primary benefit of advertising is not an increase in the advertised brand's sales to consumers, but an increase in the wholesale price of the brand, *even though its retail price decreases*.[49] The **wholesale price** is the price manufacturers charge retailers, while the **retail price** is the price retailers charge consumers.

According to this theory, advertising increases consumers' awareness of and demand for a brand. As a result, retailers are under pressure to stock the brand. Competition among retailers prompts them to promote such brands to consumers with price-cuts, in order to bring consumers into the store. As a result the average retail price of the brand decreases. Over time, highly advertised brands may even become **loss leaders**, products on whose sales retailers incur a loss. At the same time, because of increased consumer demand for the brand, the manufacturer can increase the wholesale price of the brand. The net result is that advertising increases manufacturers' revenues and profits from the brand but decreases retailers' profits. This effect has sometimes been called the **Steiner effect** after the author who developed the theory. There is substantial evidence to support the Steiner effect across a number of product categories over several decades.[50]

Conclusion

In the quest to persuade consumers and win market share, advertising is probably not a strong force but a weak force. Indeed, much advertising may be ineffective. This conclusion does not mean that *all* advertising is a waste. Advertising may be a weak force, but it is not impotent. When appropriately used, creative advertising can help launch a new product, help a smaller brand compete with a dominant brand or boost sales of a dying brand. In some favorable circumstances, creative advertising can have dramatic effects.

For example, the unusual Apple ad "1984," which mocked the dominance of IBM, may have been the critical factor in the successful launch of the Apple Macintosh. Pepsi's bold ad campaign "The Pepsi Challenge" may have been instrumental in helping the firm rise above competitors and become the major rival to Coke in the cola market. Similar aggressive advertising by MCI may have helped it gain share on AT&T after the deregulation of the telephone industry. The "Heard It through the Grapevine" campaign for California raisins may have been the primary force in creating a new identity for and reviving sales of an otherwise bland brand.

Similarly, Joe Camel was a clever modification on Old Joe that breathed new life into the Camel brand. It was rich enough to have generated a series of novel ads on the same theme of the "Smooth Character." Thus it was not only new and different, but was able to sustain its newness with novel executions over time. Indeed, in 1989, Joe Camel ranked second, behind Calvin Klein, in Video Storyboards' annual survey of outstanding print ads. By 1994, it ranked ninth, but still in the top ten of all ads. Also, in the first few years after the campaign began, the Camel brand was able to hold its market share of 4 percent when other major brands suffered market share losses.[51] The novelty of the advertising rather than the level of the advertising may have been responsible for these results.

Firms advertise with the hope that their advertising will have such dramatic effects. In doing so, they draw from the best talent and techniques available in the market. However, when all competitors have equal access to such resources, it is difficult for any one firm to always have an enormous advantage. Even when one firm breaks out from among competitors with a new approach to advertising, the effectiveness of that approach is quickly diluted by many competitors that copy it. In this sense, the market for developing creative, high-impact advertising is not different in principle from that for introducing successful new products or picking winning stocks. Many competitors strive to excel with creative and unique ads. But only a few succeed, and then too for only a short while.

Given the heavy level of competition and noise in the market, advertisers must strive to make their ads rise above the clutter. To do so they need to absorb all the knowledge available from scientific studies that show when, why and how advertising works. They need to test their ads regularly to ensure that their ads are scientifically designed for maximum effectiveness. They need to deploy their limited resources efficiently and effectively, not on the basis of assumptions and beliefs, but on the basis of scientific knowledge and tests.

These recommendations are not meant to be an endorsement of the Joe Camel advertising. The problem with cigarettes is in the product. Cigarettes, when used as recommended by the manufacturer, harm the user from the very first puff. No other legal product has such negative effects. Thus, although legal, many people consider the marketing and advertising of cigarettes to be unethical. The effort to show that cigarettes advertising has perverse effects is an indirect and difficult way to control a harmful product.

Summary

Does advertising really work? To answer this question, one needs to understand three important aspects of advertising: the variables, scientific approaches and data collection methods for researching ad effectiveness. The variables to evaluate advertising are the inputs, processes and outcomes associated with advertising.

Two traditional approaches for analyzing the effects of advertising on sales are the experimental approach and the econometric or regression approach. Neither is universally superior. Because an experiment involves a careful design of variables in an artificial environment, it provides a strong test of causality but little relevance to real markets. On the other hand, because regression uses real market data that may not be easily controlled, it is strong on relevance but weak on ascertaining causality. The field experiment is a hybrid approach that combines the strengths of these two approaches.

Researchers can collect data on advertising in two important ways: via self-report or observation. Self-report is superior to observation in that it is more accessible, flexible, sensitive, convenient and fast, and less costly. However, observation is less biased than self-reports. A large number of tools can help researchers collect information on the advertising variables. We can classify these tools as either self-report or observation, and as useful to gather data on either the input, process or outcome variables for evaluating advertising.

A vast industry of data suppliers or market research firms produce various types of information or standardized reports on advertising effectiveness. Three important standardized reports are Starch recognition tests, Burke's Day-After Recall, and Nielsen's or IRI's single-source data. Single-source data systems are gaining in popularity because they are based on observational data, and provide information on the input and outcome variables in a single system.

By using the variables, approaches and tools described above, researchers have carried out a number of studies to determine whether, when and how advertising affects sales. The main conclusions from these studies are the following:

- Decreases in the level of advertising do not lead to an immediate decrease in sales. An increase in the level of advertising by itself does not lead to an increase in sales.
- On average half of all ongoing ad campaigns are ineffective.
- Changes in the creative, medium, target segment or product itself sometimes lead to changes in sales, even though increases in the level of advertising alone do not.
- When advertising is effective, it is effective either early on or never. Advertising could have certain long-term effects.
- When advertising does affect sales, its impact is not large and is much smaller than that of price.

These conclusions suggest that advertising is not the strong force many laypeople believe it to be, and may often be ineffective. Why then do firms continue with ineffective ads? Several factors may be responsible for their behavior, including the lack of testing, role of the ad agency, competitive pressure to advertise, budget process, and indirect effects on prices.

The conclusion that much advertising may be ineffective does not mean that *all* advertising is a waste. Advertising may be a weak force, but it is not impotent. When appropriately used, creative advertising can successfully launch a new product, help a smaller brand compete with a dominant one or revitalize a dying brand.

QUESTIONS

1. Describe the key approaches used to determine how advertising affects sales.
2. What is the essential trade-off between the experimental and field approaches to determine causality? Is a marriage of these alternate approaches possible?
3. Discuss the pros and cons of obtaining information from self-reports and observation.
4. What are the problems with obtaining information through surveys? How can these problems be minimized?
5. How good is day-after recall for testing the effects of advertising?
6. Many researchers hailed the advent of scanner data as a revolution in analyzing the effects of advertising. Is the perception valid? Why?
7. What are the key findings of the effects of advertising on sales? How have these findings been supported by research?
8. Why would advertisers continue with advertising that does not seem to increase sales perceptibly within reasonable time limits?
9. Why did the *JAMA* studies stir up so much controversy and so little legislative action against Joe Camel?
10. Does advertising really affect sales? Why?

NOTES

1. Martin, Claude R. Jr. (1994), "Ethical Advertising Research Standards: Three Case Studies," *Journal of Advertising* 23 (September), 17–29.
2. Whelan, Elizabeth (1992), "Against Old Joe: It's the Final Straw," *Advertising Age*, January 27.
3. Fischer, Paul M., Meyer P. Schwartz, John W. Richards, Jr., Adam O. Goldstein, and Tina H. Rojas (1991), "Brand Logo Recognition by Children Aged 3 to 6 Years," *Journal of the American Medical Association* 266, 22 (December 11), 3145–3148.
4. *Ibid.*, 3145–3148.
5. Pierce, John P., Elizabeth Gilpin, David M. Burns, Elizabeth Whalen, Bradley Rosbrook, Donald Shopland, and Michael

Johnson (1995), "Does Tobacco Advertising Target Young People to Start Smoking?" *Journal of the American Medical Association* 266, 22 (December 11), 3154–3158.

6. *Ibid.*, 3154 and 3158.

7. DiFranza, Joseph R., et al. (1991), "RJR Nabisco's Cartoon Camel Promotes Camel Cigarettes to Children," *Journal of the American Medical Association* 266, 22 (December 11), 3149–3152.

8. *Ibid.*, 3149.

9. *Ibid.*

10. Dalrymple, Goodrum (1990), *Advertising in America: The First Two Hundred Years,* New York: Harry N. Abrams, 8.

11. This response is called a demand bias, or demand artifact, and is discussed later.

12. Some would classify DiFranza's et al.'s study as a quasi-experiment because it had no control over the 1976–1988 surveys.

13. DiFranza et al., "RJR Nabisco's Cartoon Camel Promotes Camel Cigarettes to Children," 3149.

14. *Ibid.*

15. Mizerski, Richard, Brenda S. Sonner, and Katherine Straughton (1994), "A Re-evaluation of the Reported Influence of the Joe Camel Trade Charter on Cigarette Trial and Use of Minors," working paper, Florida State University.

16. Martin, "Ethical Advertising Research Standards," 27.

17. *Ibid.*; Mizerski, Sonner, and Straughton, "A Re-evaluation of the Reported Influence of the Joe Camel Trade Charter on Cigarette Trial and Use of Minors."

18. Pechmann, Cornelia, and S. Ratneshwar (1994), "The Effects of Antismoking and Cigarette Advertising on Young Adolescents' Perceptions of Peers Who Smoke," *Journal of Marketing Research* 21, 3 (September), 236–250; Stolberg, Sheryl (1997), "FTC Reveals it has New Evidence in Joe Camel," *Los Angeles Times*, March, 27, D1, D12.

19. Religion News Service (1995), "Catholics Go to Mass Less Than They Say, Survey Says," *Los Angeles Times*, January 28, B5.

20. Note that in both the last two examples, for a particular type of respondent or researcher, the direction of the error is still known. Thus such an error is still a bias.

21. For the validity of these approaches see Hughes, David G. (1992), "Real-time Response Measures of Television Commercials," Marketing Science Working Paper 92-110; Pham, Michel Tuan, G. David Hughes, and Joel B. Cohen (1993), "Validating A Dial-Turning Instrument For Real-Time Measurement of Affective and Evaluative Responses to Advertising," Marketing Science Institute Working Paper 93-116.

22. Stewart, David W., and David H. Furse (1988), "Applying Psychophysiological Measures to Marketing and Advertising Research Problems," *Journal of Current Issues and Research in Advertising*, 285–330.

23. Rothschild, Michael L., and Yong J. Hyun (1990), "Predicting Memory for Components of TV Commercials from EEG," *Journal of Consumer Research* 16 (March), 472–478; Rothschild, Michael L., Yong J. Hyun, Byron Reeves, Esther Throson, and Robert Goldstein, "Hemispherically Lateralized EEG As A Response To Television Commercials," *Journal of Consumer Research* 15 (September), 185–198.

24. Naeye, Robert (1994), "The Brain At Work," *Discover*, July 30, 30–31.

25. Dubow, Joel S. (1994), "Point of View: Recall Revisited: Recall Redux," *Journal of Advertising Research* 34, 3, 92–106; Lipstein, Benjamin (1985), "An Historical Retrospective of Copy Research," *Journal of Advertising Research* 24, 6 (December), 11–14; Arnold, Stephen J., and Richard J. Bird (1982), "The Day-After Recall Test of Advertising Effectiveness: A Discussion of the Issues," *Current Issues and Research in Advertising*, 59–68.

26. Gibson, Lawrence (1982), "Not Recall," *Journal of Advertising Research* 23, 1, 39–46.

27. Dubow, "Point of View: Recall Revisited: Recall Redux."

28. Dubow, Joel S. (1995), "Advertising Recognition and Recall by Age—Including Teens," *Journal of Advertising Research* 35, 5, 55–60.

29. Haley, R. I., and A. L. Baldinger (1991), "The ARF Copy Research Validity Project," *Journal of Advertising Research* 31, 2, 11–32; Blair, Margaret and Karl E. Rosenberg (1994), "Convergent Findings Increase Our Understanding of How Advertising Works," *Journal of Advertising Research* 34, 3, 35–45; Lodish, Leonard M., Magid Abraham, Stuart Kalmenson, Jeanne Livelsberger, Beth Lubetkin, Bruce Richardson, and Mary Ellen Stevens (1995), *Journal of Marketing Research* 32 (May), 125–139.

30. Dalrymple, *Advertising in America*.

31. Arnold, Stephen J., and Richard J. Bird (1982), "The Day-After Recall Test of Advertising Effectiveness: A Discussion of the Issues," *Current Issues and Research in Advertising*, 59–68.

32. Lipstein, Benjamin (1985), "An Historical Retrospective of Copy Research" *Journal of Advertising Research* 24, 6 (December), 11–14.

33. Singh, Surendra N., Michael L. Rothschild, and Gilbert A. Churchill, Jr. (1988), "Recognition Versus Recall As Measures of Television Commercial Forgetting," *Journal of Marketing Research* 25, 1 (February), 72–80.

34. *Ibid.*; Dubow, "Advertising Recognition and Recall by Age—Including Teens"; Du Plessis, Erik (1995) "Recognition Versus Recall," *Journal of Advertising Research* 34, 3, 75–91.

35. Curry, David J. (1993), *The New Marketing Research Systems,* New York: John Wiley & Sons Inc.; *Advertising Age* (1995), "Top Research Companies by U.S. Research Revenues," October 30, 29.

36. Horton, Cleveland (1994), "J. D. Power Will Put Car Dealers In Driver's Seat," *Advertising Age,* July 7, 1, 50.

37. Hays, Laurie (1994), "Using Computers to Divine Who Might Buy a Gas Grill," *The Wall Street Journal*, August 16, B1, B4.

38. *Advertising Age* (1995), "Top Research Companies by U.S. Research Revenues."

39. Curry, *The New Marketing Research Systems.*

40. *Ibid.* By way of comparison, scanner data have the following features relative to the best data previously available: information on up to 70 markets versus 11 regions through Nielsen's audits; weekly reports versus monthly or bimonthly reports through audits; information on individual brand sizes versus brands in previous data sources.

41. This section is based on a paper by the author, Tellis, Gerard J. (1994), "Modeling The Effects of Advertising in Contemporary Markets: Research Findings and Opportunities," in *Attention, Attitude and Affect in Response to Advertising,* Eddie M. Clark, Timothy C. Brock, and David W. Stewart, eds. Hillsdale, NJ: Lawrence Erlbaum Associates.

42. Ackoff, Russell L., and James R. Emshoff (1975), "Advertising at Anheuser-Busch, Inc. (1963–68)," *Sloan Management Review* 16, 2 (Winter), 1–16.

43. Eastlack, Joseph O. Jr., and Ambar G. Rao (1989), "Advertising Experiments at the Campbell Soup Company," *Marketing Science* 8 (Winter), 57–71.

44. Aaker, David A., and James M. Carman (1982), "Are You Over Advertising?" *Journal of Advertising Research* 22, 4 (August/September), 57–70.

45. Abraham, Majid, and Leonard Lodish (1989), *Advertising Works: A Study of Advertising Effectiveness and the Resulting Strategic and Tactical Implications,* Chicago: Information Resources.

46. Sethuraman, Raj, and Gerard J. Tellis (1991), "An Analysis of the Tradeoff Between Advertising and Pricing," *Journal of Marketing Research* 31, 2 (May), 160–174. See also Tellis, Gerard J. (1988), "The Price Elasticity of Selective Demand," *Journal of Marketing Research* 25 (November), 331–341; Assmus, Gert, John U. Farley, and Donald R. Lehmann (1984), "How Advertising Affects Sales: Meta-Analysis of Econometric Results," *Journal of Marketing Research* 21 (February), 65–74.

47. Tellis, "Modeling the Effects of Advertising." See also Henderson Blair and Rosenberg, "Convergent Findings Increase Our Understanding of How Advertising Works."

48. Lipstein, Benjamin, and James P. Neelankavil (1984), "Television Advertising Copy Research: A Critical Review of the State of the Art," *Journal of Advertising Research* 24, 2, 19–25.

49. Steiner, Robert L. (1993), "The Inverse Association between the Margins of Manufacturers and Retailers," *Review of Industrial Organization* 8, 717–740; Albion, M. (1983), *Advertising's Hidden Effects,* Boston: Auburn House; Albion, M., and Paul W. Farris (1981), "The Effect of Manufacturers' Advertising on Retail Prices," No. 81–105, Cambridge, MA: Marketing Science Institute.

50. Steiner, "The Inverse Association between the Margins of Manufacturers and Retailers."

51. Hwang, Suein L. (1995), "Joe Camel Is Missing, But Who's Walking Miles to Find Him," *The Wall Street Journal,* July 14, A1, A6.

52. Knecht, G. Bruce (1995) "Is Big Brother Watching Your Dinner and Other Worries of Piracy Watchers," *The Wall Street Journal,* November 9, B1.

In 1987, A. C. Nielsen introduced a new technology for measuring TV audiences, which led to a substantial decline in the measured audience for TV programs. This change greatly benefited advertisers at the cost of the TV networks, who had to charge less for ads. Under pressure from the networks, in 1993 Nielsen said it had found a new set of viewers, totaling some 20 million. These changes put the company in the center of a major controversy among advertisers, research firms and the networks, and raised serious questions

Planning Mass Media

about the validity of Nielsen's entire system of measuring audiences. Why and how did this highly respected market research firm stir up such a controversy? A review of the history of the measurement of TV viewership may be helpful.

In the early 1930s two MIT professors invented a mechanical gadget called the audiometer, to better measure the audience attending to radio programs. The *audiometer* automatically recorded when a radio set was turned on and off. Six years later, Arthur C. Nielsen, who had founded the A. C. Nielsen Co. in 1923, acquired the gadget. In 1942, the company launched the Nielsen Radio Index using a greatly improved version of the audiometer. When TV became popular in the 1950s, Nielsen used a modified version of the audiometer to measure TV audiences for a sample of households who agreed to serve on a panel. This book refers to this meter as the *telemeter*. Initially, it was an electromechanical device. But with the advance of electronic technology, the telemeter got far more sophisticated. By the late 1980s it contained a computer and modem to record a household's viewing of TV programs and convey this information daily to a central computer.

However, the telemeter could not identify who in the household was watching particular programs. For this purpose, Nielsen relied on diaries maintained by panel members, which recorded the TV viewing of each member of the household for every hour and day in the month. Nielsen's ratings of TV programs were based on the combined records from diaries and telemeters.

There were several problems with this approach, especially because of its reliance on diaries for important information. First, panel members tended to be women. While projections to the population could correct this discrepancy, there were other problems. As more women entered the work force, it was harder to recruit panelists. Also, women tended to overreport the audience for shows that females in the household viewed, and underreport the audience for shows that males in the household viewed. Second, the 1980s witnessed the increasing market penetration of the VCR,

remote control and cable television. These technologies led to a proliferation of TV channels, delayed viewing of TV programs, and switching among channels. Experts questioned whether households could maintain a reliable diary of their viewing of TV programs in such a complex environment. Third, to overcome these problems, some companies in Europe were experimenting with the people-meter, a more elaborate telemeter that enabled each member of the household in the panel to record his or her individual viewing of programs. British AGB Research planned to introduce the people-meter in the United States in 1983. Two other firms, Percy and Arbitron, also planned to provide TV ratings in the United States.

In 1987, Nielsen introduced the people-meter in the United States, partly to overcome these problems and partly to forestall competition from other companies. By 1988, all other firms that had planned to operate in this market had dropped out, and Nielsen was a monopoly again. Nielsen's TV audience estimates based on the people-meter showed an immediate and systematic decline relative to those based on the previous technology. Because the cost of ad time during a program is based directly on ratings, the networks had to charge advertisers less for the time than they had initially quoted, or provide advertisers with free ad time to compensate for the lower audience than the networks had guaranteed. The shortfall in ratings cost the networks up to $200 million in revenues.

While advertisers were not displeased with the new method, the networks were outraged. The basic conflict centered on the cause for the lower ratings with the people-meter. Was it because the diaries tended to overrecord certain possibly favorite shows of the panel, while the people-meter recorded a correct count? Or was it because the people-meter systematically undercounted the audience because it relied on the efforts of many family members, including children and teens, who had to enter their numbers each time they started or stopped watching TV?

In the next few years, Nielsen came under pressure from the networks to correct this reduction in the measured TV audience. In 1993, the company claimed it had found another 20 million TV viewers. These viewers were in out-of-home locations such as hotels, motels, bars and dormitories. An increase in the audience of a prime-time program by about 1 million could add $40,000 to the price of a 30-second commercial.

The TV networks felt the change was long overdue, especially as some programs, such as soap operas, were popular during lunch breaks in offices, while sporting events were popular in taverns. Advertisers were naturally skeptical, and were not eager to pay the resulting higher costs for advertising space. For example, one senior vice president of Saatchi & Saatchi claimed that the new figures were "a network tactic to build an audience it can't get through standard Nielsen measurements," and said her company would not pay the price.

The controversy is still unsettled, while Nielsen and other data suppliers keep testing new tools and systems for measuring audiences.[1]

Why is the measurement of an audience of a medium so important? The simple reason is that it determines the rates advertisers must pay to advertise, and the revenues and profits that owners of the media earn. Nielsen's efforts to be the leader in measuring TV audiences brought it into the center of a major controversy. The two major opponents in this controversy are the TV networks and the advertisers. But two equally important parties who provide the rationale for the media are the programmers who develop the material that goes in the media, and the consumers who read, view or hear those programs. Thus, the media represent the outcome of interactions among a variety of parties with different interests.

Media planning requires an understanding of the role played by these parties as well as the technical issues involved in evaluating the media, and the sources of information needed to make these choices. This chapter discusses these issues in three parts. The first part explains the structure of the media. It explains how the market for media develops, how the media are organized, what pressures are put on programmers, and how the media are changing currently. The second part explains the process of planning the media choice for a campaign. It discusses issues such as which medium to choose for advertising, and which vehicle to choose within a medium. The third part describes the various research firms that provide information on the size of the medium, and the types of information that they provide.

THE STRUCTURE OF THE MEDIA

Media is a collective term for the channels through which programmers or advertisers communicate with individuals. **Programmers** are firms or individuals who provide material that entertains or informs individuals. The media can be classified into two broad classes: direct media and mass media. **Direct media** involve individual or personal communication with members of the audience. The major direct media are mail and telephone. Chapter 16 covers direct media, while this chapter focuses on mass media.

Mass media involve communication with a large number of individuals impersonally, without much interaction. In the United States, the major mass media include TV, newspapers, magazines, radio and outdoor media (see Exhibit 15-1). Another category of mass media are *in-store media,* which include posters, displays, signs, monitors or other equipment that can communicate messages to shoppers while they are in a store. In-store advertising is generally treated as a form of promotion and is covered in Chapter 10. The mass media can also be classified into three types: broadcast, print and outdoor media. **Broadcast media,** which include TV and radio, relay a message from a single source to the audience, who must process it while it is relayed. Of late, tape recording allows for delayed exposure to broadcast signals, but that format still constitutes a small fraction of total broadcasting. **Print media,** which include newspapers and magazines, deliver a message through hard copy that can be stored and read at the audience's leisure. **Outdoor media** deliver a message on any physical structure outside build-ings. Examples include messages on billboards, trains, buses, blimps and sports arenas.

Exhibit 15-1 shows that newspapers and TV are the most popular media in the United States, each accounting for 32 percent of all advertising expenditures. Much print advertising is for retail price promotions and classified ads, while much TV advertising is for brand image building. Thus TV is the most important medium for image advertising. Direct mail, the next most popular medium, consists primarily of appeals and offers to specific segments or individuals. Radio and magazines, which contain a mix of image-building ads and promotion offers, are the next two media in popularity. The Yellow Pages, which accounts for almost as much advertising as the latter two media, consists primarily of information on retail outlets and prices.

Outdoor advertising is distinctly smaller, accounting for only 1 percent of total expenditures. Marketers of outdoor advertising suspect that the medium may be undervalued by some of the big advertisers. For example, Edwin L. Artzt, chief executive of Procter & Gamble, made a much-publicized speech in 1994 calling for a radical change in advertisers' use of media. On that occasion, Mediacom, an outdoor advertising company, ran the ad presented in Exhibit 15-2. Pedestrians puzzled over the ad, but Procter & Gamble executives were not amused and immediately called Mediacom for an explanation. That response met the goal of Mediacom, which was to draw the attention of Procter & Gamble and advertisers like it to outdoor advertising. Procter & Gamble is one of the world's biggest advertisers, with a worldwide budget of over $3 billion, 90 percent of which is spent on TV.

Each medium has a number of outlets that carry a standard program of entertainment or information. These outlets are called **vehicles.** Examples include the newspaper *The Wall Street*

▼ **EXHIBIT 15-1.** Total U.S. advertising expenditures.*

Media	Category	1995 $ billions	Percent Share of Total	Percent Change over 1994
TV		36	23	4
	Spot	19	12	6
	Network	12	7	6
	Cable	4	1	17
	Syndicated	2	1	16
Newspaper		36	23	6
	Regional	32	20	6
	National	4	3	2
Direct Mail		33	20	11
Radio		11	7	8
	Spot	9	6	9
	Network	2	1	3
Yellow Pages		10	6	4
Magazines		9	5	8
	Weeklies	3	2	7
	Monthlies	3	2	12
	Women's	2	2	12
Outdoor		1	1	8
Miscellaneous		19	9	8
Grand Total		161	100	7

*Expenditures include media and production costs. Figures are rounded.
Source: Adapted from Coen, Robert (1996), "'96 Expected To Deliver Energetic Ad Growth," *Advertising Age,* May 20, 2.

▼ **EXHIBIT 15-2.** Outdoor ad targeting broadcast advertisers.

Source: Courtesy of Mediacom.

Journal, the magazine *Time,* or ABC's TV show *20/20.* The nonadvertising material carried by these vehicles is called the **content.** It encompasses TV programs, radio shows, magazine articles and newspaper articles. The term **programming** is also used to mean content. A vehicle's content is designed to inform or entertain various individuals. The term **audience** refers to the entire set of individuals reached by a vehicle. The term **target audience** refers to a subset of the audience of special interest to the advertiser.

We describe the structure of the media in four subsections. The first section provides the economic explanation for the existence and working of the media. The second section describes the organization of the broadcast media, which are the most complex and least understood of the media. The third section explains the pressure on editors to modify content to please various interest groups. The fourth section explains the important changes occurring in the media today.

The Market for Media

In July 1995, Disney surprised the business world by announcing a buyout of Capital Cities/ABC, the leading network television station in the United States. Initially financiers hailed the merger as a marriage made in heaven. Disney could supply super content while ABC could supply the very best distribution for the content. More probing analysts, however, questioned the wisdom of the deal.[2] The advantage to either party was not great, while the potential disadvantage was. With its distribution, ABC could always get the content it needed on the market. Similarly, with the great content it produced, Disney could always get the distribution it wanted. The merger would bind each company to the other's offerings whether or not they were good. Thus ABC might be forced to distribute Disney content that no other distributor wanted. Disney might be forced to use ABC channels or time that ABC could not sell on the open market. Saddling each firm with the poor products of its partner would just hurt each of them managerially and financially. Moreover, managing the complex conglomerate would be more difficult than managing its independent parts.

Disney's purchase of Capital Cities/ABC shows the tensions and potential synergies between programmers and media owners, while Nielsen's measurement controversy shows the tensions between the media owners and advertisers. Media owners, programmers and advertisers are the important parties who are responsible for the existence of the media. However, the market for media is rooted in consumers' need for information and entertainment. Programmers develop programs to satisfy this need. Advertisers provide information about their products through ads. Media owners provide the channel through which programmers and advertisers communicate with consumers. Thus the market for media is determined by these four parties: consumers who demand information and entertainment and the programmers, media owners, and advertisers who supply them (Exhibit 15-3).

However, the contribution of these parties is not the same across all media. In some cases, such as pay-per-view cable TV, consumers so value the programs that they are willing to pay a premium to receive them without ads. In many cases, such as broadcast radio and TV, advertisers may so value

▼ EXHIBIT 15-3. The market for media.

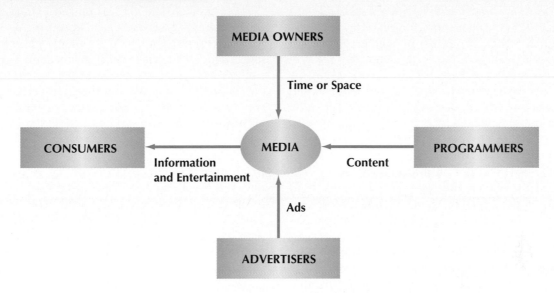

and pay for the opportunity to advertise that media owners do not need to charge consumers for their programs. In many other cases, such as most newspapers and magazines, consumers and advertisers each pay some of the costs of the media programming.

Advertisers, consumers, programmers and media owners all look at the media from different perspectives. Advertisers use the content to attract consumers to their ads. They believe they have a right to air their ads because they have bought the time or space. They want programs that attract a wide, attentive audience, with few competitors' ads, and at a minimal fee. Consumers believe they have a right to the content, either because it was promised free or because they pay some fee for it. They perceive the ads as an interruption of the content, and demand informative or entertaining programs with few ads, at minimal cost. Programmers like to design content that meets consumer demand, without any pressure from advertisers. They want media owners to pay a high price for programs that they can produce at minimal cost. Media owners have to bring the other parties together while minimizing program costs, maximizing audiences and maximizing ad rates.

The market for media programs without ads clears when media owners can supply programs to consumers at a price the latter are willing to pay. The market for media programs with ads clears when media owners can supply programs with ads at a price consumers are willing to pay, and charge for the ads a price advertisers are willing to pay. In particular, the price for ad time or space must be no more than advertisers are willing to pay for the size and type of audience that time or space attracts.

In successfully operating markets with adequate alternative media and programmers, media owners need not own programs, programmers need not own media, and advertisers need not produce programs or own media. Indeed, it is better for each of these agents to do what it does best, and resort to the market to complement its services. Nevertheless, for historical or special reasons, each of these parties may resort to integration. For example, most newspapers and magazines produce much of their news reports in-house. Indeed, the news they produce is so intrinsically linked to their unique character, and so critical to their success, that they would not do otherwise. For the same reason, many owners of broadcast media produce their own news shows. On the other hand, most of these owners resort to external programmers for their entertainment shows. In the latter case, the production of entertainment is so complex, dynamic and uncertain that media owners are better off buying it on the market than producing it in-house. For the same reasons, with rare exceptions, most advertisers neither own media nor produce shows. The few that do find it increasingly difficult for their programs or media to succeed. That is why many analysts were skeptical of the benefits of Disney's purchase of Capital Cities/ABC.

Similar mergers in the past among suppliers and buyers in properly functioning markets were also suboptimum and failed.[3] For example, Sony purchased Columbia Pictures in 1989, in part to use its digital audiotape format, which few audio programmers wanted. But putting its own content into a format the market did not want was unlikely to sell even if distributed through Columbia. Moreover, Sony was unable to manage Columbia's motion picture business, which endured a string of losses. Matsushita entered the entertainment business by purchasing MCA, seeking synergies between MCA's entertainment content and Matsushita's viewing devices. Despite MCA's phenomenal success with some movies, Matsushita failed to gain the synergies it sought. The reason is that good content by MCA could always command a price in the market equal to or higher than parent Matsushita could pay. Thus, in general, companies are better off concentrating on their core competencies, and going to the market for distributors or suppliers.

Similarly, in 1991 Procter & Gamble shut down P&G Productions, a unit that produced programs for TV.[4] Procter & Gamble started producing its own TV programs in the early 1950s when programming alternatives were scarce, because program ownership gave it exclusive rights to the ad time and independent control of the program's content. However, by the 1990s there were abundant alternative programs, each with a specific segment and fairly flexible ad slots. So Procter & Gamble did not have to undertake the risk and effort of producing its own limited programs. For the same reason, most firms today are not involved in programming, preferring to buy time on programs available in the market that have the right audience and price for their ads.

Organization of TV

This section explains the organization of TV, because of the importance and the relative complexity of the medium. This exposition should also help in understanding radio, which has a parallel organization. The owners of TV consist of a large number of TV stations scattered across the nation. Some of these stations are themselves owned by larger corporations, while others are independent. A few of these stations produce some of their own programming, especially news programs, which involve relatively low-risk investments. Most purchase their programming from suppliers in the open market. Such suppliers could be networks such as NBC, entertainment studios such as Universal Studios, or individual producers such as Phil Donahue.

A **network** is a producer of programming that has contracted with a set of stations to broadcast that programming. The major (noncable) networks in the United States are CBS, NBC, ABC and Fox. The stations are called **affiliates** when linked with their respective network, and **local stations** when contrasted with national networks. Programs are classified as syndicated or network. *Syndicated programs* are those that are broadcast at different times by different channels, such as *Wheel of Fortune* and *The Oprah Winfrey Show*. *Network programs* are those that are broadcast simultaneously to all or most channels in a network.

This relationship among networks and local stations leads to three types of advertising: network, spot and local. **Network advertising** is advertising during programs supplied by networks, and is generally aired at the same time to all affiliates in the network. The network shares the ad revenues with its affiliates. This setup greatly simplifies the purchase and management of ads for an advertiser who needs to reach a wide audience. **Spot advertising** is advertising during the private programming of local stations. Advertisers contract for such advertising directly with the local stations. Spot advertising can be national spot or local advertising. **National spot advertising** is advertising by national companies on local stations. National advertisers resort to spot advertising when they want to reach certain local audiences where their product is heavily used or can benefit from advertising. National advertisers also use spot advertising when a network program is not available during the times they wish to advertise. **Local advertising** is advertising by local firms on local stations. Because its reach is local, it is especially useful for advertisers who need the power of television but want to reach a local audience.

The amount of time advertisers can buy on TV falls into three categories: sponsorships, participation and infomercials. **Sponsorships** involve the purchase of the entire time of a program. The sponsor may use the time to air a show it has produced or purchased from a programmer, or a show produced and broadcast by the network or a local station. Sponsorship provides an advertiser control over the audience of a show and the timing of its ads, while screening out competitive ads. As the number of alternate stations and programs has ballooned, and the price of broadcast ads in each has gone up, most advertisers find sponsorships too expensive or inefficient. In **participation,** an advertiser buys some of the advertising time during a program, as do other advertisers. The advantage of participation is that the fortunes of the advertiser are not linked entirely to a particular program. The infomercial is a form of advertising that lies between these two types. The **infomercial** is an extended TV ad that lasts the length of and appears to be a regular program.[5] Infomercials are useful if an advertiser needs extended time to explain its product, the time is relatively inexpensive and the audience is not so critical as to demand particular news or entertainment. Thus infomercials have become popular during the late-night and early morning time slots.

Advertisers can buy time on TV in two ways: scatter or up-front buying. **Scatter buying** involves the purchase of broadcast time during the season. **Up-front buying** involves the purchase of broadcast time in a vehicle several months ahead of the season or quarter. Such purchases have three benefits for advertisers. First, the time costs less than in the scatter market. Second, media owners generally guarantee a minimum audience for this time. If the program does not get the guaranteed audience, the owner will provide free alternate time for the advertiser. This is called **make-good time.** Third, up-front purchases also provide an advertiser the option to select the

times it wants. However, the rate will be higher if the advertiser wants to exercise this option and reserve a certain time. The media owner may still reserve the right to change the time, unless the advertiser pays a higher *nonpreemptable rate* that denies the media owner this right. Owners of broadcast media sell the up-front time at a discount because it provides sales security as well as facilitates planning. However, very high up-front sales could be a problem.

For example, in summer 1995, the major TV networks in the United States received a bonanza in advertising commitments. They sold a total of $5.77 billion worth of advertising for the 1995–1996 television season up front. These sales covered 90 percent of their inventory of advertising time. The sales were especially welcome, as they came after many years in which advertisers scrimped on advertising. However, the up-front sales may have been a mixed blessing. They reduced time available for sales in the scatter market, which is sold at a premium of 45 percent above the up-front rate. Moreover, heavy up-front sales reduced the time available to make good on audience guarantees on up-front sales.

Cable TV Cable TV refers to TV programs transmitted through a cable instead of through the air. Like traditional TV, cable TV can also be classified into network and local stations that provide network or syndicated programs and allow for national, spot or local ads. Cable TV originated in the mid-1970s to serve small cities and localities unable to pick up signals broadcast through the air. From that time, cable TV has grown steadily mainly at the cost of network TV (see Exhibit 15-4). Several factors are responsible for the growth of cable TV at the expense of traditional broadcast TV:

▼ **EXHIBIT 15-4.** Growth of cable TV.

Annual ad revenues in millions of dollars					
	Cable TV ad revenues	Percent change	Network TV ad revenues	Percent change	Syndicated TV ad revenues	Percent change
1994	$2,970.2	27.5%	$11,893.2	9.2%	$2,358.1	45.6%
1993	2,329.0	46.4	10,892.7	1.5	1,620.1	24.0
1992	1,590.5	31.3	10,732.8	13.5	1,306.4	−29.4
1991	1,211.6	9.1	9,456.2	−6.7	1,850.4	16.6
1990	1,110.2	—	10,132.3	—	1,587.6	—

Source: Competitive Media Reporting as reported in *Advertising Age,* November 27, 1995.

- It allows for clearer reception.
- It allows for many more channels.
- Its cost per ad is generally lower.
- Its subscribers tend to be more affluent and have high purchasing power.
- Its channels have specific programming dedicated to specific topics such as sports, news, art, movies, children's shows or politics.

Thus cable TV is best suited for advertisers who want to target a well-defined segment of buyers, or who cannot afford the high costs of traditional broadcast TV. At the same time, cable TV still suffers from some limitations, which explains why it has not fully displaced traditional TV. To begin with, consumers have to pay for cable, and some cable programs are not of as high quality as traditional TV. Therefore, its penetration is not as high as that of traditional TV, which is free. In addition, there are many more cable TV channels, which each reach a smaller audience than traditional TV channels. Thus advertisers have to contract with many more media owners if they advertise on cable TV instead of traditional TV.

Pressure on Program Content

Stephen C. May, publisher of the *Times,* a general-interest weekly serving Lafayette, Louisiana, was faced with a dilemma. An editorial in his newspaper chided a local Christian group for pushing a new ABC series, *NYPD Blue,* off the air on local affiliates. The editor boasted that the *Times* always accepted political ads from any group. On reading that editorial, Roger Harris, a Ku Klux Klan member, asked to place an ad for the local chapter of the organization. The ad was free of the standard racial epithets. But it was loaded with racism. For example, it claimed "The White Race [is] the irreplaceable hub of our Nation." The Ku Klux Klan member was willing to pay $900 in cash for the ad. May was not sure whether he should reject the ad and violate his own policies of open advertising or accept the ad and antagonize his readers. The *Times* mixed investigative reporting with social consciousness and had a liberal audience.

The solution he found was to accept the ad and donate the proceeds to two groups: the local affiliate of the National Association for the Advancement of Colored People, and Klanwatch, the investigative arm of the Southern Poverty Law Center. May also ran an editorial alongside the ad that explained his dilemma and the solution he found. Members of the Ku Klux Klan were furious to learn that their Klan money had supported groups opposed to them. But Harris considered it a triumph to get his message across, even at the real and implied cost.[6]

This example shows how a newspaper has to balance its principles against the interests of its readers and its need for advertising. The First Amendment to the U.S. Constitution guarantees freedom of speech and of the press. Programmers and media owners have taken this right to mean that no government may interfere with their right to broadcast or publish whatever appeals to their audiences. Each newspaper, magazine or TV program sets its own standards for content based on its target segment. Thus the primary determinants of the content of a vehicle are the philosophy of the editor or programmer, and the tastes and interests of the audience.

However, organized interest groups have always tried to influence editors to present content that is more favorable to their own position, or to avoid content that would hurt their position or sensitivities. Editors have prided themselves on being independent from such pressures. Indeed, the audience's faith in a vehicle depends on its perception of the vehicle's independence from special interests. However independent a vehicle may be, it is vulnerable to pressures of external groups the moment it accepts advertising support. Advertisers exert implicit pressure on editors, by either buying or not buying time and space in their programs. They exert explicit pressure when they threaten to support or withdraw support for certain programs. In order to be entirely free from such pressures, certain publications, such as *Consumer Reports,* refuse to accept any advertising support. As a result, *Consumer Reports* is relatively expensive and has a relatively small subscription base, but it is highly respected and widely consulted by consumers.

Recently, however, organized interest groups have found an indirect but effective means of influencing a vehicle's content. They have threatened advertisers with boycotts of their products unless they cease their ad support for content that these interest groups find undesirable. Advertisers in turn have tried to influence the content of a vehicle either because of pressure from customers, or because of their own interests. Advertisers are most likely to successfully influence the content if they are its sole or major supporter. Exhibit 15-5 shows that pres-

▼ EXHIBIT 15-5. **Pressure in the newsroom.**

Type of Pressure From Advertisers	Percent of Editors Reporting
Attempted to influence content of story	90%
Tried to kill story	71
Withdrew advertising because of story	89
Succeeded in influencing story	37

Data Source: Marquette University study as reported in Masterson, Peg (1993), "Many Editors Report Advertiser Pressure," *Advertising Age*, January 11, 22.

sures on editors are fairly widespread, and have frequently prompted editors to change content.

However, pressures on media must not be confused with the right to free speech.[7] The media always have the right to ignore advertisers' demands if they judge them to be unprincipled. They need to attract an audience that will pay the higher price in the absence of advertising revenues. Alternatively, media can please advertisers at the cost of the audience. Advertisers will have to pay a higher price for their ads to subsidize the loss of paying customers. For the most part, the media play a major balancing act, appearing independent, thought provoking and interesting to attract audiences, while also avoiding highly sensitive material to retain advertisers and audiences.

Major Trends in Media

The evolution of the media is a dynamic process that shapes the media and substantially alters their character. Important trends in the current evolution of the media include the fragmentation of traditional media, splintering of TV ad length, increasing clutter, and growth of new media.

Fragmentation of Traditional Media Media fragmentation refers to the process by which an audience for a particular medium breaks up into smaller segments, each of which watches a different program. For example, the advent of high-quality FM broadcasts with a short range of about 100 miles led to a large increase in regional radio channels, each with a small segment of consumers with unique tastes. With the growth of cable TV, the average number of TV channels that U.S. households subscribe to rose from 10 in 1980 to 33 in 1990.[8] Recently, satellite transmission and high-capacity TV antennae has increased the number of channels accessible to house-

holds to over 100. The lower costs and higher quality of printing, together with higher disposable incomes, have also led to a proliferation of magazines and newspapers, each of which appeals to a unique segment of consumers. For example, the number of magazine titles in the United States rose from 1,450 in 1980 to 2,135 in 1990.[9]

In the past, a few TV and radio networks, major magazines and major newspapers catered to a wide audience. Today, a vast number of such outlets cater to smaller, segmented audiences. This change has major implications for advertisers. First, advertisers who need to reach certain narrow segments can do so more easily using selective outlets within the traditional media. Second, advertisers who need a wide national audience find it harder and costlier to reach. The decline in a national audience was one of the factors that aggravated the controversy surrounding Nielsen's ratings. During the 1980s and 1990s, as the national TV audience declined but TV ad rates kept increasing, knowledge of the precise audience that TV programs reached became critical for advertisers and networks. To advertisers, such knowledge meant getting a fair audience for the increasingly high price they paid for ad time. To TV networks, it meant being able to survive as the number of smaller cable TV stations and their audiences increased, squeezing their revenues and profits.

Splintering of TV Spot Length The average length of TV ads declined from 60 seconds in 1965 to 30 seconds in 1975, and is currently heading toward 15 seconds (see Exhibit 15-6). One factor responsible for this trend is the cost of TV ad time. This cost has been

▼ EXHIBIT 15-6. **Decline in ad length over time.**

Percentage of Ads By Ad-Length And Year			
Year	60 Seconds	30 Seconds	15 Seconds
1965	77%	23%	0%
1975	6	93	0
1980	2	96	0
1985	2	84	10
1990	2	60	35

Source: Erwin Ephron (1992), "He who Championed Clutter: No Easy Answers on the Question of Too Many Ads," *Inside Media*, April 29.

▼ **EXHIBIT 15-7.** Average length of network television commercials, 1965–1991.

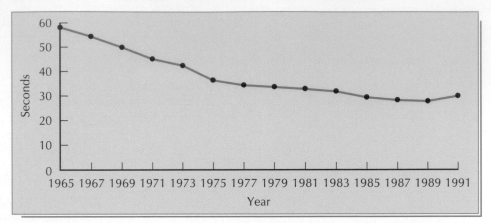

Source: Cobb-Walgreen 1990 Competitive Media Reporting as published in Robert J. Kent, "Competitive Clutter in Network Television Advertising: Current Levels and Advertising Responses," *Journal of Advertising Research,* January/February 1995, 49–56. Published with permission of the Advertising Research Foundation © 1995.

increasing as the audience's size and firms' demand for advertising time has grown. Media suppliers have reduced the minimum length of an ad to make it more affordable. Another cause of the splintering of TV ad time is a research finding that the effectiveness of a TV ad does not decline proportionally with its length. That is, an ad that is half as long as another ad may be more than half as effective. This realization has led advertisers to use TV time more efficiently by shortening ads. As a result, the average length of a TV ad has declined steadily over the last three decades (see Exhibit 15-7).

Increasing Clutter **Clutter** refers to the proliferation of ads that compete for an audience's attention within a particular time period or printed space. The amount of clutter in most media has been increasing steadily over the last three decades. For example, Exhibit 15-8 shows that the average number of network ads per prime-time hour increased from 6 in 1965 to 18 in 1991. Two forces that have triggered this increase are the proliferation of brands and the splintering of TV ads over the same time span. Note that even though total ad time has not gone up much (see Exhibit 15-9), clutter is still a major problem because the larger number of ads, messages and brands competing for consumers' attention reduces the effectiveness of any one of them.

Growth of New Media A development that has the potential to revolutionize the media is the growth of new media. A number of new media are developing simultaneously. While all are unlikely to become major media overnight, some have the potential to do so. We can classify these media into three groups: new media locations and forms, computer-based media and product placements.

New Media Locations and Forms As public transportation in the United States and some other countries has had to contend with declining revenues, it has resorted to carrying ads on public vehicles to increase revenues. Thus trains, trams, buses, and even space rockets have begun to carry ads. For example, in May 1993, Sony's Columbia Pictures plastered the rocket and booster rocket of an unmanned U.S. spacecraft with ads for its summer movie, *Last Action Hero*. Columbia Pictures claimed that by paying $500,000 for the space, it beat out dozens of competing advertisers who wanted to be the "first to be blasted off into space."[10] Blimps are not a new location for ads, but they have recently become popular. Goodyear pioneered advertising through the blimp about 70 years ago. For many decades it was the sole advertiser through this medium. Then in the last decade Fuji also attempted this form of advertising, followed by several other companies including Met Life, MCI, Blockbuster Video, Sea World, and Gulf Oil. Some companies such as Kraft and Coca-Cola have taken blimps to Europe, while Pizza Hut gained more publicity than it bargained for when its blimp crashed in New York in the midst of a 19-city tour.[11]

Another novel though more earthly outlet for ads has been turnstiles at sports and entertainment arenas.[12] Advertisers have also succeeded in selling ads in the form of posters to college students to decorate their walls. Such posters initially went on sale for $10 each in the early 1990s, with lower prices for multiple orders of posters.[13] Ads within stores have the potential to be much more effective because of their proximity to the point at which the buying

▼ **EXHIBIT 15-8.** Average number of network ads per prime-time hour, 1965–1991.

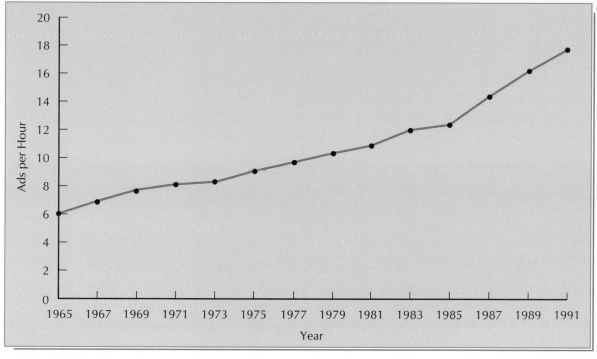

Source: Cobb-Walgreen 1990, Competitive Media Reporting as published in Robert J. Kent, "Competitive Clutter in Network Television Advertising: Current Levels and Advertising Responses," *Journal of Advertising Research,* January/February 1995, 49–56. Published with permission of the Advertising Research Foundation © 1995.

▼ **EXHIBIT 15-9.** Average network ad time per prime-time hour, 1980–1992.

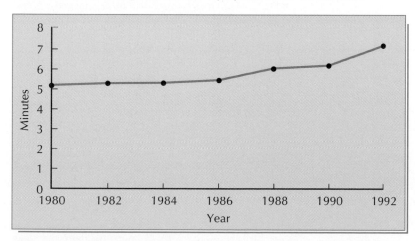

Source: Cobb-Walgreen 1990, Competitive Media Reporting as published in Robert J. Kent, "Competitive Clutter in Network Television Advertising: Current Levels and Advertising Responses," *Journal of Advertising Research,* January/February 1995, 49–56. Published with permission of the Advertising Research Foundation © 1995.

decision is made. In-store ads have appeared in new locations such as the shopping cart, the end-of-aisle monitor, the checkout conveyor belt and via storewide broadcasts. The video cart, a cart with a video monitor that carried ads, became a hot item early in the 1990s, but its popularity has since declined. Two Kroger stores in Little Rock, Arkansas, may have been the first to try ad messages on the conveyor belts at the checkout counter. The stores sold the space at the rate of $200 for a 10- × 11-inch ad for a month.[14]

Computer-Related Media In the last few years the availability of computers has increased dramatically, with a current average of one computer for every three U.S. households. This new medium has a great potential for new forms of advertising. One simple means of advertising is through the provision of free or subsidized screen savers, especially since most computers are left idle for many hours. Another important means of communication is through computer diskettes. This medium is particularly suited for consumers on the lookout for more information about the product or manufacturer. The diskette can be easily mailed to target households at a small cost and can contain audio, video and print information that fully describes a product's advantages. Perhaps the single most important impact of the computer on media is the growth of the Internet (see Chapter 16).

Product Placements Product placement involves the paid placement of a brand name or product image alongside regular programming, while not identifying the sponsor and maintaining a noncommercial character. A **noncommercial character** refers to the image of an ad made to appear like part of a program. An example is when a movie shows a scene with a hotel's brand name clearly visible, without any mention that that advertising is being sponsored by the owner of the name. Product placements can appear in movies, dramas, shows, stories, public events, and even newscasts. The potential effectiveness of product placements can be explained on the basis of implicit memory (see Chapter 6). After viewing a placement, consumers may not have explicit recall for the context of the placement, but their implicit recall of the brand name may be enhanced, leading to greater evoking and purchase of the brand than without the placement.

Product placements have a number of advantages over traditional ads. First, because consumers see the brand name in the course of some other programming, their suspicions about the trustworthiness of the exposure are not aroused. Second, the event or personality with which the brand name is associated serves as an endorsement of the product. Third, since no explicit message is communicated, consumers are less likely to develop defenses such as counterarguments against the message. Fourth, to the extent the movie or program is replayed and reaches a wide audience, the brand name achieves great exposure. Movies in particular, if they turn out to be classics, are played and replayed repeatedly on screen and via the home VCR.

Product placements also have some disadvantages. First, the placement has to be negotiated in advance without the advertiser having full knowledge of the size or nature of the audience or the details of the context in which the placement will be viewed. Second, the advertiser has little control of the program around which the placement will be developed. Third, if the program containing the placement bombs or develops a negative reputation, the advertiser does not have the option of withdrawing its ad. It remains there for the life of the program.

MEDIA PLANNING

"Enter a woman in a white bathrobe. Smiling at the men and women watching her, she turns so that her back is to them, then drops the robe to the floor. She wears nothing but body paint—a living representation of a bottle of vodka.

Performance art in SoHo? A rehearsal for an avant-garde drama Off Off Broadway?

In fact, this is no artistic endeavor. Rather, it is part of an annual spectacle that reveals a lot about the American advertising business amid one of the worst recessions in media history.

Every spring for five years, Carillon Importers Ltd., which has surfed to success on an ocean of an imported Swedish vodka called Absolut, has invited representatives from the nation's magazines and newspapers to its Teaneck headquarters just west of Manhattan. As if in a Madison Avenue version of "A Chorus Line," the publications' advertising sales executives—and occasionally, their top editors—audition for executives of Carillon and TBWA Advertising, its agency.

Like the eager dancers singing "God, I Hope I Get It," they are seeking to sell themselves in an extremely competitive business. In this case, it's to win part of the $25 million to $30 million spent each year on the witty, stylish advertising that has made Absolut's one of the best-known, most effective brand campaigns ever. In what is now a big trend in publishing, the publications hope to improve their chances by creating ads and promotions customized for the advertiser.

In they come for these "Media Meetings," involving 7 to 15 publications a day, 2 to 4 days a week, from April through June, in what has been nicknamed the Media Marathon. All told, some 200 (including *The New York Times Magazine*) pass through. Each publication gets 30 minutes to sell its ad ideas to the executives from TBWA, Absolut's agency since the campaign's inception 13 years ago, and to Michel Roux,

Carillon's president and chief executive. Mr. Roux combines the hardnosed directness of Zach, the director-taskmaster in "A Chorus Line," with a Gallic charm and playfulness.

For the first time, Carillon and TBWA allowed a reporter to attend a session of the Media Marathon. What most intrigued this outsider was the lengths to which publications will go to attract Absolut's ad dollars. The painted woman, part of a presentation by Vanity Fair magazine on a recent morning, had shock appeal. But perhaps more striking was the sight of smart, confident and aggressive people from prestigious magazines genuflecting before the mercurial godfather of liquor advertising. They flattered their host, some to the point of being obsequious. They cheered suggestions they didn't like. They spent heavily on mockups and on gifts meant to curry favor. In some cases, they even hinted at shaping their editorial content to satisfy the advertiser.

Was there really once a time when advertisers had to beg to make it into some publications? That seems a distant memory now.[15]"

Source: Reprinted from Elliott, Stuart (1993), "Advertising's Marathon Auditions," in "Themes of the Times," *The New York Times*, June 6, 1. Excerpt. Copyright © 1993 by The New York Times Co. Reprinted with permission.

Carillon's auditions of representatives from newspapers and magazines is an indication of the strong position in which advertisers find themselves as publications compete for advertising dollars. It is also an indication of the opportunities and pressures advertisers face as they develop their media plans. However, media planning is neither solely nor primarily a matter of auditioning publishers. **Media planning** involves two major decisions, media choice and vehicle choice, which are based on a thoughtful analysis of many factors and much data. Presentations by various publishers are only one input into the process. Media planners should not substitute them for their own primary research or for data from independent industry sources.

Media Choice

Media choice refers to the selection of media for an ad campaign. The term **media mix** refers to the combination of media selected. Media choice is frequently the first decision in media planning, and depends primarily on four key characteristics of the media: informative versus evocative power, focus, speed and location.

Informative versus Evocative Power **Informative** versus **evocative power** of a medium refers to its ability to communicate information relative to its ability to communicate emotion. Of the various media, the print media are best able to communicate information to an audience. The reason is that printed material remains with the reader, can be read at the reader's speed and convenience, and can be actively processed. So an advertiser can provide quite complex, detailed, or lengthy information in printed ads (see Chapter 6). In contrast, audiences generally process TV, radio or outdoor advertising under time pressure. In the case of TV and radio, a viewer's or listener's comprehension is limited by the speed of the communication. For outdoor media, a viewer's comprehension is limited by the time it takes to go past the message. For radio, TV and outdoor media, after a message is received, the recipient generally does not have the option of going back to look over it more closely. These three media also tend to stimulate passive processing by the viewer or listener (see Chapter 5). Thus the communicating of information is much easier by print than by the broadcast and outdoor media.

On the other hand, TV is an ideal medium for communicating emotion. The primary reason is that it can depict individuals in highly emotional situations, both through pictures and sounds (see Chapter 7). In addition, the audiovisual format of the medium makes for heightened attention and more effective communication of emotion. Color, light and darkness, and music can all be used creatively to arouse emotion. For the same reasons, TV is also an effective means of demonstrating key features of products. While good color and copy in printed ads can arouse emotions and demonstrate features, such arousal requires more space than does the communication of information. The arousal of emotion through print also requires more effort on the part of the reader than is required through TV.

For these reasons, the broadcast media, especially TV, can communicate an emotional ad appeal or a product demonstration more effectively and efficiently than the print media. But the print media can communicate information more effectively than the broadcast media.

Focus

In 1991 Procter & Gamble stopped producing soap operas, the format it had pioneered.[16] Soaps involve a daily or weekly series covering the lives of family members involved in various romantic or seductive plots. The goal of the soaps was to entertain women at home who had a fairly traditional lifestyle and were a ready market for the firm's brands. Procter & Gamble first aired soap operas on the radio in the early 1930s, and adapted the format for TV when that medium became popular in the 1950s. However, over the last few decades the demographics changed. More women were at work outside the home, and those that were not still had busy schedules. At the same time, talk show hosts had started presenting real-life drama with more gripping romantic or sexy plots at competing time slots. Procter & Gamble initially responded by trying to spruce up its soaps with younger actors and steamier sex scenes. But the traditional soaps targeted to the stereotypical housewife lost their original appeal.[17]

This brief history of soap operas shows how programs and media can target specific audiences. The *focus* of a medium is its ability to target distinct market segments. The various media differ dramatically in their ability to focus on intended targets. An important goal of an ad is to reach its intended target as efficiently as possible. Thus understanding the focus of a medium is an important step in media choice.

TV is the least focused medium, reaching a vast number of users. This is especially true of some TV programs such as the Olympic Games, Soccer's World Cup, the Academy Awards, or the Super Bowl, which reach hundreds of millions of international viewers (see Exhibit 15-10). The recent increase in the number of TV channels has led to some splintering of the TV audience. Now there are shows that appeal to quite specific audiences. However, compared to the other media, TV remains a classic mass medium with relatively wide, undifferentiated audiences. Popular prime-time TV programs regularly reach audiences of over 10 million adults.[18] Compare these numbers with those of newspapers. The most popular U.S. newspapers, *The Wall Street Journal, USA Today* and the Sunday edition of the *New York Times,* have circulations of under 2 million.

Although the popular daily newspapers are more focused in their audiences than popular TV programs, the difference is primarily geographic rather than demographic. With the exception of a few national newspapers, most newspapers in the United States have a regional market. As a result they attract more regional ads. For example, in 1992, newspapers attracted only $3.8 billion of the $76.3 billion that national advertisers spent.[19] Within the regional market, newspapers appeal to a large cross section of households. In general, newspapers appeal to more middle- and upper-level socioeconomic groups than does TV.

Relative to newspapers, magazines have an audience that is geographically more diverse but demographically more focused. The reason is that magazines have a larger audience that is distributed over the country. For example, the most widely distributed magazine, *Parade,* has a national circulation of 37 million.[20] Yet, magazines tend to be more highly focused than newspapers because they provide more specific content that appeals to specific audiences. For example, magazines such as *Seventeen* and *Sassy* appeal primarily to teenage girls and are a good medium for cosmetic advertisers. Similarly, magazines such as *Parenting, Modern Bride* and *Muscle and Fitness* have very precise audiences, as their names indicate.

Radio programs, especially FM broadcasts, tend to be focused both geographically, because of their small range (about 100 miles), and demographically, because of the narrow appeal of their music or talk shows. Outdoor advertising is unique in that it is geographically highly focused, but demographically highly unfocused. Only people who pass by a certain billboard are likely to see the ad it carries, but people of all demographic groups are likely to pass by most billboards.

▼ **EXHIBIT 15-10.** Most widely watched TV events (as of June 1994).

Event	Worldwide Audience (in millions)
1990 soccer World Cup championships	1,000
1993 U.S. football Super Bowl	750
1986 soccer World Cup championships	652
1991 European Cup soccer final	526
1969 American moon landing	490

Data Source: Davidson, Jean (1994), "World Cup Goal: Net Increase in U.S. Fans," *Chicago Tribune,* June 12, 5, 11.

Thus TV is an ideal medium to advertise products that have a wide appeal across demographic and even geographic boundaries. For example, Pepsi-Cola, Coca-Cola, McDonald's and Levi Jeans tend to advertise heavily to the mass international audience of major sporting events. On the other hand, manufacturers of appliances tend to use the print media to focus on the segment that is in the market for their products. The audience of the media also affects the cost of advertising, thus limiting the firms that can use that medium. Because TV reaches a wide audience, the cost per ad is relatively much more than for the other media. Thus TV may not be cost efficient for brands that do not have a large share of the market, such as In-And-Out Burger, or for product categories that have a low turnover, such as barbecue grills. In contrast, advertising in selected newspapers and magazines is relatively more affordable for such brands and categories.

The direct media, such as mail and telephone, have the highest cost per person reached. But they allow for the greatest targeting of ads. Thus these media are ideal for categories where the target market is small, well defined, geographically dispersed, but accessible by phone or mail. For example, diaper manufacturers can reach parents of newborns through the mail by obtaining addresses from the registrations of live births. Mortgage insurance companies can reach new home buyers through the mail by obtaining their addresses from the city or county recordings of new home sales. The direct media are an especially powerful medium of advertising for small companies that cannot afford mass media. For example, swimming pool services can send their mail ads to homes with pools. Such lists can be obtained from retailers of pool supplies or city registers where registration is required.

Speed The *speed* of a medium refers to how quickly it can disseminate a message to a target audience. The mass media vary substantially in speed. Radio, and especially TV, can broadcast a message to a wide audience in minutes. In comparison, periodicals such as magazines can communicate a message only on their issue dates. Because their life extends till the next issue is out, and sometimes beyond that date, magazines tend to be read at leisure. The slower reading of magazines causes a slower dissemination of the message in magazine ads. Because most newspapers have daily editions, they can also disseminate messages fairly quickly, though not as fast and

to as wide an audience as TV. The speed of message dissemination of a billboard is contingent on its location and on the frequency with which traffic passes that location.

Another factor related to the speed of message communication is the time it takes to prepare ads. In terms of preparation time, TV is perhaps the slowest, because audiovisual ads take longer to prepare, and TV ads require more approvals for content and more advance booking for appropriate time slots. Radio ads are perhaps the quickest to prepare, with ads for newspapers, magazines and billboards taking more time, in that order.

Thus, if the goal of an ad is to disseminate a message quickly across a wide audience, then TV or national newspapers are suitable, provided the ad can be prepared in time. For example, major national services, such as MCI and AT&T, or Northwest and American Airlines, often compete on special short-term promotions, which they advertise on wide-audience TV programs and in national newspapers. On the other hand, if the goal of the ad is to persuade a target segment of an enduring image or position, then magazines and specific TV programs are better suited.

Location The *location* of a medium refers to the place in which the audience normally receives messages through the medium. TV is normally viewed indoors, mostly at home. Radio is often heard outdoors, especially while driving. Print media are received and read mostly at home. In-store and outdoor media reach consumers within stores and outside buildings as their names indicate. Consumers make decisions about various products at different locations and times. Ads are likely to be most effective when placed in media that reach consumers close to the place or time at which they decide about the product.

TV, newspaper and magazine advertising is most useful for product categories in which the brand choice is made primarily in the house. Examples include automobiles, appliances and vacations. For products where the brand choice is made while traveling or commuting, outdoor or radio ads are the best. Examples include gasoline stations, auto repair shops, and restaurants. For purchases made without much previous thought and search, point-of-purchase or in-store media are the best. Examples include impulse items or nonstaple groceries. Services that are contacted primarily by phone should advertise in the Yellow Pages. Examples would be household cleaning services, auto services, restaurants, retailers, and law firms.

The traditional media differ substantially in the four important characteristics just described (see Exhibit 15-11). The choice of a medium to advertise a particular product depends on how these characteristics affect the communication of the message for that product. The evaluation of these characteristics is also primarily qualitative in contrast to that for vehicles and scheduling, which tends to be more quantitative. While, in general, the choice of a medium precedes that of the vehicle and the scheduling, the latter two decisions may also affect the choice of the medium, as we shall see next.

▼ **EXHIBIT 15-11.** Comparison of traditional media.

Medium	Informative Power	Emotive Power	Focus	Speed	Proximity to Point of Purchase
TV	Low	High	Low	High	Low
Print	High	Low	Medium	Medium	Low
Magazines	High	Medium	Medium	Low	Low
Radio	Low	Medium	Medium	High	Medium
Outdoor	Low	Low	Medium	Low	High
Mail	High	Low	High	Medium	Low
Telephone	Low	Medium	High	High	Medium

Vehicle Choice

The U.S. Super Bowl continues to attract advertisers despite the increasing cost of its ads, which in 1996 reached $1.3 million for a 30-second spot. How valuable was this buy in terms of alternatives available? One study found that ads placed in some other shows could reach a wider audience for a lower cost than a single Super Bowl ad.[21] How is this possible? If it is so, why do firms pay so much to advertise during the Super Bowl? How can one evaluate and compare two vehicle selection plans? This section provides the concepts and tools to answer these questions.

Vehicle choice refers to the selection of vehicles for an ad campaign. The choice of a vehicle depends on the evaluation of four important characteristics of vehicles: audience, cost, target market and schedule. Evaluating the audience enables advertisers to pick vehicles that reach the widest audience, the fundamental criterion in vehicle choice. However, vehicles that have a large audience also cost more. Thus evaluating costs enables advertisers to pick vehicles that reach a wide audience for the same or lower

cost. Most advertisers need to reach certain target segments of the population, rather than the whole population. Evaluating target segment ensures that the advertiser chooses a vehicle that has the widest audience per dollar within the target segment of interest. Finally, when choosing multiple vehicles in which to run a set of ads, advertisers want to ensure that the overlap among audiences of the various vehicles enhances rather than detracts from persuasion. Evaluating the schedule of ads helps the advertiser achieve this task.

Over time, researchers have developed fairly precise measures for these four characteristics. However, the measures are quite complex due to the variety of media, the unique evolution of each medium, and the variety of content provided by each vehicle. As a result, each characteristic may have multiple measures within a medium, while sometimes the same term has different meanings across the media. This section explains the most important measures of the vehicles. It then shows how the measures help to evaluate the characteristics of the various vehicles.

Evaluation of Audience The choice of a vehicle depends first and foremost on the audience of that vehicle. It is the basis by which time and space on various vehicles are sold. In the 1840s, when newspapers first began to sell space to advertisers, they did not reveal the size of the audience. Advertisers were small, regional and unsophisticated, and did not demand such information. However, by the turn of the century, newspapers began to compete with each other by touting their circulation figures, which were often exaggerated and not standardized. During the Great Depression in the 1930s, many U.S. advertisers were wiped out, and those that survived demanded to know what exactly they were buying. It was around then that George Gallup, A. C. Nielsen and others began popularizing the precise evaluation of audiences.[22] Currently, a number of measures of the audience are available. The broadcast media primarily use ratings, and to a lesser extent, share. The other media use coverage.

Ratings Ratings are often associated with Nielsen because, as the introductory example indicated, it developed many of the tools and measures for rating TV programs and currently has a monopoly of ratings. The **rating** of a program is the percentage of a population viewing the program during the average minute. The **population** for the rating may be measured in terms of individuals or households,[23] and includes the number who have ready access to a television (or radio) in their home. For example, if there are 80 million households, and 4 million households are tuned to a TV program, then the program's rating would be 5. Ratings are treated as numbers, even though they are percentages. For example, we refer to the program's rating as 5, even though it is strictly 5 percent. Audiences are likely to vary from minute to minute of the program, depending on the program's interest level, the number of ads it contains, the attractiveness of competing programs, and the time of day. The program is generally divided into quarter-hour lengths, and the rating is calculated for an average minute within a quarter hour length of the program. Since ads generally last less than a minute, the rating for an ad is the average rating of the program in the quarter-hour segment in which it appears.

Another measure for comparing the performance of competing programs is its share of audience. A program's **share of audience** is the percentage of TV users tuned to that program. The term *share* is a measure of a program's popularity or competitive performance. As such it may be calculated only from the fraction of the population that is viewing a program. The term **usage** refers to the percentage of households with their TV sets turned on (also called **HUT,** for **households using television**). So, share of audience is ratings divided by usage.[24] In other words, a program's share of audience is its ratings adjusted for the proportion of TV sets turned on.

Note that a rating measures a program's performance across all time periods, while a share measures its performance within a time period. A program with a low rating may still have a high share, and vice versa. For example, weekday morning programs generally have low ratings, but a popular morning program could have a very high share relative to its competitors. Weekday evening programs generally have high ratings, but an unpopular program could have a low share relative to its competitors.

Coverage Measures for the print media parallel those for the broadcast media, but the precise terms and definitions differ. Moreover, the definitions of some terms differ even between newspapers and magazines. The basic measures used for print media are circulation and coverage.

Circulation is the number of copies of one issue of a newspaper or magazine distributed to the population. While circulation is a precise measure that can be readily obtained, it is not very meaningful. The reason is that different magazines and newspapers have rates of readership quite different from their circulation. For example, the magazine *Consumer Reports* does not have a high circulation relative to popular magazines and newspapers. However, before purchasing products many consumers consult copies of *Consumer Reports* owned by friends or available at a library. Moreover, consumers may consult even a five-year-old issue of *Consumer Reports* if it contains the most recent review of a product category. Similarly, magazines such as *Playboy* do not have a high circulation, but are passed from reader to reader, or even resold, so that they have a long afterlife. On the other hand, some popular newspapers may have a wide circulation, but subscribers may not have the time to read every section of every issue. In addition, households have many members, who read different portions of the magazines and newspapers at different rates.

For magazines, **coverage** is the percentage of households exposed to one copy. Thus if there are 80 million households in the United States and a magazine reaches 1 million of them, its coverage is 1.25 percent. For newspapers, coverage is the percentage of households in a geographic area that receive a copy of the newspaper. Thus if .94 million copies of the *Los Angeles Times* are distributed in the Los Angeles area, which has 4.71 million households, the daily's coverage is 20 percent.

The term *coverage* is also used for broadcast and outdoor media, but with a slightly different meaning. For the broadcast media, coverage is the percentage of all households with a TV (or radio) that can receive a TV (or radio) broadcast. Thus coverage for these two media is a measure of the potential to receive messages. For outdoor media such as billboards, coverage is the percentage of the population in a region that passes that billboard.

The rating, share or coverage of various media vehicles provides the basic information for vehicle choice. In general, vehicles with higher ratings or circulation are more desirable. However, such vehicles are likely to cost more. In order to get the best value for their investment, managers need to take into account the cost efficiency of the vehicles.

Evaluation of Cost Efficiency   **Cost efficiency** refers to the coverage of a vehicle that can be bought with a fixed amount of money. Costs vary widely across media, and across vehicles within the same medium. Advertising costs have grown steeply over the last half century. When TV broadcasting originally began in the United States, advertising was illegal. On May 2, 1941, the Federal Communications Commission granted commercial licenses to 10 TV stations. For the first time, telecasters could charge fees for ads. The first TV ad may have been one for Bulova during a Dodgers-Phillies baseball game on July 1, 1941.[25] It cost $4 for airtime and $5 for station charges, for a potential market of 4,000 TV sets in the New York area. In contrast, a 30-second ad during prime time currently costs between $100,000 and $400,000.

Because of the enormous increase in the costs of advertising, today an evaluation of media costs is an essential step in choosing media and media vehicle. The broadcast and print media use different measures of cost efficiency. The broadcast media use cost per rating point (CPP), while the print media use cost per thousand (CPM).

The **cost per rating point (CPP)** for a time slot is the cost of that time slot divided by the program's rating during the time slot. In general, shows with higher ratings cost more. However, ratings may not be the only factor that determines a program's cost. The cost of a program could also be higher based on the type of audience that it commands. For example, audiences from a higher socioeconomic group may have higher disposable incomes and be more responsive to high-priced, prestigious brands. Younger consumers may spend more, or choose brands based more on advertising messages, than do older consumers. Advertisers may be more interested in programs that attract such audiences, and their demand for ad time in these programs may drive up the cost. The loyalty or attentiveness of an audience to a program's episodes may also affect the demand for its ad-time and rates.

Exhibit 15-12 compares the cost efficiency of three hypothetical programs, A, B and C. Note that in terms of absolute cost C

is the cheapest program, and would appear to be the most desirable. However, it has the highest cost per rating of the three shows. On the other hand, program A has the highest ratings of the three programs and would be the best buy in terms of ratings alone. However, after factoring in its costs, it is inferior to program B. On the basis of cost per rating, program B is the best buy.

Cost per thousand (CPM) for space in a magazine or newspaper is the cost of that space divided by the publication's circulation measured in thousands. Exhibit 15-13 compares the cost efficiency of two weeklies. Note that, even though the circulations of these two weeklies are vastly different, their costs per thousand are the same. In this case, the choice would come down to the differences in articles, readership and reading styles between the two weeklies. *Business Week* provides more newsy articles, which are more readable than those of *The Economist;* the latter provides more in-depth, analytical articles than the former. *Business Week* would appeal more to mid-level managers in the United States; *The Economist,* to economists and senior managers worldwide.

The cost efficiency of broadcast and print media may not appear to be immediately comparable with these measures. In most cases, these two media are so different in their means of persuasion that cost comparisons may not be a primary issue. However, the two measures are related by a simple formula.[26] Should managers want to compare costs across the two types of media, they can obtain the relevant figures from the media, or they can convert figures from one measure to another using the formula.

While analysis of general measures of cost efficiency is very useful, managers can greatly enhance the efficiency of the vehicle selection by focusing on programs that reach only the segments they intend to target. For this reason, they need to evaluate the target segments of an ad campaign.

Evaluation of Target Segments   In 1992, NBC dropped two of its reliable, popular one-hour programs: *In the Heat*

▼ EXHIBIT 15-12. **Cost efficiency of three hypothetical TV programs.**

Program	Absolute Cost (30-second spot)	Rating	Cost per Rating
A	$300,000	30	10,000
B	$210,000	25	8,400
C	$80,000	7	11,400

▼ **EXHIBIT 15-13.** Hypothetical cost efficiency of two weeklies.

Weekly	Circulation	Cost per Ad Page	Cost per Thousand
Business Week	1,000,000	$50,000	$50
The Economist	300,000	$15,000	$50

of the Night and *Matlock*. Both shows were performing well, running second in their respective time slots. Both did especially well among adults over age 55, ranking third and fifth in attracting this age group among all prime-time programs.

Why did NBC drop these programs? The segmented success of the programs was the problem. Both programs fared poorly with the under-50 age group. Advertisers preferred younger audiences and were buying time more heavily from rival networks ABC and Fox. The problem was that NBC had stuck with old, successful programs, while other networks had introduced new shows. As a result, the audience for NBC's programs had aged over time. The average age of NBC's audience was 42 years, compared with 44 for CBS, 34 for ABC and 28 for Fox. NBC advised show directors to try to attract younger audiences, while it also began exploring new shows that would achieve the same goal.[27]

As the NBC example indicates, advertisers are generally not interested in the whole market so much as in specific segments that are more likely to buy their product. Targeting such segments can greatly reduce the cost of a campaign. For this purpose, advertisers need to calculate the cost per person reached in the target segment, rather than in the whole market. This basis of comparison may justify the choice of certain programs that appear too costly, or it may identify inexpensive programs that efficiently reach target markets. The key tasks for this purpose are the identification and measurement of target segments.

The identification of target segments is a creative exercise that depends on good research and analysis, as Chapter 1 explains. The chapter also describes the important variables that can be used for defining segments: geographic, demographic, usage, psychographic, or benefit factors. Data to carry out such segmentation may be obtained from the advertiser's own records, primary research, secondary research or syndicated sources such as Simmons Market Research Bureau. The most commonly used measures for segmentation are location, age and gender. Other measures conveniently available from syndi-

cated sources are education, household income, employment, marital status, race, home ownership and household size. In addition, the ratings of major media vehicles are also available from syndicated sources. All of these variables are available for a large number of product categories, by major type within these categories, and by usage level for certain types.

One simple method for identifying target segments with such data is by indices. An **index** is a standardized measure of a variable. The standard that is chosen is typically the average value of the variable across segments, or the value for one important segment. The index then expresses the values of all segments as a percentage of the standard. For example, consider the analysis of nonfrozen, nonfat yogurt consumption by age in Exhibit 15-14. The first column gives one basis for potential segments, age. Columns *a* and *b* give the distribution of the U.S. adult population in each age segment in absolute and percentage terms, respectively. Columns *c* and *d* give the corresponding figures for adult consumers of this category of yogurt. The division of the percentage of consumers by the percentage of population in each age segment gives usage an index of density for yogurt consumption. On this index, the number 100 reflects average consumption density across the population of adults. The number 128 for adults 45 to 54 means that this segment of adults has a 28 percent greater *density* of yogurt users than the average segment. In general, index numbers over 100 indicate segments with heavier than average density of users, while index numbers under 100 indicate segments with lighter than average density of users.

The value of an index is that it makes comparison across segments or categories easy. Indices can be developed for entire categories (yogurt), subcategories (nonfrozen yogurt), or brands (Dannon); for entire populations (all individuals) or subpopulations (females); and for simple response (consumption) or special response (purchase with coupons). The only constraint on the development of indices is the availability of data. Indices can be multiplied or divided by other indices to yield new indices, which can then be interpreted similarly.

A density index shows relative consumption across categories after controlling for size. For the

▼ **EXHIBIT 15-14.** Analysis of nonfrozen, nonfat yogurt use among U.S. adults, by segment.

Age Segment	Adults (000)	Adults (%)	Users (000)	Users (%)	Index
	a	$b = \dfrac{(100 \times a)}{(\text{Total } a)}$	c	$d = \dfrac{(100 \times c)}{(\text{Total } d)}$	d/b
18–24	24,497	13%	1,828	12%	89
25–34	43,260	24	3,431	22	95
35–44	38,986	22	3,749	24	115
45–54	25,970	14	2,793	18	128
55–64	21,094	11	1,788	12	101
64 and older	30,310	16	1,854	12	73
Total	184,117	100%	15,443	100%	100

Data Source: Simmons (1992), *The 1992 Study of Media and Markets,* New York: Simmons Market Research Bureau, Inc., P19, 248.

yogurt example, the highest consumption occurs in ages 35–44. But that age group also has a large segment size. The highest *relative* consumption occurs in the 45–54 age group, the group with the highest density index. The advantage of relative consumption is that it shows the concentration of consumers in the category and thus the ease of accessing them when targeting the age group. Note that the marketer could be interested in targeting the low end of the index, as much as the high end. For example, a leading brand may want to target consumers who use fewer coupons because they would be more willing to pay a high price. A new brand may want to target current nonconsumers of the existing brand to get the best increase in market share.

Once the target segments have been identified, the media manager can proceed to select vehicles that better target those segments. Media vehicles can be selected in at least two ways: via an indirect approach using demographic segments, or a direct approach using usage segments.[28] To better appreciate these two approaches, we will compare them with a simple approach that does not use target segments.

Simple Approach Using Measures for the Whole Population The simple approach involves using measures of cost per rating point (CPP) for the whole population as discussed in the previous section. We can show its application in the context of the yogurt example. For simplicity, we restrict the example to only three shows: *The Price Is Right, NBA Basketball* and *Murphy Brown* (see Exhibit 15-15). The indices for each variable are calculated by dividing the specific values for each show by the mean

value for the three shows. (In a real case, the analysis would be carried out for all shows in which the advertiser may be interested). Rows *a* and *b* provide the actual cost and cost index for each show. The simple approach involves obtaining the population rating (row *c*), calculating the rating index (row *d*) and then the cost per rating (CPP) index (row *e*) for the three shows. Note that, on the basis of the CPP index for all households, *Murphy Brown* is the least expensive and the best buy. Even though its costs per ad are high, its cost per rating index is much lower because it reaches a wider audience.

But is the population of all households the appropriate audience for yogurt? Suppose most yogurt users watch some other program, such as *The Price Is Right* or *NBA Basketball*. Would not advertising on those shows be more efficient? The indirect and direct approaches also account for product usage of the market segment, such as the consumption of yogurt.

Indirect Approach Using Demographic Segments The **indirect approach** involves the use of demographic segments as an intermediate step in media choice. Product purchase or consumption levels are first analyzed by suitable demographic variables to identify demographic segments. This step was discussed earlier in this section and illustrated in Exhibit 15-14. Vehicle usage is then analyzed by those same demographic segments. The vehicles that reach those segments most efficiently are then chosen.

Take the yogurt example again. Suppose an analysis of usage by demographic groups suggests that age is the best discriminator for usage. Further, the analysis by age in Exhibit 15-14 shows that the

▼ **EXHIBIT 15-15.** Vehicle selection using three alternative approaches.

	MEASURE	UNITS	FORMULA	NBA Basketball	The Price Is Right	Murphy Brown	Avg.
					PROGRAMS		
Basic Information	Cost	000	a	$170	$250	$450	$290
	Cost index	%	$b = a/Avg\ a$	59%	86%	155%	100%
	Rating	All HH	c	2.6	5.3	14.1	**7.3**
Simple Approach	Rating index	All HH	$d = c/Avg\ c$	35%	72%	192%	100%
	CPP index	All HH	$e = b/d$	**165%**	**119%**	**81%**	**100%**
	Rating	45–54	f	2.2	7.2	10.2	**6.5**
Demo Targets	Rating index	45–54	$g = f/Avg\ f$	34%	110%	156%	100%
	CPP index	45–54	$h = b/g$	**174%**	**78%**	**99%**	**100%**
	Rating	Heavy use	i	4.5	6.5	10.2	**7.1**
Usage Targets	Rating index	Heavy use	$j = i/Avg\ i$	64%	92%	144%	100%
	CPP index	Heavy use	$k = b/i$	**92%**	**94%**	**108%**	**100%**

Data Source: Simmons (1992), *1992 Study of Media and Markets,* New York: Simmons Market Research Bureau, Inc.

45–54 age group has the highest relative consumption of yogurt, and so may be most efficient to target. To complete the analysis we need to analyze the ratings, ratings index and cost per rating index for the age group 45–54. Rows *f, g,* and *h* of Exhibit 15-15 present this information. Note that *The Price Is Right* has the lowest price per rating index, because it reaches more adults 45 to 54 years old, the segment with the heaviest density of yogurt consumption. Since advertisers are interested in reaching their target segment, the cost per rating index for this age group is more pertinent than the cost per rating in the whole population.

In the indirect approach, vehicle choice is made through an intermediate step of determining target segments based on demographics. This approach has two problems. First, it involves two steps of analysis and is more cumbersome. Second, the targeting of only one demographic group is inefficient. It does not reach all of the potential users of the product. The direct approach described next avoids these problems of the indirect approach.

Direct Approach Using Syndicated Data The direct approach chooses vehicles based directly on the viewing of these programs by product users, without resort to segmentation based on demographics. For this purpose, we need figures describing what portion of the audience of the program are consumers of the product. Fortunately, information on TV viewing directly by product consumption is also available from syndicated sources. Row *i* of Exhibit 15-15 presents ratings of the three shows among yogurt consumers or users. Rows *j* and *k* calculate the ratings index and the cost per rating index for the shows by these users. Note that when analyzed by yogurt users, *NBA Basketball* has the lowest price per rating point index, and is thus the best buy.

The third approach is the most efficient, because it is not so unfocused as to target the whole population equally, nor so focused as to target only the most promising segments exclusively. It targets by focusing directly on users. If the direct approach is so much better, why is the indirect one used? The only reason is because media time is bought and sold in bulk based on broad demographic groups. Why is media sold by broad groups in the first place? The reason is that broad demographic groups can allow targeting, albeit imprecise, across a vast cross section of products. Their use thus makes the pricing and purchase of media time and space convenient. After purchasing time and space in bulk, agencies can allocate them to different products that they handle. In actual practice, the use of broad demographic groups turns out to be the common denominator by which sales and planning take place, because of its wide applicability and convenience.

Further Improvements in Targeting With the advent of scanner data, analysts have much better information on the pattern of product purchase, consumption, and program viewing (see Chapter 14). This information can be used to provide two refinements for better selection of vehicles: new indices and weighted average indices.

1. **New Indices.** In addition to viewing of TV programs and product consumption, single-source data can be analyzed to obtain information on brand usage (brand loyalty, brand switching), response to promotion (advertising, coupons, price-cuts) or TV viewing patterns (channel surfing). Suppose a brand manager wants to target users of competing brands. He or she can concentrate on variables that describe brand usage, such as brand loyalty or brand switching. Alternatively, suppose a manager wants to advertise to consumers who respond to advertising rather than to those who respond to promotions. He or she can form segments by using the variables that describe response to advertising. While current data focus primarily on demographics and simple product usage, scanner data allow a manager to focus on more important variables.

2. **Weighted Average Indices.** A simple index is one that is developed for only one target group, such as persons aged 45–54, or users of the product. A weighted index is the weighted average of the indices for all segments, with the weights based on the importance of the segment. For example, suppose one forms four usage segments—heavy, medium, light and nonusers. The traditional approach would calculate the ratings by heavy users only, and ignore the other three segments. The weighted average index incorporates the TV ratings for all four segments, establishing weights for each segment based on the relative level of consumption, and then calculating the weighted average index for all four segments. The weighted average index ensures that all segments are included but only to the extent they are important. It is thus the most efficient approach for selecting media vehicles.

Our analysis so far has focused on measures of viewing a single episode of a program. An ad cam-paign normally involves two or more episodes of two or more programs across two or more media. We need to evaluate the efficiency of this entire set of ads, which is called a schedule.

Evaluation of Schedule A **schedule** is a set of vehicles, programs, or ad insertions over a certain time period, such as a month. The evaluation of the schedule of an ad campaign is based on three important measures: gross rating points, reach and frequency.

Gross Rating Points Gross rating points (GRPs) are the sum of all ratings for all programs in an ad's schedule. These ads may appear in different episodes of a program or in different programs. For example, suppose a brand manager chooses the ad schedule shown in Exhibit 15-16 for one month. The GRPs for this schedule are 192. Note that, although ratings are percentages, they are multiplied and added as numbers to get gross rating points. Similarly, although GRPs are percentages (for example, 192 percent), they are treated as numbers that can be compared with numbers obtained from alternative schedules. **Impressions** are the sum of all individuals or households exposed to an ad in a schedule. Equivalent to gross rating points, impressions are measured in absolute units and not as a fraction of the population. So impressions are the product of gross rating points and population.

In order to select an ad schedule, a manager must first estimate the target number of gross rating points the ad campaign should achieve in order to meet its goal. The manager can estimate this number from past experience with advertising, from published records of similar ad campaigns or from research conducted for this purpose (see Chapter 14). The manager must next choose the media for the ad campaign. Once these two decisions are made, the manager can experiment with different schedules to determine which one provides the target number of GRPs in the media best suited for the ad campaign.

▼ **EXHIBIT 15-16.** Hypothetical gross rating points for an ad schedule.

Show	Average Ratings	Episodes Selected	Gross Rating Points
Saturday Night Live	4	4	16
CBS Evening News	6	20	120
60 Minutes	14	4	56
Total			192

GRPs represent the total audience for all episodes of all programs in the schedule. A segment of this audience may watch the show once, while other segments may watch it more often. Thus GRPs do not discriminate between segments of the audience that see the program at varying frequencies. As its name implies, GRPs are a crude measure of the audience for a schedule. To better understand the meaning of GRPs we should consider the concepts of reach and frequency.

Reach The core audience for a TV program may be similar from week to week. However, variations in viewers, program content and competing programs can lead to variations in the total audience each week. Successive episodes of a program may draw loyal viewers or entirely new viewers. To plan a schedule, the similarity or variations in the audience need to be clearly measured. The measurement is especially important because some advertisers may desire a wide audience even if that means few repetitions of their ad, while others may want many repetitions of their ad even at the cost of a small audience. For example, in the early 1990s, Sears's announcement of a major change in its discount strategy needed to reach a large number of viewers, even if only once. But Kmart's switch to marketing designer labels needed repetitive advertising to persuade buyers of the attractiveness of its new label. Two measures that serve this purpose are reach and frequency.

Reach is the number or percentage of households exposed at least once to a vehicle in a given time period. The fraction of households exposed to the vehicle more than once in a given time period is called the **duplicated audience,** while the fraction exposed to the vehicle only once is called the **exclusive audience.** The term *reach* always implies no duplication in the count. For example, Exhibit 15-17 shows the audience covered by two episodes of a program. Segment B represents the duplicated audience exposed to the program on both occasions, while segments A and C reflect the exclusive audience that saw the program only once. The reach of the program is segments A and C plus segment B *counted only once,* without any duplication. For this reason, reach is also called the **unduplicated audience.** With each episode, the audience keeps growing or accumulating new viewers. The new users from each episode (segment C after two viewings) are called the **accumulation.** So reach is also referred to as **accumulated reach, cume reach** or **cumulative audience.**

The concept of reach applies to two or more vehicles within a medium. It also applies across media; for example, the reach of two issues of *People* magazine and two episodes of TV's *The Dating Game.* In these cases, the reach would be the unduplicated audience from multiple exposures to the TV show and multiple issues of *People.* The reach of a schedule that uses different media must also be calculated without including duplication of the total audience among programs or issues of the different media. The term **net coverage** refers to the reach across two or more media. In general, syndicated sources, such as Simmons Market Research, estimate net coverage from two episodes of most popular shows, or two issues of most popular publications. The net coverage of a specific schedule may not be readily available and may have to be estimated from available figures or measured by a survey specifically designed for the purpose.

Exhibit 15-18 shows the reach among U.S. adults of 10 episodes of two TV programs, the *CBS Evening News* and *The Young and the Restless.* The horizontal axis plots the episodes, while the vertical axis plots each program's reach in thousands of adults. The episodes do not have to be sequential; the numbers 1, 2, 3 do not represent the first, second or third episode, but any one, any two or any three episodes. The market for these programs is 184 million adults.

The curve highlights some important features of reach. First, both curves increase rapidly at first, but ultimately flatten out at a point well below the total population. This pattern shows that the vast majority of viewers do not watch any episode within a reasonable time frame such as a

▼ **EXHIBIT 15-17.** Duplicated and exclusive audience.

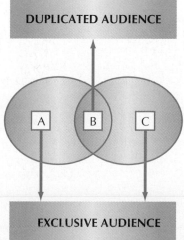

▼ **EXHIBIT 15-18.** Reach of two TV programs (U.S. adults, viewing 1–10 episodes of each program).

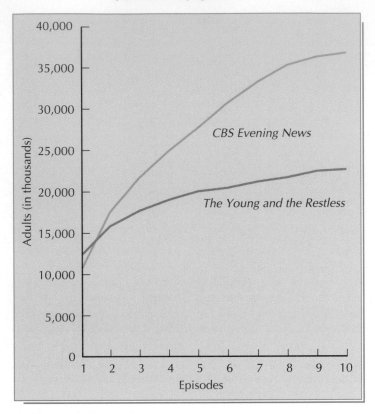

Data Source: Simmons (1992), *1992 Study of Media and Markets,* New York: Simmons Market Research Bureau, Inc., M8, 116.

the eighth episode. Thus if a manager wants to reach a wide audience, he or she is better off using few episodes of different programs rather than multiple episodes of the same program. A special type of multi-program schedule that maximizes reach, minimizes duplication and prevents the zapping of ads is a roadblock. A **roadblock** is a TV schedule that positions ads at the very same time in all or most leading broadcast channels of a medium. As a result, no matter which show a viewer turns to, he or she will see the ad.

Frequency Frequency is the number of times a household is exposed to a vehicle of a medium in a given time period such as a month. Exhibit 15-19 plots the frequency distribution of the two shows, *ABC World News Tonight* and *The Young and the Restless*. However, in this case the analysis is for adults 18–34 years old. The y-axis plots the number of adults who see multiple episodes of the program. Note that this curve is a frequency distribution, and the y-axis is not the same as that for reach in Exhibit 15-18. Nevertheless the frequency curves complement the reach curves.

The *ABC World News Tonight* presents the national and international news of the day. It typically has no serial link from one day to another. Note that a large number of viewers see only one episode. The number who see multiple episodes drops steeply and then steadily declines until no viewers see all 10 episodes. On the other hand, *The Young and the Restless* is a serial with a distinct following. It has fewer viewers (relative to the *ABC World News Tonight* who see just one or two episodes, but many viewers who watch the program regularly. The number of viewers who see multiple episodes tends to rise, with a spike at the tail (at 10). This spike represents the hard-core loyal viewers who see every episode.[29] Thus a campaign that requires repetitive viewing is better placed in *The Young and the Restless* than in the *ABC World News Tonight* . Also, an ad campaign with a serial theme is better placed in *The Young and the Restless* where consumers are likely to catch successive episodes of the serial.

The term **average frequency** refers to the frequency with which an individual is exposed to a vehicle

month. On the contrary, each program has a target segment. Although every member of this segment may not see every episode of the program, after a sufficient number of episodes, the program would reach the entire segment.

Second, any single episode of *The Young and the Restless* reaches a few more adults than any single episode of the *CBS Evening News*." But the latter program continues to reach more adults with subsequent episodes. The reason is that the *CBS Evening News*, which covers a variety of national and international events, has a broader appeal. Thus, a campaign requiring a wide audience is better placed in the *CBS Evening News* than in *The Young and the Restless*.

Third, reach increases rapidly with the first few insertions but does not increase much more with subsequent insertions. For *The Young and the Restless,* reach starts to level off from the fourth episode. For the *CBS Evening News*, it climbs until

▼ **EXHIBIT 15-19.** Frequency distribution for two TV programs (U.S. adults, viewing 1–10 episodes of each program on weekdays).

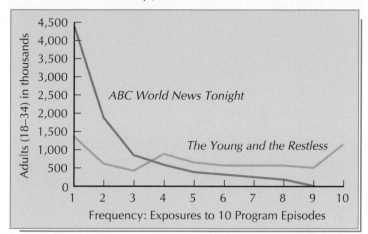

Data Source: Simmons (1992), *1992 Study of Media and Markets,* New York: Simmons Market Research Bureau, Inc., M8, 118.

or ad schedule *on average* in a particular time period. The frequency of an ad schedule is not actually measured, but derived from gross ratings points. If the reach of the schedule is known, then average frequency is given by the following formula:

Average frequency = Gross rating points/Reach

While this derived measure of average frequency is sometimes referred to as just frequency, advertisers need to keep in mind that it is a derived average number. Also, even though gross rating points are the product of reach and average frequency, that is not how they are obtained. Gross rating points are obtained by summing the ratings of all the insertions in an ad schedule, irrespective of their duplication.

Two schedules with the same gross rating points can have quite different reach and frequency figures. For example, in Exhibit 15-20, one insertion in each evening news program totals 64 gross rating points. It has minimal duplication and reaches a wide audience of 60 million households at a frequency of 1.1. But three

insertions in the *NBC Nightly News* totals 63 gross rating points. It reaches a relatively smaller audience (42 million households) for a higher frequency of 1.5 exposures. Thus for any given level of gross rating points, there is always a trade-off between reach and frequency.

Media managers can use reach and frequency analysis to evaluate and better plan an ad schedule. If they want a wide audience, they could use two or more competing programs that appeal to nonoverlapping groups of similar viewers, such as *ABC World News Tonight, CBS Evening News* and *NBC Nightly News.* On the other hand, if they want repetitions, they can use many episodes of one program that reaches the target audience, such as *The Young and the Restless* (see Exhibit 15-21). Note from this exhibit that three insertions in schedule 1 buy 19.4 gross rating points for a fairly wide reach of 36 million adults at a minimal average frequency of 1. But the same insertions in schedule 2 buy almost the same gross rating points for less than half the reach (17.6 million adults) at an average frequency of 2.1.

Ideally, an advertiser would like viewers to see the ad just enough times to get the desired response. The term **effective frequency** refers to the optimal number of exposures of an ad in a particular time period to get the response desired by the advertiser. The discussion of repetition in Chapter 4 explains the factors that influence the optimal number of exposures of an ad. Chapter 14 explains how to design tests to find out the optimal number of exposures for a particular ad. Assume the effective frequency of the ad schedule in Exhibit 15-18 is three

▼ **EXHIBIT 15-20.** Gross rating points, reach, and frequency for two hypothetical ad schedules.

	Ratings	Schedule 1 Insertions	Schedule 2 Insertions
CBS Evening News	20	0	1
ABC World News Tonight	23	0	1
NBC Nightly News	21	3	1
Gross rating points		63	64
Reach (millions of households)		42	60
Average frequency		1.5	1.1

▼ EXHIBIT 15-21. Reach and frequency for two schedules of three insertions each.

	RATING	SCHEDULE 1		SCHEDULE 2	
		Insertions	Gross Rating Points	Insertions	Gross Rating Points
CBS Evening News	6.3	1	6.3	0	
ABC World News Tonight	7.3	1	7.3	0	
NBC Nightly News	5.8	1	5.8	0	
The Young and the Restless	6.5	0	0	3	19.5
Total		3	19.4	3	19.5
Reach (millions of adults)		35.9		17.6	
Reach (%)		19.1%		9.5%	
Average frequency		1.0		2.1	

Data Source: Simmons (1992), *1992 Study of Media and Markets,* New York: Simmons Market Research Bureau, Inc., M8, 116.

exposures. If that's the case, most of the audience sees the ad too often or too infrequently. This inefficient targeting of ads is one of the major problems with the current system of using gross rating points to buy media time. Advertisers are unable to target their ads so that the right segment is exposed to the ad, just the right number of times to obtain the desired response. However, an even greater problem for advertisers is that the optimum number of exposures is not a universal constant, but must be determined for each advertising campaign. The only information we have at present is that the optimum number of exposures for a message varies by certain factors such as the complexity of the message and the familiarity of the brand (see Chapter 4).

Let us now discuss the case mentioned at the start of this section, designing the alternative schedule to advertising in the Super Bowl. One analyst found that one particular schedule of ads achieved a greater reach and higher average frequency at a lesser cost than one ad in the Super Bowl.[30] Another advantage of the alternative schedule is that it lowers risk by advertising in a number of shows instead of putting all one's investment in one show. What was this schedule? The schedule consisted of two prime-time roadblocks of inexpensive shows, one each on Sunday and Tuesday (see Exhibit 15-22). The Sunday shows consisted of the three network movies, plus *Married...With Children.* The Tuesday shows consisted of *Grace Under Fire, John Larroquette,* and CBS's and Fox's Tuesday movies. After purchasing time on these shows there was money left over to buy one spot on Fox's Saturday schedule.

So why the demand for time on the Super Bowl? Three factors may motivate the demand. The Super Bowl is especially effective at attracting a male audience aged 25–54, which is the prime target for a number of companies. It attracts a unique international audience. It is a premier advertising event, with the news media actively following and reporting on the ads that did appear during the game. So each ad, if newsworthy, may get additional coverage in the media.

Summary

Media and vehicle choice are distinct decisions often made in the order described. A manager generally determines the range of appropriate media, then examines the alternative vehicles available. However,

▼ EXHIBIT 15-22. Comparative reach: one Super Bowl ad or alternative schedule.

	SUPER BOWL (30 SEC)		ALTERNATIVE SCHEDULE (2 ROADBLOCKS: SUNDAY AND TUESDAY PRIME TIME)	
Age Group	Rating	GRPs	Reach (%)	Reach Advantage over Super Bowl
People 2 and over	37%	67	48%	30%
Adults 18–49	40	65	49	22
Adults 25–54	42	78	52	24
Men 18–49	46	63	48	7
Men 25–54	48	68	49	2

Source: Frydlewicz, Rob (1995), "Missed Super Bowl? Put Your Bucks Here," *Advertising Age,* January 30, 18.

the two decisions are interdependent because the choice of vehicles ultimately determines which media are used. For example, a marketer of a superior new word processor may decide that TV is a better medium than magazines to disseminate the value of its software to consumers quickly and effectively. However, after looking at costs of various TV and magazine programs, it may well decide that advertising in computer magazines is less costly and better targeted, albeit slower and less effective, than advertising in TV programs. Thus, the initial choice of media determines which vehicles to evaluate, but the ultimate choice of media depends on an evaluation of those vehicles. Exhibit 15 23 summarizes the stages in media planning.

Syndicated data sources

Our introductory example, Nielsen's 1987 changes in ratings of programs and subsequent discovery of new viewers in 1993, shows the critical role played by syndicated research companies in evaluating the audience for various media. The methods used by these sources are fallible, not perfect. So, the sources are under constant pressure from media owners to refine their research methods to ensure that they capture the entire audience of the various programs. On the other hand, advertisers are skeptical of any sudden increase in ratings or audiences, especially if these increases come at the instigation of media owners. Under such pressures, the independence and integrity of the syndicated data sources is a critical factor that alone can gain the trust and agreement of advertisers and media owners.

This section describes some of the leading sources for data about media audiences: A. C. Nielsen Co., Audit Bureau of Circulation, Simmons Market

▼ EXHIBIT 15-23. **Stages in media planning.**

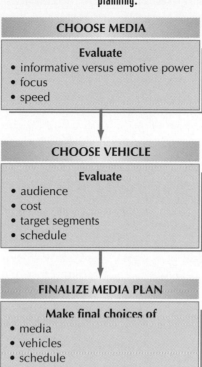

Research Bureau, and Mediamark. The section describes the methods that these agencies use to obtain their data, the key limitations of those methods, and the reports in which they are published.

The A. C. Nielsen Company

The primary source of information on the audience for television programs in the United States is the A. C. Nielsen Company, which produces the well-known Nielsen ratings. The ratings are based on self-report and observational data collected from sample households and TV stations. The data collection system involves obtaining information from two broad sources: television stations and viewers.

Using proprietary technology, Nielsen first tracks 1,700 TV stations and 11,000 cable systems daily, to obtain a census of all TV programs broadcast in the United States. It also develops a digital "fingerprint" of all commercials aired through these stations. With this information base, the company monitors samples of households to determine ratings for various programs and commercials.

For local television, Nielsen gathers viewing information using 100,000 TV diaries in 211 television markets four times a year (in February, May, July and November). These periods have come to be called the "sweep" months. Panelists report who was watching what program and what channel, by quarter-hour segments. They then mail the diaries to Nielsen, where they are pooled into a central database.

In 30 of the largest markets, Nielsen has fitted a sample of homes with telemeters, which provide the on/off status of the TV set, and the channel tuned by time of day. Within the same markets, a separate sample of households provides daily information by individual household member as described above. The company uses these two sources of information to compare alternate methods, as well as to adjust the wider individual viewing data with the set-tuning data if necessary.

Nielsen's most sophisticated system for monitoring households is the people-meter. Up to six members of a household can punch their number in this meter when they begin and stop watching each program. The meter records the channel, program and time of day and relays the information to a central computer. It thus combines the benefits of the diary and the telemeter (see Chapter 14). Currently, Nielsen has the people-meter in a sample of only 4,000 homes. While electronic reporting systems such as the telemeter and people-meter have not displaced the older diary technology, they can provide more frequent and less biased reporting of the audiences for TV programs. Nielsen ratings for various programs are available by key demographics obtained by survey from the various panelists.

The audience for the print media is evaluated by circulation and by readership surveys.

Audit Bureau of Circulation (ABC)

The Audit Bureau of Circulation (ABC) is the primary agency that collects information on circulation of print vehicles. Each newspaper or magazine has to submit a Publisher's Statement to ABC twice yearly. This statement gives the circulation of the newspaper or magazine, broken down by payment level, editions, type of issues and geographic area. These figures come from the publisher's own record and are liable to an audit. They may thus seem to be reliable and valuable information for media managers. However, circulation is an inaccurate measure of true readership. The reason is that different magazines and newspapers have different rates of pass-along readership, while subscribers themselves might vary substantially in their reading of magazines to which they subscribe.

An alternate means of gathering information on the print media is by survey. However, the survey has problems of its own (see Chapter 14). Respondents may exaggerate their readership of what they consider prestigious newspapers and magazines (*The Wall Street Journal, Atlantic Monthly*) and underreport their readership of less prestigious newspapers and magazines (*USA Today, Hustler*). Media planners need to weigh these factors when they consider the figures from these different sources. They also need to consult multiple sources to make good decisions. Two leading agencies that collect information on print readership are Simmons and Mediamark.

Simmons Market Research Bureau

Simmons Market Research Bureau collects information on consumers' brand purchases and media exposure. Simmons obtains its information primarily from annual surveys of over 20,000 adults, age 18 and over. The demographic data are obtained from two separate personal interviews. The product-use data are obtained from a self-administered questionnaire left with each respondent on the first interview and collected at the second interview. TV viewing data is obtained from a diary that a subsample of respondents keeps for two weeks. Radio listening data is also obtained from a subsample of respondents by personal interview, diary and telephone interview. Exposure to outdoor ads is derived from respondents' travel patterns. Simmons obtains data on several media including magazines, newspapers, outdoor, drive-time radio, midday radio, total radio, prime-time television, daytime television, total television and the Yellow Pages.

For magazines, Simmons has switched from the through-the-book method it used in the past, to the recent-reading method developed by Mediamark.[31] In the **through-the-book method**, respondents flip through an entire issue of a magazine they claim to have read, to indicate which articles they read and whether they found them interesting. This approach is time consuming, lasting over two hours per respondent. As a result, Simmons obtained undercounts of readership, especially among upper-income respondents, although total readership was stagnant. Faced with this inconsistency, Simmons lost some major clients in the early 1990s.

In Fall 1994, Simmons switched to the recent-reading method. In the **recent-reading method**, respondents merely state whether or not they have read a recent issue of various magazines. The interview takes only 25 minutes and leads to less inconsistent readership figures. However, the method suffers from memory lapses as respondents forget what exactly they have read, or confuse frequency with issues. For example, they may not know with certainty whether they read four issues once or one issue four times. Simmons's switch to the recent-reading method prevents it from comparing new with past figures to find trends or just to interpret findings. For newspapers, Simmons uses the read-yesterday or read-last-week method. These two methods are variations of the recent-reading method, calibrated to the previous day and week, respectively.

Mediamark

Mediamark collects information on consumers' brand purchases and exposure to media.[32] It obtains information from two waves of interviews, each covering 20,000 people and lasting five months. The respondents are adults, 18 and over, residing in the 48 contiguous states of the United States Mediamark obtains demographics and media exposure from a personal interview with respondents. The interview covers exposure to magazines, newspapers, radio, television and outdoor ads. It obtains product-use data from a self-administered questionnaire left with each respondent on the first interview and collected at a second visit.

For newspaper readership, the questionnaire method is the same as for Simmons. For magazines, Mediamark uses the recent-reading measure Simmons recently adopted. In Mediamark's method respondents are asked which magazines they have read in the last six months, which issues of each magazine they have read and how much of each issue. Other details such as the place and time of readership and source of magazines are also recorded. The interview lasts about an hour.

SUMMARY

Media is a collective term for the communication channels through which advertisers reach consumers. There are two broad classes of media: direct media and mass media. Direct media involve individual or personal communication with members of the audience. The major direct media are mail and telephone. Mass media involve communication with a large number of individuals impersonally, without much interaction. In the United States, the major mass media include TV, newspapers, magazines, radio and outdoor. The mass media can also be classified into three types: broadcast, print and outdoor. Advertising in the broadcast media can be classified as network, spot and local advertising.

The media are the outcome of four parties, each seeking its own welfare: consumers, programmers, media owners and advertisers. The market for media clears when media owners can provide programs to consumers at a price they can pay. The market for advertising through the media clears when consumers are willing to pay the price for such programs with ads, while advertisers are willing to pay the price for the space and time during those programs. Editors play a central role in the market for media, by balancing principle with the interests of their audiences and the pressures of advertisers.

The evolution of the media is a dynamic process that has shaped the media and substantially alters their current character. Important trends in the current evolution of the media include the fragmentation of the traditional media, splintering of TV spot length, increasing clutter, and growth of new media.

Media planning involves three major decisions: media choice, vehicle choice and scheduling. These decisions are distinct and are often made in the order listed. However, the decisions are not independent from each other, and choices at one stage may lead a manager to revise choices made at any earlier stage.

Media choice is frequently the first decision in media planning, and depends primarily on four key characteristics of the media: informative versus evocative power, focus, speed and location.

Vehicle choice also depends on the evaluation of four important characteristics of vehicles: audience, cost, target market and schedule. Over time, researchers have developed fairly precise measures of these four characteristics. Unfortunately, the current system of measurements is not uniform across media.

Information about media planning generally comes from either primary research or syndicated sources. The most important syndicated sources are the A. C. Nielsen Company, the Audit Bureau of Circulation, Simmons Market Research Bureau and Mediamark.

QUESTIONS

1. Today, the editor of a newspaper, magazine or TV program is at the center of many conflicting pressures. The successful execution of his or her job requires deft handling of these pressures. Explain.
2. The media are a system through which programmers and advertisers inform or entertain consumers. The media are a dynamic system

that is constantly evolving along different directions. Discuss how and why that happens.

3. How do the media differ from each other? How do these differences affect an advertiser's media choice?

4. Discuss measures to evaluate the audience and cost efficiency of the media.

5. The costs of media have grown steadily through the decades. Explain how targeting specific segments can help to make vehicle choice more cost efficient.

6. Many managers believe that gross ratings points are obtained by multiplying reach and frequency. Is that true or false? Explain.

7. What purpose do the measures of reach and frequency serve in media planning?

8. Discuss the syndicated sources for measuring the audiences of print media.

9. Measuring TV audiences with the telemeter and people-meter seems like a tremendous improvement over measuring with the diary. Is that assertion valid?

10. Discuss the controversy surrounding Nielsen's measuring of TV audiences. How can Nielsen resolve the controversy while maintaining its reputation for credibility?

NOTES

1. Curry, David J. (1993), *The New Marketing Research Systems,* New York: John Wiley & Sons; Gold, Laurence N. (1994), "Technology in Television Research: The Meter," *Marketing Research* 6, 1, 57; Piirto, Rebecca (1993), "Do Not Adjust Your Set," *American Demographics* (March), 6; Sharon, Moshavi D. (1992), "Programmers, Nielsen Disagree Over Claim People-meter Underreports Kids," *ASAP* 122, 52, 10; Mandese, Joe (1993), "TV Ratings Monopoly Faces Changing Future," *Advertising Age,* November 15, 24; Miller, Cyndee (1993), "Networks Rally Around Study That Shows Strong Out-Of-Home Ratings," *Marketing News TM,* April 26, 1; Associated Press (1993) "Nielsen 'Finds' Another 20 Million TV Viewers," *Marketing News,* April 26, 1.

2. Sisodia, Rajendran (1995), "A Goofy Deal," *The Wall Street Journal,* August 4, A8.

3. *Ibid.*

4. Stern, Gabriella (1994), "Hope For Tomorrow: P&G Aims to Salvage Soap Operas," *The Wall Street Journal,* April 26, B1, B3.

5. An **advertorial** is a print ad that appears to be an article or an editorial.

6. Wells, Ken (1993), "The Klan's Ad States Its Beliefs; Proceeds Go To The NAACP," *The Wall Street Journal,* October 21.

7. Richards, Jef I., and John H. Murphy, II (1996), "Economic Censorship and Free Speech: The Circle of Communication Between Advertisers, Media, and Consumers," *Journal of Current Issues and Research in Advertising* 18, 1 (Spring).

8. Nielsen, as reported in Shore, Andrew (1993), "When The Sun Comes Up Tomorrow, You Had Better Be Running," Speech to Retail Study Group, Paine Webber, October 11.

9. *Ibid.*

10. Goldman, Kevin (1993), "Sony's Ad Boldly Goes Where No Ad Has Gone Before," *The Wall Street Journal,* March 3, B1, B4.

11. Horovitz, Bruce (1993), "Are Blimp Ads Just Hot Air?" *Los Angeles Times,* August 13, D1, D6.

12. Goldman, Kevin (1995), "Marketers Hang New Hope on Turnstiles," *The Wall Street Journal,* August 8, B2.

13. Elliott, Stuart (1994), "In Many College Dorms, Brand Pitches Replace Che, Rock Bands and James Dean as Poster Subjects," *New York Times,* January 19, D1, D17.

14. Lawrence, Jennifer (1994), "Belted by Ad Messages," *Advertising Age,* March 14, 30.

15. Reprinted from Elliott, Stuart (1993), "Advertising's Marathon Auditions," in "Themes of the Times," *The New York Times,* June 6, 1. Excerpt. Copyright ©1993 by The New York Times Co. Reprinted with permission.

16. Sloan, Pat (1995), "P&G/Paramount Deal Likely To Be Mimicked," *Advertising Age,* March 6, 2.

17. Stern, "Hope For Tomorrow: P&G Aims to Salvage Soap Operas."

18. Simmons (1992), *1992 Study of Media and Markets,* New York: Simmons Market Research Bureau, Inc., M8, 116.

19. Glaberson, William (1993), "Newspapers in Push To Get National Ads," *New York Times,* May 10, 15.

20. *Advertising Age* (1994), "Top 100 Magazines By Gross Revenue," October 24.

21. Frydlewicz, Rob (1995), "Missed Super Bowl? Put Your Bucks Here," *Advertising Age,* January 30, 18.

22. Dalrymple, Goodrum (1990), *Advertising in America: The First Two Hundred Years,* New York: Harry N. Abrams, 39.

23. In general, either measure should give the same rating. However, if a program's viewing varies by size of the household, then ratings would vary by measure. For example, if more single-member households are tuned to late-night programs, then the programs' ratings by households would be higher than those by individual viewers.

24. Alternatively, ratings can be obtained by multiplying usage and share.

25. Dalzell, Jane (1995), "Who's On First?" *Advertising Age: 50 Years of TV Advertising* (Spring), 8.

26. CPM = 100 × CPP/POP, or CPP = CPM × POP/100, where POP is the broadcast media population in thousands. The reason is as follows:

    CPM = cost per ad/viewers in thousands by definition = (cost per ad/viewers) × 1000   (1)

    But ratings = 100 × (viewers/population), by definition. So viewers = (ratings × population)/100   (2)

    So CPM = {(100 × cost per ad)/(ratings × population)} × 1,000 = {100 × (cost per ad/ratings)/POP}   (3)

    But cost per ad/ratings = CPP   (4)

    Thus by CPM = 100 × CPP/POP.

27. Based on Goldman, Kevin (1992), "NBC Favors Youth Over Ratings, Drops Shows Older Viewers Like," *The Wall Street Journal,* March 6, B4.

28. This section is inspired by Assael, Henry, and David F. Poltrack (1991), "Using Single Source Data To Select TV Programs Based on Purchasing Behavior," *Journal of Advertising Research* (August-September), 9–16.

29. The viewers who do not see any episodes (of either program) constitute the biggest fraction of the potential audience and are not shown on the curve so as not to distort the scale.

30. Frydlewicz, "Missed Super Bowl? Put Your Bucks Here."

31. Based on Kelly, Keith J. (1995), "Simmons Research Repairs Reputation," *Advertising Age,* October 2, 48; Friedman, Wayne (1995), "Simmons: Few Surprises," *Inside Media,* June 7, 4; *Advertising Age* (1994), "Battle Over Research," October 24, S21.

32. This section is based on Mediamark Research Inc. (1990), "Ready For the 90s," New York: Mediamark Research Inc.

16 Planning Direct Media

In the 1960s and 1970s, Fidelity revolutionized personal investing by developing mutual funds that pooled investors' risk and were easy to purchase.[1] Its flagship Magellan fund was one of the most profitable funds in the 1980s and grew to be the largest mutual fund in the 1990s. The company's success fueled rapid growth, so that in 1996 it managed $405 billion in assets, four times as much as in 1990.

In the 1990s, Fidelity revolutionized direct mail with high-tech automation, to serve its large, diverse customer base

scattered all over the United States Fidelity built a $100 million facility on a 188-acre estate at Covington, Kentucky. The land was given to Fidelity by the state of Kentucky to stimulate growth in the region. At the heart of the Covington facility is a 256,000-square-foot mailing warehouse. Fidelity's managers toured manufacturing facilities and special-ordered equipment to rapidly and accurately process mail in the warehouse.

Fidelity's mailing operation is a model of efficiency. It guarantees that a request for information will be answered by mail the very next day. All requests for information at various Fidelity offices are conveyed to Covington at 2:00 A.M. EST following the day they are received. From there, the highly automated mailing system ensures that Fidelity keeps its guarantee. Robots help to store and retrieve Fidelity's 3,000 mailing kits. Computerized equipment downloads the names and addresses of customers into machines that ink-jet the data onto envelopes and apply metered postage. Scanners read the ZIP code, spray on a postal service bar code, sort the letters and put them into different trays. Postal service trucks then haul most of the sorted mail directly to the airport, which is 10 miles away, without it ever passing through a post office.

Bulk orders from brokerage firms are also automated. A computer can help execute as many as eight orders at a time. Robots retrieve and stock a rotating machine with material for the order. The machine lights up to show an employee how many of which items are needed for a particular order. A belt carries the material to another machine for least-cost routing. When the latter machine is fed the package, the ZIP code and the last date of delivery, it gives the costs that would be charged by different postal services. The employee sends the package to the service with the lowest cost.

For routine statements to customers, Fidelity uses paper that is especially chosen and aged to ensure that it creases well and stays flat. Machines spray the names and addresses of customers on the envelopes at the rate of 12,000 an hour.

Fidelity is the biggest mailer in the Cincinnati area. The Covington facility shipped 3.7 million pounds of freight and spent $40 million on postal service in 1995. The company is a service organization whose success depends on timely mail to its customers. At Covington, getting the mail out is a highly automated production operation, and an obsession with employees.

The term **direct media** is used to describe media such as mail, telephone, or the Internet that can help organizations reach individual consumers. The example of Fidelity's mailing facility shows how direct media can play a critical role in the growth and success of a service organization. However, the direct media can be a vital means of communicating and marketing for all types of organizations, not only services. For example, auto companies, publishers, computer companies, and furniture companies among others regularly send mailings to their customers in order to advertise new products and specials. Moreover, mail is not the only medium for direct communication, nor is printed material. Direct media can be classified into mail and broadcast. Mail involves private or government mail services that carry printed material, audiotapes, videotapes, samples, or CDs. Broadcast media involve fax, telephone, interactive cable TV, or the Internet, which carry printed, audio or video messages.

One characteristic of promotion through direct media is that it tries to elicit an immediate response from consumers in the form of requests for more information, purchases, commitments or sales leads. A **sales lead** is a contact that a salesperson can follow up on for a sale. The term **direct marketing** is used to describe both promoting a product and completing a sale, as long as either uses direct media. Direct marketing could occur entirely or partly through the direct media. For example, a TV ad that includes an 800 number to allow consumers to buy a product is considered by the trade to be telemarketing, a form of direct marketing, even though the advertising uses the mass media. Thus the term direct marketing is broader than the term *direct media* both because it involves promoting and selling and because it involves direct media and mass media.

This chapter covers the direct media in four parts. It first explains the reasons for the rapid growth of these media. It then evaluates their pros and cons. The third section describes the major direct media, and the fourth section explains how to evaluate the profitability of a direct media campaign.

Growth of direct media

The direct media have grown rapidly over the last few decades. For example, direct mail has grown from 14 percent of all advertising expenditures in 1980 to 20 percent in 1993, to become the third most popular advertising medium.[2] One report claims that advertising through the direct media now triggers 12 percent of consumer sales in the United States.[3] Several factors have been responsible for this growth, including advances in media technology, computerized databases, the increasing value of consumers' time, splintering of the mass market and availability of credit cards.

Media Technology Perhaps the single most important stimulus to the growth of direct media has been technology. Technology in the form of offset printing, AM and FM broadcasting and color TV broadcasting revolutionized the mass media around the middle of this century. However, more recently technological progress has enhanced the value of the direct media relative to the mass media. For example, better telecommunications equipment has made telephone service cheaper, clearer, more reliable and more freely available the world over. Further, technology has made available seller-sponsored (800) area codes, and user-paid (900) area codes, which have facilitated the marketing of goods and services. As Fidelity's Covington facility shows, better technology to sort and transport mail has also lowered the cost and improved the speed and accuracy of direct mail. The most promising of direct media today is perhaps the Internet. The launching and rapid growth of this medium has been the outcome of revolutionary progress in computer, communication, video-display and software technologies.

Computerized Databases The wide availability of inexpensive but powerful computers has been a tremendous help to business in numerous ways. One important benefit is that marketers can keep accurate records of their customers, including their addresses, demographics, purchasing behavior and response to advertising. The computerized database of customers is the heart of any direct marketing program. The computerization of customer records also allows for easy analysis of these records. In addition, computer software allows advertisers to easily customize their ads to match the customer profiles.

For example, through its telephone service AT&T has built up records of millions of customers. The records include their phone numbers, addresses, monthly use of telephone service and number of lines owned. In particular, the last three pieces of information can indicate the approximate buying power of an individual. This database became a tremendous asset to the company when it decided to enter the credit card business with its Universal Card in 1990. AT&T immediately had access to a large number of customers, could address them by name, and could tailor the incentive it offered potential customers based on their expected spending. As a result, in six months the Universal Card had more than a million owners, who spent more than $100 million with the card.[4]

Firms that do not have their own customer database can rent mailing lists from companies that own or develop these lists. For example, the College Board, which prepares the Scholastic Aptitude Test, is one of the largest suppliers of lists of students to colleges. It has the names of more than a million high school juniors and seniors who agreed to have their names included in the list. About 900 colleges nationwide buy the names of high school students from the board for their annual recruiting effort.[5]

Value of Time Most developed countries are rapidly becoming societies with "money-rich and time-poor" individuals.[6] People have a lot more income, but a lot less time. The primary reason for this change is the shift to dual-income households, where both husband and wife have jobs outside the home. As households work more, have less time, and earn higher incomes, the value of their time increases greatly. Household members have less of an incentive to shop for their purchases in the traditional way. Direct media make it possible for marketers to reach customers directly, and for customers to buy quickly, conveniently and without travel. Thus as the value of time goes up, customer demand for and response to direct media also go up.

Splintering of Mass Market

Over time the quality of manufactured goods generally goes up, and their price goes down.[7] This phenomenon has been called the experience curve. At the same time, consumers' disposable incomes have been going up. These two factors have enabled consumers to demand and purchase products that are better matched to their needs, even if they have to pay more. These factors have also motivated marketers to differentiate products from their competitors', in order to better appeal to consumers and get a higher price. As a result the mass market for products has splintered.

Mass media such as TV and newspapers are ideal for reaching a single market that wants a single product. However, when millions of consumers all over the country want products with a variety of features and specifications, marketers need to reach them directly with messages and deals tailored to their needs. Direct media are a more efficient and effective means of doing so than the mass media. Thus, the splintering of the mass market makes direct media more attractive than the mass media for communicating with consumers.

Acceptance of Credit Cards

The acceptance of the credit card as a means of payment has greatly facilitated the growth of direct media, especially telemarketing. The earliest credit card was probably introduced by Diners Club in 1950, followed by American Express and Bank of America in 1958.[8] Other banks followed in the 1960s, further promoting the acceptance of this form of payment. The credit card has three important advantages over check or cash. First, it enables consumers to buy on credit even if they do not have available cash. Second, the credit card does not require a physical presence or exchange. Third, the credit card enables instant purchase following a promotion, even a remote one through the telephone or Internet. Direct marketing can make attractive appeals and back them up with the opportunity to make instant purchases paid for by credit. This option is particularly valuable for telemarketers, who otherwise would have a difficult task collecting payments by mail.

However, to the extent that waiting and reflection may reduce unnecessary purchases by consumers, the availability of credit may hurt impulsive or less thoughtful purchasers.

EVALUATION OF DIRECT MEDIA

Advantages of Direct Media

The direct media are superior to the mass media due to their better control over the reach, frequency, and content of the ad, the convenience and easy measurement of response to the ad, and the ability to build relationships.

Precise Reach

Perhaps the greatest advantage of direct media is their reach, which is far more precise than that of mass media. The reason for this advantage is the availability of a database of individuals. At the minimum, this database must maintain the names of individuals plus one means of contact, such as a phone number or address. Typically, databases also maintain additional information on characteristics of individuals, including their past response to direct media. Advertisers can use this information to more effectively target individuals. For example, a marketer planning to mail coupons can look over a mailing list and choose precisely those individuals who do not use its brand but use coupons. In that way, it maximizes purchases of its brand without loss of revenue from consumers who already buy its brand at regular price. In practice, advertisers may not actually scrutinize every individual on the list, but may sort them by demographics or response rates into preferred segments. Nevertheless, direct media do allow for greater precision in reach than do the mass media.

Frequency Control

Consumers differ by the amount of message repetition they need to respond to an ad (see Chapter 4). By using direct media, an advertiser can better control the frequency of the message, so that each individual gets the message at the most effective frequency. Such control is possible because the advertiser may be able to obtain response rates of individuals on the list, either in detail (for each individual) or more broadly (by demographic group).

Tailored Content With mass media, an ad normally is inserted in a vehicle that carries many other programs and messages. As a result, the advertiser does not have the option to tailor the ad to each individual. However, with direct media, each message can be sent alone or with other messages. Thus the advertiser has the option to tailor the message to each individual. This tailoring may take the form of different appeals (such as informational versus emotional appeals), different content within each appeal, or more personal messages to each individual. Tailored messages are more likely to elicit a response than standard messages.

Convenient Response Direct media generally allow for more immediate and convenient response to advertising. For example, telemarketers try to elicit immediate verbal transactions, mass mailers include a postage-paid return card to facilitate the transaction, while marketers on the Internet allow transactions with a click of the mouse. In contrast, the mass media are not naturally structured for immediate response. The mass media do sometimes provide opportunities for such immediate response, but they do so by requesting that consumers use the direct media: mail, telephone or the Internet.

Response to direct media is much higher than that to the mass media. Indeed, award-winning campaigns have won very high response rates (see Exhibit 16-1). However, response rates have been declining as consumers get saturated with such appeals. Typical rates currently range from .1 to 1 percent.

Easy Measurement Direct media allow for easy, direct measurement of response from individuals. The database that maintains records about individuals can also be designed to record the amount of advertising targeted to each individual, and the nature of the individual's response. These three components can then be analyzed to determine how consumers respond to advertising far more precisely than can be done with the mass media.

Personal Relationship Direct media enable marketers to build a personal relationship with consumers more easily than do the mass media. Developing a personal relationship with consumers helps to retain consumer loyalty. The relationship could take many forms such as a newsletter, or periodic rebates, coupons or gifts sent by mail. For example, Waldenbooks has a Preferred Reader Service that tracks purchases of 1.5 million buyers of books, and mails them a newsletter tailored to their individual needs.[9]

Disadvantages of Direct Media

Direct media suffer from two key disadvantages relative to the mass media: cost and intrusiveness.

Cost Direct media reach consumers individually. Each such contact often involves human labor, as in a telephone call or delivery to a mailbox. Since labor is generally more expensive than the technology used in mass media, direct media turn out to be quite costly for each contact made. For example, a direct-mail campaign could cost at least 15 cents per household reached in postage alone. In comparison, a prime-time TV show with a rating of 14, costing $450,000 per ad would amount to about 5 cents per household reached. However, when measured

▼ **EXHIBIT 16-1.** Response rates for 1996 Echo Award for direct media campaigns.

Marketer	Type	Reach	Response Rate	Cost per Response	Conversion Rate	Revenue per Sale
Focus Software	Mail	1,000	8%	$182	35% (Gold Prize)	$975
TCI Cable Television	Mail	140,000	4%	$15	NA (Silver Prize)	NA
IBM AS/400 catalog	Catalog	125,000	29%	$155	NA	$3,274
GEO Prizm	E-mail	300,000	21%	$3	12% (Bronze Prize)	NA
USPS Elvis stamp	Mail	707,000	23%	$2	100%	NA
First Bank VISA card	Mail	1,500	8%	$476	6.3%	NA

Source: Abstracted from 1996 Echo Award entry forms.

in terms of response, direct media may turn out to be more efficient than mass media. The reason is that direct media have better reach, more effective frequency, more personalized messages, and higher consumer response. For example, Dick's Supermarket in New Orleans began mailing a 16-page brochure of specials to frequent shoppers instead of using newspaper ads. The grocery store enjoyed a 4 percent increase in sales, which more than compensated for the cost of the mailing ($100,000 more than the newspaper ad).[10]

Intrusiveness Some direct media, such as the telephone and fax, reach individuals at times or locations that they consider private. They also do so through a medium which individuals do not fully control or at times they do not expect. For example, an individual watching TV generally knows about the ads, and can predict their frequency and even their approximate time. However, a person working at home has no knowledge of when and how he or she may be reached by a telemarketer. For these reasons, direct media tend to be more intrusive. If the message in these media is not commensurate with the value of the individual's time and privacy, it may immediately turn off the individual. For example, a telemarketer asking an individual for a subscription when he or she is in the midst of a family dinner may get an immediate refusal. While better targeting can reduce the severity of this problem, it may not be able to fully resolve it.

Further, the direct media also rely on maintaining and analyzing databases. Many of these databases are built from records of customers' purchases. In all of these cases, consumers have the option to decline mailings or phone calls from firms, as explained in Chapter 2. Currently, laws do not require consumers to be informed if their purchase patterns are being recorded and analyzed for marketing purposes. However, such an activity encroaches on consumers' privacy and is likely to be an area of future regulation. Firms may also sell databases of addresses and response patterns to other firms, unless consumers explicitly request otherwise. However, a firm would violate an implicit contract of confidentiality with its customers if it sold records of customers' transactions, to another marketer.

THE MAJOR DIRECT MEDIA

This section provides a description of the three most important direct media: mail, telephone and the Internet. The mail is the oldest of the direct media, but still has enormous potential. The telephone is a relatively new medium that has become the center of an integrated marketing activity called telemarketing. The Internet is a newly emerging direct medium with enormous potential.

Mail

Advertising through the mail is very old. Many people believe that it took its current form in the late nineteenth century when entrepreneurs such as Montgomery Ward and John Sears began mailing their catalogues and offering a money-back guarantee on sales (see Chapter 1). This medium of retailing became successful because it gave consumers in small towns and villages easy access to goods available to consumers in big cities, and a cost-free option to try the product. However, much older efforts at direct mail have existed (see Exhibit 16-2). Even the money-back guarantee was offered earlier in a prim-

▼ **EXHIBIT 16-2.** **Some early direct marketers.**

Year	Direct Marketing Effort
1450	Printers and publishers issue trade catalogs.
1498	Aldus Manutius publishes a catalogue of 15 books with their prices.
1667	William Lucas publishes a gardening catalogue.
1744	Benjamin Franklin publishes a catalog of 600 books and guarantees them.
1830	Mail-order companies in New England sell sporting, camping, fishing and marine supplies.
1845	Tiffany & Co. publishes its catalog of "fancy" articles.
1886	Sears, Roebuck publishes its first catalog.
1887	The Montgomery Ward catalog offers a money-back guarantee.
1912	L. L. Bean markets rubber-soled hunting boots by mail.

Source: Muldoon, Katie (1990), "Time Flies When You Have Fun," *DM News*, March 12, 26.

▼ **EXHIBIT 16-3.** Milestones in the recent history of direct mail.

Year	Event
1863	President Lincoln introduces penny postage.
1890	USPS offers rural free delivery, an unrestricted daily mail service for rural areas.
1928	USPS establishes third-class bulk mail.
1950	Introduction of credit cards initiates purchases on credit.
1963	ZIP codes introduced.

Source: Muldoon, Katie (1990), "Time Flies When You Have Fun," *DM News*, March 12, 26.

itive form. For example, in 1744, Benjamin Franklin is supposed to have offered the following guarantee on books available on his catalog: "Those persons who live remote, by sending their orders and money to said B. Franklin, may depend on the same justice as if present."[11]

The key factor that helped the growth of direct mail in the last century was the availability of inexpensive house-to-house delivery even in hard-to-reach rural areas. Exhibit 16-3 lists the milestones in the availability of this medium. Modern direct mail was further assisted by the use of ZIP codes. They enabled easy sorting of mail, and segmentation of groups of households by a single number. Because people's wants are affected by climate and geography, and because people of similar socioeconomic status tend to reside in the same neighborhoods, segmentation by ZIP codes can be very useful. These developments, together with computerization of records and use of technology for storage and sorting of mail, enabled the setting up of high-powered direct mail systems, such as Fidelity's Covington facility.

Advertising through the mail can be considered a form of precisely targeted print advertising. Because it involves primarily the mailing of printed material, mail has all the advantages of print media such as mass production of ads, communication of detailed information, and the ability to be retained, read at leisure, and passed on to others. In addition, mail has an advantage over the print media in that it allows the marketer to target individuals.

One of the most well-established forms of advertising through the mail is the sales catalogue, which contains prices, descriptions, or pictures of items on sale. Consumers can order the featured items by

mail, telephone or fax. Annual or seasonal catalogues are shipped to households either for a fee or freely as a promotion. Sales brochures announcing items on discount are generally mailed by retailers to all households in the area served. The mail can also be used for promotions to customers who receive periodic statements or request special information, as in the Fidelity example. Typically such promotions include descriptions of special items, or the distribution of coupons, rebates and premium offers.

Mail advertisers can use the government-owned U.S. Postal Service, or any one of a number of private services. The best known of private services are United Parcel Service (UPS) which specializes in quick deliveries of parcels, and Federal Express (FedEx) which pioneered overnight delivery of letters or packages. However, most private mailing of promotion material is carried by less well-known services developed to deliver newspapers and magazines. Private services suffer from two disadvantages relative to the U.S. Postal Service. First, most households have only one box to receive mail, which is dedicated to the U.S. Postal Service and may not be used by any other service. Second, the U.S. Postal Service has great potential economies of scale in that it is the most widely established of the mail services. However, it also suffers from the disadvantage of being slower and more costly, because of its greater size and bureaucracy.[12] The number of private delivery services has grown from 88 in 1981 to over 312 in 1993, fueled in part by rate increases by the U.S. Postal Service. Yet the latter agency still has 98 percent of the $72 billion market for the delivery of promotional material.[13]

The use of mail is especially advantageous for new or small companies that know their target market. Such companies cannot afford the prices of ads in the mass media, nor do they really need the vast reach of those media. Such companies also do not get cheap or easy access to their goods and services from established retailers and distributors. By using mail to advertise and sell their products, they can bypass the regular distribution system. For example, Dell Computer Company became a multi-billion-dollar organization by marketing inexpensive computers through the mail. Thus it eliminated the costs and hurdles of an established distribution system that favored established companies, as well as the sales taxes in some states.

Currently, large established corporations, including major manufacturers, also use the mail extensively because of its more precise targeting. Consider the following examples:

- Credit card companies routinely send a variety of promotions by mail for two reasons. First, the promotions are included in the regular monthly statement for only a small incremental cost. Second, they have a good record of the purchasing habits of their customers, and so can target promotions to the appropriate consumer, with an offer tailored to elicit a response.
- Airlines routinely mail to their frequent flyers ads for their own services and those of hotels and rental car companies. The reason this operation is possible is that the airlines' frequent flyer program provides a rich database of customers' traveling patterns, which can be analyzed to precisely target various promotions.
- Some grocery stores encourage customers to use a card to purchase their groceries. This card enables the store to track consumer purchases. Consumers can then be mailed coupons and other promotions, based on their past purchasing habits in the store. To maximize the store's profits from distributing coupons, consumers should be mailed only those promotions to which they respond, and for brands they otherwise would not buy (see Chapters 9 and 12).

Telephone

The telephone is a medium of the twentieth century. Telephone service was commercialized in the early part of this century. It has grown from a simple means of two-way communication to become a major vehicle for inte-

▼ **EXHIBIT 16-4.** Consumers' rating of the importance of various attributes of telemarketers.

Attribute	Mean Importance on Six-Point Scale
Salesperson is professional and courteous.	5.3
Person rather than computer calls.	5.1
Company calling has a good reputation.	5.0
Person calls at a convenient time.	4.9
Consumer has an interest in the product.	4.7
Consumer has a good previous experience with the product.	4.5

Source: Stone, Bob, and John Wyman (1992), *Successful Telemarketing,* Lincolnwood, IL: NTC Books.

grated marketing (telemarketing). One innovation that greatly facilitated telemarketing was the introduction of toll-free 800 WATS lines sponsored by marketers. This section first covers response to telephone appeals and then the activity of telemarketing.

Response to Telephone Appeals **Telephone appeals** are vocal ads made through the telephone. Who responds to telephone appeals? How can firms enhance this response? Answering these questions is the first step in designing effective appeals. While there is extensive research on response to television and print

▼ **EXHIBIT 16-5.** Characteristics of acceptors and nonacceptors of telephone appeals.

Demographic Characteristic	Percent of Acceptors in Each Group	Percent of Nonacceptors in Each Group
Age		
18–24	21%	10%
55 and over	8	13
Education		
High school or less	46%	29%
College graduate	15	23
Annual Income		
Under $15,000	12%	7%
$35,000 to $50,000	13	22
Telephone Appeals Received (in preceding 3 months)		
3 or less	60%	48%
4 to 9	23	25
10 and above	17	27

Data Source: Stone, Bob, and John Wyman (1992), *Successful Telemarketing,* Lincolnwood, IL: NTC Books.

media, research on response to telephone appeals is very limited. A study by John Wyman was the first to study response to telephone appeals in the United States.[14] It involved a national survey of 1,000 random households to determine how consumers respond to such appeals.

One finding from the study was consumers' rating of the importance of various attributes of telephone appeals (see Exhibit 16-4). While interest in and past experience with a product are normally considered key predictors of purchase, this survey suggests that for telemarketing, the use of a courteous salesperson is the most important factor.

A more important finding from the study was the difference in demographics between consumers who accept or respond to telephone appeals, and those who do not (see Exhibit 16-5). Acceptors tend to be younger, poorer and less educated. These differences suggest that acceptors are either less sophisticated consumers, or less able or willing to shop for their needs through the traditional outlets. In either case, telemarketers need to rethink their strategy of targeting high-income segments in the hope that these segments have more disposable income and are more likely to respond. The reverse may be the case.

Perhaps the most important finding from the study was that acceptors tended to have received few (3 or less) telephone appeals, in the previous 3 months, while nonacceptors had received numerous (10 or more) such appeals. This finding suggests that consumers who receive numerous telephone appeals tend to reject them either because the number of appeals exceeds their buying capacity, or because they are tired of or disgusted with the appeals. In either case, this finding points to a dilemma for telemarketers. They must target individuals based on their past acceptance of telephone appeals. Yet, as all telemarketers tend to target the same consumers from publicly available or purchased lists, those consumers get saturated with calls and are less likely to respond. Thus an important strategy for telemarketers is to obtain new consumers who are likely to respond, yet are not on any or many public lists.

Telemarketing **Telemarketing** is an integrated system of research, promotion, generating sales leads, generating sales and providing after-sales service using the telecommunication system in conjunction with other media. In particular, telemarketing involves direct calls to consumers (proactive telemarketing), servicing of spontaneous calls by customers (passive telemarketing) or stimulation of consumers' calls by ads in other media (indirect telemarketing). Telemarketing has grown enormously in the past few years due to firms' realization that placing a telephone number in ads can greatly enhance requests for information and actual purchases. To fully exploit this benefit, firms need to set up a toll-free number, service it with skilled salespersons, and advertise the number prominently in ads in other media.

We briefly consider the use of telemarketing in conjunction with mail, print and television ads, and with sales promotions.

Mail Ads Offers through the mail get a higher response rate if they are accompanied with a toll-free number rather than a postage-paid return envelope. Catalogue directors find that average sales are 20 percent higher when executed through a listed toll-free number rather than through a mail-order card. The greater effectiveness of telephone orders may be because consumers find ordering by telephone more convenient, or they like to have the option of talking with a salesperson or executing the purchase immediately.

Print Ads Print ads frequently list a phone number for consumers to get information on the product, the dealer's location, or the terms of the sale, or to buy the product (see Exhibit 16-6). The first two pieces of information are necessary for marketing complex products such as computers, real estate or investment options. In such cases the advertiser cannot provide all the information needed in the ad, especially if it varies by individual consumer. Print ads can trigger sales through the telephone, if the products are well known and from a reputed company. For example, purchases of precious metals, commodities or mutual funds worth thousands of dollars may be executed through a toll-free number advertised in print.

Television Ads As for the mass media, TV ads for complex products could also enhance response by providing a toll-free number. In addition, TV ads for products with demonstrable features should especially use the toll-free number. TV is ideally suited for such products, and a good demonstration can elicit immediate consumer response. It is best to exploit that response with a toll-free number for consumers to get more information or make a purchase. Because time on television is

▼ **EXHIBIT 16-6.** Print ad listing a telephone number and World Wide Web address.

➤ New integrated control panel

➤ New driver's door remote keyless entry system

➤ Improved steel safety cell construction

➤ New AM/FM stereo with premium speakers

➤ Standard dual air bags*

➤ New 2.0L 4-cylinder SPI engine with 25% more power

*Always wear your safety belt. MSRP '97 Escort & '97 Escort LX with PEP 317A. Title, tax extra.

For more info: **1-800-286-1153** or *http://www.ford.com*

BUILT

IT'S PRICED REALLY NICE AND IT'S BUILT OH-SO WELL.

Smart

Source: Courtesy of Ford Motor Company.

costly, ads that provide a toll-free number must be especially designed for direct marketing. Such ads need to emphasize the urgency of consumers making the purchase immediately. Infomercials, which are generally aired at less popular and expensive times, are frequently designed for an immediate response. So infomercials should routinely list a phone number at which consumers can get more information or buy the product. Marketers of new kitchen gadgets often use this form of telemarketing, because the new gadget can be dramatically demonstrated on TV while the toll-free number allows for immediate purchase.

Sales Promotions Because sales promotions are not always clear, the provision of a telephone number for further information can ensure that they run smoothly. Such a setup is especially important for contests, sweepstakes, premiums, trials and samples. Moreover, because sales promotions require consumer participation and sometimes generate much excitement, the telephone number enables consumers to get more information about the product and purchase it if they are interested. A toll-free number can also be integrated with a promotion to enhance participation.

For example, Quaker Oats developed a promotion in which specially marked boxes of Cap'n Crunch contained a map indicating where the pirate LaFoote had buried the treasure. In a creative twist to increase interest, the company provided a toll-free number for participants to call to find out the correct location. If the taped telephone message indicated a location that matched the one on the map inside the box, the caller won a Huffy bicycle. The toll-free number was a phenomenal success, generating over 24 million calls in four months, and triggering a 33 percent increase in market share.[15]

Well-designed promotions using a prepaid (900) phone number can also work well. For example, *NBC Friday Night Videos* ran a promotion in which consumers could call one of two 900 numbers and vote for the rock video of their choice. NBC received about 100,000 calls during a 90-minute segment of the program. When the company offered a T-shirt for a lucky call, the number of calls once topped 450,000.[16]

While completing a sale is the ultimate goal of most marketing, note from the previous discussion that telemarketing need not be narrowly construed as serving only this goal. In particular, firms can also use telemarketing to provide information about products, generate sales leads or provide after-sales service. For example, marketers of the Kirby vacuum cleaner first contact potential households by phone to elicit interest in the machine, before sending a salesperson to the home to demonstrate the machine and close the sale. Telemarketing can also serve as a means to provide consumers with after-sales service. Such service is an effective means of ensuring complete consumer satisfaction with the product, and strong consumer loyalty to the brand name. Thus, while the telephone is an effective means of making offers to consumers to elicit an immediate sales response, it can also be integrated with other media and promotional tools to become a powerful means for complete marketing.

The Internet

The **Internet** is a worldwide network of computers through which individuals or institutions can communicate with each other. A key characteristic of the Internet is the great flexibility in interpersonal hookups that it allows. For example, individuals can communicate one to one, one to many, many to one or many to many.[17] In contrast, the mass media generally allow one-to-many communication, while the other direct media allow one-to-one communication. The Internet supports electronic mail, file transfers, special interest groups, conferencing, multiplayer games, and global information retrieval via the World Wide Web.

The **World Wide Web** (referred to as the Web) consists of a network of computer sites, each of which can be accessed either through its unique address or through a hypertext link. Individuals or organizations can set up sites for purposes of transactions, advertising, research, or providing news or information (for example, see Exhibit 16-7). A **hypertext link** is special text on a page of Internet material, which when clicked with the help of a mouse takes the user to a new page of information or a new site. To connect to the Internet, an individual needs a service provider. After that the individual can access one or more specific sites, conduct searches of specific topics, or randomly "surf" the Internet through hypertext links. The great flexibility of the Internet has fueled its rapid growth.

As of early 1996, the *Open Market Directory* listed about 23,000 commercial services on the Internet, while the *Yahoo Guide* listed over 42,000 companies, with the number of sites doubling every

▼ **EXHIBIT 16-7.** Two commercial uses of the Web.

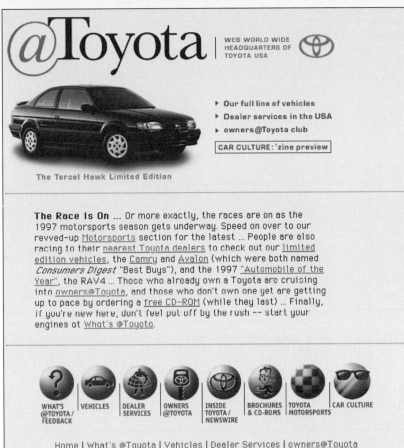

Source: Courtesy of Toyota.

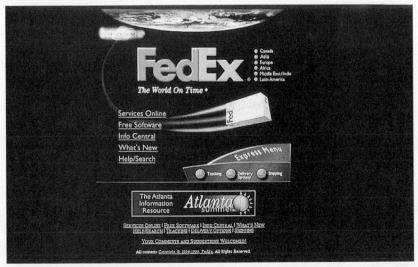

Source: Copyright FedEx Corporation.

two months.[18] Controversy surrounds estimates of the number of Internet users, because of the newness of the medium, the speed with which it is growing and the difficulty of measuring it. Based on various commercial surveys, one report estimated there were about 10 million users of the Internet in the United States alone,[19] which is ten times the number of a decade ago. Estimates of the level of trade on the Internet by the year 2000 vary between $22 billion and $50 billion.[20]

Advantages and Disadvantages of the Internet The Internet is the most promising of the direct media for several reasons.

First, it allows for multimedia presentations involving text, sound, visuals and video. Ads can demonstrate the product in use, or allow consumers to manipulate visuals to see the product from different angles. Consumers can also sample some on-line products such as books, software, CDs or videos. Thus the Internet is more flexible and powerful than the other direct media.

Second, the Internet allows individuals to access ads at their own time and pace. In this respect it is more like the print media, which a consumer can save and read at leisure. It thus avoids the intrusiveness prevalent with mail and especially the fax and telephone.

Third, the Internet allows enormous choice. Vendors from all over the world can make their goods and services available. Further, using free search services, consumers can search for information on only those categories or subcategories they want to consider. For example, using the search service Yahoo, consumers could search for vendors of chocolates in general, or of sugar-free dark chocolates with honey-roasted almonds. One study in December 1995 found 77 types of chocolates, 232 types of T-shirts, and "countless" blends and shadings of teas in one site alone.[21] There are also "malls" hosting a number of "shops," which in turn carry a number of brands. The Internet is like a worldwide Yellow Pages, only better organized and accessible.

Fourth, advertising through the Internet can be as much as 25 percent less costly than advertising through the other direct media.[22] The mere listing of a site enables it to appear on various Internet search services that consumers can easily access. Thus developing a site alone, while not costless, serves as a steady stream of advertising. In addition, advertisers can buy space on the sites of other organizations to advertise their own site and make it accessible through a hyperlink. Unlike with the other direct media, very little labor is involved in advertising through the Internet. Thus the cost per individual reached is quite low.

Fifth, buyers may be responsive to Internet ads because the Internet allows for a less costly and more private means of purchase than does store shopping. Savings can occur because the manufacturer does not have to incur costly warehouse facilities to store and display the product, and because it can eliminate the need for one or more intermediate stages of distribution. The Internet may also be less costly and more private than telemarketing. The reason is that the Internet involves no human interaction as in telemarketing.

▼ **EXHIBIT 16-8.** **PC penetration vs. TV viewing.**

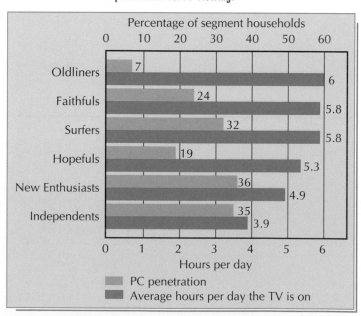

Source: Rapaport, Richard (1995), "Digitizing Desire. The New Demographics," *Forbes ASAP,* April 10, 1995, 67. Reprinted by Permission of *Forbes ASAP* Magazine. © Forbes, Inc., 1995. Reprinted by permission of Odyssey.

▼ **EXHIBIT 16-9.** Growth of on-line access.

	HOUSEHOLDS (IN MILLIONS) OWNING			
Year	TVs	PCs	PCs with Modems	PCs On-Line
1988	89	16	3	1
1989	90	21	4	1
1990	92	24	6	2
1991	93	26	7	2
1992	92	29	20	3
1993	93	31	13	3
1994	94	36	16	4
1995	95	40	20	6
1996	97	43	23	8
1997*	98	46	25	9
1998*	99	48	27	11

*Estimates
Source: Rapaport, Richard (1995), "Digitizing Desire: The New Demographics," *Forbes ASAP* 8, April 10, 72.

Sixth, the Internet allows for rapid communication. Site information can be loaded any time of the day or night, and the changes become effective immediately. Further, the listing of new sites is also disseminated fairly quickly through the on-line search services.

Seventh, Internet usage and TV viewing may be negatively correlated. One study found that those who own computers are also likely to watch less TV (Exhibit 16-8). If Internet usage is also negatively correlated with TV viewing, then the Internet may be a good medium through which to reach consumers not easily accessible through TV.

The Internet suffers from some disadvantages that do not make it the medium of choice for marketers at the present. First and most important, the Internet's reach is quite small and selective. Despite rapid growth, only a fraction of current computer owners access the Internet, while computer ownership itself is not universal (see Exhibit 16-9). Moreover, the typical Internet user tends to be male, college educated, young and wealthier than the average American.[23] Cruising the Internet is not an activity that everyone enjoys. Many people are computer illiterate, and even those who are not find the Internet too slow and cumbersome. Third, privacy and security on the Internet are not thorough. Marketers can electronically track inquiries and purchases made by individuals. Also, computer hackers may be able to get access to accounts or credit card numbers communicated through the Internet. Because of the select nature of Internet users and the companies they attract, Internet sites are highly skewed by industries. As of mid-1995, the highest proportion of firms with sites was in the telecommunications and computer industries, while the lowest was in the food and drug industries (see Exhibit 16-10).

However, all the disadvantages of the Internet are likely to diminish with better technology and increasing popularity of the medium. Thus the promise of the Internet remains bright.

▼ **EXHIBIT 16-10.** Proportion of various industries with Internet sites.

Most Internet-Oriented Industries	Percentage of Firms with Sites
1. Telecommunications	43%
2. Computers and office equipment	41
3. Electronic entertainment equipment	24
4. Publishing	20
5. Financial services	17
6. Insurance and real estate	12

Least Web-Oriented Industries	Percentage of Firms with Sites
6. Drugs and remedies	3%
5. Food and food products	3
4. Apparel and footwear	3
3. Retailing	3
2. Building materials	3
1. Toiletries and cosmetics	<1

Source: *InterAd* (1995), "Webtracking," 1.1, July, 5.

EVALUATING THE PROFITABILITY OF DIRECT MEDIA

Determining whom to target in a direct media campaign, or whether even to run a campaign, depends on an analysis of the profitability of the campaign.

There are two important stages in the evaluation of the profitability of using the direct media: collecting data and computing profits.

Collecting Data

Data are essential for evaluating the profitability of direct media. The promoter needs information on at least three aspects of the campaign: the costs of the campaign, contribution margin from each transaction and response rate of the campaign. Once a marketer has run a campaign and obtained these data, he or she can relatively easily analyze the profitability of the campaign using a spreadsheet based on the table in Exhibit 16-1. Gross profit is revenue minus cost per response. Net profit is gross profit minus the cost of the item sold.

However, knowledge that a campaign has not been profitable is not so useful after its completion. Most marketers want to know whether a campaign will be profitable *in advance* of its execution. For this purpose the marketer has to separate direct costs from indirect or fixed costs.

Direct and Indirect Costs **Direct costs** are the costs that change with each additional contact made through direct media. Examples are the costs of postage or a phone call to contact each individual, or the cost of reshelving returns. On the other hand, **indirect costs** are costs of the campaign as a whole, and do not change by the number of contacts or sales. An example would be the rental of the database. Exhibit 16-11 lists common direct and indirect costs of direct media. Indirect costs are separated from direct costs because they relate to the overall decision of undertaking a campaign. Once such a decision has been taken, these costs are sunk, and must no longer be considered when deciding whom in the database to target.

Contribution Margin Advertising through direct media is often used in conjunction with marketing a product through the same media. Thus the payoff from using the direct media depends intrinsically on what the marketer gains from the sale. That gain is called the contribution margin. The **contribution margin** is the difference between the price at which a unit is sold to consumers and the variable cost of producing that unit. The term *contribution margin* is used because the difference between the two figures makes a *contribution* toward the fixed costs of producing that unit. Note that the indirect costs of the campaign, or the fixed costs of manufacture, must never be included when computing the margin. The reason is that those costs are incurred at some earlier point in time. They are *sunk* costs and are generally not affected by the decision to use direct media to market to consumers. So fixed costs of production are analogous to indirect costs of the campaign, while variable costs of manufacture are analogous to direct costs of the campaign.

Response Rate The unique and most important element in evaluating the profitability of direct media is the expected response rate. The **expected response rate** is an estimation of the proportion and type of consumer response expected relative to the total number of consumers to be contacted. The response rate consists of three proportions or probabilities: the

▼ **EXHIBIT 16-11.** Costs of direct marketing.

A. Direct and indirect costs in direct-mail campaigns.

DIRECT COSTS		INDIRECT COSTS
Dispatch Costs	**Return Costs**	
Packaging	Postage for returns	Development of campaign
Labeling	Unusable returns	Administration of campaign
Handling	Reshelving usable returns	Purchase of the database
Postage		Internet site costs, if any
Phone or fax costs		
Internet contact costs		

B. Variable and fixed costs of a sale.

Variable Costs	Fixed Costs
Material to manufacture each item	Management time
Labor to manufacture each item	Office supplies
Purchase of the item	Buildings
Utilities to produce each item	Plant and equipment

purchase probability, the return probability and the nonresponse probability.

The **purchase probability** is the probability that a contacted individual will buy the marketed product and not return it. The purchase probability is the number of unreturned purchases of an individual divided by the number of times he or she was contacted. This probability can be obtained from past experience that this marketer or others have had with that individual. The **return probability** is the probability that an individual will buy the product and return it. The **nonresponse probability** is the probability that the individual will not respond to the campaign. Like the purchase probability, the latter two probabilities can also be calculated from the past purchase history of the individual. Note that an individual must either buy and keep, buy and return or not buy the product. So by definition, the sum of the three probabilities must equal 1.

For example, consider an individual who has been contacted six times, and has bought and kept the product twice, bought and returned the product once, and not responded thrice. His purchase probability is .33, return probability is .17, and nonresponse probability is .5.

In practice, marketers work with huge databases using complex programs with multiple mailings. Thus they may not be able to compute the response rate for each individual as simply as shown in the example. For this reason, researchers have developed statistical models that estimate the response rates accurately after taking into account the complexity of the marketing program and the multiplicity of the contacts.[24]

Estimating Profits

When estimating the profitability of a campaign in advance of its occurrence, the marketer has to consider the profitability of two components of the campaign: contacting each individual, and running the entire campaign. For the first component, the marketer has to determine whether or not to contact specific individuals in a database. For this purpose, the marketer does not include the indirect costs of the entire campaign, because it has not yet decided to proceed with the campaign. The key issue in the first stage is to determine which individuals, if any, it can profitably contact given their expected purchas-

es. For the second component, the marketer has to determine whether to proceed with a campaign. To do so, the marketer must take into account the fixed costs of the campaign. The key issue in this stage is whether the responsiveness of some individuals in the database is strong enough to justify the costs of the whole program. We next explain how to carry out the analyses in each of these stages.

Profitability of Contacting an Individual When will it be profitable to contact an individual through direct media? It is profitable to contact an individual if the expected profit from sales to that individual exceeds the expected direct costs of doing so. The **expected profit** from a sale is the contribution margin from a unit sold to that individual multiplied by the probability of that sale. The **expected direct costs** from a sale are the direct cost of contacting that individual *plus* the expected cost of a return should that individual buy a unit and return it. The **expected cost of a return** is the probability of a return multiplied by the cost of returns. So a marketer should consider contacting an individual if:

Expected profit > Direct cost of sale + Expected cost of returns, i.e.

$$p_p \times m > p_p c_d + p_r \times c_r$$

where p_p = probability of purchase

m = margin per unit

c_d = direct costs per unit

p_r = probability of returns

c_r = return costs per unit.

Note that in this formula, the marketer should not take into account any indirect costs of actually conducting the campaign. The reason is that the latter decision depends on the responsiveness of the entire sample of individuals who will be contacted, and not on any single one. We now consider the profitability of that decision.

Profitability of Entire Campaign Suppose the marketer has determined that there are N individuals in a database whom it can profitably contact. The profitability of actually running an entire campaign depends on whether the total expected profits from contacting the N individuals will exceed the total expected costs of contacting them, plus the total indirect costs of the campaign, such as acquiring or maintaining the database containing the N individuals. So, the entire campaign is profitable if:

Total expected profit > Total expected cost of sale + Expected cost of returns + Total indirect costs, i.e.

$$(N \times P_p \times m) > (N \times P_p \times c_d) + (N \times P_r \times c_r) + C_i,$$

where P_p = mean probability of purchase in the whole sample

P_r = mean probability of returns in the whole sample

C_i = the indirect costs of the campaign.

In summary, the marketer has first to consider whether there are any individuals worth contacting, then it must consider whether it is profitable to run the entire campaign.

Recontacting those who did not respond after the first contact may yield a positive response for several reasons. First, the initial contact may have reached the wrong person in the household, may have been misplaced (as in a print campaign) or may have reached the right individual at an inopportune moment. Second, recontacting may serve as repetition of the message that persuades or reminds the individual about the merits of the offer. Third, in a recontact, the marketer could increase the incentive or reduce the price in order to make the offer more attractive. The marketer can estimate the profitability of recontacting individuals the same way it evaluates the profitability of contacting individuals (the first-stage analysis). However, when doing so, it must take into account (as a direct cost) the cost of any additional incentives it may offer.

SUMMARY

Direct media describe means by which firms can reach consumers as individuals, such as mail, telephone or the Internet. A key characteristic of promotion through direct media is that it tries to elicit an immediate response from consumers in the form of requests for more information, purchases, commitments or sales leads. Direct marketing refers to both promoting a product and completing a sale, as long as either activity uses direct media. Direct mail

has grown rapidly to become the third most popular advertising medium, accounting for 20 percent of all advertising expenditures in 1993. Several factors have been responsible for this growth, including advances in media technology, computerized databases, splintering of the mass market, increasing value of consumers' time and availability of credit cards.

The direct media are superior to the mass media due to their better control over the reach, frequency, and content of the ad, the convenient and easy measurement of response to the ad, and the ability to build relationships. On the other hand, direct media suffer from two key disadvantages relative to the mass media: cost and intrusiveness. The mail is the oldest of the direct media, but one which still has enormous potential. The telephone is a relatively new medium that has become the center of an integrated marketing activity called telemarketing. The Internet is a newly emerging direct medium with enormous potential.

Data are essential for evaluating the profitability of direct media. The promoter needs information on at least three aspects of the campaign: the costs of the campaign, contribution margin from each transaction and response rate of the campaign. It is profitable to contact an individual if the expected profit from sales to that individual exceeds the expected direct costs of doing so. The profitability of actually running an entire campaign depends on whether the total expected profits from contacting individuals exceeds the total expected costs of contacting them, plus the total indirect costs of the campaign, such as renting or maintaining the database.

QUESTIONS

1. What are the direct media? How do they compare to the mass media?
2. Why have the direct media grown rapidly in the last two decades?
3. Telemarketing has grown to become one of the most important means of direct marketing. Discuss.
4. What are the advantages of advertising through the Internet?
5. How does the Internet serve as a means of advertising?

6. How can a firm determine whether it should undertake a direct marketing campaign?

NOTES

1. Adapted from Hirsch, James S. (1996), "A High-Tech System For Sending The Mail Unfolds at Fidelity," *The Wall Street Journal*, March 20, A1, A6.

2. Miller, Peter (1993), "Changing Consumers Spark Mail's Growth," *Advertising Supplement to Advertising Age,* September 27, P4.

3. Endicott, R. Craig (1995), "Direct Ads Spur 12% of Consumer Sales," *Advertising Age*, October 9, 34.

4. Blattberg, Robert C., and John Deighton (1991), "Interactive Marketing: Exploiting the Age of Addressability," *Sloan Management Review* (Fall), 5–14.

5. Singer, Penny (1987), "Can Colleges Be Sold Like Cars?" *New York Times*, December 27, C8.

6. Sheth, Jagdish N. (1983), "Marketing Megatrends," *Journal of Consumer Marketing* 2, 1 (Summer), 5–13.

7. For example, see Curry, David, and Peter Riesz (1988), "Prices and Price-Quality Relationships: A Longitudinal Study," *Journal of Marketing* 52, 1 (January), 36–51.

8. Muldoon, Katie (1990), "Time Flies When You Have Fun," *DM News*, March 12, 26.

9. *Direct* (1990), "Walden Gets to Know Millions of Customers through Reader Clubs," March, 6.

10. Zimmerman, Denise (1996), "Brodbeck Data Base Marketing Cuts Pickers Lifts Volume," *Supermarket News* 46, 10, 25.

11. Muldoon, "Time Flies When You Have Fun."

12. Schlossberg, Howard (1994), "Marketers are Bypassing the Postal Service," *PROMO* (March), 25.

13. Fisher, Christy (1994), "Postal Hikes Fuel Alternate Services," *Advertising Age*, January 17, 25.

14. Stone, Bob, and John Wyman (1992), *Successful Telemarketing,* Lincolnwood, IL: NTC Books.

15. *Ibid.*

16. *Ibid.*

17. Hoffman, Donna L., and Thomas P. Novak (1996a), "A New Marketing Paradigm for Electronic Commerce," working paper, Owen Graduate School of Management, Vanderbilt University.

18. Hoffman, Donna L., and Thomas P. Novak (1996b), "Marketing in Hypermedia Computer-Mediated Environments: Conceptual Foundations," working paper, Owen Graduate School of Management, Vanderbilt University, February.

19. *Ibid.*

20. *Ibid.*

21. Akst, Daniel (1996), "For Shoppers, Internet Beats Big Online Services," *Los Angeles Times*, December 6, D4.

22. Hoffman and Novak, "Marketing in Hypermedia Computer-Mediated Environments."

23. *InterAd* (1995), "Who's Out There," (July), 2–3.

24. Rao, Vithala R., and Joel H. Steckel (1994), "Selecting, Evaluating, and Updating Prospects in Direct Mail Marketing," Marketing Science Institute, Technical working paper, No. 94-121; Bult, Jan Roelf, and Tom Wansbeek (1995), "Optimal Selection For Direct Mail," *Marketing Science* 14, 4, 378–394; Basu, Amiya K., Atasi Basu, and Rajeev Batra (1995), "Modeling the Response Pattern To Direct Marketing Campaigns," *Journal of Marketing Research* 32 (May), 204–212.

The introduction of Microsoft's new operating system, Windows 95, on August 24, 1995, was the most eagerly awaited event in the history of business. The product had been extensively covered in the lay, business, and professional press for months ahead of time. In addition, numerous software companies that planned to introduce products linked to the new operating system gave further exposure to Windows 95. Retailers also prominently featured the product in their ads. Some analysts estimated that retail-

17

Budgeting:
Setting the Level and Timing of Promotion Expenditures

ers and related manufacturers all over the world spent over $1 billion on promoting Windows 95 with related hardware and software. Retail stores ran ads in local papers, and announced the product's availability on storefronts with dancers, balloons, strobe lights, giant displays and other promotional gimmicks.

All the same, Microsoft spent heavily on promoting the product's global introduction. For example, in the United States, a new Windows 95 light show glowed over the Empire State Building. In

Australia, Microsoft floated a four-story-high Windows 95 balloon over Sydney Harbor, accompanied by musicians and dancers. All babies born in Australia on August 25 got a free copy of the operating system. In England, Microsoft fully sponsored a free edition of the *Times* of London, a first in the newspaper's 307-year history. Microsoft chairman Bill Gates himself took an active part in the promotion, appearing in commercials, at promotional parties and for public interviews. Many analysts estimated that Microsoft's total promotional budget for the introduction was as much as $200 million. Explaining the logic for his company's promotional strategy, Gates commented, "You have to create a lot of excitement to overcome inertia."[1] What he did not state was that Microsoft was flush with funds and expected to sell 30 million copies of Windows 95 in the first three months at a retail price of $95 a copy.

On August 23, 1995, many retail stores the world over stayed open through midnight to be able to sell the product at 12:01 A.M. the following day, the moment they were licensed to do so. Customers lined up outside stores to buy the product in cities across the globe. One Computer City store in East Hanover, New Jersey, sold 200 copies in one hour. A market research firm, ARS Inc., found that 43 percent of 42 stores in the United States reported higher-than-expected sales, while only 14 percent had disappointing sales. Overall, sales were brisk. An estimated 8 million copies of the product were sold within the first 24 hours, over 18 million copies in the first four months and 40 million copies in the first twelve months. The introduction was a great success.

For Brad Chase, general manager of Windows 95, responsible for planning the introductory campaign, the results were sweet success. However, interviews with him indicated that a more important strategic decision may have really lain behind the success of the introduction. Chase and his team decided to give 1 million copies of the beta or test version of the product to computer experts, journalists, and influential customers to preview. The risk in doing so was that bugs in the program could create adverse publicity. The potential payoff was that these opinion leaders would be so enamored with the product that they would recommend it to their customers, readers or friends. Similarly, the company decided on a single international launch date several months in advance. The risk was that the company would not be able to meet that date. The potential payoff was that global hype would feed on itself, creating enormous publicity and building up heightened expectations. The results justified the risky strategy. The advance publicity was immense. One report estimated that the proposed introduction gathered 3,000 headlines, 6,582 stories and over three million words between July 1 and August 24, 1995.[2]

Why did Microsoft spend $200 million promoting the introduction of Windows 95, a product that was eagerly sought by consumers and widely discussed in the press? How did it come up with a budget? More generally, how does one determine the promotion budget and schedule for a product? This chapter addresses these questions. It is divided into two parts. The first part discusses the different methods for determining the promotional budget. It presents the pros and cons of each and describes industry practice. Once a firm has decided upon the promotion budget, it has to schedule this budget over the planning period, which is usually the financial year. The second part discusses this topic of promotion scheduling.

METHODS FOR DETERMINING THE PROMOTION BUDGET

There are six important methods of determining the promotion budget: affordability, percentage-of-sales, competitive parity, objective and task, profit maximization, and ratio of elasticities. These six methods are listed in order of increasing sophistication required by the planner, and thus of increasing difficulty. The first three approaches are relatively simple because they use simple heuristics or rules of thumb. The last three are relatively complex because they require analysis of data. This section explains each of these methods, discussing their pros and cons, and their relevance to industry practice.

An important concept necessary to compare these different methods is that of the optimal level of promotion. Suppose two variables, such as promotion and profits, are related by a bell-shaped curve, so that profits in response to promotion first increase, then level off and finally decrease. The level of promotion at which profits reach a maximum is called the **optimal level of promotion.** More generally, when the output of a system first increases and then decreases in response to an input, the **optimum** is the point at which the input to the system gets the highest returns or output.

Affordability

In the **affordability** method of budget setting, a firm spends as much on promotion as it can afford. It first determines how much money is available after other expenses are paid. It then determines to spend some fraction or all of that amount on promotion. The great advantage of this approach is its simplicity. It involves no complicated analysis beyond what a firm normally does in financial analysis for the year. However, it suffers from a key limitation: the cost of foregone opportunities.

Consider a small firm with a product that is distinctly superior to competitive products in the market and has a latent market demand. The challenge for the firm is to develop the market for the product, perhaps through promotion. In that case

the firm may benefit from spending heavily on promotion, even if it has to obtain that money by borrowing from the outside. However, if the firm uses the affordability method, it foregoes a great opportunity. Alternatively, consider a large, dominant firm in a market with a well-known, mature brand, such as Wrigley chewing gum. Because of the equity in its name, the brand can generate ample revenues even without much promotion. Indeed, promotion for this brand does not do much to enhance its current image or sales. In this case, the firm can afford to advertise, but its resources could be better spent in developing alternate products or brand names. If the firm advertises the mature brand based on affordability, it foregoes better alternate uses of its money.

Although the affordability approach seems simplistic and runs contrary to prudent investment practice, it often drives promotion decisions. Affordability rather than need may have been the main factor motivating Microsoft's promotion budget for the product. Microsoft did not have a budgetary problem, especially given the rapid growth of the company, its steady increase in profits over the years, and its enormous increase in stock value. Other firms may also determine their promotion budget like Microsoft. For example, a number of studies find a positive relationship between profit margins and advertising expenditures (expressed as a fraction of sales), possibly because more profitable firms have more resources to spend on advertising.[3] More to the point, surveys of management practice find that the affordability method is one of the most popular especially in Europe, and among firms involved with services and business-to-business marketing.[4] The reason for its popularity is that it is an easy, spontaneous reaction to a firm's budgetary fortunes. When firms are under budgetary pressure they tend to cut back on advertising. When they are flush with funds, they tend to spend liberally on advertising, even beyond what seems necessary or desirable.

Affordability may be one reason why firms tend to cut back on advertising during a recession. Recessions generally lead to lower profits, if not actual operating losses, because firms' revenues decline but their fixed costs do not decline without a planned effort. When squeezed for profits, firms tend to cut back on advertising, especially as the damage from such a move may not be immediately apparent.

Percentage of Sales

In the **percentage-of-sales method**, a firm spends a fixed proportion of its sales revenue on advertising or promotion. The proportion that it spends is called the *advertising-to-sales ratio* or the *promotion-to-sales ratio,* respectively. This ratio may be based on past experience, a manager's belief, a published study or a consultant's recommendation. The firm projects its sales for the year ahead, and calculates the percentage of sales to budget for promotion. For example, the 1995 report on advertising expenditures indicates that the advertising-to-sales ratio for the computer software industry is 1.6 percent.[5] Let us assume that Microsoft advertised its products in the same proportion as the software industry, which it leads. For Windows 95, the company expected sales of 30 million copies, or $1.5 billion.[6] At the rate of 1.6 percent, its advertising budget for the product should have been $24 million. However, the company probably spent much of its $200 million 1995 promotion budget on advertising. Clearly, the company did not determine the advertising budget as a percentage of sales, probably because Windows 95 was a new product with great sales potential and had an owner with deep pockets.

The advantage of the percentage-of-sales method is its simplicity. The advertising-to-sales ratio is obtained without much effort from the firm's accounting records. Sales forecasts for the year ahead are also routinely prepared. The future advertising budget can be determined easily by multiplying the advertising-to-sales ratio by the forecasted sales. Another advantage of this method is that advertising is linked to the pattern of sales. As a result, advertising would be higher during periods when sales are higher, and lower at other times. When sales are high, consumers are in a spending mood, and are most responsive to advertising. The opposite occurs when sales are depressed. So the percentage-of-sales method ensures that advertising is targeted at times when it is most likely to be effective.

The disadvantage of this method is that it could lead to self-fulfilling prophecies for products, especially those whose sales are sensitive to advertising. A forecast of lower sales may prompt a cutback in advertising, leading to a realization of lower sales. Another disadvantage of this method is that it uses advertising to reinforce the cyclical or seasonal pattern in sales, rather than to even out the sales pattern, if possible. Seasonal and cyclical patterns in sales create manufacturing dislocations and inventory problems, adding to the overhead costs of firms. A third disadvantage is that this method also involves the cost of missed opportunities, as does the affordability method. Finally, the percentage-of-sales method requires a history of advertising and sales covering periods of stable market conditions, and cannot be used for new products.

The percentage-of-sales method is one of the most popular budgeting methods, sometimes being used by as many as 50 percent or more of surveyed respondents.[7] Further, firms may underreport their use of this method, partly because it may represent only a starting point, not the primary method for budgeting. An analysis of actual industry figures for advertising-to-sales ratios indicates that these figures remain fairly constant over time within industries, firms and brands, but vary dramatically across these categories within a year (see Exhibit 17-1). Thus firms probably use the percentage-of-sales rule implicitly far more than they admit to doing.

Competitive Parity

One of the most intense competitive battles ever fought has been that between Coca-Cola and Pepsi-Cola. The story begins with Dr. John Pemberton, a pharmacist in Atlanta, Georgia, who formulated Coca-Cola in 1886. Initially he sold the formula as a refreshing drink at the fountain counter of his pharmacy. As the drink grew in popularity, the ownership of the brand changed hands, and it began to be marketed more aggressively. In the early decades of the twentieth century the brand became the most popular beverage in the United States In 1920 the Supreme Court granted the Coca-Cola Company exclusive rights over the name "Coke."

Pepsi-Cola was formulated by another pharmacist, Caleb Bradham, in New Bern, North Carolina, in 1893. This drink was initially not as popular as Coca-Cola, and in the early 1900s the company owning the formula was on the brink of bankruptcy. However, Pepsi-Cola began to be aggressively marketed, and by the end of World War II it turned out to be Coca-Cola's primary rival.

The rivalry between Coca-Cola and Pepsi-Cola became intense in the 1950s due as much to the similarity of their formulas as to the chief executive of Pepsi-Cola, who was bent on beating his rival. Exhibit 17-2 shows the recent market share and share-of-voice histories of these two brands. One of the most important events in this history is the "Pepsi challenge." The challenge grew out of the efforts of a Pepsi-Cola sales manager in Dallas, Texas. In 1974, the manager ran some blind taste tests in which 58 percent of consumers preferred Pepsi. In the next few years, results of these and similar tests began to be advertised as the Pepsi challenge. From 1975 to 1980, Pepsi-Cola more than doubled its advertising, from $15 million to $39 million, to advertise, the challenge. Coca-Cola also responded with increases in advertising (from $20 million in 1975 to $36 million in 1980) and with price discounting. Yet the novelty and impact of Pepsi-Cola's ads probably advanced Pepsi-Cola's market share relative to Coca-Cola's, as can be seen in Exhibit 17-2.

In 1982, Coca-Cola introduced Diet Coke to combat the growth in market share of Diet Pepsi. By 1984, Diet Coke had grabbed a 5.2 percent market share relative to 1.6 percent for Tab, an earlier sugar-free version of Coke, and 3.7 percent for Diet Pepsi. The growth of the diet and caffeine-free segments led to a steady decline in the market shares of regular Pepsi-Cola and Coca-Cola.

In 1985, to the surprise of many analysts, Coca-Cola introduced New Coke, a sweeter drink, to combat Pepsi's appeal especially among the younger generation. Pepsi capitalized on Coca-Cola's move by declaring victory in the contest of formulas. The market's reaction did not help Coca-Cola. Many Coke drinkers preferred the old formula, while some publicly protested the change. In response to the strong appeal of the traditional formula, and the lukewarm appeal of the new formula, Coca-Cola reintroduced the old formula as Coca-Cola classic. For the rest of the decade Coca-Cola tried to reposition the two brands as best it could to stem consumer displeasure and confusion, and to reduce the costs of manufacture and inventory management. Finally, in 1992 Coca-Cola changed the name of New Coke to Coke II.

In the meantime, Pepsi continued its attacks on Coca-Cola, though less directly, with creative advertising that emphasized its youthful image. Pepsi's ads generally rated more highly than those of Coca-Cola on recall and liking. However, Pepsi-Cola was less suc-

▼ **EXHIBIT 17-1. Variation in advertising-to-sales ratios.**

A. Advertising-to-sales ratios across industries over time.

Category	1982	1985	1989
Wood products	0.3	0.3	1.8
Bakery products	1.7	1.5	1.7
Apparel/clothing	2.8	2.3	2.9
Dairy products	4.3	5.1	4.7
Soft drinks	5.7	6.6	7.4
Pens and office supplies	5.9	5.3	5.4
Soaps and detergents	6.8	7.9	7.7
Perfumes and confectioneries	8.4	13.1	10.4
Toys	10.5	10.0	14.2

B. Advertising-to-sales ratios across firms over time.

Firm	1984	1985	1986	1987
Borden dairy	2.4	1.7	2.0	1.6
Campbell Soup	6.7	6.4	5.8	6.3
Heinz	8.6	9.5	7.9	8.0
Pillsbury	10.1	8.8	9.0	8.9
Colgate-Palmolive	12.8	11.7	11.3	11.3
Procter & Gamble	15.3	15.6	12.7	11.2
Kellogg	17.1	17.6	16.4	21.1

Source: Sethuraman, Raj, and Gerard J. Tellis (1991), "An Analysis of the Tradeoff between Advertising and Price Discounting," *Journal of Marketing Research* 28 (May), 160–174; original figures from *Advertising Age*'s annual report of advertising expenditures.

cessful with its choice of endorsers. Madonna, Mike Tyson and Michael Jackson were all embroiled in controversy, rendering Pepsi's association with them a liability. However, the controversies caused little immediate damage to the market share. Indeed, through all of the upheavals, controversies and radical changes, the market shares of both Coca-Cola and Pepsi-Cola declined almost steadily through the decade.[8]

Both Coca-Cola and Pepsi-Cola went through fairly tumultuous events in the 1980s, including new product introductions, a brand renaming, and controversies involving their endorsers (see Exhibit 17-2). Yet both brands seemed to maintain similar advertising budgets (see Exhibit 17-3). The parity of the ratios over the years is amazing given that firms may not explicitly collude to set their advertising-to-sales ratios. Moreover the ratios are based on estimated sales, market share and advertising, and so are unlikely to be the same by accident. Thus the firms must have made a conscious effort to maintain

▼ **EXHIBIT 17-2.** Share of market and voice of Coke and Pepsi over time.

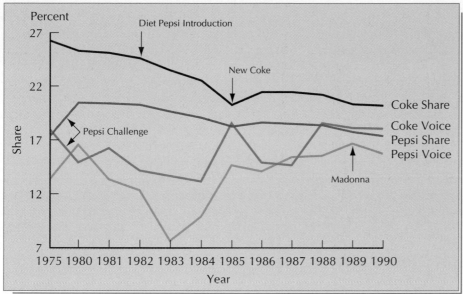

Source: Prepared from data in Porter, Michael E. (1989), "Coca-Cola versus Pepsi-Cola and the Soft Drink Industry in 1986," Boston, MA: Harvard Business School Publishing Division, Case 9-391-179.

sumers, Coke and Pepsi, or Diet Coke and Diet Pepsi, are close enough substitutes that they constitute the market for colas or diet colas, respectively. Markets may be organized in a hierarchy of decreasingly substitutable products. For example, the market for diet colas would fall within the market for all colas, which in turn would fall within the market for all soft drinks, which would fall within the market for all beverages. Which market is the appropriate one? For this method of budget-

competitive parity in advertising budgets. Indeed, this is one of the most important methods for budgeting, especially for close competitors like Coke and Pepsi. The method is fairly popular in the United States, although not used much in Europe. The following discussion explains the method in three parts: definition of terms, decisions to be made, and evaluation of method.[9]

Definition of Terms In the **competitive parity method** a firm chooses an advertising or promotion level relative to the level of one of its competitors in the market. A *market* is a set of brands consumers consider similar enough to be substitutes. For example, for most con-

▼ **EXHIBIT 17-3.** Advertising-to-sales ratios of Coke and Pepsi.

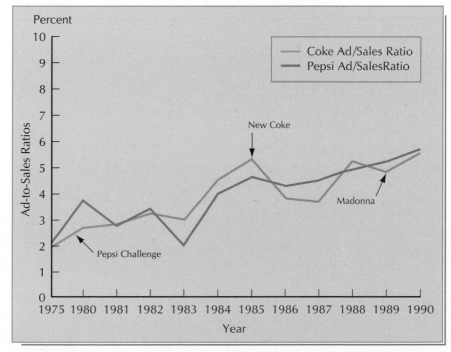

Source: Prepared from data in Porter, Michael E. (1989), "Coca-Cola versus Pepsi-Cola and the Soft Drink Industry in 1986," Boston, MA: Harvard Business School Publishing Division, Case 9-391-179.

ing, firms should define the market in terms of the brands that are advertised separately. For example, since the diet colas are advertised separately from colas, they constitute a market that is different from the colas. Once it has defined its market, the firm obtains the advertising and sales figures of its competitors from one or more industry reports or syndicated data sources (see Chapter 14). It then calculates share of market and voice. *Market share* is the sales of a brand divided by the sales of all brands in its market. *Share of voice* is the advertising spending of a brand divided by all advertising spending in its market. In the competitive parity method, the firm determines its advertising budget by projecting its competitor's advertising spending for the year ahead and choosing a matching level.

Decisions to Be Made The firm has to make three strategic decisions when choosing this method: which competitor to focus on, what advertising measure to use, and what parity level to adopt.

The firm should focus on the competitor most similar to itself, rather than on the market leader or the most aggressive competitor. In this way the firm ensures that it matches a budget that is most relevant to its own situation. The firm can measure advertising in terms of either the absolute advertising level or the advertising-to-sales ratio. The latter measure is more relevant because it adjusts for differences in size of different firms. The firm can choose a level of advertising that is either higher, lower or even with its competitor. Which one is appropriate?

To answer that question, we need to address a fundamental premise about marketing effectiveness. It states that a brand's share of market is proportional to its share of marketing effort.[10] As advertising is an important marketing input, a corollary of this premise is that a brand's share of market is proportional to its share of advertising, holding other marketing variables constant. The rationale for this premise is that a firm that has a larger share of advertising is able to attract, persuade and retain a larger share of consumers. However, two factors may cause deviations from this gen-

eral rule: economies of information and the growth rate of a firm.[11]

Economies of information means that a brand's cost of advertising per consumer goes down as its market share goes up. Because of the level of noise from competing messages, brands need to advertise at some minimum level just to be heard. The large-share brand can better cope with this barrier, because it can spread this cost among the large number of consumers it serves. Moreover, greater familiarity with the brand name or message of the large-share brand may enhance attention to or persuasiveness of its advertising (see Chapter 4). So, the cost of advertising per consumer or per market share point is lower for the large-share brand. Thus the large-share brand can achieve the same effectiveness with less advertising than a small-share brand. Support for this phenomenon comes from a study of 666 brands in 117 markets (see Exhibit 17-4).[12] Note from the exhibit that brands with a large share of market (over 21 percent) have a share of voice lower than their market share by 3 to 5 percent. On the other hand, brands with small market share (below 19 percent) have a share of voice which is above their market share by 1 to 5 percentage points. Also, the degree to which the share of voice exceeds market share increases as the share of market declines.

The *growth rate* of a brand refers to the rate at which its sales increase from year to year. One study

▼ EXHIBIT 17-4. Average market share compared to share of voice.

Share of Market	Percentage by Which Share of Voice Is Above (+) or Below (–) Market Share
1 to 3%	+ 5%
4 to 6%	+ 4%
7 to 9%	+ 2%
10% to 12%	+ 4%
13 to 15%	+ 1%
16 to 18%	+ 2%
19 to 21%	No difference
22 to 24%	–3%
25 to 27%	–5%
28 to 30%	–5%

Source: Jones, John Philip (1990), "Ad Spending: Maintaining Market Share," *Harvard Business Review,* January–February, 38–41.

finds that when a brand spends more than twice as much as its competitors for over 18 months, its market share begins to increase,[13] if other factors are held constant. For example, in the 1980s, Pabst and Old Milwaukee beers held leading market positions in Iowa. By advertising Busch more than twice as much as these leading brands, Anheuser-Busch was able to gain share on them (see Exhibit 17-5). A brand that wants to grow purely by advertising expenditure needs to estimate whether it has the capacity to maintain this level of expenditure, and whether it can outlast competitors if they try to match this level of expenditure. On the other hand, a firm that lets its competitors double its ratio of share of voice to market share is likely to lose share. Such a firm needs to evaluate whether it wants to cede its share of market to save on advertising expenditures, rather than hold its share of the market by matching the level of its competitor's advertising.

▼ **EXHIBIT 17-5.** Change in market share in response to advertising.

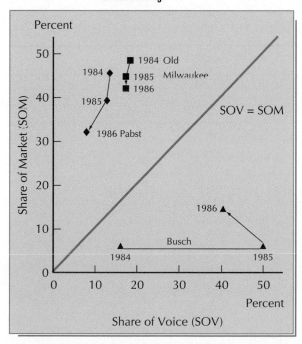

Evaluation of Method The competitive parity method has several advantages. First, like the previous two approaches it is fairly simple to execute. Second, it ensures that the firm is in line with its competitors. If competitors determine their level of advertising expenditures based on special experience, proprietary research or the creative insight of one or more managers, then the firm would reap the same rewards by copying their percentage. Third, in mature markets, sales increases come primarily from increases in market share. Sometimes such increases may be the result of higher levels of advertising relative to competitors. If a firm follows competitors' levels of advertising, it is unlikely to be vulnerable to sales losses due to the heavier advertising of its competitors. Fourth, when all competitors in an industry strive to follow the competitive parity approach, they are less likely to trigger an advertising war that could lead to wasteful overadvertising by all.

However, the competitive parity approach suffers from many limitations. First, the method is relevant for a brand that has a history of advertising in a mature, stable market. New brands could use the method only if they had as parity the percentage of sales of similar brands during their introduction. However, for brands such as Windows 95 that are unique, the competitive parity approach may not be valid. Also, if the market is racked with new entrants, price wars, advertising wars, or big fluctuations in industry sales, the method is not useful.

Second, the method assumes that the firm has the same goal as its competitor. This assumption is sometimes invalid. For example, the targeted competitor may advertise heavily to increase price, motivate the sales staff to work harder, or motivate retailers to better stock the brand.

Third, the method assumes that the targeted competitor has determined the optimal level of advertising and is advertising at that level. Because of the difficulty of determining the optimal level, and because politics may prevent a firm from budgeting at the optimal level, such an assumption may not be valid. Thus an advertiser's following a competitor unsure of the right advertising level, might be like the proverbial blind leading the blind.

Fourth, the competitive parity approach may lead firms to match the competitor's level of advertising in a simplistic way without taking into account the relative advantage of firm size. In particular, because of economies of information, large firms may be able to sustain their market share with less advertising than small firms need.

Objective and Task

The **objective-and-task method** sets the promotion budget at the level needed to achieve a goal or task set by the firm. To execute this method, the firm needs clear goals and clear knowledge of the factors needed to achieve those goals. Goals may be set in terms of a hierarchy of desired effects (see Chapter 13). For example, one such hierarchy would be:

Advertising \$ → Awareness → Purchase intention
→ Sales → Market share

An important aspect of this hierarchy is knowledge of the transition probabilities that indicate how each variable in the chain relates to or translates into the next variable (see Chapter 13). Once it has this knowledge, the firm can work backwards from goals to needed input. For example, a firm can set a market share goal, and then determine the level of promotion that it would need to achieve that goal.

The objective-and-task approach is a rational way of setting the ad budget. It follows directly from the philosophy of beginning the planning process by first setting goals, as explained in Chapter 13. This approach is especially useful for new products, when a firm may have no history of its own or competitive promotion to guide it. However, the approach suffers from some key limitations.

First, as discussed in Chapter 13, firms need detailed knowledge of the way promotion works. They need to know the key variables that promotion affects, the hierarchy through which the variables are related, and the transition probabilities that describe this relationship. Firms that have a long history of promotion, such as General Electric, General Motors or Procter & Gamble, may have this knowledge. However, newer firms may find it difficult to obtain. Even large firms such as Microsoft that regularly introduce new products may be unable to use this method, because they do not have a long or detailed history of promotion and its effects.

Second, the method by itself makes no attempt to determine the optimal level of promotion. A firm may decide that it needs to spend \$10 million to achieve a 5 percent market share to yield a profit of \$14 million. However, market tests could reveal that it can achieve a 4 percent market share yielding \$13 million in profits for only \$6 million of promotion. Thus the objective-and-task method does not guarantee the optimum or best level of promotion. On the contrary, it assumes that the firm has deep pockets and is willing to spend what it takes to achieve its goals. In this respect it resembles the affordability approach. This assumption may be valid for products such as new car models that cost a great deal to develop, and are likely to last a long time if successfully launched. For example, Chrysler spent \$100 million on advertising during the first three months of the launch of the Neon in 1994.[14] The method is also relevant for a firm that has a large discretionary budget and is willing to use it to achieve its goals. Indeed, a survey indicates that the use of the objective-and-task method is higher among firms with large budgets, being used by as many as 80 percent of large consumer products firms.[15] Overall, the method appears to be the most popular method in the last few decades, both in Europe and the United States.[16]

Profit Maximization

In the **profit-maximization method** the firm chooses the optimal promotion budget that most increases its profits.

To use this method, the firm needs to know its sales-response function. The **sales-response function** describes how sales are related to different levels of advertising or sales promotion (see Chapter 14). Sales can be measured either in units or in dollars. The level of advertising can be measured in dollars, gross rating points or frequency of individual ads. The level of sales promotion can be measured in dollars or frequency of each promotion. The level of advertising or promotion is also called the *advertising intensity* or *promotion intensity*, respectively. In general, it is much easier to find the sales-response function to sales promotions than to advertising, because the former have immediate and pronounced effects. Chapters 10, 11 and 12 have short sections that show how to evaluate the profitability of retail, trade and consumer promotions, once one has the sales response function for these promotions. By using such analyses, a manager can find the level of sales promotion that maximizes profits. The rest of this section shows how to determine the advertising budget to maximize profits.

The sales response to advertising is assumed to follow an *S*-shaped curve (see Exhibit 17-6). This response seems the most reasonable from a theoretical standpoint. At one extreme, a very low level of advertising is unlikely to achieve any response from consumers because it would be drowned out in the sea of noise from competing ads and messages. As the level of advertising increases, beyond some critical point (Point A), consumers are likely to notice the ads and begin responding to them. This point is called the **threshold**. Beyond the threshold, the response may increase sharply as the level of advertising increases. However, the response is unlikely to increase without limit. Beyond a certain point (Point B), the rate of increase is likely to slow down. Ultimately, increases in advertising may not lead to any increase in response. The point at which this occurs is called **saturation**. Let us call this Point C.

Assume that we measure the investment in advertising in terms of the dollars it takes to buy media time and space. And assume we measure advertising response in terms of the sales revenue in dollars that results from that advertising. If these two variables are plotted on the horizontal and vertical axes of a graph, we get the *S*-shaped sales-response curve described in Exhibit 17-6. One of the major goals of advertising testing is to measure this advertising-response function (see Chapter 14). In the absence of formal tests, some managers may be able to propose a rough response curve from their experience.

If we subtract all the variable costs, such as for materials or sales commissions, from the sales revenue, we get the *gross profit* associated with each level of advertising. The *net profit* or *final profit* also requires the subtraction of fixed costs such as advertising and overhead expenditures from the gross profit. Assume that the gross profit curve for a particular

▼ **EXHIBIT 17-6.** S-shaped response to advertising.

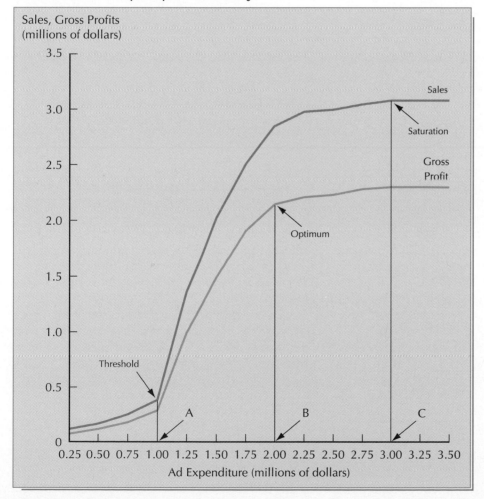

brand is the one plotted in Exhibit 17-6. The gross profit curve shows the dollar increase or decrease in gross profits from each additional dollar spent on advertising. Assume that points A, B and C occur at advertising expenditures of $1 million, $2 million and $3 million, respectively, as shown in the graph. Given this scenario, what would be the ideal point at which to advertise? Clearly, advertising below Point A or above Point C would be futile, because such advertising does not enhance profits. The desirable advertising level would be somewhere between the two points.

Note that the gross profit curve keeps rising steeply, between points A and B, and then begins increasing, but less steeply, between B and C. Before Point B, the firm earns more than a dollar for every dollar spent on advertising. At B, the firm earns exactly a dollar in profits for every dollar in advertising. After B it earns less than a dollar in profits for each dollar spent on advertising. So, whatever the firm's budget, the best level at which it should advertise would be Point B, or $2 million. This point at which the firm's return from advertising is the best is called the **optimum level of advertising** or the *optimal advertising intensity.*

The major limitation of the profit-maximization approach is that it requires knowledge of the response function. This function is very difficult to determine accurately. Chapter 14 describes the different types of research that can be carried out to determine this function. Because of the expense of the research, determining the response function can be costly. However, in most cases, lack of knowledge of the response function may lead a firm to advertise at less or more than the optimal level, leading to far greater costs than the cost of the research. Thus, the cost or difficulty of determining the response function is a weak excuse for not obtaining this important piece of information.

Another limitation of profit maximization is that it involves a technical, short-term orientation. The returns to advertising may not all accrue in the short term. In particular, the introduction of new products may be an important investment for the future. To the extent that advertising helps such introductions, the sum of all future returns may be intangible or not immediately obvious. So, the profit-maximization approach should make adequate allowances for long-term returns to advertis-

ing, or should be used in conjunction with other approaches that do so.

The profit-maximization approach is the best approach for determining the advertising budget for firms interested in short-term profitability. The profit analysis of advertising expenditures is also useful for firms that do not have short-term profits as their goal, because they get an idea of the monetary returns to advertising. The use of this type of research is increasing, especially among U.S. firms with large advertising budgets.[17] Such firms have the most to gain from a profit-maximization approach, and can best afford the expenses that it involves.

However, the use of this method is limited by the ability and willingness of firms to carry out research such as experimentation or historical analysis to determine the response function. Also, the approach may indicate a budget level that is radically different from the one the firm is currently using. In that case, the firm's managers may be unwilling to make such a big change from their past practice.

Matching the Elasticity Ratio

Matching the elasticity ratio involves adjusting the current advertising budget by the ratio of the advertising to price elasticities. This is a new method for budgeting proposed by the author and his co-researcher.[18] Advertising and price elasticities are indicators that measure to what extent a brand's sales respond to changes in advertising or price, respectively (see Chapter 14). This method is suitable for allocating the promotional budget between advertising and price promotions, or for determining the advertising budget relative to the price of a product.

By this approach, if the market were more responsive to advertising than to price discounts in the current period, then in the next period the manager would spend more on advertising relative to price discounts. But if the market is more responsive to price discounts than advertising, the manager should spend more on price discounts. The firm can estimate its advertising or price elasticities by the experimental approach, or, as is more commonly done, by regressing a brand's past sales on its past price and advertising (see Chapter 14). The precise change in the advertising budget is given by precise formulas that relate the two elasticities to the advertising-to-sales ratio, the margin per unit and market conditions.[19]

Using the ratio of elasticities to set the advertising budget involves a blend of the percentage-of-sales and the optimization approaches. Like the percentage-of-sales approach it starts off with the current budget of the firm. Like the optimization approach it involves attention to market response. The approach has several appealing features.

First, like the percentage-of-sales approach, this approach is based on past practice of the firm. Second, unlike the optimization approach, the manager does not look for a single, theoretically best budget, which is difficult both to find and to implement. Rather the approach suggests the direction of change from current practice—whether the firm should increase, decrease or maintain the current advertising budget for the next period. These changes do not have to be radical, but could be small exploratory steps. Third, the small adjustments to current budgeting levels can over time help the firm to approach or even reach the optimum budget. Fourth, offering price discounts is generally the most effective marketing tool to increase sales, and one that is often considered as an alternative to increasing the advertising budget (see Chapters 9 and 10). The sales staff, retailers and distributors often put pressure on marketing managers for price discounts. Thus, setting the advertising budget in the context of the market's response to price and advertising takes into account such pressures in a scientific way.

The main disadvantage of this method is that the estimation of advertising and price elasticities is difficult and may be controversial (see Chapter 14). Many small firms do not have the data or expertise to estimate these elasticities accurately. For this reason, the authors who proposed this approach argue that differences in the price-to-advertising elasticities lead to four major generic strategies[20] (See Chapter 18).

The elasticity-ratio approach to setting the advertising budget is rarely used in industry because of its newness. However, the growing popularity of single-source data may enable firms to better estimate the advertising and price elasticities of their brands. In that case, more firms may begin to use the method as they realize its advantages.

SCHEDULING ADVERTISING EXPENDITURES

In the 1950s, Hubert Zielske, a manager of the research department at the Foote, Cone and Belding ad agency, carried out what has become a classic study in advertising scheduling. He mailed an ad for a food staple 13 times to each of two groups of women. One group received the ad in a burst of one ad a week for 13 consecutive weeks. The other group received the ad in pulses of one ad every 4 weeks for a whole year. Every week Zielske measured the aided recall of the ad of a sample of respondents from each group. To avoid the effects of heightened attention to the ad after the first questioning, no respondent was questioned twice. The curve Zielske obtained for recall was dramatically different for the two groups (see Exhibit 17-7). He found that the burst of advertising achieved a relatively high recall that peaked at the time of the last ad and quickly died out after that. The pulsing schedule of ads achieved a lower overall recall peak, but one that kept increasing with each pulse of advertising and was spread out over the entire year. The average weekly recall rate was 21 percent with the advertising burst, and 29 percent with the advertising pulse.[21]

▼ **EXHIBIT 17-7.** Recall as a function of ad repetition.

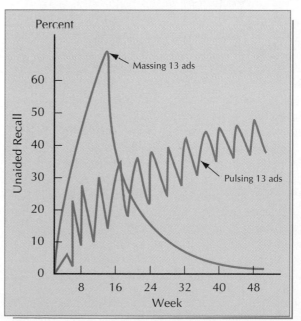

Source: Hubert A. Zielske, "The Remembering and Forgetting of Advertising," *Journal of Marketing* 23, 1, 1959, 239–243. Reprinted with permission of the American Marketing Association.

Scheduling refers to the timing of promotion expenditures or the sequencing of promotions within a time period. The profitable scheduling of promotions depends closely on the response of sales to promotions. Sales response to advertising is much more complex than that to sales promotions, because advertising has many subtle and dynamic effects. So, this section discusses scheduling in the context of advertising.

While an infinite variety of sequences of ads is possible, analysts generally identify four prototypical patterns: massing, flighting, pulsing and even scheduling (see Exhibit 17-8). Scheduling is a dynamic activity, and the meaning of these four terms is dependent on the *planning horizon,* or time frame, being considered for the advertising plan. The most common planning horizon is one year. Scheduling involves the timing of ads during short units of time, such as a week or a month, within this planning horizon of a year. In this context, the four patterns of scheduling can be defined as follows:

Massing involves the scheduling of all ads within one short period of time such as a week or a month. The rest of the year no advertising is done. Zielske's scheduling of advertising for 13 consecutive weeks in one experimental group is an example.

Flighting involves irregularly scheduling ads in bursts for short periods of time within the year, separated by long periods of time with no advertising. Flighting may also be called **bursting.**

Pulsing involves regularly scheduling ads on and off during fixed periods of the year. One example would be a schedule of one week on and one week off throughout the year. Zielske's scheduling of ads once a month in his other experimental group is an example. Pulsing also applies to a schedule of ads with regularly placed highs and lows. Note that pulsing and flighting are similar concepts. The key difference is that flighting refers to a less regular pattern, with short periods of advertising interspersed with long periods without advertising.

▼ **EXHIBIT 17-8. Four alternative ad schedules ($20 million over 10 weeks).**

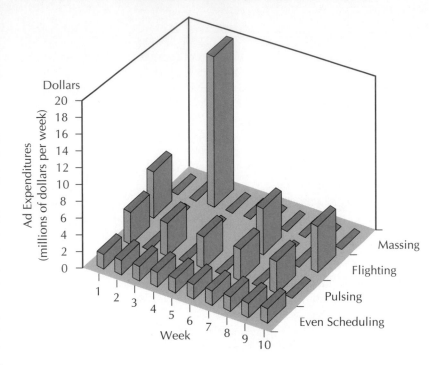

Even scheduling involves a constant level of advertising through the year. Even scheduling is also called **continuity.**

These terms also apply if we change the units of analysis to two weeks, or to a month. For example, flighting describes the following pattern: three weeks on, two months off, two weeks on, three months off, etc. Pulsing also describes the pattern of one week on and three weeks off right through the year. Scheduling can be carried out hierarchically, with one schedule nested within another. For example, the massing of ads in one month of the year still requires the scheduling of ads within that one month. That schedule could again involve massing, flighting, pulsing or even scheduling of ads on weeks or days within the month.

Factors Affecting the Choice of Scheduling

During the 1993 Super Bowl 22 advertisers sponsored a total of 43 ads. Pepsi bought five 30-second ads for about $4.25 million. Master Lock bought one 30-second ad for $.85 million.[22] Pepsi spent only a fraction of its annual budget on the five ads. Master Lock spent its entire annual budget on the one ad. With its five ads

Pepsi won the highest recall (49 percent) of the 22 advertisers, based on a telephone survey of 300 individuals by one research firm. Master Lock had the worst recall (0 percent) of all advertisers—no individual could recall the advertiser.[23]

Why did Master Lock choose a mass strategy and spend its entire advertising budget on one ad? Was that a wise decision? Why did Pepsi choose to buy five ads in one show? Was that a wise decision? Which one of the four scheduling patterns should an advertiser choose? The answer to these questions depends on several factors, including the goal of the ad campaign, the pattern of sales, the optimal ad frequency relative to available budget, and the dynamic effects of advertising.

Goal of the Campaign

As Chapter 13 explains, ad campaigns can have one of several goals: gain attention/provide information, persuade or remind. An attention-getting/informative campaign is one that alerts consumers about some new, important development. Such developments could include a radical change in the sales policy of a company, the introduction of a new product, change in the name of a brand or company, or change in the design of an existing product. Firms need to alert consumers of these changes quickly and surely. Of the four scheduling patterns, massing may achieve this goal most effectively. It can more easily rise above the clutter of competing ads, and as long as consumers need only to be aware of the change, and not be persuaded of it, the scheduling of repetitive ads through the year may not be necessary. The need to rise above the clutter of advertising and draw attention to its name may be one reason why Master Lock spent its entire annual advertising budget on one Super Bowl ad. Was that a good strategy? Perhaps the company should have also taken into account its response function.

Persuasion requires time and effort. For this purpose, a mass campaign would not be effective. A persuasion campaign would require one of the other three patterns: flighting, pulsing or even scheduling. Which one of these three patterns is preferable depends on the available budget and on the manner in which consumers are persuaded by the ads. These factors are discussed in the next section.

A reminder campaign requires a relatively lower level of advertising than the other two types, but one that is regular throughout the year. For this purpose, pulsing or even scheduling is the best. Here again, the choice between the two depends on the available budget and the response to the ads.

Sales Pattern

The most obvious factor that affects ad scheduling is the pattern of sales. Sales for many products are seasonal. Typical examples include swimsuits, barbecue grills, Christmas cards, turkey and movies. Even items that appear to have a relatively constant use during the year, such as movie tickets or TV sets, have a seasonal sales pattern. Moviegoing peaks during the summer, Thanksgiving, and winter holidays. Sales of TV sets peak just before the Super Bowl and during the winter holiday season. Advertising needs to be scheduled to take advantage of these seasonal patterns. The best schedule for advertising seasonal goods is flighting.

Should the flight of ads coincide with the peaks or the troughs of the sales curve? The motivation to advertise during the trough is to even out a sales pattern. However, an advertiser could benefit more by scheduling flights during the peak. First, consumer behavior is resistant enough that advertising during a trough is not likely to even out the seasonality. Second, retailers are unlikely to stock the item during a known trough, even if one advertiser were to flight its ads. Third, and most important, the advertiser of a particular brand of the seasonal product is likely to get the most response to advertising when sales are naturally at their peak, rather than when sales are naturally at their trough.

For the same reasons, advertising may be more beneficial when concentrated during an economic boom, rather than during a recession, although advertising agencies and the media would prefer advertisers to believe otherwise. For example, during the recession of 1991 R.H. Macy & Co., a New York–based retailing chain, ran a huge $150 million advertising campaign to spruce up its image and increase sales. The campaign did not help the company much, and sales continued to be sluggish due to the recession, as were sales for other retailers. Macy suffered over $150 million in losses for the fall quarter of 1991, a loss that was aggravated by its heavy advertising.[24]

However, advertising when sales are close to their maximum may not be productive. The case of Windows 95 is a good example. Because of the advance publicity associated with the introduction of the product, and availability of the product only from August 24, 1995, advertising right before the release date was unlikely to increase sales. Those who had already decided to buy would do so even without the advertising. Those who wanted to wait until enough consumers had bought and tested the product would most likely wait even with exposure to some advertising.

Optimal Ad Intensity Relative to Available Budget

A firm's advertising schedule also depends on its optimal ad intensity relative to the annual budget available for advertising. To demonstrate the interactive role of these two factors, consider again the example shown in Exhibit 17-6. Assume that the firm has an S-shaped response function as shown in that exhibit. Now assume that response function applies to the level of advertising spending *within any single week*. In this case, how should advertising be scheduled during the year?

If the firm's annual advertising budget is below $1 million, it should not advertise at all, because even if it spent all its budget in one week it would get no response and earn no profits. For an advertising budget between $1 million and $2 million, the firm should mass all its advertising in one week. Splitting the amount over two or more weeks would lead to suboptimal scheduling, because the profits from the smaller amount spent in each of those weeks would be much less or nonexistent. Consider again the case of Master Lock. It spent its total advertising budget on one ad probably to draw consumers' attention. However, given the poor recall it obtained, one may well ask whether the amount it spent was below the threshold level for the firm.

If the firm has an annual ad budget ranging from $2 million to $40 million, the firm should flight its advertising. Each flight should use the optimum $2 million in advertising a week. The number of flights would depend on the budget. These flights would best be spread out over the year to ensure adequate presence throughout the year.

For an annual ad budget of around $50 million to $100 million, the firm should pulse, running ads on and off for a week each. The week with ads would still involve spending the optimum $2 million on advertising. For an annual ad budget over $104 million, the firm should adopt an even advertising

schedule, advertising right through the year at the optimum level of $2 million a week.

One may well ask whether the available budget should drive the schedule, or whether the available budget should itself be determined by the optimal response function. Ideally, the latter situation should prevail. However, in many firms, brand managers have a certain budget that was predetermined at the start of the year from negotiations with senior managers. In other firms, advertising is driven by the available budget as discussed earlier. In these cases, the combination of the available budget and the optimal advertising intensity could be used to determine the best advertising schedule.

This framework of scheduling assumes that the other three factors (sales pattern, ad goals, dynamic effects) are controlled. In particular, the dynamic effects of advertising affect the sales response to advertising on which this discussion is based. Thus taking into account these dynamic effects is also important in scheduling.

Dynamic Effects of Advertising

The **dynamic effects of advertising** are changes in advertising response over time. There are three types of dynamic effects: wearin, wearout and delay. Each of these effects is distinct and has differing implications for scheduling. Wearin and wearout are opposite effects and will be discussed together.

Wearin and Wearout Suppose laboratory research indicates that the optimum frequency to advertise a brand is three times a week. Consumer response in actual markets may vary from the laboratory optimum because of lower attention and higher noise. For example, consumers may barely notice the ads in the first week of advertising. By the third week they may find them familiar. By the fifth week they may begin to enjoy them. By the twentieth week they may be sick of them. Wearin and wearout refer to the change in response to the frequency of the ads *from week to week* (see Exhibit 17-9).

Wearin is the increase in the effectiveness of advertising intensity from period to period. It is also called **buildup**. An ad is said to have worn in when it first begins to be effective. **Wearout** is the decrease in the effectiveness of advertising intensity from period to period. An ad is said to have worn out when it ceases to be effective. Note that these

▼ EXHIBIT 17-9. **Wearin and wearout of an ad campaign over time.**

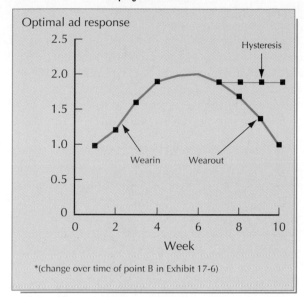

*(change over time of point B in Exhibit 17-6)

wearin and wearout. The duration of the flight should be long enough to capitalize fully on wearin, but short enough to prevent the onset of wearout. Once the campaign has begun to wear out, advertising should be terminated. The duration between flights should be long enough to induce wearin and not wearout.

Delayed Effects of Advertising   The **delayed effect of advertising** refers to the sales resulting from a single ad or advertising campaign *after the advertising stops.* The effect of advertising is generally believed to be non-instantaneous and to persist beyond the period of the advertising. For this reason this effect of advertising is also called the **long-term** or **carryover effect of advertising.** For example, Exhibit 17-10 shows how a single burst of advertising in week 3 causes an immediate spike in sales, which then declines over the following six weeks to the base level of week 1. Most experts suspect that the delayed effect of advertising follows a declining exponential curve as shown in Exhibit 17-10. For this reason, this effect of advertising is also called **advertising decay.** Note that advertising carryover is quite different from advertising wearout. Ad wearout occurs from the repetition of a campaign over time, while ad carryover refers to the persistence of the effect of advertising *after* the campaign is terminated. **Hysteresis** is a particular form of advertising carryover, in which

dynamic effects are different from response to ad intensity. Ad intensity deals with *how much or at what level to advertise within a given period such as a week.* Wearin and wearout deal with *how many periods to sustain that level of advertising.* Analysis of response to ad intensity tries to determine the shape and optimum point of the ad response curve, as shown in Exhibit 17-6. Analysis of dynamic effects of advertising tries to determine how that optimum changes from week to week, due to repetition of the advertising content.

What causes wearin and wearout? At the individual level, wearin is probably caused by habituation, which is the increase in liking as consumers get used to or familiar with a stimulus (see Chapter 4). At the aggregate level of a market, wearin is probably due to the higher likelihood of consumers being exposed to or noticing an ad as it is repeated. At the individual level, wearout is probably due to the increase in tedium with repetition of a stimulus (see Chapter 4).

What implications do wearin and wearout have on the scheduling of ads? In the presence of wearin and wearout, an even schedule would be ineffective. The right approach would be to use flighting. Flights of advertising can be scheduled to take advantage of

▼ EXHIBIT 17-10. **Carryover effects of advertising.**

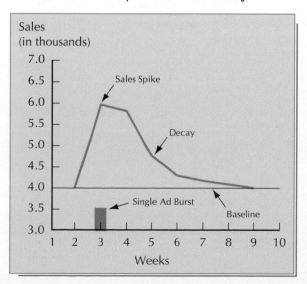

advertising propels sales to a higher level or plateau, at which they remain even after the campaign ends (see Exhibit 17-9).

What causes delays in advertising effects? We can identify at least four causes: long-term memory, delayed purchase, delayed persuasion and word-of-mouth. First, long-term memory for an ad may enable some consumers to recall its message even when the advertising stops. Because of this recall they may continue to buy the advertised brand even without renewed advertising. Second, a delayed purchase occurs when consumers *decide* to buy a brand in response to an ad, but *actually buy* it only when their inventory of the product runs down, or they have the resources to make the purchase. So they may respond to the ad several periods after viewing it, when the occasion for purchase comes along. Third, delayed persuasion occurs when consumers need to think about the message, get more information about the product or discuss it with others before they decide to buy the brand. In this case, their response to the ad may be delayed due to delays in persuasion. Fourth, word-of-mouth diffusion of the message in the ad may cause new consumers to learn about the advertised products. This learning may result in product sales after the advertising has been terminated.

In addition to these four causes, there are at least two other causes of the delayed effects of advertising due at least partly to variables other than advertising. First, if the brand is out of stock, response to advertising may not be instantaneous even if the decision to purchase it is made on viewing the ad. The purchase of the brand may occur only when the brand is in stock. In this case, the delayed response is due to both advertising and distribution. Second, consumers may be very pleased with the quality of a brand they first purchased in response to advertising, and they may continue to buy it. In this case, their continued purchase of the brand is due to both advertising and product quality.

The best scheduling strategy in the presence of delayed effects of advertising is pulsing. Each pulse of advertising should occur about the point at which the bulk of the effect from the previous pulse of advertising has fully decayed. In this way, a firm would not be wasting its budget by advertising when the effect of the previous advertising is still good.

Exhibit 17-11 summarizes the appropriate scheduling pattern depending on the level of the factors discussed here: sales pattern, campaign goals, response relative to budget and dynamic effects.

Summary

There are six important methods of determining the promotion budget: affordability, percentage of sales, competitive parity, objective and task, profit maximization and matching the elasticity ratio. These six methods are listed in the order of increasing sophistication required by the planner, and thus of increasing difficulty. In particular, the

▼ EXHIBIT 17-11. Scheduling as a function of key factors.

Determining Factor	Level of Factor	Scheduling Pattern
Sales pattern	Seasonal sales	Flighting
	Even sales year round	Even
Campaign goals	Attention/Information	Mass
	Persuasion	Pulsing, flighting
	Reminder	Even
Response relative to budget	Budget less than threshold level	No advertising
	Budget between threshold and optimum level	Mass
	Budget moderately above optimum	Flighting
	Budget several times larger than optimum	Pulsing
	Relatively huge budget	Even
Dynamic effects	Wearin	Flighting
	Wearout	Flighting
	Carryover effects	Pulsing

first three approaches are relatively simple because they use simple heuristics. However, they suffer from the cost of foregone opportunities when the budget selected is either too high or too low relative to the optimum. The optimum is a point at which the advertising budget gives the best returns in terms of a firm's profits. The profit-maximization method is the only one that gives the optimal promotional budget.

In the affordability method a firm spends as much on promotion as it can afford. This is the simplest method but also the most likely to be suboptimal.

In the percentage-of-sales method, a firm spends a fixed percentage of its sales on promotion. Besides simplicity, the advantage of this method is that promotion is budgeted at times when it is most likely to be effective. The disadvantages of this method are that it reinforces cyclical or seasonal sales patterns, and could lead to self-fulfilling prophecies.

In the competitive parity method a firm chooses a promotional level that matches the level of one of its competitors. This is a simple method that ensures that a firm stays in line with its competitors, especially in stable or declining markets. However, the method assumes that the competitor has the same goal, knows the right level of promotion, and is promoting at that level.

The objective-and-task method sets the promotion budget at the level needed to achieve certain goals. It is especially useful for new products, when a firm has no history or competitors to serve as guides. But it requires detailed knowledge of the hierarchy of effects.

In the profit-maximization approach the firm chooses the optimal promotion budget, or the budget that maximizes its profits. The major limitation of the profit-maximization approach is that it requires knowledge of the consumer or market response to promotion. This function is very difficult for firms to determine accurately.

Matching the elasticity ratio enables a firm to improve on its past budget allocation between advertising and price promotion. It also allows a firm to improve the fit between its advertising budget and the price it charges. The advantage of this method is that it is sensitive to consumer response to price and advertising. The disadvantage is that it requires technical knowledge about price and advertising elasticities.

Scheduling involves the decisions about the frequency and timing of promotions. The choice of scheduling depends on four key factors: the sales pattern of the product, the goals of the ad campaign, the sales-response function relative to the available budget and the dynamic effects of promotion. Various levels of each of these factors suggest one of four typical schedules: massing, flighting, pulsing and even scheduling.

QUESTIONS

1. Close rivals such as Coke and Pepsi or Miller and Budweiser may be prone to use the competitive parity method for budget setting. What precautions should such firms take when using this method?

2. Explain in depth the profit-maximization method for budget setting. Experts often rate this method as the best. Why? Is it the most practical or popular? Why?

3. The affordability and percentage-of-sales methods use simple heuristics to set the promotion budget. What are these heuristics? What are these methods' advantages and disadvantages relative to the profit-maximization method?

4. Consider a firm that is trying to determine its promotion budget for the introduction of a new durable product in a new category. The introduction may open up a major mass market for the product. Which method should it use? Why?

5. Explain the elasticity ratio method for allocating the promotion budget. What are its advantages and disadvantages?

6. Compare and contrast the different methods of setting the promotion budget.

7. How do the different methods of budget setting differ in management practice? What are the reasons for these differences?

8. Explain the different methods of scheduling the promotion budget.

9. What factors determine which advertising schedule a firm should use?

10. Advertisers would like to see the effects of their advertising immediately. However, ad agencies claim that the effects of advertising are noninstantaneous, and may take years to fully play out. Explain this issue.

NOTES

1. Helm, Leslie (1995), "Global Hype Raises the Curtain on Windows 95," *Los Angeles Times,* August 24, A1, A8.

2. Based on Maites, Alan and William A. Robinson (1995), "Windows 95 Ad Blast Missed A Major Step," *Advertising Age* 10, 9, 14; Clark, Don (1995), "Windows 95 Buzz Will Get Even Louder," *The Wall Street Journal,* August 18, B1; Johnson, Bradley (1995), "Windows 95 Opens With Omnimedia Blast," *Advertising Age,* August 28, 1, 32; *Ibid.*; AAII Staff Roundup (1995), "Is Microsoft Getting Its Bang For Buck, Peso or Rand?" *Advertising Age,* September 18, I3; Jaben, Jan (1995), "'Eighth Wonder of the World,'" *Advertising Age,* September 18, I3; News Roundup (1995), "For Microsoft, Nothing Succeeds Like Excess," *The Wall Street Journal,* September 25, B1; Clark, Don (1996), "Windows 95 Birthday Isn't Gala for All," *The Wall Street Journal,* August 22, B1, B3.

3. Farris, Paul, and Mark S. Albion (1981), "Determinants of the Advertising-to-Sales Ratio," *Journal of Advertising Research* 21, 1, 20–26. Alternate explanations for the positive relationship may be that firms that have a higher profit margin have more to gain from advertising than those with a lower profit margin. Still another although less compelling explanation is that higher advertising leads to higher profits.

4. Bigné, Enrique (1995), "Advertising Budget Practices: A Review," *Journal of Current Issues and Research in Advertising* 17, 2, 17–33; Lynch, James E., and Graham J. Hooley (1990), "Increasing Sophistication in Advertising Budget Setting," *Journal of Advertising Research* (February/March), 67–75; Hooley, Graham J., Christopher J. West, and James E. Lynch (1994), *Marketing in the UK: A Survey of Current Practice and Performance,* London: Institute of Marketing.

5. Advertising Factbook (1995), *Advertising Age,* January 2, 12.

6. This number is based on the assumption that Microsoft realized 50 percent of the retail price of $100 of Windows 95.

7. Bigné, "Advertising Budget Practices."

8. Based on Porter, Michael E. (1992), "Coca-Cola Versus Pepsi-Cola and the Soft Drink Industry," Case No. 9-391-179, Boston, MA: Harvard Business School Publishing Division; Winters, Patricia (1992), "Coke II Enters Markets Without Splashy Fanfare," *Advertising Age,* August 24, 2.

9. Bigné, "Advertising Budget Practices."

10. Little, John D. C., et al. (1975), "A Market Share Theorem," *Journal of Marketing Research* Vol. 12 (May), 136–141.

11. Schroer, James C. (1990), "Ad Spending: Growing Market Share," *Harvard Business Review,* (January-February), 44–48. The subsection is based on this article.

12. The study of the 666 brands is by Jones (cited below). Although a study by Balasubramanian and Kumar (cited below) seems to find the opposite relationship, that study used firm-level data. Moreover, a review by Farris and Albion ("Determinants of the Advertising-to-Sales Ratio") indicates that two other studies also found a negative relationship between market share and the ratio of advertising to sales. Citations: Ailawadi, Kusum L., Paul W. Farris, and Mark E. Parry (1994), "Share and Growth Are Not Good Predictors of the Advertising and Promotion/Sales Ratio," *Journal of Marketing* 58 (January) 86-97; Balasubramanian, Siva K., and V. Kumar (1990), "Analyzing Variations in Advertising and Promotional Expenditures: Key Correlates in Consumer, Industrial, and Service Markets," *Journal of Marketing* 54 (April), 57–68; Jones, John Philip (1990), "Ad Spending: Maintaining Market Share," *Harvard Business Review,* January–February, 38–41.

13. Schroer, "Ad Spending."

14. Underwood, Elaine and Warner Fara (1994), "Interactive List Vows Chrysler," *Adweek,* February 7, 10; Lazarus, George (1993), "Budget VP Shift Marketing Gears," *Chicago Tribune,* October 25, 4.

15. Bigné, "Advertising Budget Practices."

16. *Ibid.*

17. Lynch and Hooley, "Increasing Sophistication in Advertising Budget Setting."

18. Sethuraman, Raj, and Gerard J. Tellis (1991), "An Analysis of the Tradeoff Between Advertising and Pricing," *Journal of Marketing Research,* 31, 2 (May), 160–174.

19. *Ibid.*

20. *Ibid.*

21. Zielske, Hubert A. (1959), "The Remembering and Forgetting of Advertising" *Journal of Marketing* 23, 1, 239–243.

22. *USA Today* (1993), "Super Bowl Admeter," February 1, 3B.

23. *Ibid.*; Goldman, Kevin (1993), "As Ad Clutter Becomes Tradition at Super Bowl, Viewer Recall Slips," *The Wall Street Journal,* February 3, B8.

24. Lipman, Joanne (1991), "Was Macy's TV Ad Campaign A Mistake?" *The Wall Street Journal,* December 23, B6.

The Gillette company markets razors and blades, toiletries, cosmetics, stationery products, small appliances and dental products. Yet the company is best known, and rightly so, for its razors and blades. King Gillette, a 40-year-old inventor, launched the company in 1903, by popularizing a razor with a safe, inexpensive, disposable blade. With this pioneering innovation, consumers could shave at home daily without the hassle of having to sharpen the blade. Since then, Gillette has remained the leader in the safety

Integrated Advertising and Sales Promotion Strategy

blade market (see Exhibit 18-1). Many analysts attribute the success of Gillette to consumer loyalty to the Gillette name.

However, a closer look at the safety razor market reveals two phenomena that undermine this thesis. First, the razor and blade market is a dynamic one in which aggressive competitors continually introduce new products. Gillette's product line itself has steadily and regularly changed as new products were introduced (see Exhibit 18-2). Second, many of Gillette's products are better known by their specific brand name than by the Gillette name. Thus Gillette's great stability in market leadership and market share has been achieved in the midst of, and perhaps because of, continual change.

Gillette has aggressively introduced new products, having been responsible for every major innovation in the safety razor market, except two: stainless steel blades, introduced by Wilkinson, and the injector, introduced by Schick. Moreover, Gillette has introduced new products regularly, even though they cannibalize its own older products. Gillette's promotion strategy also reveals some interesting patterns. New products typically are heavily promoted, while older products are not (see

Exhibit 18-3A). Newer products also have heavy support in terms of advertising and consumer promotions, while older products have heavier trade promotion (see Exhibit 18-3B).[1]

The history of Gillette raises a number of questions. For example, why does Gillette regularly introduce new products even at the cost of cannibalizing its established ones? Why are consumers loyal to Gillette if the firm regularly introduces new products with different brand names? Is Gillette's pattern of promotion expenditures good strategy or mere accident? This chapter addresses these and related issues.

Integrated advertising and sales promotion strategy means the blending of one promotional variable with one or more marketing or promotional variables to achieve and possibly enhance the effect of each. Integration is vitally important for two simple reasons. First, marketing and promotional variables are intrinsically interdependent. Knowing and exploiting these interdependencies can enhance the effectiveness of these variables. Second, firms currently work in a highly competitive environment with scarce resources. Integrating promotion and marketing variables can enhance the effectiveness of advertising and promotion while conserving resources.

This chapter discusses three broad areas in which integration is vital to success: integration of advertising and sales promotion variables over different stages of the product life cycle and in successive product life cycles, and integration of marketing and promotion variables for market defense.

PROMOTION STRATEGY OVER THE PRODUCT LIFE CYCLE

The **product life cycle** refers to the cyclical pattern in sales that describes the evolution of a product from its introduction to its demise. Typically, researchers categorize this evolution into four stages: introduction, growth, maturity and decline (see Exhibit 18-4). The product life cycle greatly influences the planning of advertising

▼ **EXHIBIT 18-1.** Gillette's shares of the blade market.

Year	Unit Market Share %	Year	$ Market Share %
1964	58%	1980	64%
1965	56	1981	63
1966	56	1982	64
1967	59	1983	61
1968	60	1984	62
1969	59	1985	62
1970	60	1986	64
1971	58	1987	64
1972	57	1988	65
1973	57	1989	
1974	57	1990	64
1975	57	1991	65
1976	56	1992	64
1977	54	1993	67
1978	54	1994	64

Data Source: Salomon Brothers Analyst Report, September 24, 1990, as cited in Ghemwat, Pankaj (1991), "Gillette's Launch of Sensor," Boston, MA: Harvard Business School Publishing Division, Case No. 9-792-028; Kummel, Charles M., and Jay E. Klompmaker (1982), "The Gillette Company," case written when the authors were at the University of North Carolina; Sloan, Pat (1992), "The People Behind Today's Marketing Success Stories," Advertising Age, July 6, S-12.

▼ **EXHIBIT 18-2.** Life cycles of Gillette's razor blade products.

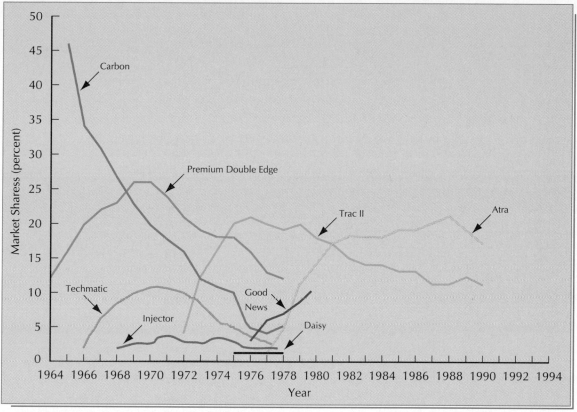

Note: The figures do not show market shares for most brands, beyond 1978.

Sources: Chakravarty, Subrata N. (1991), "We Had to Change the Playing Field," *Forbes,* February 4, 82–86; Ghemwat, Pankaj (1991), "Gillette's Launch of Sensor," Boston, MA: Harvard Business School Publishing Division, Case No. 9-792-028; Kummel, Charles M., and Jay E. Klompmaker (1982), "The Gillette Company"; ASAP (1995), "Retailers Take Twofold Approach to Shaving Category; Industry Overview," *Chain Drug Review,* January 30, 17, 3, 36; Sloan, Pat (1992), "The People Behind Today's Marketing Success Stories," *Advertising Age,* July 6, S-12.

and promotion expenditures. Yet the product life cycle is a misunderstood concept that has generated much controversy among researchers.[2] Thus a thorough understanding of the phenomenon is important for planning advertising and promotion expenditures.

The two major drivers of the product life cycle are technology and consumer preferences. These two factors relate to the two principal agents responsible for the existence of products, the seller and the consumer of the product, respectively. Consumer preferences determine what is desired in the market, while technology determines how that desire can be met. The distinction between preference-based and technology-based life cycles is important for planning advertising and promotion. Technology-based

life cycles are somewhat more predictable and controllable by managers than are preference-based life cycles. For example, Gillette controls the rate and direction of technology within the firm. To the extent it is ahead of competitors, it can also determine the timing of new product introductions. In such a situation, advertising and sales promotion can be carefully balanced over stages of the life cycle of a given product, as well as the life cycles of succeeding products. Such planning may not be as easy or necessary for preference-based life cycles.

Technology affects the life cycle of every product through the mining, manufacture or marketing of the product directly or (indirectly) of its substitute or complement. For example, it is technology that directly drives the life cycles of shaving systems (see

▼ **EXHIBIT 18-3.** Gillette's promotional strategy for a portfolio of products.

A. A Product's Promotion Budget versus Its Contribution to Sales

Item	Atra	Trac II	Double Edged	Techmatic	Other	Total
Product's budget as % of total budget	34%	38%	8%	0%	20%	100%
Product's sales as % of total sales	21%	42%	17%	2%	18%	100%

B. Allocation of Product's Budget to Advertising and Trade Promotion

Item	Atra	Trac II	Double Edged	Techmatic
Allocation to advertising and consumer promotions	56%	29%	5%	0%
Allocation to trade promotions	42	70	92	53
Other	2	1	3	47
Total	100%	100%	100%	100%

Source: Kummel, Charles M., and Jay E. Klompmaker (1982), "The Gillette Company."

▼ **EXHIBIT 18-4.** The product life cycle.

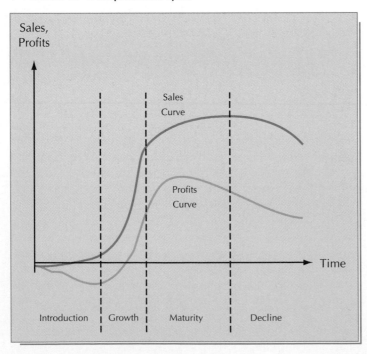

Exhibit 18-2). Similarly, technological progress made possible the video recorder, which led to the new life cycle of the complementary product, movie videos.

Consumer preferences affect product life cycles by influencing demand. Firms supply products to consumers to meet consumer demand. When this demand changes, firms change their offering in the market, resulting in the introduction of new products and the demise of old products. Consumer preferences change either because of changing fashions, satiation with existing products and the desire for novelty, or information about new products.

A **fashion** is an arbitrary design entirely dependent on consumer tastes and not on any functions it serves. The degree to which a product is prone to fashion depends on how much of its design is taste driven versus functional. Examples

▼ EXHIBIT 18-5. Dependence of products on technology and fashion.

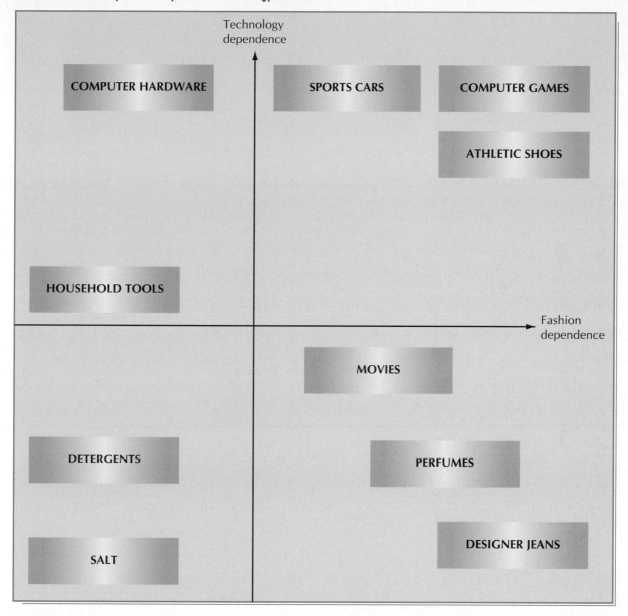

of products susceptible to fashions are perfumes, designer clothes and hairstyles. Such products are often called fashion goods. A large component of the design of these products appeals to the arbitrary tastes of consumers. Other products, such as gadgets, tools and appliances, are utilitarian, not fashionable, because their design primarily meets a functional consumer need. Most products probably lie between these two extremes, in that they serve a basic function yet are sold with a large stylistic component. Exhibit 18-5 classifies a range of products along two dimensions: technology and fashion dependence.

Novelties are a class of products whose appeal depends on their newness. While some repetitive exposure to the product may increase its appeal, the appeal wears off fairly soon. As a result, the products have low repeat usage. Examples of such products are board games, computer games, music recordings, novels and movies. These products have life cycles driven by the speed of consumer satiation with their use. While the life cycle of any particular movie, book, musical piece or game may vary, and while perennial favorites may seem never to die, as a rule most items within these categories have relatively short and distinctive life cycles. For example, most consumers read a novel or see a movie only once.

Even though novelties and fashions represent different classes of goods, the same principles of promotion probably apply to both. At first glance, fashions may seem like social phenomena over which firms have little control. For example, Bloomingdale must stock short or long dresses depending on what's in fashion. On the other hand, Addison-Wesley must find original creations to publish as books. However, this difference is probably exaggerated. Just like music recordings and movies, books are also prone to fashions. At particular times, certain book genres come into vogue and publishers scramble to sign up authors who can write a book to fit that style. The same is true of music and movies. Sometimes a movie or musical piece may itself trigger a new trend, just as a creative designer could initiate a new fashion in clothes. Thus the difference, if any, between these classes of goods is one of degree rather than of character. Fashion goods are more prone to fash-

ion than originality, while the reverse is true of novelties.

Information can influence the preference for any product, and thus its life cycle. For example, in the last four decades, evidence has accumulated that smoking or chewing tobacco causes lung cancer, mouth cancer and other diseases. The spread of this information caused a decline in the use of tobacco-related products such as cigarettes, chewing tobacco and pipe tobacco (see Exhibit 18-6). Information that cholesterol is bad for health has caused lower consumption of food products rich in cholesterol, such as red meats, milk, cream and eggs. On the other hand, information can also lead to the introduction or growth of new product categories. For example, in the last few decades knowledge about cancer prevention has led to the growth of exercise machines, exercise clubs, yogurt and high-fiber foods.[3] Knowledge about the causes of tooth dis-

▼ **EXHIBIT 18-6.** Impact of information on sales of cigarettes.

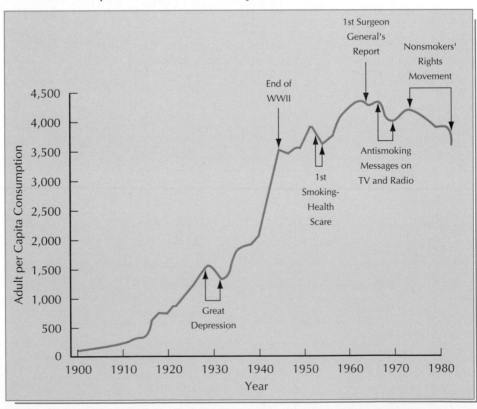

Source: Rangan, Kasturi V. (1992), "Smoke Wars: The Case For and Against The Tobacco Industry," Case No. 9-590-040, Cambridge, MA: Harvard Business School Publishing.

ease led to the growth of dental floss, fluoride tooth-paste and fluoridated water supplies. Information can also influence the life cycles of fashions and nov-elties. For example, certain clothes and hairstyles become popular among ethnic groups when they learn that their ancestors wore that style.

The important question for promoters is how the product life cycle affects promotion strategy. This chapter addresses this question in three parts, based on three important aspects of the product life cycle: stages of the life cycle, succession of life cycles, and the speed of the product's takeoff.

Promotion Strategy over Stages of the Product Life Cycle

Stages of Life Cycle Analysts typically identify four stages in product life cycles: introduction, growth, maturity and decline (see Exhibit 18-4). **Introduction** represents a period following a product's commercial-ization when sales remain low or increase only slowly. **Growth** refers to a period following the introduction when sales increase rapidly. **Maturity** is a period when sales are stable or flat. **Decline** refers to a stage when sales decrease either slowly or rapid-ly until the product ultimately dies out.

All products that have ever been commercialized have had an introductory stage. Further, all com-mercial products no longer in existence had a decline. Many products go directly from introduc-tion to decline. The most famous example is the Edsel, a heavily publicized and much-awaited new car introduction of the mid-1950s that flopped.[4] Such products never really catch on with consumers. All other products that have been introduced, and especially successful products, go through a growth stage. Rapid growth is not sustainable forever. Every product that goes through the growth stage will also go through maturity. Exhibit 18-2 shows that this is true for every one of the products introduced by Gillette in the last 40 years. Some of these products passed through a new growth phase, others remained in maturity for a long time, while still others eventually died out.

An important issue when identifying the stages of the product life cycle is the level of aggregation. Products can be analyzed at the level of functional need (transportation systems, shaving systems), cat-egory (cars, disposable razors), model or formula

(four-door coupe), or brand name (Chevrolet, Toyota). This ordering of aggregation is from the broadest to the narrowest.

Life cycles may not be fully evident at the func-tional need level because consumer needs are fairly basic and persistent. For example, people have a perennial need for food, drink, clothing and trans-portation. Thus total sales of products that serve these needs are unlikely to show neat increases and declines that match typical life cycles. On the other hand, as technology reduces the cost and improves the quality of various products that meet these needs, total sales are likely to go up over time. For example, total transportation in person-miles keeps increasing as the cost of air and road travel decreas-es, even though better communication is supposed to reduce the need for transportation.

Life cycles may not be clearly evident at the brand level, because firms can modify the product without changing the brand name. Indeed, product modifi-cation in response to changes either in consumer tastes or in technology is a primary means by which a firm can extend a brand's life and prevent its demise.[5] For example, the name Tide has been kept alive and dominant even though its formula has changed with technological innovation. Such changes may mask the maturity, decline or demise of brand names.

Product life cycles are most evident at levels between these two extremes, for categories and models. Indeed, specific categories and models are no more than technological solutions to consumer needs. An immutable fact of market economies is that *technology continually progresses*. The progress is the result of advances in human knowledge that lead to more efficient means of meeting consumer needs. This technological progress is the most impor-tant cause of the distinctive patterns in product life cycles, especially for technology-driven products. For example, successive technologies of double-edged razor blades, twin razor blades, and pivoting head razors drove the overlapping life cycles of Premium Double Edge, Trac II and Atra, as seen in Exhibit 18-2.

The important question for firms is how much to invest in promotion across each of the stages, and how to allocate that amount between advertis-ing and sales promotion. A related issue is how to price the product, because price determines the margin for advertising and the leverage for sales promotions.

Promotion Strategy Managers have to make three important decisions about promotion strategy: how large the whole promotional budget should be, how that budget should be allocated between incentive and informative promotions, and how to price the new product.

Total Promotional Budget The total promotional budget should generally decrease over the life cycle, for several reasons. First, consumers are generally not well informed about a new product. They have limited or no experience with it. Thus a primary purpose of promotion is to disseminate information about a new product. This can be done with advertising or with sales promotion, such as sampling and trial. The latter two methods are expensive but effective means of introducing new products.

Second, consumers generally are familiar with mature products, having experienced them directly or indirectly in one context or another. Some may be heavy users or even habituated to mature products. So firms do not need to inform consumers about these products. At the same time, consumers who are habituated to a product are unlikely to change easily. Thus, promotion of these products is unlikely to be very effective.

Third, products decline either because of innovations that render them obsolete, or because they go out of fashion. In either case, promotions at this stage represent a costly means of stemming the decline in sales. On the other hand, declining products still retain a core of loyal buyers, who need little promotion to sustain their loyalty. So promotions of products in decline need to be kept to a minimum. For all these reasons, firms should promote most heavily in the earlier stages of the life cycle.

Informational versus Incentive Promotions *Informational promotions* include advertising or sampling to give consumers more information about products. *Incentive promotions* include coupons, rebates, price packs and premiums, which give consumers a monetary incentive to buy the product (see Chapter 9). Managers should invest in informational promotions in the early stages of the life cycle, and in incentives in the latter stages, for two reasons.

First, as stated, information dissemination is more relevant in the earlier stages of the product life cycle

than in the later stages. Second, by the time a product reaches maturity, the technology to produce it is standard and widely adopted. Differences between brands become few and less significant. A fairly large segment of consumers is also well aware of the attributes and prices of alternative products. As a result, these consumers are more price sensitive. Moreover, fairly often, generic or private-label brands offer comparable products at lower prices. At the same time, established brands have a large clientele of loyal purchasers. In this scenario, an established brand is better off price discriminating among consumers. Firms can use coupons, rebates and temporary price discounts to attract switchers without lowering the price to all of their consumers. It is probably for these reasons that Gillette typically advertises its new products more intensely than its older products (see Exhibit 18-7).

Pricing Pricing plays a critical role in the overall strategy for new products. It determines the margin that the firm can earn on the new products to support the promotional effort and to reward shareholders for supporting the firm's innovative efforts. At the same time, price also determines the degree to which a new product penetrates the market and may serve as a signal of quality to consumers.

A simple strategy for pricing new products is to price well above costs to take advantage of consumer demand for the innovation. This pricing strategy is called **price skimming**. Price skimming has many advantages. First, consumers normally assume that a new product is better and costs more to produce, so they are willing to pay more for it. Second, to the extent that a high price signals quality to consumers, the high price of the new product may reinforce consumers' belief in its quality. Third, many markets include a segment of innovators who like to own the latest innovations, even if, and sometimes because, they are high priced.[6] Finally, when a firm is unsure of the optimum price, setting a high price gives it leverage to lower the price to the optimum point. Starting with a low price does not give such an advantage (see Chapter 9).

However, some situations may justify the use of a **penetration pricing** strategy. This is a price strategy for new products in which the price is set low to quickly attract new buyers. It has some advantages. First, a low price ensures rapid penetration of the market, with the potential for economies of scale.[7] If

▼ **EXHIBIT 18-7.** Gillette's advertising allocation by product over time.

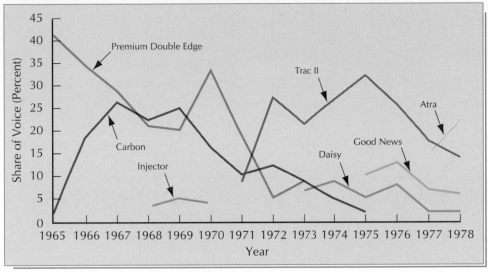

Source: Kummel, Charles M., and Jay E. Klompmaker (1982), "The Gillette Company."

such economies of scale are great, the firm may well find that marketing at a small margin to a large segment of consumers is more profitable than doing so at a high margin to few consumers. Second, a firm may adopt a low price to discourage competitors from entering the market, thus decreasing the intensity of rivalry and ensuring a more steady stream of profits in the long term. This strategy is particularly relevant if economies of experience are important.[8] That is, by introducing the new product with a low price, a firm can readily gain experience manufacturing the product, ensuring that its costs drop well below that of a competitor who lacks the same experience.[9] Third, for certain lifesaving products, such as drugs, high prices could limit the benefit of the product to market segments who need the product and can afford it. In this case, the broader goal of meeting long-term consumer welfare suggests that a firm not exploit consumer need with unfairly high prices.

Advertising, promotion and pricing strategies should be mutually consistent. Thus if a firm chooses a price-skimming strategy, it should adopt an image-boosting ad campaign that can justify the high price. In such a case, sales promotions should be more informative than incentive oriented. On the other hand, if the firm chooses a penetration strategy, the ad campaign should emphasize value, and sales promotions should be more incentive oriented.

In particular, sales promotions that discriminate between price-sensitive segments would be appropriate so that the firm need not charge all consumers one low price.

Promotion Strategy over Successive Life Cycles

Life Cycle Succession The life cycle of a given product does not occur in isolation. Extensive research, especially with technology-driven products, indicates that life cycles are dynamically linked over time.[10] The dynamic linkage of technology-driven life cycles is due to the S-curve of technological progress. Research on the progress of technology over centuries indicates that each new technology follows a distinct S-curve (see Exhibit 18-8). For example, the field of lighting progressed through a succession of technologies: wood, oil, gas, incandescent, and fluorescent technology,[11] each with its own S-curve. A new technology, such as incandescent lighting, emerges as a possibility to solve a human need. At first, this technology must struggle against a superior existing technology, such as gas, adopted by existing firms and perfected through years of experience. The inventors of the new technology, convinced of its potential, keep working to eliminate its weaknesses. As their experience with the new technology accumulates, it begins to meet consumer needs more efficiently.

▼ EXHIBIT 18-8. The S-curve of technological progress.

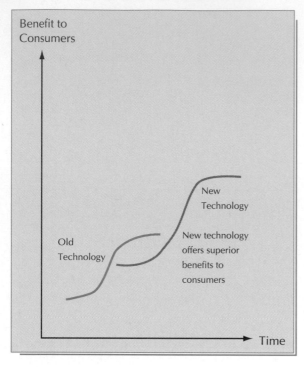

Source: Utterback, James M. (1994), *Mastering the Dynamics of Innovation,* Cambridge, MA: Harvard Business School Press.

However, growth cannot endure forever. There are limits to all advances. Progress in the new technology reaches a point at which further experience or research yields diminishing returns in terms of better quality or lower price of the new product. As a result, sales of the new product cease to increase rapidly and begin to level off. The new product has reached maturity. Maturity could last forever, with ever smaller and more costly increases in the sales of the product. However, at some time, experience and research give rise to a new technology, and the cycle is repeated with a new product. The development of successive technologies (wood, oil, gas, incandescent, fluorescent), each with its own *S*-curve, is responsible for the life cycle of lighting products. Similarly, successive technologies (carbon, double edge, pivoting head, etc.) drive the life cycle of razor blades, as seen in Exhibit 18-2.

The major error that firms make is to underestimate the potential of a new technology and overestimate that of an old one. When threatened with a new technology they strive to improve the old technology with a burst of research, or they intensify promotions to maintain sales against the advances of the new technology. Such efforts probably bear fruit, but the rate of progress is too small and the cost too high relative to corresponding efforts invested in the new technology.[12] For example, the gas companies did try to innovate when faced with incandescent lighting, producing the Welsbach gas burner. But that was not sufficient. Firms that have invested in the old technology are either unaware of the *S*-curve, or find it hard to break away from past investments in equipment, expertise and operating routines.[13] As a result, products based on the old technology, and brands and firms wedded to them, frequently die out with the old technology.

A point is reached at which the new technology can solve consumer needs far better than the old technology. At that point, products based on the new technology turn out to be cheaper or better than those produced with the old technology. Consumers readily adopt these products, leading to rapid growth of the new products and a corresponding decline of the old products. The growth phase begins. Because of the relative superiority of the new technology, products based on it are cheaper or better than the old products ever were (see Exhibit 18-9). So the new product not only replaces the old but expands the market for it. Thus, successive generations of technology lead to ever larger markets for products that meet a particular consumer need.

▼ EXHIBIT 18-9. Productivity of basic lighting technologies.

Technology	Brightness in Candlepower
Gas flame or kerosene lamp	7
Welsbach gas burner	250
Tungsten filament lamp	1,500

Source: Utterback, James M. (1994), *Mastering the Dynamics of Innovation,* Cambridge, MA: Harvard Business School Press.

The *S*-curve has important lessons for firms:

- Every technology, however radical and promising, has limits at which progress occurs more slowly at increasing cost.
- When introduced, a new technology may look inferior to the existing technology. However, it often has far greater potential, because it can progress further than the existing technology.
- Initial progress with the new technology is slow. But rapid progress is possible. When it occurs, the new technology surpasses the old in efficiency, and sales of products based on it grow rapidly.
- Once this point is reached, advertising of products based on the old technology is likely to be ineffective and inefficient. On the other hand, advertising of products based on the new technology can be very rewarding.

Gillette's real success is probably due to the fact that it understands these principles. The firm is committed to relentless innovation, and regularly introduces new products wedded to new technology, even though they end up cannibalizing its own prod-

ucts.[14] In the short term there is an apparent loss. But in the long term, Gillette stays ahead of its competitors. Indeed, when Wilkinson introduced stainless steel blades before Gillette, the latter saw its market share drop dramatically in one year. Ironically, Wilkinson had to license some of that technology from Gillette, which held most of the patents. That lesson underscored for Gillette the importance of relentless innovation. This is the rationale behind the popular recommendation to managers about the importance of cannibalization: "Eat your own lunch before somebody else does."[15]

Life cycles influenced by consumer tastes probably also have *S*-curves. However, these *S*-curves are driven by fashion or novelty, which in turn is influenced by social, economic and political factors. As such, the latter curves are shorter, more erratic and less predictable. For example, books, songs, and especially movies have life cycles that last months or, frequently, only weeks (see Exhibit 18-10). Popular books, songs and movies sometimes have sequels, which correspond to updated versions of products based on the same technology. The sequels have instant name recognition and appeal but are gener-

▼ **EXHIBIT 18-10.** Life cycles of some movies.

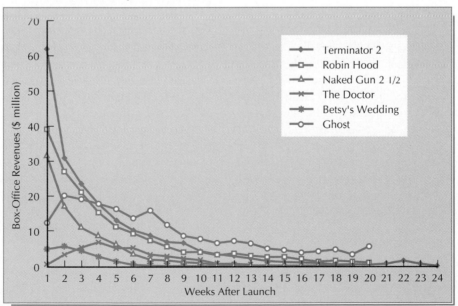

Source: Sawhney, Mohanbir S., and Jehoshua Eliashberg (1996), "A Parsimonious Model For Forecasting Gross Box-Office Revenues Of Motion Pictures," (*Marketing Science* 15, 2, 113–131) or Working Paper, University of Pennsylvania.

▼ **EXHIBIT 18-11.** Promotional strategies as a function of price and advertising elasticities.

ADVERTISING ELASTICITY	PRICE ELASTICITY	
	High	Low
High	I. *Build strategy:* for growing products	II. *Image strategy:* for introductory products or image products
Low	III. *Mass strategy: -* for mature products or price sensitive products	IV. *Harvest strategy:* for declining products

Source: Adapted from Sethuraman, Raj, and Gerard J. Tellis (1991), "An Analysis of the Tradeoff Between Advertising and Price Discounting," *Journal of Marketing Research* 28 (May), 160–174.

ally popular only with an ever smaller core of loyals, until the series of sequels finally dies out.

Promotion Strategy The important question for firms is how to budget for advertising and promotion given a portfolio of products with interrelated life cycles.

We discuss the strategy in terms of overall promotion budget, allocation of advertising and sales promotion and pricing.

Total Promotional Budget The total promotional budget should be highest for new products, and gradually reduced as the product moves through the life cycle. Besides the advantages stated earlier, this strategy is consistent with the *product portfolio theory* for managing products.[16] According to this theory, firms need to maintain a mix of products, each in different stages of the life cycle, for efficient management of resources. Older products provide a steady stream of income and cash, as the mature product has less room for technological advance but a core of loyal consumers who need little promotional support. Newer products need heavier investment for product and market development. Thus an ideal cash flow would arise from a mix of mature or declining products and new or growing products. By also trimming promotion for older products and increasing that for newer products, the firm can approach the ideal cash flow suggested by the product portfolio theory.

Allocation to Advertising and Sales Promotion The advertising and sales promotion budget can also be allocated over a portfolio of products based on their related life cycles. Suppose a category of goods has a fixed distribution of advertising and sales promotion. When faced with a portfolio of products, a firm should invest more of the advertising dollars for the newer products, and more of the sales promotion

dollars for the mature products. As stated earlier, the reason for such an allocation is consumers' differing response to advertising and sales promotion over different stages of the product life cycle.

Based on these principles, one study argues that managers have a choice of four distinct strategic investments for a portfolio of products at different stages of the life cycle.[17] Exhibit 18-11 presents these strategies as four regions or markets defined by two axes representing price or advertising elasticity.

- Market I has high advertising and price elasticity. An example would be the market for a growing brand. Consumers are responsive to advertising to define the brand, and also to price discounts because the brand is not yet a necessity. So the firm can build the brand's position by spending heavily on both advertising and price discounts.
- Market II has high advertising elasticity and low price elasticity. This is a market for new brands that need extensive information dissemination, such as Windows 95. Such a brand should spend heavily on advertising and avoid price discounts.
- Market III has low advertising elasticity and high price elasticity. A brand in such a market should spend relatively less on advertising and more on price promotions. Examples are mature brands that have fallen to a commodity status and suffer competition from cheap private labels (peanut butter, laundry detergents, toasters).
- Market IV has low advertising and price elasticity. An example is the market for a declining product category, such as tape decks or double-edged razors. In such a market, all consumers know about the brand, many have moved to alternative products, but some consumers are very loyal to a brand or the product and will con-

tinue to buy it even in the face of better alternatives. So, a firm could harvest a brand in this market by cutting back on both advertising and promotion.

Besides helping to balance a portfolio of products, a differential allocation of advertising and sales promotion ensures that these products appeal to different segments. Such differentiation decreases cannibalization within the portfolio, while increasing competition with rival products.

Pricing As stated earlier, price skimming is generally a good strategy for pricing new products. The existence of a portfolio of products at different stages of the life cycle reinforces the advantage of price skimming, for the following reason. New products generally cannibalize sales of related old products. The cannibalization is very high if the new product represents a new generation of the old product, and is perfectly substitutable. This was the case for Gillette's shaving systems. In that case, the firm faces a dilemma. Should it introduce the new product and suffer cannibalization, or hold back the new product and suffer the threat of competitive innovation?

A strategy of price skimming can resolve the problem. The firm should introduce the new product, at a high enough price so that the margin from the new product is higher than that from the existing product it replaces. In that case, all cannibalization in sales results in increasing margins and profits for the firm. The firm could reduce price as its costs of producing the new product drop, or as competitors threaten the firm with their own product innovations.

Promotion Strategy Depending on Speed of Takeoff

Speed of Takeoff The **takeoff,** the point that demarcates the introductory and growth stages of the product life cycle, is characterized by the first rapid increase in sales of the product. Extensive research on new products indicates that most become popular exhibit a takeoff.[18] In the case of technology-driven products, the reason for the takeoff is the *S*-shaped curve. With technological progress, a new product continues to improve until a point at which its value to consumers exceeds that from older products. At that point, sales of the new product take off. Predicting when the takeoff will occur is vitally important to managers because it requires enormous manufactur-

ing, distribution, and promotion resources. Moreover, managers may discontinue a new product or miss a great opportunity by wrongly assuming the product will not take off. Research by the author and his colleague indicate that the takeoff of new products can at least partly be predicted.[19]

For promoters, the key question is, how does the takeoff affect the planning of promotion? Promotion strategy depends critically on the speed of takeoff. Product life cycles take on distinct shapes depending on the speed of takeoff. Consider the life cycle patterns in Exhibit 18-12. The first, an immediate hit or blockbuster, shows an instantaneous takeoff and, thereafter, continuous decline. The second shows a normal or bell-shaped pattern of growth and

▼ **EXHIBIT 18-12. Three typical life cycles.**

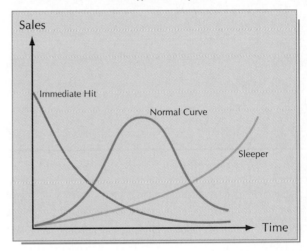

decline, while the third, a sleeper, shows a long, slow takeoff. Are these three life cycles realistic? They are probably valid for novelties. Durable and nondurable products may also have distinct life cycles due to the speed of takeoff, though in their case, the decline of the curve may not be visible because maturity lasts a long time (see Exhibit 18-13).

To understand how promotion strategy should vary by speed of takeoff, consider the histories of the three books: *Sex* by Madonna, *Men Are from Mars, Women Are from Venus* by John Gray, and *Jonathan Livingston Seagull* by Richard Bach. *Sex,* which portrayed erotic images of celebrity Madonna, stirred tremendous prerelease publicity and motivated a

▼ **EXHIBIT 18-13.** Life cycles of some durables.

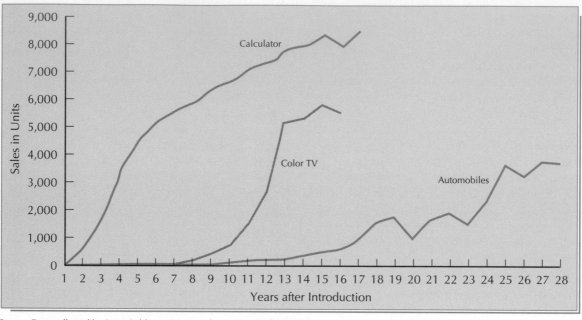

Source: Data collected by Peter Golder, assistant professor, New York University.

first printing of 835,000 copies, the biggest first printing ever of any book of that type.[20] However, subsequent printings were much smaller and sales rapidly declined, because the book had little substantive value. Its life cycle resembles the immediate hit in Exhibit 18-12. On the other hand, Richard Bach found a publisher for his book only after 20 refusals.[21] The first printing was only 6,000 copies. However, the book, which describes the struggle of a little bird to fly, slowly caught on with the public all over the world and sold 10 million copies in over 23 languages.[22] Its curve resembles that of the sleeper in Exhibit 18-12. *Sex* was all hype and had no "legs." *Jonathan Livingston Seagull* had no hype but strong legs. Between these two extremes was the best-seller *Men Are from Mars, Women Are from Venus*. It had a steady rise, long maturity and slow decline. Should promotion strategy differ for these three different life cycles? How?

Promotion Strategy Both the intensity and content of advertising and sales promotion need to vary for each of these three life cycles. The first type of life cycle needs intense advertising and little promotion prior to release. Since the product lacks substance,

its success depends on piquing consumer curiosity before word-of-mouth reveals its true substance. Sales promotion, especially price promotion, needs to be limited, since those who want to buy the product will do so even at a high price. In contrast, the third type of life cycle needs little or no advertising. Word-of-mouth, although slow, will be an efficient means of disseminating the value of the product. However, the product may benefit from sales promotions, such as free or discounted copies for influential people, who may talk about it and promote its appeal to the general population. The success of *Jonathan Livingston Seagull* may have been due to the inspirational nature of the story, which had universal appeal to people of many countries. Mass promotion of the book with one or two messages may have been unnecessary, and may have limited rather than heightened its appeal.

Movies represent a special case of novelties because their life cycles are very short. Moreover, most movies follow the first life cycle pattern, which is characteristic of novelties—instantaneous takeoff. The height of the takeoff depends on the popularity of the movie, but most movies have their highest ticket sales in the first weekend after release. Indeed, movies are perhaps the most perishable product made.[23] On average, producers release eight to ten movies each week. One or two of these movies attract the most attendance. Such attendance gets reported by the press, and reinforced by word-of-mouth, encouraging more theaters to run the movie. That in turn leads to increased attendance. The other movies introduced each week quickly die out.

Relaunching a failed movie is very difficult because the first failure sends a negative signal to consumers and distributors, while competition from new movies is likely to be at least as intense as it was the first time around. Indeed, if many producers relaunched their failures, the market for movies would become even more crowded and the competition more intense. Because of the nature of movies, and the promotion strategy adopted for most, ticket sales for most movies follow the first of the three life cycles of novelties. They peak in the first or second weekend and then decline until they eventually close, on average, 15 weeks later (see Exhibit 18-10).

Advertising and promotion play a critical role in the success of a movie. They determine what aspects of the movie should be emphasized, to whom, and through which medium. TV remains the medium of choice, because the perishability of the movie makes it imperative to reach a vast audience instantly, while the audiovisual nature of TV can best depict its content. However, in practice, the industry spends slightly over half its advertising budget on newspapers, and slightly under half on TV.[24] Movie distributors advertise in newspapers, because they reach a mass audience and provide a guide to the availability of the movie.

INTEGRATION OF ADVERTISING AND SALES PROMOTION IN EVERY LIFE CYCLE STAGE

All promotion variables are related to each other either as substitutes or complements. Many variables are obvious substitutes. For example, a price-cut can be offered either as a coupon or a rebate. A direct advertising campaign can use either telephone or mail. Managers have to make trade-offs among such substitutes. The previous chapters emphasize the choice among such substitutes when discussing the various forms of promotion. This section presents some less obvious but important relationships among substitutes and complements. These relationships are universal and hold in every stage of the product life cycle.

Trade-Offs among Promotion Components

Three important trade-offs between advertising and sales promotion merit our attention: a direct trade-off between advertising and trade promotion, an indirect trade-off between advertising and trade promotion and a direct trade-off between advertising and price promotion.

Direct Trade-Off between Advertising and Trade Promotion
A subtle but very important trade-off between advertising and trade promotion occurs because of the way these variables are budgeted. Advertising is an expense that must be incurred in expectation of sales. As explained in Chapter 17, a firm should continue to spend on advertising as long as margins from each additional unit sold due to the advertising exceed the cost of that advertising. In contrast, trade promotions are generally proportional to the units sold. Thus, as a manager increases the trade promotion budget, unit margins decrease, and advertising becomes less profitable. Therefore, as trade promotion increases, advertising should decrease. On the other hand, increases in advertising tend to increase consumer demand for the product (even without trade promotion). In such a case, trade promotion leads to opportunity costs as this demand would have occurred at the regular price. So increases in advertising should be accompanied by decreases in trade promotion. Thus advertising and sales promotion are substitutes directly through their impact on sales and margins.

Indirect Trade-Off between Advertising and Trade Promotion
Advertising has a very important indirect effect on retailers, which leads to an indirect trade-off between advertising and trade promotion. Advertising creates a brand identity for a product. Consumers then begin to demand that product, and retailers begin to stock it. The better the quality and advertising of the product, the more consumers demand it and the greater the firm's returns from advertising. As advertising for such products increases, retailers begin to compete among themselves to promote the product. They may even sell these products as loss leaders to get consumers into stores. Thus, advertising could help to reduce the retail

price of high-quality products. Consumer demand for the product is transferred up through the distribution system, when retailers and wholesalers increase their demand for the product. As a result, advertisers profit because they can increase the sales or price of the product or decrease trade promotions. Thus, higher advertising can substitute for sales promotions. In contrast to the first trade-off, this one occurs indirectly, through the effect of advertising on retailers' behavior.

Direct Trade-Off between Advertising and Price Promotion Advertising has the potential to differentiate one brand from another. This effect is especially true of advertising based on emotional and endorsement appeals (see Chapters 7 and 8). It is also true of advertising based on informational appeals that communicate differences among brands (see Chapter 6). As such advertising makes brands appear less similar to each other, consumers become less price sensitive and more willing to pay a higher price for a brand. As a result, advertisers need to offer fewer price promotions. Price promotions are promotions such as coupons or rebates that involve some reduction in the net price of the brand(see Chapter 9). Thus increases in brand-differentiating advertising can be accompanied by decreases in price promotions.

However, some advertising decreases differences among brands. This effect is especially true of advertising that compares attributes or prices of brands. As brands appear more similar to each other, consumers are more motivated by differences in price. As a result they become more sensitive to or even expect price promotions. Thus comparative advertising increases pressure on the advertiser for price promotions.

Reinforcement among Promotion Variables

One of the important goals of manufacturers is to increase the pass-through of trade promotions to consumers. Two means by which they can do so are by stimulating double couponing and by offering cooperative advertising. Chapter 11 explains these two aspects of sales promotion. This section explains how manufacturers can use these two types of promotion to reinforce the effects of advertising, consumer promotions and trade promotions.

Advertising, Manufacturer Coupons and Trade Promotions *Double coupons* are offers by retailers to double the face value of a manufacturer coupon (see Chapter 10).

The retailer has to pay only the incremental cost of doubling the face value of the coupon, while the manufacturer reimburses the retailer for the initial face value of the coupon and the processing cost. The manufacturer also pays the distribution costs as it does for regular coupons. Double coupons have benefits for retailers, consumers and manufacturers.

Consumers benefit from double coupons for the simple reason that they offer twice the savings that would normally accrue from coupons. Retailers benefit from double coupons for two reasons. First, because of the higher savings and higher visibility and excitement they generate, double coupons create a higher sales response relative to retail coupons of the same face value. Second, because they take the form of coupons, double coupons have a higher price discrimination effect relative to price-cuts of the same total value. Manufacturers benefit from double coupons in two ways. First, they stimulate higher sales than would normally occur from coupons. Second, retailers may use some of the trade promotions they receive to pay for double coupons, thus increasing the pass-through.

Thus it is in the interest of manufacturers to encourage double coupons. They can do so by simultaneously scheduling advertising, coupons, and certain forms of trade promotion. The availability of coupons provides an opportunity for retailers to offer double coupons. Advertising increases the visibility of the brand, stimulating retailers to compete among themselves to promote it. Trade promotions such as trade deals or trade allowances enable retailers to pay for the cost of the double coupons. Thus simultaneously scheduling these three variables enhances the individual effectiveness of each.

Advertising and Trade Promotions *Cooperative advertising* is an offer by the manufacturer to pay some fraction of the retailer's advertising costs (see Chapter 11). Typically retailers advertise the availability and special promotion of a brand in newspaper or direct-mail ads. Manufacturers can gain a lot by offering some of the trade promotion in the form of cooperative advertising, instead of offering it entirely or partly in the form of trade deals, for several reasons.

First, advertising by the retailer gets added exposure for the manufacturer's brand. Thus the manufacturer's willingness to pay some of these costs is not only fair but will motivate the retailer to undertake more of such advertising. Second, retailers generally sell much more on a price-cut if they advertise the price-cut with a newspaper ad or store display (see Chapter 10). If the manufacturer pays for some of these costs with cooperative advertising, the retailer is more likely to advertise the product, which will benefit them both. Third, retail advertising draws consumers into stores, and prompts other retailers to increase their advertising. This process can trigger inter-retailer price competition and ensure that more of the manufacturer's trade deal is passed on to consumers. Fourth and most important, the increase in retail sales with an advertised discount is sometimes so much greater that a retailer can be better off passing on a trade deal with a retail ad than pocketing it. Thus a preferred promotional strategy for the manufacturer is to split its promotional support into a trade deal and cooperative advertising, rather than offering a trade deal alone. By the same logic, the manufacturer could also split its advertising budget into media advertising and cooperative advertising, rather than using all of it for media advertising.

INTEGRATING PROMOTION AND MARKETING FOR DEFENSE

Each year firms introduce thousands of new products. Most of these are minor variations of existing products, while some are radical innovations. How should incumbent firms react to these new entrants? Should incumbents "blast them off the face of the earth, or just hope they go away?"[25] In particular, how should incumbents integrate promotion with the other marketing variables to effectively defend their market position?

John Hauser, a professor of marketing at the Massachusetts Institute of Technology, and his associates developed a model that addresses this problem.[26] The model suggests precise allocation of the marketing budget for specific situations, as well as general strategies of defense. This section first explains the model and then presents some generic defense strategies.

The Defender Model

The **Defender Model** finds the optimal mix of key marketing variables for an incumbent brand to defend against a new entrant or the attack of a competitor. The marketing variables used are promotion, price, product design and distribution. The model combines perceptual maps used in marketing with indifference curves used in economics to identify the optimal mix of these variables. Like perceptual maps, the model can place specific brands and consumer segments on graphs defined by two or more dimensions (see Chapter 1). The dimensions are the most important attributes on which consumers evaluate brands. However, unlike perceptual maps but like indifference curves, the dimensions are represented as the benefit that consumers perceive in an attribute *per unit price* they pay to buy that attribute (Exhibit 18-14). Such scaling makes brands located farther from the origin of the graph more desirable to consumers. Thus the model can estimate a brand's theoretical market share given its price and perceived attributes, relative to a set of competing brands and a distribution of consumer preferences. The actual market share is further affected by the number of consumers who are aware of that brand and likely to evoke it when making a choice.

An important feature of the model is that it shows how the key marketing variables affect a brand's position and thus its market share:

- Promotion is considered in terms of advertising and salespromotion. Advertising itself is broken into two components: content and intensity. Ad content determines the image of the brand, and thus its position on various dimensions at equal distances from the origin. The brand's position in turn determines the range of segments the brand would attract. Ad intensity determines how many consumers are aware of the brand, and thus the actual share of market given the brand's position. Sales promotion affects the brand's price, because most sales promotions involve price promotions.
- As the denominator of a dimension, price affects a brand's distance from the origin. A brand with lower price or superior benefits than competitors on any one dimension would lie farther from the origin on that dimension. Thus it would attract more consumers interested in that dimension than would competing brands.
- Product design and quality affect the position of the brand, just as they do the content of advertising.

▼ **EXHIBIT 18-14.** Brand location from Defender Model analysis of the analgesic market.

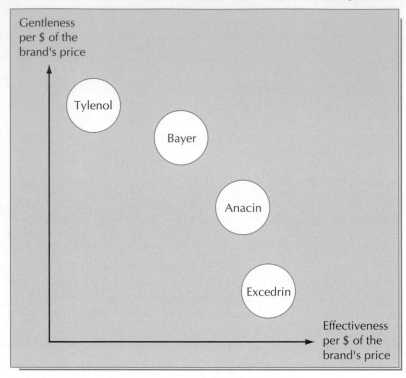

Source: Hauser, John (1986), "Theory and Application of Defensive Strategy," in *The Economics of Strategic Planning,* Lacy Glenn Thomas, ed. Lexington, MA: Lexington Books.

■ The model incorporates distribution only as availability. As such, it affects consumers' awareness just as much as ad intensity does.

Note that the model assumes fairly simple effects for the marketing variables so as to make the analysis manageable. If the model had to incorporate the entire range of effects associated with each marketing variable, the analysis would be too complex to carry out and interpret.

The key advantage of the Defender Model is that it captures a brand's market share as a function of its position, and the joint impact of key marketing variables. Managers can see how their brand's share changes as they change each of these variables, or as competitors change their marketing efforts. Given the costs per unit of sales, managers can determine the impact on profits of changing these variables. By simulating the impact of alternate strategies, the model can show the best marketing strategy in terms of profits. Thus the Defender Model is a powerful tool for developing optimal integrated marketing strategy.

An important purpose of the model is to determine the optimal defensive strategy for an incumbent faced with new entry or aggressive moves of competitors. To do so, a firm would have to carry out the research necessary to identify the dimensions, place competing brands and consumers on those dimensions, and estimate how marketing variables affect its position on those dimensions. The model can then present that data in a way that suggests the brand's optimal strategy. However, for firms that do not have the time or resources to carry out such detailed research, the model also suggests principles of defense in varying situations.

For example, what should AT&T do when MCI attacks its position by claiming to be lower priced (see Chapter 6)? One common response of incumbent firms to an attack is to ignore it. Another reaction of an incumbent to an attack, especially by a well-known rival, is to hit back. The former response may be an underreaction, while the latter may be an overreaction. The Defender Model suggests more rational defenses, which we summarize as three generic strategies: deflection, tit-for-tat, and counterattack.[27]

Deflection

Deflection is a defense strategy in which the incumbent moves away from an attack in the direction of its strengths. In particular, the incumbent needs to redesign the product to emphasize its strengths. The advertising should not refute the attack but emphasize these strengths. Such a defense is possible only if the attack occurs under the following conditions: the market is segmented, the attack is against the incumbent's weakness and appeals to a different segment than the incumbent does, and the segment sizes are stable. When these conditions are met, an incumbent can safely deflect an attack away from its weakness and toward its strengths.

This scenario probably reflects the situation that AT&T faced when MCI first entered the market. MCI attacked AT&T's position by claiming to be lower priced. At that time demand was relatively stable, but the market probably had at least two segments: one put more weight on service quality or was content with the status quo; the other was receptive to appeals based on price. AT&T had a well-entrenched position and was well known for its high-quality products and service. However, it also had a huge bureaucracy with the disadvantage of higher costs from years of being a monopoly. MCI was a new entrant with lower service, costs and prices. MCI wisely attacked AT&T's greatest weakness—high cost and prices. In this scenario the best strategy for AT&T was deflection. It should neither have lowered its price, nor disputed the issue by suggesting how small the price difference really was. Its best response was to move in the direction of its strength, stressing its long record of superior service. There are several reasons for such a recommendation.

First, AT&T had a large segment of loyal consumers. It would be futile for AT&T to compete with MCI for a small segment of price-conscious consumers, whom it may not entirely win over anyway. Moreover, AT&T would suffer opportunity losses to the extent that AT&T's loyal consumers would gain from any price-cut to the price-sensitive segment. Second, comparative advertising that disputed the price issue would increase all consumers' awareness of the comparability of the two service providers and sensitivity to price. Third, advertising comparing AT&T's and MCI's prices would enhance the visibility and prestige of the latter and give its claim further credibility.

In general, a deflection strategy requires the following integrated mix of marketing variables:

- The incumbent should reposition its brand to better meet the needs of its primary segment.
- The incumbent's ads should stress the strengths of the brand relative to the attack. If possible, the incumbent should consider redesigning the product along its strengths.
- The incumbent's ad appeals should use endorsements or emotion rather than arguments. If they use arguments, the ads should adopt supportive or framing arguments that emphasize the strengths of the incumbent, without mentioning

the attack. They should avoid any type of comparison with or refutation of the attack.
- The incumbent should consider curtailing advertising intensity and distribution coverage. Since the attack is likely to take away one or more consumer segments among which the incumbent is weaker than the attacker, the incumbent should cut advertising and distribution expenses that serve those segments. It can then refocus its efforts on its core segment.
- The incumbent could raise its price to its core segment, especially if its former price was low to appeal to multiple segments.

Tit-for-Tat

Tit-for-tat is a strategy in which the incumbent matches or betters the attacker's offer. So if an attacker enters with a lower price, the incumbent matches the price, or further lowers its own price. If the attacker enters with superior quality, the incumbent matches or betters that quality. Tit-for-tat is an aggressive strategy that can lead to an escalating price or advertising war between incumbent and attacker. A price war can lead to deteriorating profits for both attacker and incumbent. An advertising war can lead to a deteriorating image for both brands, especially if the advertising involves claims and counterclaims. Thus, incumbents should not resort to such a strategy unless they have a clear advantage in costs or resources, or they hope to discipline the attack. In particular, this strategy is relevant if the attack is head on, claims to offer the same or better benefits than the incumbent, and either the market is unsegmented, or both brands appeal to the same segment.

The authors of the Defender Model analyze the case of Tylenol and Datril, as a classic example of a successful tit-for-tat strategy. At the time, Johnson & Johnson's Tylenol had a reasonable share of the market for analgesics (pain relievers). Tylenol was formulated with acetaminophen, a pain reliever that did not irritate the stomach as did aspirin. Thus Tylenol was positioned as a more soothing alternative to aspirin-based products such as Bayer aspirin and Anacin. Then Bristol-Myers introduced Datril, another acetaminophen product, as "just as good as Tylenol, only cheaper." With that positioning, Datril had the potential to steal a big slice of Tylenol's market share. Perhaps the only good response for Johnson & Johnson was tit-for-tat. The company matched Datril's price, persuaded the television networks to discontinue Datril's advertising (which was no longer true) mobilized its sales force to combat Datril's attack, and began heavy advertising to reinforce Tylenol's superiority. As a result, Tylenol stopped Datril's attack.

Another example of tit-for-tat is AT&T's response to the growth of MCI in the 1990s. In the last decade, MCI grew its share of the long-distance telephone service market with cleverly packaged programs that promised big savings in telephone bills. Consumers became increasingly price conscious and MCI's market share steadily increased. AT&T could no longer ignore MCI, when by mid-1993 MCI's share had grown to 20 percent, Sprint's share to 11 percent and AT&T's had dropped to 60 percent. So in August 1993, AT&T launched a massive advertising campaign tied to the word "true." It challenged MCI's claims to lower price programs, pointing out hidden costs in MCI's offer, and refuting MCI's claims (see Chapter 6). At the same time, AT&T offered customers its own premiums, frequent flyer miles and long-distance credits tied to the theme "True Rewards." AT&T also spent over $400 million on advertising, twice as much as MCI. The competing programs confused some consumers and the war of words irritated others. However, the campaign tarnished the luster of MCI's plans and ultimately stopped the firm's growth in market share.[28]

A consistent tit-for-tat defense requires the following integrated strategy:

- The incumbent should position its brand to be superior to the attacker's.
- The incumbent should lower its price to be even with or below the attacker's price.
- The incumbent's ad should use argument, preferably a comparative, inoculative or framing argument. The ads should provide clear and strong evidence showing the comparative superiority of the incumbent on the *same* dimensions.
- If possible, the incumbent should redesign the product to emphasize its superiority on the *same* dimensions as the attack.
- In the short run, the incumbent should consider using advertising intensity and distribution coverage to completely block the attacker's entry and drown out its appeals. If the attacker persists in the long run, the incumbent may have to trim advertising and distribution expenditures to conserve resources.

A tit-for-tat strategy is expensive, risky, and certain to reduce profits. If the attack persists, the incumbent will have to be resigned to lower market share and profits, despite increasing marketing expenditures.

Counterattack

Counterattack is a defensive strategy in which an incumbent responds aggressively to an attack by positioning a new brand near the attack, while moving its existing brand away from the attack. With the advantage of two brands, the incumbent adopts a tit-for-tat strategy for the new brand, and a deflection strategy for the existing brand. When does a counterattack make sense? A counterattack is relevant when the attack is along dimensions on which the incumbent is weak and appeals to another segment that is growing at the cost of the incumbent's primary segment. Because the incumbent is already well positioned toward one segment, it should move its existing brand to fully exploit its strengths as in a deflection strategy. However, since the attack identifies a segment with high potential, the incumbent must address its previous oversight. It could do so most effectively by introducing a new brand that differs as much as possible from its existing brand, but resembles the attacking brand closely. Such a counterattack is expensive in the short run but the incumbent's best response for the long run.

The Defender Model provides a good framework for analyzing the strategy of Coke vis-à-vis that of Pepsi. Pepsi attacked Coke first, with the "Pepsi Challenge," that in blind taste tests more people preferred Pepsi to Coke. That attack led to a steady increase in Pepsi's market share through the 1970s. Given Coke's strength as the original cola flavor and its strong loyalty among a core group of consumers, it could then have used a deflection strategy: ignore that attack, not challenge the claims, and reinforce its strength—"the real thing," the traditional flavor. Coke's response may have followed that strategy at least some of the time. There was loss of market share, but alternative strategies would have been costly. Indeed, Coke also used comparative advertising and increased advertising and sales promotion in those years, without clear benefits.

However, in the 1980s Pepsi gained market share by stressing its theme of youthfulness that appealed to the younger generation (see Chapter 17). In particular, its formula was sweeter than Coke's and preferred by youth. Moreover, the segment of young drinkers who like a sweeter formula was growing, while that of older consumers who preferred the older formula was shrinking. Coke's own research indicated as much. What should Coke have done?

As the earlier discussion suggests, the best strategy in such a situation is to counterattack: reposition the original Coke as the traditional drink, preferred by experienced drinkers. Introduce a sweeter formula, perhaps with a different name, to attack Pepsi's position more directly. The ideal plan would have been to have the two Coke brands positioned far from each other, while the new brand was positioned close to Pepsi. That way Coke could have protected its position among loyal drinkers, while attacking Pepsi's segment with a comparable drink.

Instead, Coke never seemed to have analyzed the situation correctly, and made repeated errors. Dropping the old formula, which had a strong franchise, was a mistake. Branding the new formula with the name "Coke" was also a mistake, as it cannibalized sales of the old formula. Carrying two brands with similar names was a mistake, as it increased costs, confused consumers and did not attack Pepsi strongly enough. Some people assumed that Coke intentionally adopted the strategy to gain press coverage for its brands. However, numerous analysts with inside information confirmed that the company never had a goal of gaining press coverage, and the net cost to the company of its 1980s strategy exceeded its benefits. Coke began to recover from its mistakes only when it devised a radically new advertising campaign with creative themes and novel images (see Chapter 3).

This example shows how the generic strategies of defense can be used fruitfully to develop insightful responses to various attacks.

Summary

Integrating advertising with sales promotion and other marketing efforts is vitally important to exploit the interdependencies among these variables, enhance their effectiveness and conserve scarce resources. Such integration is especially important over stages of the life cycle and to defend against attacks by competitors.

The total promotional budget for any one product should generally decrease over successive stages of its life cycle. Within the budget, managers should allocate more resources to informational promotions in the early stage of the life cycle, and to incentives in the latter stages. For new products, a strategy of price skimming is preferable to one of penetration pricing.

Given a portfolio of products, a firm should budget more for new or growing products, and less for mature or declining products. Within any product's budget, a firm should allocate more of the budget for newer products to advertising, and more of the budget for older products to sales promotion. When determining price, a firm should set a new product's price high enough so that its margin is higher than that of the product whose sales it is likely to cannibalize.

The faster a new product takes off, the more a firm should budget to promote it. A firm should spend more on advertising for products that are expected to take off rapidly, and more on sales promotions, especially sampling, for products that are likely to take off slowly.

Advertising and sales promotion have three important trade-offs for any product within any stage of its life cycle: a direct trade-off between advertising and trade promotion, an indirect trade-off between advertising and trade promotion and a direct trade-off between advertising and price promotion. Advertising directly substitutes for trade promotions because advertising involves fixed expenses that are independent of unit sales, while trade promotions involve unit expenses that reduce the margin for the brand. Advertising indirectly substitutes for trade promotions, because it encourages retailers to compete among themselves in promoting the brand to consumers, increasing sales even with fewer trade promotions. Advertising directly substitutes for price promotions when it increases brand differentiation and reduces consumers' need for price promotions.

Advertising has some important reinforcement effects on some promotions. When advertising is accompanied by coupons and trade promotions, competition among retailers pressures them to pass through more of the trade promotion to consumers as double coupons. Similarly, when cooperative advertising accompanies trade promotions, it prompts them to pass through more of the trade promotions, because consumers respond more strongly to retail promotions accompanied by advertising.

The Defender Model is an analytical framework that suggests precise allocation of the marketing budget to defend against attacks in specific situations. The key advantage of the model is that it captures a brand's market share and profit as a function of its position in reference to rival brands, and the joint impact of key marketing variables. The Defender Model also suggests three generic defensive strategies: deflection, tit-for-tat and counterattack. The use of these strategies depends on market segmentation, market growth and the direction of the attack relative to the defender's position.

Questions

1. Why do products go through life cycles? Explain fully.
2. How should firms budget promotion through various stages of the life cycle?
3. Why does Gillette regularly introduce new products even at the cost of cannibalizing its own products?
4. Why are consumers loyal to Gillette if the firm regularly introduces new products with different brand names?
5. Is Gillette's pattern of promotion expenditures for its succession of new products good strategy or mere accident? Explain.
6. How does the speed of takeoff affect the planning of promotion?
7. Explain the trade-off between advertising and sales promotion within any stage of the product life cycle.
8. How should incumbents deal with new entrants? Should incumbents "blast them off the face of the earth, or just hope they go away?"
9. How should incumbents integrate promotion with the other marketing variables to design an effective defense of their marketing position?
10. How did AT&T respond to the various moves of MCI over years? Was it good or bad strategy?
11. Explain the differences between a strategy of deflection and one of tit-for-tat. When should each be used?
12. What is a counterattack? When does it make sense?
13. Why did Coke discontinue its original formula and introduce New Coke in 1985? Why did it subsequently reintroduce its original formula? What should it have done?

Notes

1. Tellis, Gerard J., and Golder, Peter N. (1996), "First to Market, First to Fail? The Real Causes of Enduring Market Leadership," *Sloan Management Review* 37, 2, 65–75; Kummel, Charles M., and Jay E. Klompmaker (1982), "The Gillette Company," Case written when the authors were at the University of North Carolina; Chakravarty, Subrata N. (1991), "We Had To Change the Playing Field," *Forbes,* February 4, 82–86.
2. Tellis, Gerard J., and C. Merle Crawford (1981), "An Evolutionary Theory of Product Life Cycle," *Journal of Marketing* 45 (Fall), 125–132.
3. Hwang, Suein L. (1993), "Yogurt Makers' Stress On Health and Science Bears Fruit," *The Wall Street Journal,* October 7, B8.
4. Green-Armytage, Johnson (1995), "Edsel 95?" *Computer Weekly,* September 14, 38.
5. Tellis and Crawford, "An Evolutionary Theory of Product Life Cycle."
6. Tellis, Gerard J. (1988), "The Price Sensitivity of Competitive Demand: A Meta-Analysis of Sales Response Models," *Journal of Marketing Research* 15, 3 (November), 331–341.
7. *Economies of scale* refers to reduction in costs per unit as a firm produces in large quantities to meet higher demand. These economies are due to the fact that all costs of equipment do not have to increase proportionally as the quantity produced increases.
8. *Economies of experience* refers to decreases in costs per unit as the firm accumulates experience in producing the product over time. The decreases in costs are due to knowledge that managers and employees gain to produce the product more efficiently. The reduction can be substantial in the first few years of a new product.
9. Tellis, Gerard J. (1986), "Beyond the Many Faces of Price: An Integration of Pricing Strategies, *Journal of Marketing* 50 (October), 146–160.
10. Foster, Richard (1986), *Innovation: The Attacker's Advantage,* New York: Summit Books.
11. Based on Utterback, James M. (1994), *Mastering the Dynamics of Innovation,* Cambridge, MA: Harvard Business School Press.
12. Foster, *Innovation.*
13. Chandy, Rajesh (1996), "Organizing for Radical Product Innovation," Unpublished dissertation, University of Southern California.
14. Tellis and Golder, "First to Market, First to Fail?"

15. Nault, Barrie R., and Mark B. Vandenbosch (1995), "Protection Through Preemption," working paper, Graduate School of Management, University of California; Deutschman, A. (1994), "The Managing Wisdom of High-Tech Superstars," *Fortune,* October 17, 197–206.

16. For example, see Wind, Yoram, and Vijay Mahajan (1981), "Designing Product and Business Portfolios," *Harvard Business Review* 59 (January-February), 155–165.

17. Sethuraman, Raj, and Gerard J. Tellis (1991), "An Analysis of the Tradeoff Between Advertising and Price Discounting," *Journal of Marketing Research,* 28 (May), 160–174.

18. Golder, Peter N., and Gerard J. Tellis (1996), "When Will It Fly? Modeling The Growth of New Consumer Durables," Working Paper, Stern School of Business, New York University.

19. *Ibid.*

20. Shapiro, Eben (1992), "Edging Into Madonna's Limelight," *New York Times,* October 19, D6.

21. Bauer, Barbara, and Robert F. Moss (1985), "Feeling Rejected? Join Updike, Mailer, Oates . . . ," *New York Times,* July 21, 7, 1.

22. Slung, Michele (1982), "Book World; Book Report," *The Washington Post,* April 11, 1982; Coleman, Terry (1995), "Living To Tell The Tale," *The Guardian,* February 15, T2.

23. Quote by Tom Scherak as reported by Tellis, Gerard J. (1996), "Marketing *Last of the Mohicans:* A Case Study," University of Southern California, Los Angeles.

24. Eliashberg, Jehoshua (1996), "Research Opportunities in Movie Marketing," talk presented at University of Southern California, May 21, 1996.

25. Hauser, John (1986), "Theory and Application of Defensive Strategy," in *The Economics of Strategic Planning,* Lacy Glenn Thomas, ed. Lexington, MA: Lexington Books.

26. *Ibid.*

27. These names and strategies are proposed by the author and do not appear in the papers that describe the Defender Model. The strategy of "tit-for-tat" was originally proposed by Anatol Rappaport as a means by which one player in a two-player prisoner's dilemma could discipline the other player to cooperate. The author has extended the use of the strategy to the current context, without asserting that it necessarily is the same as the one proposed by Rappaport.

28. Fitzgerald, Kate (1995), "How AT&T Finally Found Its True Calling," *Advertising Age,* January 30, 3, 6; Fitzgerald, Kate (1995), "AT&T's 'True'-ly Effective Campaign," *Advertising Age,* January 2, 10.

Glossary

Ability, competence of an individual to engage in the mental effort to evaluate an argument-based message.

Accessibility, ability to obtain information on difficult-to-observe issues.

Account review, a full-scale evaluation of a current agency, against the record or proposals of prospective new agencies that are interested in serving an account.

Accounts, an agency's clients who advertise.

Accounts management, the solicitation and servicing of an agency's accounts.

Accounts-based organization, an organization form in which an agency's staff is organized in teams, each of which serves one account.

Accumulated reach, see Reach.

Accumulation, see Reach.

Active meter, an electronic device worn by panelists or embedded under their skin to record when and what they watch on TV.

Active processing, state in which consumers think about information they receive, although they do not make an effort to get this information on their own.

Ad campaign, a series of ads linked by a single theme.

Ad-intensity, advertising level.

Ad-weight, advertising level.

Adaptation-level theory, explanation of how individuals perceive and react to patterns of stimuli. The central premise is that individuals adapt to the stimuli they have experienced in the past to form certain standards of comparison or *adaptation levels.*

Advertising, communicating a firm's offer to customers by paid media time or space.

Advertising agency, an organization that solicits clients, creates ads, or places ads in the media.

Advertising decay, see Delayed effect of advertising.

Advertising effectiveness, the possibility of a positive effect of advertising.

Advertising level, amount of advertising in terms of number of exposures, gross rating points or dollars spent.

Advertorial, 1. a print ad that appears like an article or an editorial; 2. long print ad in a magazine or newspaper that resembles an editorial or regular feature article and provides detailed information about the attributes, use, or purchase of a product.

Affective, dealing with emotions.

Affiliates, stations that contract with a network to broadcast the network's programs.

Affirmative disclosure, provision of new, clear and conspicuous information by an advertiser to compensate for a past deceptive promotion.

Affordability method, a method of budget setting in which a firm spends as much on advertising as it can afford.

Agency brand, an independent or merged agency that is primarily involved in agency work and not in owning subsidiary agencies.

AIDA, an acronym for the four variables involved in an early learning hierarchy:

Attention → Interest → Desire → Action

Aided recall, subject's recall with some help.

Analysis, stage of individual's perception in which he or she compares external stimuli with images stored in memory to identify patterns.

Arbitrage, action of agents who buy a product at a lower price intended for price-sensitive consumers, and sell to consumers who would have bought the product at a higher price.

Argument strategy, forms of reasoning a communicator uses to persuade consumers.

Art direction, the development of visuals and sound for ads, which may be print, audio or video.

Art director, an individual within an agency who is responsible for the design of ads.

Association, linking of one piece of information with another stimuli or piece of information.

Associative mode, arousal of emotions with stimuli that are only tangentially related to the product.

Associative thinking, a process of thinking in which an individual puts together unrelated ideas.

Asymmetry in response, opposite but unequal reactions of consumers to positive and negative stimuli.

Attention, act of focusing one's senses to receive external messages or stimuli.

Attitude, underlying predisposition to act.

Attribution theory, a theory that posits that consumers develop reasons for their observed behavior after observing it, even though such reasons may not have motivated the behavior.

Audience, the total set of individuals reached by a vehicle.

Audiometers, a device that is hooked to a radio to record when and to which channel it is tuned.

Average frequency, the frequency with which an individual is exposed to a vehicle or ad schedule *on average* in a particular time period.

Avoidance, state in which consumers consciously avoid ads.

Bait and switch, a promotional strategy by which a retailer draws customers into a store with an unusually low discount price on an item, then encourages them to buy a substitute item at a higher price, either through personal selling pressure or by not stocking the discounted item.

Baseline, estimated sales in the absence of a promotion.

Behavioral research, field of study covering consumer behavior, managerial decision making and social psychology.

Benefit segmentation, segmentation on the basis of the unique benefits that consumers seek in a product.

Bias, an error with a known direction but of unknown magnitude.

Bill-back, a manufacturer's discount off the list price that a retailer may claim based on the number of units the retailer sells to consumers on the discount.

Bonus plans, programs in which a buyer can accumulate points towards free purchases of the same or other products.

Brain-wave recordings, electrical recordings of electromagnetic activity in the brain.

Brand choice, consumer's selection of a brand, which can be decomposed into trial, repurchase, or switching.

Brand switching, consumer's purchase of a different brand from one he or she regularly buys.

Broadcast media, media that relay a message from a single source to the audience, which must process it while it is relayed.

Buildup, see Wearin.

Bursting, see Flighting.

Buyer, an individual or organization who may potentially buy products from a firm.

Cable data, records with a TV meter of a household's exposures to TV advertising.

Carryover effect of advertising, see Delayed effect of advertising.

Casting, the selection of individuals for characters in an ad.

Categorization, mental process of organizing information in chunks.

Cease-and-desist order, an order by a federal agency that requires a firm to stop a promotion that the agency found to be deceptive.

Celebrities, individuals or characters who are known to a large portion of the general population because of the publicity associated with their lives.

Centers, large areas of a store dedicated to displaying one or more products.

Central route of persuasion, one of the paths of the elaboration likelihood model, by which an individual responds to a message based on his or her evaluation of its pros and cons.

Cents-off, price pack.

Channel, path through a distribution system.

Channel conflict, friction, mistrust and open conflict among members of a distribution system.

Character, human role in a drama.

Characterization, the portrayal of characters in an ad.

Checkout scanner, device that a store uses to record items sold; it reads a laser beam that bounces off the item's universal product code.

Chunk, integrated mental unit of stored information.

Circulation, the number of copies of one issue of a newspaper or magazine distributed to the population.

Classical conditioning, relatively enduring change in behavior that results from perceived associations among two stimuli.

Clutter, a proliferation of ads that compete for an audience's attention within a particular time period or printed space.

Cognition, individual's process of thinking.

Cognitive consistency, individual's desire for consistency between incoming information and prior beliefs, preferences, and behavior.

Cognitive involvement, involvement characterized by thinking.

Cognitive, relating to thought processes.

Cognitive learning, change in opinion, attitude or behavior caused by exposure to information.

Commission, a compensation method in which an advertiser pays an agency a fixed percentage of the media bill for its services.

Communication, persuasion, or transfer of information between two parties.

Comparative advertising, advertising that compares a brand to some competitive standard.

Comparative argument, message comparing the target brand to some competitive standard.

Competitive parity method, a special type of percentage of sales method in which the percentag of sales chosen for advertising is the same as that used by competitors in the industry.

Complex argument, argument that uses several reasons or pieces of evidence, some in favor of and others against the advocated position.

Complex message, message that is sufficiently difficult, rich or ambiguous that the receiver cannot absorb all the information it includes in a single exposure.

Compressed ad, shorter ad that drops a portion of a longer ad.

Conative, relating to consumer's mental activity that is proximate to behavior.

Condition, a state of an experiment in which subjects are exposed to one or more treatments.

Conditioned response, response elicited by a conditioned stimulus due to its association with the unconditioned stimulus.

Conditioned stimulus, stimulus that does not initially elicit the desired (unconditioned) response.

Consideration, something of value.

Consumer, individual or organization who may potentially buy products from firms.

Consumer orientation, an attitude of setting consumer satisfaction as a firm's primary goal.

Consumer promotion, promotion that a manufacturer offers a consumer directly.

Consumer shows, conventions open to the general public.

Content, 1. the nature and form of a message that is communicated through an ad; 2. the nonadvertising material carried by vehicles.

Contests, games or a combination of games and sweepstakes in which winners are at least partly determined by rules.

Contextual stimuli, stimuli that form the background to the focal stimuli.

Continuity, see Even scheduling.

Contribution margin, the difference between the price at which a unit is sold to consumers and the variable cost of producing that unit.

Control group, an independent sample comparable in every way to an experimental sample, except that it is not subjected to the treatment.

Convenience, ease with which information can be obtained from respondents.

Conventions, periodic (generally annual) meetings at which members of an association exchange views, plan events or examine new products.

Cooperative advertising, an offer by the manufacturer to pay some fraction of a retailer's advertising.

Copy, main verbal component of an ad.

Copywriting, development of the verbal component of ads, whether spoken or written.

Corrective advertising, advertising meant to correct any untruthful information or impressions that consumers may have gotten from some prior deceptive promotion.

Cost basis, a compensation method by which an agency charges a client an amount that covers its cost plus an agreed-upon profit which may be related to the margin an advertiser earns on an advertised brand.

Cost efficiency, coverage of a vehicle that can be bought with a fixed amount of money.

Cost per rating point (CPP), cost of a program's time slot divided by the program's rating during the time slot.

Cost per thousand (CPM), cost of space in a magazine or newspaper divided by its circulation measured in thousands.

Count-recount, a discount off the list price that a manufacturer computes and pays a retailer, for units the retailer sells to consumers at the discount.

Counterarguments, reasons against a premise.

Counterattack, a defensive strategy in which an incumbent responds aggressively to an attack by positioning a new brand near the attack, while moving its existing brand away from the attack.

Coupon drop, commencement of coupon distribution.

Coupon redemption, a consumer's claiming of the cash value of a coupon at the time of purchase.

Covariation, similar variation between two variables.

Coverage, proportion of a population exposed to a medium; for a magazine, percentage of households exposed to a copy; for a newspaper, percentage of households in a geographic area that receives a copy; for outdoor media, percentage of the population in a region that passes that billboard; for the broadcast media, percentage of all households with a TV (or radio) that can receive a TV (or radio) broadcast.

CPM, see Cost per thousand.

CPP, see Cost per rating point.

Creative boutiques, small agencies that specialize in developing the creative for ads.

Creative, 1. unique design of an ad; 2. productive divergence.

Creatives, people responsible for the function of designing an ad's creative.

Creativity, productive divergence.

Credibility, the expertise and trustworthiness of the source of a message.

Cross-ruff coupons, on- or in-pack coupons that may be used only for the purchase of another product.

Cume reach, see Reach.

Cumulative audience, see Reach.

Customer, individual or organization who may potentially buy products from firms.

Day-after recall, measure of the proportion of a sample of the audience for an ad that can correctly recall it one day after viewing it.

Dealers, wholesalers, distributors or retailers that are the target of trade promotions.

Deceptive, a material, unsubstantiated claim that misleads a significant segment of a population.

Decline, a stage of the product life cycle when sales decrease either slowly or rapidly until the product ultimately dies out.

Decomposing a promotional bump, breaking up a sales increase from a promotion into its components.

Defender Model, an analytical framework that finds the optimal mix of key marketing variables for an incumbent brand to defend against a competitor's attack.

Defense reaction, state of mind in which an individual ignores or denies a piece of evidence or a message in order to protect himself or herself from the pain of the implications.

Deflection, a defense strategy in which the incumbent moves away from an attack and in the direction of its own strengths.

Delay purchases, retailer's postponement of purchases just prior to a deal, to run down their inventories, and restock them at the lower deal price.

Delayed effect of advertising, sales resulting from a single ad or advertising campaign *after the advertising stops*.

Demand artifact, demand bias.

Demand bias, tendency of respondents to guess the hypothesis of the researcher and adjust answers to please the researcher.

Demographic segmentation, segmentation on the basis of demographics such as gender, age, education, income, or race.

Dependent variable, effect of an independent variable that is being researched.

Design, plan of a research study.

Designers, see Creatives.

Diary, a periodic record of an individual's activity.

Direct costs, costs that change with each additional contact made through direct media.

Direct marketing, promoting a product and completing a sale through direct media.

Direct media, media that involve individual or personal communication with members of the audience.

Direct-mail coupons, coupons mailed directly to households based on general or specific mailing lists.

Disaggregate data, data recorded at the smallest reasonable level such as by brand, store or week.

Disguise, a task given to subjects who are recruited for a research study, so as not to alert them to the hypotheses.

Displays, in-store arrangements that give greater visibility to a brand relative to competing brands

Dissonance theory, a theory that posits that consumers adjust their thoughts and feelings to be consistent with their behavior.

Dissonance/attribution hierarchy, a model of consumer decision making that can be explained either by dissonance theory or attribution theory.

Distributors, wholesalers, retailers and other agents who undertake the physical transfer of goods from firms to consumers.

Divergent thinking, a process of thinking in which thoughts flow in all directions from one starting point, even if the path seems illogical.

Diverting, dealer's buying a product in a region with a deal, to sell in another region without a deal.

Dominant brand, brand that has a large market share and strong loyalty.

Double coupons, offers by retailers to double the face value of a manufacturer coupon.

Dual entitlements, principle about perception of fairness in pricing, by which consumers are assumed to think that sellers are entitled to ongoing profits while consumers are entitled to ongoing prices.

Duplicated audience, fraction of households exposed to a vehicle more than once in a given time period.

Dynamic effects of advertising, changes in advertising response over time.

Economies of information, decline in a firm's cost of disseminating information to each consumer as the number of its consumers increases.

Effect of advertising, a change that advertising causes on the mental or physical state or activity of the recipient of an ad.

Effective frequency, optimal number of exposures of an ad in a particular time period.

Efficient consumer response, a management system that tries to eliminate inefficiencies in the distribution and promotion of goods.

Efficient product introduction, new product introductions in which manufacturers coordinate with retailers the introduction of products consumers want and that are likely to succeed.

Efficient product replenishment, quick and timely movement of goods from manufacturers through distributors to retailers.

Efficient promotion, a program that eliminates forward buying and diverting, by applying a manufacturer's discount only to goods that a retailer sells to consumers on discount.

Efficient store assortment, efficient stocking, storage and withdrawal of goods to eliminate waste, speed transactions and give more space to fast-moving or high-margin products.

Elaboration, process by which an individual evaluates or reasons about a message.

Elaboration likelihood model (ELM), theory that predicts the probability (likelihood) that individuals will be persuaded by a message by reasoning about (elaborating on) the message.

Electronic displays, displays using one or more new media, such as a TV monitor, video player, or computer.

Electronic distribution, system of distributing coupons to consumers based on an electronic gadget.

Electronic processing, system of processing coupons from consumers based on an electronic gadget.

Emotion, state of arousal indicated by specific types and levels of biochemical activity in the brain and the body.

Emotional involvement, involvement characterized by feeling.

End-of-aisle displays, displays located at end of a store's aisles.

Endorsement, any advertising message, that consumers are likely to believe, reflects the opinions, beliefs, findings or experience of a party other than the sponsoring advertiser.

Endorsement process, the identification, selection and use of endorsers to communicate with a target segment.

Endorser, a person, character or organization that speaks or appears in an ad in support of the advertiser or its claim.

Ennobling emotions, emotions that inspire audiences to difficult action with feelings such as pride, courage or dedication.

Even scheduling, a constant level of advertising through the planning horizon; also called *continuity.*

Everyday-low price, strategy by which a firm routinely sells a product at a price generally as low as the discounted price offered by other firms.

Evocative power, ability of a medium to communicate emotion.

Evoke, spontaneously bring to mind.

Exchange, the give-and-take among individuals about a problem and its solutions.

Exclusive audience, fraction of households exposed to a vehicle only once in a given time period.

Execution, the specific form of communication that an ad adopts.

Exhibits, displays that manufacturers set up at conventions to show their products.

Expected cost of a return, probability of a return multiplied by the cost of a return.

Expected direct costs, the direct cost of contacting an individual *plus* the expected cost of a return should that individual buy a unit and return it.

Expected profit, the contribution margin from a unit sold to an individual multiplied by the probability of that sale.

Expected response rate, estimation of the proportion and type of consumer response expected relative to the total number of consumers to be contacted.

Experiment, a setup that manipulates one or more independent variables to observe their effect on a dependent variable of interest.

Expert, an individual or organization the target population perceives as having greater knowledge about the advertised product than the average consumer.

Expertise, the ability of the source to make valid claims, as perceived by the audience.

Explicit lie, a claim that unambiguously contradicts fact.

Explicit memory, retrieval of information to which an individual has been previously exposed along with the context in which exposure took place.

Explicit mode, arousal of emotions with stimuli together with direct statement or argument of the message.

External agency, an organization independent of an advertiser that carries out one or more of the major advertising functions: accounts management, creative, research, media planning.

External validity, ability of a study to replicate the natural environment.

Extinction, ultimate loss of a conditioned response due to the occurrence of either the conditioned or the unconditioned stimulus alone.

Eye camera, a device that records how the eye moves in response to a visual stimulus.

Face value, dollar amount clearly printed on the coupon, which a consumer can save by meeting certain purchase conditions.

Factor, a suspected cause of a particular phenomenon.

Fairness doctrine, a policy that required broadcasters to provide time for opposing views in ads or programs that took on a strong advocacy position.

Familiarity, the audience's knowledge of the source from prior exposures.

Fashion, an arbitrary design entirely dependent on consumer tastes, not on functions served.

Features, retail ads announcing a product's availability at a low price, or a temporary price-cut.

Federal regulation, laws of the federal government, rules of various federal agencies, and rulings of federal courts.

Feeling attributes, characteristics of products that are preference-, not reason-, based, on which two or more individuals could reasonably differ.

Field approach, research method in which a researcher analyzes relationships among variables based on naturally occurring data.

Field experiment, an experiment conducted in the field or natural setting.

Financial harm, loss of property or money.

Fixed costs, costs that do not change per unit of the item sold.

Fixed fee, a compensation method by which an advertiser negotiates with an agency a fixed payment for its services.

Flanking attack, argument that indirectly opposes a brand or premise by emphasizing dimensions on which it is weak.

Flexibility, ability to adapt to a respondent's needs.

Flighting, irregularly scheduling ads in bursts for short periods of time within the planning horizon, separated by long periods of time with no advertising.

Focal stimuli, key stimuli in the environment on which individuals focus.

Focus group, a sample of respondents who are led through a group discussion by a facilitator with an agenda of research issues to be addressed, but no complete set of questions.

Foot-meter, a device that lets a respondent move a lever with his or her foot to express response to an ad.

Forward buying, 1. retailers' purchases of future requirements in a current period to take advantage of a current trade deal; 2. consumer's purchase of an item earlier than planned.

Forward conditioning, process in which the conditioned stimulus precedes the unconditioned one.

Framing, the presentation of information in a context that provides it with new meaning.

Framing price increases, raising consumers' reference price so as to reduce the perceived loss from a price increase.

Freelancers, specialists who carry out design or production jobs for advertisers or their agencies, as demand arises, frequently working out of their homes.

Freestanding inserts (FSIs), separate advertising sections of a newspaper, typically the Sunday newspaper.

Frequency, 1. number and pattern of repetitions in a time period; 2. number of times a household is exposed to a vehicle in a given time period such as a month.

Front-of-store displays, displays located in the lobby space near the store's entrance.

Full-service agency, an agency that performs all of the major agency functions.

Functional organization, an organization in which an agency is divided into departments, each of which serves one of the core functions of an agency.

Gain, extent to which a consumer's reference price exceeds actual price.

Gang clipping operations, groups of people who fraudulently redeem coupons.

Generic brands, brands with no specific name and very simple packaging.

Geographic segmentation, segmentation on the basis of geographic location of consumers.

Goal, statement of a desired result.

Gross rating points (GRPs), sum of all ratings for all programs in an ad's schedule.

Gross up, a computation by which an advertising agency increases the media bill of its client by its commission rate.

Growth, a stage of the product life cycle following the introduction, when sales increase rapidly.

Habituation, increase in liking and decrease in uncertainty for a message due to repeated exposure.

Hand-meter, a device that lets a respondent move a lever with his or her hand to express response to an ad.

Hard thinking, exact, analytical, logical and focused thinking.

Hard-sell message, direct request for a behavior change accompanied with some pressure or urgency.

Head-on attack, argument that directly criticizes a brand or position.

Headline, first or most prominent printed line of an ad or statement of a video or audio ad.

Hierarchy of effects, models that describe the effects of advertising as intermediate stages in a chain of events ranging from a consumer's first exposure to an ad to his or her ultimate purchase of a brand.

High-low pricing strategy, maintaining a high regular price and intermittently offering price promotions.

Holding company, a firm that owns two or more autonomously run agencies.

Households using television, see Usage.

Humor, painless incongruity.

HUT, see Usage.

Hypertext link, special text on a page of Internet material, which when clicked with a mouse takes the user to a new page of information or a new site.

Hypothesis, an expected relationship between a dependent and independent variable.

Hysteresis, a particular form of advertising carryover, in which advertising propels sales to a higher level or plateau, at which they stay even after the campaign ends.

Ideal points, consumer preferences for specific combinations of product attributes.

Identification, a receiver's perception of himself or herself as similar to a source of a message because of the latter's attractiveness.

Immersion, a metaphor for the process of burying oneself in the data about a phenomenon.

Implicit memory, retrieval of information to which an individual has been previously exposed, but without retrieval of the context of exposure.

Implicit mode, arousal of emotions with stimuli that implicitly suggest the message.

Impressions, sum of all individuals or households exposed to an ad in a schedule.

In-aisle displays, displays located in a store's aisles.

In-pack coupons, coupons in a package that may be used only on subsequent purchases of the same product.

Incentive, practical motive to buy a brand, involving a cut in price or an increase in value.

Incremental consumption, a consumer's higher use of a product relative to the normal level.

Incremental profits, increase in profits due to incremental sales.

Incremental sales, increase in sales from the regular level due to a promotion.

Incubation, setting aside a problem to leave time for ideas to germinate.

Independent agency, an agency that provides full service but is not owned or has not merged with any other agency.

Independent variable, factor.

Index, a standardized measure of a variable.

Indirect approach, use of demographic segments as an intermediate step in media choice.

Indirect costs, costs of a campaign as a whole, which do not change by the number of contacts or the number of sales.

Individually addressable tap, a gadget that enables a central computer to send a cable TV signal directly to a specific household.

Inertia, lack of consumer response to stimuli.

Infomercial, long television ad that resembles a regular program and provides detailed information about the attributes, use, or purchase of a product.

Information processing, how the mind receives, deals with, and stores information.

Informative power, ability of a medium to communicate information.

Informed consumers, consumers who are fully informed about the value (price and benefits) of a product.

Injury, harm that consumers suffer from deceptive advertising.

Inoculative ad, argument that protects the current standing of a brand or position by alerting the audience about and helping it defend against an impending attack by a rival.

Input variables, independent variables of a system or process.

Inquiries, efforts by consumers to contact an advertiser.

Instantly redeemable coupons, coupons found on the package that may be used for the current purchase of the product.

Integrate losses, strategy of joining together several potential price increases so as to reduce perceived loss to consumers.

Integrated advertising and sales promotion strategy, blending of one promotional variable with one or more marketing or promotional variables to enhance the effect of each.

Intensity of emotions, range of emotions on a continuum going from positive to negative.

Interactive displays, displays involving various manipulatives for obtaining or providing information.

Interactive effect of two or more variables, change caused by those two variables on some third variable beyond what either of them causes individually.

Internal agency, a department or business unit within a firm that carries out the functions of an advertising agency.

Internal validity, ability of a study to test causality between dependent and independent variables.

Internalization, a mental process by which a receiver integrates a message with his or her belief system, because he or she finds the source of the ad sufficiently credible.

Internet, a worldwide network of computers through which individuals or institutions can communicate with each other.

Interview, a structured dialogue in which a researcher probes the responses or knowledge of the respondent through a set of open-ended questions.

Introduction, a stage of the product life cycle following its commercialization, when sales remain low or increase only slowly.

Just-in-time inventory, a system in which a manufacturer or retailer retains just enough inventory to meet current demand, through efficient communication with buyers or suppliers.

Laboratory experiment, an experiment conducted in an artificial environment.

Lay endorser, defined by the FTC to be an individual who appears in an ad, and is neither well known to the general public, nor considered by the latter to be an expert.

Leading question, question that prompts a specific answer.

Leakage, phenomenon in which consumers who would have bought a product at a higher price targeted to them, buy the product at a lower price intended for price-sensitive consumers.

Learning, relatively enduring change in behavior that results from experience.

Learning hierarchy, a model of consumer decision making in which a consumer buys a product only after learning about it, such as the AIDA model.

Learning theory, explanation for consumer behavior that posits that consumers learn from past actions.

Lifestyle segmentation, psychographic segmentation.

Likability, an audience's positive regard for the source because of his or her physical appearance and behavior.

Line ads, features (ads) that are just one or two lines.

Local advertising, advertising by local firms on local stations.

Local stations, a term used to describe radio or TV stations when contrasting them with the national networks.

Logical thinking, a process of thinking in which one reasons step by step to a conclusion that is indisputable.

Long-term memory, individual's ability to remember information for long periods of time after receiving it.

Long-term effect of advertising, see Delayed effect of advertising.

Loss, extent to which a price exceeds a consumer's reference price.

Loss leaders, brands that retailers sell below cost, to get shoppers into stores, whose other purchases may increase the retailers' sales and profits.

Loss of benefits, the act of buying a product with inferior quality or features.

Low-involvement hierarchy, a model of consumer decision making in which a consumer begins to like a product he or she heard about and tried.

Low-involvement processing, 1. passive processing; 2. state of message reception in which consumers notice ads but do not process or think about them extensively.

Lucky loyals, consumers who would be willing to pay a regular price for a product, but get a discounted price when they buy it.

Magazine coupons, coupons in the pages of periodicals.

Main effect of a variable, a change that that variable alone induces in some other variable.

Major ads, features (ads) that cover a half or full page.

Make-good time, free alternate time that media owners offer advertisers, if a program in which they advertise does not get the guaranteed audience.

Manufacturer, see Firm.

Manufacturer coupons, certificates from manufacturers, redeemable at a retail store, offering consumers some fixed saving off the retail price of the product if they meet some conditions.

Market outcome, a measure of a firm's performance in relationship to other firms in the market.

Market research, a process of obtaining information about a client, and its customers, competitors and environment to make good advertising decisions.

Market segmentation, a conceptual breakup of a market into groups of relatively homogeneous consumers, to better serve each of them.

Marketing, identifying needs of consumers, and designing, pricing, promoting, distributing and selling products to meet those needs.

Mass marketing, selling a standard, undifferentiated product to the whole market.

Mass media, media that involve communication with a large number of audience members impersonally, without much interaction.

Massing, scheduling of all ads within a short period within a planning horizon.

Matching-the-elasticity ratio, a budgeting method that adjusts the current advertising budget by the ratio of the advertising to price elasticities.

Material claim, relates to the purchase decision of a consumer.

Maturity, a stage of the product life cycle following growth, when sales are stable or flat.

Meaning transfer model, a theory of the effectiveness of endorsers that posits that a celebrity encodes a unique set of meanings that can, if the celebrity is well used, be transferred to the endorsed product.

Media buying, the purchase of time and space on various media to advertise.

Media choice, the selection of one or a combination of media for an ad campaign.

Media companies, organizations that own one or more media.

Media coupons, coupons sent through the media, typically print media.

Media mix, the combination of media selected for advertising.

Media owners, organizations that own one or more media.

Media plan, consists of a mix of time slots on and spaces in various media.

Media planning, choice of media and vehicle for and scheduling of the ad or ad campaign.

Media planning, the design of the media plan and the purchase of media time and space.

Media, a collective term for the channels, such as TV and magazines, through which advertisers or programmers communicate with individuals.

Medium-size ads, features (ads) that use a portion of a page.

Memory, individual's mental coding of information for future use.

Memory lapse, respondent's forgetting aspects of his or her past.

Mere exposure, repetition of stimuli that initially have no meaning.

Message repetition, repetition of stimuli that are immediately intelligible.

Message sidedness, whether a message contains a one-sided or two-sided appeal.

Misleading claim, suggests a meaning that contradicts fact, by omission or choice of words.

Mixed shows, conventions open to the trade or the public.

Mockup, a demonstration of a product benefit with artificial ingredients or unnatural props.

Mode, a presentation style in which endorsers in ads appear.

Model, 1. an endorser chosen primarily for his or her physical attractiveness or beauty; 2. a graphical depiction of a process; 3. a theory of a phenomenon.

Mood, transitory, generalized emotional state that is not directed at any particular object or activity.

Morals clause, a statement that gives an advertiser the right to terminate a contract with a potential endorser.

Motivation, willingness of an individual to evaluate a message.

Multicollinearity, a condition in which two or more independent variables change in the same way, so it is unclear which influences the dependent variable.

Multiple regression, a statistical procedure that attempts to determine the effect of two or more independent variables on a dependent variable.

Narrative, the presence of some spokesperson who describes or interprets the action.

National brand, a brand that has a national reputation and is owned by a manufacturer.

National spot advertising, advertising by national companies on local stations.

Negative option mail-order plans, practice by which marketers send merchandise to consumers at regular intervals unless the consumer explicitly indicates he or she does not want it.

Net coverage, reach across two or more media.

Network, a producer of programs that has contracted with a set of stations to broadcast those programs.

Network advertising, advertising during programs supplied by networks, generally aired at the same time to all affiliates in the network.

Niche marketing, a strategy in which a firm identifies and markets a unique product to a market niche.

Noise, 1. prevalence of errors of unknown size and direction; 2. high level of competing ads.

Non-price promotions, sales promotions not involving a price change.

Noncommercial character, image of an ad made to appear like part of a program.

Nonresponse probability, probability that an individual will not respond to the campaign.

Novelties, a class of products whose appeal depends on their newness.

Objective evidence, data about which two or more people would come to the same conclusion.

Objective-and-task method, method of budgeting that sets the promotion budget to achieve a certain goal.

Observation, collection of information by a researcher by noting the phenomenon and not asking any questions of subjects.

Off-invoice discounts, a direct reduction in the manufacturer's invoice or list price to retailers, per unit of the product.

On-air tests, Field experiments of an ongoing TV ad.

On-pack coupons, coupons on a package that may be used only on subsequent purchases of the same product.

One-sided appeal, argument that lists all pros about the advertised brand or position or all cons about the rival brand or position.

Opportunity cost, loss incurred by not taking advantage of an occasion to earn a profit.

Optimal level of promotion, level of promotion at which profits reach a maximum.

Optimum, point at which the input to the system gets the highest returns or output.

Optimum level of advertising, level of advertising at which a firm's return from advertising is the best.

Outcome, change in consumer behavior desired by an advertiser.

Outdoor media, media that deliver the message on physical structures outside buildings.

Package coupons, coupons on packages of products.

Participation, purchase of advertising time during a program, together with other advertisers.

Pass-through, the fraction of the trade deal that retailers pass on to consumers.

Passive meter, an electronic device hooked to a TV set to record when the set is on, which program is on, and who is in the room.

Passive processing, state in which consumers receive information or stimuli but do not actively process it; they also neither seek out nor avoid such information.

Patent medicine, a drug or medicine sold prior to U.S. regulation of drugs, that claimed to provide some cure or health benefit to consumers.

Pay-for-performance, various trade deals by which manufacturers pay the discount only for units that the retailer actually sells to consumers on discount.

Penetration pricing, a pricing strategy for new products, in which the price is kept low to quickly attract many new buyers.

People-meter, a partly interactive electronic device connected to a TV set that records who in the household is viewing which TV program.

Percentage proven recall, percentage of the sample audience who recall, without any help, specific information about an ad.

Percentage related recall, percentage of the audience who recall the ad but are unable to provide specific information.

Percentage-of-sales method, an approach to advertising in which a firm spends a fixed percentage of its sales on advertising.

Perception, individual's process of forming mental patterns and drawing meaning from external stimuli.

Perceptual mapping, a procedure for graphically depicting consumers' perceptions of competing brands and consumers' ideal points.

Perceptual priming, form of implicit memory in which an individual shows behavior favorable to a brand or position about which information has been received but without retrieval of that information or its context.

Performance basis, a compensation method in which an advertiser pays an agency to the extent its advertising campaign meets the advertiser's stated goals.

Periodic discounting, strategy of periodically offering discounts to discriminate among consumer segments based on their temporal demand for a product.

Peripheral route of persuasion, path of the elaboration likelihood model by which an individual responds to a message based on the cues associated with the message.

Permanence, extent to which the change due to persuasion endures.

Personal scanner, device that a household uses to record items purchased; it reads a laser beam that bounces off the item's universal product code.

Personal selling, communicating a firm's offer to consumers through the sales staff.

Persuasion, the act of changing an opinion, attitude, or behavior by some communication.

Physical displays, assortments of a product with signs, flyers or gadgets that better explain it to consumers.

Physical harm, damage to body or health.

Physical stimuli, things that can impact the five human senses (sight, hearing, smell, taste, and touch).

Pitch, organization of notes in a musical piece.

Plot, sequence in the action that leads to increasing tension due to some unknown outcome, which is then resolved.

Pocket the deal, practice of retailers retaining a fraction of a trade deal that they do not pass on to consumers.

Poll, a study consisting of a short questionnaire.

Population, for a TV or radio program, total number of individuals or households with ready access to a television (or radio) in their home.

Positioning, projecting a distinct image for the product in the consumer's mind.

Premium, a gift or reward that promoters give consumers for purchasing a product.

Preparation, the collection and analysis of all the facts relating to the current situation.

Price discount, a price-cut.

Price discrimination, charging different prices to different consumers so as to better match the price each is willing to pay.

Price discriminatory theory, explanation for firm behavior that posits that a firm acts to distinguish consumers based on their price sensitivity.

Price packs, new packages on which a manufacturer offers a temporary lower price to consumers.

Price promotion, sales promotion that involves a change in price.

Price skimming, a pricing strategy for new products, in which the price is kept much above costs, to take advantage of demand for the new product.

Price-based trade deals, reductions in the price of a product that a manufacturer offers a retailer for a limited time.

Price-cut, temporary reduction in list price of a product.

Princliple of relativity, evaluation by consumers of a gain or loss in purchase in reference to the price of the item purchased.

Print media, media that deliver the message through a printed page, which can be stored and read at the audience's leisure.

Private labels, brands owned by and labeled after the store in which they are sold.

Process variables, measures of consumer's mental activity in response to an ad.

Product, a good, service, idea, time or candidate that an individual or organization offers to another individual or organization.

Product life cycle, cyclical pattern in sales that describes the evolution of a product from its introduction to its demise.

Product orientation, a firm's focus on its own products as the key to success.

Product placement, 1. paid placement of a brand name or product image alongside regular programming, without identifying the sponsor and while maintaining a noncommercial character;

2. a planned and paid appearance of a brand message in a movie or TV program.

Production houses, agencies that specialize in producing the final form of ads.

Profit orientation, a firm's focus on short-term profits as the key to success.

Profit-maximization method, approach in which the firm chooses the advertising budget that maximizes its profits.

Profits, revenues less costs.

Program tie-in, an arrangement by which a program provides exposure to a particular brand in exchange for a commitment by the brand's owner to advertise during that program.

Programmers, firms or individuals who provide material that entertains or informs individuals.

Programming, see Content.

Promotion, advertising and sales promotion.

Promotional bump, increase in sales in response to a promotion.

Prototypical brand, brand that is the best example or is typical of a category.

Psychographic segmentation, segmentation on the basis of consumers' lifestyles.

Publicity, communicating a firm's message to consumers through unpaid news releases.

Puffery, exaggerated, nonspecific claim.

Pull strategy, use of consumer promotions to create primary demand for a product that pulls it through the distribution system.

Pulsing, regularly scheduling ads on and off during fixed periods of the planning horizon.

Pun, word with two meanings.

Pupillometer, a device that records the dilation of the pupil in response to a stimulus.

Purchase probability, probability that a contacted individual will buy the marketed product and not return it.

Push money, a manufacturer's cash payment to a retailer to earn the retailer's goodwill or encourage it to promote the manufacturer's brands.

Push strategy, use of retail promotions to push a product to consumers through the distribution system.

Q-ratings, the percentage of those familiar with the public figure who rate him or her as "one of my favorites," prepared by Marketing Evaluations Inc. of Port Washington, New York.

Qualifying discounts, strategy of offering discounts to a new segment of consumers that is independent and demographically distinct from the primary consumers of the product.

Questionnaire, a list of questions asked of a respondent.

Quota incentives, cash rewards or percentage rebates that a manufacturer offers retailers if they meet certain targets.

Random, with an equal chance.

Random discounting, strategy of randomly discounting prices to discriminate among consumer segments, based on their costs of information about price.

Rating, percentage of a population viewing the program during the average minute.

Reach, number or percentage of households exposed to a vehicle at least once in a given time period.

Real incremental sales, increase in sales due to a price promotion, that *would not have taken place at all* in the absence of the price promotion.

Rebates, guarantees by firms to reimburse consumers directly for the purchase of a product, subject to certain conditions.

Rebuttal, argument that immediately refutes a rival's claim.

Recall, an individual's bringing to consciousness a previously encountered stimulus or a previously generated thought.

Recent-reading method, a method of testing readership of a magazine or newspaper by asking respondents if they have read a recent issue.

Recognition, an individual's claim that he or she has previously been exposed to a stimulus.

Reference price, price that a consumer uses as a standard for comparing current prices of products.

Refund, Rebate.

Refutational appeal, message that first presents a counterargument to a position being advanced, then destroys it.

Refutational argument, argument that first presents a counterargument to an advertised brand or is position and then destroys it.

Regression analysis, a statistical procedure that attempts to determine the effect of two or more independent variables on a dependent variable.

Regret theory, belief that consumer's actions are motivated by fear of regretting *not* taking the action rather than by the intrinsic satisfaction of taking it.

Regular sales, sales that take place in the absence of a promotion.

Rehearsal, strengthening of mental paths linking information nodes.

Relevance, meaningfulness because of similarity to the natural environment.

Repetition, exposure of some stimulus to a subject two or more times in succession.

Repurchase, choice of the same brand a second consecutive time.

Residual stimuli, accumulated experiences of individuals with stimuli that form a standard for evaluating current stimuli.

Resistance, extent to which change due to persuasion survives attacks based on new information.

Resonance, form of humor that creates an echo or multiplication of meaning between a picture and associated text.

Restitution, compensation for damage caused by deceptive promotion.

Retail coupons, similar to manufacturer coupons except that they are offered from retailers to consumers.

Retail price, a price a retailer charges consumers.

Retail promotion, promotion that a retailer offers a consumer.

Retail promotions, sales promotions that a retailer offers consumers.

Retailer-distributed coupons, manufacturer coupons distributed through retail stores.

Retrieval, individual's mental function that brings information from long-term memory to consciousness (short-term memory).

Retrieval cues, stimuli with which the individual stores a piece of information to facilitate retrieval.

Return probability, probability that an individual will buy the product and return it.

Revenues, sales in dollars.

Reverse causality, situation in which a dependent variable affects or causes an independent variable.

Roadblock, a TV schedule that positions ads at the very same time in all or most leading broadcast channels of a medium, so that a viewer will see the ad irrespective of which show he or she turns on.

Run-of-press newspaper coupons (ROP newspapers), coupons printed on the pages of newspapers.

Sale, a price-cut.

Sales conferences, manufacturer-sponsored private meetings of all retailers in a region at a planned time and place.

Sales in units, sum of all quantities purchased by all consumers within a particular time period and region.

Sales lead, a contact that a salesperson can follow up on for a sale.

Sales orientation, a firm's focus on increasing sales as the key to success.

Sales promotion, time-bound program of a seller that tries to make an offer more attractive to buyers and requires their participation in the form of an immediate purchase or some other action.

Sales-response function, pattern of sales that result from different levels of advertising.

Sample, item distributed through sampling.

Sampling, free or subsidized availability of a product for consumers' trial.

Sampling coupons, higher value coupons that motivate product trial.

Saturation, level of advertising at which increases in advertising do not lead to any increase in sales even though lowering advertising causes decreases in sales.

Scan-down, a type of bill-back based on a retailer's sales that are recorded electronically by a checkout scanner.

Scanner data, laser scanner records of consumer purchases at a store's checkout.

Scatter buying, purchase of broadcast time during a season.

Schedule, a set of vehicles, programs, or ad insertions over a certain time period, such as a month.

Scheduling, timing of ads, or their sequencing within a time period.

Seal of approval, a logo of the certifying organization that appears on the product's package or ad and states that the certifying organization vouches for the merits of the product.

Search, state in which consumers make an explicit effort to collect information about the products they plan to purchase.

Second market discounting, strategy of offering discounts to a new segment of consumers that is independent and geographically distinct from the primary consumers of the product.

Segmentation, a conceptual breakup of a market into groups of relatively homogeneous consumers to better serve each of them.

Segregating gains, strategy of separating several price cuts (or increases in benefits) so as to increase perceived gain to consumers.

Selective attention, systematic pattern of consumer preference for some stimuli.

Self-enforcement, marketers' avoidance of pricing as high as the trade will bear, in deference to consumers' perception of unfair pricing.

Self-regulation, control of advertising by advertisers themselves or their organizations.

Self-reports, statements made by subjects in response to questions posed by a researcher.

Self-serving bias, a misperception of reality that prompts individuals to believe that their own possessions are better than others perceive them to be.

Sensitivity, willingness of respondents to provide information.

Share of audience, percentage of TV users tuned to that program.

Shelf-talker, sign or display fixed onto the shelf, typically close to the product.

Shipments, sales of manufacturer to dealers.

Short-term memory, individual's ability to remember information for up to 20 seconds after receiving it.

Similarity, the likeness between source and receiver.

Simple regression, statistical procedure that attempts to determine the effect of one independent variable on a dependent variable.

Single-source data, a combination of precise data on sales and all the marketing variables that influence sales.

Slapstick humor, form of humor which uses very simple or overplayed forms of incongruity.

Social desirability bias, tendency of respondents to respond to questions in a manner that they think is desired by society.

Soft thinking, reasoning by metaphor, paradox, ambiguity and fantasy.

Soft-sell message, subtle message that allows for different interpretations, persuades by suggestion, or makes no direct request for action or change.

Source, the originator of a message.

Source attractiveness model, a theory of the effectiveness of an endorser that posits that the acceptance of a message depends on the attractiveness of the source or the endorser.

Source credibility model, a theory of the effectiveness of an endorser that posits that a receiver's acceptance of a message depends on the credibility of the endorser.

Specialized agency, an organization that performs some but not all of the major functions of an agency: accounts management, creative design, media planning, research.

Spiffs, incentives offered by a manufacturer to the retailers' sales force to motivate them to sell more of the manufacturer's brand.

Split cable test, an experiment in which matched samples of households are sent different levels or executions of an ad campaign, without their knowledge of the research design.

Spokesperson, an endorser who is a person or a character.

Sponsorship, purchase of the entire time of a program.

Spot advertising, advertising during the private programming of local stations.

Stand-alone department, a separate department with its own cost structure and a department head who reports to a marketing or divisional manager.

State regulation, laws of state governments, rules of various state agencies, and rulings of state courts.

Steiner effect, increase in wholesale price and decrease in retail price of a brand due to manufacturer's advertising the brand.

Stereotype, a perception or depiction of an individual based on a simplistic, biased image of the group to which the individual belongs, rather than on his or her own individual characteristics.

Stimulus novelty, extent to which a focal stimulus appears different to an individual from the contextual and residual stimuli.

Stockpiling, consumer's purchase of excess quantities of a product for future consumption or to reduce purchases at a future period.

Storage, individual's mental function that retains information in long-term memory.

Store switching, a change of store that a consumer frequents.

Street money, push money.

Subjects, participants in a research study.

Subliminal advertising, ads that contain imperceptible messages embedded in overt material.

Subordinate brand, brand that has a small market share and weak loyalty.

Substantiation, evidence from laboratory or field studies that provides reasonable support for a claim.

Success trap, the tendency to assume that today's business successes will automatically continue well into the future.

Support arguments, reasons in favor of a premise.

Supportive argument, affirmation of the positive attributes of a brand without any comparison, refutation, inoculation, or framing.

Survey, a study that obtains information through self-reports, typically through a long questionnaire.

Sweepstakes, drawings in which winners are determined purely by chance.

Switch, consumer's choice of a different brand from that bought on a previous purchase.

Synthesis, stage of individual's perception that draws appropriate meaning from patterns based on the context of their occurrence.

Tagline, last sentence or statement of an ad.

Takeoff, a point that demarcates the introductory and growth stages of the product life cycle, characterized by the first rapid increase in sales of the product.

Talent houses, agencies that represent endorsers, performers and other artists.

Target audience, a subset of the audience of special interest to the advertiser.

Target marketing, a strategy in which a firm markets variations of a product to various segments.

Tedium, growing boredom with repetitive exposure to a message.

Telemarketing, 1. an integrated system of research, promotion, generating sales leads, generating sales and providing after-sales service using the telecommunication system in conjunction with other media; 2. promotion of any good or service over telephone lines.

Telemeter, a device that is hooked to a TV set to record when and to which channel it is tuned in.

Telephone appeal, a vocal ad made through the telephone.

Testimonial, a type of implicit endorsement in which the endorser describes his or her experience with the product.

Texture, qualitative richness of a musical piece.

Theater tests, laboratory experiments for screening TV ads.

Thinking attributes, product characteristics based on reason, on which consumers are likely to agree.

Threshold, a level of advertising beyond which increases in advertising cause increases in sales, and below which lower levels of advertising cause no change in sales.

Through-the-book method, a method of testing readership of a magazine or newspaper by evaluating a respondent's reading of various articles in the magazine or newspaper.

Tie-ins, joint promotions for two or more items by one or more firms.

Timing, temporal organization of the components of a musical piece.

Tit-for-tat, a defensive strategy in which the incumbent matches or betters an attacker's offer to consumers.

Total effect of two or more variables, sum of the main and interactive effects of variables on some other variable.

Total familiar score, a measure of Q-ratings computed as the percentage of the respondents who rate a candidate from "one of my favorites" to "never seen or heard of before."

Trade allowance, short-term cash or other benefit that a manufacturer makes to wholesalers, distributors or retailers so that they may buy more of the product, or promote it more heavily to consumers.

Trade contests, manufacturer-organized competitions among retailers, who are rewarded if they meet certain sales targets.

Trade deal, any sales promotion that a manufacturer offers a retailer that involves a price reduction, more favorable terms or cash, to enable them to more easily buy, stock or sell the manufacturer's product.

Trade games, manufacturer-organized games for retailers in which the winner is determined after meeting certain conditions, with or without a drawing.

Trade promotion, promotion that a manufacturer offers a wholesaler, distributor, or retailer.

Trade shows, conventions open only to the trade.

Trade sweepstakes, manufacturer-organized drawings for retailers in which the winner is determined purely by chance.

Transition probabilities, fraction of consumers who pass from one stage to another of a hierarchy of effects.

Treatment, level of the independent variable in an experiment.

Trial coupons, sampling coupons.

Trial, 1. consumer's first choice of the brand; 2. testing or experiencing a product without actually buying it.

Trustworthiness, willingness of a source to make honest claims.

Two-factor theory, explanation for the nonlinear response to repetition due to the interplay of habituation and tedium.

Two-sided appeal, argument that states both pros and cons about an advertised brand or its rival.

Unaided recall, subjects' recall of an ad without being offered any clue or help.

Unconditioned response, natural response to the unconditioned stimulus.

Unconditioned stimulus, one to which an individual already has a natural predisposition to respond.

Unduplicated audience, see Reach.

Unfair ads, ads that can harm consumers but *are not deceptive.*

Uninformed consumers, consumers who are not fully informed about the value (price or benefits) of a product.

Universal product code, a unique 10-digit number that firms assign to every manufactured product.

Unlucky loyals, consumers who pay the regular price for a product that is sometimes on discount.

Up-front buying, purchase of broadcast time in a vehicle several months ahead of the season or quarter.

Usage, percentage of households with their TV sets turned on. Also called HUT, for households using television.

Usage segmentation, segmentation on the basis of consumers' usage of products.

Value pricing, a manufacturer's strategy of offering lower prices to dealers in exchange for greatly reducing trade promotions; similar to the everyday-low-price strategy offered by retailers to consumers.

Vehicles, standardized media outlets that carry a set program of entertainment or information.

Verification, testing an idea on a small scale to determine whether it is feasible and productive.

Wearin, increase in the optimal level of ad intensity from period to period.

Wearout, decrease in the optimal level of ad intensity from period to period.

Weber's law, theory about human perception of stimuli that states that a perceivable change in a stimulus increases at a constant rate with the level of that stimulus.

Wheeler-Lea Amendment, a change in Article 5 of the Sherman Act passed in 1938 to read, "unfair methods of competition and unfair or deceptive acts or practices in commerce are hereby declared unlawful."

Wholesale price, a price manufacturers charge a wholesaler, dealer or retailer.

World Wide Web, a network of computer sites, each of which can be accessed either through its unique address or through a hypertext link.

Zapping, consumers' avoidance of TV ads by switching among channels.

Zipping, consumers' avoidance of TV ads by fast-forwarding through them when replaying taped programs that contain the ads.

Company Index

ABC, 350
Disney buyout of, 348, 350
Absolut ad campaign, 109
Addison-Wesley, 419
Adidas, 128–129
Admarketing, fee negotiations with
Home Depot, 80, 81
AdTel, experiments evaluating
advertising's effect on sales, 336,
337
American Airlines, 286, 334, 359
AAdvantage program of, 287, 288
American Express Co., 112, 144,
332, 379
computer usage to gather cus-
tomer data, 333
American Home Products, 41
Ammirati Puris Lintas, 62
AMR Corp., 334
Amstar Corp., corrective advertising
of, 42
Anheuser-Busch, 74, 203, 401
Bud Bowl ad campaign of,
119–120, 125
experiments evaluating advertis-
ing's effect on sales, 336, 337
O'Doul's brew promotion, 214,
214
Apple Computer Company,
Chiat/Day's "1984" Macintosh
introductory ad campaign for,
3–4, 5, 65, 83, 86, 340
Aribitron, 345
AT&T, 73, 139–140, 141, 151, 186,
333, 340, 359, 378
deflection strategy and MCI
attacks on, 432
MCI negative advertising against,
145, 146, 152

refutational ad of, 108, 108
tit-for-tat strategy and MCI, 433
Audit Bureau of Circulation (ABC),
and circulation of print vehicles,
372
Avis, 26
Ayer, N. W., 14
DeBeers Consolidated Mines
account and, 73

Backer Spielvogel Bates Worldwide,
63
Bank of America, 379
Bartles and Jaymes, 186
BBDO Worldwide, 62
Beatrice Cheese, Inc., Reddi-wip ad
and, 172
Beauty-Rama Carpet Center, correc-
tive advertising of, 42
Benetton, 75, 129, 129, 201
controversial ads of, 76, 163, 163
social themes in advertising of, 86
Blockbuster Video, 354
Bloomingdale, 419
BMW, ad refuting Mercedes-Benz,
150, 150, 151
Boase Massimi Pollitt, 74
Boise Tire Co., corrective advertising
of, 42
Borden's Eagle Brand Condensed
Milk, 13
Bozell Worldwide, 67
National Fluid Milk Processor
Promotion Board campaign
of, 99–100, 100, 102, 103,
108, 109, 110
Bridge Shop N Save, 273
Bristol-Myers, 432–433
British AGB Research, 345

British Airways, 63, 73
Buffalo Bills, 223–224
Bugle Boy, 201
Burger King, Lion King figurine promotion of, 283, 284, 287
Burnett, Leo, Co. Inc., 63, 64, 74
as agency brand, 73
appealing ad personalities of,
86–87, 87
and GM Oldsmobile account, 79
outstanding creative and dedicated
client service of, 66, 66
Busch theme parks, 285

Calvin Klein, 75, 189, 201, 340
sexual themes in advertising of,
83, 86
Camay soap, 27
Campbell's Soup Company, 13, 187
advertising's effect on sales and,
336, 337
deceptive advertising by, 34–35,
36, 37, 38, 41–42
demonstration by, 45
puffery by, 39
Capital Cities/ABC, Disney buyout
of, 348, 350
Carillon Importers Ltd., and Media
Marathon for Absolut advertising, 356–357
CBS, 350
Chevron Corp., 56
Chiat/Day, 65–67, 72, 74, 75, 151
Apple Macintosh "1984" introductory campaign of, 3–4, 5,
83, 86, 340
creative and accounts management
functions of, 65
creativity of, 86

weak accounts management of, 66
Chrysler, 127, 150, 151, 186, 402
  and Iacocca endorsement demon-
      strating expertise, 188, *189,*
      191–192
  CNA Insurance Cos., 334
  Coca-Cola, 13, 65, 82, 114–115,
      150, 197, 201, 340, 354, 358
  advertisement for, *12*
  analysis of strategies used against
      Pepsi attacks, 433–434
  Diet Coke Roman era ad of, 125
  flanking used against, *141*
  and humor in advertising, 169,
      170
  music in Diet Coke ad, 173, 175
  Pepsi-Cola and, 397–398, 399
  polar bear ad campaign of, 27
  types of agencies representing, 68
College Board, 378
Columbia Pictures, 350, 354
Computer City, 395
Connector Set Toy Co., 285
Continental Airlines, Wells Rich
    Greene BDDP ad error and, 77
Converse, 199, 200
Coors Light Beer, *23*
Cordiant, *63,* 64, 73. *See also*
    Saatchi & Saatchi
CoreStates Financial Corp., tie-in
    with Disney's Premier Cruise
    Lines, 284–285
Costco, 247, 251
Creative Artists Agency (CAA), 72
  Coca-Cola campaign of, 68
  Coca-Cola classic's polar bear icon
      of, *71*
  as specialized agency, 71
Crest toothpaste, *26,* 185
CRK Advertising, 75

D'Arcy Masius Benton & Bowles,
    74
  advertising campaign for Qantas,
      77
DDB Needham Worldwide, *62*
DeBeers Consolidated Mines, Ltd.
    Ayer, N.W., and, 73
  emotional appeal ad of, *166*
Dell Computer Company, 15,
    382–383
Dentsu Inc., *63*
Dick's Supermarket, 381

Diners Club, 379
Disney, 187
  buyout of Capital Cities/ABC,
      348, 350
  Premier Cruise Lines tie-in with
      CoreStates Financial Corp.,
      284–285
Disney Channel, 312
Dixons Group PLC, 63
Dove Soap, 26, *193*
DuPont, 128, *128*
Duxiana, 126, *127*

Energizer, 187
  Chiat/Day's Bunny campaign and,
      65
Energy Star, 186, *187*
Erickson, Company, The, 73
Euro RSCG, *63*

Fallon McElligott, 68
Federal Express (FedEx), 186, 382
  Web usage of, *387*
Fidelity, high-tech automated direct
    mail facility at Covington,
    376–377, 378, 382
Fingerhut Cos., 333
Firestone, deceptive advertising by,
    38–39, 40
First Alert, 178
First Bank System, 334
Fleming, 255
Folgers, puffery by, 39
Foote Cone and Belding (FCB)
  classification of products by, *164*
  scheduling study by, 405, *405*
Ford Motor Company, 73, 145, 286
  Model T, 25
  print ad with telephone number
      and Web address, *385*
Fox, 350
FreshenUp, 37, 40
Frigidaire Company, emotional
    appeal ad, *167*
Fuji, 354
Fuji Heavy Industries, 300, 302,
    305, 309. *See also* Subaru of
    America

Gainesburgers, 37
Gallaher Tobacco Ltd., 63
Gallup, 17
Gartner Group, 333

General Electric, 402
General Foods, Oscar Mayer sub-
    sidiary of, *41*
General Mills, 187, 251, 288
  everyday-low-price strategy of,
      279, 280
General Motors, 73, 254, 265, 402
  Oldsmobile account with Leo
      Burnett Co. and, 79
  psychographic segmentation and,
      22–23
  value pricing strategy of, 264
Gillette
  PETA's campaign against, 162
  promotional strategy and product
      development of, 414–415,
      415, 416, *416, 417,* 420, 421,
      422, 424, 426
Gold Blend Campaign, 123, 128
Goodby, Silverstein and Partners, 86
Goods for Guns Foundation, *179*
Goodyear Tire and Rubber, 354
  Infitreds, 46
  warranty of, 46
Grey Advertising, *63*
Guess, Inc., soft-sell ad, 108, *109*
Gulf Oil, 354

Hakuhodo, *63*
Havas Advertising, *63*
Health Insurance Association of
    America, Harry and Louise ad
    campaign of, 187, 194
Hewlett-Packard, stimulus use in
    DeskJet ad, 123, *124,* 126
Home Depot, fee negotiations with
    Admarketing, 80, 81
Honda, 67
  Civic, 39
  puffery by, 39
Hoover Vacuum Cleaners, trip pro-
    motion debacle, 214–215
Hutton, E. F., 27, 190

IBM, 73, 333
  central route of persuasion ad,
      112
  computers of, 21
IKEA, 113, *113*
Information Resources Inc. (IRI),
    266
  experiments evaluating advertis-
      ing's effect on sales, 336–337

scanner data system of, 332–334, 335

Intel, exhibit at COMDEX (fall 1993), 260, *260*

International Business Machines Corp. *See* IBM

International Manufacturer Technology Show, 260

International Winter Consumer Electronics Show, 260

Interpublic Group of Companies, 62

Isuzu Motors, 186–187

ITT Continental Banking, corrective advertising of, *42*

Ivory Soap, 8–10, *9, 10,* 13
niche marketing of, 27

Jockey, psychographic segmentation and, 25, *25*

Johnson & Johnson, 432–433
fear and resonance in dental floss ads, *181*
Tylenol ads of, *11*
Tylenol cyanide poisoning disaster, 151

Johnson & Johnson-Merck, Pepcid AC of, 43

JWT Worldwide, 73

Kellogg's, 187, 288
humor in advertising and, 169, 170

Kmart, 35, 248, 334, 367
competition with Wal-Mart, 233–234, 240

Kodak, *12,* 285

Korean Airlines, warmth-arousing ad of, *178*

Kraft, 354
Cheez Whiz ads of, *41*
misleading claims by, 37
singles, 37
sweepstakes offer of, *289*

Kroger, 264, 355

LA Gear, 199, 200

Land O'Lakes, ad encouraging display usage, *263*

Lee jeans, 25, 145
ad using unique selling proposition, 92

Lens Craft Research, corrective advertising of, *42*

Lever Brothers, 251
Lever 2000 and, 28–29
positioning by, 27

Levi jeans, 358

Levi Strauss Overalls, 13

Lion Brand, 284

Lipton Cup-a-Soup, *53*

Listerine, *17*

Little Caesar's, 187

Lowe Group, 62

Luckys grocery store, 234

Macy, R. H., & Co., 407

Magic Wand, demonstration by, 45

Malaysia Airlines, 148, *148*

Marketing Evaluations Inc., Q-ratings of, 195–196

Marlboro Man, 64

Marriott Hotels, product placement and, 50

Martin and Woltz Agency, and Virginia tourism campaign, 88, *89, 92*

Master Lock, 406–407, 408

Matsushita, 350

Matsushita Electric of Hawaii, corrective advertising of, *42*

Maxwell House Coffee, 145

Maytag Corporation, 215

MCA, 350

MCA Advertising, 74

McCann, H. K., Company, 73

McCann-Erickson, Inc.
merger of H. K. McCann Company and The Erickson Company, 73

McCann-Erickson Worldwide, 62
accounts of, *69–70*
Coca-Cola account of, 68
as full-service agency, 71

McDonald's, 74, 157–158, *158,* 160, 190, 358
Chicken McNugget ads of, *41*
combating "worm meat" rumors, 136, 137

MCI, 151, 340, 354, 359
AT&T negative advertising against, 145, *146,* 152
AT&T refutational ad of, 108, *108*
AT&T tit-for-tat strategy and, 433
deflection strategy and attacks on AT&T, 432

Friends and Family program of, 287

Mediacom, 347, *348*

Mediamark, as syndicated data source on consumers' brand purchases and media exposure, 373

Mercedes-Benz, BMW's ad refuting, 150, *150,* 151

Met Life, 354

Michelin, 157–158, *158,* 160, *161,* 165, 179
XH4 tires, 46

Microsoft, 65
Internet Explorer promotion, 212, *212*
Windows 95 promotional sampling strategy of, 289–290
Windows 95 worldwide promotion of, 394–395, *396, 397,* 407–408

MicroVision, 22

Miller Brewing Co., 74

Minnesota Valley Canning Company, 186

Mirror Group Newspapers, 63

Montgomery Ward & Co., 233
catalog of, 13–14

Mr. Clean, ad for, 45, *45*

Nabisco Inc., 266, 286

National Carpet, corrective advertising of, *42*

National Fluid Milk Processor Promotion Board, 99
Bozell Worldwide milk campaign for, 99–100, *100,* 102, 103, 108, 109, 110

Nature Valley, 122

NBC, 125, 350
audience target segments and, 362–363

NEC, 133

Nestlé, 162–163
Butterfingers promotion of, 272–273
Gold Blend advertising campaign of, 123, 127–128
Taster's Choice campaign of, 123

New Saatchi Agency, 63, 65. *See also* Saatchi & Saatchi
creation of, 63–64

Nielsen, A. C., 17

controversial TV viewership measurement, 344, 353
history of radio/TV audience measurements, 344–346, 360–361
as syndicated data source for U. S. television programs, 371–372
Nielsen Marketing Research, 266, 332, 334
Nike, 144, 163, 185, 198, 199, 200, 299, 305
  arousing ennobling emotions in ads for, 180
  matching celebrity to consumer segments, 197
  Wieden and Kennedy advertising campaign for, 86
Nissan, 65, 67
  Chiat/Day ad campaign for, 86
Northwest Airlines, 359
  Mall of America promotion and, 211, 212

Ocean Spray Cranberries, corrective advertising of, *42*
Ogilvy & Mather Worldwide, *62, 73*
Old Milwaukee, 401
Omnicom Group Inc., *62, 65*
Oneida, 128
Oral-B Laboratories, two-sided ad for, *107, 108*

Pabst, 401
Pampas, *63*
Payless Drug Company, corrective advertising of, *42*
Pearl Drops toothpaste, *26,*
Penney, J C, 233
People Panel, The, 195
Pepcid AC, 43
Pepsi-Cola, 65, 68, 102–103, 114–115, 150, 151, 169, 170, 172, 197, 198–199, 288, 340, 358, 406–407
  analysis of Coke's strategies used against, 433–434
  competitive parity with Coca-Cola, 397–398, 399
  compressed ad of, 109
  flanking used by, *141*
  Jackson, Michael, as celebrity endorser for, 169, 170, 198–199, 200, 398
  Madonna as celebrity endorser for, 184–185, 186, 199, 398

Percy, 345
Peter Pan Peanut Butter, *23*
Piggly Wiggly Stores, *19*
Pillsbury, 264
Pizza Hut, 284, 285, 354
Polar bear ads. *See* Coca-Cola
Post, C. W., 273
Power, J. D., Associates, 332
Premier Cruise Lines, tie-in with CoreStates Financial Corp., 284–285
Price Club, 247
Procter & Gamble, 8–10, 62, 73, 77, 185, 264, 265, 266, 347, 402
  Ivory soap and, 9–10, *9, 10*
  organization for advertising, *78*
  P&G Productions of, 350
  promotional plan for detergents, 213–214, *214*
  self-regulation by, 54
  soap brands of, 27
  soap operas and, 357–358
  value pricing strategy of, 251–252, 254

Qantas, D'Arcy Masius Benton & Bowles advertising campaign for, 77
QTest, 168
Quaker Oats, *12*, 82, 264, 266
  Cap'n Crunch contest of, 288, 386
  value pricing strategy of, 252, 254

Raibow toothpaste, 37
Ralphs grocery store, 234, 255
Reebok, 65, 151, 198
Renault, 190
Reynolds, R. J. (RJR), Joe Camel ad campaign of, 311–313, 317–318, 319, 322, 331, 340
Rhode Island Carpets, corrective advertising of, *42*
Richards Group, 77
RJR. *See* Reynolds, R. J. (RJR)
RJR Foods, Inc., corrective advertising of, *42*
Rover Group Ltd., 333
Royal Caribbean Cruises Ltd., 334
Royal Crown, *141*

Saatchi, M&C, Agency, 64. *See also* New Saatchi Agency; Saatchi & Saatchi

Saatchi & Saatchi, 67, 74, 346
  client contact and, 67
  conflicting views in, 62–63
  as Cordiant agency, 64
  development of, 61–62
  as holding company, 73
  New Saatchi Agency as rival of, 63–64
Safeguard soap, 27
Sam's Club, 251
Samsonite Corp., informational appeal ad, *166*
Sam's Warehouse, 247
Sara Lee, Bryan's bacon and bologna ads of, *41*
Savon Drugs, price advertising of, 37
Schick, 415
Seagram, 55
Sears, Roebuck & Co., 15, 233, 367
  auto-services practices of, 20–21
  pricing strategy of, 244, 247, 248, 251
Sea World, 354
7-UP, *141*
Shangri La Industries, corrective advertising of, *42*
Simmons Market Research Bureau, 363, 367
  as syndicated data source, 372–373
Smith Barney, 190–191
SmithKline, 264
  Tagamet HB of, 43
Sony, 350, 354
Spray 'n Wash, 163
Spring Mills, 127
Stouffers Red Box frozen entrees, *23*
STP Corp., corrective advertising of, *42*
Subaru of America
  hierarchy of effects and, 309–310
  Wieden & Kennedy ad for Impreza, *303*
  Wieden & Kennedy campaign for, 299–302, *301*, 304–306, 307
Sucrets throat lozenges, 264
Sugar Information, corrective advertising of, *42*
Sun Country Classic, 190
Sun Microsystems, 333
Super Sports Wide Oval Tire, 38
SuperValue, *255*

Tagamet HB, 43
Target, 35, 248
Taster's Choice campaign, 123
TBWA Advertising, and Media
    Marathon for Absolut advertis-
    ing, 356–357
Texaco, CleanSystem3 campaign by,
    56
Thinking Machines Corp., 333
Thompson, J. Walter, Co., *62*
Tide, self-regulation of, 54
Tony the Tiger, 64
Toshiba, 189–190, 192
Toyota, 62, 67, 73
    Corolla, 44
    endorsements for, 44
    Web usage of, *387*
Transmedia, 287
Tums, 43
TWA, 73
Tylenol
    irritating ad of, 175
    poisoning with, 151

UltrAir, 129
United Colors Communication, 75
    controversial ad by, *76*
United Parcel Service (UPS), 382
U. S. Postal Service (USPS), 382
    catalog delivery by, 14
    mail advertising regulation by,
        51–52

mail and, 382
    manufacturer coupons and, 273
Universal Studios, 350

Video Storyboard Tests Inc., 100,
    198
"Virginia is for lovers" campaign,
    88, *89*, 92
VISA, 285, 286
VLI, Today contraceptive sponge ads
    of, *41*
Volkswagen, Bernbach's provocative
    ad for, *90*
Volvo, 178
    demonstration by, 45
Vons supermarket chain, 234
    electronic distribution system of,
    281

Waldenbooks, 380
Wal-Mart, 248, 251
    competition with Kmart, 233–234,
        240
    deceptive advertising by, 35, 36,
        37
Ward, Montgomery, & Co. *See*
    Montgomery Ward & Co.
Warner-Lambert
    corrective advertising of, *42*
    e.p.t. TV ad campaign, 157–158,
        158, 160, 165, 168–169, 188,
        194

Waserns Inc., corrective advertising
    of, *42*
Wawa Food Markets, 286
Wells Rich Greene BDDP, error in ad
    for Continental Airlines, 77
Wetterau, *255*
Wide Oval Tires, 38–39
Wieden & Kennedy, 64, 68
    ad for Impreza, *303*
    and Nike advertising campaign, 86
    Subaru advertising campaign of,
        299–302, *301*, 304–306, 307,
        309–310
Wilkinson, 415, 424
Winn Dixie, 264
Wonder Bread, 37
WPP Group, 62

Yamaha International, corrective
    advertising of, *42*
Yellow Pages, 359
Young & Rubicam, 63

Zest soap, 27

Name Index

Aaker, David A., 176, 177, 179, 183n, 343n
Abelson, Robert P., 134n, 155n
Abraham, Magid, 267, 342n
Abraham, Majid, 310n, 343n
Ackoff, Russell L., 343n
Adams, John, 104
Agassi, Andre, 197
Ailawadi, Kusum L., 412n
Akhter, Syed H., 131
Akst, Daniel, 393n
Albion, Mark S., 343n, 412n
Alden, Dana L., 183n
Alwitt, Linda F., 111, 117n
Amit, Ghosh, 134n
Anand, Punam, 135n
Andrews, Craig J., 117n, 131
Antin, Tony, 95n
Antonini, Joseph, 234
Aradhna, Krishna, 250n
Arnold, Stephen J., 342n
Artzt, Edwin L., 347
Ashmore, Richard D., 207n
Assael, Henry, 156n, 375n
Assmus, Gert, 343n
Atler, Stewart, 94n
Azcuenga, Mary L., 35

Bach, Richard, 426, 427
Balasubramanian, Siva K., 60n, 412n
Baldinger, A. L., 342n
Ball, Benjamin F., 271n
Barkley, Charles, 197
Barton, R., 135n
Basu, Amiya K., 393n
Basu, Atasi, 393n
Batra, Rajeev, 182n, 393n
Bauer, Barbara, 436n

Bauer, Raymond A., 183n
Baum, Laurie, 295n
Bawa, Kapil, 294n
Bayor, Leslie, 95n
Beatty, Sally Goll, 117n
Bellizzi, Joseph A., 208n
Beltramini, 207n
Bennett, Peter, 135n
Bennett, Tony, 100
Berger, Paul D., 207n, 208n
Berkowitz, L., 156n
Bernbach, William, 66, 88, 90
Bernstein, David H., 59n
Bierley, Calvin, 117n
Bigné, Enrique, 412n
Bird, Larry, 160
Bird, Richard J., 342n
Bishop, Jerry E., 155n
Bither, Stewart W., 156n
Blair, Adams, 338
Blair, Margaret, 342n, 343n
Blalock, Cecelia, 293n
Blasko, Vincent J., 94n, 95n
Blattberg, Robert C., 231n, 240, 250n, 270n, 271n, 280, 293n, 294n, 393n
Block, Timothy C., 117n
Boone, Pat, 44
Bowes, Elena, 135n
Bradham, Caleb, 397
Bradley, Johnson, 32n
Brock, Timothy C., 183n, 310n, 343n
Brodsky, Terry, 162
Brown, Ronald H., 32n
Bruner, Gordon C., II, 173, 174, 183n
Bruzzone, Donald E., 176, 177, 179, 183n

Bryant, Jennings, 183n
Bucklin, Louis P., 134n
Buesing, Thomas, 294n
Bult, Jan Roelf, 393n
Burke, Bill, Sr., 33n
Burke, Raymond R., 95n
Burnett, Leo, 86–87
Burnkrant, Robert E., 135n
Burns, David M., 341n
Burns, Greg, 270n, 271n
Bush, George, 40, 152
Buzzell, Robert D., 270n, 271n

Caballero, Marjorie, 207n
Cacioppo, John T., 111, 113, 114, 115, 117n, 193
Calder, Bobby J., 155n
Calfee, John E., 59n
Campbell, Leland, 183n
Carlson, Eugene, 32n
Carlson, Les, 207n
Carlton, Jim, 250n
Carman, James M., 343n
Carroll, Lewis, 310n
Carton, Barbara, 162
Cavendish, James, 319–320
Celsi, Richard L., 117n
Chakravarty, Subrata N., 416, 435n
Chandy, Rajesh, 95n, 435n
Charles, Marj, 271n
Chase, Bradley, 289–290, 395
Chaves, Mark, 319–320
Chevalier, Michel, 270n, 271n
Chiat, Jay, 65
Churchill, Gilbert A., Jr., 342n
Clancey, Maura, 134n
Clark, Don, 412n
Clark, Eddie M., 183n, 310n, 343n
Clarke, Darryl G., 310n

Clemons, D. Scott, 117n
Clinton, Bill, 152, 153, 186, 187
Clow, Lee, 65, 86
Coen, Robert, 347
Cohen, Dorothy, 38n, 59n
Cohen, Joel B., 342n
Cole, Catherine A., 294n
Coleman, Terry, 436n
Colford, Steven W., 60n, 156n,
    207n, 271n
Colley, Russell H., 310n
Collins, Pat, 255
Collis, David J., 94n
Connors, Jimmy, 186
Cooper, Gordon, 44
Cooper, Lee G., 24n
Cosby, Bill, 185, 190, 192, 198, 204
Craig, C. Samuel, 117n
Crawford, C. Merle, 435n
Creno, Glen, 230n
Cronin, Jerry, 305
Crowley, Ayn E., 156n
Cuinan, Mary, 333
Cuneo, Alice Z., 95n
Cunningham, Michael, 183n
Curhan, Ronald C., 270n, 271n
Currim, Imran S., 231n
Curry, David J., 33n, 342n, 343n,
    374n, 393n

Dalrymple, Goodrum, 94n, 95n,
    135n, 207n, 342n, 374n
Dalrymple, Helen, 32n
Dalzell, Jane, 374n
Davidson, Jean, 358
Davis, Murray, 126
Davis, Scott D., 294n
Day, Guy, 65
deBono, Edward, 84
Decker, Cathleen, 140
Deighton, John, 117n, 168, 182n,
    393n
Dérze, Xavier, 231n
DeSarbo, Wayne, 196
Deutschman, A., 436n
Deveny, Kathleen, 33n, 183n, 236,
    276, 293n, 294n
Dhar, Sanjay K., 294n
Dickson, Peter R., 231n
DiFranza, Joseph R., 313, 317–318,
    321, 331, 342n
Dimeo, Joan, 208n
Dodson, Joe A., 294n

Dolich, Ira J., 156n
Donahue, Phil, 350
Donofrio, Nicholas, 333
Doughty, Heidi, 162
Dreze, Xavier, 250n
Drogin, Bob, 295n
Drucker, Peter F., 23, 33n
Dubow, Joel S., 331, 342n
Duff, Christina, 250n
Dugas, Christine, 41n, 59n
Dukakis, Michael, 152
Du Plessis, Eric, 329, 342n
Durairaj, Maheshwaran, 156n
Durvusula, Srinivas, 131
Dwyer, Paula, 41n, 59n

Eastlack, Joseph O., Jr., 343n
Ehrenberg, A. D. C., 294n
Elders, Joycelyn, 152, 153, 312
Eliashberg, Jehoshua, 95n, 424,
    436n
Elliot, Stuart, 117n
Elliott, Stuart, 94n, 374n
Elyse, Tanouye, 59n
Emerson, Ralph Waldo, 18
Endicott, R. Craig, 393n
Engle, Randall W., 117n
Englis, Basil G., 207n
Enshoff, James R., 343n
Eovaldi, Thomas L., 59n, 60n
Evans, Bergen, 32n

Fader, Peter S., 250n
Farley, John U., 343n
Farmer, Kenneth M., 182n
Farris, Paul W., 156n, 343n, 412n
Fawcett, Adrienne Ward, 32n, 59n
Feldman, Paul, 231n
Fera, Warner, 412n
Ferri, Gian Luigi, 53
Festervand, Troy A., 208n
Field, Harry, 142, 143
Fischer, Paul M., 312
Fisher, Christy, 393n
Fitzgerald, Kate, 156n, 250n, 294n,
    436n
Fizdale, Rick, 95n
Flynn, Julia, 95n
Folkes, Valerie S., 33n
Ford, Gary T., 59n
Ford, Henry, 25
Fornell, Claes, 33n
Foster, Richard, 435n

Fox, Michael J., 109
Franklin, Benjamin, 382
Franz, Julie, 295n
Friedman, Milton, 227
Friedman, Wayne, 375n
Frydlewicz, Rob, 370, 374n
Furse, David H., 95n, 183n, 342n

Gabler, Neal, 207n
Gaidis, William C., 294n
Gallup, George, 329, 360
Gamble, James, 8, 9
Gardner, Meryl P., 183n
Garfield, Bob, 32n, 135n, 182n
Garnett, Katrina, 333
Gates, Bill, 395
Gatty, Bob, 59n, 60n
Gellene, Denise, 59n
Gerstner, Eitan, 250n, 270n
Ghemwat, Pankaj, 415, 416
Gibson, Lawrence, 342n
Gibson, Richard, 238, 294n
Gillette, King, 414
Gilmore, Robert F., 135n
Gilpin, Elizabeth, 341n
Glaberson, William, 374n
Gleason, Mark, 117n
Glionna, John M., 294n
Glover, John, 95n
Godin, Helene, 207n
Goetzinger, Charles, 104
Gold, Laurence N., 374n
Goldberg, Marvin E., 183n
Goldberg, Stephen M., 94n
Golder, Peter N., 32n, 427, 435n,
    436n
Goldman, Kevin, 79n, 94n, 156n,
    207n, 208n, 374n, 375n, 412n
Goldstein, Adam O., 341n
Goldstein, Robert, 342n
Goll, Beatty, 60n
Goodhardt, G. J., 294n
Goodman, Charles S., 231n
Goodrum, Charles, 32n
Gorn, Gerald J., 156n, 183n
Gray, John, 426
Green, Corliss L., 294n
Green-Armytage, Johnson, 435n
Greene, Bob, 155n
Grev, Rita, 183n
Grewal, Dhruv, 231n
Greyser, Stephen A., 183n
Guilford, J. P., 84

Gundlach, 173
Gupta, Kamal, 33n
Gupta, Sunil, 250n
Gupta, Udayan, 33n
Gurumurthy, K., 231n

Ha, Young-Won, 117n
Habern, Glenn, 333
Hagerty, Michael R., 183n
Haley, R. I., 342n
Hamilton, Ian, 197, 199
Hammond, Kathy, 294n
Haran, Leah, 250n
Harris, Richard Jackson, 59n
Harris, Roger, 352
Harshman, Richard, 196
Hatfield, Tinker, 200
Hauser, John, 430, 431
Hawkins, Scott A., 117n
Hays, Laurie, 334, 342n
Heasley, Philip, 334
Heitsmith, Glenn, 274, 294n
Helm, Leslie, 412n
Helson, Harry, 125
Henderson Blair, Margaret, 338
Henthorne, Tony L., 183n
Hess, James D., 250n, 270n
Hevner, 173
Hewitt, Jean, 162
Hewson, Edward, 104
Hirsch, James S., 208n, 393n
Hoch, Stephen J., 117n, 182n, 231n
Hoch, Steve, 250n
Hoffman, Donna L., 393n
Hofmeister, Sallie, 294n
Holmes, Larry, 204
Hooley, Graham J., 412n
Hope, Bob, 196
Hopkins, Claude, 171
Horovitz, Bruce, 156n, 183n, 374n
Horton, Cleveland, 32n, 342n
Houseman, John, 190
Houston, Whitney, 186
Howard, Daniel J., 155n
Hoyer, Wayne D., 59n, 155n, 156n, 183n, 231n
Hughes, David G., 342n
Hume, Scott, 253, 293n
Hwang, Suein L., 343n, 435n
Hyun, Yong J., 342n

Iacocca, Lee, 150, 186, 188, *189,* 191–192

Inman, James E., 59n
Inman, Jeffrey J., 231n, 294n
Ippolito, Pauline M., 60n

Jaben, Jan, 295n, 412n
Jackson, Bo, 200
Jackson, Michael, 169, 170, 198–199, 200, 398
Jacoby, Jacob, 59n, 155n
Jaffe, Lynn J., 207n, 208n
Janiszewski, Chris, 117n
Jaworski, Bernard J., 117n, 118n
Jaynes, John, 334
Jensen, Jeff, 207n
Jensen, Thomas D., 207n
Jobs, Steve, 20
Johnson, Bradley, 250n, 271n, 295n, 412n
Johnson, Earvin "Magic," 198, 199, 204
Johnson, Michael, 341n–342n
Johnson, Richard D., 156n
Jones, Charles, 295n
Jones, John Philip, 400, 412n
Jordan, Michael, 86, 160, 185, 197, 198, 199, 204

Kaatz, Ronald B., 134n
Kahn, E. J., Jr., 60n
Kahneman, Tversky, 231n, 232n
Kalapurakal, Rosemary, 231n
Kalmenson, Stuart, 342n
Kalwani, Manohar U., 231n
Kamins, Michael A., 156n
Kamp, Edward, 182n
Kassarjian, Harold H., 117n, 118n
Keller, Bruce P., 59n
Keller, Kevin Lane, 155n
Kelly, Keith J., 375n
Kent, Robert J., 354, 355
Keough, Donald, 68
Kerwin, Kathleen, 95n
Key, Janet, 58n
Kim, Byung-Do, 231n, 310n
Kimble, Gregory A., 117n
King, Charles, 137–138
King, Karen Whitehall, 117n
King, Thomas R., 94n, 207n
Kinnear, 173
Kinsman, F. G., 13
Klein, David M., 183n
Klompmaker, Jay E., 415, 416, 417, 422, 435n

Kneale, Dennis, 135n
Knecht, G. Bruce, 343n
Knetsch, Jack L., 232n
Koop, C. Everett, 185, *186*
Koresh, David, 54
Kover, Arthur J., 94n
Krishna, Aradhna, 231n
Krishnan, Trichy V., 250n
Kristof, Kathy M., 59n
Krugman, Herbert E., 106, 110, 134n
Kudrow, Lisa, 100
Kuhn, Thomas S., 95n
Kumar, V., 134n, 412n
Kummel, Charles M., 415, 416, 417, 422, 435n

LaBarbera, Priscilla A., 55n, 56n, 59n
Laczniak, Russell N., 117n
Landler, Mark, 95n
Langmeyer, Lynn, 208n
LaTour, Michael S., 183n
Lawrence, Jennifer, 270n, 288, 293n, 374n
Lazarus, George, 95n, 412n
Lears, Jackson, 208n
Leavitt, Clark, 117n
Lee, Angela, 155n
Lehmann, Donald R., 343n
Leigh, James H., 132
Lemmon, Jack, 195–196
Leno, Jay, 169, 170
Leone, Robert P., 294n
Levin, Gary, 207n
Levine, Joshua, 59n, 60n
Lieber, Janet, 278
Liesse, Julie, 95n
Limbaugh, Rush, 186
Lipman, Joanne, 60n, 79, 94n, 135n, 207n, 208n, 412n
Lipstein, Benjamin, 310n, 342n, 343n
Little, John D. C., 231n, 412n
Livelsberger, Jeanne, 342n
Lloyd, Chris Evert, 186
Lodish, Leonard M., 250n, 267, 310n, 342n, 343n
Lord, Kenneth R., 135n
Loren, Sophia, 191
Louis-Dreyfus, Robert, 62
Lubetkin, Beth, 342n
Luhr, David, 300

Lumpkin, James R., 207n, 208n
Lynch, James E., 412n
Lynch, Peter, 185

MacDonald, Alice, 214, 291
MacInnis, Deborah, 117n, 118n, 182n
Madden, Charles S., 207n
Madonna, 184–185, 186, 197, 199, 398, 426–427
Magiera, Marcy, 94n
Mahajan, Vijay, 436n
Maites, Alan, 412n
Major, John, 223
Mandese, Joe, 207n, 374n
Marmorstein, Howard, 231n
Martin, Claude R., Jr., 341n, 342n
Martin, Edward J., 273
Martin, Ingrid M., 33n
Masterson, Peg, 353
Mathios, Alan D., 60n
May, Stephen C., 352
Mazis, Michael B., 42n
McAlister, Leigh, 231n, 250n, 294n
McCarthy, Michael, 23n
McCracken, Grant, 117n, 190–191, 207n
McEnroe, John, 197
McGill, Ann L., 135n
McGuire, William J., 118n, 156n
McNeill, Dennis L., 42n
McQuarrie, Edward F., 170, 171, 172, 183n
McQueen, Josh, 168
McSweeney, Frances K., 117n
Meyers, Janet, 95n
Mick, David Glen, 170, 171, 172, 183n
Miller, Cyndee, 207n, 374n
Miller, Julia, 59n
Miller, Karen Lowry, 270n, 271n
Miller, Peter, 393n
Milliman, Ronald E., 183n
Millington, Elizabeth, 162
Milner, Laura, 208n
Mitchell, Andrew A., 111n, 117n, 182n
Mittal, Banwari, 134n, 294n
Mizerski, Richard, 342n
Mokwa, Michael P., 94n, 95n
Mondale, Walter, 177
Monroe, Kent B., 59n
Montogomery, Alan L., 231n

Moriatry, Sandra E., 95n
Morrison, Donald G., 24n, 294n
Moss, Kate, 100, 202
Moss, Robert F., 436n
Muehling, Darrel D., 117n, 131, 156n
Mueller, Frederick H., 32n
Muldoon, Katie, 381, 382, 393n
Mulhern, Francis J., 294n
Murphy, John H., II, 374n
Myers-Levy, Joan, 135n, 156n

Nader, Ralph, 40
Naeye, Robert, 342n
Narasimhan, Chakravarthi, 135n, 294n
Natarajan, Rajan, 183n
Nault, Barrie R., 436n
Neelankavil, James P., 343n
Nell, Elaine B., 156n
Nelson, Emily, 59n
Neslin, Scott A., 231n, 240, 250n, 270n, 271n, 280, 293n, 294n
Newman, Joseph W., 135n
Nielsen, Arthur C., 17, 344–345, 360
Nixon, Richard M., 40
Nord, Walter R., 95n
Novak, Thomas P., 393n
Novella, Antonia, 311

O'Brien, Louise, 295n
Ogilvy, David, 79, 80, 81, 84–85, 88, 91, 94n, 129
Olsen, Douglas, 135n
Olson, Jerry C., 117n
Olssen, Jonathan, 162
Ortega, Bob, 58n, 250n
Oshinsky, 173
Ostrom, Thomas M., 117n
Ovitz, Michael, 68

Packard, Vance, 105
Parker-Pope, Tara, 94n
Parry, Mark E., 412n
Parsons, May L., 183n
Patzer, Gordon L., 135n
Pavlov, Ivan, 101–102
Peacock, Peter, 294n
Pechmann, Cornelia, 117n, 156n, 342n
Pehrson, John D., 326
Peller, Clara, 198

Pemberton, John, 397
Peracchio, Laura A., 135n
Percy, Larry, 135n, 155n
Petty, Richard E., 111, 113, 114, 115, 117n, 193
Petty, Ross D., 59n, 60n, 156n
Pham, Michel Tuan, 342n
Pierce, John P., 312
Piirto, Rebecca, 374n
Pippin, Scottie, 197
Poltrack, David F., 375n
Pomice, Eva, 208n
Pope, Kyle, 94n
Porter, Michael E., 94n, 399, 412n
Power, Christopher, 33n
Presley, Priscilla, 191
Preston, Ivan L., 59n
Price, Nicholas, 312
Prince, Greg W., 94n
Procter, William, 8, 9
Purk, Mary, 231n, 250n

Quayle, Dan, 186
Quelch, John A., 78n, 214, 270n, 271n, 291

Rabinowitz, David, 207n
Rajendran, K. N., 231n
Raju, Jagmohan S., 294n
Rangan, Kasturi V., 419
Rangaswamy, Arvind, 95n
Rao, Ambar G., 343n
Rao, Ram C., 250n
Rao, Vithala R., 393n
Rapaport, Richard, 388, 389
Rappaport, Anatol, 436n
Ratchford, Brian T., 174, 183n
Ratneshwar, S., 342n
Raven, Peter, 156n
Ray, Michael, 182n, 308
Reagan, Ronald, 40, 177
Reeves, Byron, 342n
Reeves, Rosser, 88, 91
Reid, Leonard N., 207n, 326
Reynolds, Christopher, 295n
Richards, Jef I., 59n, 374n
Richards, John W., Jr., 341n
Richardson, Bruce, 342n
Richins, Marsha L., 202, 203
Richmond, Howard, II, 333
Richter, Paul, 248
Rickard, Leah, 207n
Ridley, Matt, 231n

Ries, Al, 33n, 141
Riesz, Peter, 393n
Rinne, Heikki J., 231n
Ripley, M. Louise, 95n
Robertson, Thomas S., 117n, 118n
Robinson, David, 197
Robinson, William A., 412n
Rogers, John C., 149
Rogers, Stuart, 117n
Rojas, Tina H., 341n
Romer, Daniel, 168
Rosbrook, Bradley, 341n
Rosenberg, Karl E., 338, 342n, 343n
Ross, Chuck, 59n
Rossi, Peter E., 231n
Rossiter, John R., 135n, 155n
Rotfeld, Herbert J., 59n, 60n, 183n
Roth, Joe, 80
Rothenberg, Randall, 95n, 310n
Rothschild, Michael, 294n, 342n
Roux, Michel, 356–357
Rubel, Chad, 117n

Saatchi, Charles, 61
Saatchi, Maurice, 61–64, 65, 66–67
Sabatini, Gabriela, 191
Salem, D'Jamila, 60n
Salmon, Walter J., 270n, 271n
Sampras, Pete, 100, *100*
Sanger, Steve, 279
Sawhney, Mohanbir S., 424
Sawyer, Alan G., 117n, 155n, 231n
Scherak, Tom, 436n
Schiller, Zachary, 270n, 271n, 274
Schlossberg, Howard, 255, 271n, 294n, 393n
Schmittlein, David C., 24n
Schroer, James C., 401, 412n
Schulberg, Jay, 102
Schumann, David, 113n, 114n, 117n, 193
Schwadel, Francine, 250n
Schwartz, Meyer P., 341n
Scott, Charles, 62
Scott, Cliff, 183n
Scott, George C., 190
Scott, Linda M., 155n, 183n
Sears, John, 381
Secunda, Eugene, 135n
Segal, Erich, 88
Selinger, Iris Cohen, 83n
Sen, Subrata, 294n
Serafin, Raymond, 208n

Sethuraman, Raj, 343n, 398, 412n, 425, 436n
Shapiro, Eben, 436n
Sharkey, Betsy, 208n
Sharon, Moshavi D., 374n
Sheldon, Esther K., 183n
Shelton, Debbie, 88
Sherer, 173
Sheth, Jagdish N., 135n, 393n
Shields, Brooke, 189–190, 192
Shimp, Terrence A., 117n
Shoemaker, Robert W., 231n, 294n
Shopland, Donald, 341n
Shore, Andrew, 374n
Shriman, David, 156n
Silk, Alvin J., 94n
Silverstein, Rich, 86
Silverstein, Stuart, 59n
Simpson, Bart, 272
Simpson, O. J., 140–141
Singer, Penny, 393n
Singh, Surendra N., 342n
Sisodia, Rajendran, 374n
Skillern, Frank, 333
Sloan, Alfred, 22
Sloan, Gleason, 94n
Sloan, Pat, 94n, 374n, 416
Slung, Michele, 436n
Smith, Adam, 227
Smith, Amie, 294n
Smith, Dave, 95n
Smith, Martin J., 182n
Snyder, Wally, 59n
Soley, Lawrence C., 134n, 207n
Solomon, Caleb, 60n
Solomon, Michael R., 207n
Somoroff, Michael, 83
Sonner, Brenda S., 342n
Sorbara, Joseph A., 273
Spotts, Harlan, 183n
Springs, Elliott, 127
Srinivasan, Srini S., 294n
Stafford, Edwin R., 207n
Stannard, Charles I., 182n
Starch, 330
Starr, Ringo, 190
Stayman, Douglas M., 183n
Steadman, Major, 135n
Steckel, Joel H., 393n
Steinberg, Jeff, 183n
Steiner, Robert L., 339, 343n
Stem, Donald E., Jr., 156n
Stern, Barbara B., 182n

Stern, Gabriella, 374n
Stern, Louis W., 59n, 60n
Sternthal, Brian, 117n, 155n, 294n
Stevens, Mary Ellen, 342n
Stewart, David W., 95n, 117n, 156n, 182n, 183n, 310n, 342n, 343n
Stewart, Jimmy, 187
Stipp, David H., 155n
Stolberg, Sheryl, 342n
Stone, Bob, 383, 393n
Strathman, Alan J., 118n
Straughton, Katherine, 342n
Strauss, Neil, 232n
Streisand, Barbra, 228–229
Stuart, Elliott, 94n, 95n
Stuart, Elnora W., 117n
Sugita, Yoshi, 231n
Swasy, Alecia, 32n
Swinyard, William R., 149
Synodinos, Nicolaos, 117n

Taylor, Elizabeth, 191
Teinowitz, Ira, 79n, 94n, 208n, 271n
Tellis, Gerard J., 32n, 117n, 134n, 231n, 294n, 310n, 343n, 398, 412n, 425, 435n, 436n
Thaler, Richard, 231n, 232n
Thatcher, Margaret, 223
Thomas, Lacy Glenn, 436n
Throson, Esther, 342n
Tripp, Carolyn, 207n
Trout, Jack, 33n, 141
Tucker, Sharon, 95n
Tversky, Amos, 231n
Tybout, Alice M., 155n, 156n, 294n
Tyson, Mike, 398

Underwood, Elaine, 412n
Unnava, Rao H., 118n
Urbany, Joel E., 231n
Ursic, Anthony C., 205
Ursic, Michael L., 205
Ursic, Virginia L., 205
Utterback, James M., 423, 435n

Valencia, Humberto, 208n
Vandenbosch, Mark B., 436n
Veechi, Christa Van Anh, 59n
Vicary, James McDonald, 105
Vinovich, 173
Von Oech, Roger, 84

Waldholz, Michael, 183n
Wallas, Graham, 95n
Wallenstein, Andrew, 94n
Walton, Sam, 234
Wanamaker, John, 313–314
Wansbeek, Tom, 393n
Ward, Montgomery, 13, 381
Warlop, Luk, 117n
Wascoe, Dan, Jr., 293n
Watson, 173
Wattenberg, Ben J., 32n
Weber, Ernst, 123–125
Wedlin, 173
Weigold, 156n
Weinberg, Charles B., 156n
Weinberger, Marc G., 183n
Wells, George, 271n
Wells, Ken, 374n

Wells, Melanie, 95n
Wentz, Laurel, 94n, 95n
West, Christopher J., 412n
Whalen, Elizabeth, 341n
White, Vanna, 100
Whitehill King, Karen, 326
Whiteman, Charles, 310n
Whitney, Craig, R., 231n
Whittler, Tommy E., 208n
Wieden, Dan, 300, 305
Wilkes, Robert E., 208n
Wilkie, William L., 42n, 156n
Williams, Terrell G., 149
Willigan, Geraldine E., 207n
Wind, Jerry, 95n
Wind, Yoram, 436n
Winer, Russell S., 231n
Winters, Patricia, 412n

Wisniewski, Kenneth J., 250n, 271n
Wonder, Stevie, *170*
Woods, Robert J., 195–196
Woodside, Arch, 135n
Wyman, John, 383, 384

Yao, Dennis A., 59n
Yim, Chi Kin, 231n
Young, James Webb, 84

Zajonc, Robert, 104
Zeithaml, Valerie, 231n
Zielske, Hubert, 405, 406
Zimmerman, Denise, 393n
Zinkhan, 183n
Zinsser, William, 133

Subject Index

Accessibility, of information, 320
Accessible segment, 26
Accountability, in political advertising, 44
Accounting measures of performance, *28*, *29*
Accounting variables, 307
Account review, 79
Accounts, 66
Accounts-based organization, 74–75
Accounts management, 66–67
  at Chiat/Day, *65*, 66
  at Leo Burnett Co., 66
  at Saatchi & Saatchi, 66–67
Accumulated reach, 367
ACORN, 22
Active meter, 324
Active processing, 122
Activism
  emotion and, 161–163
  PETA and, *162*
Ad appeal, 31
Adaptation-level theory, 125–126
Ad campaign. *See* Campaigns
Ad-intensity, 336
Ad meter, 325–326, *326*
Ads, ineffective, 338–339
AdTel Experiments, 336, *337*
Advertisement, copy in, 132–133
Advertisements
  components of, 131–133
  context of, 110
  effectiveness of distinctive, *131*
  placement of, 133
  quick cut, 125
Advertiser-agency relationships, 79, *79*
Advertisers, leading national, *8*

Advertising, 6. *See also* Advertising-sales relationship; Integrated advertising and sales promotion strategy; Truth in promotion
  budget allocation to, 425–426, *425*
  carryover effect of, 409–410
  challenges to claims of, 41
  claims in, 17, *17*
  collecting data on, 319–328
  controversies over role of, 14–16
  cooperative, 260–261, *261*
  corrective, 42–43
  delayed effects of, 409–410
  dynamic effects of, 408–410
  early agency, *14*
  early media for, 13–14
  early newspaper, *11*
  effectiveness of, 311–314
  evaluation methods, 315–319
  expenditures on, 6, *7*
  history of, 8–18
  for innovative new products, *12*
  integrated strategy for, 414–415
  integration in life cycle, 428–430
  judgments about, *5*
  laboratory experiment on, 315
  market share and, *401*
  measurement of, 17, *306*, 328–335, *328*
  political, 44
  and price promotion, 429
  principal agents of, 6–8
  Procter & Gamble's Ivory soap and, 8–10, *9*
  resonant, 170, *171*
  scheduling expenditures for, 405–410

  setting goals for, 299–302
  S-shaped response to, 403, *403*
  subliminal, 105–106
  substantiation of, 38–39
  systematic measurement of, 17
  on television, 350–352
  theme of, 27
  time devoted to television, 51
  and trade promotion, 428–429
  U.S. expenditures on, *347*
  from U.S. independence to Civil War, 10
  World War I to World War II, 16–17
  after World War II, 17–18
Advertising Age, 50 best TV ads of, 91
Advertising agencies. *See also* Campaigns; Goals
  accounts management at, 66–67
  choosing, 75–80
  compensating, 80–83
  creative function of, 65–66
  early, *14*
  functions of, 65–68
  growth of, 14–16
  locating, 75–76
  market for, 64–65
  market research and, 67–68
  McCann-Erickson Worldwide as, 68, *69–70*
  media planning by, 67
  organization of, 74–75
  organizing advertising function and, 76–77
  ownership of, 72–74
  relationships with advertisers, 79
  Saatchi & Saatchi, 61–64

structure of, 64–75
types of, 68–72
Wieden & Kennedy's Subaru
  account, 299–302, *301, 303*
world's largest (1995), *62–63*
Advertising associations, with advertising regulations, *55*
Advertising effects, 306–308
Advertising elasticities, promotional
  strategies and, *425*
Advertising function, 76–77
Advertising level, 336
Advertising organization. *See*
  Holding company
Advertising program, *30*
Advertising regulation
  comparative, 43–44
  demonstrations, 45
  endorsements, 44–45
  loans and leasing, 46
  warranties, 45–46
Advertising-sales relationship,
  335–340
  studies on, 336–338
Advertising-to-sales ratio, 397, *398*
  of leading colas, *399*
Advertorials, 126
Ad-weight, 336
Affective goals, 28, *28*
Affective processes, 307
Affiliates, 350
Affirmative disclosure, 41–42
Affordability, budget and, 396
African-Americans, racial stereo-
  types of, 204
Age group, segmentation by, *22*
Agencies, 6–7. *See also* Advertising
  agencies
  early, *14*
  growth of, 14–16
  ineffective ads and, 339
Agency brand, 73
Agents, of advertising, 6–8
Age stereotypes, 204–205
AIDA (attention, interest, desire,
  action), 308
Airline industry
  bonus plans in, 286
  mail promotions and, 383
Alcohol, labeling of, *54*
Alcohol manufacturers, slotting
  allowances and, 258
Alcohol and Tobacco Tax Division,
  of Internal Revenue Service, 17

Allowance, display, 261–262
Allowances, slotting, 258
American Bar Association
  ban on member advertising, 56
  FTC and, 40
  self-regulation by, 55
American Dental Association
  self-regulation and, 55, 57
American Medical Association, self-
  regulation and, 57
Analysis, 137
Anheuser-Busch experiments, 336,
  337
Animals
  for attention, *128*
  PETA and, *162*
Anorexia, female models and,
  202–203
Antitrust division, of Justice
  Department, 35
Appeal, *30*
  of unconditioned stimulus, 103
Apple Macintosh computers, introduction of, 3–4
Arbitrage, 219
Argument
  components of, *168*
  effectiveness of, 168
  framing in, 152, *154*
  inoculative, 152–153
  refutational, 150–152
  supportive, 152
Arguments. *See also* Argument strat-
  egy; Argument strength
  AT&T "Reachout and touch
    someone" campaign and,
    139–140, 141
  comparative, 147–150, *147, 148,
    149*
  counterarguments, 139, *142*
  number vs. strength of, 112
  strength of, 141–142
  support, 139, *142*
Argument strategy, 137, 145–153
  in deregulated telephone industry,
    145, *146*
Argument strength, 112, 113, *114*
Arousal, 158
Art direction, 65–66
Association, 102–103, 143
Associations, with advertising regu-
  lations, *55*
Associative mode, emotion and, 160
Associative thinking, 84

Assumptions, contradicting, 126
Asymmetry, 228
  in promotions and, *243*
  in response, 225–227
Attention, 120
  ad components and, 131–133
  ad placement in medium and, 133
  animals for, *128*
  emotions and, 126–129
  gaining, 123–131
  headlines for, 131, *131*
  humor and, 172
  information and, 126, *127*
  message and, *130*
  methods for gaining, 130–131
  Nestlé Gold Blend and Taster's
    Choice campaigns, 123
  physical stimuli and, 123–126
  providing information and, 126
  receptivity and, 121–123
  selective, 120–121
  stimulus intensity and, *124*
  value offer and, 129
Attention-getting/informative campaign, 407
Attributes, product, 165
Attribution theory, 278, 308
Audience. *See* Syndicated data
  sources
  endorsers and, 192–193, *192*
  humor and, 171–172
  involvement of and emotion for,
    165
  mood of, 165–166
  reach and, 367
  responses to attractive models,
    203
  share of, 361
  truth in promotion and, 37–38
  vehicle choice and, 360–362
Audiometer, 344
Audit Bureau of Circulation, 17
Automobile industry
  BMW's refutational argument and,
    150–151
  General Motors in, 22–23
  Japanese exports and, 305
  Wieden & Kennedy's Subaru cam-
    paign, 299–302, *301, 303*
Automobile leases, 46
Automobile retailing, 264
Average frequency, 368–369
Avis rental car, 26
Avoidance, 122

Bait and switch, 49

Banks and banking, draft fraud and, 51

Bargains, 48

Baseline, 267

BATF. *See* Bureau of Alcohol, Tobacco, and Firearms (BATF)

Behavior. *See also* Consumer
hierarchy of effects and, 306–310
music and, 174

Behavioral price response curve, *223*

Behavioral research, 217

Beliefs, 126

Benefit segmentation, 23–24, *26*

Better Business Bureau, self-regulation and, *55*

Bias
demand, 321–322
in recognition measurement, 330
of self-reports, 320–321
self-serving, 20
social desirability, 321

Big Brother, data collection and, 324, *325*

Bill-back, 258

Black Bag experiment, 104

Black box, consumer behavior and, 307

Bonus plans, 286–288

Boutiques, 71

Brain, memory, retrieval, and, 142–143

Brain-wave recordings, 327

Brand and branding, 13, 15–16
comparative advertising by, 149–150
competition and, 400–401
displays and, *236, 238*
dominant and subordinate, 149–150
growth rate of, 400
message familiarity and, 107, *107*
private labels and generic brands, 242–243
proliferation of, 253–254
prototypical, 144–145
similarity of, 253
stimulus link to, 128
switching, 242–243

Brand choice, 306
as strategic goal, *28, 29*

Brand loyalty, 24, 141, 275
association and, 143

Brand switching, 269

Broadcast media, 50–51, 347

Brokers, advertising, 14

Brown's iron bitters, *16*

Bud Bowl campaign, 119–120, 125

Budget and budgeting
affordability method, 396
for Coca-Cola and Pepsi-Cola, 398–399
competitive parity method of, 399–402
determining, 396–405
elasticity-ratio approach to, 404–406
Gillette's allocation, by product, *422*
ineffective ads and, 339
for Microsoft Windows 95, 394–395
objective-and-task method of, 402
percentage-of-sales method, 397
over product life cycle, 421
profit-maximization method of, 402–404
total promotional, 425

Bulimia, female models and, 202–203

Bureau of Alcohol, Tobacco, and Firearms (BATF), 35, 54, 258

Bursting, 406

Business associations
with advertising regulations, *55*
self-regulation by, 55–57

Buyers, 6, 247

Cable data, 332

Cable TV, 351–352, *351*

California, Sears deceptive practices in, 20–21

Caller ID, data collection and, *325*

Calvin Klein jeans ad, 189–190

Camel cigarettes. *See* Joe Camel advertising campaign

Campaigns, 109. *See also* specific campaigns
goals of, 302–306, 407, *410*
message repetition in, 109
speculative, 80
wearin and wearout of, 408–409, *409*
Wieden & Kennedy's Subaru campaign, 299–302

Campbell's Soup experiments, 336, 337

Carryover effect, of advertising, 409–410

Casting, 200

Catalog advertising, 13–14

Catalog direct marketing, 381–382

Categorization, 144

Causality
reverse, 319
testing, 316–317

Cease-and-desist order, 41

Celebrity endorsers, 44, 112, 184–185, 186–187, *191. See also* Endorsers
conditioning and, 102
matching to consumer segments, 197
overuse of, 197–198

Centers, as displays, 237

Central route of persuasion, 111–112, *112*, 114–115

Cents-off packs. *See* Price packs (cents-off packs)

Chain letters, 52

Channel characteristics, of promotions, 215–216, *216*

Channel conflict, 264

Character, 168

Characterization, 200
irritation and, 176

Charities, fictitious, 52

Check kiting, 52

Checkout scanners, 327–328, 332

Children, infomercials and, 50

Children's Television Act (1991), 51

Choice, on Internet, 388

Chunks of information, 143–144

Cigarettes. *See also* Joe Camel advertising campaign
information on, *419*

Circulation, 361
figures for, 17

Civil War period, advertising and, 10–16

Claims
challenges to advertising, 41
material, 39
misleading, 37
substantiated, 17, *17*

Classical conditioning, 101–104

Clayton Act (1914), price discrimination and, 47

ClusterPLUS, 22

Clutter, 354

Codes. *See* Self-regulation

Cognition, 137, 139–142. *See also* Cognitive consistency
argument strength and, 141–142
defined, 139

mood and, 142
repetition and, 142
Cognitive consistency, 120–121, 140–141
brand loyalty and, 141
O. J. Simpson trial and, 140–141
Cognitive goals, 28, *28*
Cognitive involvement, 110
Cognitive processes, 307
Cognitive responses, 139
Commercials. *See also* Television
degrees of irritation with, *176*
length of television, *354*
music in, 173–175
Commercial speech, First Amendment protection of, *56-57*
Commission compensation method, 14, 80–81
Communications. *See also* Attention; Copy; Meaning; Perception
modes of endorsers, 193–194
print, 138–139
sales promotions and, 216
television, 138
Comparable market price, 48
Comparative advertising, regulation of, 43–44
Comparative argument, 147–150, *147, 148*
competitive position and, 149–150
effectiveness of appeal, *149*
trends in use of, *149*
two-sided appeals and, 148–149
Comparative reach, *370*
Compensation, 18
for advertising agencies, 80–83
Home Depot, Admarketing, and, 80
percentage of advertisers using various types, *83*
Competition
among agencies, 65
AT&T and MCI, 433
bonus plans and, 286
Coca-Cola and Pepsi-Cola, 397–398
comparative arguments and, 147–150
ineffective ads and, 339
retail promotions and, 235
Competitive parity, between Coca-Cola and Pepsi-Cola, 397–398
Competitive parity method, 399–400

strategic decisions in, 400–402
Competitive position, 149–150
Complex argument, 108
Complexity, of message, 108–109, *108*
Comprehension levels, 138–139
Compressed ad, 109
Computerized databases, 378
Computer market, IBM in, 21
Computers. *See also* Personal computers
data mining and, *333–334*
media and, 355–356
Conative goals, 28, *28*
Conative processes, 307
Conditioned response, 102
Conditioned stimulus, 102
Conditioning
classical, 101–104
factors favoring, 103–104
process of, 102–103, *102*
source attractiveness and, 189
Consideration, sweepstakes, lotteries, and, 49
Consistency, cognitive, 140
Consumer, 6
endorsers and, *193*
information processing by, 137–145
matching celebrities to, 197
meaning and, 138
mistrust of promotion by, 40–41
price promotions and, 222–223
price-sensitive, 247
prior experiences of, 138
product life cycle and, 417–418
role of, 8
shopping changes by, 254
Consumer attention
distinctive ads and, *131*
gaining, 123–131
Consumer orientation, 18–21
product orientation and, 20
profit orientation and, 21
sales orientation and, 20–21
self-serving bias and, 20
success trap and, 20
Consumer promotions, *30, 213,* 215, 272–273
bonus plans as, 286–288
comparing, 292, *292*
manufacturer coupons as, 273–281
Nestlé Butterfinger promotion, 272–273

premiums as, 283–284
price packs as, 282–283
rebates as, 281–282
sampling as, 289–291
sweepstakes and contests as, 286–287
tie-ins as, 284–286
types of, *273*
Consumer Reports, advertising in, 352
Consumer shows, 260
Consumption, 29
Content, 348
creativity and, 88–90
direct media and, 380
Content pressure, and media advertising, 352–353, *353*
Contests and sweepstakes, 49, 286–287, *289*
consumer promotions and, 272–273
guidelines for, *290*
by Quaker Oats, 288
trade, 263–264
Context, of ad, 110
Contextual stimuli, 125
Continuity, 406
Contracts, with external agencies, 77–79
Contribution margin, of direct media, 390
Control group, 105
Controversial issues, 51
Convenience, of self-reports, 320
Conventions, 260
Cooperative advertising, 260–261, *261,* 429–430
Copy
in ad, 132–133
effective, 139
Copywriting, 65–66
Core competencies, external agency and, 76
Corrective advertising, 42–43
history of cases of, *42*
Cosmetics, 13
Cost(s). *See also* Budget and budgeting; Compensation
of direct marketing, 390, *390*
direct media and, 380–381
fixed, 246
of Internet advertising, 388
of internal vs. external agency, 75
price promotion profitability analysis and, 244–246

of sampling, 291
of trade promotions, 264–266
Cost-basis compensation method, 82
Cost effectiveness, of endorsers, 194
Cost efficiency, and media selection, 362, *362, 363*
Cost per rating point (CPP), 362, 364
Cost per thousand (CPM), 362
Counterarguments, 139, *142*
Counterattack strategy, 433–434
Coupon(s), 221, 239–240. *See also* Coupon redemption
  evaluating strategy of, 279–281
  expenditures on, *279*
  life span of, *277*
  long-term effects of, 277–278
  manufacturer, 273–281
  misredemptions of, 52, 278–279
  purpose of, 275
  redemption costs of, *280*
  in sales promotions, 214
  trends in, 280–281
Coupon drop, 275–276
Coupon redemption, 274, 275–279
  rate in U.S., *276*
  redeemer characteristics, 277
Covariation, 319
Coverage, 361–362
Creative, 5
Creative boutiques, 71
Creative function, 65, 67
Creative styles, 86–88
  examples of, by agency, 86–87, *87*
Creative thinking, 83–84
  fostering, 84–85
Creativity, 27. *See also* Creative thinking
  Apple's introductory Macintosh ad, 83
  Bernbach and, 88–90, 91
  Calvin Klein ads, 83
  content or execution and, 88–90
  management of, 83–92
  Ogilvy and, 91
  organizing for, 85–86
  Reeves and, 91
  science and, 5
  "Virginia is for lovers" campaign and, 88, *89*, 92
Credit cards
  data collection and, *325*
  direct media growth and, 379
  mail promotions, 383
Cross-ruff coupons, 274

Culture
  advertising and, 18
  music and, 175
Cume reach, 367
Cumulative audience, 367
Curiosity, 127–128
Customer, 6. *See* Consumer
Customer Satisfaction Index, 332
Customized research, 196

Data, disaggregate, 241
Databases
  computerized, 378
  direct media, 381
Data collection. *See also* Measurement
  on advertising, 319–328
  Big Brother and, 324, *325*
  on Catholics' church attendance, 319–320
  methods for, 320–322
  on outcome variables, 327–328
  on profitability of direct media, 390–391
  syndicated data sources and, 371–373
  tools for, 322–328
Data mining, *333–334*
Day-after recall, 329
Dealer, trade promotions and, 252
Deal price, 254–255
Deceptive, use of term, 39
Deceptive advertising. *See also* Truth in promotion
  by Campbell Soup Company, 34–35
  criteria for, 37–39
  price cuts and, 239
  puffery, miscomprehension, unfairness, and, 39–40
  by Wal-Mart, 35
Deceptive practices, of Sears, 20–21
Deceptive pricing, regulation of, 48
Deceptive value, 48–49
Decline period, 420
Decomposing
  of promotional bump, 242–244, 246, *246*
  trade promotion profitability and, 267, *268*
Defender Model, 430–434
  analgesic market and, *431*
  Coca-Cola/Pepsi-Cola competition and, 433–434
Defense reaction, fear and, 179

Defense strategies
  counterattack as, 433–434
  Defender Model and, 430–431
  deflection and, 431–432
  tit-for-tat strategy, 432–433
Defensive marketing, 152
Deflection strategy, 431–432
Delayed effects, 409–410
Delivery, of catalogues, 14
Delivery services, 382
Demand, consumer preferences and, 417
Demand bias (demand artifact), 321–322
Demographic segments, 21, *22, 25*, 364–365
Demonstration, 45, 168, *168*
Density index, 363–364
Dental floss ads, 181
Dependent variable, 315
Deregulation, of telephone industry, 145
Design, of experiment, 315
Design function. *See* Creative function
Detergents, sales promotions of, 213–214, *214*
Diary, 323, 327
Differentiation, 18
Direct approach, and demographic segments, 364–365
Direct costs, direct media and, 390, 391
Direct mail, costs of, *390*
Direct-mail coupons, 274
Direct marketing, 377–378, *381*
Direct media, 346
  campaign profitability, 391–392
  direct costs and, 390, 391
  Fidelity and, 376–377
  focus of, 359
  frequency and, 379
  growth of, 378–381
  Internet and, 386–389
  mail, 381–383
  planning of, 376–377
  precise reach and, 379
  profitability of, 389–392
  telephone as, 383–386
Direct trade-offs, 428
Disaggregate data, 241
Discounts and discounting, 217, *220*. *See also* Price-cuts
  against former or regular list price, 48

off-invoice, 256–257
  periodic, 219–220
  qualifying and second market, 222
  quantity, 257
  random, 220–222
Discrimination. *See* Price discrimination
Diseconomies of scale, 25
Disguise, 315
Displays, 235–237, *235*
  Disney's "The Lion King," *236*
  encouraging, *262, 263*
  location of, 236–237
  sales of popular brands and, *238*
  sales performance of brands and,
    236
  types of, 237
Display support, 261–262
Dissonance, 28, 308
Dissonance/attribution hierarchy,
  308
Distilled Spirits Council, self-regula-
  tion and, *55*
Distinct stimulus, 103
Distribution, trade promotions and,
  252–253
Distributors, 7–8
Divergent thinking, 84
  creativity and, 83
Diversity, as advertising goals, 300
Diverting, 255, *255*
  costs of, 265
Dominant brand, 149–150
Double coupons, 235, *235,*
  239–240, 429
Draft fraud, 51
Drama
  components of, *168*
  emotion and, 168–169
  fear and, *180*
Dream Team, Reebok, Nike, and,
  197
Drugs
  advertising of ethical, 52-53
  Pure Food and Drug Act and, 16
Dual entitlements, 227–229
Duplicated audience, 367, *367*
Dynamic effects, of advertising,
  408–410, *410*

Early advertising, by Sears, Roebuck
  and Co., 15, *15*
Echo Award-winning direct media
  campaigns, *380*

Economies of information, 400
Economy of scale. *See* Diseconomies
  of scale
Economy size, 49
ECR. *See* Efficient consumer
  response (ECR)
Effective frequency, 369
Efficient consumer response (ECR),
  266
Elaboration, 111–115
  and IBM ad, 112, *112*
  and IKEA ad, 113, *113*
Elaboration likelihood model
  (ELM), 111–114, *111*
  Edge disposal razors and, 113,
    113
Elasticity-ratio approach, to budgeting, 404–406
Elderly endorsers, 204–205, *205*
  casting and characterization of,
    206
Electronic coupons, 275
Electronic displays, 237
Electronic distribution, 280–281,
  281
ELM. *See* Elaboration likelihood
  model (ELM)
Emotion
  action and, *161*
  advantages of, 161–163
  appropriate use of, 165–166
  attention and, 126–129
  Benetton ads and, 163
  classification of, 159–160, *159*
  curiosity as, 127–128
  defined, 158–160
  disadvantages of, 165
  drama and, 168–169
  ennobling, 180–181
  fear as, 127, 178–180
  humor and, 169–173
  irrationality of, 159
  irritation as, 175–177
  kitchen appliance appeal and, *167*
  logic and, 160
  methods of arousing, 166–175
  music and, 173–175, *173, 174*
  Nike ads and, 163–165
  persuasion through, 160–165
  reason and, *162*
  role of, 115
  sex as, 127, 128, 129
  Spray 'n Wash Stain Stick ads and,
    163

on TV, 357
  warmth as, 177–178
  Warner-Lambert and, 157–158,
    158, 165
Emotional involvement, 110
Empathy, 160
End-of-aisle displays, 236
Endorsements
  Coca-Cola, Pepsi, and, 197
  process of, 185
  regulation of, 44–45
  by testimonials, *193*
Endorsers, 44–45
  application of models of, 191–192
  audience and, 192–193, *192, 203*
  celebrities as, 186–187
  communication modes of,
    193–194
  cost effectiveness of, 194
  elderly, 204–205, *205*
  evaluation of, 194–196
  experts as, 185–186
  Jackson, Michael, as, 198–199
  Johnson, Earvin "Magic" as, 198,
    199
  Jordan, Michael, as, 198, 199
  lay, 187–188
  meaning transfer model of,
    190–191
  Nike Air and, 185
  overuse of, 197–198
  Pepsi "Make a Wish" ad and, 184
  persuasion and, 114, *114*
  race of, 204
  role of, 188
  screening candidates for, 198–199
  source attractiveness model of,
    188–190
  source credibility model of, 188
  stereotyping of, 200–205
  strategic implications of, 196–200
  types of, 185–188, *191*
  use of, 192–194
Ennobling emotions, 180–181
  Nike ads and, 180–181
Entry, into agency market, 64–65
Ethnicity
  ethnic jokes and, 170
  sensitivity to, 18
Even scheduling. *See* Continuity
Everyday-low price (EDLP) strategy,
  247
Evidence, objective, 160
Evocative power of medium, 357

Exchange, creative thinking and, 85
Exclusive audience, 367, *367*
Execution, creativity and, 88–90
Exhibits, 260, *260*
Expenditures
  on advertising, 6
  on research, 18
  scheduling, 405–410
Experience curve, 379
Experiment, 315, *316. See also*
    Research; Testing
  evaluating, 316–317
  field, 319
  multifactor, *316*
Expert endorsers, 44–45, 185–186,
    188
Expiration dates, on coupons, 276
Explicit lie, 37
Explicit memory, 144
Explicit mode, emotions and, 160
Exposure, 145
  repetition and, 104–105
External agency, 75
  selecting, 77–80
External stimuli, perception and,
    137–139
External validity, 316
Extinction, 102
Eye camera, 326–327

Face value, of coupon, 239, 274
Factory price, 48
Fairness
  in media broadcasting, 51
  in pricing and promotion, 227
Falsehood, 37
Familiarity
  exposure and, 104
  of message, 107, *107*
  with source attractiveness model,
    188
Fashion, 417–418, *418*
FCC. *See* Federal Communications
    Commission (FCC)
FDA. *See* Food and Drug
    Administration (FDA)
Fear, 178–180
  in dental floss ads, 181
  drama used for, *180*
  First Alert ads and, *178*
  response to, 178–179, *179*
Features, retail promotions and,
    235, *235*, 237–238

Federal Communications
    Commission (FCC)
  media regulation by, 50–51
  promotion and, 35
  television advertising and, 362
Federal Food, Drug and Cosmetic
    Act (1938), 52
Federal regulation, 35
Federal Reserve Board, automobile
    leases and, 46
Federal Trade Commission (FTC).
    See also Regulation; Truth in
    promotion
  Campbell's Soup Company and,
    34
  changes in criteria for, 40–41
  comparative ads and, 148
  history of, 36
  implementing policy of, 41–43
  infomercial regulation by, 50
  labeling regulation and, 52, 53, 54
  mail advertising regulation by, 51
  price-cuts and, 239
  price discrimination and, 47
  responsibilities of, 35
  unfairness definition and, 40
Federal Trade Commission Act,
    Wheeler-Lea Amendment to
    (1938), 17
Federal Truth in Lending Act, 46
Feeling attributes, 165, *166. See also*
    Emotion
Fees. *See* Compensation
Feminine hygiene ads, 175, 177
Fibermunchies, 37
Field experiments, 319. *See also*
    Field studies
  on advertising-sales relationship,
    336–337
Field of Dreams (movie), 18
Field studies, on advertising-sales
    relationship, 337–338
Field testing, 318–319
Figures of speech, in magazine ad
    headlines, 132, *132*
Financial harm, 39
Financing, 259
Firearms, labeling of, 54
Firm, use of term, 6
First Amendment, protection of
    commercial speech by, 57
Fixed costs, of promotions, 246
Fixed-fee compensation method,
    81–82

Flanking attack, 141, *141*
Flexibility, of self-reports, 320
Flighting, 406
Focal stimuli, 125
Focus, of media, 357–360
Focus group, 324–325
Food, labeling of, 52–54
Food and Drug Administration
    (FDA)
  Campbell's soups and, 35
  labeling regulation by, 52–54
  promotion and, 35
Food industry, 13
Foot-meter, 325–326
Forgetting, 143. *See also* Memory;
    Memory lapse
Forward buying, 243–244
  costs of, 265
  trade promotions and, 255
Forward conditioning, 103
Framing, 152
  Elders, Joycelyn, and, 152, *153*
Framing price increases, 227
Fraud
  coupon misredemption and, 278
  draft, 51
  via mails, 51–52
"Free" goods, as attention getter,
    129
Freelancers, 71
Free speech, protection of, 57
Frequency, 306, 368–370, *369*
  for ad schedules, *369*
  direct media and, 379
  of message repetition, 106–107
  for two schedules, *370*
Frequent flier plans, 286
Front-of-store displays, 236
FTC. *See* Federal Trade Commission
    (FTC)
FTC v. Raladam, 36
Full-service agency, 71–72, *72*
  McCann-Erickson Worldwide as,
    68
Functional MRI, 327
Functional organization, 74

Gallup Poll, 17
  data from, 320
Games, trade, 263–264
Gang clipping operations, 278
Gender, sensitivity to, 18
Gender stereotypes, endorsers and,
    201–204

Generic brands, 242–243
Geodemographic segmentation, 21–22
Goals
  attainable nature of, 305
  involvement in, 305–306
  precise nature of, 304–305
  of promotion, 27–29
  setting, 29, 302–306
  strategic, 28–29, *28, 30,* 31
  of Subaru campaign, 304–306
  tactical, 28, *28, 30*
  ultimate, *28,* 29, *30*
Great Depression, 17
Grocery stores, 234
  mail promotions, 383
  segmentation by, *23*
Gross profit, 403–404
Gross rating points (GRPs), 366–367, *366*
  for ad schedules, *369*
Growth period, 420, 422–423
Growth rate, of brand, 400–401
Guides Against Deceptive Pricing (FTC), 48

Habituation, 104
Hand-meter, 325–326
Hard-sell message, 108–109
Hard thinking, 84
Harm
  from misleading advertising, 39
  proof of, 44
Harper's Illustrated Weekly, 13
Headline, attention and, 131–132
Head-on attack, 141
Health. *See also* Joe Camel advertising campaign
  endangering, 39
Hidden Persuaders, The (Packard), 105
Hierarchy, 27
Hierarchy of effects, 306–310
  models of, 308–309
  uses of, 309–310
High-low pricing strategy, 247
Hispanics, racial stereotypes of, 204
History of advertising, 8–18
Holding company, 73–74
Home pregnancy kit, 157–158, *158,* 165
Household purchases, in response to TV ads, *107*
Humor, 169–173
  Coca-Cola and, 169

Kellogg's Crispix and, 169
  role of, 171–173
  slapstick, 170
HUT (households using television), 361
Hyperlink. *See* Internet
Hypertext link, 386
Hypothesis, 315
Hysteresis, 409–410

IAT (individually addressable tape), 334
Ideal points, 27
Identification, with source attractiveness model, 189
Illustration, irritation and, 176
Immersion, creative thinking and, 84
Implicit memory, 144
Implicit mode, emotions and, 160
In-aisle displays, 236
Incentive, 216. *See also* Sales promotion
  pay-for-performance, 257–258
  quota, 257
Incentive promotions, 421
  comparing, 292, *292*
Incentive system, 21
Incremental consumption, 269, 242n
Incremental profits, 245
Incremental sales, 245–246
Incubation, creative thinking and, 84
Independent agency, 72, 73
Independent variable, 315
Index, 363–364
  new, 366
  targeting and, 366
  weighted average, 366
Indirect approach, and demographic segments, 364–365
Indirect costs, of direct media, 390
Indirect trade-offs, 428–429
Industry groups, with advertising regulations, *55*
Inertia, 225
Infant formula, Nestlé and, 162–163
Infomercial, 50, 126
Information
  attention and, 126, *127*
  memorizing and retrieving, 142–145
  preferences, product life cycle, and, 419–420
Informational promotions, 421
Information collection, search and, 121

Information processing, 137–145
Information Resources Inc. (IRI) experiments, 336–338
Informative power, of medium, 357
Informative trade promotions, 259–262
In-house agency. *See* Internal agency
In-house self-regulation, 54
Injury, materiality and, 39
Innovation, lifestyle changes and, 11–13
Inoculative argument, 152
In-pack coupons, 274
In-pack premiums, 283
Input
  measuring, 322–324
  variables, 322
Inquiries, 331–332
In-store displays, 235–237, 262
In-store media, 347
Integrated advertising and sales promotion strategy
  for defense, 430–432
  of Gillette company, 414–415
  over product life cycle, 415–430
Integrated advertising setup, 76–77
Integrating losses, 226–227
Integration, 115
Intensity
  of advertising or promotion, 402
  of choice, *28,* 29
  of emotions, 159
  scheduling and, 408
  of stimulus, *124*
Interactive displays, 237
Interest groups, and advertising effectiveness, 314
Internal agency, 75
Internal Revenue Service, Alcohol and Tobacco Tax Division of, 17
Internal validity, 316
Internet
  advantages and disadvantages of, 388–389
  direct media and, 386–389
  growth of on-line access, 389, *389*
  industries with sites, 389, *389*
Interview, in data collection, 325
Introduction period, 420
Introductory offers, 49
Intrusiveness, of direct media, 381
Inventions. *See* Innovation
Inventory, trade promotions and, 253, 265
Invisible hand concept, 227

Involvement. *See also* Attention
persuasion and, 110–111
Irritation, 175–177
causes of, 176
degree of, by commercial, *176*
effectiveness of, 177
in Stayfree and Tylenol ads, 175
Issues, Tylenol poisoning and, 151

JAMA. *See* Journal of the American
Medical Association (JAMA)
Japan, automobile exports from,
305
Joe Camel advertising campaign,
311–313, 317–318
recognition and, 331
Journal of the American Medical
Association (JAMA), on Joe
Camel ads, 311–313, 317–318
Justice Department
antitrust division of, 35
price discrimination and, 47

Kitchen appliance, emotional appeal
for, *167*
Klanwatch, 352

Labeling
of alcohol, tobacco, and firearms,
53–54
of ethical drugs, 52–53
of food, 52–54, *53*
regulation of, 52–54
Laboratory experiment, 315. *See
also* Experiment
Lanham Act (1946), 36
amendment to, 41, 43, 44
Lateral thinking, 84
Laws. *See* Regulation
Lawsuits, about rival advertising,
43–44
Lay endorsers, 44, 187–188
Leading question, 321
Leakage, 219
Learning, conditioning and,
103–104
Learning hierarchy, 308
Learning theory, 278
Leasing, truth in lending and, 46
Lies, explicit, 37
Life cycle. *See* Product life cycle
Lifestyle
innovation and changes in, 11–13
segmentation by, 22

Lighting technologies, *423*
Likability, of source attractiveness
model, 188–189
Limited time price, 48
Line ads, 238
Link
with products, 144
between stimuli, 103
List prices, 226
Loans, truth in lending and, 46
Local advertising, 350
Location, of medium, 359–360
Logic, emotion and, 160, *166*
Logical thinking, 84
Long-term memory, 142
Loss leaders, 15–16, 244
Loss of benefits, 39
Lottery, 49
Low-involvement hierarchy,
308–309
Low-involvement processing, 110,
115
passive processing as, 122
Loyals, 221, 245
Loyalty. *See also* Brand loyalty
to bonus plans, 287

Macintosh computers, 3–4
Magazine advertising, resonance in,
171
Magazine coupons, 274
Magazines, 13–14
circulation of, 361
focus of, 358
Magnetic resonance imaging. *See*
Functional MRI
Mail
catalogues as, 14
as direct medium, 381–383
fraud via, 51–52
regulation of advertising via,
51–52
unordered merchandise and, 52
Mail ads, telemarketing and, 384
Mail-in premiums, 283
Mail-order firms
fraud and, 51–52
negative-option plans and, 52
prompt shipping by, 52
unordered merchandise and, 52
Major ads, 238
"Make a Wish" ad, Madonna and,
184

Make-good time, 351
Management, trade promotion as
distraction to, 264–265
Manufactured goods, market for, 13
Manufacturer, use of term, 6
Manufacturer coupons, 239–240,
273–281
annual distribution of, *274*
popularity of coupon vehicles, *274*
Mapping, perceptual, 26–27
Market(s), 6
for advertising agencies, 64–65
for budgeting, 399–400
development after Civil War,
10–16
for media, 348–350, *349*
Marketing
direct, 377–378
mass, 21
niche marketing and, 25
and promotional planning, 27–31
strategic, 18–27
Marketing Evaluations, Inc.
celebrity rankings of, *196*
Q-ratings of, 195, *195*
ratings framework of, *195*
Marketing planning, process of, *30*
Market outcomes, 307
Market position, 29
as strategic goals, *28*, 29
Market research, 67–68. *See also*
Research; Testing
firms, 71
Market segmentation, 21
Market share
advertising and, *401*
budgeting and, 400
of Coca-Cola and Pepsi-Cola, *399*
Defender Model and, 430–431
effect of repeating old and new
ads, *338*
of Gillette blades, *415*
share of voice and, *400*
Mass campaign, 407
Massing, 406
Mass marketing, 21, 24
proliferation of brands and, 254
splintering of, 379
television and, 18
Mass media, 346–347. *See also*
Media
Mass production
advertising and, 15
branding and, 13

Material claim, 39
Materiality, and injury, 39
Maturity stage, 420, 423
Maximization. *See* Profit maximization
Meaning, perception and, 137
Meaning transfer model, 190–191
Measurable segments, 24–25
Measurement. *See also* Advertising; Data collection; Research; Testing
  of advertising effectiveness, 328–335
  direct media and, 380
  of TV viewership, 344–346
Media, 7. *See also* Media planning; specific media
  for accessing segments, 26
  agencies and, 80
  broadcast, 50–51
  comparison of, *360*
  computer-related, 355–356
  defined, 67
  early, 13–14
  expenditures on, *347*
  fragmentation of, 353
  growth of new, 354–356
  mail, 51–52
  market for, 348–350, *349*
  Nielsen measurements and, 344–346
  regulation of, 50–52
  structure of, 346–356
  supplier-buyer mergers and, 348–350
  trends in, 353–356
Media associations, with advertising regulations, *55*
Media bill, 80–81
Media-buying agencies, 71
Media choice, 357
  vehicle choice and, 370–371
Media companies, 7
Media coupons, 274
Media mix, 357
Media owners, 7
Media plan, *30, 31*
Media planning, 67, 344–346, 357–371
  direct media, 376–377
  focus and, 357–360
  media choice and, 357
  vehicle choice and, 360–370
Media vehicles. *See* Vehicle choice

Medical agencies, 72
Medicines, patent, 16
Medium, ad placement in, 133
Medium-size ads, 238
Memorization, 142–145
Memory, 137
  brain and, 142–143
  explicit, 144
  implications of, 144–145
  implicit, 144
  organization of, 143–144
  perception and, 137–138
  structure of, 142–143
Memory lapse, 322
  hand-meter and, 326
Merchandise, unordered, 52
Mere exposure
  Black Bag experiment and, 104
  repetition and, 104–105
Merged agency, 73
Mergers
  Disney-Capital Cities/ABC merger and, 348
  Matshushita-MCA merger and, 350
  Sony-Columbia Pictures merger and, 350
Message
  attention and, *130*
  cognition and, 139–142
  complexity of, 108–109, *108,*
  familiarity of, 107, *107*
  frequency of, 106–107
  print, 138–139
  repetition of, 106–107
  selective acceptance of, 140
  simplicity of, 145
  stimulus link to, 128
  television, 138
Meters, for data collection, 323–324, 325–326, 327
Milk mustache campaign, 102
  by Bozell Worldwide, 99–100
  low involvement and, 110
Minorities, ethnic jokes and, 170
Minority agencies, 72
Miscomprehension, 39–40
Misleading claim, 37
  suits over, 43–44
Misrepresentations, 37, 43
Missing-heir swindles, 52
Mixed compensation method, 82–83
Mixed shows, 260
Mockup, 45

Model, for customized research, 196
Models (endorsers), 185
  responses to attractive, *203*
Mood
  of audience, 165–166
  cognition and, 142
Motion Picture Association, self-regulation and, 57
Motivational trade promotions, 262–264
Movie, advertising of, 427–428
MRI. *See* Functional MRI
Multicollinearity, 241, 318–319
Multidimensional scaling, 27
Multifactor experiment, *316*
Multimedia presentations, on Internet, 388
Multiple regression analysis, 318
Music
  culture and, 175
  emotions and, 173–175, *173, 174*

NAACP. *See* National Association for the Advancement of Colored People
Name recognition, exposure and, 104
Narrative, 169
National Advertising Division, of Better Business Bureau, *55*
National Association for the Advancement of Colored People, 352
National Association of Broadcasters, self-regulation by, 55
National spot advertising, 350
Natural sciences, 18
Negative option mail-order plans, 52
Negatives, in refutational advertising, 151
Net (final) profit, 403–404
Network, 350
Network advertising, 350, *355*
"New" goods, as attention getter, 129
New products. *See* Product(s); Product life cycle
Newspapers
  advertising in, 13
  circulation of, 17, 358, 361
  early ad in, *11*
Niche marketing, 24, 25
  perceptual mapping and, 27

Nielsen indices, 17
Nielsen polls, 321
Nielsen Radio Index, 345
900 numbers, 386
Noise, in self-reports, 321
Noncommercial character, of ad, 356
Nonpreemptable rate, 351
Non-price promotions, 216
Non-price trade deals, 258–259
Nonresponse probability, for direct media sales, 391
Northridge earthquake, dual entitlements and, 227
Novel stimulus, 125
Novelties, 418–419
Nutritional Labeling and Education Act (1990), 53
Nutrition labeling, 52–54, *53*

Objective-and-task method, of budgeting, 402
Objective evidence, 160
Observation, 320. *See also* Research
Offensive marketing, 152
Off-invoice discounts, 256–257
One-sided appeal, 148
On-line access. *See* Internet
On-pack coupons, 274
Open Market Directory, 386
Optimal advertising intensity, 404
Orientation
   product, 20
   profit, 21
   sales, 20
   service, 20
Outcome variables, measuring, 327–328
Outdoor media, 347, *348*

Package coupons, 274
Packaging, 13
Participation, 351
   in sales promotion, 212
Passive meter, 324
Passive processing, 122
Pass-through, 215–216
   brand switching and, 248
   of trade deals, 255–256
Patent medicine, 16
   ad for, *16*
Pavlovian conditioning, 101–102
Pay-for-performance incentives, 257–258

PCs, and TV viewing, *388*
Penetration pricing strategy, 421–422
People-meter, 323–324
People Panel, The, 195
Percentage-of-sales budgeting method, 397
Percentage proven recall, 329
Percentage related recall, 329
Perception, 137
   cognition and, 139–142
   external stimuli and, 137–139
   selectivity of, 138
   stages of, 137–138
   symmetry and asymmetry of, 228
Perceptual bias, 84
Perceptual mapping, 26–27
Perceptual priming, 144
Performance basis compensation method, 82
Periodic discounting, 219–220, *220*
Peripheral route of persuasion, 111, 112
Permanence, 114
Personal computers. *See also* Computer market
   advertising of, 5
   Apple Macintosh "1984" ad and, 3–4
Personal relationship, direct media and, 380–381
Personal scanners, 328
Personal selling, 6
Persuasion. *See also* Emotion; Endorsers
   argument strategy and, 145–154
   classical conditioning and, 101–104
   defined, 101
   elaboration and, 111–115
   emotion and, 157–158, 160–165
   with endorsers, 184–186
   hierarchy of effects and, 306–310
   information processing and, 137–145
   integration and, 115
   involvement and, 110–111
   McDonald's rumor and, 136–137
   milk mustache campaign and, 99–100
   processing route of, 114–115
   repetition and, 104–109
   scheduling and, 407

PETA
   activism of, *162*
   Gillette and, 162
Phone calls. *See* Telemarketing
Phonograph, *12*
Physical displays, 237
Physical harm, 39
Physical stimuli, 123–126
   adaptation-level theory and, 125–126
Pictures
   attention and, 133
   in catalogue advertising, 14
Pitch, 173
Placement
   of ads, 122
   in medium, 133
Planning
   marketing, 30
   marketing and promotional, 27–31
   media, 356–371
   of promotions, 29–31
Planning horizon, 406
Plot, 168–169
   irritation and, 176
Pocket the deal, 254
Political advertising, 44
Politicians, fairness doctrine and, 51
Polls, 17. *See also* Audience; Gallup poll
   Gallup, 321
   Nielsen, 321
   vehicle choice and, 360–361
Ponzi schemes, 52
Population
   for rating, 361
   target segments and, 364
Population growth, 11
   trade promotions and, 254
Pornographic material, 52
Positioning, 26–27
Post Office Laws, 17
Pragmatism, 120
Precognitive commitment, 84
Prediction, conditioning and, 103
Preference, selective attention and, 120
Premiums, 49, 283–284
Preparation, creative thinking and, 84–85
Presidential campaign
   inoculative argument in, 152
   refutational argument in, 152
   warmth of Reagan-Mondale, *177*

Pretests, television ads used in, *326*
Price and pricing. *See also* Discounts and discounting
  asymmetry in response and, 225–226
  comparable market, 48
  deceptive, 48
  fairness in, 227
  former or regular, 48
  ineffective ads and, 339
  for limited time only, 48
  lowest, 37
  new products and, 421, 426
  penetration, 421–422
  reference, 223–225
  self-enforcement and, 229
  suggested retail, 48
  value pricing, 290
  wholesale or factory, 48
Price-based trade deal, 256–258
Price-cuts, 235, *235*, 238–239
Price discount, 238. *See also* Discounts and discounting
Price discrimination, 46–47, 219, *220*
  theory of, 278
Price elasticities, promotional strategies and, *425*
Price packs (cents-off packs), 48, 282–283
Price promotion, 46, 217–229
  comparing, 292
  consumer responses to, 222–223
  idealized sales response to, *245*
  profitability of, 244–248
  by Sears, Roebuck & Co., 244
  timing of, 247
  trade-offs with advertising, 429
Price response curve, *225*
Price-sensitive consumers, 247
Price skimming, 421, 426
Pricing strategy, of Sears, Roebuck & Co., 248, *248*
Print advertising
  mail and, 382
  telemarketing and, 384, *385*
Printer's Ink, state regulation of advertising and, 16
Printing, color, 13–14
Print media, 347
  information and, 357
  milk mustache campaign and, 99–100
Print messages, miscomprehension of, 138–139

Private labels, 242–243
Prizes. *See* Contests and sweepstakes
PRIZM, 22
Probability
  nonresponse, 391
  purchase, 391
  return, 391
Problem solving. *See* Creative thinking; Creativity
Processing, active and passive, 122
Process variables, 307, 324
Product(s), 6
  ads for innovative new, *12*
  attributes of, 126, 165
  innovations in, 11–13
  market for, 13
  mass production and, 13
  misrepresentations about, 43
Product classes, elderly endorsers and, *205*
Product classification, by Foote Cone and Belding (FCB), *164*
Production, dislocations of, 265
Production houses, 71
Productivity, creativity and, 83
Product life cycle, 415–420, *417*
  of durables, *427*
  of Gillette's razor blade products, *416*
  integration of advertising and sales promotion in, 428–430
  life cycle succession and, 422–426
  movies and, *424*
  promotion strategy and, 420–422, 427–428
  speed of takeoff and, 426–428, *426*
Product orientation, 20
Product placement, 50, 356
Product portfolio theory, 425
Profit, 29
  defined, 307
  dual entitlements and, 227–228
  incremental, 245
Profitability
  coupon strategy and, 279
  of direct media, 389–392
  for levels of advertising, 403–404
  of price promotion, 244–248
  of trade promotions, 267–269
Profit centers, bonus plans as, 287–288
Profit maximization, 227
  as budgeting method, 402–404
Profit orientation, 21

Programmers, 346. *See also* Media
Programming, 348
  television messages and, 138
Program tie-in, 50
Prohibition, self-regulation of alcohol and, 54
Pro-life activists, 162
Promoters, 6
Promotion(s), 6, 34–57. *See also* Consumer promotions; Sales promotion(s); Trade promotion(s)
  asymmetric draw of, 243
  budget allocation to, 425–426, *425*
  consumer, 30, 272–273
  costs of, 247
  fairness in, 227
  Gillette's strategy for, *417*
  goals of, 27–29
  integrated strategy for, 414–415
  integration in life cycle, 428–430
  and marketing planning, 27–31
  meaning of truth in, 36–43
  optimal level of, 396
  planning of, 29–31
  price, 46
  over product life cycle, 415–420
  reinforcement among variables, 429–431
  sales, 46–49
  strategies as function of price and advertising elasticities, *425*
  strategy over product life cycle stages, 420–422
  trade, *30*
  truth in, 35
Promotional bump, 242–244
Promotion-to-sales ratio, 397
Prototypical brand, 144–145
Psychographic (lifestyle) segmentation, 22
  Jockey ad based on, *25*
Psychology
  creative thinking and, 84
  mere exposure effect and, 104
Publicity, 6
Publisher's revenues, 14
Puffery, 39
Pull strategy, 215
Pulsing, 406
Pupillometer, 327
Purchase frequency, 29
Purchase intensity, 306
  as strategic goal, *28, 29*

Purchase probability, for direct media sales, 391
Pure Food, Drug and Cosmetic Act (1934), 17
Pure Food and Drug Act (1906), 16
Push money, 259
Push strategy, 215

Q-ratings, 195–196, *195*
Qualifying discounts, 222
Quantity, 306
Quantity discounts, 257
Questionnaires, 323, 327. *See also* Experiment; Research; Testing
Quick cut, 125
Quota incentives, 257
Quotas, on Japanese automobile exports, 305

Race
  sensitivity to, 18
  stereotypes of, 204
Radio. *See also* Media
  focus of, 358
Railroads, expansion of, 11
Random assignment, 317
Random discounting, 220–222
Rates, for advertising, 351
Ratings, 360–361
  of endorsers, 195–196, *195*
  gross rating points (GRPs) and, 366–367
  of telemarketer attributes, *383, 384*
Reach, 367–368
  for ad schedules, *369*
  comparative, *370*
  of direct media, 379
  for two schedules, *370*
  of two TV programs, *368*
Reading methods, 372–373
Reason, emotion and, *162*
Rebates, 221, 281–282
  misredemption of, 52
Recall, 329–330
  as function of ad repetition, *405*
  and recognition, 330–331
Recency, 145
Recent-reading method, 372
Receptivity, attention and, 121–123
Recognition, 330–331
Redemption. *See* Coupon redemption

Reference prices, 223–225
  ads with, *224*
Refund, 282
Refutational advertising
  attacks by rivals in, 151–152
  negatives in, 151
  unambiguous issues in, 151
Refutational argument, 150–152, *150*
  in AT&T-MCI advertising, 151, 152
  by BMW, 150–151
  by Chrysler Corporation, 150
Regression analysis, 318
Regulation, 16
  business associations and, *55*
  of comparative advertising, 43–44
  of demonstrations, 45
  of endorsements, 44–45
  federal, 35
  of labeling, 52–54
  of list or regular prices, 247
  of loans and leasing, 46
  of media, 50–52
  of price packs, 283
  of promotion, 34–57
  Pure Food and Drug Act and, 16
  of sales promotions, 46–49
  self, 35, 54–57
  state, 16, 35
  of sweepstakes and contests, 288–289
  of time devoted to ads, 51
  of warranties, 45–46
Regulatory agencies. *See* Regulation; individual agencies
Rehearsal, 143
Relativity principle, reference prices and, 224–225
Relevance, 317
  of ads, 317–318
Religion, sensitivity to, 18
Remembering. *See* Memory
Repetition, 104–109, 115
  cognition and, 142
  involvement and, 110
  message, 106–107
  recall as function of, *405*
Repurchase and repurchasing, 29, 275, 306
Research, 18. *See also* Experiment; Market research; Testing
  behavioral, 217

customized, 196
data collection tools, 322–328, *322*
field approach to, 318–319
memory lapse and, 320–322
self-reports and, 320–322
Residual stimuli, 125
Resistance, 114
Resonance, 169–170
  in dental floss ads, 181
  in magazine advertising, *171*
  in Reddi-wip ad, *172*
Response, 102
  asymmetry in, 225–227
  budget and, *410*
  cognitive, 139
  direct media and, 380
  for 1996 Echo Award-winning direct media campaigns, *380*
Response curves, *223, 225*
Response rate, for direct media, 390–391
Retail coupons, 239
Retailer-distributed coupons, 274–275
Retailers
  brand promotion by, 253
  trade deal and, 254
Retailing, growth of power, 254
Retail prices, advertising and, 16
Retail promotions, *213, 215, 234–235. See also* Sales promotion(s)
  by automobile manufacturers, 264
  degree of response to, 241–242
  effects of, 240–244
  Kmart and, 233–234
  promotional bump and, 242–244
  types of, 235, *235*
  Wal-Mart and, 233–234
Retail sales, promotions and, *241*
Retail stores. *See* Retail promotions; Sales promotion(s)
Retrieval, 142–145
  cues for, 144
Return probability, for direct media sales, 391
Revenues, 29, 307
  in Great Depression, 17
Reverse causality, 319
Reverse sexism, 202
Risk, creativity and, 86
Rivals, advertising by, 43–44

Roadblock, 368
Robinson-Patman Act (1936), price discrimination and, 47
Rules, creative thinking and, 85–86
Rumors, about McDonald's, 136–137
Run-of-press newspaper coupons (ROP newspapers), 274

Sales
  advertising and, 335–340
  incremental, 245
  measurement data on, 332–335
  pattern of coupon responses and redemptions, 275–277, *276*
  retail, *241*
  use of term, 29
Sales bump, 242–244
  decomposing of, 246, *246*
Sales conferences, 262–263
Sales in units, 29, 307
Sales lead, 377
Sales orientation, 20–21
Sales pattern, scheduling and, 407–408, *410*
Sales promotion(s), 6, 31, 211–215. *See also* Integrated advertising and sales promotion strategy; Retail promotions; Trade promotion(s)
  advertising effectiveness and, 314
  budget for, 396–405
  characteristics of, 216
  classification of, 217
  contests, sweepstakes, and, 49
  with coupons, *214*
  contests and sweepstakes and, 49
  deceptive pricing and, 48
  deceptive value and, 48–49
  defined, 212, *213*
  dual entitlements and, 227–229
  goals of, *215*
  by Hoover Vacuum Cleaners in Britain, 214–215
  key dimensions of, 215–216
  by Northwest Airlines, 211, 212
  price discrimination and, 46-47
  price promotions and, 217–229
  over product life cycle, 415–420
  regulation of, 46–49
  setting goals for, 299–302
  of software, *212*
  spending on (1960-1994), 7
  telemarketing and, 384, *385*

timebound nature of, 212
trade allowances and, 47–48
of Windows 95, 394–395
Sales-response function, 402
Sales responses, and coupons, 275–276
Sampling, 289–291
  of Windows 95, 289–290
Sampling coupons, 291
Saturation point, 403
Scaling, multidimensional, 27
Scan-down, 258
Scanner data, 332
  suppliers of, 266
Scanners
  checkout, 327–328
  personal, 328
Scatter buying, 351
Schedule, 366–370
Scheduling
  ad intensity, budget, and, 408
  of advertising expenditures, 405–410
  campaign goal and, 407
  choice of, 406–407
  defined, 406
  as function of key factors, *410*
  sales pattern and, 407–408
  Zielske's study of, 405–406
Science
  advertising strategies and, *5*
  natural and social, 18
Screening, of endorsers, 198–199
S-curve
  product takeoff and, 426
  as response to advertising, 403, *403*
  of technological progress, 422–425
Seal of approval, 186
  ENERGY STAR and, 186, *187*
Search, information collection and, 121
Search vehicles, for Internet, 388
Second market discounting, 222
Securities and Exchange Commission, 17
Segmentation, 21–24. *See also* Targeting
  by age group, *22*
  benefit, 23–24
  demographic, 21, *22*
  diseconomies of scale and, 25
  by grocery store, *23*

market, 21
media for accessing, 26
psychographic (lifestyle), 22
schemes for, 22
segment evaluation and, 362–363
segment size and, 22, *24*
usage, 22
yogurt use and, 363–364, *364*
Segregating gains strategy, 226
Selective attention, 120–121
Selectivity, of perception, 138
Self-enforcement, sales promotion and, 228–229
Self-liquidating premiums, 283
Self-regulation, 35
  by business associations, 55–57
  in-house, 54–55
  subject matter addressed by, *56*
Self-reports, 320
  advantages of, 320
  disadvantages of, 320–322
Self-serving bias, 20
Selling, personal, 6
Senses, 137
Sensitivity, of self-reports, 320
Sequencing, 144
Service orientation, 20
Sex
  appeals, in ads, 201
  as attention getter, 127, 128, 129
Sexism, gender stereotyping and, 201–204
Share of audience, 361
Share of voice
  budgeting and, 400
  market share and, *400*
Shelf-talkers, 236–237
Sherman Act, 36
Short-term memory, 142
Significant audience, truth in promotion and, 37–38
Similarity, of source attractiveness model, 189
Simplicity, of message, 145
Single-source data, 332–335
Situation analysis, 30, *30*
Skimming. *See* Price skimming
Slapstick humor, 170
Slotting allowances, 258
Smoking. *See* Joe Camel advertising campaign
Soap operas, Procter & Gamble and, 357–358

Soaps
  Dove, 26
  Ivory, 8–10, *9*
  niche marketing of, 27
Social desirability bias, 321
Social sciences, 18
Soft-drink market, flanking attacks
    in, *141*
Soft-sell message, 108, *109*
Soft thinking, 84
Sound, attention and, 132-133
Source attractiveness model,
    188–190
Source credibility model, 188
Southern Poverty Law Center, 352
Specialized agencies, 68–71
Speculative campaigns, 80
Speech, protection of, *57*
Speed, of medium, 359
Spiffs, 259
Spokesperson, 185
  fictitious characters as, 186
Sponsor identification, broadcast
    media and, 50
Sponsorships, 350–351
Spot advertising, 353–354, *353, 350*
Stand-alone department, 76
State regulation, 35
States, advertising in, 16
Statistics
  field testing and, 318–319
  variables and, 240, 241
Stayfree, irritating ad of, 175
Stereotyping
  by age, 204–205
  of endorsers, 200–205
  racial, 204
  sensitivity to, 18
Stimulus, 102
  contextual, 125
  emotion and, 158–159
  focal, 125
  intensity of, *124*
  perception and, 137–139
  physical, 123–126
  residual, 125
  Weber's law and, 123–125
Stimulus novelty, 125
  of Bud Bowl ad, 125
Stockpiling, 29, 243–244, 268–269
  trade promotions and, 255
Storage, 142, 143
Store switching, 244, 269
Story
  components of, *168*

effectiveness of, 168
  narrative and, 169
Strategic goals, 28–29, *28, 30,* 31
Strategic marketing, 18, *30*
  consumer orientation and, 18–21
  positioning and, 26–27
  segmentation and, 21–24
  targeting and, 24–26
Strategies. *See also* Defense strate-
    gies; Integrated advertising and
    sales promotion strategy;
    Promotion(s)
  penetration pricing, 421–422
  promotional, *425*
  science and, *5*
  value pricing, 251–252
Street money, 259
Subjects, 315
Subliminal advertising, 105–106
Subordinate brand, 149–150
Substantiation, of claims, 38–39
Success trap, 20
Suggested retail price, 48
Sunk costs, 390
Super Bowl, *358,* 360, 370
  Apple Macintosh "1984" ad
    during, 3–4, *5*
  Bud Bowl campaign and, 119–120
  celebrity and brand recognition
    during, *194*
  scheduling choices and, 406–407
Supportive arguments, 139, *142,*
    153
Supreme Court, on freedom of com-
    mercial speech, *56-57*
Survey, 320
Sweepstakes. *See* Contests and
    sweepstakes
Swindles. *See* Deceptive advertising
Switch, 28, 306
Switchers, 221
Symmetry, 228
Sympathy, 160
Syndicated data sources, 371–373
  Audit Bureau of Circulation
    (ABC), 372
  Mediamark, 373
  Nielsen, A. C., Co., 371–372
  Simmons Market Research
    Bureau, 372–373
Syndicated programs, 350
Synthesis, 137

Tactical goals, 28-29, *30*
  affective, *28, 28*

cognitive, 28, *28*
  conative, 28, *28*
Tagline, of Ivory Soap, *9,* 28
Takeoff, 426–428
Talent houses, 68, 71
Targeting, 24–26
  adequate size segment and, 25
  for bonus plans, 287
  target segments and, 362–366
Target marketing, 24
Target of emotions, 159
Technical information, in-house
    agencies and, 75
Technology
  life cycles and, 422–423
  media growth and, 378
  product life cycle and, 416–417
  products and, *418*
  S-curve of progress, 422–425
Tedium, 104
Telemarketing, 51, 384–386
  ratings and acceptors of, *383,* 384
Telemeters, 323, 345
Telephone. *See also* Telemarketing
  acceptors and nonacceptors of
    appeals, *383*
  as direct medium, 383–386
  telemarketing and, 51, 384–386
Telephone and Consumer Protection
    Act (1991), 51
Telephone industry
  AT&T, MCI, and, 145, *146*
  deregulation of, 145
Television, 17–18. *See also*
    Commercials; Music
  ads used in pretests, *326*
  cable, 351–352, *351*
  events watched on, *358*
  focus of, 358–359
  household purchases in response
    to, *107*
  length of commercials, *354*
  low-involvement processing and,
    110
  measuring viewership, 344–346
  miscomprehension of messages on,
    138
  network ads per prime-time hour,
    355
  organization of, 350–352
  PC penetration and, *388*
  program content and, 352–353
  time devoted to ads on, 51, *355*
Television ads, telemarketing and,
    384–386

Testimonials, endorsement by, *193*
Testing, 18. *See also* Experiment;
   Research
  of causality, 316–317
  of endorsers, 194–196
  ineffective ads and, 338–339
  of Joe Camel ads, 317–318
Texture, in music, 173
Theater tests, 315
Thinking. *See* Creative thinking
Thinking attributes, 165, *166*
Threshold, 403
Through-the-book method, 372
Tied-houses, 258
Tie-ins, 284–286
  CoreStates Financial Corp. and
    Disney's Premier Cruise Lines,
    284, 285
  examples of, *285*
Time, direct media and, 378–379
Time-bound nature of sales promo-
    tions, 212
Time frame, 406
Timing, 173, 306
  of price promotions, 247
Tit-for-tat strategy, 432–433
  AT&T-MCI competition and, 433
  Tylenol-Datril competition and,
    432–433
Tobacco. *See also* Joe Camel adver-
    tising campaign
  labeling of, 54
Toiletries, 13
Toll-free numbers, telemarketing
    and, 384–386
Toothpaste, benefit segmentation
    for, *26*
Trade allowances, regulation of,
    47–48
Trade associations, with advertising
    regulations, *55*
Trade contests, 259
Trade deal, 256
  non-price based, 258–259
  price-based, 256–258
Trade games, 263–264
Trade-offs, among promotion com-
    ponents, 428
Trade promotion(s), *30*, *213*, 215,
    235, 251–252
  brand switching and, 269
  characteristics of, 252–256
  classification of, *256*
  costs of, 264–266

description of, 256–264
dynamics of, 254–256
goals of, 252–253, *252*
incremental consumption, store
    switching, and, 269
informative, 259–262
manufacturers' expenditures on,
    255
motivational, 262–264
problems of, 264–267
profitability of, 267–269
stockpiling and, 268–269
trade-offs with advertising,
    428–429
Trade show, 260
  COMDEX and, 260, *260*
  International Manufacturer
    Technology Show, 260
  International Winter Consumer
    Electronics Show, 260
Trade sweepstakes, 263–264
Traditional media. *See also* Mass
    media; Media; Media planning;
    specific media
  comparison of, *360*
Transportation, advertising on, 354
Treatment, of ad, for experiment,
    315–316
Trial, 29, 290–291, 306
Trial coupons, 291
Trial promotion, 291
Trial samples, 290
True Lies (movie), product place-
    ment in, 50
Trustworthiness, of endorser, 188
Truth in lending, 46
Truth in promotion
  criteria for, 37–39
  deception versus puffery, miscom-
    prehension, and unfairness,
    39–41
  evaluation of, 36–41
  meaning of term, 35, 36–43
Turnstile advertising, 354–355
Two-factor theory, 104, *105*
Two-sided appeal, *107*, 108,
    148–149

Unconditioned response, 102
Unconditioned stimulus, 102
Unduplicated audience, 367
Unfairness, 40
U.S. Department of Agriculture, reg-
    ulation by, 52

U.S. Health Department, 52
U.S. Postal Service (USPS), 35
  catalogue delivery by, 14
  mail advertising regulation by,
    51–52
  mail and, 382
  manufacturer coupons and, 273
U.S. Treasury Department, BATF in,
    54
Universal product code (UPC), 328
Unordered merchandise, 52
Up-front buying, 351
Usage, of medium, 361
Usage segments and segmentation,
    22, 364
USP (Unique Selling Proposition), 91
  Lee Jeans ad and, *92*
USPS. *See* U.S. Postal Service (USPS)

Validity, of experiment, 316
Value
  as attention getter, 129
  deceptive, 48–49
Value pricing, 290
  by Procter & Gamble, 265
  by Quaker Oats, 252
Variables
  effects of, 240–241, *240*
  in experiments, 315
  input, 322
  process, 307
Vehicle choice, 360–370
  media choice and, 370–371
Verification, creative thinking and,
    85
Vertical thinking, 84
Voice-over, by celebrity, 187

Warehouse clubs, 234, 247
  value pricing by, 251
Warmth
  ad arousing, *178*
  emotion and, 177–178
Warranties, 45–46
Wearin, 408–409, *409*
Wearout, 408–409, *409*
Web. *See* Internet; World Wide Web
Weber's law, 123–125
Web sites, 389, *389*. *See also*
    Internet; World Wide Web
Weighted average indices, 366
Wheeler-Lea Amendment to Federal
    Trade Commission Act (1938),
    17, 36

Whites, racial stereotypes and, 204
Wholesale or factory price, 48
Windows 95, 394–395
Women
  changing perception of, *19*
  cosmetics for, 13
  gender stereotyping and, 201–204
  portrayals of, *202*

World War I, advertising after, 16–17
World War II
  advertising after, 17–18
  advertising before, 16–17
World Wide Web, 386. *See also* Internet
  commercial uses of, *387*

Yahoo Guide, 386–388
Youth theme, of Pepsi advertising, 102–103

Zapping, 122
Zest soap, 27
Zipping, 122